RAILROAD GAZETTEER.

HAMBURG-AMERICAN PACKET CO.

ALLEMANNIA, CIMBRIA, FRISIA, GELLERT, HERDER, LESSING, SILESIA, SUEVIA, WIELAND, WESTPHALIA.

DIRECT WEEKLY MAIL STEAMERS TO

ENGLAND, FRANCE AND GERMANY.

LEAVING NEW YORK EVERY THURSDAY AT 2 P. M. FOR
PLYMOUTH, CHERBOURG AND HAMBURG.

Avoiding the discomforts of trans-shipment across the English Channel.
Passengers landing at Plymouth are forwarded FREE OF CHARGE TO LONDON or any station in the South of England. The distance by rail from Cherbourg to Paris is only 7 hours.

☞ Steamship Orders of the Central Pacific R. R. will be accepted from passengers booked through to Europe from Japan, China and Australia.

FOR FURTHER PARTICULARS, APPLY TO
C. B. RICHARD & CO., Gen. Pass. Agts.,
61 Broadway, New York.

J. F. MEINKE & CO., Gen. Agts. Pacific Coast, A. MALPAS, Agt.
401 California Street, cor. Sansome,   Overland Ticket Office,
SAN FRANCISCO.   SAN FRANCISCO.

OCCIDENTAL AND ORIENTAL STEAMSHIP COMPANY,
FOR
JAPAN AND CHINA. Leave Wharf, cor. First and Brannan Sts. AT 2 P.M.
YOKOHAMA AND HONG KONG,
Connecting at Yokohama with Steamers for
SHANGHAE.

Gaelic,	Oceanic,	Belgic,
Friday, July 1st.	Tuesday, July 19th.	Friday, Aug. 19th.
Saturday, Sept. 17th.	Thursday, Oct. 6th.	Friday, Nov. 4th.
Saturday, Dec. 3d.	Wednesday, Dec. 21st.	

EXCURSION TICKETS TO YOKOHAMA AND RETURN AT REDUCED RATES.

PASSAGE TICKETS,—Cabin Plans on exhibition and Passage Tickets for sale at Room No. 74, Offices Central Pacific R. R. Co., cor. 4th and Townsend Sts.

For Freight, apply to Geo. H. Rice, Freight Agent, at the PACIFIC MAIL S. S. Co's Wharf, or at No. 202 Market Street, Union Block.

LELAND STANFORD,   T. H. GOODMAN,
President.   General Passenger Agent.

New York, Co

The six largest S.

OCEANIC, ATLANTIC, BALTIC,
ARCTIC, PACIFIC, ADRIATIC.

6,000 Tons' Burden; 3,000 Horse-power each

These magnificent Steamships have been built especially for the Transatlantic trade, with a view of offering to all classes of passengers greatly-increased comfort and accommodations.

The midship section of each ship (where least motion is felt) is devoted solely to saloon passengers. This section comprises main saloon, smoking-room, ladies' boudoir, state-rooms, hot and cold baths, etc. A piano and library are provided, in order to render the voyage more enjoyable. Fresh water laid on to each state-room.

The ventilation is perfect, and each section is thoroughly warmed. Wines, etc., of the best qualities, to be procured on board.

RATES.
Saloon, $80, Gold; Excursion, $140, Gold;
Steerage, outward $30 Currency.

For full particulars, apply at

"WHITE STAR LINE"
Offices, 19 Broadway N. Y.

J. H. SPARKS, Agent.

| CITY OF RICHMOND, | 4,607 | CITY OF NEW YORK, | 3,500 |
| CITY OF CHESTER, | 4,566 | | |

BETWEEN
NEW YORK AND LIVERPOOL,
CALLING AT
QUEENSTOWN (Cork Harbor).
From NEW YORK every THURSDAY or SATURDAY.
From LIVERPOOL every TUESDAY or THURSDAY.

PASSENGERS BOOKED TO AND FROM
ALL POINTS IN GREAT BRITAIN AND IRELAND,
AND ON THE CONTINENTS OF EUROPE AND AMERICA.
Steamers Sail from Pier 37,   North River, New York.

RATES OF CABIN PASSAGE.
$80 and $100 gold, according to accommodation, all having equal saloon privileges. Children between two and twelve years of age, half fare. Servants, $40.

ROUND-TRIP-TICKETS AT REDUCED RATES.
TICKETS TO LONDON $7, and to PARIS $12, gold, additional.

The Steamers of this line, built in watertight compartments, are among the strongest, largest and fastest on the Atlantic. The saloons are large, luxuriously furnished, amidships, well lighted and ventilated, and take up the whole width of the ship amidships. The principal staterooms are amidships, forward of the engines, where least noise and motion are felt, and all are replete with every comfort, having double berths, electric bells, and all latest improvements. Ladies' Cabins and Bath Rooms, Gentlemen's Smoking and Bath Rooms, Barbers' Shops, Pianos, Libraries, &c., provided.

A. MALPAS, Agent,   JOHN G. DALE, Agent,
Central Pacific R. R. Office, San Francisco.   29 and 31 Broadway, New York.

PACIFIC MAIL STEAMSHIP CO.'S
Through Line
TO
CALIFORNIA, CHINA, AND JAPAN.
Touching at Mexican Ports, and carrying the United States Mail.

Steamships on Atlantic and Pacific Oceans.

ARIZONA,	COLORADO,
HENRY CHAUNCEY,	CONSTITUTION,
NEW YORK,	GOLDEN CITY,
OCEAN QUEEN,	SACRAMENTO,
CHINA,	GOLDEN AGE,
RISING STAR,	MONTANA,
ALASKA,	GREAT REPUBLIC, &c.
JAPAN,	

One of the above large and splendid Steamships will leave Pier No. 42, North River, foot of Canal Street, at 12 o'clock noon, on the 1st, 11th, and 21st of every month (except when those dates fall on Sunday, and then on the preceding Saturday,) for ASPINWALL, connecting via Panama Railway with one of the Company's Steamships from Panama, for SAN FRANCISCO, touching at ACAPULCO.

Departures of the 1st and 21st connect at Panama with Steamers for SOUTH PACIFIC and CENTRAL AMERICAN PORTS. Those of the 1st touch at MANZANILLO.

Departure of 11th each month connects with the new steam line from Panama to AUSTRALIA and NEW ZEALAND. Through tickets sold.

One hundred pounds of baggage allowed to each adult. Baggage-masters accompany the baggage through, and attend to ladies and children without male protectors. Baggage received on the dock the day before sailing, from steamboats, railroads, and passengers who prefer to send down early.

An experienced surgeon on board. Medicine and attendance free.

Pacific Coast Steamship Company,

Will despatch, every Five Days, until further notice, for
PORTLAND AND ASTORIA,
one of their new A-1 Iron Steamships, viz: "COLUMBIA," "OREGON," and "STATE OF CALIFORNIA,"
Connecting at PORTLAND, Oregon,
with Steamers of River Division and Railroad, and their connecting Stage Lines, for all points in OREGON,
WASHINGTON and IDAHO Territories, BRITISH COLUMBIA and ALASKA.

North American Steamship Co.
NASSC.

OPPOSITION TO MONOPOLY.
THROUGH LINE TO
CALIFORNIA,
VIA PANAMA OR NICARAGUA.

SAILING AT NOON FROM
PIER 29 NORTH RIVER,
FOOT OF WARREN ST.,
ON THE FOLLOWING FIRST-CLASS STEAMSHIPS.

ON ATLANTIC OCEAN.	ON PACIFIC OCEAN.
Santiago De Cuba,	Oregonian,
San Francisco,	Moses Taylor,
Dakota,	Nebraska,
Arago,	Nevada,
Fulton,	America.

Passage and Freight at Reduced Rates.

For further information apply at
Company's Office, 177 West St., N. Y.

CUNARD LINE.
ESTABLISHED 1840.

Lane Route.   Royal Mail Steamers.

FAST EXPRESS MAIL SERVICE BETWEEN
LIVERPOOL, BOSTON AND NEW YORK
CALLING AT CORK HARBOR.
TWO SAILINGS EVERY WEEK.

IN ATLANTIC SERVICE:

CAMPANIA,	CATALONIA,	SCYTHIA,	LUCANIA,
ETRURIA,	UMBRIA,	AURANIA,	SERVIA,
GALLIA,	BOTHNIA,	PAVONIA,	CEPHALONIA.

From NEW YORK every Saturday and alternate Tuesday.
From BOSTON every Saturday.

Rates of Passage, $50 and upwards, according to steamer and accommodation.
Second Cabin, $35 and upwards, according to steamer and accommodation.

RETURN TICKETS ON FAVORABLE TERMS.
Steerage Passengers booked to and from all parts of Europe at very low rates.

VERNON H. BROWN & CO., Agents,
4 Bowling Green, New York.

GUION LINE.
UNITED STATES MAIL STEAMERS.

This Line has always sailed the safest route ; as a proof of this, it has not lost a soul by accident since it commenced. The "Guion Line" and "Old Black Star Line" have been established over 25 years.

The following or other first-class full-powered Steamships will be despatched from Liverpool to New York every Wednesday and Saturday, calling at Queenstown the day following to embark passengers.

	TONS.	CAPTAIN.		TONS.	CAPTAIN.
IDAHO,	3131,	C. J. Bridoe.	WYOMING,	3720,	Jas. Price Junr.
NEVADA,	3125,	T. Jones.	MONTANA,	4000,	Jas. Guard.
WISCONSIN,	3700,	T. W. Freeman.	DAKOTA,	4000,	Wm. Forsyth.

Rates of Cabin Passage, 12, 15, 17 and 20 guineas, according the size, situation, and accommodation of the steamer, all having the same privileges in the Saloon. Children under twelve years of age, half-fare; Infants free. The Saloon and all Cabin Sleeping Berths being on the main deck, these Steamers are unsurpassed for comfort, light, and ventilation.

Intermediate Passage, including bed, bedding, and mess utensils, £8 8s.
Steerage Passage to New York, Boston and Philadelphia, £5, including a plentiful supply of provisions, cooked and served up by the Company's Stewards. Passengers forwarded to all parts of the United States and Canada; also to San Francisco, China, Japan, India, New Zealand, and Australia, by Pacific Railway and Mail Steamers, at lowest through rates.

An experienced Surgeon is attached to each Steamer, also Saloon and Steerage Stewardesses.

Drafts issued on New York for £1 and upwards, free of charge.

The Steamers of this Line leave Pier 46, North River, New York, for Queenstown and Liverpool every Tuesday and Friday.

Wet Britches & Muddy Boots

Railroads Past & Present

GEORGE M. SMERK, EDITOR

A list of books in the series appears at the end of this volume.

Wet Britches and Muddy Boots

A History of Travel in Victorian America

JOHN H. WHITE, JR.

INDIANA UNIVERSITY PRESS

Bloomington & Indianapolis

This book is a publication of

Indiana University Press
601 North Morton Street
Bloomington, Indiana 47404-3797 USA

iupress.indiana.edu

Telephone orders   800-842-6796
Fax orders   812-855-7931

© 2013 by John H. White Jr.

All rights reserved

No part of this book may be reproduced or utilized in any form or by any means, electronic or mechanical, including photocopying and recording, or by any information storage and retrieval system, without permission in writing from the publisher. The Association of American University Presses' Resolution on Permissions constitutes the only exception to this prohibition.

♾ The paper used in this publication meets the minimum requirements of the American National Standard for Information Sciences–Permanence of Paper for Printed Library Materials, ANSI Z39.48–1992.

*Manufactured in the
United States of America*

*Library of Congress
Cataloging-in-Publication Data*

White, John H., [date]
  Wet britches and muddy boots :
a history of travel in Victorian
America / John H. White, Jr.
    p. cm. – (Railroads past and present)
  Includes bibliographical
references and index.
  ISBN 978-0-253-35696-3 (cl : alk.
paper) – ISBN 978-0-253-00558-8 (ebook)
  1. Travel–United States–History–19th century. 2. Transportation–United States–History–19th century. I. Title.
  HE203.W45 2012
  388.0973'09034–dc23
                    2011044593

1 2 3 4 5   18 17 16 15 14 13

THIS BOOK IS DEDICATED TO THE MEMORY OF CHRISTINE.

Contents

FOREWORD by Andrew Cayton *ix*

PREFACE *xiii*

ACKNOWLEDGMENTS *xxv*

1 Transportation for Hire: From Human Burden to Taxis *3*

2 Down That Long & Dusty Road: Stagecoach Travel in America *21*

3 The Omnibus: Travel for All Citizens *65*

4 Streetcars: That Most Democratic Conveyance *87*

5 Ferryboats: Crossing the Rivers and Bays *131*

6 Canals: The Low & Slow Way to Go *155*

7 River Steamers: White Swans on the Inland Rivers *179*

8 Lake Steamers: On the Inland Sea *223*

9 Coastal & Sound Steamers: Close to Shore *249*

10 Ocean Sail: At the Mercy of the Wind *297*

11 Ocean Steam: The Triumph of Technology *327*

12 Emigrant Travel: A Nation of Nations *371*

13 Passenger Trains: Coach Class *407*

14 Passenger Trains: First Class *447*

Appendix: Travel Words & Tales *487*

INDEX *501*

Foreword

ONE OF THE MOST ARRESTING IMAGES IN THE HBO ADAPTATION of David McCullough's best-selling biography of John Adams is the departure of the president from Washington, D.C., in March 1801. A huge horse-drawn coach pulls up in front of the White House. With some difficulty, the sixty-seven-year-old Adams climbs onto it, taking a seat among a group of ordinary Americans. Then the coach pulls away, launching Adams on his long journey back to his home in Quincy, Massachusetts.

The scene startled me because it was so unfamiliar. I knew I could hold forth at length on why Adams was leaving Washington against his will and the significance of his mingling with his fellow citizens. But I had no idea what this form of public transportation was, how long it had been in operation, how much it cost, how long it took to get from one place to another, and what it felt like. Like most of my academic peers, I was so used to thinking about large-scale questions of power and change that I had virtually no idea of what it was like to get around in the United States in 1800. It quickly dawned on me, of course, that I had just experienced the gap between the kind of knowledge constructed by academic specialists and the kind of knowledge most people want to know. The latter included the details of the Adams's family life, especially the relationship between John and Abigail, which had made McCullough's book so popular. It is, after all, the specifics of what we call material culture – the sights, sounds, and texture of ordinary life – that most satisfies a human curiosity about the concrete and personal aspects of the past.

When John Adams left Washington, most human beings traveled as their ancestors had traveled for centuries. They walked. But as the coach he boarded suggested, ordinary people were slowly joining the powerful and privileged in being carried, either by other people or by animals. The major exception to this rule was waterborne commerce. Then suddenly in the space of a couple of generations everything changed. The development of steam engines, telegraphs, railroads, and steel made it easier and cheaper to move people, goods, and ideas over long distances and to congregate in rapidly expanding urban areas. The new technology also made it possible for Europeans and North Americans to fight more wars, conquer more territory, and dominate much of the rest of the world. The pace of progress was astonishing, even in retrospect. The United States was a loose confederation of states in 1800, most of them hugging the Atlantic Ocean as they had as British colonies. By 1900, Americans had supposedly settled all of the inhabitable land within the borders of the present-day United States. The continental republic was an industrial behemoth poised to pass Great Britain as the world's greatest economic power, its great cities sprawling concentrations of people, wealth, information, and power.

None of this change would have been possible – at least not in the same way – without the sudden ubiquity of relatively cheap forms of transportation, not only from coast to coast, mines to factories, fields to markets, but also from suburbs to cities and workplaces to homes. A new breed of capitalist entrepreneurs rushed to exploit these developments, setting up streetcar companies and railroad corporations that would redefine American life and rearrange the structures of power in local communities as well as the nation as a whole. In the early twentieth century there were no greater incarnations of the wonders of modernity than Grand Central Station in New York City and Victoria and Waterloo in London or the traveling palaces of Pullman cars and Cunard liners. Journeys that had once taken weeks, if not months, were accomplished in days or even hours.

The technological revolution had enormous and largely unanticipated social and political consequences. Almost overnight the possibility of a daily commute accelerated the rearrangement of burgeoning urban landscapes into distinctive neighborhoods defined by class, ethnicity, and race, widening the difference between workplace and home and accentuating the separation between family and commercialized leisure. The same men and women who traveled several miles to work every day were also able to attend baseball games, visit amusement parks, and go to the theater. By the second half of the 1800s, trains and steamers encouraged Americans to travel to distant places as merchants, sailors, missionaries, and increasingly as tourists. They went to places famous for their culture (Italy), power (Great Britain), spirituality (the Holy Land), or natural beauty (Niagara Falls). Americans traveled in such large numbers that Mark Twain's 1869 satire, *Innocents Abroad,* became a runaway best seller.

Americans were not alone. Around the world people were dealing with the impact of railroads and telegraphs, repeating rifles and photographs, sewing machines and steamships.[1] Improvements in transportation and communication made men and women more directly aware of cultural, religious, and political differences. Unexpectedly, they also promoted a convergence in customs. From Shanghai to Boston, people

---

1. Jan de Vries, "The Industrial Revolution and the Industrious Revolution," *Journal of Economic History* 54 (1994): 249–70. See C. A. Bayly, *The Birth of the Modern World, 1780–1914: Global Connections and Comparisons* (Oxford: Blackwell, 2003).

were wearing dark suits, ties, bowler and stovepipe hats, or the latest Paris dresses and bonnets; eating beef and pork, breads and rice; drinking coffee and tea sweetened with sugar; speaking standardized languages; living in cities that in terms of appearance and organization were variations on a global theme; and finding refuge from dirty, crowded public streets in the domesticity of elaborately decorated private homes. Writing of the Young American in 1859, Abraham Lincoln remarked on the interconnectedness and homogeneity produced by a revolution in transportation:

> Look at his apparel, and you shall see cotton fabrics from Manchester and Lowell; flax-linen from Ireland; wool-cloth from Spain; silk from France; furs from the Arctic regions, with a buffalo-robe from the Rocky Mountains, as a general out-sider. At his table, besides plain bread and meat made at home, are sugar from Louisiana; coffee and fruits from the tropics; salt from Turk's Island; fish from New-foundland; tea from China, and spices from the Indies. The whale of the Pacific furnishes his candle-light; he has a diamond ring from Brazil; a gold-watch from California, and a Spanish cigar from Havana.[2]

All this I knew as I watched John Adams take his seat among his fellow citizens. I had a sense of the overarching narrative of progress, of the writings of its proponents and critics, of the arguments about whether it should be financed publicly or privately. What I did not know was how this transportation revolution actually unfolded. I had no sense of the sights, sounds, and smells, let alone the specific origins, of the omnibus or the steamer.

Luckily for me – and a host of curious readers – Jack White has answered these and other similar questions in his engaging history of travel in nineteenth-century North America. Jack White brings to this task expertise accumulated during a long career as a distinguished historian of transportation, particularly railroads. As important, he possesses an infectious enthusiasm for the workings of trains and boats and buses. Informative as this book is, it is also a labor of genuine love. I cannot imagine anyone who knows more about travel in nineteenth-century United States than Jack White. He has mined an abundance of newspapers, magazines, and books for anecdotes and stories of travel. But he wears his erudition well. Readers not only learn about every possible mode of human transportation, but they also get as strong a sense as the written word can convey of the tactile experience of travel. Jack White introduces us to steamers and trains, buses and taxis, showing us the origins of a wide variety of conveyances that revolutionized life in North America.

When John Adams took leave of the White House in 1801 and climbed aboard a public conveyance, he was entering a modern world in which travel would become normal and available to anyone who could pay the fare and meet the schedule. Neither Adams nor any of his contemporaries could have anticipated how this revolution in transportation would

2. Abraham Lincoln, "Lecture on Discoveries and Inventions," in *Lincoln: Selected Speeches and Writings*, ed. Don E. Fehrenbacher (New York: Vintage, 1992), 200.

transform the United States and indeed the world. But they knew something big was happening; they knew that these were exciting and unsettling times and that their grandchildren would live very differently from their grandparents. Meanwhile, they marveled at the explosion of new contraptions that conveyed them farther and faster almost every year. Jack White invites us to experience what nineteenth-century Americans experienced, not from the remote perspective of the detached historian but from the personal perspective of a man or woman standing on the deck of a lake steamer, entering a cabin on a canal boat, feeling the texture of a seat and the rush of a crowd, or simply marveling at rapidly shifting landscapes through the smoke-stained windows of a passenger train. John Adams, hero of the political revolutions of the eighteenth century, rode into retirement on a vehicle that signified the coming and far more encompassing revolutions of the nineteenth century.

ANDREW CLAYTON

Preface

THE PURPOSE OF THIS BOOK IS TO DESCRIBE THE TRAVEL experience in nineteenth-century America. What was it like to ride in a stagecoach, a riverboat, or a train 150 years ago? Were the seats comfortable? Was heating provided? Was the ventilation adequate? How were tickets purchased, and at what cost? How fast did vehicles and ships travel? Why was the passage to Europe faster than the return trip to North America? Why did stagecoaches ride so miserably and railroad cars ride so smoothly? How safe was travel at the time? Is it true riverboats were one of the most dangerous modes of travel? How large was passenger traffic on the various modes of travel? What were the duties of stagecoach drivers, transatlantic sea captains, or railroad train conductors? How did a locomotive engineer drive his iron steed? Were great fortunes made in the transportation business? Did government attempt to regulate the travel industry? Did the rich ride in comfort while the poor traveled in less-well-appointed accommodations, or was there a greater mix of social and economic classes? These and many other topics are explained in the fourteen chapters of this volume.

But surely the history of early American travel has been handled in many other books. That is true, but almost all deal only with one mode of travel such as railroads, seagoing ships, or canals. Very few have attempted to handle all types of transport systems, other than juvenile or pictorial accounts. There have been a few volumes of a serious nature that deserve mention. John L. Ringwalt's *Development of Transportation Systems of the United States* appeared in 1888. It is a detailed and rich source of data, but it says rather little about the travel experience and a great deal about the network or system of transportation. Seymour Dunbar's *A History of Travel in America* appeared in 1915 and is a monumental work of fifteen hundred pages. It is more anecdotal in nature than Ringwalt's book and tends to wander off the subject with long detours into American Indian history. George R. Taylor's *Transportation Revolution* is a far more sophisticated study that is rightly considered a classic in American economic history.

It is concise, literate, and scholarly. However, Dr. Taylor's focus is freight transportation, and he says less about passenger travel, since its effect on the national economy was less important. A more recent volume is *Transportation in America* by William L. Richter, which was published in 1995. Because the book is organized alphabetically rather than by mode or date, I feel it presents a disjointed story that fails to provide a narrative that is understandable by the general reader. It is an excellent collection of data but lacks the organization to be read as a story. Each of these four studies offers considerable information, and all were valuable to my research. None are now in print, so I felt justified in offering the present volume to the public. My book is not documented in the traditional manner, though I try to make my sources clear within the text. This volume is not for scholars or specialists but was written for students and the general reader.

This study covers all forms of public transport, but it does not include individual travel on foot or horseback, nor any form of private conveyance. The time period covered is largely limited to the 1800s, but when appropriate, early or later time periods are included. Chapter 1, for example, addresses ancient and primitive travel. This study does not pretend to be a complete account of public travel in America and is intended only to create a general picture of what occurred.

Humans found travel necessary before agriculture led to settlements and the raising of crops. We were scavengers who picked up food en route as hunters and gatherers. Grain, fruit, and small animals were consumed when and where they could be found, but it was soon necessary to move on, always seeking fresh fields to explore in our quest for sustenance. Long, muscular legs made man an ideal creature for walking. We could walk day after day from twenty to forty miles if necessary. Even after mankind developed civilizations that included dwellings and cities, the attraction to travel remained powerful. Writers of the past commented on the subject often. Seneca wrote that travel and a change of place imparts vigor. Centuries later, Samuel Johnson advised travelers to visit a country better than their own and to copy its virtues. He also contended that the most wonderful experience was to travel in the company of a pretty woman. Other wise men believed movement was the essence of life. It was a force deep within us; we are nomads drawn to the open road that winds through the distant hills and forest. We are by nature wayfarers. Robert Louis Stevenson declared, "I travel not to go anywhere but to go ... I travel for travel's sake."

A major reason to travel is to get away, to break up the routine of everyday life. This is the purpose of a vacation, to go on a holiday and see new places and faces. People dream of seeing the nation's capital, Niagara Falls, Rockefeller Center, or the Grand Canyon. Others become romantic about foreign sights in the faraway Pacific or the wilds of Africa. Limited budgets often preclude such adventures, and the would-be world travelers settle for a week in a nearby state park or fishing lake. More-determined persons go on budget vacations to see exotic places. We give examples of hearty souls who would go emigrant class to achieve their travel dreams or needs in chapter 12.

Thousands of trips were made to attend family events such as graduations, weddings, and funerals. In some cases, people just wanted to spend time with a parent or relative. Public events were also traffic generators: athletic games, rodeos, and the Kentucky Derby would put thousands in motion. Washington, D.C., required a very large railroad station to handle the crowds that came to witness the presidential inauguration once every four years. National meetings of the Freemasons and other fraternal organizations were widely attended. Churches, business groups, and veterans moved en masse for regional or national conclaves, and special trains were operated specifically for these meetings. Hotels were solidly booked and restaurants were crowded.

A few traveled to escape the law. Burglars, murderers, swindlers, and other criminals got out of town and traveled afar to establish themselves elsewhere with a new identity. Mexico and South America were favored hideouts. Henry Meiggs left the United States in 1854 to escape legal action and spent his remaining years in Peru building railways. Boss Tweed left the country for Cuba in 1875 to escape prison.

Others traveled for more noble reasons. Herodotus traveled the ancient world gathering information on a variety of cultures and peoples. His systematic recording of these facts made him, some claim, the first historian. Scientists such as Charles Darwin traveled thousands of miles seeking new information on the natural world. Many explorers went to the Arctic regions seeking to expand our knowledge of these icy terrains. Some of these explorers died in the service of science. In chapter 7 we discuss the travels of artists such as George Catlin, who recorded the American Indian in the 1830s, and James Audubon, who, like Catlin, traveled up the Missouri River to study animal and bird life.

Juan Ponce de Leon had perhaps the best reason to travel. In 1512 he went to Florida seeking the fountain of youth. Since ancient times many have traveled to hot springs hoping to regain their health. Hotels and resorts were built in many parts of the United States, and many became fashionable destinations. This subject is discussed in chapters 9 and 14. Upper-class families generally left their city townhouses for country retreats or mountain hotels to escape the heat. Southerners would summer in Newport, Rhode Island, or White Sulphur Springs, Virginia, to avoid the hot weather in Dixie. The White Mountains and the Adirondacks were favored by eastern residents. Part of the summer exodus was prompted by outbreaks of cholera and yellow fever common to port cities such as

Baltimore and New York. In the winter, northerners were attracted to Florida, Southern California, and some Caribbean islands. Here again, much of this migration was limited to the more affluent classes.

Business travel can be traced back to trade among primitive peoples before humans crossed over to the western hemisphere. Flints and bits of native copper were carried hundreds of miles and exchanged for food or other commodities. By the Victorian era, European salesmen crossed the Atlantic to sell woolens while Americans peddled grain or lumber in the Old World. Domestic salesmen known as drummers traveled the United States to sell a variety of products from shoe polish to steam boilers. Executives visited suppliers to negotiate better terms. Bankers journeyed across states to sell bonds or open new branches. Trade was aggressive and competitive and involved much person-to-person contact. This meant going to Chicago, Rochester, or wherever opportunity or profitable connections could be made.

America had a reputation for movement. It became known as a nation of travelers. "Let's go" was a common expression. In 1855 a French visitor reported, "They are in such a hurry – these sons of the New World." We were a "locomotive people," restless, impetuous, and ready to roll. An anonymous author wrote in the 1830s that Americans were born in haste, take our education on the run, marry on the wind, make a fortune at a stroke, and lose it quickly. Our soul is a high-pressure engine and our life is like a shooting star. So is the business mentality. Even so, the real joy of travel is the delight of getting home. Can anything be sweeter?

Happy travelers tended to be cheerful, carefree people who were ready to overlook the problems inherent in most journeys. Delays, missed connections, broken seat springs, too much or too little heat did not bother them greatly. Such folks laughed off accidents as just another inconvenience. However, although there are sunny accounts of travel, most firsthand reminiscences dwell on the hardships. The list is a long one. When traveling by stagecoach, the chief complaint was the roughness of the ride – it was bad enough to shake your guts loose – but also the coach stopped every ten miles to change horses, and passengers were told to stay in their seats or be left behind. The inns were crowded, and no one had a private room. As many as six people shared a bed. The food was often poor and expensive. Speeds were slow. It took days to go any distance. The overland stage required 25 days to go from Arkansas to California in 1858. But this was far faster than going by ship around South America's Cape Horn, which generally required about 150 days. Fares were high, generally 5 cents a mile and sometimes much higher. Stagecoach accidents resulted in injuries but few deaths, hence it was a relatively safe way to travel.

It is easy to see why so many people had a negative view of travel during the Victorian period, especially in the first half of that age. It was uncomfortable, slow, costly, and dangerous. Why not just stay at home, where it was the complete opposite? There was your fireplace, a good chair, your books, your family, and your own bed. Life was quiet and secure. It might be a little dull, but was that all so bad? You needed to go south to settle your late sister's estate, but your liver had been acting up, so you put it off as long as possible. Now the lawyers were hounding you. Fortunately, your younger brother was foolhardy – he loved to travel – make him do it. Pay his expenses; it would be a bargain.

Canal boats were pleasant for daytime journeys, but the sleeping arrangements were medieval and the interior space was limited. They were incredibly slow, rarely traveling more than 4 miles per hour. Riverboats offered good interior space plus small sleeping compartments and good food. The packets moved along at about 15 mph, which was fast compared to stagecoaches and canal boats. By the 1850s steamers made the trip from New Orleans to Louisville in six days. Fares were cheap at a penny per mile. The accident rates were high, making steamers a dangerous way to travel.

Railroads proved superior for speed and outran all of their competitors. By around 1850, 25 mph was a typical train speed. To our ancestors it seemed like flying. Western lines tended to run slower; the Union Pacific Railroad rarely topped 18 mph until 1880. As the rail system grew to 30,000 miles by 1860, most eastern canals and stage lines lost their passenger trade. Riverboats began losing the long-distance travel market at the same time. The cars were fairly roomy and offered heating in winter; they also offered toilets and drinking water. The seats were adequate for daytime passengers but made a poor bed for sleeping. Periodic stops were made for meals, but generally only first-class passengers could afford a berth and meal on the train. Coach fares were around 3 cents a mile, which was moderately high but still affordable to all but the poorest citizens. The safety record of railroads was also only moderately good and was a topic of public discussion that led to regulation of the industry. By 1890 railroads dominated intercity travel in the United States.

Public travel in America at the opening of the nineteenth century was an infant industry. There were no scheduled ships leaving our ports. Passengers waited for a ship's captain to announce his intent to go to England, France, or Brazil. In 1818 a line opened between New York and Liverpool, the first to sail on a fixed schedule. Stagecoach service was limited to the East Coast and often presented problems; some lines ran only one day a week, and many roads had no bridges over major streams. Ferry boats, too, were troublesome, as they did not operate in winter and before the introduction of the steamboat in 1807 usually only went downriver. It was almost impossible to make a long trip by one conveyance. Typically the trip began by carriage, then by ferry boat, with another transfer to a

PREFACE xvii

stagecoach or a ship. As late as the 1850s Horace Greeley complained, "The chief miseries of traveling are changing cars and crossing ferries." Getting on and off repeatedly with baggage, such changes in transportation mode remained a vexation well into the nineteenth century.

One traveler recorded her experience in going from Staten Island to the Pennsylvania Railroad station in Jersey City in 1893. The Staten Island Rapid Transit took her to the ferry station, where she boarded a boat to South Ferry. It was blocked from landing by another passing vessel. Minutes were lost. It was then a race to the elevated station to transfer uptown to another ferry to Jersey City. Once inside the sprawling station, there was a goodly walk to the gate of the train. Four transfers and several hikes on foot were needed to go just about 8 miles. Today airlines offer fewer direct flights, and passengers now commonly change planes at a second airport. If everything is on schedule, the exchange works well – even the bags are transferred from one flight to the other. We have all experienced missed connections, however, which in some cases can mean a delay until the next day.

Modern travelers understand money problems when they travel abroad. These normally concern handling strange currencies and the exchange rate. But in early America such problems occurred inside the United States. Our national banking system was eliminated by Andrew Jackson in 1832. In its place rose a chaotic nonsystem of state banks that issued their own bills. Many failed after a few years, but their currency remained in circulation. Even the bills of the more stable state banks were of little value outside of their immediate location. Pittsburgh bank notes had almost no value in Chicago and vice versa. The state bank bills were easy to counterfeit; indeed, some counterfeiters issued notes for banks that did not exist. Paper money understandably was not wanted. Gold coins became the only trusted medium of exchange, but they were in short supply. Specie, or money in coins, was so scarce that foreign coins were legal for exchange in the United States until 1857. All of this had a great impact on travelers. They needed a way to pay for meals, lodging, and fares en route, and this could only be done with coins. Finding a supply of them became a problem for any journey, one that had to be solved before leaving home. In some cases, travelers would carry jewelry or sterling silver household items such as tableware to pay their way along the road. To make change it was sometimes necessary to cut coins or jewelry into pieces. Spanish dollars minted in Mexico were very popular in the United States during this period. When cut into "two bits" this wedge-shaped piece was worth 25 cents, or one quarter. All of this nonsense ended in 1863 with a new national banking act that included paper currency produced by the U.S. Treasury. It was legal tender accepted throughout the nation. However, most citizens continued to prefer gold coins, which were minted by the federal government in great enough number to end the Jackson-era money madness.

The national economy was subject to periodic panics, or depressions. These were often the result of liberal loan policies. Too much debt led to bank failures and economic bad times in 1819, 1837, 1857, 1873, and 1893. The panic of 1857 was of rather short duration, but its effects were international. Everyone suffered to some degree. Investors were ruined and working people lost their jobs. Bankruptcies and foreclosures were commonplace. Even in good economic times the average person worked long hours for modest pay. A typical workday was ten to twelve hours. Unskilled workers made a dollar a day. Skilled workers such as machinists and locomotive engineers were paid between $2 and $3 a day. Women and children of poor families worked part-time to supplement the family budget, many women taking in laundry or sewing. Widows supported themselves by taking in boarders. Children left school at the eighth grade to find low-paying jobs as messengers or water boys; boys sold newspapers on street corners; girls peddled pencils or apples. Saturday was a workday, so only Sunday was a holiday. Vacations were only for the more affluent classes. If you were sick or injured, your job and paycheck ended as well. Charity hospitals did what they could to help poorer people. Private charity organizations cared for orphans, the aged, and homeless people, and some cities operated such institutions as well, but there was no large-scale public safety net. Families cared for their own aged and infirm kin to the best of their ability.

Modern America has lived with inflation since the end of World War II. The declining value of the dollar is accepted as normal. The rate varies from year to year, but it is steadily downward. This was not true in Victorian times. The dollar tended toward deflation – that is, it crept up in value as a general trend. Debtors were forced to repay loans with more valuable currency. The only significant inflation in the United States during the nineteenth century was during the Civil War. Federal income tax was not established until 1913. Before that time, excise taxes funded the national government. Modern readers will be more surprised to learn that the revenue from customs duties and other sources actually created a surplus in the federal treasury during the latter part of the Victorian era.

Nature created many obstacles to easy travel in North America that are no longer obvious. The earliest settlers traveled along the eastern coast by ship as the only easy way to get around. They went up rivers, bays, and natural harbors to establish settlements. The way west was blocked not only by the Alleghenies but also by dense forests of giant trees, some dating back before the time of Columbus. The great forest that covered the eastern half of the United States effectively blocked travel until about 1825. Animal trails offered only a narrow pathway for men on foot or pack

PREFACE xix

animals. Wagon roads came at a tremendous price in human labor. Roads were built a few miles at a time with little government aid. Most early settlers went west via the Ohio River or Lake Erie. Until the 1820s there was little public transportation west of the Alleghenies, as will be revealed later in this book.

There was an enormous amount of talk about internal improvements that would build roads and canals and make rivers more navigable. Albert Gallatin, the secretary of the treasury, prepared a comprehensive plan in 1808 that would create a fine national transportation system. Much of the plan was eventually completed long after Gallatin's death. During his life there was no political will to do very much. Political parties were very divided on this matter. Put simply, those in favor believed in federal funding for the transportation plan; those opposed did not. State governments made an effort to complete certain projects – the Erie Canal as built by New York State was an outstanding success – but most other state projects were far less successful. Some were such failures that the state government was bankrupted by these efforts. Private investors were involved in toll road construction and railroads. The private highways had rather mixed results. The railroads were generally efficient carriers and good investments. There were strong anti-tax feelings in the nation at a time when private enterprise was seen as the only solution. Small local taxes were tolerated, but the federal government was expected to live off of revenues generated by tariffs and excess taxes. The federal government worked directly to build a national road to Wheeling, West Virginia, from Cumberland, Maryland. It was a partner in building the transcontinental railroad, harbor and river improvements, and a few other projects, but in general it stood clear of transport involvements until after 1900. The bicycle and automobile rapidly grew in popularity by this time, and both local and federal governments funded road building.

Where possible, statistics on travel have been included in the following chapters. The U.S. census of 1880 is the first solid source for such data on a national scale. Before that time, traffic and revenue numbers can be found for a few states. Individual corporations would also include statistics in their annual reports, which are useful but do not answer the need for national statistics. The census fails to provide such information for such basics as the number of horses in the United States; it offers figures for horses on farms but not in urban areas. (Readers who assume the census offices published numbers on every subject, even those that would be of general interest, are under a false assumption.)

Travel in early America was largely a male enterprise. This is documented indirectly by the space allocated to men and women on ships and boats. In almost every case, the number of cabins for women was a fraction of the number reserved for men. The same was true on railroads. One car might be reserved for ladies while the rest of the train was open to both sexes. Women generally stayed home to tend to children; however, circumstances sometimes dictated that they travel long distances under difficult conditions. Emigration might be the most extreme example. Here, not just women but children and infants, too, were at sea or on the road. Crossing the ocean was a major trial for travelers, and millions of women proved themselves ready and able to embark on such journeys. We discuss this in chapter 12. Once on shore, women once again went by wagon or river rafts and set up housekeeping in frontier settlements. Middle-class and upper-class ladies had a somewhat easier time. The idea of separate accommodations for women dates back to the sailing ship era. By the early 1800s separate cabins were set aside for them, though they generally dined with male passengers in the main cabin. This tradition was extended to ferry boats, river steamers, and railroad stations. Railroads provided ladies' cars in a less consistent fashion, which is outlined in chapter 14. Lodging was a greater problem for ladies traveling alone. Inns were often too crowded for the luxury of separate accommodations, so women were well advised to write ahead for arrangements with friends or family. Matters in this regard became easier after hotels became more common. It should also be noted that transport workers, ships' captains, stewards, railroad conductors, and station agents could be counted upon to assist single women and children who were traveling unescorted. It is also true that a few women traveled the world and wrote about their adventures. Miss Isabella Bird and Fredrika Bremer and Frances Trollope are well-known examples, and America can claim the fearless female traveler and journalist Anne Royall.

The Victorian era is likely unfamiliar to most readers. It is so far in the past and so different from modern life, a brief summary seems necessary. Technically, it is bounded by the reign of Queen Victoria, 1837–1901, but it is sometimes understood as the entire nineteenth century. Its namesake was the British monarch who reigned for sixty-three years when England was a world power with an empire so widespread that the sun was always shining on some segment of it. It was a time of great prosperity, emigration, and population growth. Democracy expanded in Western Europe and North America while colonialism grew elsewhere in the world. New fortunes were made in a few years and as quickly lost as factories replaced craftsman and small workshops. People left countryside homes and small towns for cities. Populations that were once largely rural became urbanized. The very rich found life as cheerful and breezy as a Strauss waltz and were portrayed as rich and carefree; yet, as in present-day America, even the wealthy can be troubled and unhappy. The upper classes were wedded to comfort, sentimentality, and an appearance of breeding and good manners. Self-control, propriety, and a good public appearance were important. A growing middle class held that hard work, sobriety, and living the Protestant ethic were essential to the creation of the good life. Working-class people struggled to exist on low wages and harsh working conditions. Some succeeded in moving upward economically and socially; others turned to trade unions and socialism as part of a necessary class struggle to improve their lives. Capital and labor became combatants; the government generally sided with capital, but labor continued its battle for better wages and shorter hours and eventually succeeded to win some concessions from management. Oddly enough, protective tariffs so favored by capitalists helped to protect jobs for the working class.

The Victorian era was also a time for incredible technical advances. The steam engine was greatly improved and refined, and its effect on transportation is illustrated in the main body of this book. The limitations of human and animal traction are discussed in the early chapters. How steam power and electricity, which was dependent on steam, revolutionized everyday life is explained in almost all chapters in this book. Steam replaced sail on the seas, and electricity replaced the horse on street railways.

There is much that is not so obvious or easy to explain, and that is how different everything was in the time of Queen Victoria. Appearance was much more important. Dress was more elaborate and formal. One was always fully covered. This was necessary to look proper. The fabrics were heavy, and there were layers of clothes, even in the summer. Hats were always worn. We explain in chapter 7 how one young woman lost her life because she would not be seen in public without a hat. People dressed up to go to work, shop, or travel, even to go on a picnic. A vest, tie, jacket, and hat were required. This tradition of formality carried over to housing, conversation, and most social events.

On the other hand, everyday comforts such as indoor toilets, central heating, air conditioning, and electric lighting were unknown. Only important streets and roads were paved. Street lighting was not common. Tap water was not treated and could be unsafe. Bathing was done once a week, usually on Saturday evening. Water was heated on the kitchen stove and poured into a large metal tub placed near the stove. Young girls went in first – they were the cleanest members of the family. Then the women would bathe, followed by the men. The water would now be cloudy, but it was good enough for the boys, who were the dirtiest members of the family. By the end of the next week, most people were smelling a little rank. There was no deodorant at this time, so body odor was common, especially in warm weather.

Medical care was well intended but rather ineffective. The only method to stop serious infections was amputation. High blood pressure was untreatable, as were most other common illnesses. Infant deaths were common. Parents were lucky to see half of their children reach adulthood. Few adults kept their teeth. In 1850 life expectancy was thirty-eight years. By 1900 it was up to forty-six, showing that some progress was being made in health care and sanitation.

A reading list will be found at the end of each chapter. Many of the books listed can be found in larger public or university libraries. My research went well beyond these books and included other similar volumes as well as magazines and newspapers of the period. Travelers' guidebooks were also a useful source of information, but such material is widely scattered. The earliest guide I consulted was published in 1835 by Mitchell and Hinman in Philadelphia. Appleton Guides appeared in about 1850. Curran Dinsmore of New York began the *American Railway Guide* at the same time; the title is somewhat misleading, because the small volume also includes information on lake and river steamers. Other early guides were published by Henry S. Tanner, John Disturnel, John Ashcroft, and Joseph H. Colton. In June 1868 the *Official Railway Guide* printed its first issue and rather quickly eclipsed its competitors. This monthly publication soon added steam navigation lines to its format and continued until 1995. Karl Baedeker's 1893 guidebook to the United States is useful for late-Victorian subjects. The literature on travel, tourism, and transportation is huge. I examined around two or three thousand books, articles, and newspapers in the course of my research, but that is only a small fragment of the total literature available on the subject.

Acknowledgments

I AM INDEBTED, FIRST AND FOREMOST, TO MRS. JANET STUCKEY of Miami University's King Library Walter Havighurst Special Collections for encouraging me to complete this book. Whenever I was ready to abandon the project, she would insist it was not too large or broad; we could and would finish it. Mrs. Stuckey found time in her busy schedule to type and retype the chapters. Because she would not stop, I was forced to continue as well.

Several faculty members at Miami University were also supportive. Dr. Andrew Cayton prepared an elegant preface; Dr. Mary Cayton and professors Allan Winkler and Osama Ettouney offered advice on publishing the manuscript. Betsy Butler helped Mrs. Stuckey type several of the early chapters. Dean Judith Sessions provided support and desk space in the rare book room. Ralph E. Via Jr. found books and periodicals not available at local libraries. I am also indebted to Jenny Presnell, history bibliographer, and members of the staff of the Walter Havighurst Special Collections for their assistance, including Jim Bricker, Jamie Brinkman, Barbara Schutte, and Suzanne Haag for their efforts in the production of this book.

The late Ronald Shaw, a veteran teacher at Miami University, spent many hours with me discussing canals and early travel history, all of which proved valuable as I proceeded with my text.

Dr. Paul Johnston, curator of Marine Collections at the Smithsonian Institution, read one of the chapters, as did Herbert H. Harwood of Baltimore. Both offered detailed criticism that led to revisions of the text.

There were many individuals who were able to offer specific information, direct me to a source, or simply suggested a likely source. These include M'lissa Kesterman, Cincinnati Museum Center Library; Kurt Bell, Railroad Museum of Pennsylvania; C. W. Hauck of the Railway and Locomotive Historical Society; William Middleton, independent author; Kyle Wyatt, California State Railroad Museum; Wendell Huffman, Nevada State Railroad Museum; Gregory Ames, Mercantile Library in St. Louis, Missouri; and Thomas T. Taber, compiler of railroad historic and index reference works. Carl Swabe and Daniel Finfrock of Hamilton, Ohio, offered data on travel in southwestern Ohio; and Jim Wilke of Los Angeles offered expert advice on Victorian color schemes.

Andrew Dow, former director of the National Railway Museum in York, U.K., went to considerable trouble to send me copies of articles on American railway travel that appeared in British journals. Jim Harter, whose illustrated volumes offer a useful picture of travel in the Victorian era, has provided me with excellent copies of several images for this book. Edward T. Francis shared his expert knowledge of early New York and New Jersey transportation with me over the years.

To my past and present colleagues at the Smithsonian Institution, I wish to thank Robert M. Vogel, Robert C. Post, William Craig, Jeffery Stine, and Roger White for their advice and help over the past half century.

Finally, thank you to Linda P. Oblack, Nancy L. Lightfoot, and Peter C. Froehlich at Indiana University Press, who worked very diligently to make this volume a reality.

Wet Britches & Muddy Boots

1.1. Tunis bearer and passenger, ca. 1890.

(Marshall M. Kirkman, *Classical Portfolio of Primitive Carriers*, 1895)

Transportation for Hire № 1

From Human Burden to Taxis

THE EARLIEST HUMAN TRAVEL WAS SELF-LOCOMOTION. Mankind was blessed with very strong legs, and we could transport ourselves over very long distances. These day-by-day perambulations could carry one across a continent, if such a long trip was necessary. The average person can complete between 20 and 25 miles in a day, with the actual walking time totaling only six to eight hours. Someone who was determined to cover more ground could walk for a few more hours and do 30 miles in a day. Hence crossing North America could be done on foot in a little less than three and a half months. This optimistic schedule would depend on favorable weather, a certain degree of good fortune, and no unforeseen difficulties. In reality, however, when we consider crossing the country's several mountain ranges and rivers, which would impede travel considerably, it would likely take twice as many days to march across the vast expanse of what is now the United States. Most early travel was actually more local in nature and involved the search for food when our ancestors subsisted as hunters and gatherers of cereals, fruit, and small game.

With the establishment of agriculture about ten thousand years ago, mankind settled down into a less ambulatory lifestyle. Walking remained the chief mode of getting around, until the domestication of animals opened a new era in travel. The donkey proved itself a reliable, if slow-moving, beast of burden. The introduction of the riding horse from Central Asia in about 1400 BC offered Europeans the first really fast way of getting around. Speeds of 25 mph could be reached, but the animal could sustain such velocities for only very short distances.

Every community included certain members who were unable to walk very far because of advanced age, physical disabilities, or illness. For these same reasons, they could not stay on horseback for long. A few were simply too lazy to do so, but if they had the means they could hire a human bearer to carry them. A few strong men in need of money were ready to hoist people up on their back and march out to wherever their patrons

1.2. Turkish bearer and passenger, ca. 1890.

(Marshall M. Kirkman, *Classical Portfolio of Primitive Carriers*, 1895)

cared to go. It can be assumed that most such journeys were relatively short. This practice continued in certain parts of the world until late in the nineteenth century. Marshall M. Kirkman included engravings of human burden bearers in his 1895 volume on primitive carriers. He shows such a carrier in Tunis and a second example from Turkey (figs. 1.1 and 1.2). Figure 1.2 shows a Turkish human bearer fitted with a folding chair strapped to his back. The passengers sit facing backward on the seat. The rear legs of the chair are inserted into sockets on the bearer's trousers. The passenger has a foot rest, a sun shield, and a wraparound handrail. In a similar fashion, ferrymen would carry patrons across creeks and small rivers piggyback style. This practice goes back to ancient times, for Saint Christopher was a human-bearer ferryman in Syria in the third century AD. After his

1.3. Ferrymen in Formosa, ca. 1890.

(Marshall M. Kirkman, *Classical Portfolio of Primitive Carriers*, 1895)

martyrdom in about 250 AD, he became a hero to early Christians. Many centuries later he was canonized as the patron saint of travelers and ferrymen. However, his feast day, July 25, is no longer celebrated by the Roman Catholic Church. Figure 1.3 shows ferrymen in Formosa carrying patrons across a shallow river in the 1890s.

One-on-one transport surely had its limitations, especially if the passenger was very large, the trip very long, or the terrain very difficult. The use of a portable bed allowed two or more men to transport a single passenger for longer distances with greater ease, since the burden was divided among multiple bearers. The bed was similar to a modern stretcher, as the frame extended beyond the limits of the bed itself. The use of removable poles attached to the frame's sides worked even better. If the poles were made long enough, up to eight men could serve as bearers. A lightweight compartment was made by adding upright posts, a roof, and draw curtains at the sides and ends. The curtains kept out sun and offered the occupant a degree of privacy. Conveyances of this type are believed to have originated in Asia. The Greeks adopted them for invalids and women, but in general the litter was not fashionable for regular travel. It became so in Rome around 190 BC. The Romans called them *lectica*, the Latin word for "bed." A soft mattress and bolster, plus easy pillows, added to the traveler's comfort. The more luxurious litters were made from precious woods and decorated with ivory, silver, and gold. The curtains were fashioned from the most costly textiles (fig. 1.4). Less ornamental litters could be found near the city gates of most towns. They were available for hire by anyone

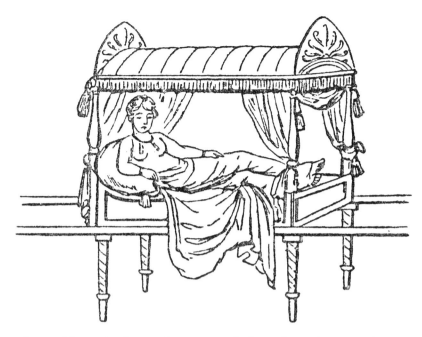

1.4. A Roman litter, or lectica.

(Johann Christian Ginzrot, *Die wagen und fahrwerke der Griechen und Römer und anderer alten Völker*, Lentner, 1817)

who could pay the fare and represented about the only form of public transit available in ancient times. The remains of one of these simple litters were discovered in Rome on Esquiline Hill in 1874, offering the best record yet found for such a conveyance.

For longer journeys, litters were slung between two mules in a fore and aft position. The compartment was somewhat more substantial than the litters carried by human bearers. An attendant walked beside the *basterna*, as such conveyances were named in Roman times, to guide and manage the mules. Riders or postilions, one on each mule, were sometimes used in place of the walking attendant. If nighttime travel was attempted, torch bearers walked ahead to light the way. Figure 1.5 shows an illustration of a French horse litter of the fourteenth century.

A chair fitted with two horizontal poles allowed two men to carry a passenger. It also offered the passenger a more comfortable ride. Where labor was cheap, the use of two rather than one bearer made little difference in the operating cost. Just when and where the traveling chair was introduced cannot be determined, but they were used by all societies. In Madagascar four rather than two bearers were employed. The poles were carried on the men's shoulders – Asian style – rather than at waist level, which was typical in the west.

The chair was improved during the 1500s by a lightweight enclosure as the sedan chair. Italy was the apparent home of this improved form of chair, and the name likely comes from the Latin word *sedes,* meaning "to sit." The compartment was large enough for only one occupant and measured about 30 by 30 by 60 inches. The enclosure offered privacy to

1.5. A French horse litter, or *basterna*, fourteenth century.

(Ezra M. Stratton, *The World on Wheels*, 1878)

the traveler and protection from the sun and rain. The entrance door was placed at the front of the enclosure. The sedan chair spread from Italy to Spain and finally to England in the late sixteenth century. After 1630, sedans were commonly used in London as taxis. During the eighteenth century they were frequently used by ladies and gentlemen in the cities of England and France for transportation. During Queen Anne's reign the fare was fixed at 1 shilling per mile. Wealthy families might own their own sedan, often handsomely painted by a notable artist. The exteriors were decorated with gilt and fine carvings. The interiors were lined with silk, and the bearers wore elegant uniforms.

The sedan chair was used to a more limited degree in the major cities of North America in colonial times. In 1770 Philadelphia was the largest city, yet its population was only twenty-eight thousand. Ben Franklin mentions riding in a sedan chair nineteen years later. Efforts to introduce this form of city transit in Boston were less successful. The Puritans found the very idea abhorrent. A remarkably elaborate chair, covered in costly silk and festooned with solid silver ornamentation, was offered to John Winthrop (1588–1649), the governor of the Massachusetts Bay Colony. It had been found on a Spanish galleon captured off the coast of Mexico. Its Yankee capturers thought the governor would be delighted to receive this glittering prize, but the frosty old Winthrop snorted that he had no need for such a frivolous thing.

The sedan chair was put on wheels sometime later in the eighteenth century by French carriage makers. How widely used such vehicles became is uncertain. The vehicle's body was considerably larger than the typical sedan chair, big enough possibly for two passengers. It rode on spoke wheels about 4 feet in diameter. A single man pulled it along using

1.6. A sedan chair, eighteenth century.

(Thomas A. Croal, ed., *A Book about Traveling: Past and Present*, 1877)

a pair of shafts attached to either side of the body. This vehicle was actually nearly identical to rickshaws once used in Asia and Africa except for its enclosed body. They were called *vinaigrettes* because of their resemblance to bottles of smelling salts once so popular in genteel households.

INTRODUCTION OF THE TAXI CAB

The ancient ancestor of the modern taxicab can also be traced back to water taxis on the River Nile in the time of the pharaohs. Similar services were offered on the Thames from London Tower and upriver to what is now London's West End in Shakespeare's time. Imperial Rome offered hackney service using a four-wheeled carriage invented by the Gauls called the *rheda*, or *redae* or *reda*. It sometimes had a cloth roof to fend off the sun or rain and was generally powered by a team of oxen (fig. 1.8). These sturdy beasts were slow but steady and were not so easily fatigued as horses nor as likely to run amok. Figure 1.8 is likely a more pristine example of a *rheda* while still in like-new condition. In about 1625, horse-drawn vehicles called hackney coaches appeared on London's streets that offered to carry city dwellers around town for a modest fee (fig. 1.9). These for-hire carriages were generally elderly, unkempt, and rather soiled. Some of these same vehicles had once been elegant showpieces belonging to a royal family. But now they were near the end of their service life. The drivers were of a similar unsavory nature. Worse yet, they tended

1.7. A British sedan chair with a lift-up roof, eighteenth century.

(Author's collection)

to be rude, drunken, and inclined to overcharge their patrons whenever possible. Because some hackmen drove in a fast and reckless fashion, they were called "Jehu" after the Tenth King of Israel, Jehu (d. 816 BC), who drove his chariot in a fury against the king of Judah. Even so, they offered ready transport when most people needed to – and could, if the occasion demanded it – fly across town like frightened rabbits.

The word *hackney* is said to have come from a medium-size riding horse with an ambling gait that was once popular in England. While too small for hunting or military use, the hackney proved suitable for pulling light vehicles. Other etymologists contend the term comes from the word *hack*, which meant any article for sale or hire. The driver of the first hacks rode on the back of the horse as postilions rather than on the vehicle. *Hackney* was often shortened to *hack* and came to mean any overworked horse. Indeed the word *hackneyed*, connoting an overworked phrase or saying, comes from the same source. It is also claimed that the name is derived from a borough situated about 3.5 miles northeast of the London Bridge, but most etymologists deny this theory.

1.8. A Roman *rheda* used for both private and taxi service.

(Ezra M. Stratton, *The World on Wheels*, 1878)

The growing popularity of the public coaches alarmed Charles I, who felt they were damaging the city roads and thus diverting public money that might be better spent maintaining his royal court in greater luxury. In 1635 Charles ordered that their number be limited to fifty and that the hackneys be licensed and regulated, not so much to protect the public as to discourage their use. London was growing so fast, however, that traffic congestion and an increasing number of people created a greater demand for improved urban transit. London was becoming the largest city in world – between 1600 and 1700 it grew from 200,000 to 675,000 residents – and the number of hackneys grew with the population. By 1662 there were 500 hackneys in the British capital. In 1694 the count was up to 700, and by 1771 there were 1,000 in service. The hackneys might be shabby in appearance, but they were a fast way to get around for those who could afford to pay. Fares varied over the years, from 3½ pence per mile to a zone fare system set up inside a 4-mile circle with Charing Cross at its center. Within the circle a flat fare of 1 shilling prevailed; outside the circle the rate was 1 shilling per mile or fraction of a mile beyond the first. Drivers were allowed to charge a small fee for luggage as well. The coaches were governed by laws going back to the time of Richard I's first year as king, 1189, when ferrymen, innkeepers, and flour mill operators became the subject of standards of service and price regulations. This became part of British common law that was copied in the American colonies of today's United States. The hacks faced increasing regulations in the Victorian era. In 1843 the London Hackney Act required drivers to wear badges and to refrain from using profane language,

1.9. An English hackney wagon of about 1650.

(Author's collection)

driving too fast, drinking on the job, and overcharging their passengers. Their vehicles were subject to annual vehicle inspections. The drivers were tested for driving skills and an expert knowledge of the city street system. They were required to display lighted lamps at dusk and during the dark of night. This law became the model for other cities around the world.

Yet nothing seemed to discourage the growth of the taxi fleet. By 1860 there were more than forty-three hundred hacks operating in London. Early in the next century, the number grew to over eleven thousand. The rustic old hackney coach had long since passed out of fashion by this time and had been replaced by specialized vehicles designed and built specifically for taxi service.

The first of this new breed appeared in London in 1823. It was a light, springy, two-wheel carriage called the *cabriolet* that had been popular in Paris since the early 1700s (figs. 1.10 and 1.11). It required only a single horse, which made it far more economic than the heavy hackney coaches, which needed two horses. The cabriolet could turn and maneuver easily in traffic, swinging around and dashing off in the opposite direction with ease. Its name came from a Latin root word for a young goat or kid that had a frisky, capering motion to it. The passenger seat was covered by a fold-down top that could be raised or lowered according to the weather. Waterproof curtains could be closed to protect the occupants on rainy days. The driver sat on the right side of the body, on an outrigger seat, with no protection from the elements. The harness of these lightweight taxis often had small bells attached that set up a jolly serenade as the cabriolet bounced along the streets. By mid-century four-wheel cabriolets were introduced. The name was quickly shortened to "cab" and so has come into modern usage.

In 1834 a Leicestershire architect named Joseph A. Hansom (1803–1882) patented a unique style of carriage for taxi service. It featured two very large wheels, a narrow boxlike body with two side-by-side seats and

TRANSPORTATION FOR HIRE   11

1.10. A British cabriolet of the 1820s.

(H. C. Moore, *Omnibuses and Cabs: Their Origin and History*, 1902)

a low front-door passenger entrance. The driver sat on a roof above the passengers. A test vehicle was driven around the streets of London. Hansom offered rights to his design for £10,000, but no buyer came forward until John Chapman, secretary of the Safety Cabriolet and Two-Wheel Carriage Company, secured right to the patent for a small fraction of Hansom's asking price. Chapman improved the design by moving the driver's seat behind the passenger compartment for better balance and devised a lever system to open and close butterfly doors on the front of this enclosure (figs. 1.12 and 1.13). The Hansom cab proved a success as modified and became the "gondola of London." Later in the nineteenth century it was popular in New York as well. *Munsey's* magazine claimed in June 1898 that the Hansom had captured New York. They were as thick on Fifth Avenue as in Piccadilly. The whole avenue was alive with them. For reasons not explained, the Hansom was the joy of the feminine heart.

Not long after the introduction of the Hansom, a prominent Scottish jurist, Henry P. Brougham (1778–1868), became interested in carriage design. How this very busy lord of the realm found time for such a trivial occupation is difficult to imagine, for he was a Member of Parliament, Lord Chancellor, and the founder of London University (fig. 1.14). Yet in 1838 Lord Brougham's contribution to the betterment of horse-drawn transport was unveiled (fig. 1.15). It was a light four-wheel vehicle with a drop floor, making entry and exit safe and easy. The driver sat out front on an open seat. The passenger compartment seated two comfortably.

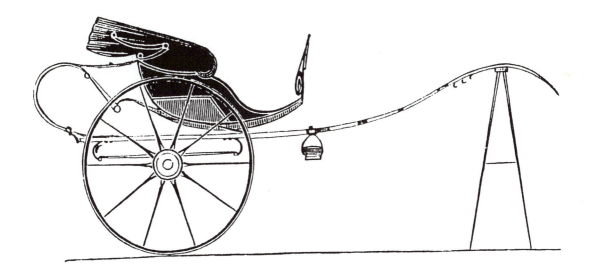

1.11. An American cabriolet of about 1830.

(Ezra M. Stratton, *The World on Wheels*, 1878)

A third passenger could ride right up front with the driver – this was a favored place for young boys. Brougham had intended it as a gentleman's carriage, yet it had features that recommended it for hack service. It was described as discreet, simple, practical, and dignified. It was the most popular closed carriage in Victorian England. Ease of access and a better ride because of the four wheels made it a strong competitor to the Hansom, and many a London cab was soon built to Lord Brougham's plan. It, too, traveled across the Atlantic to find favor in New York City among taxicab operators.

THE TAXICAB APPEARS IN THE NEW WORLD

It is likely that cab service originated in the United States in March 1840. By mid-April of that year, twenty-five such vehicles were operating in Manhattan. A watercolor rendering of one of these two-wheel conveyances was prepared by a contemporary Italian artist, Nicolino Calyo (1799–1884), who prepared a series of paintings based on New York street scenes. The cab was very similar to Hansom's design, except that the wheels were smaller and the entrance was made through a rear door. By 1866 there were approximately fifteen hundred cabs in this great city near the sea. *Leslie*'s magazine, in its issue of January 6, 1866, offered an appraisal of the local service and found much to critique. The light and handy cabs of the 1840s had been replaced by lumbering secondhand coaches that were slow and clumsy. They were manned by "one of the most insolent sets of men in the city." Two horses were needed, and the seating for four to six was wasteful. Most cab patrons traveled alone and hardly required such ponderous vehicles. Passengers were ready to pay for fast, courteous service, yet the New York system charged high for the rather sluggish travel. *Leslie*'s editor went on to note the contrast between taxi

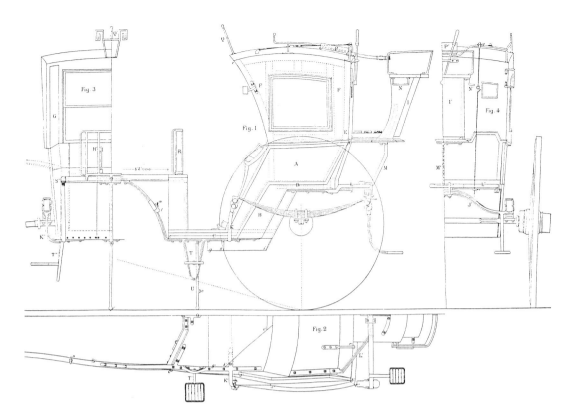

1.12. A Hansom cab of 1898.

(*The Hub*, August 1898)

operation in New York with those of its European counterparts. New York cabs charged 50 cents for short trips plus 25 cents for each additional passenger. London fares were fixed at 18 U.S. cents a mile or 72 cents per hour. Things were cheaper yet in Paris, where the 6-mile-circle zone fare was just 37 U.S. cents or 60 cents per hour. Both London and Paris had small and nimble vehicles that could thread their way quickly through the worst traffic. When would New York catch up with the great cities of Europe?

There was a gradual shift to Hansom cabs, but the old flat-rate fare of 50 cents remained in place until the early twentieth century. Some years earlier the 1871 *Scientific American* noted that Manhattan cabs were painted dark red and striped in broad vermillion lines and thin black lines. Some details on cab operations were given in *Outing Magazine* of November 1906. It noted that the two thousand taxis that roamed the city's pavement were sent out each day from forty-five stables. Some would ply the streets looking for customers. Others lined up at designated stands near railway or ferry terminals. Others yet waited outside hotels, prominent churches, or city hall. Hotels often required a commission or kickback to use stands outside their entrance. Police put up stanchions and rope lines to limit the number of cabs that might wait at any stand in the center city.

Some years earlier, some of the drivers founded an association called Liberty Dawn. It was a mutual benefit group that paid sick and death

1.13. A London Hansom 1895.

(Smithsonian Institution, Neg. 34, 417–E. Courtesy of the National Museum of American History, Smithsonian Institution)

benefits; the latter payment would guarantee the member a decent funeral. This association later joined the Teamsters International Union as Local 607. Before the union was formed a driver worked twenty-hour days and slept in a stable. After the union came about, his workday was fourteen hours and he could afford a small flat or accommodations in a rooming house. He generally earned $2 a day plus tips and drove a new carriage pulled by good horses.

A few words should also be offered on the patrons of these sometimes-not-so-genteel conveyances. Many passengers were rich or respectable, it is true. A fair percentage were businessmen hurrying to an appointment or a concerned parent needing to getting home quickly to a check on the children. But there was a strong belief that less savory members of our society were frequent users of these public carriers as well. Thieves, bootleggers, and gamblers seemed drawn to the taxicab. There was also the cheating husband who left his paramour in the privacy of a taxi rather than show his face on the streetcar. The bank thief might elude the police by hopping into a cab. Drunks too tipsy to navigate a short walk home would hail a cab. And then there was the prostitute, whose trade seemed to flourish even in the supposedly sanctimonious Victorian era. A Cincinnati newspaper of June 7, 1866, reported that a harlot "as gay and fashionable in dress and fair in face as she is deformed morally, flings herself into the hack and order[s] the nonchalant driver, who well knows her and all women of her class, to exhibit her on Fourth Street between Main and Elm, and then make for the Avenue." The morality of American society showed

TRANSPORTATION FOR HIRE   15

1.14. Portrait of Henry P. Brougham.

(*Harper's Weekly*, June 13, 1868)

no signs of improvement, but the size of the republic was definitely on the rise.

As the new century dawned, New York and Brooklyn were consolidated, making New York City the second largest city in the world, with a population of 3.4 million. The U.S. census for 1900 reported a total of 36,794 taxi drivers in the nation. Most American cities had cab service, supplementing street railways, which remained the preferred mode of urban transport. But this status quo would radically change over the succeeding decades as strange new vehicles became more and more popular.

THE HORSELESS AGE

The motorized taxi carries us into the twentieth century, and because the focus of this book is the Victorian era, our discussion on this modern

1.15. A Brougham of 1890.

(*The Hub*, October 1890)

period of for-hire vehicles will be brief. Efforts to develop a practical horseless carriage had been under way since the eighteenth century. Nicolas Cugnot's steam wagon of 1770 was among the first of a long line of experimental vehicles that led to the present-day automobile. Battery-powered electric carriages were first tried for taxi service in London and New York in 1897 (fig. 1.16). They were silent and odorless, but they were also slow and heavy. The clumsy wet-cell batteries weighed 800 pounds and required frequent recharging. A fairly sizable electric fleet was installed in New York, but gasoline motor cars proved faster and more reliable and soon replaced the Edison dream for an all-electric world. By 1903 Manhattan had three thousand petrol taxis in service, running a combined 5,000 miles a day. Several years later, London's gasoline-powered taxi fleet was nearing sixty-four hundred vehicles. The horse-drawn Hansoms and Broughams were soon made obsolete.

In Chicago, John D. Hertz (1879–1961) began to manufacture the famous Yellow Cab in 1905 (fig. 1.17). They would become familiar in most American cities. Harry N. Allen introduced a German invention, the taxi meter, in New York at about the same time. The Checker Cab Manufacturing Company began production in Kalamazoo, Michigan, in 1922. Its large, roomy sedan was designed specifically for taxi service. It became a favorite with the traveling public because it was so easy to get in and out of, compared to the typical American car. Drivers and operators liked them because of their durability. The last Checker was produced in 1983 and so ended, for many taxi patrons, the golden age of the American taxicab. Whatever the comfort level of modern motor cars might be, the taxi remains an active component in all major cities of the world today.

1.16. A New York electric taxi of 1897.

(Georges Dary, *A travers l'électricité*, 1903)

SUGGESTED READING

Armstrong, Anthony. *Taxi!* London: Hodder and Stoughton, 1930.
Belloc, Hilaire. *The Highway and Its Vehicles.* Ed. Geoffrey Holme. London: Studio Limited, 1926.
Berkebile, Donald H. *American Carriages, Sleighs, Sulkies, and Carts: 168 Illustrations from Victorian Sources.* New York: Dover Publications, 1977.
———. *Carriage Terminology: An Historical Dictionary.* Washington, D.C.: Smithsonian Institution Press, 1978.
———. *Horse Drawn Commercial Vehicles: 255 Illustrations of Nineteenth-Century Stage Coaches, Delivery Wagons, Fire Engines, etc.* New York: Dover Publications, 1989.
Casson, Lionel. *Travel in the Ancient World.* London: Allen and Unwin, 1974.
Croal, Thomas A., ed. *A Book about Traveling, Past and Present.* London: William P. Nimmo, 1877.
Dollfus, Charles, et al. *Histoire de la Locomotion Terrestre.* 2 vols. Paris: Société nationale des enterprises de presse: Editions Saint Georges, 1935.
Geogano, G. N. *A History of the London Taxicab.* New York: Drake Publications, 1973.
Gilbert, Gorman, and Robert E. Samuels.

1.17. Advertisement for a Yellow Cab, model "O," 1921.

(Lad G. Ahren collection)

The Taxicab: An Urban Transportation Survivor. Chapel Hill: University of North Carolina Press, 1982.

Green, Susan, ed. *Horse Drawn Sleighs.* 2nd ed. Mendham, N.J.: Astragal Press, 2003.

Hazard, Robert. *Hacking New York.* New York: C. Scribner's Son, 1930.

King, Edmund F. *Ten Thousand Wonderful Things.* 1859. London: G. Routledge and Sons, 1860.

Kirkman, Marshall M. *Classical Portfolio of Primitive Carriers.* Chicago: World Railway Publishing, 1895.

Kouwenhoven, John A. *The Columbia Historical Portrait of New York.* Garden City, N.J.: Doubleday, 1953.

Lay, Maxwell G. *Ways of the World: A History of the World's Roads and of the Vehicles That Used Them.* New Brunswick, N.J.: Rutgers University Press, 1992.

Maresca, James. *My Flag Is Down: Diary of a New York Taxi Driver.* New York: E. P. Dutton, 1948.

Mooney, William W. *Travel among the Ancient Romans.* Boston: R. D. Badger, 1920.

Moore, H. C. *Omnibuses and Cabs: Their Origin and History.* London: Chapman and Hall, 1902.

Papayanis, Nicholas. *Horse Drawn Cabs and Omnibuses in Paris: The Idea of Circulation and the Business of Public Transit.* Baton Rouge: Louisiana State University Press, 1996.

Scrimger, D. L. *Taxicab Scrapbook: A Pictorial Review of the Taxi.* Charles City, Ia.: Scrimger, 1979.

Stratton, Ezra M. *The World on Wheels.* New York: B. Blom, 1878.

Vidich, Charles. *The New York Cab Driver and His Fare.* Cambridge, Mass.: Schenkman, 1976.

Wakefield, Ernest H. *History of the Electric Automobile.* Warrendale, Penn.: Society of Automotive Engineers, 1994.

Down That Long & Dusty Road № 2

Stagecoach Travel in America

A FEW RIDERS SPOKE WITH ENTHUSIASM ABOUT STAGECOACH travel. Dr. Samuel Johnson, the English lexicographer, said his greatest pleasure was to travel on a mail coach accompanied by a pretty woman. Mark Twain found freshness, a breeziness, in stage travel that liberated one from daily cares and responsibilities. The stage was not just a great swinging, swaying vehicle but also an imposing cradle on wheels. From the abundant travel literature available on the subject, however, it would appear that these two literary giants were very much in the minority. The nearly universal opinion about stagecoach travel was negative. It was in just about all ways the most uncomfortable and disagreeable method of human locomotion ever devised, short of the slave ship. Contemporary accounts emphasize the jolting ride, the lack of interior space, the hazards of rolling over, and the need to get out and walk or help push when a steep grade was encountered. There were numerous other complaints. Some of the grumbling might be discounted as the normal human penchant to complain about everything, but there appears to be good reason for unhappiness in stage travel. Stagecoaches were referred to as "mud clippers"; some were never cleaned and remained earth-colored for their entire working lives. A guidebook of 1851 said they were a most "incommodious means of conveyance." A traveler claimed that his body was a perfect jelly after a trip in a Pennsylvania coach. At the end he was too tired to stand and too sore to sit. It was generally a rather miserable way to get from here to there. Why, even Mark Twain was less than enthralled with this mode of travel when he reached the end of his western stage trip in 1861. Travelers used the stage despite its drawbacks, because it was often the only way to go – there was no alternative. In 1830 if you wanted to go by public conveyance – for example, from Cincinnati to Xenia, Ohio – there was no other choice.

Before exploring road coach history we should explain a fundamental characteristic of its operation. The term *stage* must be examined, for it explains the basis of how road coaches were run. One did not simply hook up a team and dash across the country. Horses were not capable of running long distances with a heavy vehicle. After about 10 miles they were winded and tired. They needed rest, water, and feed before they were ready for another run – and we are not speaking of high-speed racing; just a trot was about all any driver could expect from a team. Starting and stopping at regular 10-mile intervals would allow the coach and its passengers to get nowhere, so the system of taking on a new team at these periodical stops was devised. Passengers stayed inside the coach and the driver remained on his seat box while hostlers detached the used team and then quickly attached a fresh team. Off the coach would go after only a few minutes delay. About every 50 miles or so the coach would stop for a longer interval so that the passengers might refresh themselves at a tavern (fig. 2.1). It was also time to switch drivers after nearly ten hours on the road. Highway travel was a series of short hops, or stages. A little progress was made at a time. A long journey such as Boston to Savannah would involve more than one hundred changes of horses and so was made in many stages.

Stagecoach service began in what is now the eastern United States early in the eighteenth century. The colonial population remained small – about 434,000 in 1715 – and even the largest cities were hardly more than towns. Yet there was sufficient settlement to generate at least a modest demand for public transit. A line running from Burlington to Perth Amboy, New Jersey, in 1706 appears to have been the first in North America. About a decade later Boston and Newport, Rhode Island, were connected by stage service. In the 1730s Philadelphia and New York were connected by stages. Actually that route began as an awkward water-highway operation. Passengers boarded a small sailing ship in New York and proceeded to Perth Amboy, where they took a stage to Bordentown, New Jersey, and were once again required to transfer to a sailing vessel that navigated the Delaware River to Philadelphia. This patchwork system required three to five days and was dependent on favorable wind and weather. In 1771 a faster overland stage began running between these major centers that was considered so revolutionary it was named the Flying Machine, with perhaps just a little exaggeration considering its schedule of thirty-six hours. Coaches ran three days a week in the summer but only twice weekly in winter. Such limited operations were typical of most early stage lines. Passengers became accustomed to layovers at transfer stations, which added to the cost, time, and frustration of traveling. About the first daily service offered in colonial America was the Boston-to-Salem line in 1770, yet it was understood that "daily" service actually meant six days a week, as the Sabbath could not be violated. Daily runs were normally made only on the more heavily traveled routes throughout the stagecoach era. Some lines advertised that more coaches would be put on if the traffic demanded it, while others cautioned they would run only when the weather

2.1. The Boston stage arrives in Concord, New Hampshire, winter 1810. Hostlers unhitch the horses as the passengers alight to enter the tavern.

(Author's collection)

was favorable. Experienced passengers were prepared to accept the vicissitudes of coach operations.

In 1823 ticketing was consolidated by the Stevens family of Hoboken, who were pioneers in steamboat transport. It was now possible to travel with a single ticket by steam from the sixth ferry in New York City and land at Perth Amboy. It was then by stagecoach to Bordentown and a Delaware River boat to Philadelphia. Baggage was checked through at each transfer, so travelers could go from Wall Street to Market Street with ease. By the 1820s about two thousand passengers traveled this route each week.

The water/road route continued until the 1830s when the Camden and Amboy Railroad took over the road section of the trip and deposited passengers in Camden, directly across the river from Philadelphia. Travelers between Philadelphia and Baltimore followed a similar route via Newcastle, Delaware, then overland to the Chesapeake Bay and by water to Baltimore. A boat was taken from Philadelphia down the Delaware River to Newcastle.

2.2. "Newark stage for New York," about 1800. Powles Hook became Exchange Place, the Pennsylvania Railroad's Jersey City Station.

(E. T. Francis collection)

After the American Revolution, stagecoach operations continued to grow. By 1784 service was available between Boston and Richmond, Virginia. Within five years a postal route ran all the way along the eastern seaboard from Maine to Georgia. The establishment of postal routes did much to stimulate stagecoach operations, although much mail continued to go via agents on horseback. Even so, by 1802 one could go 1,200 miles by stage from Boston to Savannah in twenty-two and a half days at a cost of $70. This works out to about 53 miles a day, which is not terribly fast, nor was the ride very comfortable, but it was a considered a remarkable achievement at the time.

As the young republic grew stronger, eastern stage operations became denser and more competitive. Lines that began with weekly service went biweekly, then triweekly, then daily. Popular routes were serviced by several lines so that patrons might pick and choose between the Swiftsure, the National, the Good Intent, or the June Bug line. In 1810, Philadelphia, by then a sizable metropolis of around one hundred thousand, could boast of thirty-eight stagecoach lines. In 1829 just the lines between Philadelphia and New York were carrying two thousand passengers a week.

Even the old Boston Post Road was so improved that it no longer took thirteen days to go from Boston to New York. The coaches ran the 250-mile route via Worcester, Massachusetts, and Hartford and Stamford, Connecticut, in just three days in 1806. The Eastern Stage Company operated 77 lines out of Boston in 1829 and sent out 1,600 coaches a week. Three years later they had 106 lines in operation. It should also be understood

Cincinnati and Dayton
MAIL STAGE.

THIS STAGE will run once a week, between Cincinnati and Dayton, as follows:

Leave Cincinnati every Monday at 4 A. M:— arrive at Hamilton same day by 6 P. M. Leave Hamilton every Tuesday at 4 A. M: arrive at Dayton same day by 6 P. M. Leave Dayton every Friday at 4 A. M.: arrive at Hamilton same day by 6 P. M. Leave Hamilton every Saturday at 4 A. M.: arrive at Cincinnati same day by 6 P. M.

STAGE OFFICES.

Cincinnati, *Hezekiah Fox.* Hamilton, *Thomas Blair.* Dayton, *Timothy Squires.*

As this line will generally be managed by the owners, they assure the public, that every possible attention shall be given to render passengers comfortable and easy.

HENDERSON & SQUIRES.

April 12, 1825.   37tf

2.3. Advertisement for the Cincinnati and Dayton Mail Stage.

(*Liberty Hall Newspaper,* April 12, 1825)

that coach service served not just as a go-between for major eastern cities but that operations extended to some smaller towns as well. Resorts were favored destinations. In 1767 vacationers seeking the spa at Stafford Springs, Connecticut, could take a coach from Boston. Just seven years later biweekly stages carried New Yorkers from Jersey City to that natural wonder, the Passaic Falls at Paterson, New Jersey. As an added accommodation, passengers need not assemble at the hotel or tavern but would be picked up at their home if they so desired. Over the following generations hundreds of resort hotels opened in all areas of the United States. Just about everyone was served by the stagecoach, even into the railroad era, because railroad tracks only rarely came within walking distance of the hotel. In some cases the stages were owned and operated by the hotel itself.

Stagecoach operations, as we have seen, began in the northeastern colonies and gradually spread to the west and south. Operations tended to concentrate in the built-up and populous areas, because this is where the greatest traffic and revenues could be found. Hence, southern New England and the Middle Atlantic states had the greatest density of stagecoach operations. As the population of the Midwestern states grew dramatically after about 1820, so, too, did the stage operations.

Travelers going west faced a greater challenge. A pair of young travelers set out for Pittsburgh in 1802 only to find that stage service ended in Shippensburg, Pennsylvania, 170 miles short of their destination. This part of the trip took three days. They faced the alternatives of either buying horses or going ahead on foot. Horses would fetch only half their value in Pittsburgh, so the pair elected to buy one horse. They took turns walking or riding and made Pittsburgh in just nine days. It was only two years before regular stage service began between Pittsburgh and the East. By 1806 a stage line opened between Lexington, Kentucky, and Pittsburgh. Very soon Cincinnati, Dayton, and Columbus, Ohio, were linked into an expanding stagecoach system (fig. 2.3).

William Neil, a Columbus banker, became interested in stagecoaches in 1822. He skillfully expanded the local system to offer service as far north as Michigan. By 1831 more than seventy coaches a week entered Columbus. The line from Wheeling, West Virginia, to Columbus offered twenty-four-hour service. The 535-mile trip from Wheeling to St. Louis, Missouri, required five days and eighteen hours, including stops. The fare was $25.00. Neil's drivers were described as men of good sense, hard, steady, and taciturn, but always gallant to the ladies. By 1843 Neil's Ohio Stage Company operated 1,500 route miles. Express coaches ran from Baltimore to Columbus in sixty hours. This included six half-hour stops and one one-hour stop in Wheeling. The mail coach made the same run in just forty-four and a half hours. The time saving was made up by eliminating the rest stops and by driving the teams at a faster pace. William Neil's reign as the Ohio stagecoach king was hardly trouble free. Robberies were frequent and most involved the U.S. mail. In 1850 it was discovered that one of the company's own agents was a confederate of the robbers. Three years later the affairs of the Ohio Stage Company were wound up; the railroads of the area had rendered the road coaches obsolete. As an astute businessman, however, Neil had already invested in this new form of overland transportation.

As late as 1817 one of Indiana's pioneers lamented on the primitive conditions of his state. He claimed, not with complete accuracy, that

NEIL, MOORE & CO.'S STAGES,

LEAVE DAILY FOR

Columbus, Zanesville & Wheeling,

At 8 1-2 and 10 1-2 A. M.

ALSO,

For Dayton and Piqua,

At 2 P. M.

Through to Dayton in 7 hours. Fare to Dayton, Two Dollars.

P. CAMPBELL, Ag't.

Office in Cincinnati,
On Front Street,
Two doors below Cincinnati Hotel.

2.4. Neil, Moore, and Co. stage line advertisement from a J. F. Kimball and Company business directory, 1846.

(Miami University Libraries, Special Collections)

Indiana possessed not a single bridge, turnpike, or carriage. All travel was by foot or on horseback. Families rode as a group on a single horse. The father sat up front on the saddle with one to three youngsters in his arms; the wife rode just behind him holding the smallest child on her lap. This picture of pioneer travel was perhaps a decade or more out of date, for the stage lines were already pushing across Indiana's borders by this time. Service between Vincennes, Indiana, and Louisville, Kentucky, began in May 1820. A few months later stages rushed westward to St. Louis. By 1837 stagecoach service had spread to Iowa. The western United States grew greatly after Mexico ceded half of its land to Uncle Sam in 1848; previously it had been largely untouched by stagecoach lines. All of that changed very quickly after the discovery of gold in California. Suddenly there was a clamoring for overland transport.

The earliest line in California opened between San Francisco and San Jose in 1849 just as the gold rush got under way. The pioneer western lines were often run by experienced stagecoach operators from the East such as James E. Birch and John Butterfield. Birch ran stages out of Sacramento directly to the gold fields and charged whatever the traffic would bear, which in this case was twenty times the going rate back East. Birch soon managed to consolidate stage operations in California, but his fortune-making career was cut short by an untimely death at sea in 1857. This was at the very time that long-distance stage travel was about to begin in the western territories. Getting to California by sea was too slow and far too indirect. The trip via Cape Horn was 13,000 miles long and required about 140 days to complete. The water route via Panama was shorter and faster, but it involved crossing the isthmus, which was home to a dreadful jungle and the ever-present danger of tropical diseases. And travelers could be stuck in Panama City for up to two weeks awaiting passage to San Francisco. Why not just head overland and make the journey entirely on U.S. soil?

An overland route faced many difficulties. It would be very long – 2,800 miles – making it surely the longest stagecoach route ever attempted. It would go through unsettled territory, some of which was supposedly set aside permanently as Indian land. There were no roads, bridges, ferries, and no settlements, wells, nor really much of anything that would sustain a stage line. At the same time, building a road, albeit a primitive road, would be comparatively easy, because there was no forest in the way. Since much of the land was arid, rivers and streams were not the major barriers they were in the eastern half of the nation. But of greater consequence is the fact that there was a real determination to have a transcontinental stage line. The spirit of manifest destiny willed that it be done and be done quickly.

A line between San Antonio and San Diego, popularly called the Jackass Mail, opened in July 1857. Passengers were obliged to leave the coach and go by mule back across the desert portion of the journey. The Jackass Mail proved too slow, requiring up to sixty days, or double the time required by the Panama route. A federal subsidy was needed to encourage the development of a faster overland route. A $600,000-a-year mail contract was more than veteran stagecoach owner John Butterfield (1801–1869) could resist. Because the postmaster general was a southerner, a southern route to California was specified. Butterfield organized the Overland Stage Company in 1857. The first coach from California arrived in St. Louis on September 16, 1858. Ironically, the offices of the company were on the south end of Broadway in New York City. The stage route began in Tipton, Missouri, and swung south through Fort Smith, Arkansas, across Texas to El Paso, then west to Tucson and Los Angeles, and then north to the final terminal in San Francisco.

The Ox Bow Route, as it was popularly called, represented an investment of nearly $1 million. Roads were built or rebuilt. Wells were drilled to supply water for men and animals. One hundred thirty-seven stations were constructed to shelter hostlers, agents, and horse feed. One thousand

2.5. Stagecoach crossing the Rocky Mountains at Guy's Gulch in a snowstorm.

(*Harper's Weekly*, Feb. 8, 1868)

horses and 500 mules plus 250 stagecoaches were purchased. Butterfield hired 800 men to operate the line. On September 16, 1858, the route began with biweekly service. At first twenty-five days were required, but by 1860 the time was down to twenty-one days and fifteen hours. On average the coaches covered 120 miles a day (running twenty-four hours per day) at an average speed of about 5 mph. Passengers were expected to ride through the few layovers. A newspaper account from February 1866 said the Overland Company operated the longest stage route in the world. At this time the company employed 825 men; 356 coaches and express wagons; and 8,530 horses and mules. The stage fare from Atchison, Kansas, to Placerville, California, was $200, while the railroad fare to Atchison was only $41. Stagecoach stations were about 13 miles apart and offered meals for 60 cents. Telegraph offices were open all along the line. The Overland Company also operated a northern line via Boise City, Idaho, to Dalles Falls on the Columbia River in Oregon; steamer then carried passengers

DOWN THAT LONG & DUSTY ROAD   29

to the Pacific Ocean. In 1865 the company carried 4,288 passengers over its Atchison line. The coaches carried $2.4 million in specie and 46,000 pounds of express.

Western stage lines faced the wrath of winter on the more northerly routes such as the Sweetwater stage line that ran from Green River to Fort Washakie in the Wyoming Territory. In January 1862 a storm overtook a coach near Pacific Springs. The passengers and driver abandoned the vehicle after cutting the horses free. Those on board began walking back toward the last station. A few days later the driver was found frozen to death standing upright in the snow. The superintendent of the line, Thomas Scott, was also standing upright, alive but immobile. He lost his hands and feet to frostbite. The single passenger was lost and presumed dead. Travelers were well advised not to travel by stage lines during the winter (fig. 2.5).

Western travel could be boring, for the roads out west seemed to go from no place, through nothing to nowhere. The stations were not set up for overnight passengers, but some who simply could not take another day in a coach, or travelers who became ill, were put up on a provisional basis. Most stops were limited to changing animals; only a few stops were scheduled for food or other more personal matters. Those who booked travel on the Butterfield Overland Mail were expected to ride straight through. It was rough on the passengers, the animals, the coaches, and the drivers. The comfort level was well below zero, but for all of its drawbacks, the Butterfield operation was very effective. At its slowest, the overland stage was ten days faster than the Panama route. By 1860 Butterfield was moving more mail than the ocean routes. The stagecoach seemed ready to triumph. But in the spring of 1861 the Civil War broke out, and the U.S. mails and Butterfield's coaches were no longer welcome in Confederate territory. After a few months the southern route was abandoned. The stagecoach mail route shifted to the north and ran over the so-called Central Route that ran from Independence, Missouri, to Pacerville, California, via Salt Lake City.

The California Stage Company monopolized road travel in its home state and in Nevada and Oregon. It was established in early 1854 by James E. Birch. Headquarters was in Marysville, California, a small town north of Sacramento. An article appearing in the *Sacramento Union* early in February 1865 offered some details on the operation of this firm. Service to Virginia City, Nevada, was carried by the Pioneer line. The running time in the summer was about eighteen hours, but in the winter it took around thirty-two hours and could vary greatly depending on the weather. A second line to Virginia City went via the Central Pacific Railroad as far as Newcastle Gap, California, then by stages to Virginia City. Travel time was equal to that of the Pioneer line. A much longer line connected Sacramento to Portland, Oregon, a distance of 710 miles. The California Central Railroad took travelers as far as Lincoln in Placer County, California. The trip continued by stage to Marysville. It was then back on to a train; the Northern Railroad carried passengers to Oroville, then by coach to Chico, Red Bluff, Shasta, Yreka, and Roseburg in California and Eugene, Salem, and Portland in Oregon. The time was six days and five hours with sixty station stops; the mail coach, by contrast, took seven days. Several independent stage lines operated out of Sacramento at this time with service to Sonoma, Jackson, Georgetown, Ophir, and Stockton, California.

In 1862 Ben Holladay (1819–1887), a native of Kentucky and a man experienced in every frontier occupation from Indian trading to cattle driving, entered the stagecoach business. Holladay, a powerfully aggressive sort of man, came to dominate the western stagecoach operations. He was running stages and freight wagons over 3,100 route miles with 15,000 employees; 20,000 vehicles; and 150,000 draft animals. Holladay's eastern terminal was Omaha. Some idea of his operation can be gleaned from a pamphlet about transport in Nebraska. The fare from Omaha to Denver was $175 and the time was seventy-two hours. Once the railroad opened between the two cities a decade later, the fare was reduced to $25 and the time to one day. The fare to Salt Lake City was $300 and the time was six days. To San Francisco the fare was $500 and the time sixteen to eighteen days. Prices in the far West were very inflated – a meal cost $60 in San Francisco, or sixty times what it would cost back East. If passenger service seemed slow, sending goods was slower yet. Omaha to Denver required forty-five to sixty days by oxen, and the wagon would be en route to Salt Lake for six months. The size of business was no guarantee of profits, and within a few years Holladay – aka the King of Hurry, or the Napoleon of the Plains – was financially overextended. In late 1866 he sold out to Wells, Fargo, and Co., a major express business that had formerly been one of Holladay's best customers. The monopoly of the western stage business proved a poor investment, for in May 1869 the First Transcontinental Railroad opened and most of the through-passenger business deserted the dusty stages for the comparatively clean and fleet trains. Stagecoaches remained important to long-distance and local travel in the West and elsewhere long after the coming of the railroad, because many communities remained far from the tracks, especially before 1890.

ROADS AND THE RIGORS OF TRAVEL

Roads were uniformly bad in early America. That is no exaggeration; it is a fact and one that is repeatedly noted in just about every travel account of the time. With all the bumping, jolting, and rocking, travel was intolerable. There was an old saying about roads of the time: "Be sure to choose your rut carefully. You will be in it for a very long time." The stagecoach was described as a torture chamber and the most uncomfortable vehicle ever devised by man. Yet the vehicle itself rode quite well on good surfaces. Its big wheels and leather thoroughbrace springs offered a pleasant enough ride over any decent roadway, such as the ordinary crushed-stone secondary roads still found today in some rural areas. I base this opinion on my personal experience after riding in several stagecoaches across open fields or on country lanes. The narrow, unpaved county roads that today we regard as so primitive and tedious would have been seen as a marvelous highway by our ancestors. They were accustomed to little more than a pathway hacked through the forest. The tree stumps were not even removed and were cut down just low enough for the coach axles to pass over them. One had to shift and turn to avoid the stumps while driving along lest the vehicle be overturned or a wheel broken. The route was not selected by a transit or level but instead followed a natural path established millennia ago by rabbits, deer, or buffalo. Indians came to follow these animal traces, as did the white settlers, until they became established roads. Many existing roads still follow these ancient pathways.

Such avenues of travel would hardly be recognized as roads by a contemporary observer. We might see them as a crude lane cut through the forest by loggers seeking a temporary way to remove logs. The lane curved this way and that to avoid a large tree or clump of rocks. There were no cuts or fills to level the route; it merely followed the natural rise and fall of the land. Nor was there any pavement, not even a bushel of gravel. The bare earth surface turned into dust when it was dry and into a soupy quagmire when it was wet. Spring rains could turn an earth road into a sea of mud; leaving vehicles to sink into as much as 2 feet of muck. Mild winters were an impediment to travel because of the mud. Earthen roads were more passable when they were frozen. The measure of a middling-good road was said to be one where the mud did not quite get over the tops of your boots. Traffic and nature combined to create troublesome ruts and low spots. Roots and fallen branches added to the bumpiness of the ride, but a fallen tree put a stop to any stage's journey until or unless the passengers aided the driver in removing the obstacle.

Considering the unrefined nature of our pioneer highways, the quality of the ride was very deficient. Passengers spoke of being tossed around inside the coach like ivories in a dice box. One rider said the ride was so rough it came near to shaking out his liver. Indeed one stage line on the old National Road unapologetically called itself the Shake Gut Line. The jostling and lurching made many a traveler "seasick," even though they were far away from the ocean. The largest bumps threw some passengers against the roof. The damage might be no more than a crusted hat or bonnet, yet John Marshall was not so lucky while on a Richmond-bound stagecoach in 1835. The elderly chief justice suffered a serious bruise after bouncing against the ceiling. The contusion hardly helped a man approaching his eightieth year and already in poor health. Marshall died that July. Younger, more athletic passengers were tempted to ride up on the roof to escape the cramped interior and have a better view of the passing scene. Such adventurers were well advised to grab a good hold, for the lurching of the coach could unexpectedly send them over the side. Injuries depended on how and where the projectile landed. It is no wonder that one passenger lamented that his transfer from a steamer to a stagecoach was like the descent from paradise into hell. Yet another victim of stage travel, Irish poet Thomas Moore (1778–1852), describes his experience in these words:

> Dear George, though every bone is aching
> > after the shaking
> I've had this week, over ruts and ridges
> > and bridges
> Made of a few uneasy planks,
> > in open ranks
> Over rivers of mud whose names alone;
> Would make the knees of the stoutest man knock.

Why were the roads so bad? Was it a matter of ignorance, perversity, or indifference? Surely these factors played a part in the bad roads of early America, but it would appear that the chief explanation was economics. The country's population was small – in 1700 only three hundred thousand – hence the tax base was very limited. In addition there seemed little reason to build elaborate highways when traffic was so light. Only when the land was more densely settled and when larger cities developed could better roads be justified. Yet they were slow in coming, largely because the colonists wanted to talk about good roads but did not want to pay for them. Following British law, roads were managed by local parishes, which might levy taxes for the purpose and require local citizens to work so many days on road construction and repairs. Because neither method was popular, the parishes tended to ignore roadwork. In some cases townships took over this duty, but most proved no more effective than the parish system. Most locals apparently thought if the road allowed passage to the nearest settlement, that was good enough. The colonists were discouraged from taking up any ambitious road-building schemes because of the dense forest that blanketed the eastern half of North America. We are not speaking of just a few big trees here and there; it was a solid wall of trees standing side by side, mile after mile. To cut a pathway before the time of chainsaws and other power machinery, the work had to be done by hand, and it was hard, heavy, and slow work. Because road building was so labor intensive, it was also expensive. So it is no surprise that few parishes were eager to get into the road-building business.

After the Revolution it was hoped the new government might take on what had been left undone as far as transportation in the colonial era. Surely the population had grown remarkably – by 1800 there were 5.3 million – and with that came larger cities and greater demand for transit. Yet federal involvement was more a matter of grandiose plans derailed by political bickering. Albert Gallatin, the secretary of the treasury during the Jefferson and Madison administrations, was an ardent supporter of internal improvements and wrote a brilliant plan for improving U.S. transportation. His comprehensive plan included coastal canals, an intracoastal waterway, the Erie and James River canals, and a system of roads and bridges. The scheme would be financed by the sale of public land. John C. Calhoun was a supporter, yet there were equally powerful politicians who opposed any federal involvement in Gallatin's plan. Even so, most of the projects Gallatin proposed were eventually completed. After years of talk, the Cumberland or National Road, America's first federal highway, was finally opened between Baltimore and Wheeling in 1817. It was a well-made highway with a crushed-stone base topped off with gravel. The National Road was slowly pushed westward and around 1852 stopped just short of St. Louis in another instance of too little, too late.

Several states took up the good roads crusade. By 1821 New York could boast 4,000 miles of decent roads while Pennsylvania claimed 1,800. By 1802 a coastal highway was finished between Boston and Savannah. A connecting system of independent stage lines carried passengers over the 1,200-mile route in twenty-two and a half days for a cost of $70. Virginia showed the greatest enthusiasm for producing a comprehensive statewide road system by creating a Board of Public Works in 1817. It created a miniature version of Gallatin's plan and agreed to pay up to 40 percent of the capital for approved projects. The state would share the cost of bridges with county governments. In fact, Virginia had been a pioneer in road improvements long before establishing its public works board. In 1785 the state enacted a turnpike law based on the British system established during the reign of Charles II. The Little River Turnpike was the first fruit of the new law. It was built between Alexandria and Bluemont, Virginia, where it crossed over Snicker's Gap and went north and west, ending at Aldie, Virginia, in 1802. It is now part of U.S. Interstate 50. Virginia was fortunate to employ a skillful French engineer, Claude Crozet, to manage its public works. Crozet was a graduate of the Polytechnique School of Science in Paris. He served Napoleon in Germany and Holland and then immigrated to the United States in 1816 and was a professor of engineering at West Point. After surveying the James River and the Kanawha Canal, he

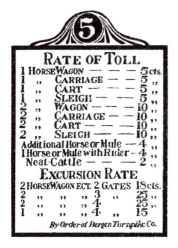

oversaw the creation of a fine road system in Virginia starting in 1837 and later built the longest railroad tunnel at Blue Ridge between 1849 and 1858.

Because the public purse seemed largely closed to the cause of good roads, private enterprise stepped in with the toll road. The era of the turnpike moved ahead in 1794 when the Philadelphia-to-Lancaster road opened. All were welcome to use the hard-surface road – pedestrians, equestrians, freight wagons, carriages, and stagecoaches. Each paid a fee every 5 to 10 miles at a tollhouse. A horse and rider might pay only 4 cents while a private coach would pay 25 cents. Stagecoaches, as regular customers, usually worked on a reduced toll, payable quarterly. The idea of the turnpike was appealing, because good roads would be provided at no cost to the taxpayer – the user, in effect, paid the freight (figs. 2.6a and 2.6b).

Charters for turnpike companies were freely granted. By 1820 about 40,000 miles of toll roads were in service. Stagecoach speeds almost doubled on the better-built roads. Coaches rumbled along at 8 mph; the ride was vastly improved and the certainty of travel was much enhanced. Yet not all turnpikes enjoyed the traffic of the Lancaster road, so rather few made money. Construction costs, including bridges, tollhouses, and the road itself came out to around $7,000 a mile. This fairly high capital cost, plus regular maintenance, meant that a substantial procession of travelers and wagons had to pass over its gravelly surface in order to pay for it. Alas, the required traffic never developed. Turnpikes came to be seen as a poor investment, and once this reputation was established, fewer citizens were ready to invest in them. The turnpike solution proved to be only a half solution to the nation's transport needs, and bad roads remained a fact of life well into the nineteenth century.

In 1842 Charles Dickens wrote about the inferior roads he encountered in northern Ohio. The day before, he had traveled over a fine macadam road, probably a toll road, but now he was being thrown about on

2.6. *Above left,* Toll rate board from Bergen (New Jersey) turnpike, ca. 1820. *Above right,* Toll gate on the National or Cumberland Road in West Virginia, 1888.

(Above left, E. T. Francis collection. Above right, J. G. Pangborn, *Picturesque B. and O.: Historical and Descriptive,* 1882)

DOWN THAT LONG & DUSTY ROAD 35

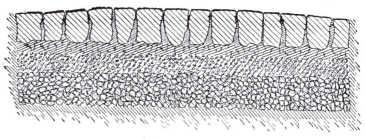
Ancient Roman Road.

Early Eighteenth Century Road.

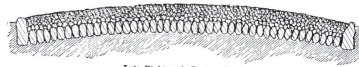
Late Eighteenth Century Road.

Modern Macadam Road.

2.7. *Above,* John L. Macadam perfected a cheap but durable road surface made from crushed stone in about 1820. *Right,* The four road surfaces here represent hard surfaces from classical times to the early twentieth century.

(Harwood Frost, *The Art of Road Making*, 1910)

an extremely rough corduroy road. On the last stretch of the journey to Sandusky, the path was so narrow that tree branches rattled and scraped along both sides of the coach. Even a decade later, Frederick Olmsted, then a *New York Times* correspondent, found road conditions just as bad, if not worse, in North Carolina. The road there was so poor that the trees slowed the coach to a hesitant walk, and the driver drove the coach alongside of it whenever possible. At one point the coach rolled over – no one was hurt, but the passengers were required to help set the vehicle upright. The westbound stage on the same route upset while crossing the Eno River. All of the passengers survived, but the baggage and mail were lost in the swift-flowing muddy water. Stagecoach travel, even in the eastern states, remained a pretty miserable experience in the 1850s.

The great hope for good roads in the western world was a Scot named John Loudon Macadam, who was born in Ayr, Scotland, in 1756 (fig. 2.7). His father died when he was fourteen, and he was sent to live with a merchant uncle in New York. The uncle was a conscientious guardian; he trained his ward in the mercantile trade and introduced him to better families of New York society. Macadam married into the richest family on Long Island. His future in colonial America seemed assured; however, the outbreak of war, when he was just twenty, threatened that golden future. Yet as a loyal subject of George III, he was made prize master of captured American ships. He fled to England when the British surrendered to the American patriots in 1783 and returned home a wealthy young man. He was able to live the life of a gentleman but took up road building as a hobby. After many years of study he devised an inexpensive method for creating compacted crushed-stone road surfaces (fig. 2.7). The material could be laid over subsoil without a stone foundation and was watertight. The Macadam road was extensively used in Europe and America and should not be confused with modern-day tarmac. Macadam died in Scotland in 1836 at the age of eighty.

FERRIES

The crossing of streams showed some improvement during the early years of the republic. Even so, Thomas Jefferson noted in 1801 while traversing the 120 miles separating his home from the capital that he crossed no fewer than eight rivers. Five of these had no bridges and no ferries. One might spend hours searching up and down small streams and shallow rivers for a safe place to ford. Bigger streams required a ferry boat or a bridge, with the latter being the cheaper alternative. Some ferries were nothing more than a rowboat large enough for a few passengers and their luggage. Several trips might be required to transfer a coach load of passengers and their belongings. A second coach would be boarded on the far side. Larger ferries could take the whole coach, of course, thus saving considerable transit time and the everlasting annoyance of getting off and back on. Some ferry operations became rather sophisticated. In 1825 an enterprising ferry master offered two boats – one for heavy wagons and a smaller, cheaper sister vessel for light carriages. Both were operated across the Wabash River at Vincennes, Indiana, by "experienced and trusty hands."

At about the same time, team or treadmill ferry boats were being operated back East. Horses – usually eight in number – powered the treadmill. The team boat at Burlington, New Jersey, promised to run every half hour across the Delaware River, whether full or empty. Passengers were advised that the crossing time was eight minutes with the tide, but fifteen against it. The boat ran only during daylight hours and shut down once the ice set in. Those who insisted upon travel in the depths of winter faced up to walking across frozen rivers. One group of determined travelers crossed the broad Susquehanna River near its mouth in the winter of 1832. It was a bitter-cold night with a blowing snowstorm. The empty coach, mounted on sledge runners, pulled by a single horse, and pushed by several workmen, led the way. The passengers followed on foot. Partway across the party became lost and were about ready to accept their fate when a distant bell began to ring, guiding them to the opposite shore. The distance covered was only 3,500 feet, but it must have seemed like ten times that distance to the frightened passengers as they clambered up the south bank of the river.

Warm weather brought the return of ferry service, yet the stage traveler's problems were far from over. Spring also brought on flash floods and high water. A pioneer ferry on the Kentucky River was swept downstream during a time of high water and swift currents. The craft got stuck far from shore, and the stage and its passengers were stranded overnight. A British traveler named Basil Hall came to a ferry landing in about 1827 only to find the boat swept away by the river. A young man in a canoe was carrying the passengers across one by one. The baggage followed next and then the horses were led across. When all of the passengers were united with the driver, they pulled the coach across using an old rope. All went well until the coach reached the bank, where it proved too heavy for the volunteer stevedores. At last someone thought to hitch up the horse, and the soggy coach was reluctantly drawn ashore.

Ferries demonstrated their shortcomings in nearly every season, for even when all went well, they were a slow and inefficient way to cross a stream. A bridge was the direct way across the water. The coach might need to slacken its speed, but the transit was made in so many seconds. There was a problem, however, in replacing ferries with bridges. Bridges, even wooden bridges, were expensive to build and maintain. They could only be justified where a goodly traffic warranted their construction. Because the national and local governments were so reluctant to involve themselves in internal improvements, many early bridges were built privately as toll bridges. The small charge collected from each traveler or vehicle wishing to pass over was expected to pay off the mortgage, repair costs, and yield a profit to the owners of the bridge. Most of these bridges were fairly modest wooden truss affairs, covered over with a roof and side walls to protect the frame.

Now viewed as a quaint relic, the covered bridge was in its time a vital part of America's highway system. A few, in fact, were considered engineering marvels of their day. The Market Street Bridge over the Schuylkill River at Philadelphia was a wooden colossus measuring 750 feet long and 42 feet wide. It opened in early 1805 at a cost of $300,000. A similar structure was completed during the following year at Trenton, New Jersey, over the Delaware River. But less traveled roads waited decades to see a bridge erected over major streams. It was not until 1855 that a bridge crossed the Shenandoah River on the main road to Winchester, Virginia.

This structure lasted only seven years before it was burned during the Civil War. A ferry resumed service at some inconvenience to regional travelers – an inconvenience that lasted until 1894 when a second bridge was opened.

A few stages managed to operate over good stretches of road and solid bridges. Plank roads offered a partial solution to the pothole dilemma. In New England roads were often rolled, rather than plowed, so that the snow became a smooth if not a frigid surface. Yet even where the awful bump and bounce was moderated, stage travel remained a mighty uncomfortable way to go.

IT'S GOING TO BE A BUMPY RIDE

Passengers on stagecoaches were forced into a small space where each person touched his or her seatmate. In most cases they were strangers and might not have cared for the appearance or smell of their fellow passengers. Everyone wiggled and squirmed to arrange their body parts for the least possible contact, but the motion of the coach was such that all were jumbled back and forth in a regular collision of elbows, shoulders, and hips. Those riding on the front and rear seats had upholstered back cushions, while those unlucky enough to sit on the center or jump seat had only a broad leather strap for back support (fig. 2.8). Sit anyway and anywhere you wished, but no adult could claim more than his allotted 15 inches of space. You could turn and shift a little, but after so many hours your legs would swell, a foot would go dead, or your joints would ache. The crowding was exacerbated by passengers who insisted on bringing some of their baggage inside rather than placing it on the roof or rear boot of the coach. Such intrusions sometimes prompted rather heated arguments, as was the case when a young woman entered a full stage at Vernon, New York, with an enormous hatbox. After a prolonged argument that included not just the passengers but also the lady's boyfriend and a host of loafers standing around the coach stop, the box was placed outside of the coach. On the other hand, the driver could become very insistent on placing mailbags inside the coach. Sam Clemens and his brother rode in a coach so full of mailbags that they could only rest on top of them, because the seats were completely covered.

Most passengers were pleased by the large window openings that made the interior of the coach well lit and amply ventilated. Yes, there was lots of fresh air – maybe even too much on less temperate days. There were no windows, and the only way to close up the openings was to roll down leather curtains mounted on the outside of the coach body. It tended to be an all-or-nothing sort of closure. The interior was now plunged into a deep gloom, for the only light came from small glass panels built into the

2.8. Interior of 1848 coach in the collection of the Smithsonian Institution, Washington, D.C. Note the jump seat in the foreground.

(Smithsonian Institution Neg 78-1872. Courtesy of National Museum of American History, Smithsonian Institution)

doors, or in some cases along the sides of the doors. One traveler described the coach with its curtains down as being hot and dark; or, as Twain said, it was as dark as the inside of a cow. It was like being in a dungeon. Those who suffered from claustrophobia were made to feel even more miserable. Worse yet, the curtains were not very effective. Rain, snow, and sleet would blow in around their edges, wetting the passengers' garments and feet. If the road was more than a little wet, mud would also spray inside. On a dry day during the winter the side curtains did an equally inefficient job of keeping out the cold. The coach had no heat source, but a few experienced travelers learned to carry hot bricks wrapped in rags. As a heat source they would soon expire, but foot stoves filled with hot coals lasted awhile longer. The use of foot stoves was not encouraged, however, because they could set a highly combustible stagecoach on fire.

One of the great miseries of stage travel was insistence on straight-through, nonstop traveling. This made sense when travel time was considered, and if the passengers were nothing more than mail pouches it would have worked well. But most were bone weary after ten hours in this miserable, cramped, rough-riding vehicle, and they wanted a break. A meal and a night's rest at an inn were a necessity. Was that too much to ask? It was if the coach ran only once or twice a week. Few passengers cared to lay over in some out-of-the-way country tavern for so many idle days. So it was up and off before dawn each day or up and off after only a hasty meal and no bed rest at all, depending on the stage line's schedule. As stage operations grew over the years and competing lines served the more popular routes, passengers began to find a few options. In 1832, for instance, the Swiftsure line – from New York to Philadelphia – offered daylight service three days a week. Other lines offered express stages, which made the trip in two and a half days, or longer, slower four-day service for Philadelphia-to-Pittsburgh runs. Those wanting room and comfort went on the slow schedule.

There are no statistics on how many stage travelers were killed or injured. In fact, there appear to be very few statistics of any sort regarding this industry. We therefore can offer only anecdotal evidence on the dangers of stage travel. One can imagine the number of sprained ankles and skinned knees resulting from passengers clambering up and down the high iron steps of a coach. Just a slight misstep and you could take a good fall. At night the chances of this happening only increased. How many passengers had their hands smashed in the entrance door? There are enough reported incidents to suggest that rollovers and upsets were fairly common. The vehicle itself could fall apart under its passengers. Wheels collapsed, wheel bearings burned out, thoroughbraces could and did break down after so many years of hard use.

If the vehicle presented hazards, so did the mode of power. Anyone who has spent time around horses knows they are large, powerful, and nervous. When they sense danger, their instinct is to flee. It can be something as small as a blowing leaf or as startling as a gun discharging. Off they go in a mad dash to get away. If they are attached to a coach, it goes with them. If you are in the coach, you go too! Around 1870 a coach running along the edge of a high bluff was ready to descend a long grade that led down to the Kentucky River, about a dozen miles southeast of Lexington. The bluff was 300 feet above the river. Something spooked the horses and they dashed directly over the hillside. The coach became airborne, passing over treetops until it crashed at the bottom, where it rolled over several times. All of the passengers were injured but all recovered. In most cases, the end result of a runaway was far less dramatic or destructive. Often as not, the driver could rein the team in, or if he had fallen from his seat box – which did happen – one of the passengers might be able to climb up and out from inside the coach and man the reins. Or the team would just run from fright and stop running when their wind was gone.

There was one place of travel where the horses tended not to ever run away – in fact, they hardly ever performed much stage service at all there – and that was in the American desert. Mules were the mainstay of these dry regions, and everything moved mighty slowly over the parched ground. Why, an active volcano would have difficulty in stirring up a team to run off. On the Central Route, about 100 miles west of Salt Lake City, it was so dry and hot that the mules would hardly move. They would go 300 to 600 feet and stop; then they would sneeze and chew their bits and refuse to go until the driver's insistent whip cracking drove them on for another short hop. At the end of ten hours they would have covered 2¼ miles. There was no water for the team or the passengers. Only alkali dust was in abundance.

Horses were a remarkable draft animal, and America was dependent on them for propulsion. Drivers bonded with their steeds – their voice and smell calmed the powerful animals. In return, the team quickly learned the road and after a few trips needed little guidance. They were excellent at staying on the road after sunset, because their night vision was superior to that of humans. They could follow the edge of the road and keep the coach rolling along where it belonged in the center of the lane. Nighttime running was dangerous. The side lamps were to warn pedestrians and other vehicles that a stagecoach was approaching. The amount of light they projected was too small to be useful in seeing ahead. The driver or his assistant would blow the coach horn as an additional alert that they were on the road.

Since ancient times highwaymen have preyed upon the public. It was not a trade invented in the western United States; eastern stages were set upon by robbers as well. A favorite place to stick up New York stages was just across the Harlem River Bridge on the road leading to New Haven, Connecticut. The trees offered good cover here. The same held true for a pine forest between Baltimore and Washington. Some highwaymen were active into the 1880s, but it is the American West that first comes to mind for this particular style of crime. Holdups were not daily occurrences, but they were common enough that a rider or armed guard accompanied most stagecoaches. Valuables were placed in a strongbox bolted to the coach's floor. The box was too heavy and bulky to be easily carried off by men on horseback. As a further discouragement, silver was shipped in large, heavy ingots for the same reason. These weighty bars sometimes proved a hazard

2.9. Indian attack on a stagecoach of the Butterfield line, resulting in a high-speed chase.

(*Harper's Weekly*, April 21, 1866)

to passengers, especially if the coach rolled over, because the bars were placed loose on the floor.

In 1883 a mail stage was held up near Keene, Montana, on a mountain road surrounded by a wood. Highwaymen had felled a large tree to block the road. Around noon the stage stopped by the huge log. Three masked men stepped out with shotguns aimed at the driver and passengers. Two of the passengers were ladies, one of whom burst into tears, certain that her end had come. One of the ruffians assured her that no harm would come if everyone remained calm and cooperated. One of the male passengers hid a pocketbook containing $270 in bills in the folds of a curtain. It went unnoticed. Another man wearing kid gloves fumbled with his fingers – this was noticed, and the wily highwayman told him to remove his glove. A gold ring was revealed – the robber turned the man's finger over and noticed a brilliant glitter in the sunlight. "This is a shiner," he exclaimed and "a perfect daisy." With that he removed the ring and dropped it into his boot.

Black Bart, aka C. E. Bolton and Charles E. Boles, was the greatest and yet mildest of all the stage robbers. Between 1875 and 1883 he held up twenty-eight California stages. He was a small, dapper man only 5 feet, 8 inches tall and wore size 6 shoes. He worked alone, traveling on foot, and did not use a horse to make his getaway. His place and date of birth are uncertain, but he was around fifty when captured. All of his robberies were in Northern California – the first took place on July 26, 1875, near Copperopolis. He waited at a sharp curve in the road, and when the stage came around it he stepped out with a double-barrel 12-gauge shotgun. His voice was surprisingly deep – "Throw down the box," he ordered. This scene was repeated twenty-eight times. Finally in November 1883, Bart was wounded by a driver during a stickup, and his days as a road agent were over. After spending five years in San Quentin prison, Black Bart disappeared without a trace to become a legend among western outlaws.

The western routes had a nearly complete monopoly on Indian problems (fig. 2.9). Most of these attacks were hit-and-run raids with few passenger fatalities, although some stage line employees were wounded and killed. Service was sometimes shut down when the hostilities became widespread. In August 1862, during the Sioux War, the Central Overland shut down for three weeks. Over the next two years Ben Holladay's operations were halted for several weeks by raids that included burning stagecoach stations. Stages were run in convoys and protected by army troops, but some of these were attacked as well. In 1865 a stage line running out of Denver experienced Indian interference and lost several employees during these raids. Two years later Indians attacked a coach running along the Platte River, killing the driver. The lone passenger then tried to climb up into the seat box and take the reins, but while trying to make his way from inside the coach to the roof the stage hit a rut and the passenger was thrown to the ground. By some miracle he was not hurt, and by a double miracle his accidental ejection was not noticed by the Indians, who rode on chasing the empty runaway coach.

※ ※ ※

The American stagecoach traveler was by necessity a stoic. He learned to endure danger and hardship as a matter of course. He was obedient as well; when the driver said to get out and walk or get out and push, he did so. He calmly endured mosquito attacks, hailstorms, prairie fires, floods, Indian wars, and holdups. He was patient, yes, and tolerant of his fellow passengers, some of whom were pretty disagreeable. He did not bore them with long stories. He never spit to windward. He never drank by himself, but always offered to pass his bottle around. He never fired his pistol out the window, because it might frighten the horses. The model stage passenger was in effect a gentleman of the old school.

LIFE ALONG THE ROAD

The arrival of the daily stage was a big event in many communities. The sleepy town square came to life when the post horn sounded in the distance. A single long, clear note rang across the hills, and then the bright red or yellow Concord coach would be seen approaching. The deserted streets and sidewalks came alive with people hurrying toward the inn in search of visiting relatives or friends. Some gathered just out of curiosity or idleness; others came expecting some important piece of mail, a letter from a loved one, or a special package. The high-pitched call of the post horn had hardly faded away when the heavy coach, headed by four sweating horses, came down the dusty street and stopped in front of the inn. The innkeeper came down to greet his new guests. He offered assistance to the ladies as they attempted to negotiate the narrow, folding iron steps. Meanwhile the padlocked mail pouch and selected pieces of luggage were unloaded. Parcels, express, and newspapers were pulled out of the rear and front boots. The exhausted team was unhitched and led back to the stables. The town square once again returned to its normal laconic state as a busy hubbub of gossip and conversation blossomed inside the common room of the inn. The stage had arrived. The high point of the day was now past.

The room-and-board side of stagecoach travel was a highly variable one, ranging from the homey to the horrible. In remote areas travelers could expect nothing more than a log hut, while in big cities one-hundred-room hotels offered elegant accommodations with hot and cold running water and gas lighting. In between were the country or small-town inns and taverns that provided an acceptable bed, plain but decent food, and a comfortable bar for drink and conversation. In some places only an "ordinary" was available; these establishments were more on the order of a guesthouse, and travelers dined with the proprietor and his or her family. The comfort level depended greatly on the location and efficiency of the owner. Inns in remote, unsettled areas tended to be crude and uncomfortable. There was rather little business to encourage a first-class establishment, nor was there likely any competition, so the place could be a nasty hovel, but it was take it or do without. Such places were described as almost barren of any furniture. In winter they were Arctic cold, and in summer, Sahara hot. Flies seemed to swarm in all seasons, as did the mingled odors from the kitchen and fireplace.

The rustic one-room tavern of the frontier was replaced in time by better facilities. Multistory and multiroom establishments became typical. Most had a dining room and a barroom or common room on the first floor and bedrooms above. Some were well furnished with attractive furniture, rugs, and tableware. A few taverns, such as the Cross Keys Tavern of Shelbyville, Kentucky, grew into mansions with great white columns supporting the front porch. Most bathing was done with the traditional bowl and pitcher placed on a marble-topped dresser in the bedroom, but a few places offered separate bathhouses where troughs were filled with fresh springwater and a high fence was provided for privacy. Only in big cities, such as Philadelphia, where waterworks were available could hotel guests expect to find the luxury of running water in the rooms.

Along busy roads the number of taverns multiplied as the traffic proliferated. Every few miles would be another inn; they often took on the name "mile house," so almost every community had a Four-Mile House or a Six-Mile House. Others were more original, so travelers of the time might stay at the Eagle, the Indian Queen, the Golden Lamb, or even at places with such fanciful names as the Fried Meat. Inns became so dense that there were four hundred of them along just 271 miles of the road between Baltimore and Wheeling. In the Old South things were different, for there were almost no big towns or taverns. Hospitality was an integral part of southern living, and travelers there were simply taken into private homes.

The quality of inns varied greatly but tended to get more rustic as one got farther from the eastern seaboard. One of the more aristocratic commentators on American taverns was Louis Philippe, the Duke of Orléans (1773–1850). He was a direct descendent of Louis XIII and heir to the French throne. However, in the late eighteenth century France was not a healthy place for noblemen, so Louis Philippe spent much of 1796–1799 touring the United States. He decided it was safer to stay on the move, even at this distance from France, and therefore spent considerable time at roadside inns. The inn at Staunton, Virginia, in the fertile Shenandoah Valley was a fine establishment, but its counterpart at Natural Bridge was a true hovel. Others Louis Philippe described as beggarly or squalid boozing kens. As he went west, they only became worse. This once fabulously rich and pampered young man, who had enjoyed the best food in the world, was reduced to such meager fare as cornmeal and bacon, which he had to beg for, when he came upon a miserable place that had no better food to offer. He ended up in Bardstown, Kentucky, in July 1798 to find no chamber pot in his room. The innkeeper insisted they were not necessary, saying it was fine to pee out the window: no one would care or notice here in the backwoods. But the future king was disinclined at such an arrangement and insisted on a chamber pot! In short order the innkeeper produced a pot from the kitchen.

Upon reaching an inn most travelers hardly knew what to do first: eat, drink, or sleep. If rest was uppermost on your mind, the tavern was hardly the best place to find peace and quiet. It was busy and noisy with people coming and going at all hours. A few too many hot toddies might generate a good deal of loud talking and singing down in the bar, and at least some of the ruckus would drift up to the bedrooms. The heavy *clomp, clomp, clomp* up the steps as new guests arrived could wake all but the soundest sleeper. The speaking of other guests, even when in low voices, and the constant opening and closing of doors throughout the building upset the tranquility. The changing of horses tended to go on during most of the day and night. Because the stables were next to the inn, the noise of the horses snorting, clomping, and shaking their harnesses, plus the coarse language of the hostlers while guiding their steeds to and from the stable, welled up in the yard just below the bed chambers.

Private rooms were unknown at the typical stage taverns. Guests were expected to share a room with strangers, though of course in compliance with the Victorian morals of the day – the sexes were never mixed. When travel was brisk you could expect to share your bed with up to six other lodgers. No one undressed; you slept in your street clothes and did not bother to remove your hat and overcoat. The bed itself might have a straw mattress (the worst), a corn husk mattress (a little better), or a good feather bed with clean sheets (heavenly). Bearskin blankets were warm enough but tended to attract vermin. While traveling in northern Ohio in the early 1830s, one guest found the bedbugs so intolerable at his rough lodging place that he went out and slept in the coach. Yet even when a good bed was found, sleep was short. Old coachmen were insistent about being up and off just before dawn so that they might have maximum time on the road during daylight. There was no place for sleepyheads among the stage passengers. All were awakened at some ungodly predawn hour and required to stumble down the steps, out into the chilly morning air to board the unheated coach. Normally there was no time for breakfast; that could wait for a few stops down the road. The charge for a night's lodging was from 12½ cents to 25 cents, but considering the comfort level encountered at most taverns, it hardly seemed like much of a bargain. There was a suspicion of kickbacks, because some taverns were built by the stage lines and leased to contract operators, and passengers were directed only to taverns owned by, or at least friendly to, the stage company. To counter the worst abuses, the need for some form of government regulation was evident from the earliest colonial times. In 1634 Massachusetts licensed the state's tavern operations. Most of the rules concerned food prices – for example, a meal might not exceed 6 pence, or a quart of beer might not exceed 1 pence.

Before retiring, many travelers went to the bar to wash the dust out of their throats and to generally unwind after too many hours inside the bouncing coach. Some would enjoy conversing with the tavern keeper – always ready for gossip from either end of the stage line – or other guests seated around the tables of the taproom. A game of cards might start up at one table, or if a fiddler was present, the younger guests might start up a dance. Most country musicians performed tolerably well, but not always so. In 1807 a traveler visited a log cabin tavern and suffered through a fiddle contest between three brothers who scraped away at their instruments without mercy. Some years earlier the proprietor of a resort hotel at Passaic Falls, New Jersey, promised his guests "the genteelest treatment" and a convenient room for dancing, with a fiddler always ready to play for the ladies and gentlemen who requested one. The same obliging host ran a twice-weekly coach for his New York City patrons.

Entertainment was surely a minor function for tavern keepers, but the same cannot be said for food. The subject of dinner fare was an important topic among travelers of the past and in travel journals was eclipsed only by the roughness of the roads one had traveled on. Food fell into the same category as the quality of the inns themselves, ranging from the very good to the terrible. In the frontier setting meals were rough and simple and often consisted of little more than bacon, Indian bread, and whiskey. No one thought of a balanced diet, fat content, or ingesting the correct amount of green leafy vegetables. Diners were more intent on filling up rather than in counting calories or getting the right mix of vitamins. On some stage routes, if you got two meals a day you were doing well.

At most, ordinary food was served family-style in large bowls or platters. Diners sat at long tables, and food was passed around so that everyone could help themselves. People tended to eat quickly and with little conversation. When finished, they would leave the table. If you lingered it meant you wanted more food, and the kitchen generally prepared an ample supply. However, latecomers might find that certain items were no longer available; the fried chicken and raisin pie were all gone. Food was available only at specific times, and there was no menu or choice of entrees. Drinks were available at all times, however. In the West, especially, many meals were salt pork, fried cornbread, dried fruit, coffee with sugar but no milk. At a better stop you might find bacon and greens, bread, applesauce, and pie. Elsewhere the best you could hope for would be stewed meat, fried potatoes, canned tomatoes, and warm rolls. Game was served in many taverns, and not just in the far West. Travelers might find venison, wild turkey, squirrel, and bear. The cook might even slip in a mule steak when no one was watching.

Seasoned travelers kept informal good and bad lists. On the good list were taverns that served two or three kinds of pie at breakfast. Around Washington, D.C. one could expect a delicious breakfast of fried chicken, hominy cooked as hominy should be prepared, corn waffles and cakes, and muffins light and flaky, all served in the deftest manner. This, too, was on the good list. At Weldon, North Carolina, however, the southern magic failed at one stop where travelers were sold coffee that was a nightmare and biscuits that brought on low spirits for two days. In other places no bread was served and travelers faced wheat cakes described as lumps of paste. Johnnie cake was common fare going back to colonial times.

It was quick, cheap, and easy to make: Combine cornmeal, water, and a little salt, then mix vigorously until it is light and spongy. Spread it on a board or shingle, and bake it upright in the fireplace near the fire. Some cooks called it journey cake, because it was hard and could stand up well to rough handling and travel. It was plain and good.

Nasty-looking meat and coarse food put other establishments on the bad list. It was, of course, difficult to avoid bad list inns completely, for the stages stopped where they would, irrespective of travelers' wishes. In the better taverns the innkeeper appeared at the head of the table smartly dressed in a fine suit, complete with ruffles on his white shirt. Guests were called to the dining room by a large roof bell. In 1807 an inn in Frankfort, Kentucky, had a dining room 72 feet long. Green silk fans, manually powered, kept the flies away. At this time travelers expected to pay 50 cents for breakfast or supper and $1 for the main meal at lunchtime.

During the stagecoach era, tavern keepers were men. Women might serve as cooks, chambermaids, or waitresses but almost never as managers of the establishment. One exception to this rule was Aunt Hannah Fisher, proprietress of the Wayside Inn in Eastchester, New York, about 15 miles north of New York City. Aunt Hannah was described as a stalwart maiden, standing about 6 feet tall. In the 1830s she had the reputation of being able to whip any man on the route between New York and Boston. Should a guest become disorderly, Miss Fisher was ready to demonstrate her reputed powers by dispatching the troublesome person out to the street. Her normal exit route was the half-open Dutch door in the barroom. However, the troublesome patron was not just escorted out the door; he was picked up and thrown over the lower panels into the street. All of this was reported in the May 19, 1880, *New York Times,* some fifty years after Aunt Hannah's no-nonsense career at the Wayside Inn had come to an end.

Life around the tavern involved more than sleeping, meals, and entertainment. It also encompassed a large number of smells, most of which would be on the bad list. The barroom was often very close and overheated, smelling of yesterday's beer and onion stew. Adding to the scent were horse droppings just outside the front door that trailed all the way around to the stables. There were other pungent odors around such as the privies, whose locations were no mystery on a warm and windy day. Your fellow passengers were another likely source of smells. Like you, they had little opportunity to bathe. Bathtubs were few and required some labor to fill from kettles heated on the kitchen stove. Because rest stops were so brief, travelers would use the time to rest rather than wash up. Some individuals attempted to mask their body odors with perfumes, but the combination of scents was sometimes more disagreeable than

2.10. Arizona Mail and Stage Company advertisement (*Railroad Gazetteer*, June 1881) and stagecoach ticket, San Jose and Santa Cruz, 1870s–1880s.

(Jim Wilke Collection)

Arizona Mail & Stage Co.

THE ONLY LINE RUNNING

SIX-HORSE CONCORD COACHES DAILY,

AND CARRYING THE U. S. MAIL AND WELLS, FARGO & CO'S EXPRESS.

—TO—

TOMBSTONE, BISBEE,

Contention City,

Charleston, Patagonia (or Harshaw),

WASHINGTON, CAMP HUACHUCA,

And all Mining Districts in SOUTHERN ARIZONA

Passengers for the above Points leave Daily

SAN FRANCISCO, via S. P. Atlantic Express, at	....	9.30 A. M.
SACRAMENTO, " "	........at........	11.50 "
LATHROP, " "	........at........	2.00 P. M.
LOS ANGELES, " "	........at........	8.00 A. M.

Connecting at BENSON

WITH THE COMPANY'S COACHES DAILY

—FOR—

CONTENTION CITY, TOMBSTONE,

BISBEE,

CHARLESTON, CAMP HUACHUCA, PATAGONIA and WASHINGTON.

Passengers by this route have the privilege of STOPPING OVER AT ANY POINT, resuming the trip at their pleasure.

☞ For Through Tickets and further particulars, inquire at the

Principal Ticket Offices of the Central Pacific Railroad.

And at the Company's Office,

2 New Montgomery Street, under Palace Hotel, San Francisco.

J. KNOWLTON, Jr., - - - - Ticket Agent, San Francisco.

dealing with a single smell. Because deodorant was unknown until comparatively recent times, travelers had to just screw up their noses and endure the malodorous atmosphere as an unavoidable part of the travel experience.

Taverns were more than a place to eat and sleep; they were in effect the local depot for the stage line. Potential passengers came to the inn seeking schedules, fares, and other basics about stage travel. The stage company maintained an office in a corner of the barroom that rarely consisted of more than a table, a cash box, a ledger, and a few pens. The tavern keeper doubled as the agent. Passengers were booked for a certain stage on a certain date; their name, destination, and fare were written into the ledger kept by the tavern keeper, himself very often a tenant and quasi employee of the stage line. In some cases a waybill or manifest was kept by the stage driver, who would record names, destinations, and fares as passengers boarded. He also collected the fares, which were turned in to an agent at the end of the run. Printed tickets were not issued until rather late in the stagecoach era (fig. 2.10).

It is difficult to generalize on the subject of fares because of the capricious nature of the industry. Rates might be cheap one season and unreasonably expensive the next. Actual costs and a fair return seemed to affect the operations rather little. Stage lines were more driven by competition and what the market would bear. If a competing stage line started up, fares would fall. If the coaches ran full, stage managers were tempted to raise their prices. In the late colonial times we find examples of fares ranging from 2.4 pence per mile to 4 pence per mile. During the 1820s and the 1830s many stage lines were charging around 10 cents a mile. This was not a bargain. Ten dollars to go from New York to Albany, for example, or $17.50 to go from Baltimore to Wheeling was a tidy sum at the time. It limited travel to the businessman and the middle class; poor folks were essentially excluded. By the late 1840s rates appear to have dropped somewhat. On well-traveled routes such as Philadelphia to Pittsburgh, one could go for 5 cents a mile. Where the traffic was less dense you could expect to pay more; hence, those going between Mobile and New Orleans paid 7½ cents a mile.

Figuring the cost of going from A to B was sometimes more complicated than just calculating the mileage. Summer rates were somewhat cheaper than winter rates on some lines. Food and lodging were generally the traveler's responsibility, but one line in northern New York included these costs in its passage. On at least one occasion during a rate war, passengers were treated to free meals – the rival line added a bottle of wine to the gratis vittles. Where traffic was large enough to warrant express coaches, passengers could expect to pay a 2-cent-a-mile premium over the slower stages. In a few places even the direction of travel could materially affect the rate. Because the prevailing direction of travel was toward the Pacific, $200 was the fare for going west, while the return rate was half that figure, because almost no one was making the return trip. Perhaps the strangest system devised for fares was that used by the Louisville-to-St.-Louis line in the 1820s. Rates were determined by the passenger's weight, with 100 pounds being the basic fare. A petite 90-pound lady went for a 10 percent discount while a beefy 200-pound man paid double fare. Western lines in general tended to gouge their customers, but they usually tried to find an inventive excuse for doing so. The normal western rate of 12 cents a mile was about double that charged back East. Indian trouble prompted a line run out of Atchison, Texas, to jump its fare to over 34 cents a mile. If a new gold field should open, stage fares in the area were sure to skyrocket, but at least there was a certain logic to western operators' rate adjustments. They ran long routes through sparsely settled territories, some of it controlled by hostile Native Americans, so the costs and risks were greater than in the populous East.

Of course nothing knocked down fares so quickly as an old-fashioned rate war. Operating costs real and imagined were ignored as one line cut its fares to take over the business. In the 1860s two lines slugged it out between Denver and Central City – hardly a major route, but one that blew up into a major battle. The normal rate was $6; eventually this was beaten down to $2. The public enjoyed a fine bargain, but only briefly, for when the rival line, exhausted and broken, abandoned service, the victor raised the fares to $12. Rate wars were not waged to benefit the public but to control traffic and eliminate competition.

Most travelers carried some luggage. Even the most economic packer required a hand-carried bag. Stage operators advised their patrons to travel light; in fact, they insisted upon it and imposed a heavy tariff upon those who arrived at the depot burdened with multiple valises and bags. From the beginnings of stage travel on the continent until around 1820, the free baggage per passenger was around 20 pounds. Some lines would permit only 14 pounds and charged $1 per pound for anything in excess of this limit. Fourteen pounds did not amount to a very large quantity of personal effects, considering the weight of the bag itself. Near the middle of the nineteenth century, the baggage limit went up to 25 pounds, but even so, in an era of heavy clothing and multiple layers for women, a passenger was lucky to take one or two changes of clothes. Yet travel journals of the time advised travelers to take half of their household when taking to the road. Men heading west were advised to pack a pair of thick boots, wool pants, six pairs of socks, three wool shirts, a hat, a coat, an overcoat, blankets, an India rubber cloth, two pairs of drawers, towels, toilet goods, a Sharp's rifle, a Colt revolver, a knife, and plenty of ammunition. Another traveler's list suggested such items as a mosquito net, a small lantern, a good stock of candles, a tinderbox, a medicine chest complete with scales, a teakettle, and a selection of bedding from pillows to blankets. Such a well-equipped passenger could almost set up a general merchandise shop at each stop if he or she was not already bankrupt because of extra luggage charges.

Stage operators had good reason to limit the carriage of baggage on their vehicles. The capacity was limited in cubic space, and every additional pound slowed the horses down. In addition, space had to be reserved for the mails. On some lines the post office revenues for the carriage of mails meant the difference between profit or loss. Mail contracts required on-time delivery, so stage operators tended to think more about the timeliness of the letters than the schedules of their passengers. Leather mail pouches were placed in the front boot of the coach, directly below the driver's seat. This was considered the most secure place on the coach and was under the watchful eye of the driver.

We tend to think only of the western mail coach operators, such as Ben Holladay and John Butterfield, but in the East, James Reeside (1789–1842) of Baltimore, a major stagecoach owner and operator of the region, also relied heavily on U.S. postal contracts. Reeside was born in Scotland and brought by his parents to Baltimore County, Maryland, as an infant. He grew up as an unusually tall (6 feet, 5 inches) and strong man. His quick wit and friendly and capable manner won him many friends. He began as a teamster and hauled goods between Baltimore, Philadelphia, and Pittsburgh. During the War of 1812 he moved artillery for the army. After the war he got into stagecoaching and ran a line from Hagerstown, Maryland, to McConnellsburg, Pennsylvania. This included his first mail contract. In 1818 he joined with Stockton and Stokes of Baltimore and several other stage operators to form a regular line to carry mail along the Cumberland Road. Nine years later the U.S. postmaster general asked Reeside to relocate to Philadelphia and manage mail transport between New York and Philadelphia. This was the number-one mail route in the nation. Reeside shortened the delivery time from twenty-three to twelve hours and became the nation's largest mail contractor, with four hundred employees and one thousand horses. The press nicknamed him the "land admiral" and went on to claim that the admiral would leave Philadelphia on a six-horse coach with a hot Johnny cake in his pocket and reach Pittsburgh before it got cold.

Reeside made quite an appearance in his bright red vest, a color that matched the paint of his coaches. He was active in politics and on friendly terms with members of Congress. They could always depend on their good friend James for a free pass when traveling home. This patronage surely helped direct many contracts to Reeside; however, all of these good feelings and generous earnings came to an end with a prolonged lawsuit between the contractor and the post office. The courts award a $190,000 settlement to Reeside in 1841. He died in September of the following year and did not live long enough to fully enjoy his winnings.

At every turn travelers were expected to pay up. Be it a pint of beer, a plate of roast beef, or a ticket to Tomahawk, the wayfarer had to produce the requested amount of cash. Personal bank checks and credit cards were a luxury available only to future generations – even wiring home for money was not possible until very late in the telegraph era – so it was necessary to have a well-calculated and ample stash of cash before setting out on a journey. With the end of British colonial control, the United States slipped into something of a currency no-man's-land. Gone were all of those solid pounds, shillings, and pence. Efforts to establish a stable national currency had failed for political reasons, resulting in an erratic system of state banks. Two short-lived national banks were opened and then closed in the early years of the republic, and the United States had no national bank notes until 1864. Those who stayed at home were less affected by the local bank system, but for those who traveled, the state banking system proved troublesome because the value of the currency tended to decline the farther away from home one ventured. A $20 note issued by a Richmond bank might be worth only $3 in Cincinnati. It might well have no value at all once it reached Indianapolis.

Paper currency was generally suspect, although notes issued by a major bank such as Nicholas Biddle's Philadelphia institution, the Second Bank of the United States, would hold their value fairly well because the bank was so recognizable. Gold or silver coins were the only currency that was universally acceptable and were normally taken with no discount. Veteran travelers knew to carry coins and not paper money. The nationality was not too important; Spanish pieces of eight (worth $1.25) were a fairly common medium of exchange and stayed in circulation until foreign coins were declared invalid for domestic use in 1857. Why not just obtain a good supply of gold or silver coins before leaving home? This jolly good idea was thwarted by the simple fact that such coinage was in short supply. Yet even having a good purse of coins did not completely solve the traveler's money problems, because making change was difficult. When it came time to settle with the tavern keeper and he owed you, say, 30 cents in change, he might offer you a metal token or a small denominational paper note in that amount. If you refused this – and not without reason, because once again such semi-official, privately issued currency had no value outside of the immediate area of issue – then there was only one alternative: the chopping block. A pie-shaped section would be cut out of a good coin, in the amount of 30 cents. Thus came into the language some once literal terms such as "two bits" or "four bits," each bit being a wedge-shaped bit or piece cut from a coin.

A LONG FINALE: THE END OF STAGECOACH TRAVEL

The end of stagecoach travel was a long time in coming. This slow recessional lasted for nearly half a century. The big intercity runs were the first to go as more railroads opened for business. The new steam cars possessed every advantage from speed to comfort. Compared to the stage, the railroad coaches were large, roomy, and offered smooth riding. There was a stove for warmth and candles for light; upholstered seats and drinking water added to the passenger's comfort. Many cars even had a dry closet where one might relieve himself en route. When it came to speed, most pioneer rail lines ran along easily at 25 mph, nearly five times the speed of a stagecoach. The rail fares were much cheaper, especially in the West, where stage fares were often six times greater than railroad fare. The stagecoach was beaten on just about every count that mattered to travelers; hence the old form gave way to the new mode. Yet the railroad didn't run everywhere, nor were all terminals reached at any one given time. While the railroad system expanded year by year, many communities remained unserved for some time. In the interim the old-fashioned stagecoach remained the principal form of public transport. The stage was increasingly used to get from the main street to secondary places. It was no longer New York to Albany but rather Albany to Middletown, New York. Stage lines tended to start at railroad depots and go off into the hinterland, becoming the backwoods carrier serving the small and the obscure. In the East most of the major or long-distance stage lines were gone before 1865. As branch line railroads developed in the area, even the short-haul routes disappeared. As the nineteenth century drew to a close, the stagecoach continued to run on very short hauls, such as runs between railroad depots and resort hotels. In the Catskill Mountains, for example, in 1905 there were fifty-one stage lines serving the hotels of the area. The average trip was only about 6 to 10 miles, so the stages were performing only local portage service.

In the far West the stage maintained its importance as a front-line carrier somewhat later. In a July 1874 *Harper's Weekly* magazine the stagecoach was remembered as a thing of the past. It remained important in the West as the advance guard of civilization. The old-fashioned stage was still common in Arizona, New Mexico, Texas, Wyoming, and Montana. Where no passengers wanted to exit or get on, the coach did not stop. The

2.11. Throwing out the mail and catching a postal bag without stopping. Somewhere in the southwestern United States, 1874.

(*Harper's Weekly*, July 4, 1874)

mail pouch was thrown off and the vehicle's speed was scarcely checked (fig. 2.11). The driver would dexterously catch the bag tossed up to him by the station agent. The main-line rail system was not complete until around 1890; hence many passengers continued to take connecting stages for hundreds of miles across Wyoming, Dakota Territory, and the like. One by one these long routes were eliminated by parallel railroads. When the Santa Fe Railroad reached Trinidad, Colorado, in April 1879, the local paper said few travelers would miss the tedious and unpleasant excursion on the coaches. It was adieu to the old-fashioned stagecoach and welcome to rapid transit by steam power. After 1910, gasoline-powered buses began to take over the short haul and secondary runs, yet it is claimed that one stagecoach operation lasted as late as 1926. The rustic stagecoach proved a stubborn survivor, having lasted for more than two centuries.

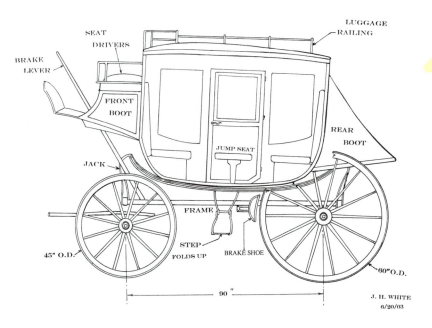

2.12. The interior of a typical stagecoach is shown in the cutaway drawing, ca. 1880.

(Author's drawing)

THE STAGECOACH AS A VEHICLE

The stagecoach was a four-wheel passenger vehicle generally of a rather heavy pattern. The coach is believed to have appeared around 1400 AD (the exact date is uncertain) in the Hungarian town of Kocs, which is about 50 miles south of Vienna, Austria. The name of the vehicle, too, was based on the town's name, Kocs, which became *coach*, in English. The coach gradually spread to the west and was finally adopted in England around 1550. Sixty years later coaches were used for public transport. The first vehicles used in the North American colonies for public passenger transport were not really coaches, but were more like covered wagons. The body was a simple rectangle much like a farm wagon. Simple boards formed bench seating; the top of the wagon was a cloth stretched over arch bows. The driver sat on the front bench; the passengers entered from the front and stepped over the series of seat benches as they moved to the rear (fig. 2.12).

Around 1770 true stagecoach-style vehicles came into use. The body curved at both ends. Passengers entered through side doors, and the driver sat outside the body on a box or perch seat (fig. 2.13). The arched roof was part of the body. By around 1820 the American stagecoach body became more oval in shape. A few years later prominent coach builders such as Abbot and Downing and Eaton and Gilbert produced an improved version of the stagecoach known respectively as the Concord and the Troy coach

2.13. A driver on his seat box dressed for winter in a great coat that falls to his heels.

(*Scribner's Monthly*, August 1874)

(fig. 2.14). The roof was somewhat flattened and outfitted with iron railings so that it might carry luggage on top of the vehicle. The ends were flattened and parallel to each other; the side wall of the lower body was less curved. The stagecoaches were built in several sizes, styles, and levels of finish; hence they ranged in price from a hack passenger wagon costing $600 to the largest twelve-passenger Concord costing $1,200. The interiors were upholstered in cloth or leather, though padding was none too generous. An Omaha newspaper reported in 1877 that experienced travelers always choose the front seat directly below the driver. It offered the best ride and the least dust. The exteriors were lavishly painted and decorated with rich scrolls and ornaments in bright colors. The lettering was often in gold leaf. All surfaces were heavily varnished to give the coach a glossy finish and protect the paint.

2.14. Troy coach, the Maggie Gray; engraving from a catalog issued by Eaton and Gilbert of Troy, New York, ca. 1859.

Just why stagecoaches and other horse-drawn vehicles had such large wheels may puzzle some modern people. At 60 inches in diameter the larger rear wheels were as high as some adults. They were made that size for good reason. Large wheels helped get the coach over the poor roads of the day. Small wheels tended to fall into holes and ruts, while large wheels could bridge or more easily climb out of depressions and irregularities in the road surface. Big wheels also raised the axle height and made it possible to clear tree stumps, large rocks, or other obstacles that might be in the roadway. When it came to fording a stream, having the coach floor as high off the ground as possible helped to avoid flooding the vehicle's interior. It should be clear that the Concord's big wheels were more than just for show – they had a real purpose.

Only the best lumber was used by coach builders. They favored white ash for body frames, wheel fellies, poles, axle beds, and perches. The body panels were of basswood or clear poplar. The wheel spokes were made from white oak and the hubs from elm or black cherry. A nine-passenger coach weighed about 1 ton.

THE STAGECOACH BUILDERS

Many shops built stagecoaches, but the larger makers were located in the northeastern United States. Most of the manufacturing was by Abbot, Downing, and Company of Concord, New Hampshire. The location of the business gave the coach its popular name, the Concord coach. The first production of coaches started in 1825. The company built vehicles for operators all over North and South America and exported coaches to

2.15. Melon-shaped stagecoach with horses at a gallop, ca. 1825.

(Printer's cut, author's collection)

Australia and South Africa. The design was remarkably consistent over the years, and when the last coach was finished in 1910, it did not differ greatly from its ancestors. In all, Abbot, Downing, and Company built about three thousand coaches.

Another major builder was Eaton and Gilbert of Troy, New York. The firm started in 1815 as a small carriage shop belonging to Charles Veazie. Around 1825, Orsamus Eaton joined the firm. Stagecoach building started at this time. The early Troy coaches, as they were called, were more egg- or melon-shaped than those built in later years (fig. 2.15). Uri Gilbert joined the business in 1830 and became the prominent partner. Eaton and Gilbert were as large as Abbot, Downing, and Company; they may have built even more coaches than the Concord manufacturer. By 1860 Gilbert was deeply involved in the railroad car building trade; hence most of the late modern coaches were likely made in Concord. This is why the Concord coach is better remembered than the Troy coach. The far West had one large-scale coach builder, M. P. Henderson of Stockton, California. The shop opened in 1869 and continued until about 1910 when the automobile put an end to carriage and coach manufacturing.

Interest in early travel and horse-powered vehicles has prompted a number of small woodworking shops to reproduce coaches. The market may be small, but the enthusiasm for these replicas is strong. A number of original stagecoaches have been preserved and can be seen in museums such as the New Hampshire Historical Society in Concord; the Pioneer Village in Minden, Nebraska; and Carillon Park in Dayton, Ohio.

THE DRIVERS AND THEIR TEAMS

Young boys viewed the stage driver as a dashing hero who raced his coach over dusty highways in a reckless and carefree fashion. Ideally he had a different girl in every town along his route. He dressed as a dandy, smoked the best cigars, and drank the smoothest whiskey. He hogged the middle of the road, using the excuse that "the mail must get through," and reveled in his reputation as the wind-splitting demon of the highway. Road racing was actually a problem, and many stage companies prohibited the practice, yet some passengers encouraged it despite the obvious danger. One stage line running out of Paterson, New Jersey, in 1823 could guarantee that there would be no reckless driving or racing, because the proprietor was also the stage driver. A European traveler several years earlier praised American stage drivers for their dogged determination in getting their passengers through to their destinations despite miserable roads and bridges. They were resourceful and dexterous and managed to get over roads that no European driver would even attempt. Sometimes, however, the driver didn't make the complete run. One driver was thrown from his seat, but his horses continued on until they stopped out of habit at the next tavern. The driver was found 3 miles back on the road, seriously injured but alive.

The driver's seat, high above the road, was fully exposed to whatever the weather had to offer. On a fine day it must have been a grand place to view the passing countryside; the sight of other carriages and wagons ambling along or cows and sheep being driven to market must have been a delight. It was best for the driver to hold on somehow, for the stage would lurch and bounce unpredictably. But if both hands were full of reins – hold on to what? If it rained, the driver would be soaked from top to bottom; on a dry day he would be coated inside and out with dust. But the winters were worst. Sitting out on top of the boot he was exposed to all the fury of Old Man Winter. Hats, scarves, great coats, gloves, blankets, boots, nothing could really keep out the chill or the wetness. It was simply a miserable station and one that few men could endure without a little boost from John Barleycorn. A French visitor said in 1794 that American drivers were almost always slightly drunk. It was not always an inebriated driver who caused an accident on the road, however. One such operator made it to the end of his run but turned the team over to the stable boy rather than a hostler. The boy was unable to control the team, and the horses took off wildly down the road. The coach rolled over and several passengers were injured. Then again, there are stories of drivers who stuck to their posts to the end. Consider the driver in Kentucky who labored to get his passengers through a winter storm. He would not stop or turn back. Partway through the journey, when the stage pulled up at a post office stop, the driver was found frozen to death in his seat. The life of a stage driver was certainly not easy, safe, or well paid. It surely was nothing as glamorous as that imagined by young boys of the time.

Commonplace workhorses or heavy harness horses were used for stagecoach service. These were the type of animals found on the farm and used to pull wagons or plows. They were not the light and fleet Arabians or fancy thoroughbreds. Such animals weighed about 1,100 pounds and had the strength of five men. James Watt calculated horsepower to be 33,000 foot-pounds per minute, but this required a very large draft horse. The typical 1,100-pound horse could generate only about 16,500 foot-pounds per minute, or one-half a unit of horsepower. Such an animal could carry a rider for about 25 miles. That daily limit declined markedly when it came to stage service, and 10 or perhaps 15 miles was the maximum. Horses needed considerable rest, grooming, and veterinary care. They generally were rather fussy eaters and, unlike cattle, demanded only the best hay and feed. The coach usually moved along at a trot, or approximately 6 mph. In the East, four-horse teams were generally adequate to meet schedules. When a long or unusually steep grade was encountered, an extra team was hitched on to go over the slope. These tow teams were managed by a young boy who rode bareback on one of the horses as a postilion. When the crest of the hill was reached, the boy would unhitch from the stage horses and ride the team to the bottom of the grade to await the next stage.

Out West most stage lines used six-horse teams, figuring the extra motive power was needed because of rougher road conditions, greater distances, and the possible need to put on some extra speed in the event of an Indian raid. Western operators were apparently hard-pressed to find animals locally and sometimes used half-wild stock that even the best drivers had trouble controlling. The Butterfield line ran some mustangs that were said to be as wild as deer.

SUGGESTED READING

Beebe, Lucius Morris, and Charles Clegg. *U.S. West: The Sage of Wells Fargo.* New York: E. P. Dutton, 1949.

Berkebile, Donald H. *Carriage Terminology: An Historical Dictionary.* Washington, D.C.: Smithsonian Press, 1978.

Coleman, J. Winston. *Stage-Coach Days in the Bluegrass: Being an Account of Stage-Coach Travel and Tavern Days in Lexington and Central Kentucky, 1800–1900.* 1935. Louisville: University Press of Kentucky, 1995.

Colton, J. H. *Colton's Traveler and Tourist's Guide-Book through the New-England and Middle States and the Canadas: Containing the Routes and Distances on the Great Lines of Travel by Railroads, Stage-Roads, Canals, Lakes and Rivers: Together with Descriptions of the Several States, and of the Principal Cities, Towns and Villages.* New York, 1850.

Conkling, Roscoe P., and Margaret B. Conkling. *Butterfield Overland Mail, 1857–1869; Its Organization and Operation over the Southern Route to 1861; Subsequently over the Central Route to 1866; and under Wells, Fargo and Company in 1869.* 3 vols. Glendale, Calif.: A. H. Clark and Co., 1947.

Dunbar, Seymour. *A History of Travel in America, Being an Outline of the Development in Modes of Travel from Archaic Vehicles to Colonial Times to the Completion of the First Transcontinental*

Railroad; *The Influence of the Indians on the Free Movement and Territorial Unity of the White Race; The Part Played by Travel Methods in the Economic Conquest of the Continent; And Those Related Human Experiences, Changing Social Conditions and Governmental Attitudes Which Accompanied the Growth of a National Travel System.* New York: Tudor Publishing Co., 1937.

Earle, Alice Morse. *Stage-Coach and Tavern Days.* 1900. Bowie, Md.: Heritage Books, 1997.

Forbes, Allan. *Taverns and Stagecoaches in New England: Anecdotes and Tales Recalling the Days of Stagecoach Travel and the Ancient Hostelries Where Strangers Tarried.* 2 vols. Boston: State Street Trust Co., 1953–1954.

Frederick, J. V. *Ben Holladay, The Stagecoach King: A Chapter in the Development of Transcontinental Transportation.* 1968. Lincoln: University of Nebraska Press, 1989.

Holbrook, Stewart Hall. *The Old Post Road: The Story of the Boston Post Road.* New York: McGraw-Hill, 1962.

Holmes, Oliver W., and Peter T. Rohrbach. *Stagecoach East: Stagecoach Days in the East from the Colonial Period to the Civil War.* Washington, D.C.: Smithsonian Institution Press, 1983.

Hulbert, Archer Butler, ed. *Crown Collection of Photographs of American Maps: Series V: The Great Western Stage-Coach Routes.* Cleveland, 1930.

Ierley, Merritt. *Traveling the National Road: Across the Centuries on America's First Highway.* Woodstock, N.Y.: Overlook Press, 1990.

Lane, Wheaton J. *From Indian Trail to Iron Horse: Travel and Transportation in New Jersey, 1620–1860,* intro. Thomas Wertenbaker. Princeton, N.J.: Princeton University Press, 1939.

Lay, M. G. *Ways of the World: A History of the World's Roads and of the Vehicles That Used Them.* New Brunswick, N.J.: Rutgers University Press, 1992.

Meyer, Balthasar Henry. *History of Transportation in the United States before 1860; Prepared under the Direction of Balthasar Henry Meyer,* by Caroline E. MacGill et al. Washington, D.C.: Carnegie Institution of Washington, 1917.

Rose, Albert C. *Historic American Roads: From Frontier Trails to Superhighways,* illustrated by Carl Rakeman. New York: Crown, 1976.

Searight, Thomas B. *Old Pike: A History of the National Road, with Incidents, Accidents, and Anecdotes Thereon.* Uniontown, Pa.: Thomas B. Searight, 1894.

Strahorn, Carrie Adell. *Fifteen Thousand Miles by Stage: A Woman's Unique Experience during Thirty Years of Path Finding and Pioneering from the Missouri to the Pacific and from Alaska to Mexico,* illus. Charles M. Russell and others. New York: G. P. Putnam's Sons, 1911.

Stratton, Ezra M. *World on Wheels; or, Carriages, with Their Historical Associations from the Earliest to the Present Time, Including a Selection from the American Centennial Exhibition.* 1878. New York: B. Blom, 1972.

Twain, Mark. *Roughing It.* Hartford, Conn.: American Publishing Co., 1872.

Yoder, Paton. *Taverns and Travelers: Inns of the Early Midwest.* Bloomington: Indiana University Press, 1969.

3.1. Typical omnibus used in most American cities, 1850s.

(Author's collection)

The Omnibus № 3
Travel for All Citizens

INNOVATIONS IN THE PRACTICAL FIELD OF TRANSPORTATION IS normally accomplished by mechanics or businessmen, and yet the introduction of the omnibus is credited to a French philosopher and scientist, Blaise Pascal (1623–1662). Late in life this learned man, best known for his work in calculus and fluids, decided to establish public transit in Paris. He advocated horse-drawn carriages that would run over a fixed route to carry ordinary folks around town at low fares. Five routes were established and service began during his final year. However, Pascal's democratic notions that the service would be open to all citizens was thwarted by a government charter prescribing that only "people of merit" might ride in such coaches and excluded soldiers, pages, servants, and laborers. Uniformed drivers and conductors were provided, but the vehicles were slow and the fares high. This pioneer operation expired by about 1675. The concept was reintroduced in 1823 by the operator of a hot bath in Nantes, a suburb of the French capital, who sought an inexpensive way of carrying patrons to his establishment from Paris. The bus proved so successful that service was expanded to other routes, and within five years more omnibus lines were organized. By mid-century thirteen hundred buses were running in Paris. The system, consolidated by royal decree in 1855, was carrying 40 million passengers. That number rose to 120 million by 1867. By this time Paris was a large metropolitan area, having overflowed its ancient walls in the seventeenth century and spread well into the countryside. Great boulevards and broad avenues replaced the crooked medieval streets in the 1850s and 1860s. The population had grown to more than one million by 1850 and would more than double over the next half century. The old "walking city" was obsolete, and Parisians were unwilling to trek for miles from one destination to the next. While the buses were not much faster than a walk, they allowed travelers to rest as the horses plodded along.

In November 1860 the *American Railway Review* described an orderly and well-regulated Paris bus system whose operations greatly contrasted with those elsewhere in the world. No intoxicated or poorly dressed person, nor anyone carrying a large package that might annoy other passengers, was allowed to board. The conductor also would not allow women, young children, or infirm persons to occupy the roof seats. There were no standees, and waiting passengers were not allowed to board if all seats were taken; they had to wait for the next bus. Seats inside the main compartment had arm rests so that each of the fourteen occupants had a distinct and separate space. Ten more spaces were on the longitudinal roof bench. Visiting American and British travelers must have been astonished at how things were handled in France, where transit riding was not ruled by the law of the jungle.

The omnibus was introduced in London by George Shillibeer, an English carriage builder, who had worked in France building omnibuses for the Parisian market. He started operations in July 1829 with a bus that ran from Paddington into the center of London. It was a large, heavy vehicle with twenty-two spaces inside and no roof seats and was pulled by three horses harnessed abreast. Uniformed drivers and conductors attended the largely middle-class patrons of the Paddington coach line. Shillibeer soon had many competitors, and the London system was soon without any "system" at all as individual operators filled the city streets with more buses, few of which followed any schedule or regular routes. The fine uniforms were replaced by casual dress and rude manners. The six million visitors to the Great Exhibition of 1851 complained about poor service and high fares. The protests eventually led to reform. The London General Omnibus Company was organized in December 1855 by the same capitalists who were operating the Paris systems. They bought out owners of 610 old buses and purchased many new vehicles. Fares were lowered and made consistent, and the snappy uniforms were restored. This system was taken over by British management a few years later.

A remarkably detailed account of the London omnibus system and its operation was compiled by Henry Mayhew in 1861 as part of his monumental study of London labor and London poor. Mayhew was a journalist and founded the satirical magazine *Punch*. According to his report, in 1838 there were 620 buses in service, or double the number just four years earlier. Roof seats were added in the 1840s, giving the buses a seating capacity of twenty-five. The interiors were too small for standees. The hours of operation were fourteen hours per day, seven days a week. Each bus made six round trips per day of about two hours' duration. Two-man crews were standard, unlike in the United States, where a single man served as both driver and conductor. In England the conductor stood on a small shelf or step to the left side of the rear door.

The London horse bus plodded along with little change into the twentieth century when the sudden introduction of the motor bus made it obsolete. The horse-powered bus reached its peak in about 1905 when the

3.2. Abraham Brower's Broadway omnibus of 1831.

(Ezra M. Stratton, *The World on Wheels*, 1878)

London omnibus company owned seventeen thousand horses and fourteen hundred buses. In 1914 the final London omnibus rolled into history.

THE OMNIBUS MAKES ITS APPEARANCE
IN THE NEW WORLD

It is likely that American visitors to London or Paris returned home with admiration for what they had seen in the capitals of Europe: a transit system that featured fixed routes, continuous service, and a single fare would spark admiration and the obvious notion that the same system should be created for the home market. But it is just as likely that city transit evolved from suburban stagecoach lines that served communities situated just outside the city limits. In 1798 Bernard de Klyne began stage operations from Wall Street to Greenwich Village in New York City. He would run only when customers presented themselves. Similar service ran along Broadway to Harlem and Manhattanville, but the fares were high. It was 18¾ cents to Harlem and 25 cents to the next village named. A savings of one-third was possible by buying tickets in lots of six or twelve. There was no service on Sunday. New York City was expanding ever northward up Manhattan Island so that villages such as Harlem were swallowed up by townhouses, tenements, stores, factories, and pavement. In fact, New York was now the fastest-growing city in the United States – between 1840 and 1850 its population increased by 130 percent. For all the talk about moving west, it appeared more people were moving off the farm and into the city. The Erie Canal and Hudson River delivered huge cargoes of grain and lumber to New York Harbor. Trade and commerce flourished; the city prospered and outpaced all other East Coast ports. The demand for intracity transit kept the omnibus business profitable and growing. The streets were surging with life, and no one wanted to walk when they could ride. Why become sweaty on a hot day and soil your fancy duds? It was better to pay a few cents and let the horses sweat.

3.3. The Lady Clinton, a side-entrance omnibus, tried on the Broadway line in 1831.

(*Harper's Monthly*, August 1893)

Abraham Brower began omnibus operations on Broadway in 1827 in an effort to promote urban mobility. It was not long before the line ran as far as Bleecker Street. No fixed vehicle design seemed apparent, so a variety of plans were tested. In a short time the European or long coach design was adapted. An early example was Brower's *Omnibus* of 1831 that featured large windows, longitudinal bench seats, and an end entrance (fig. 3.2). While this vehicle seemed to satisfy the wants of the operators, its design was defective in many ways: It was high above the streets, requiring a difficult ascent for all but the most athletic. The old and infirm would find it a serious challenge. The narrow entrance door made it difficult for ladies with their wide hoop skirts to squeeze through. Women with babes or packages in arms definitely required assistance. It was necessary once inside the bus to tramp to the forward end to pay your fare through a hole in the roof near the driver's seat – he was required to extend his hand down and back to receive the coins or bills. In all, it was a most awkward arrangement.

A better plan was exhibited in July 1831 by the Lady Clinton, built by a Newark carriage builder for William Niblo, proprietor of the famous

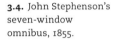

3.4. John Stephenson's seven-window omnibus, 1855.

(Clarence Hornung collection)

theater and garden at Broadway and Prince Streets. It was described by a New York newspaper of the time as being superbly finished with a dark blue broadcloth interior and silk curtains. Better yet, this "improved bus" had low entrance doors on the sides so that everyone could enter and exit easily and safely (fig. 3.3). Sadly for the traveling public, the Lady Clinton established no excitement among carriage builders, and the pattern created for Brower remained the standard plan throughout the omnibus era in the United States.

John Stephenson (1809–1893) came to dominate the production of American omnibuses. He started in a small shop in the rear of Abe Brower's stable on Lower Broadway in May 1831. Later he moved uptown to

Harlem and opened a proper factory on Fourth Avenue, and by 1856 he employed two hundred men and produced three hundred buses a year. Many were for local lines, but others were made for other U.S. cities, and some were shipped to South America, New Zealand, and South Africa. Stephenson was extremely fussy about the woods used in his coaches; only top-grade lumber was selected. It had to be carefully dried and inspected. White oak or ash was used for the frames, elm for the wheel hubs, and Spanish cedar or white poplar for the body panels. Considerable furniture glue and wood screws held the pieces together. Light weight and strength were the primary goals of the construction. The painting, lettering, and decorative artwork were done by the best craftsmen available. Local carriage shops elsewhere competed with Stephenson, and although they produced vehicles of good quality, no one ever succeeded in taking over the old New York master's dominance of the omnibus trade (fig. 3.4).

During the early years of bus operation, small independent line operators named each coach. Asa Hall, proprietor of the Greenwich Village line, seemed to favor military leaders such as General Andrew Jackson, the Marquis de Lafayette, Commodore David Porter, and Baron Friedrich von Steuben. He threw in one president, James Madison, for good measure. Other lines picked more commonplace names such as Comet, True Blue Mechanic, Forget-Me-Not, and Good Intent. The Broadway line was content with a simple number for each bus. A photograph for one such Stephenson bus in the 900 series is preserved in the photographic files of the Smithsonian Institution.

In 1834 the *New York Gazette* said the metropolis might be renamed the City of Omnibuses. The streets seemed to be paved with them – a slight exaggeration certainly, for there were only 97 in service. But the numbers would grow along with the population, and New York was already home to around 300,000 people and getting more populous by the day. The bigger the crowd, the greater the need for an easy, cheap way to get around town. The number of buses did grow – to 255 by 1846; 425 by 1850; and peaking in 1853 at 683. There were twenty-seven routes making 13,420 trips and collecting 120,000 fares each day. Yet the world of business is never trouble-free, and the bus trade had its downside as well. The financial panic of 1837 killed off a number of the more marginal operators. A general consolidation took place after the economy slowly recovered during the next four or five years. A second amalgamation took place in April 1854 when the New York Consolidated Stage Company absorbed about a dozen of the smaller omnibus lines. This was not because of hard times, but because of the advent of new competition. The street railway had become fashionable and offered larger, more comfortable conveyances that ran at slightly faster speeds. But most of all, it was new and

hence attractive to a nation that consistently valued the new over the old. In time the horse-drawn street cars would all but replace the now old-fashioned omnibus.

In general, the public appeared grateful for the convenience of public transit, yet it is normal to find fault with every aspect of daily life, so the omnibus also had its detractors. As early as October 2, 1864, the *New York Herald* referred to the modern martyrdom of riding an omnibus in which the driver quarrels with the passengers. He reported that there were quarrels getting on and getting off. The quarreling continued about change and ticket swindling. Drivers would swear at the passengers, and the passengers would harangue the driver through the roof hole. And so the omnibus rolled along, a veritable bedlam on wheels. Sometime later the *Tribune* sarcastically claimed the arrangement for pushing passengers out into the mud was unsurpassed. It was said the bus was never full, and there was always room for one more, no matter that every seat was taken. There was a place for the peddler and his large pack, or the German woman with a basket of stale fish, or the wench with her bundle of soiled linens. *Puck*, the American humor magazine, had some fun satirizing the "Broadway Sardine Line" in an 1881 cartoon illustrating the many hazards faced by regular travelers on the well-patronized, if not well-loved, public carrier (fig. 3.5).

3.5. A satire of omnibus travel was presented by a New York humor magazine. Note the fare box depicted in the center row, second sketch from the left side.

(*Puck*, March 10, 1881)

THE OMNIBUS 71

3.6. Interior of a New York omnibus, 1840s.

(George G. Foster, *New York in Slices*, 1849)

The gifted and productive British novelist Anthony Trollope visited New York in 1861 and reported firsthand on the perils and pleasures of omnibus riding. Trollope tried to be more tolerant and kindly in his commentary on American manners than his caustic mother, Frances. In many ways he found the buses to be excellent: they were plentiful, one never had to wait long for the next one to arrive, and they were surprisingly clean. Yet one needed to be a native to understand their mode of operation, and these were not obvious to a foreigner like Trollope. There was no conductor at the rear door to accept payment, make change, or offer directions. It took some time for the alien passenger to understand that the driver seated on the roof at the front of the bus was also the conductor. When it was necessary to walk to the front of the vehicle, one had to take care not to trample feet or the overflowing dresses of the day while moving forward (fig. 3.6). Then you called up through a small opening in the roof, just behind the driver's seat, to communicate with said driver. Through the same hole you handed up your money and received back the change. It was all very confusing. Heaven forbid you should need to ask for directions from the driver, or where to change lines or get off. He attempted to shout back at you through the same obscure hole – most of which you could not understand, because the driver was preoccupied with managing the team of horses through the street traffic. You were no sooner seated when the bus stopped and a lady entered. She came straight to you and without a word or gesture handed you a coin. You wondered why. Then the other passengers said she wanted you to pay her fare with it. Ladies never wanted to reach up through that nasty hole in the roof or possibly be touched by the rough hand of the driver, so supposedly everyone understood that she expected a male passenger to do this for her, without any need to ask for this service. Now that he knew, Trollope, of course, obliged.

He had a new surprise coming when he saw that it was time for him to exit – his stop was coming up. He could not open the rear door and called to the driver to stop, but the coach moved on. He called again – still no response – and then one of the passengers told him to ring the bell. There was a cord running along the upper wall, front to back. Once the bell was sounded, the bus stopped and Trollope hopped off. He found that some buses had no bell signal and that a tug on the leather door strap signaled the driver to stop by pulling on his leg. The strap had a loop at the front that engaged the driver's right leg or foot, and this is how the door was opened and closed. The strap was visible inside the omnibus, for it rang along or near the roof line inside the body. Trollope found dealing with horsecars much less puzzling, because they had a proper conductor who was stationed inside the car or on the rear platform. He had less trouble with the coinage, too, because an English penny equaled 2 American cents and a shilling was worth 24 cents.

The drivers were a curious part of city life, for they were so public being out on the streets in plain view most of the day, yet they had very little actual contact with the passengers or the thousands of other inhabitants who walked by them on the sidewalks. There were a few words exchanged during fare collection, and half of that was unintelligible to both parties. Most of the drivers were rough men with little or no education who lived brutal, uncaring lives far removed from elegant, upper-crust residents, who might as well have lived in a different world. James McCabe, in his 1882 book *New York by Sunlight and Gaslight*, described the driver as a large, heavy man with large hands whose dress ranged from the nasty to the eccentric. They tended to be middle-aged or older and had weather-beaten faces. They smelled like old horse blankets, McCabe said, because they likely slept in stables and were well wrapped in these coverlets during most winter days. Being outside fourteen hours a day in all seasons required a strong constitution and an indifference to comfort, as was related in *Railway Age* of July 1880. In summer the sun beat down relentlessly, save for the shade offered by a small cotton umbrella fastened to the roof or seat back. If there was a breeze, the driver hoped to catch some of that, being high above the street. On rainy days he tried to stay dry by wrapping up in oilskin and a rubber coat. Winter was the worst season, for the cold wind off the river seemed to penetrate even the heaviest coat.

Just sitting in one position most of the day caused cramps, and most men were happy to jump off the seat box to pavement at the end of the run and change the team for a fresh pair of horses. These artless fellows would often board near the stables. There they would have a quick breakfast at daybreak and be off to work. Lunch and dinner were sent over to the stable by the landlady. Here the driver would bolt down his food in twenty minutes and then be back to his roof perch. If he was married, his wife took care of meals and one of the children made the delivery. He would get home at about midnight and fall into bed. If he could afford to take a day off, he would spend it filling up on beer. The major drawback to the job was not the long hours or the tedium of work, but the door strap. If jerked hard from inside, it could almost knock him off the bus. At other times, young men would run up behind the bus and before it stopped would pull the door open with all of their might – this would pull the driver's leg with a jerk that could lay him flat out on the roof. Yet the job suited most drivers, who were happy to have steady employment at $2 a day.

A reporter for the *New York Times* found some of the drivers observant and even wise. He noted that Walt Whitman spent many hours seated next to drivers on the Broadway buses and gained insights into human nature from this lofty perch. The drivers tended to be uncommunicative around strangers but would open up after the offer of a chew of tobacco or a good cigar. They could be an amazing source of information about what was going on around town, particularly any good scandal. They were masters of chatting and became eloquent when denouncing the drivers of rival lines. The less philosophical drivers tended to go a little too fast and would dash ahead of a rival bus to pick up fares. Racing was a common, if unsafe, practice. The men would spend hours decorating the buses and horses with flags and streamers for holidays like the Fourth of July. They took pride in driving down the great avenues with matched pairs of grays or bays. On very cold days they showed concern for the passengers on long trips up to Harlem by stopping at Cato's tavern for drinks, smiles, and a warm-up. They were good fellows at heart, but few could claim to be saints.

The less-than-saintly side of the drivers was evident when it came to fare collection. So much coinage passing through the hands of these poor men surely was a temptation that tested their honesty. Many simply could not resist and would keep a certain percentage of the money, since there was no way for owners to account for the total. Spotters were only partially successful in stopping the pilferage. Sometime around 1870 the old cash box was replaced by a fare box inside the passenger compartment up near the front and placed so it was visible to the driver. This device had a glass front window and was securely locked. It was an old idea that had been patented by John B. Slawson in 1857. (Slawson obtained more patents and purchased those of other inventors until he basically monopolized this device.) The fare box did not entirely end "knocking down" on the fares, because the drivers still had to make change and had some access to the cash exchange, but the fare box helped keep them honest. Eventually the omnibus lines were forced to reduce their fares from 10 cents to a nickel because of the competition of the horsecars and, later still, that of the elevated railways.

At the beginning of the twentieth century, the only omnibus line still running in Manhattan was on Fifth Avenue. It was no longer just wagons and carriages; there were now a few motor cars mixed in with the surging traffic. Most of the time the horses moped along as if half asleep. Then the driver would see a break in the traffic and urge the team along to dodge out into the center lane around an obstinate coal wagon. These fuel haulers were the meanest cusses on the streets and seemed to take pleasure in blocking traffic. They were especially hard to get around. The omnibus driver had an advantage in being so high up that he could see ahead and spot breaks in the congestion, but he had to move quickly before the traffic closed up again. A driver being interviewed by a reporter for *McClure's* magazine was a veteran at the reins who had started as a youngster. Now sixty-eight years of age, he still liked driving and refused offers to take an easy job back at the stable. He preferred the hum and rumble of the streets and hoped to stay on the seat box for just a few more years.

Omnibus drivers faced a special challenge during certain winters. Every ten years or so New York, Boston, almost every northern city on the continent was hit by a massive snowstorm. It could pile up to 2 feet. Removal in those days was unlikely, so most transit systems were ready to bring out the sleighs. These were not the quaint little cutters pictured in Currier and Ives prints, but giants pulled by twelve or more horses. Most people, even the drivers, seemed to accept the appearance of the immense sleds as a holiday event, possibly because they often showed themselves around Christmastime. The sleighs were outfitted with small harness bells that served to warn pedestrians and other vehicles that it was approaching, for they ran smoothly and almost noiselessly over the compacted snow. Even the sounds of the horses' hooves were muffled, so a sleigh could be on top of you in a matter of seconds. The tinkling little bells were just enough of a signal to alert one and all to look about and be aware. Men and children seemed to love the big sleighs and would shout and laugh with much merriment. Poor boys would pelt them with snowballs, but this only seemed to add to the festive spirit of travelers. The largest specimens that ran on Broadway were called the "man-of-war"

3.7. Huge sleighs temporarily replaced omnibuses during times of heavy snows.

(*Illustrated London News*, April 10, 1852)

sleighs. They seated up to sixty passengers and had high, rolled-back front ends with fine scrollwork and lettering. One of those that operated on the Fulton Ferry line was pictured in the *Illustrated London News* in 1852 (fig. 3.7). They continued to run until late in the nineteenth century.

Large sleighs much like those just described were used to ferry passengers across the Hudson River at Albany before the railroad bridge was completed in 1866. The river tended to freeze over every year by December. The ferry boats could not deal with thick ice, so the sleds were put into service. The northern terminal of the Hudson River Railroad, located at East Albany, was a busy station. Most passengers desired to cross the river because their destination was the state capital, so the ferries – or sleds, depending on the severity of the winter – were generally very busy.

After the introduction of streetcars, the omnibus entered a lengthy Indian summer. Their numbers and importance declined greatly by the last year of the Civil War, when only 231 of them were still operating. The 1880 census reported on the New York omnibus system, which continued to serve on Broadway, Fifth Avenue, and other major streets. The Madison Avenue line ran uptown to Grand Central Station. The fare was 5 cents and the several lines pooled their earnings. There were a total of 215 buses; 1,460 horses; and 427 men in this service. They carried 41,800 passengers a day, but did not operate on Sunday. Owners paid a yearly license fee of $25 to the city, and the drivers paid an annual permit fee of 25 cents. By the early 1880s only three lines were running where there had once been thirty. The Fifth Avenue and Fulton Ferry lines were owned by two

3.8. Fifth Avenue double-deck omnibus, 1890.

(Harper's Weekly, July 11, 1891)

wealthy brothers, S. W. and S. M. Andrews. One of the Andrews brothers was active into the early 1880s. Drivers claimed he had a net worth of $4 million but that he kept an eye on the buses to make sure not one nickel was stolen. He would wait for the last bus to check in around 1:00 AM and oversee the counting of the day's receipts. Any driver who was short would be docked 50 cents for each missing nickel. The drivers had a special hand signal they would flash to buses passing in the opposite direction to indicate that the boss was out spotting. Francis A. Palmer, a bank president, controlled the Broadway line, and was apparently content to stay in his office and allow his drivers to work in peace. Efforts to replace this busy line with a street railway had been stopped by the department store giant Alexander T. Stewart. His death in 1875 helped the horsecar advocates, but it required almost another decade to put tracks in the lower end of Broadway. In July 1885 a sale of the defunct omnibus line attracted a large crowd, but the bidding was anything but lively. Seventy-two buses were sold for as little as $20 each. Only the Fifth Avenue line persisted, and its future was hardly secure.

Fifth Avenue was the most fashionable street in the city. Mansions of the richest families in America fronted on the pavement; so, too, did the grandest churches, the Metropolitan Museum of Art, and the west border of Central Park. The ridership was a mix of upstairs-downstairs with servant girls and top-ranking corporate leaders seated on the same bus. By the early 1890s the double-deck buses, called Jumbos, paraded down the avenue (fig. 3.8). There were seats going across the roof, widthwise, in place of the more common longitudinal variety. A high railing made passengers feel secure, though the back staircase might have deterred less adventurous travelers. The combined seating on these double-deckers was thirty-five. There was a conductor, who wore a white cap in the summer, and hence no need for the driver to use the old-fashioned door strap system. The driver sat up front at roof level, as in the first days of omnibus operation. A three-horse team harnessed abreast gave the rig a dashing appearance. The clientele were almost all beautifully dressed – men in top hats and ladies decked out in high fashion that included some very pricy headgear. Late in the afternoon on a summer day the buses took on a more colorful look. The children at play in the park would board with their floppy hats covered in flowers; they gathered on the top deck and as the bus came down Murray Hill Street, it would sway from side to side, making the flowers nod and move as if blown by the passing wind. Such lovely, almost poetic scenes are rarely associated with city transit, and indeed the lovely scene would not continue for many more years. In 1905 the first motor bus appeared, and three years later the Fifth Avenue line said farewell to the last of its old-fashioned horse-powered omnibuses.

THE OMNIBUS BEYOND MANHATTAN

The American omnibus originated in New York City and surely reached its apogee in that location, but they were found in other urban areas as well. Philadelphia opened its first omnibus line on Chestnut Street in December 1831 and soon had a second, longer route connecting the navy yard with the city's Kensington neighborhood. By 1848 the city had eighteen lines and 138 buses; a decade later the number of buses had more than doubled. The central omnibus terminal was at the Merchant's Exchange on Dock Street, two blocks above the Delaware River and just below Spruce Street. The Exchange was a handsome Greek Revival building designed by William Strickland and completed in 1834 (fig. 3.9). The buses congregated in a plaza at the front entrance. On busy routes, a bus left every five minutes. The convenience of a single central terminal was undeniable, but the concentration of so much activity in one area caused inordinate congestion, so the city required some lines to find a new end terminal. Fares in Philadelphia started at a shilling, or 12½ cents, in the 1830s, but began to decline over the following decades. Some short routes charged only a nickel, and in 1852 competition was so fierce that most lines charged only 3 cents for a ride. In addition, an annual pass was available that reduced fares to 1 cent, but the cardholder might make only four trips per day. Extra trips beyond this limit had to be paid for at the cash-fare rate. In about 1890 Philadelphia's Broad Street line acquired some double-deck omnibuses that featured a very substantial rear stairway and a canvas canopy for the driver. These yellow-and-white vehicles were locally made and used a three-abreast team of horses like New York's Fifth Avenue line.

Boston adopted the city bus in 1835, but it already had a fairly well developed system of suburban stage lines running to nearby suburbs such

3.9. Philadelphia's Merchant Exchange was the site of the central downtown omnibus terminus.

(*Gleason's Pictorial*, May 6, 1854)

as Roxbury and Cambridge. The line to Roxbury opened in early 1826 with hourly service. By April of that year the line was carrying eleven hundred travelers a week.

St. Louis, Missouri, was hardly a major city in the 1830s, but it showed an eagerness to catch up with its larger eastern counterparts by adapting the latest ideas in urban transit (fig. 3.10). Limited taxi operation started in 1838, but the inauguration of bus service depended on some curious circumstances. Erastus Wells came west in 1843 from New York to settle in St. Louis. He joined several other young men, including Calvin Case and James B. Eads, in salvaging steamboat wrecks. Among the items salvaged was an army ambulance. Wells and Case decided to convert the ambulance into an omnibus and began offering service along Broadway to the northern city limits. The experiment worked so well that new buses were ordered from a Troy, New York, manufacturer and a second line was

3.10. Andrew Wight had been an ornamental painter for John Stephenson and started omnibus production in St. Louis in about 1858.

(*National Car Builder*, June 1881)

opened. Their success began to build, and by 1850 they had 90 buses, 450 horses, and 100 men in service. In 1859 Wells expanded into street railways and went on to become a successful business leader in his adopted hometown. He also served several terms in the U.S. Congress. His one-time partner, James Eads, went on to become one of the most prominent engineers in the nation.

In addition to providing intercity and intra-city travel, omnibuses were commonly used by hotels and resorts that needed a cheap vehicle to move clients short distances. This was especially true for passengers arriving at the depot, very often as small groups. A small bus was just right to convey them to the hotel. Even small communities had a hotel bus. Oxford, Ohio, for instance, was a small college town with about seventeen hundred residents in 1870, yet it was large enough to have a hotel and its own omnibus. Big-city hotels might have more than one bus because of greater traffic and multiple stations common in larger metro areas. The bus did not just pick up incoming guests, but those departing the hotels as well.

Resorts also found omnibuses useful because they, too, had guests arriving in groups, for even a single family could be six or more people, too many for a common carriage. The great rushes that were common at the open or close of the summer season saw a gigantic scuttling of vehicles carrying crowds to and from the railroad station. Saratoga Springs, New York, was one of the nation's most popular summer resorts in the nation. New York City's wealthier class seemed to spend most of July and August in this pleasant retreat just a few miles from Albany. The crowds were always on the move to the racetracks, the steamboat landing on the Hudson River, or the boat races on the nearby lake. A fleet of omnibuses were ready to move the crowds. Such a scene in front of the Grand Union Hotel was depicted by *Leslie's Illustrated* in the middle 1870s. It shows half a dozen omnibuses surrounded by a sea of people. One unusually long bus is lettered for the Steamboat line, which indicates an effort to find ways to handle seasonal visitor surges. An even larger bus was built in 1875 by John Stephenson for service in Brooklyn. It was 36 feet long, seated 120 passengers, and was likely too big for regular service. The more typical four-window bus seated 12 passengers and could be powered by just two horses, though in some cities where hills were more common, four horses were needed. Their short wheel base allowed them to turn and dodge in and out of traffic.

3.11. Omnibuses provided a convenient and affordable way to transport guests to and from hotels and resorts.

Resorts often purchased larger buses, since they were not running through congested big-city streets. Among the preserved Stephenson photographs in the Smithsonian's collections is an undated print of an eight-window bus from the White Sulphur Springs Hotel. This venerable West Virginia spa dates back to the 1770s. Somewhat shorter buses were proposed for use on the Mount Washington, New Hampshire, carriage road in the 1850s, where a resort hotel named the Tip Top House was the destination of tourists heading toward the summit of the highest mountain in New England. One can only wonder how the horses endured this exhausting climb. An engraving illustrating this line is reproduced in figure 3.12 from *Ballou's Pictorial* magazine of August 9, 1856. The elegant buses and the fine hotel shown were in fact never completed. The carriage road was not opened until 1861, and Concord coaches were employed. The cog railway opened up the formidable grade to the Tip Top House eight years later. It might be assumed that the horses were retired from their arduous hill-climbing duties, however. *Harper's Monthly* reported in its August 1877 issue that the road coaches remained in service and were well patronized.

A few retail establishments employed omnibuses as a way to bring customers to the door. This was true for stores not placed in the prime shopping areas of downtown. Reluctant buyers would complain that it was too far to walk or that they would not spend extra car fare to patronize any store outside the very center of town. This was exactly the problem faced in the 1880s by the partners William and Frederick Alms and William D. Doepke in Cincinnati. These enterprising men had opened a dry goods store on Main Street at Twelfth Street in 1865. They built a fine new store nearby at Main and the canal some six blocks north of the fashionable department stores clustered around Fountain Square. Frequent sales and aggressive advertising helped to attract buyers, but in the fall of 1887 Alms and Doepke decided to offer a free ride to all who desired to ride uptown (fig. 3.13). A handsome wagonette, as smaller omnibuses were generally called, made its circular way through the busy streets. Roof seats

THE OMNIBUS 81

3.12. Mount Washington in New Hampshire planned an omnibus line for its carriage road in the 1850s.

(*Ballou's Pictorial*, August 9, 1856)

were available, much to the joy of youngsters and sun worshippers of the day. When the horse was superseded by the gasoline engine, a private bus took over the duties of the wagonettes. The bus, too, would disappear from the center city as shoppers gravitated to the suburban shopping malls. Alms and Doepke itself shut its doors in 1954.

The lumbering horse-drawn buses had one more unexpected use, and that was as a party vehicle. An early instance of such employment happened near St. Louis in the early fall of 1867. *Leslie's Illustrated Newspaper* reported a Sunday picnic organized by D. R. Hart for his family at Breese Lake between Venice and Brooklyn, Illinois. A city bus was hired to carry the picnickers to the lake. All went well at first, but soon after leaving the ferry landing on the east side of the Mississippi River, the omnibus slipped off the road and rolled over several times as it slid down an embankment. The driver, horses, and passengers all escaped without serious injury. The only victim of this mishap was the old turtle-roof bus, which was smashed to pieces.

About a decade later, a group of east-side New Yorkers calling themselves the Macrelville Old Social Club hired an elderly omnibus, pulled by four equally used-up steeds, for a New Year's Eve party. The members of this ad hoc social club were not from Gotham's first families, but they were intent on consuming a goodly number of cocktails during their evening perambulations. The horns and rattles, plus the vehicle's own jingles as it bounced along the pavement, set up a merry, if not always melodic, concert. Before the sun showed its red glow in the eastern sky, the club members grew silent and ready for sleep. The sponsors of the party were

3.13. A few department stores operated free bus service to accommodate their customers.

(*Cincinnati Gazette*, October 12, 1887)

content that the event ended without a scrimmage. *Leslie's Weekly* reported on this excursion in its issue of January 12, 1878.

Yet another omnibus party was recorded by an anonymous artist in a watercolor rendering preserved by the Maryland Historical Society in Baltimore. Sometime in 1856 a large group of young toughs, forty or fifty in number, came riding through the center of town intent more on mischief than on merrymaking. They were members of the Know-Nothing Party, a group that hated immigrants and all foreigners who happened to take up residence in the United States. Each man had a rifle, pistol, or knife in plain sight. There was no spirit of tolerance or brotherly love in this nasty group, and every German or Irishman was well advised to take cover as this omnibus made its way through the city.

THE OMNIBUS AS A VEHICLE

Coach and carriage building was a well-established trade by the time the omnibus came into production. The body shape presented no great problems, and the seating and interior upholstery were comparatively simple and utilitarian. Yet the vehicle's demanding work schedule, in operation more than the typical carriage, required special care in its construction. Strength and durability were essential. Some omnibuses had extra-heavy wheels for this reason. The standard four-window bus had a body just over 9 feet long. The front wheels were generally 40 to 44 inches in diameter while the rear wheels measured between 56 to 58 inches in diameter. The wheel base was about 7 feet. The ceiling was just 6 feet, meaning tall men needed to stoop. The floor was almost 4 feet above the street level. Omnibuses weighed about 2,500 pounds and cost between $600 and $700. Seating was limited to twelve to fourteen passengers. A simple candle lamp provided just enough illumination to move around inside

3.14. Chicago omnibus well loaded leaves town in the evening rush hour.

(*Scribner's Magazine,* September 1875)

the compartment. The iron stairway at the rear door was more like a ladder than a staircase. It was often fitted with a flap or a cover to keep the treads clear of mud or snow. The paint jobs were elaborate and attractive. They featured small portraits or scenery, elegant scrolls, handsome letters, stripes, and shading or outlining in several colors.

A few of these robust and attractive vehicles have been preserved and may be seen on exhibit at the Smithsonian Institution, Shelburne Museum (Vermont), Stony Brook Long Island Carriage Museum, and a few local historical societies elsewhere in the United States.

SUGGESTED READING

Abraham Brown Obituary, *New York Times,* May 2, 1890.

Abraham Brower's Obituary, *Pioneer Omnibus Operator,* ca. 1804–1890.

Barker, T. C., and Robbins, M. *A History of London Transport: Passenger Travel and the Development of the Metropolis.* London: Allen and Unwin, 1963.

"The Beginnings of Mass Transportation in Urban America," *Smithsonian Journal of History* 1 (Summer) 1966.

Berkebile, Donald H. *Carriage Terminology: An Historical Dictionary.* Washington, D.C,: Smithsonian Institution Press, 1978.

"The Carriage Road Mt. Washington," *Ballou's Pictorial,* Aug. 9, 1856.

Davidson, Marshall B. *Life in America*, vol. 2. Boston: Houghton Mifflin, 1951.

"The Departing Omnibus," *New York Times*, Nov. 13, 1881.

Dunbar, Charles S. *Buses, Trolleys, and Trams*. London: Paul Hamlyn, 1967.

"Fifth Avenue Bus Driver," *McClure's Magazine*, April 1903.

"Fifth Avenue Omnibuses," *Harper's Weekly*, July 11, 1891.

Hornung, Clarence P. *Handbook of Early Advertising Art*. New York: Dover Publications, 1956.

"How Omnibus Drivers Live," *Railway Age*, July 8, 1880.

Lay, Max G. *Ways of the World*. New Brunswick, N.J.: Rutgers University Press, 1992.

Mayhew, Henry. *London Labour and the London Poor*. London: Griffin, Bohn, 1861.

McCabe, James D. *New York by Sunlight and Gaslight*. Philadelphia: Douglass Bros., 1882.

McKay, John P. *Tramways and Trolleys: The Rise of Urban Mass Transport in Europe*. Princeton, N.J.; Princeton University Press, 1976.

Miller, John A. *Fares Please*. New York: Appleton-Century, 1941.

Moore, H. C. *Omnibuses and Cabs: Their Origin and History*. London: Chapman and Hall, Ltd., 1902.

"More About the Omnibus," *New York Times*, Dec. 4, 1881.

Nevins, Alan. *British Travelers in America*. New York: Henry Holt, 1923.

"Paris Omnibus," *American Railway Review*, Nov. 22, 1860.

Scharf, John T. *History of St. Louis*. Philadelphia: L. H. Everts and Co., 1883.

———. *History of Philadelphia, 1609–1884*. Philadelphia; L. H. Everts and Co., 1884.

White, John H., Jr. *Horsecars, Cable Cars, and Omnibuses*. New York: Dover Publications, 1974.

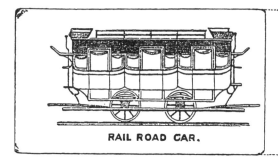

4.1. New York and Harlem Railroad ticket issued about 1838. The car was made by John Stephenson in 1831.

(*Scribner's Magazine*, September 1889)

Streetcars № 4

That Most Democratic Conveyance

THE OMNIBUS PROVIDED ADEQUATE PUBLIC TRANSIT IN MOST cities by the middle of the nineteenth century. Yet transit operations, especially in the larger urban centers, were looking for ways to increase vehicle capacity and lower operating costs. The solution was the streetcar. It was a very low-tech scheme that used old and familiar methods. The track plan was the old-fashioned strap-iron rail scheme that performed poorly on steam-powered lines but was sufficient for small, light city cars. Its big advantage was cheapness. The cars were undersized and devoid of heating or power brakes. The driver's right arm powered the brake lever. Lighting was minimal, with one small oil lamp at each end of the car. The motive power was the horse, a creature enslaved for drayage since the beginning of civilization. They were a serviceable, if unenthusiastic, street motor but were costly and inefficient. Horses were expensive to buy, capable of working only a few hours a day, and subject to illness. They were always hungry. They also presented a health hazard to all city dwellers, because the street was their toilet. Because thousands of horses were needed to power the cars, the pavement was always covered in urine and feces. Labor costs were high as well. It took a two-man crew to operate each car; one managed the horses and the hand brake while the second looked after the passengers and collected the fares. This rudimentary form of transit was clearly hard on both man and beast.

With so many shortcomings, why did the horsecars last for fifty years? Why were thousands of miles of track and millions of dollars invested in these hopelessly inefficient little vehicles? The simple answer was that they worked. They could move millions of passengers during all seasons, and they did so cheaply enough that fares remained low and investors received a decent return. Countless inventors tried to replace the horse with steam, cable, and other forms of power, but with little effect. Electricity would finally begin to unseat the old-fashioned horsecar in the late 1880s. It seemed curious even to observers of the time that in an age devoted to science and industrial progress, the antiquated horsecar prevailed for half a century.

IT STARTED IN NEW YORK CITY

The street railway was not consciously invented. Its conception was accidental and cannot be credited to any one person. It is certain, however, that it started in New York City and so was a very American innovation. The New York and Harlem Railroad was incorporated in 1831 to build an ordinary steam railroad the length of Manhattan Island and head northward after crossing over the Harlem River (fig. 4.1). Its southern terminal was at Broadway and Chambers Street, near the city hall and situated at the southern end of the island. The Harlem railway began at Prince Street near the old St. Patrick's Church and followed several streets to Bowery Street. The tracks went up Bowery to Union Square then northbound on Fourth Avenue and on to Yorkville and Harlem. The tracks were buried under the street surface with only the tops of the rails exposed. Granite stringers were capped with thin iron bars that served as the rails. The first segment to Fourteenth Street opened in mid-November 1832. A local newspaper reported, "The horses trotted off in a handsome style, with great ease at twelve miles an hour. Crowds of spectators greeted the passage of the cars with shouts and every window on the Bowery was filled." The cars were described as spacious and convenient, being divided into three compartments. This style of car remained in service on the Harlem line as late as 1887. The following year it progressed to Thirty-Second Street, where Murray Hill blocked the right of way. A ten-block-long tunnel was commenced that required four years to complete. A second tunnel was built at Ninety-Second Street but was only two blocks long.

On January 1, 1837, the New York and Harlem Railroad issued a report that reflected on the operation of the company during the previous year. During the winter, service began at 7:00 AM and continued until 10:00 PM. During the summer, operations started two hours earlier. The round trip to Yorkville (near Eighty-sixth Street) required ninety-six minutes for a distance of roughly 5½ miles. The fare to Yorkville was 12½ cents – the fare below Forty-second Street was 6 cents. The winter of 1836–1837 was a heavy snow season, and the railroad tracks were blocked for several weeks. The railroad was obliged to purchase sleighs to maintain service and spent $2,000 in clearing the track to resume service. In a subsequent report for 1841 it was noted that the service between Prince Street and Twenty-Seventh Street now operated every five minutes, so this portion of the railroad was operated as a quasi streetcar line. Late in 1837 that railroad entered Harlem at 125th Street, which was near the end

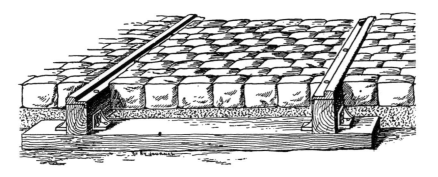

4.2. The typical horsecar track was buried in city streets so that only the top of the rail was visible.

(C. B. Fairchild, *Street Railways: Their Construction, Operation and Maintenance*, 1892)

of Fourth Avenue. It was located on the east side of the cucumber-shaped island. Near this place the railroad crossed the Harlem River and would eventually reach Chatham, which is a little southeast of Albany.

Franz Anton Ritter von Gerstner offered many interesting details on the railroad in the late 1830s. It was built entirely for passenger service and as such was an enormous success. The New York and Harlem Railroad carried one million passengers in 1839 and expected that number to grow by 50 percent the following year. Few European lines had such patronage, and no other U.S. railroad was doing as well. On Sundays each car was packed with one hundred riders; however, the four-wheel double-deckers had seats for only fifty, so many people had to stand during most or all of the trip. In September 1838 the railroad ran a special train of thirty cars to carry thirteen hundred soldiers. It was pulled by two locomotives. Most of the traffic was on the lower end or that part of the line below Fourteenth Street. Horses propelled the cars from this stop to city hall. Steam locomotives operated on the northern end of the line.

On July 3, 1839, a locomotive named the New York derailed at Fourteenth Street adjacent to Union Square. The engineer and superintendent of the line worked to re-rail the engine, with a large crowd gathered to watch. The men became so involved in shifting the locomotive that they neglected to check on the water level of the train's boiler. Low water is a common cause for boiler explosions, and after a time the boiler blew up with a tremendous roar. A New York newspaper provided a gory description of the incident, reporting that two men were killed. Legs were seen flying into Union Square, arms went into a pile of lumber, the engineer's head was split in two, and the intestines and organs of other victims were splattered on the pavement. A mob gathered and reacted to the horror before them by pulling up and destroying the railroad track on Bowery Street. The city fathers reacted by banning locomotives below Thirty-second Street. In 1858 that limit was moved up to Forty-Second Street at Fourth Avenue. This is how the site of Grand Central Station was established. The Harlem line built its own terminal at Fourth Avenue and Twenty-Seventh Street in 1832. This modest wooden structure burned in

STREETCARS

1845 and was replaced with a larger masonry structure in the Italianate style. After being remodeled in 1851 and 1858, it became a theater in 1871 and was demolished in the late 1880s for the new Madison Square Garden.

The forty-minute headway on which the cars initially ran was increased rather quickly to ten minutes, effectively making it become a street railway style of operation on the city end of the line. This portion of the railway was divided into four parts with a 6¼cent fare for each segment. Twenty-five cents was the fare to Harlem. The horses on the south end of the Harlem line averaged 5,692 miles a year in the late 1830s. Operations continued on a steady and profitable basis through the next two decades. In fiscal year 1861–1862 the city portion of the railroad carried 3.5 million passengers with a total mileage of 5.29 million. A decade later the city cars transported 12.2 million for a distance of 12.27 million miles. In 1871 the Harlem line had 106 horsecars in service.

The sedate and old-fashioned Harlem line showed little ambition to expand over its first thirty years, but that was about to change. The only part of the railroad that made money was the streetcar end. The upcountry line had little traffic and produced no profit. The stock had a par value of $50, but sold for only $3 by 1857. Seeing real value in the New York and Harlem property, Cornelius Vanderbilt lent the company money and began to buy up its stock in 1857, often at 50 cents on the dollar. By April 1863 he and his son-in-law, Horace Clark, had enough shares to take over the company. Vanderbilt became president, and the Wall Street traders went crazy speculating in its shares. Daniel Drew, the Great Bear, stood to lose almost $2 million. The New York and Harlem was no longer a Cinderella railroad but the new darling of the bulls. Vanderbilt had begun his entry into the world of railroading, and the little Harlem line was the first stepping-stone in what would become an empire.

The value of the New York and Harlem to Vanderbilt was that it offered an entry onto Manhattan Island and that that it owned terminal property at Forty-Second Street that could be redeveloped into a grand station. The city end of the line was operated as a separate subsidiary known as the Fourth Avenue Railway. It paid a dividend of 2–3 percent to the parent company, which was leased to the New York Central and Hudson River Railroad in April 1873 for 401 years. In 1876 the Fourth Avenue line had stock valued at more than $20 million and revenue of nearly $800,000, which was good for a line just 5½ miles long. By 1888 *Poor's Manual of Railroads* reported that the track mileage had grown to 8¼ miles. Some 1,389 horses propelled 162 cars that carried 16.6 million passengers. In June 1896 the Fourth Avenue line was leased to the Metropolitan Street Railway. This last named corporation was organized in the summer of 1892 as the Metropolitan Traction Company by Peter Widener, William Whitney, and Thomas Ryan to consolidate New York

City's street railways, exclusive of the elevated lines. It was an ambitious and costly scheme. The partners showed their positive intentions by replacing the antiquated horsecar system with cable and electric traction. The Fourth Avenue line, for example, was partially converted to electricity in March 1898. New cars were purchased, and some lines, trying to gain a competitive edge, offered free transfers between the lines, although they were often reluctant to grant such privileges. At the same time, the partners were plundering the assets of the Metropolitan and enriched themselves by around $100 million between 1893 and 1902. The collapse of the company in 1907 represented one of the great corporate swindles in American history.

Street railways in New York and elsewhere could not build tracks in the city streets without a degree of regulation by the city government. Almost every municipality demanded a formal plan outlining the route, fare structure, and the details of operations. Some cities, such as Cincinnati, passed a general ordinance in 1859 outlining such basics. The city engineer was involved in the details of the route and track construction. The privilege of using the city streets was not free. The railways paid a 2½ percent tax on their gross earning; this was later revised to 12½ percent. There was a car tax of $4 per foot of the body's length; hence a standard 16-foot-long body was taxed at $64 a year. The railways were responsible for maintaining the pavement between and beside the rails. They were required to offer "owl car service" between midnight and 6:00 AM. There were to be no seat cushions between May 1 and November 1, when the weather was warmer and customers would not mind sitting on the cooler wooden seats. Harness bells were not permitted. The track gauge was fixed at 62½ inches so that ordinary railroad cars could not be used. Cash fares were set at 5 cents in 1859. In 1879 tickets could be used at these prices: six for 25 cents; ten tickets for 48 cents; and twenty-five tickets for $1. Later children could ride for a cash fare of 3 cents; two children could ride for 5 cents. Few other industries were subject to municipal regulations in the Victorian era. However, starting around 1901 the Progressive movement ushered in an era of statewide oversight in the form of public utilities commissions that covered electric power, gas, and transit companies.

Two men were particularly prominent in their development and progress of the New York City horsecars. No other lines were built after the opening of the Harlem line until 1851. The Sixth Avenue Railroad was chartered in September of that year. It ran from the Astor House hotel at Vesey Street and Broadway to Central Park. Alphonse Loubat (1799–1866), a French engineer living in New York at the time, took over as chief engineer and devised a grooved rail that became popular on American horsecar lines. Loubat was so excited by his success in the United States, he returned to France in 1853 with the mission of introducing the

American city railway to Paris. He received permission to build a line from Sèvres into the center of Paris by way of the Place de la Concorde and on to Vincennes on the east side of the city. But after construction had started, the city authorities reneged on their promise and would not allow him to lay track inside the city center. It would be some time before Paris would open its avenues to tram cars.

George Law (1806–1881) is generally associated with the construction and the steamship trade, but he, too, became involved in city railways by 1850s. Law was born in upper New York State near the Vermont border to a poor Irish immigrant family. He received no more than a perfunctory education and left rural life at the age of eighteen to become a hod carrier and a stone cutter. He worked building locks on the Erie Canal and became a contractor three years later. His rise to fame and fortune was swift from that time on; by 1834 he had saved $28,000. In 1839 he won a contract to build the High Bridge aqueduct that carried water across the Harlem River for the Croton Waterworks. This magnificent structure stands proudly today as a monument to its long-forgotten builder. In 1842 Law became the president of the Dry Dock Bank in New York City after saving it from insolvency. In 1854 he took over the Eighth Avenue Railroad when it, too, was about to fail. Its lackluster manager could not seem to complete the line, and the city was ready to void its charter. Law went to work with his usual vigor and completed the track in ten weeks. He purchased fifty cars and advanced the ailing line $800,000. It proved a good bargain, paying dividends averaging 12 percent. Law remained president of the railroad until his death. He also financed and built the Ninth Avenue Railroad in 1859, but it proved to be a poor investment and never made money. Law's son took over management of both horsecar lines after Law's death in 1881. Within a few years both the Eighth and Ninth Avenue lines were absorbed by the Metropolitan Street Railway.

THEY SPREAD LIKE WILDFLOWERS

It was not long after the first lines in Manhattan began operations that similar horse railways began to appear elsewhere in the United States. Some historians claim New Orleans was the second city in the world to open a street railway. The New Orleans and Carrollton Railroad opened a branch line from Magazine Street in January 1835. It was horse powered and used groove rail. Brooklyn, being the second largest city in New York and a close neighbor of the birthplace of the street railway, organized a city railway in late 1853. Construction began the following spring, and the first segment opened between the Fulton Ferry terminal and city hall. By 1860 there were five major lines radiating out of Brooklyn; some went as far as Green Point, the Hamilton Ferry, and Greenwood Cemetery. The

American Railway Review published a detailed account of the system in its September 27, 1860, issue. It explained that the Brooklyn system had 21 miles of double track, 120 cars, and 920 horses. The employees included 95 conductors, 120 drivers, and 20 blacksmiths of the total 339 employed. In 1859, 9.2 million passengers were carried for a total of 2.4 million miles. As Brooklyn grew in population and spread out over the landscape, the street railway grew steadily. By 1875 the system had expanded to 44 miles, a figure that would grow to 324 miles by the early 1890s. The system had by this time 5,500 horses, 29 steam dummies, 714 open cars, and 815 closed cars. Its gross earnings were $3.5 million, its assets $9.8 million, and its regular dividend was 8 percent.

Boston was only a few years behind in adopting horsecars for urban transit. The city's narrow and crooked streets were ill adapted to street railways. Unlike most major U.S. metropolitan cities, Boston failed to build on the grid system and was laid out much like a European town of the Middle Ages. Despite this handicap, Boston would develop a sizable and efficient rail transit system. The suburbs were well served by the steam railroad that radiated out from the city hub in all directions. Trunk lines, such as the Boston and Worcester and the Old Colony, carried thousands of commuters to and from the hub. The narrow-gauge Boston, Revere Beach, and Lynn Railroad transported commuters along the Atlantic shore to Lynn, 9½ miles to the north of Boston. It expanded in 1875 and within a dozen years was carrying an astonishing 2.1 million passengers a year in its diminutive wooden coaches.

Boston's pioneer horsecar line was chartered in the spring of 1856 and began running cars to Cambridge by June of that year. It not only carried commuters to the city but also transported them in and around Boston itself. The two communities were united by a 6,190-foot-long bridge on the west side of the city. When service began, fifteen cars generated revenues of $40 a day. The 5-mile line cost $300,000 and was declared a benefit to all economic classes because it offered cheap and convenient transport. Its cars were painted a straw color and burned lamps with green lenses at night. A second line opened to Roxbury during 1856; its cars were painted blue, edged in gold; the nighttime running lights were red. This was the Metropolitan Railroad, which started at the Tremont House hotel and ran three miles out to Roxbury's Granary Burial Grounds. In this soil can be found the graves of John Hancock, Samuel Adams, and Paul Revere. By 1860 Boston's 57 miles of horse railways were moving 13.6 million passengers a year.

The Metropolitan Railroad became Boston's largest street railway. By the early 1870s it was carrying more than 16 million passengers a year. In 1888 this one company owned 85 miles of track; 3,720 horses; and 764 cars. It hauled 42.9 million passengers, registered over $2 million in gross

4.3. Boston's Highland Street Railway operated deluxe cars for its Back Bay patrons. Each car was named for a former state governor. This car was built in about 1880 by J. M. Jones of Troy, New York.

(*National Car Builder*, June 1881)

earnings, and paid a 10 percent annual dividend. It became part of the West End Street Railway at this time. Within a few years the West End was said to be the largest street railway in the world and controlled two-thirds of the horsecar lines in Boston. Eight thousand horses were needed to power the West End Street Railway.

The Highland Street Railway was part of the West End by January 1887. This line served the wealthy Back Bay neighborhood of Boston and, unlike most streetcar operations, was managed in first-class fashion (fig. 4.3). The conductor and drivers were handpicked – only the most courteous and intelligent applicants were hired. They were outfitted in fine gray uniforms similar to those worn by postmen and were paid higher than usual salaries. The cars were large and beautifully finished inside and out. They featured double clerestory roofs and an elaborate paint scheme that looked like Scotch plaid. Some years after the fact, the *Street Railway Journal* of May 1890 reported that John Stephenson, the pioneer streetcar builder of New York, had refused to consider the plaid paint scheme, so the cars were built by Walter Jones in Troy, New York.

Boston's first electric streetcar line opened in January 1890. Its performance was so superior to the animal-powered cars that the West End company moved ahead with an electrification program. Ninety percent of its lines were converted by 1895, and the few remaining horsecars were retired within five years. Because of growing congestion, the Tremont Subway was opened in September 1897. It was the first underground railway in the United States and the fourth in the world. Later in the same year, the Boston Elevated Railway Company acquired the assets of the West End Street Railway. All streetcar service in Boston was run by Boston Elevated until 1947, when a public agency, the Metropolitan Transit Authority (MTA), took over the property.

Philadelphia was the largest American city during colonial times. Its order, broad streets, and tolerance attracted many diverse people. But as the new nation expanded and trade patterns shifted, New York took the lead and soon left its rival behind in the dust of its magical rise to greatness. Yet Philadelphia always hoped it might resume its rightful place in the order of things. Even in such mundane matters as public transit, the city seemed always a few years behind New York. Philadelphia's first horsecar line opened in January 1858, two years behind stodgy and intolerant Boston. What the city lacked in primacy, it made up for in being quick to expand its systems. By late 1859 there were cars running on Tenth, Eleventh, Spruce, Pine, Race, and Vine Streets. It was not long before Philadelphia had eighteen separate street railway companies and 155 miles of track.

An alliance was formed in 1859 between the city's competitors to coordinate fares, transfers, and other matters of operating practices. This cooperative spirit was generally not followed in other U.S. cities. Transfers were made free on New Year's Day in 1880. This allowed passengers to change cars on different lines at no extra cost and facilitated long-distance travel. Sunday service was made legal in 1867 by a court decision. During the same year, the state legislature passed an act requiring that black passengers be treated on equal terms with white passengers. The merger movement caught up with the City of Brotherly Love in 1895 by way of the Union Traction Company. Within three years the city had 448 miles of streetcar track in operation. The Philadelphia Rapid Transit Company, with an authorized capital of $30 million, succeeded the Union Traction Company in 1902. This company was one of the playthings of the Widener-Elkins Traction Syndicate.

Peter Arrell Brown Widener (1834–1915) was a native of Philadelphia who started life as a butcher. In time he was able to open his own shop, and being unusually energetic and ambitious he acquired a chain of shops. He was also active in the Republican Party; his political connection helped him land a large army contract for mutton during the Civil War. The profits from this arrangement allowed him to buy an interest in a local street railway in 1862. At the same time, he joined a partnership with William L. Elkins to acquire more transit properties. Elkins was an attorney and a sharp businessman, so the two men were a dynamic duo. They gradually gained control of all public transportation in Philadelphia and then began buying up streetcar lines elsewhere. They became associated with Thomas F. Ryan in New York City and bought the Metropolitan Traction Company in 1886. This firm merged with the Interborough Rapid Transit Company and so controlled New York City Transit. In 1897 the partners – now known as the Widener-Elkins Traction (or Transit) Syndicate, or more simply as the Philadelphia Syndicate – bought out the Charles Tyson Yerkes transit empire in Chicago. Yerkes had been successful in consolidating the Windy City's transportation system but in the process had alienated just about everyone of any prominence in the city. He was considered a robber baron par excellence; he cheated his partners, stockholders, and

Table 4.1. Basic Statistics for U.S. Street Railways in 1881

415	street railways in operation
18,000	cars
100,000	horses
150,000	tons of hay consumed each year
11,000,000	bushels of grain consumed each year
3,000	miles of track
1,212,400,000	passengers carried
35,000	employees
$150,000	invested

Source: *Railway Review*, December 23, 1882.

customers; and for good measure he had bribed or attempted to bribe most government officials of the area. Unable to continue in business in this community, he went to England. Yerkes became the prototype for the antihero in Theodore Dreiser's *Trilogy of Desire*, which includes *The Titan, The Financier,* and *The Stoic.*

Widener and Elkins moved across the nation scooping up transit, gas, and electric companies that amounted to an investment of $1.5 billion. The personal fortunes of the partners were enormous, and most of it came from 5-cent streetcar fares. Whoever contends that the transit business was never profitable does not know its history. Widener's estate at the time of his death in 1915 was $50 million.

Leslie's Illustrated Newspaper offered its opinion of the benefits of the streetcar in an editorial appearing in its December 15, 1860, issue. The nation was only carrying forward its passion for railways as the cure for all transportation problems. French writer Michel Chevalier had commented on this in his 1835 book about the American people. He said if they could not have a railway upon the earth, they could make one in the air. America had trains running through the wilderness that terrified the bear and buffalo and amazed the Indians. The street railway had rendered the omnibus as obsolete as the sedan chair. Streetcars reduced traffic and street noise by their greater carrying capacity. The system raised property values by 30 to 50 percent in the central business districts of New York and Philadelphia. Central Park was more accessible to every New Yorker now, because the cars were so much faster than the old-fashioned buses. One-fifth of the U.S. population now rode tram cars each day. It was amazing to think that the great cities of Europe remained content with omnibuses. When would they catch up with America's progressive ways?

Horsecar transit was a basic part of American life, so much so that the San Francisco city directory of 1875 opened with this statement: "[The] horse car is among the most indispensable conditions of modern metropolitan growth. It is to the city what the steam car and the steam ship lines are to the state and country. In these modern days of fashionable

Table 4.2. U.S. Street Railways in 1890

Miles of track	5,783.47
Cars	32,505
Employees	70,764
Passengers	2,023,010,202
Cost	$389,357,288.87
Animal-powered	2,633.87 miles
Electric	485.76
Cable	159.72
Steam	378.28
Mixed	718.18

Source: *U.S. Census*, 1890.

effeminacy and flabby feebleness which never walks when it can possibly ride, the horse car virtually fixes the ultimate limits of suburban growth."

After the big eastern seacoast cities had embraced the horsecar, municipalities in the more western states began to copy the actions of their big brothers. Actually Mexico City and the Indonesian island of Java opened lines in 1857 and 1858, respectively, before any Midwestern U.S. cities had cars running. Chicago had its State Street line running in very early 1859. St. Louis began limited service in July, and Cincinnati did the same in September of that year. Other U.S. cities entered the horsecar era more cautiously: Milwaukee, 1860; Washington, D.C., 1862; Louisville, 1864; Dayton, Ohio, 1870; and Los Angeles, 1874. Smaller communities such as Maysville, Kentucky, opened a 3½-mile mule-powered line in 1883. Table 4.1 offers a concise overview of the industry as it was in 1881.

Most street railways were built by local contractors who were familiar with either road or railroad building. An exception to this general rule was Charles Hathaway (1820–1903), a native of Grafton, Massachusetts. He entered railway building in 1844 and built rail lines in New York and Pennsylvania. In 1857 he constructed several streetcar lines in Philadelphia, and from that time on he specialized in car lines and real estate speculation. In 1860 he went to England as the protégé of George Francis Train (1829–1904) to build a street railway or tram line in Birkenhead, across the Mersey River from Liverpool. Train was likely one of the most eccentric individuals in American history, yet his odd ways and curious opinions did not hamper his success in business, which he conducted on an international basis. He became famous for his round-the-world travels, which were well publicized; his first trip took eighty days, but the fourth was made in just sixty days.

Just why Train felt it was his mission to introduce street railways to Britain is unclear, but he intended to do it independent of governmental approval. He ordered Hathaway to lay track. The cars, made in Philadelphia, were broken down in sections and shipped to Birkenhead, where

Hathaway's men reassembled and painted them. The line opened in August 1860. The local vestryman agreed to the project, but so many wagons and carriages had problems with the rails in the street that the authorities had both Train and Hathaway arrested and jailed for "breaking up the Queen's highway." Both men paid bail and were freed. Train went on to build lines in London and other European cities. By 1890 Britain's city railway system had almost 1,000 miles of line; 3,800 cars; 27,000 horses; and carried 526 million passengers a year.

Hathaway returned to the United States during the summer of 1862 and resumed building streetcar lines in this country and Canada. In 1873 he moved to Cleveland to build several lines. He decided to make Cleveland his home and bought an interest in the Superior Street Railway. Four years later one of Hathaway's sons-in-law, Frank De Haas Robinson, became a partner in the family business. Together they built scores of lines in Philadelphia, Rochester, Minneapolis, and other major and minor cities in North America. Hathaway himself claimed he had built, owned, or operated seventy street railway lines before retiring in 1890. The old railway builder lived in a fine house on Superior Street and spent his last years traveling, hunting, and fishing. He died at the age of eighty-three on July 1, 1903. His old friend George Train lived on until early in the next year, but as a pauper with a park bench as his daytime abode. He refused to speak with adults, but happily chatted with children and squirrels. Apparently, he had never been happier.

TRAFFIC, OPERATIONS, AND SAFETY

Do not assume that city railways operated in a leisurely or informal fashion. They were run much like mainline railroads in a military manner with definite procedures, schedules, and considerable discipline. The driver and his car were to leave the car house at a specific time and proceed over a definite route, and it was to reach intersections or corners at definite times. The timetable was designed to work within normal traffic conditions with a little slack time added for minor emergencies such as derailment, rain, snow, or fire. Rush hour often ruined the most carefully constructed schedule. The car's progress was monitored by supervisors stationed at major junctions throughout the city. If car 13 was more than a few minutes late, this was noted and the crew was asked to explain their lateness at the end of the trip. Drivers who were habitually tardy were soon let go. It was necessary to keep the cars in a regular order in case they bunched up in groups and thus disrupted the scheduled time interval or "headway." If everyone out on the line was where they should be at the correct time, patrons could count on a car arriving at a particular stop at three-minute intervals.

In most cities streetcar service ended at 11:00 PM or midnight. Most working people were already at home in bed. Younger folks, and a few too old for such activities, would stay out for a little more nightlife. Midnight owl service was offered in larger urban cities, but each line might be served by only one car and the wait could be very long. Regular service began around 6:00 AM, and by 7:00 AM rush hour was under way with cars at two- to three-minute intervals; this continued until around 10:00 AM. Service would then be cut back somewhat but would pick up again between 3:00 and 8:00 PM for the evening rush hour. New York City and Brooklyn, however, had many lines offering twenty-four-hour service. The busiest line in the nation was the Church Street line in Lower Manhattan, served by 120 cars an hour. With so many cars running, it must have been extremely difficult to maintain a one-half-minute headway. The hectic nature of New York horsecars inspired newspaper journalist Junius H. Browne to include a derisive essay on the subject in his 1869 book, *The Great Metropolis*. He contended the street railway was invented to kill time while its owners swindled and incommoded the traveling public. Their purpose was to make sure people did not get home too soon and to render their customers as uncomfortable as possible in the process. The more money the lines made, he said, the meaner they got. "They complain that their employees rob them. Why should they not? The owners plunder the public; why deny to their servants the same privilege?" Browne continued on in this fashion for a full seven pages. Apparently the rigors of big-city life were becoming too much for him to bear, or he just felt the need to ventilate his special hatred for the slow-moving hay burners.

The slow horsecar might seem immune to accidents, yet injuries were possible even at five miles an hour. The city newspapers reported streetcar accidents on a daily basis. The *Cleveland Plain Dealer* offered this sampling of mishaps in 1864: February 23, a boy was run over, breaking his leg; July 4, a driver fell from the car, breaking both arms; July 5, a passenger jumped from the car, his arm was badly crushed and was amputated; July 14, a man was seriously injured upon falling from a car; September 2, a runaway down a west-side hill – the passengers jumped, one was killed and several were injured. A Cincinnati newspaper reported that a boy's foot was crushed on the city's opening day for street railway service, September 14, 1859; he slipped and fell while boarding and one of his feet was run over by the wheels of the car. Less than a year later, another Cincinnati paper reported that a man lying down on the track at Fourth and Elm Street was run over and killed; not surprisingly, the incident was deemed a suicide. In May 1866 a seven-year-old boy was run down on Walnut Street; his hand was severed and his left arm and leg were crushed, resulting in his death. An older man stepped off a car in March 1877 on Colerain Pike; the car jerked forward, the man fell under the wheels, and his ankles were crushed. In February of the following year, a car came to the city end of the line at Third and Lawrence. The conductor noticed that one of the passengers had remained in his seat after the car had stopped. He discovered the man was dead. Back East in Hoboken, New Jersey, a horsecar bounced over a switch so vigorously that a passenger standing on the front platform was jolted over the end handrail. He broke his neck when he landed on the pavement and was dead a few minutes later.

Less obvious dangers were present on streetcars. Pickpockets found the crowded cars a convenient place to pinch wallets and pocket watches. The thieves worked in pairs and stood beside each other, remaining silent and pretending not to know each other. Their M.O. worked best during rush hour, when the cars were full. A passenger would push his way toward the rear platform to exit the car. As he attempted to squeeze past the thieves, one of them would slam his elbow into the victim's ribs and snarl, "Who are you pushing?" His accomplice would deftly reach around and grab the victim's diamond stickpin while the man in front grabbed both the wallet and watch. The victim would get off a little dazed and upset. Within minutes he would notice he had been robbed, but the car would already be blocks away. Other crooks used a similar scheme to grab the car's cash box. One of the robbers would run alongside a car and ask the driver for directions, and while this conversation went on, a second man would pull the cash box loose from its mounting. The thieves would race off and divide up the cash they had purloined.

CONDUCTORS AND DRIVERS

The workers who operated America's early transit systems are largely an anonymous group; individual biographies are nearly nonexistent, so their story must be told in generalities rather than in specifics. Thousands of photographs of horsecars and their crews have been preserved in local historical societies across the nation. Yet in only a few cases can the individuals depicted be named, and even then their life stories are almost never recorded. It is possible, however, to reconstruct a group portrait of the everyday lives of a typical driver and conductor from reports in the daily press and magazines. Their duties, work habits, hours, interaction with passengers, and other details were fairly well recorded by reporters of the time. It was not a glamorous, comfortable, or well-paid trade, yet the trials and tribulations of these ordinary workingmen won a certain sympathy from newsmen of that era. It is difficult not to have some compassion for the lot of common humanity, since we are all part of that same fabric.

It should be explained that of all the unskilled jobs available during the nineteenth century, there were many that were worse. Mining, lumbering, and seafaring were far more dangerous. Farming offered less pay

4.4. City railways expanded rapidly throughout the United States during the 1850s. Urban transit encouraged commuting to the near-in suburbs.

(*Ballou's Illustrated*, December 13, 1856)

and was of a more mind-numbing routing. Most factory jobs involved heavy lifting and greater confinement. Railroad work was not only dangerous but also involved nights or even days away from home. During bad economic periods many workers lost their jobs, but the street railway tended to run in good times or bad. Steady work had its attractions, such as regular pay and a full stomach.

There were two men on the car. We will start with the driver standing on the front platform just behind the horses. Because not much of the population came from farming communities, most country boys were handy with horses and mules, which were used to plow, cultivate, harvest, and power wagons and buggies. If a lad could drive a wagon, he could soon learn how to guide his team through busy streets filled with vehicles and pedestrians. All of this was surely different from the farm and required diligence and quick responses. Yet slow traffic speeds mitigated some of the difficulties of navigating the streets. The driver and his team learned to work together and were intentionally paired. The horses came to recognize their driver by his voice and smell. They would respond to his voice commands – sometimes little more than a grunt or clicking of his tongue got the team moving. A gentle pull or slackening of the reins signaled when to go or stop. Some teams would respond to the sound of the conductor's bell signal – they would start at two rings of the bell – while the driver held the reins loosely in his hands. A stubborn team might require more direct measures to start or stop, and a few might need the touch of a whip or a harsh giddy-up or whoa. Some horses simply were not suited for city railway work and even experienced drivers could not control them.

The driver's second duty was to manage the car's brakes. It was a simple manual system that forced iron shoes against the car wheels to stop the vehicle. A large, polished-brass goose-neck handle was mounted on the right side of the platform handrail. It wound up a chain that was attached to levers and rods of the brake gear. The driver furnished the power to work the handle. The horses could slow the progress of the car's movement by holding back, but the brake was needed to control the heavy car, especially on downgrades. So the driver stood out under the roof of the front platform all day, handling the team and the handbrake. He rarely dealt with the passengers, for they were instructed to board the car's rear platform, and this was understood by all but the most uninformed traveler as the car's entrance. Few modern readers would appreciate the importance of the front dashboard that separated the driver from his team. A horse might urinate or defecate while in motion, and whatever the animal expelled would fly backward toward the driver. The dashboard served as a very useful shield to deflect whatever was sent back toward it.

The life of the driver was predictable and dull – day after day of slow motion over the same streets and trackage. The wheels grinding over too-familiar rails and past identical stores, homes, and schools. Even the passengers all looked alike to a driver after years of handling the leather reins. And then at an unexpected moment the job became exciting and sometimes dangerous. One day in October 1889 a horsecar was crossing over a railroad track on the west side of Cincinnati. Suddenly the railroad gates dropped, blocking the horsecar's way. A train was fast approaching, but the driver whipped up his team and they crashed through the gates and dashed to safety. Had the driver or team hesitated, everyone in the car would have been killed or injured. Children playing in the streets would occasionally get run over, and it became the sad duty of the driver to pick up the injured or dead child and walk to the home of the parents. Given horses' penchant to run away when excited, a number of horsecars were wrecked in this manner. Such a runaway was reported by a Cleveland newspaper in early September 1865. A west-side horsecar team ran away going downhill, and the passengers jumped. One was killed and several others were injured. So the dull existence of the horsecar driver was punctuated by moments of excitement and death.

The duties of the conductor were more complex and demanding than that of the driver. He was required to collect fares, make change, call out street stops and connecting lines en route, and answer the many questions posed by passengers. He would assist people in getting on and off the car, including the elderly and lame, young mothers with children, or matrons overwhelmed with shopping bags or boxes. The conductor also signaled the driver when to start or stop by pulling an overhead rope attached to a small bell mounted under the roof at each end of the car. This system was used to prevent the car from starting while people were still boarding or exiting. The conductor was expected to maintain his balance as the car bounced and swayed along over rough places in the track or bumped over a switch or crossing. While the speeds were rarely more than 5 mph, the curves were often at 90 degrees, so everyone standing needed to hang on. Yet with the conductor passing out change, tickets, transfers, or working his bell punch or fare register, it was difficult for him to hang on while transacting his normal duties, so from time to time he would inadvertently bump into patrons and offer a quick "excuse me" before colliding with the door post or yet another passenger.

4.5. Crowded conditions emphasized the smallness of the horsecar interiors. The conductor stands to the center right in this engraving.

(*Daily Graphic*, November 5, 1875)

Such a job called for a patient and enduring man. He had to be self-effacing and humble as well, for to confront a passenger often meant dismissal, should the passenger report him to the front office. It didn't matter who was right or wrong – the conductor was expected to somehow mollify the passenger and smooth over every situation. No pets were allowed; this was a rule on many lines. Still passengers would bring them aboard, as in this example: *The conductor informs a lady passenger holding a small lap dog that pets are not allowed on the streetcar. She insists the dog is so small that he is bothering no one. "But Madam, I am sorry, the rule is no pets," he says. Nearby passengers begin butting in and offering advice. Meanwhile, other passengers are boarding the car, their fare must be collected, and they also have questions or need a transfer. Finally, the conductor insists that the lady and her dog must leave the car. She does so, but the chances are good that she will report the "rude" conductor's ill treatment of her to his supervisor. If he is disciplined or discharged remains a question; yet, if he doesn't enforce the rules, he is also likely to be in trouble.*

Ladies were known to cause delays when they were traveling together. A conductor in Boston placed a placard on his car that read: "This car cannot wait for ladies to kiss each other good-by." Similar disputes resulted from drunken passengers, arguments over getting correct change for $5 bills, or for being ejected for refusing to pay the fare. Once again, who was right or wrong in these small squabbles mattered not, yet it was the conductor who was expected to suffer in silence and work his long hours without complaint or offense.

One of the conductor's most important duties was to make sure each patron paid a fare. Normally the quick exchange of a nickel or a ticket satisfied this requirement. Yet no trip was free from riders trying to avoid the fare payment. Some would claim they had forgotten their wallet or purse. Others would be a penny short, as if that were okay. However, at the end of the run the conductor would be responsible for such shortages, so each short-change incident set off another argument. Other passengers attempted to use counterfeit coins or tickets. The counterfeit ticket became a special problem during the Civil War when there was a shortage of coins. Many merchants and ordinary citizens began using streetcar tickets to make change. For the purposes of trade the tickets were traded at face value – that is, a cash fare cost about 1 cent less when a customer purchased a packet of tickets or a punch card. These cardboard tickets were simple in design and hence easy to counterfeit. It became necessary to call in the old tickets and issue ones of a more elaborate pattern that were more difficult to duplicate. By 1862 the federal government began to issue small-denomination scrip to eliminate the small-change problem.

If the passengers were looking for a way to cheat the transit lines, so were the employees. There was a prevailing belief that conductors regularly stole a certain percentage of the cash fares. It was so simple to slip a few coins into one of his pockets rather than into the company's change box. And who was to know? It was done so quickly. One estimate claimed a dishonest conductor might keep $3.00 or $4.00 a day. This was well above his regular pay of $2.00 to $2.50 a day. It surely was a temptation for a poor man to handle so much loose change. The conductor was more or less a free agent. Supervisors rarely rode on cars, and the driver was too busy with the horses, brake, and traffic to closely observe the actions of the conductor. Besides, even if he noticed a stray coin being slipped into the conductor's vest, he would not likely tattle on a coworker. Instead, he might expect to get a cut of the take.

Street railway managers were so obsessed with the notion that they were being robbed by their employees that they set various safeguards to discourage thievery. The bell punch was one such precaution introduced around 1870. The introduction of the bell punch prompted the creation of a jingle that was reproduced in city papers across America in the mid-1870s:

> Conductor, when you receive a fare,
> Punch in the presence of the passenjare!
> A blue trip slip for an eight-cent fare,
> A buff trip slip for a six-cent fare,
> A pink trip slip for a three-cent fare,
> Punch in the presence of the passenjare!
> CHORUS
> Punch, brothers! Punch with care!
> Punch in the presence of the passenjare!

4.6. This series of small engravings shows car parts and other items necessary for horsecar operations. All date from around 1880.

(*The Car-Builder's Dictionary*, 1888)

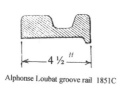
Alphonse Loubat groove rail 1851C

Girder Rail. 1875C

Bell-strap Guide, with Screw-top.

Signal-bell.

Bell-punch.
A, combination lock; B, aperture in which trip-slip or ticket is inserted; C, door inclosing bell; D, receptacle for counters.

Centre-Lamp. (For Street Cars.)

Bell-strap Guide.

Driver's Change Box.

Front View.   Back View.
Open-plate Wheel, for Street Cars.

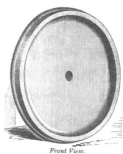
Front View.   Back View.
Single-plate Wheel, for Street Cars.

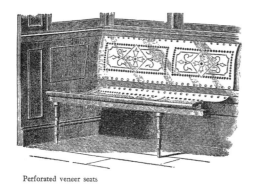
Perforated veneer seats

B. Front View.

Slawson farebox 1878

B. Back View.

    Mark Twain was so taken with the rhyme that he used it in a short article written for the *Atlantic Monthly* in February 1875. The newspapers picked up on the "Punch" by alluding to streetcar conductors as Knights of the Punch. This handheld device looked like a heavy-duty paper punch and worked in that fashion, but it also had a built-in bell that would ring.

Each ring indicated that a fare had been received and was being recorded. A dial fastened to the side of the punch would register another fare. At the end of the day the little register would total the number of fares collected. If the cash and tickets turned in at the end of the run agreed, all was well with the company and the employee. If not, the conductor was expected to pay the difference or explain the surplus.

The bell punch was not foolproof. A mechanic from Colt Arms Company conspired with conductors on the Girard Avenue Line in Philadelphia to alter the register so that it would record fewer fares than were actually collected. The fraud was discovered, and the twenty conductors involved were fired. A clock register was adopted to replace the bell punch by some Philadelphia lines. Over the years a general average of what a car was expected to earn was calculated, and this was used as a benchmark for receipts. If the total turned in was much below this average, the conductor was under suspicion. The Third Avenue Railway in New York expected each car to gross about $25 per day. Based on this average, it was calculated that if just one fare per car were stolen each day, loss in revenues would equal $50,000 per year. In theory, at least, the potential loss was substantial, so measures beyond the bell punch seemed necessary.

Spotters were employed to check up on the employees' honesty while on the job. The spotters tried to blend in with other passengers and often dressed like common laborers or, in a few cases, like an old woman. They would observe collection practices and how accurately the bell punch or fare register was operated. The car men were generally alert to the presence of a spotter and used sign language to send a silent signal to fellow employees. Spotters were difficult to identify, because the company learned to hire new ones frequently. At first it was found that women working in pairs were better at the job than men. But as early as the 1860s, some New York lines found that male spotters were quicker and apt to notice than women. Spotters tended to be overly zealous at their jobs and learned that the more fraud they reported, the greater the reward, so they would make false charges that were readily accepted by suspicious transit managers. Store clerks were also recruited to spy on the plundering conductors. Clerks at corner stores were in a prime lookout place to watch and report on passing cars. They kept a log on the time the car passed, its number, how many passengers it carried, or an approximation of same, and any suspicious activity on the part of the conductor. Crews that ran off-schedule were subject to suspension or dismissal. It was also made clear from the first day that stealing would not be tolerated. The new recruits were sternly lectured about honesty and the safeguards of the bell punch and spotters. Some companies required a $1,000 bond and a deposit of $25 as a safeguard against stealing on the job. Some men simply declined the job, because where was a poor man to find $25? Yet even conductors who wanted to remain honest were under pressure from fellow employees to steal on the job and share the spoils with various foremen or subordinates.

The foremen involved were the starters and the receivers. The former assigned crews to certain cars and established starting times. These fellows made it clear to the conductor that they required kickbacks in the form of a cigar, a drink, or even a meal. If such gratuities were refused, the unresponsive conductor was sent out early or was assigned the less desirable routes. The receiver was another petty tyrant who collected the fares and tickets at the end of each run. He would declare the driver's account short by a small sum and demand, say, 15 cents to square the shortage. The fares were collected four or five times a day, so the receiver could hope to improve his income by 60 to 75 cents each day by each car, and if he collected from twenty cars, his wages were considerably increased. If the conductor refused to pay up, he was reported as being short so much each trip and would be in trouble with the management. Because the managers presumed the conductors were petty thieves, the receivers were believed. It was a neat swindle and one the stablemen hoped to copy on a smaller scale. And soon the conductor found that all of his fellow workers expected him to kick back a certain share of his purloined income. Because of these curious customs, the conductor was forced into petty thievery. Some felt the job was degrading and shameful because it was universally assumed that those who performed it were scoundrels.

There were extra costs borne by the lowly car men. They were expected to buy a uniform hat, and even a secondhand one cost $1.50. A chain for the bell punch sold for 50 cents. The car man was to be clean shaven and have nicely blackened boots. A neat appearance and honesty did not shield him from the company's many rules, however. He was subject to three days off without pay for such infractions as forgetting to note on his daily report the car number or the name of the driver. If his car fell behind schedule, he was suspended for one to two weeks. Others were waiting to take his position should he resign or be fired. Men learned not to complain or become "growlers." In a statement made to the *Baltimore American* in 1880, a conductor on the Citizens Passenger Railway in Baltimore said he was grateful to have a steady paying job despite its difficulties. He said he worked a sixteen-hour day. His noon and evening meals were delivered by one of his children, who passed a lunch basket to him as his car passed by en route to Druid Hill. He ate standing up whenever traffic permitted it, and he was lucky to get home by midnight. The only time he had with his family was his day off, and that, of course, was unpaid. Some men worked seven days a week because they could not afford to take a day off.

Not all car men were so accepting of their situation, and the street railway industry had its share of strikes. There had been small work stoppages almost since the beginnings of street railway service, but the first large-scale strike started on April 11, 1866, when drivers struck the Third and Sixth Avenue lines in New York. The stablemen were put on cars with police escorts, but the service was not very good and the few cars running were very crowded. The loads were so great the weary horses would stop to rest. Taxis were doing a brisk business. There was some union violence and talk of tearing up the tracks, but overall the men were sober and well-behaved. They did, however, intercept and turn back drivers brought down from Albany. Matters got rougher by the seventh day and new drivers were attacked by the strikers; only the police were able to prevent bloodshed. Harnesses were cut to stall the cars. The conductors were then ordered by the various lines to take over the duties of the drivers. Those who refused to do so were dismissed. By April 19 the strike was over. The strikers had lost and capital had prevailed.

But much more violent strikes were to come. The Knights of Labor engineered a walkout in St. Louis in the fall of 1885 that partially shut down the local streetcar system. A few union members decided to give riders and strike-breaking operators a good scare. On October 23 they blew up a horsecar on the Washington and Eighteenth Street line, killing one passenger. The gang proceeded to dynamite four more cars before being apprehended. Strikers in New York and Brooklyn the following spring were content to derail cars or block the tracks with piles of lumber, coal, or bricks. Sixteen thousand men were on strike and presented a force too large to defeat. After a weeklong battle with police, the New York State Railroad Commission worked out a peace plan. The workers won a twelve-hour day with a half hour off for lunch. The men staged a victory parade with cars decorated with flags and upturned brooms.

Horsecar workers were like most laborers in the Victorian era: part of a large economic and social underclass. They were paid a living wage but had no paid holidays, vacation, or health or retirement benefits. Having little political power, they were largely ignored by business and political leaders. Yet a few journalists were moved to speak sympathetically of these downtrodden men. Newspaper editorials appeared during the second half of the nineteenth century asking the traveling public to consider the unfortunate men who labored such long hours for such modest pay. A Newark paper suggested that a word of kindness from the passengers would be appropriate for these public servants who endured so much each day.

The *Cincinnati Gazette* offered an editorial titled "Slaves of the Rails" in January 1876 and declared the conductors as the hardest-working persons in the city. A conductor was on his feet most of the day and night. He was exposed to rain, snow, and sun as the seasons progressed and was offered only the partial shelter of an open-sided roof. He had to bolt down his food while on duty. His off hours were spent sleeping, so he might as well not have a wife or family. Anyone who spent most of his time on that machine of discomfort commonly known as a streetcar was deserving of our collective sympathy. Shorter hours and more humane treatment were surely reforms very much needed.

Another representative of the Cincinnati press presented the same workers as cheerful, bluff men who never complained about their jobs. One driver, a German immigrant named Joseph Hettel, claimed he and his fellow workers slept well and ate like bears. Another veteran of the reins admitted to serious problems with rheumatism, but said his comrades got up a benefit to support him over the previous winter when he was confined to his bed. A young conductor named William Leist brushed aside the rigors of his job to explain some of the problems faced by his passengers on the Pendleton line. Much of the trackage ran along the Ohio River on the east side of town. When floods covered parts of the track, passengers would kneel on the seats to escape the muddy water. Leist told of a car that ran away when the brakes failed. The panicked passengers rushed to the door to jump off, but Leist pushed them back inside. The car came to a stop at the bottom of the hill and everyone was safe after an exciting ride, but only because of the conductor's quick thinking and forceful action.

Certain members of the clergy took an interest in the problems of the working class. One who cared was the pastor of a fashionable church in a wealthy neighborhood. He attempted to educate his flock on the plight of the horsecar conductor. Early in 1879 the Reverend D. W. Rhodes, spiritual leader of the Church of Our Savior, an Episcopal church in Cincinnati's posh Mt. Auburn suburb, urged his parishioners to consider the lives of these much-maligned men. He had gone out of his way to talk with them and learn more about them. While most laborers put in a ten-hour day, the car men worked for fifteen or even seventeen hours. Only the Main Street line allowed them thirty minutes for a meal. Dr. Rhodes found that some were only boys, wise beyond their years no doubt, but still far too young to put in such long hours. Rhodes said it would be a kindness to smile and say hello when paying them the fare. After all, they were fellow human beings, not some machine collecting money for the transit monopoly, whose one purpose seemed to be extracting ever more cash from the traveling public.

The Consolidated Street Railroad in Cincinnati earned a healthy $16 \frac{2}{3}$ percent on its investment in the previous year; surely its profits were sufficient to allow slightly better pay and shorter hours for its car men. Yet Reverend Rhodes's plea for greater understanding and compensation were ignored by both the Consolidated and at least one of the city's wealthiest citizens. Henry Probasco lived in a house that resembled a

Norman castle and was crammed full of great art and rare books. In May 1884 Mr. Probasco was riding downtown on a Clifton Avenue horsecar. He purchased a coupon ticket that allowed him to transfer between the car and the city's incline railway for one fare. After transferring to a second car, this grand gentleman was busy with pencil and paper; the boy conductor asked for his fare, but Probasco could not find the remaining part of the ticket, which was needed for the second leg of the trip, so he gave the boy a nickel instead. When he later found his ticket stub, he showed it to the boy and asked for his nickel back, but the boy explained that it was too late; he had already recorded it as a cash fare. A few minutes later, when Probasco got off the car, he had the boy arrested and locked up in the stationhouse overnight. Although thirteen years earlier Probasco had presented the city of Cincinnati with a magnificent bronze fountain that became its centerpiece, peevish actions like harassing young conductors did little to enhance Probasco's reputation as a public benefactor.

The horsecar era came to an end in the 1890s with the advent of electric trolleys. By this time working hours had been reduced to a more manageable twelve-hour day. Within a few years, front and rear platforms were enclosed and electric heaters made the motorman's station on the car more comfortable. Seats were provided for him as well. At the same time, a strong national union evolved that lobbied for better wages and benefits. The job would never be ideal, but it surely had improved greatly as the Victorian era came to a close.

HORSE POWER: A LIVING MOTOR

The Victorian era was the Age of Steam, which prided itself on being modern and up to date. Yet curiously almost everything that moved within the city was animal propelled, be it transit cars, milk wagons, moving vans, or doctors' carriages. There was much discussion about the need to substitute some form of mechanical power, the brutality of working draft animals to their death, and the unsanitary state of the streets because of urine and feces deposited by so many horses. The inefficiency of animal traction bothered businessmen and accountants. Yet it continued into the first quarter of the twentieth century; little had changed since the beginning of civilization many centuries before.

The horse and man first came together about five thousand years ago in central Asia when it was discovered that the horse could transport a human rider. It was not long before the horse that camel, oxen, and other beasts were trained to pull a vehicle. The horse became the favored beast for drayage and there were many breeds to choose from. The Arabian was small and fast but rarely used for drayage. The Clydesdale, Dutch, and Flemish horses were large creatures of considerable power but too expensive for most large-scale uses. These giants stood a foot taller than a typical horse and weighed a ton or more, which is as much as an American bison. The Hunter was fast and durable but remained largely the property of wealthy sportsmen. The common working horse, which is of mixed breed and suitable for all purposes from plowing to drayage, was perfect for street railway work. Such horses stood 15 to 16 hands high and weighed around 1,100 pounds. (A hand equals 4 inches, and the height is measured from the ground to the top of the horse's shoulder, [called the withers, or about 60 inches.)

Many names were used and misused as generic names for a horse. *Quadruped* and *equine* are the proper scientific designation while *nag* and *dobbin* are not. Some specific names were misused when referring to horses in general – for example, *filly* (young female), *mare* (female), *pony, bay, dapple gray, show horse, gelding* (neutered male), *stallion* (male), *hack* or *hackney*. (The origin of the latter was given in chapter 1.) *Steed* was a good general term and can be traced back to the Old English word for *stallion*.

In transit service the horses normally walked at their normal speed of 5 mph. If the car they pulled was empty or lightly loaded and the streets were relatively clear of traffic, the driver might put them into a trot, which was 8–9 mph. The sex or color of the animal seemed to make little difference as to which horses were preferred. Mares tended to live longer but were not as docile as stallions. Grays, browns, and bays were the most popular colors. It was generally believed that grays took the heat best and that black horses died early. Buyers looked for a "blocky" animal – that is, one not too leggy or with too much sunlight under him. Age was a big factor in horse selection; the best age was five to six years. Most were worn out by the time they reached fourteen years of age. Street railway service was especially hard on horses because of the arduous work, the hard road surfaces, and the nervous strain of working in crowded and noisy streets. Few worked longer than four or five years. They were so used up that no one would pay more than $70 for one. Many sold for $25. There were exceptions, however, such as a Boston Metro horse named Billy still living at age thirty after nineteen years in service. He never missed a day's work. A Jersey City line horse named Old Frenchy, whose age was uncertain, had been pulling cars for fifteen years. The old rascal would slip out of his stall to forage around the stable and eat the other horses' grub. Frenchy had a stable mate named Rocket that was faster than the best trotting horse. A line in New England had a horse named Calico that proved so fast, he performed well at a local racetrack.

A new horse was sold with a ten-day-trial guarantee; if a horse proved to be unsatisfactory it could be returned for a full refund. Some railways had a private track where the new horses could get used to pulling a car.

That being accomplished, they were worked for a few hours in regular service. It took about two months for a horse to get accustomed to street traffic. These animals were usually fresh from an Ohio or Kentucky farm and had never been in a large city. It took time for the new steed to bond with his driver; the animal got used to the man's scent and voice and, once familiar with them came to trust the driver. After about a year in regular service the horse was considered seasoned.

Temperament was a major factor in deciding if the animal was right for streetcar service. He might be fine for rural or small-town America. Biters and kickers cannot be changed, and such horses were returned to the dealers. In April 1887 the *Railroad Gazette* reported that twenty to twenty-five thousand horses were retired each year as being worn out. Some were sold for fertilizer or glue at $1 each. The better ones might fetch $70 and be used for a peddler's wagon or go to a farm if they were lucky. A new horse cost $125 to $160 depending on the market demand. During the Civil War the price of horses went up by 50 percent, as did wages, and the price of feed doubled.

The horse was the single most expensive cost of city railways, generally figured at 40 to 50 percent of total expenses. It took a lot more horses than you might assume to operate a single car. A full-size car was powered by two horses. The pair could be worked for only about four hours a day, or 10 to 12 miles. Horses required a lot of rest and worked only a six-day week. Some lines would work them 14 or 15 miles a day, knowing they would not last long in service and would be retired sooner. Because service was offered for around eighteen hours a day, it took several sets of horses to keep the cars moving, since each team worked only four hours. The New York City Railway required many more steeds – about fifteen thousand – because of their twenty-four-hour service. Almost all lines reduced mileage and hours during the summer. New York's Second Avenue line reported losing only 3 horses during the summer of 1890, out of a stable of 1,938, because of a relaxed schedule. Extra horses were needed to cover for those on the sick list. Others were needed for doubling on hills, where extra power was required to surmount a steep grade. These extra teams were operated by "hill boys," who rode bareback on one of the mounts; after helping a car uphill, the boy would ride the team downgrade to help the next car. More horses were needed in winter to pull snowplows and sweeper cars to clear the tracks.

There were other costs involved with equine power. The horses ate three meals a day and generally had an excellent appetite (fig. 4.7). Being large animals, they required about 26 pounds of grub a day plus 10 gallons of water. A typical diet for these herbivores was 16 pounds of grain and 10 pounds of hay. In nature they ate grain, grass, roots, twigs, and

4.7. Horses were well fed and groomed because they represented a street railway's largest single investment. Good care was simply good business.

(C. B. Fairchild, *Street Railways: Their Construction, Operation, and Maintenance,* 1892)

fruit. In captivity they were fed cheaper grains, such as oats, corn, and barley. Wheat was too expensive and too rich for their consumption. The Cincinnati Street Railway gave their horses 15 pounds of cornmeal and 7 pounds of cut hay (it was easier to eat) but no oats. Some lines fed their horses steamed potatoes. Oats were served only after a year or more in storage. A horse can survive on hay and water, but he won't have much energy. Green grass and corn gave them energy. Horses will overeat and so must be fed accordingly. Feeding times were typically 8:30 AM, 3:30 PM, and 12:30 AM. It was bad practice to work a horse soon after a meal, so the schedule of some of the herd was varied so that some were ready for the first shift, which began generally at 5:00 or 6:00 AM.

The food served was generally cheap. Corn was one of the less expensive grains, and hay was not costly either. But when horse railways needed gigantic quantities of both to feed one hundred thousand animals, the cost was equally large. On a small scale we should consider the City Passenger Railroad of Cincinnati, one of several independent transit companies in that Ohio city. For seven months ending December 31, 1864, these figures were offered by the *American Railroad Journal* in March 1865 (table 4.3).

The company posted a modest profit of $1,777.55. The point of this discussion is that because of their "fuel" costs, horses were not an economic form of power for street railways.

A dozen years after the Cincinnati report was published, the Franklin Institute printed a similar report in its journal for running a two-horse car in Philadelphia for one day (table 4.4).

Although the list of expenses was long, animal traction offered an unexpected source of revenue from that bad-smelling by-product, manure. Because of their high-bulk diet, horses produced a goodly amount of offal.

STREETCARS 113

Table 4.3. Operating Costs of City Passenger Railroad

For feed	$28,770.18	Labor, repairing track and materials	8,713.43
Stable labor and expenses	9,836.06	Car repairs	10,228.80
Conductors	9,694.49	Building repairs	1,811.09
Drivers	9,742.43	Rent	780.15
Taxes	3,605.46	Gas and oil	600.16
Smith shop	3,731.60	Car license	720.00
Legal expenses	1,975.00	Harness and repairs	1,589.01
Insurance	857.15	Stationery and printing	591.49
Transportation incidents	1,408.03	Damages	1,706.62
Salaries of officers	2,939.16	**Total**	**$102,252.36**
Horses	2,554.75		
Car washing	398.00		

Source: *American Railroad Journal*, March 1865.

However, what was a nasty waste product to the average city dweller was an excellent plant fertilizer to farmers, and street railways had no problem in selling it. Each horse could be counted on to produce about 22 pounds of manure a day. Considering the thousands of horses in drayage service in a large city, the total amount could only be measured in tons. The city of Boston employed ninety-one men and forty-two wagons to clean the streets. In 1880 they collected twenty-six thousand wagon loads that sold for just over $25,000. The Third Avenue Railway of New York reported revenues of $14,000 a year from this source. It was necessary to remove the manure because it was a breeding ground for flies. It also carried a virus of tetanus that was deadly to humans. In addition, the thousands of gallons of urine spread on the pavement were hardly beneficial to the environment.

The horse is a well-designed creature except for his feet. Eighty percent of a horse's health problems can be traced to his hooves. Cutting away the excess from the hoof will allow the horse to walk comfortably. Bathing the hoof in a solution of chloride soda can cure lameness. The chief caregiver was the hostler working in the stable. Each such worker cared for around eighteen horses. If one of his charges was not eating well, it was a sure sign the horse was sick. The hostler would check its feet; a stone caught under the shoe or a loose shoe was often the problem. Sometimes a nail would get embedded in a hoof. At the big Fourth Avenue stable, fourteen men were employed to replace shoes. They serviced 130 horses a day and replaced 265 shoes. A new shoe would normally last only twelve to sixteen days. The Fourth Avenue stable also served as a car barn. It was located at Fourth and Thirty-Second Street. Like everything in New York, it was built on a high scale. The two-story brick structure contained almost 1,000 stalls, with additional space for 120 cars. The upper story was reserved for the storage of grain and hay. There was a hospital

Table 4.4. Philadelphia Daily Horse Care Costs

9 horses–first cost $140 each	$1,260.00
Feed & stable expenses–46¢ each	4.14
Shoeing–6¢ each	0.54
Maintenance harness	0.18
Horses, depreciation per year	1.15
Maintenance car	0.40
Wages for driver	1.75
Daily interest on the car and horses	0.37
	$8.53

Source: *Journal of the Franklin Institute*, April 1877.

with room for 75 ill horses and a full-time veterinarian to treat them. One hundred hostlers and stablemen and boys cared for the horses. They fed, washed, and brushed the animals. An addition to the building in 1876 cost $150,000. It was designed by J. B. Snook, the architect of Grand Central Station. Once the need for an army of horses was eliminated by the electric trolley, the street railway's need for so much storage space was reduced considerably. Thus another wasteful feature of animal traction was eliminated.

Like all mammals, horses were subject to periodic epidemics, the causes of which were poorly understood until rather late in the Victorian era when scientists such as Louis Pasteur finally convinced the medical profession that germs, tiny organisms too small to be seen, were the cause of most infections and diseases. While the human population in large cities was visited periodically by yellow fever and cholera epidemics, the equine population was attacked by flu or grippe-like infections. In the summer of 1871 New York City horses experienced a distemper that paralyzed their legs. The veterinarians said it was a form of cerebrospinal meningitis. Hundreds of horses were affected, some died, and others were transported to Rikers Island. Street railway stables became giant horse hospitals; service on most lines was greatly reduced until the scourge went away as silently as it had appeared. Late in the fall of the following year a far more serious epidemic broke out that would prove to be the worst such health issue faced by domestic horses since they first emigrated to the western hemisphere. It was an influenza strain peculiar to equines, known as the epizootic.

This acute inflammation of the respiratory tract and lymph system originated in North Africa, spread to Europe, and then landed in North America in 1870. The symptoms were a hacking cough and a general weakness, cold ears and legs, and a watery discharge from the nose that became green or yellow as the infection worsened. It could last from seven to ninety days, but only about 1 percent of those afflicted died. The first case

4.8. Horses disabled while working were rescued and returned to the stable's hospital by special ambulance.

(C. B. Fairchild, *Street Railways: Their Construction, Operation, and Maintenance*, 1892)

was noticed in Toronto in October 1872, and within days it had spread to Montreal and Ottawa. It crossed the border at Buffalo, New York, and in three days reached Rochester on October 25. The street railway and livery stables in that city closed down. New York waited fretfully, and by the first week of November the Great Epizootic, as it was by then named, hit Gotham. Within twenty-four hours seven thousand out of eighteen thousand streetcar horses were stricken. Sick horses were well wrapped in blankets and withdrawn from service. They were given light rations of food that included warm mashes, bran with a little oats, small amounts of hay, and lots of water. Flaxseed tea and linseed oil and turpentine were rubbed on their throats. Compounds of nitrated potash and tartionized antimony made a powder that was administered twice a day.

By November 16, streetcar service was all but suspended. Express companies and fire and police departments depended on horses for vehicular power. Oxen were pressed into service so that a few deliveries were possible. Laborers plus furloughed drivers and conductors were hired to pull a few cars through the streets. It required about ten or twelve men to pull a car, since an adult man can develop about one-tenth of a horsepower. Cars were run in this fashion in Boston and Philadelphia, but most citizens found the man-powered cars far too crowded, smelly, slow, and ill ventilated to warrant their patronage. The masses were on the sidewalks, and Gotham was once again a walking city.

The city government relaxed its prohibition on steam power in the streets, and a Remington steam car was placed on the Bleecker Street line. Plans were under way for a cheap water taxi along the Hudson and East Rivers. Philadelphia lost a fairly sizable number of its horses to the plague. Commodore Vanderbilt lost one of his prize carriage horses, Mountain Boy, to the epizootic; this magnificent specimen was valued at $20,000. By late November the worst of the epizootic had passed and enough horses had recovered or been replaced that service got better each day. The epidemic progressed as far south as New Orleans and as far west as St. Louis.

City lines in the Old South preferred mules to horses; more than eight thousand could be found in cities such as Louisville, Atlanta, and New Orleans as late as 1890. There were few mules in this country when it was organized in the 1780s. A few had been imported from the West Indies, but they were too small to handle American-size work needs. After retiring in 1788 George Washington began to study the matter. He discovered that while mules were smaller than a common farm horse, they lived longer, ate less, and were less prone to diseases. The typical mule weighed between 700 and 800 pounds and stood a few hands lower than a horse. When the king of Spain learned of Washington's interest, he sent a jack (ass or male donkey) and two hinnies (offspring of a male horse and female donkey) selected from the Royal Stud estate in Madrid. The jack was gray, heavy-built, and stood 16 hands high. This giant specimen was named by Washington as Royal Gift. His old friend the Marquis de Lafayette had a jack and several hinnies sent from Malta. Washington bred these animals with his coach mares to produce a strain of American mules that were tall and strong. And so began the introduction of the mule into American farming and transportation.

Mules were bred long before the discovery of the New World and were in existence in Roman times. Some experts considered them more intelligent than either horses or donkeys. Mules seemed to know when rain was on the way and would prick up their long ears as a signal. They were quick to sound the alarm if a predator or enemy was approaching. They were sure-footed and could be worked for twenty-five years or more; some authorities claimed forty years of service. Unlike horses, mules could be toilet trained. Workers on the Louisville streetcar system would walk them to a designated station near the car barn to defecate and then to a second station to urinate. Having done their duty, the mannerly beasts were taken to their stalls for a meal and rest. There was little need to clean the streets or the stalls. In addition to having a strong gastric system, mules eat less food than horses. They were seldom sick or off their food and did not suffer from hoof or leg problems. They could work 20 miles a day, compared to the horse's limit of 10 to 12 miles, and did this in climates as hot as San Antonio, where 100-degree days are common in the late summer. Their only defect was the difficulty in selling them at the end of service.

Considering the advantages of the mule over the horses, it is a wonder they were not more extensively used outside the south. Writer C. B. Fairchild hints at one reason: the horse was a more beautiful creature, so the public was more attracted to the steed. One poignant, if not beautiful, story tells of the death of an old mule that died in service on Walnut Street in Cincinnati. The mule was pulling a car up a steep grade that ascends from the river to Fourth Street when he slipped and fell. The animal regained his feet after a struggle but toppled over again, and after casting a parting glance at his old partner in harness, closed his eyes and died. Heart failure was the verdict.

The horse railway was a brutal business that overworked and wore out the men and beasts needed to keep it operating. Most passengers tried not to think about it. They closed their eyes and minds to the suffering of the horses, creatures used up and broken in body and spirit by overwork. The public indifference toward the routine beating and abuse of draft animals was not shared by certain reform-minded persons like Matthias N. Forney, editor of the *Railroad Gazette*. He complained that horses were literally tortured to death, for overwork is torture of the worst kind. On the opposite side of the country, a San Francisco wire rope manufacturer, Andrew Hallidie, was so shocked by the daily injuries to city railway horses that he introduced the cable railway in 1873 in order to put an end to animal traction. An even more zealous champion of horse flesh emerged from the diplomatic corps to found a national society to prevent the cruel treatment of any dumb animal. His name was Henry Bergh, a wealthy New Yorker who discovered his life's work at about fifty years of age. His father ran a shipyard on the East River that generated ample funds, so Henry went to college but never graduated, instead wandering around Europe with no real purpose. He held some diplomatic posts, as a literary envoy, which was largely honorary in nature. Yet he was an observant and sensitive person. In his travels he was greatly revolted by bullfights in Spain and by the cruelty to draft animals he witnessed in Russia and elsewhere.

On his way home from Russia in about 1865, Bergh spent some time in England, where he learned about the Royal Society for the Prevention of Cruelty to Animals. This group had been established in 1824 and was performing admirable service in the British Isles. Bergh met with the group's director and was encouraged to form a similar organization in the United States – the tall, serious dilettante now had a noble mission. Once back in New York he began to speak to any group who might aid him in establishing a society to improve the life of our fellow creatures. At these lectures he picked up support from such notable citizens as Peter Cooper, Horace Greeley, and John Jacob Astor. The mayor of New York also endorsed Bergh's idea, and Bergh spent hours cajoling the editors of New York's fifteen newspapers to write about his dream project. The support thus generated was substantial, and in April 1866 the New York state legislature passed an act chartering the American Society for the Prevention of Cruelty to Animals (ASPCA). Those who would abuse their livestock, draft horses, turtles, or household pets had best beware. Henry Bergh had the legal authority to have them arrested for such action and could remove said creature to a hospital for care and rehabilitation. He would soon have uniformed agents patrolling the streets on the lookout for violators of the new law. Bergh himself could step in and order a teamster to stop beating his horse; if the teamster refused, a policeman would be summoned to arrest the misanthrope. Bergh organized a streetcar raid one cold winter day on what is now Park Row, where six horsecar lines converged near city hall. It was rush hour, and everyone wanted to get home and out of the wet, cold streets. Bergh, however, was more concerned about the misery of the sick and lame steeds straining to move the heavy cars. Each one was stopped and seized, the harness unsnapped. The street was soon a blockade of unpowered cars, with hundreds of commuters having no alternative but to proceed on foot. When asked who was responsible for creating such an outrage, the answer all around was "Bergh."

When New York stewed, the ASPCA opened branches in Ohio, New Jersey, and California. The Cincinnati chapter offered a report in July 1886 that addressed the condition and treatment of streetcar horses. Most of the complaints concerned the two longest lines in the city: the Pendleton line to the east and the Sedamsville line to the west. Both ran along the Ohio River. Poor track conditions were a major problem. The city had neglected to repair street pavements, which in turn had warped, buckled, and squeezed the track. The rough and uneven track greatly increased the power requirements to move the cars, making the horses labor much greater. The city taxed the gross earnings of the street railway by $12\frac{1}{2}$ percent; the revenue was to pay for street repairs, yet these repairs were delayed year after year. The Pendleton line responded to the ASPCA complaint by sending twenty horses to pasture and buying replacements. It also added ten minutes to the Sedamsville schedule. The company made street and track repairs in several places and put on extra hill horses. The public had to share the blame for overworking the horses, since they demanded to be picked up or dropped off nearer their homes and refused to walk to the nearest regular stop. This meant the cars stopped and started up two or three times per block. Starting required the greatest amount of power and did more to tire the animals than anything else. If a conductor refused a request to stop at the patron's door, the passenger was likely to file a complaint with the management. The ultimate solution was to replace animal power with mechanical power, and as it happened that would be rather soon. Meanwhile the ASPCA was doing what it could to make a bad situation better. Henry Bergh remained a hands-on style of manager and would search the city for animals of all types in need of assistance. He also turned his attention to abandoned and neglected children. He died at home during the great blizzard of 1888 knowing he had made a difference by making the public more sensitive to animal rights. Single-minded and eccentric people like Bergh both alienated and inspired the public, but in the end they became heroes in the humanitarian movement.

4.9. The decorative nature of Victorian transit is illustrated by this selection of engravings. The upper set depicts engraved glass used in clerestory windows as end side lights. The lower set shows striping designs for the exterior car body panels.

(*Street Railway Journal*, Feb. 1890, and C. B. Fairchild, *Street Railways: Their Construction, Operation and Maintenance*, 1892)

CARS FOR SUMMER AND WINTER TRAVEL

Essentially the horsecar was a wooden box supported by four cast-iron wheels. Platforms at both ends were just 21 inches above street level; a step made boarding easy. The 30-inch-diameter wheels projected up into the body, keeping the car low to the ground. The short wheel base, generally 6 feet, allowed the vehicle to go around sharp curves easily. This close spacing of axles also made the cars bob up and down, even at slow speeds. Most full-size cars had a 16-foot-long body that was 7 feet, 6 inches wide at the window level but tapered down to just 6 feet at the floor. Long bench seats offered space for twenty-two passengers. Thin pierced veneer was used for the seat itself, although a better quality car had upholstered seats. The windows could be opened by dropping them down inside a cavity formed by the inner and outer walls of the body. Wooden louvered

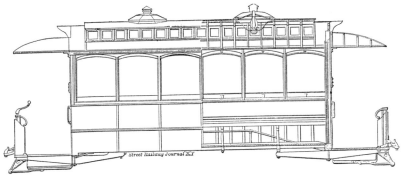
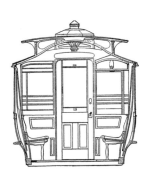

4.10. This late-model Stephenson horsecar was of a lightweight construction. It weighed just under 2 tons, including its wheels and hardware. The body was 16 feet long.

(C. B. Fairchild, *Street Railways: Their Construction, Operation and Maintenance*, 1892)

window shades were raised or lowered in a similar fashion. Additional light and ventilation was offered by small clerestory windows (fig. 4.9 and 4.10). The windows in the upper sashes were made from colored glass that was etched or engraved in a decorative manner. In some cases the glass surface was chipped to form decorative shapes or letters. The only illumination on most cars came from small corner lamps at the end of the car. These built-in lamps had a colored bull's-eye lens on the outside of the end panel. The illuminated lens could be seen for some distances and alerted passengers that a Red, Blue, or Green line car was approaching. In larger cities a dozen or more colors might be used to designate the various lines. The exterior paint scheme of the body would repeat the color-code systems, making it easier for illiterate or non-English speaking patrons to board the correct car.

The first streetcars were actually side-door cars built in 1831 for regular railroad service on the New York and Harlem Railroad. They were not easy to enter or exit but worked well enough during the first years of operation. Cars with large end platforms designed for easy access were introduced around 1850. These rectangular vehicles were simple and compact but much too heavy for two horses when fully loaded with passengers. Car builders looked for ways to produce a lightweight design. Floor frames were made simpler and slimmer. Wheels and other castings were made as thin as possible, and malleable iron was used in place of cast iron to save weight. India rubber springs saved a few pounds. By late 1860 Kimball

4.11. Passengers found a space on the end platforms during rush hour. Cars seated twenty-two passengers but carried around ninety when standees crowded aboard.

(*Frank Leslie's Illustrated Newspaper*, November 16, 1872)

and Gorton of Philadelphia had almost cut horsecar weight in half. They were offering a twenty-seat car that weighed just 3,300 pounds. Cars of this type were supplied to Cincinnati, Pittsburgh, Baltimore, and Boston.

John Stephenson cut the weight of his standard twenty-two-seat car to just under 2 tons, and it was still strong enough to withstand the rigors of New York City service (fig. 4.11). Stephenson used a considerable variety of woods to achieve strength and weight reduction. He invested in the very best lumber and would search the countryside for prime trees. Those growing alone in a pasture were his first choice. Once cut, the wood was air dried for three to four years. He contended that American wood was stronger than most imported varieties, and it was generally cheaper. He could sell a first-class car for just $1,000 and still make a profit. (To put this cost in perspective, a five-room house in those days sold for the same amount.)

During rush hour thirty passengers would squeeze into the bench seats, a space intended for twenty-two; forty more would stand inside with another ten or so on each platform. The theme was that the car was never full; pack them in, move up and squeeze in with your boxes, bundles, valises, and market baskets. The horsecar was likely the most overloaded vehicle in service, since its load at rush hour could be 6¾ tons. Double-deck

4.12. Bob-tail cars were designed for lightly traveled lines and were about half the size of a standard car. This car was built for Wilmington, Delaware, by J. G. Brill in Philadelphia around 1880.

(*Street Railway Journal*, November 1884)

cars were introduced in an effort to offer more seats and ever more room for standees, and several cities tried them with moderate success. In the 1880s Stephenson offered such cars with seating for forty-six passengers that weighed as little as 4,600 pounds. However, the narrow, curving stairway to the top deck discouraged many patrons. It also slowed loading and unloading the car, so although European lines used with them with success, the double-decker was never widely used in this country.

While higher-capacity cars remained an unanswered need, transit managers were quick to devise a compact style of car for more lightly traveled lines. John B. Slawson was central to the introduction of the one-man, one-horse streetcar, commonly called the bob-tail or fare-box car. This style of car used a fare box installed inside the car just behind the front bulkhead that separated the platform from the car body. The box was a self-service device that replaced the conductor. The driver could see the box by turning his head occasionally as the car rolled along (figs. 4.12 and 4.13). Slawson patented the device in 1857. At the time, he was a part-time omnibus operator in New Orleans. He had gone south in 1840 to manage a cotton press but found time to engage in transit. In 1860 he organized a city railway and equipped it with very small cars that were about half the size of a standard two-horse car. Most such cars seated ten passengers and weighed only 1 ton. Passengers entered through a rear door, walked forward to the fare box, and took a seat after depositing the fare.

The fare-box car was unpopular with the public because it was so small and lacked a conductor. The sole man on duty was too busy watching out for traffic and managing the horse to spend time attending to the passengers' needs. Operators, however, were delighted with the cost

4.13. The interior of a bob-tail car is shown by this engraving. Note the fare box next to the passenger with a bowler hat. The driver can be seen through the front door glass panel.

(*Daily Graphic*, January 19, 1884)

savings of Slawson's inventiveness. Bob-tails were soon in service on lines across the nation. Slawson returned to New York City after the end of the Civil War, ending a self-imposed exile after an encounter with General Butler during the Union occupation of New Orleans. He invested in several crosstown lines and equipped them, to the disgust of New Yorkers, with tiny fare-box cars. Late in 1888 the bob-tails were replaced by a fleet of handsome, full-size cars that brought considerable joy to the crosstown travelers.

The everyday maintenance of the cars involved a sweep-out after every round trip and washing them down each night. The interiors were cleaned and windows were polished. The wooden veneer seats were covered with Axminister carpets during the winter. Most cars had wood mats on the floor; however, some used cocoa mats. The car's exterior was varnished once a year to preserve the paint, lettering, and striping. Wheels lasted eighteen months on busy lines and twenty-four months on less-traveled routes. The bodies and running gears were rebuilt so extensively that after fifteen years almost every part had been replaced.

LOOKING FOR A MORE PERFECT STREET RAILWAY MOTOR

By the last decades of the nineteenth century, horsecars were seen increasingly as obsolete and inefficient. Traffic volumes in larger cities were overwhelming the tiny cars. New York transit continued because cable and elevated lines took over the major routes. Animal rights groups pushed to end horse traction, and champions of labor demanded more humane hours for drivers and conductors. Capitalists wanted better dividends for

4.14. Cable cars replaced horsecars in a few locations but usually only on heavily traveled routes because they were so costly to build. This scene shows Geary Street at Lotta's Fountain in San Francisco.

(*Harper's Weekly*, October 24, 1891)

investors in street railway shares; the public wanted faster and more comfortable service; and health experts sought cleaner, more sanitary streets. Only horse breeders and feed suppliers still advocated the old-fashioned power source.

Since 1860 inventors and mechanics labored to find a more perfect street railway motor. The most conservative group was certain that steam would offer an easy solution as it had for just about every power requirement in the Victorian world. The technology was so well proven and successful, it was all just a matter of adopting and fine-tuning it. A Cincinnati fire engine builder, A. B. Latta, produced a 6 horsepower dummy locomotive in March 1860 specifically for street railway service that condensed its exhaust steam and thus operated silently. The horses were not fooled by this noiseless motor and could scarcely be coaxed to pass it. Steam dummies were used with some success on suburban lines but were not tolerated within the central business district – so much for the ability of steam to solve every problem. Even the fireless locomotives devised by Emil Lamm operated only to the edge of downtown New Orleans. Horses pulled the cars into the city center.

The cable railway offered an indirect way to harness steam power for city railway service. Stationary engines in power plants, generally at the center of the line, powered endless wire rope cables. The cable ran continuously just below the street's surface in a shallow conduit. A slot way allowed a grip connected to a car to grab the moving cable and propel the track-borne vehicle. The grip was released and brakes applied to stop the car. The inventor of this ingenious scheme was Andrew Hallidie, an emigrant from Britain who had settled in California during the gold rush. By

1858 Hallidie was making wire rope in San Francisco. He was also active in suspension bridge and overhead ropeway construction. The ropeway ore carriers were similar to the technology needed for a cable railway. Hallidie's first line opened in August 1873 on Clay Street. The little cars easily ascended the steep streets of San Francisco. More such lines were built over the next decade (fig. 4.14). By 1890 twenty-nine American cities had cable lines. They were very costly to build and operate, so they were economic only when heavy traffic was present. Most of their power was lost through the friction of the machinery and the enormous weight of the cable itself. Their operating cost was figured at about $21 a mile, or just $3 less than horsecars. Cable lines were quickly abandoned in most cities soon after the introduction of electric traction. By 1902 half of the cable mileage was abandoned. At its peak there were just 488 miles of cable lines, or just 8 percent of the total street railway mileage; however, these lines carried 400 million passengers out of an industry total of around 2 billion.

New York's first elevated line opened in 1868 with a steam-powered cable line on Greenwich Street in Lower Manhattan. The company failed in the fall of 1870, but new owners gained permission to reopen it with very small steam locomotives. The elevated structure was about 20 feet above the congested streets; this allowed the trains to operate unimpeded. The locomotives proved reliable and were nearly smokeless, because anthracite coal was used for fuel. By 1878 the west-side line had expanded its tracks from the Battery to Sixty-first Street. Three more lines were built the length of the island along and above Second, Third, and Ninth Streets. By 1880 there were 32 miles of elevated railways in New York City. They carried 190,000 passengers a day and introduced rapid transit to America. Speed was the key to their success. They were more than twice as fast as a horsecar and became so popular that by 1893 they were transporting 200 million passengers a year. They were also the most profitable passenger-carrying railroads in the nation. The steam locomotives were replaced by electric-powered cars by 1903. The Manhattan elevated railways were gradually replaced by subways because the "El" was unsightly and noisy. Despite the obsolescence of elevated rail systems, Chicago continues to use this form of public transport extensively. The elevated railways made economic sense only for the very largest cities and were too costly to be built elsewhere.

The need for an effective, clean, and economic street railway motor had been investigated as early as the 1830s. Electricity was a subject best understood by scientists in the early nineteenth century, yet practical mechanics hoped to apply it to everyday uses such as lighting and power. The transition from the theoretical to the utilitarian was long and arduous. It involved dozens of investigators in as many nations. Battery-powered cars

4.15. Boston was one of the first large cities to adopt the electric trolley. The scene shown here is Park Street in downtown Boston.

(*Scribner's Magazine*, May 1892)

were too feeble to receive serious consideration, but in 1879 Werner von Siemens opened a small line in Germany powered by a generator. With this strong electrical source the trolley car gained the muscle it needed to succeed. Other pioneers labored to perfect the electric trolley. Frank Sprague succeeded in getting the details right in 1888. He built an electric railway in Richmond, Virginia, that was a commercial success. Despite poor track and grades as steep as 10 percent, forty cars ran over the system in a dependable fashion. One Richmond paper reported, "It's a success. It is a revolution." The news of Sprague's triumph traveled quickly in the transit world. Boston's West End Street Railway abandoned plans for a new cable line and hired Sprague to build an electric line. The Edison Electric Light Company, sensing large profits in the traction business,

4.16. In this artist's rendering, the horsecar is overwhelmed by a lightning storm symbolizing the triumph of the electric trolley.

(*Electrical World*, October 31, 1891)

purchased a controlling interest in Sprague's firm. In short order General Electric took over Edison, and the trolley revolution was under way (fig. 4.15).

Few industries showed such enthusiasm for the new form of motive power. Within a decade the horsecar vanished from the American scene, but although operating costs were reduced by 60 percent, the capital cost to convert from horse to electric power was substantial. A power plant with substations and power transmission cables was needed. New cars were purchased because the horsecars were generally not suitable for conversion to the new power source. The new cars were larger and much heavier because of the motors and their electrical apparatus; hence new track was required. A mile of double track, including trolley wire, poles, and feeder lines, cost around $100,000. By 1900 the nation's street railway system had a little over 20,000 miles of track, at a cost of $2 billion. Except for a few miles powered by animals, steam, or cable, it was an all-electric system. Ridership continued to expand until 1929, despite the growing popularity of the automobile. By the 1970s public transit required a government subsidy to sustain operations. The excellent profits so common in the Victorian era had long since vanished. Today, when our society faces an energy deficit, transit may once again become our best hope for efficient urban transport.

One might assume that a horse can generate 1 horsepower (hp). In a world full of contradictions, however, we must report than an average 1,100-pound horse can exact only about ½ hp as defined by James Watt in 1782. Watt selected a very large and powerful horse for his test example, and this noble specimen was able to lift 33,000 pounds to 1 foot in one minute. This number remains the standard for a modern horsepower today. Hence the two-horse cars of Victorian America were actually powered by animals that together could generate only one-horse power.

SUGGESTED READING

Note: We have not included the numerous histories of individual street railways that generally included only a cursory mention of pre-electric operations. A comprehensive listing can be found in Thomas R. Bullard, *Street, Interurban, and Rapid Transit Railways of the United States: A Selective Historical Bibliography*. Forty Fort, Penn.: Harold E. Cox, 1984.

Buckley, R. J. *History of Tramways from Horse to Rapid Transit*. Newton Abbot, U.K.: David and Charles, 1975.

Browne, Junius H. *The Great Metropolis: A Mirror of New York*. New York: American Publishing Co., 1869.

Chevalier, Michel. *Society, Manners, and Politics in the United States: Letters on North America*. Paris, 1835.

Clark, D. K. *Tramways: Their Construction and Working*. London: C. Lockwood and Co., 1878.

Dowson, J. E., and A. Dowson. *Tramways Their Construction and Working*. London: E. and F. N. Spon, 1875.

Easton, Alexander. *A Practical Treatise on Street or Horse Power Railway*. Philadelphia: Crissy and Markley, 1859.

Fairchild, C. B. *Street Railways: Their Construction, Operation and Maintenance*. New York: Street Railway Publishing Co., 1892.

Haupt, Herman. *Street Railway Motors*. Philadelphia: H. C. Baird and Co., 1893.

Hilton, George. *The Cable Car in America*. Berkeley, Calif: Howell-North, 1971.

Middleton, W. D. *Time of the Trolley*. Milwaukee: Kalmbach, 1967.

Middleton, W. D., and W. D. Middleton III. *Frank Julian Sprague*. Bloomington: University of Indiana Press 2009.

McShane, Clay, and Joel McShane. *The Horse in the City: Living Machines in the Nineteenth Century*. Baltimore: Johns Hopkins University Press, 2007.

Miller, J. A. *Fares, Please*. New York: Appleton-Century, 1941.

McKay, John P. *Tramways and Trolleys: The Rise of Urban Mass Transit in Europe*. Princeton, N.J.: Princeton University Press, 1976.

Post, Robert C. *Urban Mass Transit*. Westport, Conn.: Greenwood Technographics, 2007.

Reed, Robert C. *The New York Elevated*. New York: A. S. Barnes and Co., 1978.

Rowsome, F., Jr. *Trolley Car Treasury*. New York: McGraw-Hill, 1956.

Steuart, William M. *Street and Electric Railways*. Bulletin. U.S. Census. Washington, D.C.: U.S. Government Printing Office, 1903.

Train, George F. *Observation on Street Railways*. London, 1860.

White, John H. *Horsecar, Cable Cars and Omnibuses*. New York: Dover Publications, 1974.

Wright, Augustine W. *American Street Railway*. Chicago, 1888.

5.1. An elementary scow ferryboat of about 1800 by Thomas Bewick, a British engraver.

Ferryboats № 5

Crossing the Rivers and Bays

EVERY LARGE CITY OR TOWN ON A RIVER, LAKE, OR BAY WOULD likely have had a ferry at some time in its history. We discuss only some of these conveyances that helped travelers cross over the waters of America. The methods of propulsion – oars, poles, horses, river currents, and steam – illustrate the inventiveness of our ancestors. The type of boats and the nature of their operation will constitute the third general area of our discussion.

The ferry has been described as a floating section of highway. It has been useful but hardly ever beautiful. It has lacked the majesty of a great liner, the grace of a square rigger, and even the briskness of a tugboat. It has no knife-edge prow to cut through the ocean waves and almost no beauty of line or symmetry of proportion. The ferryboat emerged as a meek and lowly vessel, squat, humble, and often rather dingy in appearance. Its oval shape and rounded roof made it resemble a giant turtle. Even so, the humble ferryboat had its admirers. America's great poet Walt Whitman found the Brooklyn ferry a source of inspiration. He rode it daily to and from Manhattan in the 1850s and 1860s. In 1882 he recalled, "I have always had a passion for ferries; to me they afford inimitable streaming, never failing, living poems." He would ride in the pilothouse, having made friends with the men at the wheel. In this elevated station he could view the fine harbor and its enormous maritime traffic. He would revel in the great tide of humanity in motion. The sights of the sloops, skiffs, and ocean steamers and the majestic sounds of the boats offered him a refreshment of spirit not found elsewhere. And all of this for a 2-cent fare. Other commuters on these "people's yachts" shared Whitman's appreciation for the ferry as a cruise ship and an opportunity to be out in the sun and fresh salt air. The view of the skyline, seagulls, and the wonderful variety of watercraft made this part of the commute pleasurable. Even the passage of a garbage scow reinforced an appreciation of the great cities' complexity and many services. The ferry's steady motion offered a little quiet time to reflect and daydream.

Not all observers of the American scene agreed with this rosy view of ferryboat travel. Brian Cudahy reminds us of O. Henry's short story "The Ferry of Unfulfillment," wherein the heroine is described as part of that "sad company of mariners" who commute to and from work each day aboard a crowded ferry. She is one of the thousands who cannot afford to live inside the great city but comes in early each morning like a dejected slave to toil away in some miserable workshop and repeat the journey that evening out into the back reaches of New Jersey or Long Island. Yet perhaps once or twice a year even these downtrodden folks experienced a moment of elation while crossing the waters as the ferry steamed toward its distant landing.

The exact details of the first North American ferry cannot be determined, other than that it was established by an anonymous American Indian and that others were established by these same people at many locations throughout the continent. The earliest European ferry in what is now the United States was likely organized in 1630 to connect Boston and Charlestown, Massachusetts. The 1-pence fare was not sufficient because of the limited traffic and was soon doubled. This operation was established by charter following British law, and other colonies at once encouraged the creation of local ferry service but also collected an annual fee amounting to £40 or about $200 U.S. A Brooklyn-to-New-York ferry was established in 1642 or 1643. A second New York ferry was organized in 1661 to connect Jersey City with Manhattan. Philadelphia's first ferry ran across the broad water of the Delaware River in about 1687 so that travelers might cross over to New Jersey. Its charter was continued by a royal act of King George I in 1715. There was little settlement west of the Alleghenies until after independence from Britain, but by the late 1780s charters were given to ferry operators in Cincinnati, Detroit, and other western locations. St. Louis opened a ferry line in 1795, for example. These grants almost always included specified fares. Those established in February 1792 for the Cincinnati ferry were rather high for such a frontier settlement. A passenger was charged 6 cents, pigs went at the same rate, a man and horse cost 18 cents, cattle went at the same rate, and a team and wagon were charged $1.

Most of these pioneer ferries consisted of a small boat propelled by oars or poles (fig. 5.1). For wider crossings a sail would be rigged up. Some ferries were too small for wagons or cattle, and many ran only in daylight hours. Some were seasonal and made no effort to operate during the winter; those that did might be forced to temporarily suspend operations if rivers froze over or heavy ice floes were experienced. Flooding could also shut down service or lead to accidents. During a period of high water in 1819 on the Great Miami River in western Ohio, the operator of Balls Ferry at Trenton was ready to shut down, but a group of passengers insisted he take them across. Halfway across the boat turned over in the raging water, and five of the eight aboard, including the ferryman, were drowned. Sail-powered ferries could be even more accident prone, for a big blow could cause the boat to capsize. A drunk ferryman might refuse to trim the sails and thus bring on disaster. Sometimes the boat was blown off course and might land miles away from the intended terminal. No schedule was maintained on lightly traveled ferries. The boat ran on demand, and its owner/operator would go off to tend to other matters. A horn or bell was placed next to the ferry, and customers would sound one or both to summons the ferryman.

It was common to have a tavern or inn at the ferry, and this facility was often operated by the ferryman and his family. Such establishments out in the wilderness or other remote places could be rustic. But even the most humble was certain to have a bar, because most passengers seemed to require a drink before making the crossing. In some cases the state or colonial charter might require the ferry operator to maintain an inn for convenience of the public. Food and lodging were thus available for those not desiring to go on with their journey. Their horse might require rest and feed as well. So the inn might be more profitable than the ferry itself. The tally might come to $1.50 per customer when all the small charges for dinner, whiskey, a bed, breakfast, and the stable fees were totaled. A ferryman might easily gross $15,000 a year, which was an attractive sum to a small businessman in early America.

Vincennes, Indiana, was on the main road west to St. Louis. A ferry was established in Vincennes to assist travelers in crossing the Wabash River. In an advertisement dated August 13, 1825, the ferryman alerted patrons that he could furnish all types of animal feed from hay to corn. He also was associated with a grocer ready to supply food, liqueurs, salt, and patent medicine for human travelers. Two boats were at the ready – a large one for heavy wagons and a smaller one for carriages and light wagons. The boats had banisters, or handrails, to prevent passengers from falling overboard. Not all of the ferry taverns were so humble, however. The Brooklyn ferry house was a two-story brick building erected in 1700. It had five chimneys, a fine dining room, and a well-stocked bar. It was replaced by an even larger stone edifice in 1748 and was well regarded by the traveling public. Some ferry taverns marked the beginnings of new towns such as Zanesville, Ohio; Harper's Ferry, West Virginia; Harrisburg, Pennsylvania; and Dobbs Ferry, New York.

TEAM AND STREAM BOATS

Manual power would remain a common means of ferry propulsion for ferries throughout the Victorian era as it had since ancient times. More inventive men looked for ways to harness other common power sources for a variety of tasks. Horses, mules, and oxen had been reliable motors for vehicles, pumps, and mills. The Romans devised a plan for a horse-powered vessel, but it is uncertain if it was ever executed. Experiments were conducted with such a vessel on the River Thames during the reign of Charles II. (The idea was reinvented in the New World by John Fitch, who is generally associated only with the introduction of steamboats. At the very time he was involved with the force of mechanical propulsion, Fitch built a steam boat for use at Philadelphia in 1791.) The general plan for horse-powered or team boats was a circular table that was geared to paddle wheels. The horse would walk on the surface of the table and cause it to revolve, thus turning the paddle wheels. Up to eight horses could be employed, so a fairly sizable boat could be propelled. The horses, in effect, stayed in place, as the motion of their feet and legs caused the turn table to move. Since the animals did not leave their confined compartment, they really did not need to see. Blind horses were available cheap, so ferry operators found employment for these otherwise worthless animals.

Boats of this type were found in all regions of the United States – at work on the Hudson River; the inland rivers; and in major cities such as New York, Philadelphia, Detroit, and Cincinnati (fig. 5.2). A preserved example was found in 1983 near Burlington, Vermont. Skin divers may still see it, as it resides quietly below the surface of Lake Champlain. The 63-foot-long open-deck vessel appears to be similar in design to a plan patented by Barnabas and Jonathan Langdon in 1819. It had side wheels and was powered by two horses. Burlington was served by a network of ferries; one of the lines traveled to the north end of the lake, landing at Rouses Point near the Canadian border.

Another steamboat pioneer, Captain Moses Rogers (1780–1821), master of the transatlantic steamer *Savannah* of 1819, also began his maritime career with team boats. In 1814 one of Rogers's team boats began service on the Brooklyn ferry line. It was a large vessel powered by eight horses and crossed the river twelve times a day. The crossing was made in just eight minutes under good conditions, but if the winds and tides were unfavorable it could require eighteen minutes. A normal passenger load was 200 passengers, plus an unspecified number of horses and vehicles. On one trip 543 passengers were carried across the East River by this boat. Rogers soon had another team boat working on the Hoboken line across the Hudson River. A vendor was allowed to sell cakes and candy on one of these Hoboken ferries and did so with little notice until he decided to add fireworks to his wares. It was not long before a group of mischievous boys purchased a supply of firecrackers from this stand and discharged their stock to their own merriment. The horses were not so amused, however,

> # CINCINNATI
> ## Horse Ferry Boat.
>
> THE Horse Ferry Boat, No. 1, is now in complete operation between Cincinnati, Newport, and Covington. It is so constructed as to accommodate passengers with a safe, speedy and very comfortable passage ; and will carry, with perfect safety, at least two wagons and teams, and ten or fifteen horses, with any rea-reasonable number of persons.
>
> The boat will leave the mouth of Licking, every morning at sunrise, and continue to run during the day, except a sufficient time for refreshment at breakfast and dinner, staying fifteen minutes at each shore. The bell will ring at her arrival and departure. The fare will be the same as in other boats.
>
> PLINY BLISS.
>
> June 15, 1818   11 3w

5.2. A Cincinnati newspaper advertisement for team-boat horse power.

(*Western Spy*, June 15, 1818)

and in their fright and panic the crazed animals demolished the boat's machinery. Moses Rogers's proud creation began to drift with the current until it grounded on Governors Island. This incident presumably ended the sale of fireworks on the Hoboken ferry.

In April 1816 the Philadelphia papers carried advertisements for a team-boat ferry to Camden, New Jersey, patented by a Mr. Hart. The line engraving accompanying this notice shows a circular cabin with a domed roof near the center of the hull. Eight horses furnished power to the vessel, which measured 66 feet long by 40 feet, 10 inches wide. The fare was listed as $6¼$ cents.

Many other examples of team boats elsewhere in the nation might be noted, but we will close our discussion with the thought that this preindustrial form of propulsion persisted well into the motor age. A fair number of team boats were found on some of the smaller Ohio River ferries into the early years of the twentieth century.

The origins of the stream or current boat are less clear, but water was another clever power source harnessed by our ancestors to propel ferryboats across narrow rivers. A side board or rudder was used to catch the current or flow of a stream and use its force to push the boat across. The rudder or board was set at a 30-degree angle to catch the flow of the water current. By reversing the angle of the rudder, the boat could be propelled in the opposite direction, so two-way propulsion was possible. The system was considerably aided by a rope or cable guidance. The rope was slung across the stream at a low level; a pulley and second rope attached to the boat itself completed the system.

A winch at either end of the rope was used to maintain tension, for the rope needed to be above the stream. It also helped to keep it out of the water, thus preserving the rope. The introduction of wire rope cable in 1842 offered a material that permitted a longer stretch to the current-driven ferry. It is difficult to determine just how quickly the new technology was adopted by ferrymen, but it was likely in widespread use by the 1860s.

The efficiency of the stream ferry was dependent on the flow of the water. In a sluggish stream the boat would move slowly, but the ferryman could assist with a pole or oar. He could also reach out from the front of the boat, grasp the rope, and pull the boat along in a hand-over-hand fashion. The rope or cable, it should be noted, also served as a guidance device; the ferryman did not have to steer the boat, for the rope and the attachment pulley would deliver it to the designated landing automatically. An early example of a rope ferry was observed by an English visitor over the Muskingum River at Marietta, Ohio. The stream was about 600 feet wide; the current ran at between 3 and 4 mph. The boat made the crossing in just one minute. A rope 2 inches in diameter served to guide it. Ferries on this old system remained in service on the Oconee River in Georgia as late as 1941.

A variation on the rope ferry that also used the power of the stream current was observed in operation at Chattanooga, Tennessee, in about 1870. It might best be described as a pendulum ferry, for the boat swung on a cable anchored on a small island in midstream. This allowed the use of current power across a fairly wide river. Several small boats fitted with small towers kept the rope from dragging in water. It was a very makeshift-looking affair, but it operated with apparent success for some years.

A more elaborate variation on rope or cable ferry was established at Rouses Point, New York, in September 1851. To satisfy marine interest intent on maintaining navigation on Lake Champlain, it was necessary to maintain an open channel of 300 feet near the center of the long railroad-bridge crossing at this point. The solution was to make the center section of the bridge float, making it, in effect, a boat. A small steam engine powered a drum that pulled on an endless chain that normally lay on the bottom of the lake. The boat-bridge would thus pull itself from one end of a 300-foot opening until it touched the opposite pier so that trains could make the crossing. Since there was little traffic on this line, the channel was normally open for navigation.

STEAM CONQUERS ALL

The steam engine was introduced for commercial use in 1712 and was largely used by the mining industry until the beginning of the following century. Numerous efforts to harness this new force of transportation power proved more difficult than most engineers had expected, and it was an artist, rather than a mechanic, who had the first success commercially. Robert Fulton had been trained as a portraitist but sensed that his real passion was for invention. In truth, though, he was not a remarkable technician but, rather, a gifted promoter. With the backing of a wealthy New York diplomat, Robert Livingston, Fulton managed to assemble a workable steamboat in 1807. Fulton and his partner had plans to create a national steamboat monopoly but never succeeded with this ambitious scheme beyond New York state. Their first few boats were built for Hudson River service to Albany. Fulton developed plans at the same time for ferry operations to and from Manhattan Island and organized a company for this purpose in 1809.

The first boat, named *Jersey,* was put into operation in late July 1812. It was to run from the Jersey City community of Paulus Hook to Cortlandt Street in Lower Manhattan. The paddle wheel of this double-hull vessel was placed in the space between the hulls. It was a double-ender that could load passengers and vehicles from either end. This meant the boat need not turn around when landing at its opposite terminal. Most subsequent ferryboats followed this plan. Many inland river ferries, however, were single-enders with a bow and a stern and were loaded from either side of the deck. The deck of the *Jersey* was 80 feet long and 30 feet wide. The passenger cabin was fitted with bench seating and a stove. Passenger capacity was said to be three hundred, but this likely included both standing and seated passengers. The boat could handle six carriages and considerable luggage. She made the 1-mile crossing in fourteen minutes on a calm day and in twenty minutes against a strong tide. This was a great improvement over the sailing ferries that might require three hours to cross against headwinds and strong currents or tides.

Yet these pioneer steam ferries proved to be somewhat underpowered. A sister boat, the *York,* was taken involuntarily by the ice in February 1818 toward New York Harbor's Narrows and appeared headed for the Atlantic Ocean when it fortunately went aground on Governors Island. There her thirty passengers spent several miserable hours before being received by another boat.

In 1814 Fulton started a second ferry line to Brooklyn. The first boat, the *Nassau,* was a near duplicate of the Jersey City boats. The fare was 4 cents, or twice that of the established sail-powered boats, but passengers seemed ready to pay the price for the relative certainty of steam transit.

5.3. Fulton's steam ferryboat, the *Nassau* of 1814, connected Brooklyn and New York. It is depicted here on a ticket of that time.

(*Harper's Weekly*, November 2, 1872)

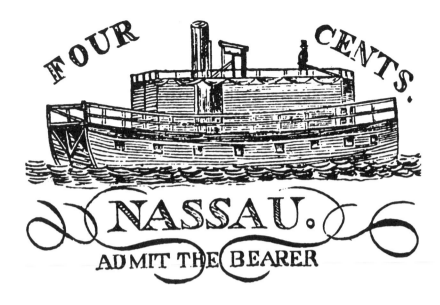

(An illustration of a ticket for the *Nassau* is reproduced in figure 5.3.) When this pioneer was retired a few years later, it was tied up at a wharf to become a dockside chapel. Fulton died somewhat prematurely in February 1815, and his business, including the two ferry lines, was carried on by his partners. Both of these operations continued as among the most popular of the New York ferries and over the years carried millions of passengers.

The advantages of steam propulsion were obvious to ferryboat operators elsewhere in the nation, but steam likely made economic sense only for well-patronized lines. The older manual- or animal-powered methods tended to prevail in many areas despite their technical obsolescence. *Harper's Weekly,* in its issue of October 20, 1866, depicts a sizable barge ferry loaded with a horse, a wagon, two oxen, and several passengers being rowed through Berwick Bay, Louisiana, by two stalwart oarsmen (fig. 5.4). The old-fashioned stream-powered boats could be found in America's byways well into the twentieth century. But steam soon found its champions as well. Philadelphia was home to a steam ferry simultaneously with Fulton's first ferry. Cornelius Vanderbilt adopted steam for his Staten Island ferry in 1817. Detroit had one a decade later, and St. Louis and Cincinnati soon followed. When Leavenworth, Kansas, finally received a new steam ferry built in Pittsburgh in 1854, it could make no claim about being a first-generation user of steam power, but it did boast that the city's latest acquisition had a paddle wheel that could "knock all creation out of the river."

FERRYBOAT CAPITAL

New York City had the largest U.S. ferryboat system, and perhaps the longest in the world, during the Victorian era. This was true primarily

5.4. Oarsmen propel a scow ferry across Berwick Bay, Louisiana, to Brashear City.

(*Harper's Weekly*, October 20, 1866)

because Manhattan was an island, a major population center, and much of its population commuted from outlying residential areas to the center city. It should also be understood that many of these commuters were factory workers because so much manufacturing was still being conducted in old parts of New York City. Brooklyn was an independent city until 1898, and a very large one. The traffic between two large cities separated by the East River created sizable ferryboat traffic that was only partially relieved in 1883 with the opening of the giant suspension bridge. There were upward of seventy ferryboat lines in and around New York City. The busiest were the lines from Jersey City and Hoboken to Manhattan Island and the Wall Street and Fulton Street lines to Brooklyn (fig. 5.6). A few lines, such as Fulton, Cortlandt and Barclay Streets, were so busy they ran twenty-four hours a day. Most ran from 6:00 AM to midnight with little or no late evening service. Less heavily traveled lines might offer much more limited operations in terms of hours and frequency of runs. The trustees of St. Patrick's Cathedral operated ferry service to a cemetery located on an island in the East River. There were boats to the navy yard, Wards Island, and the New York State mental hospital, all of which operated on a very limited basis indeed. We will describe only that part of this large and complex system that served the more populous southern end of Manhattan Island.

The system was summarized in 1882 in J. D. McCabe's book about Manhattan as consisting of twenty-six lines that carried 125 million

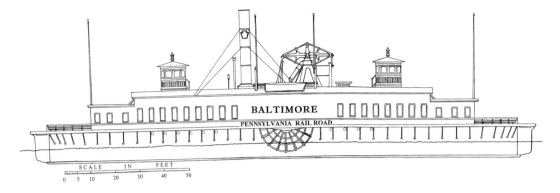

5.5. The *Baltimore*, Pennsylvania Railroad's ferry from Jersey City to New York, was an iron-hull double-ender built in 1882.

(After a drawing in J. E. Watkins, *History of the Pennsylvania Railroad*, 1896)

passengers plus an unspecified number of vehicles. The typical crossing was made in a few minutes, and each boat carried about 1,000 passengers. On the well-patronized routes a boat left every ten minutes. Separate cabins for men and women were placed on either side of the deck. Men might ride in the women's cabin as long as they did not smoke. These rooms were long, narrow, and built on a curve that followed the shape of the vessel. Two more passageways toward the center line were reserved for wagons, carriages, and horses. The very center was reserved for the engine and boiler. A pilothouse was located at either end of the top or hurricane roof, and a large marker light was mounted on the top of each pilothouse. The pilot communicated with the engine room via a signal bell system and speaking tubes. The latter were not considered very useful unless the person using them had a very powerful voice.

The ferry lines were located along both the Hudson and East Rivers, but the greatest concentration was at the lower end of Manhattan Island, because this was the most developed part of the city. The 1886 map in figure 5.6 will help readers find the lines and terminals of the New York system near its peak. By the beginning of the Civil War, many of the New Jersey–based ferry lines had been taken over by the owners of railroads that terminated along the shore of this mighty harbor. Starting in the north at Weehawken, New Jersey, was the New York Central West Shore terminal opposite Sixtieth Street in Manhattan. Well down the Hudson was the Delaware, Lackawanna, and Western rail and ferry terminal in Hoboken. A few blocks down from that was the Erie Railway's station. Nearby in Jersey City was the Pennsylvania Railroad's (PRR) facility, and to the south of this important terminal were the Lehigh Valley and Central of New Jersey stations.

Of those just named, the PRR ferry system was the most significant. It had started as the Paulus Hook ferry in colonial times and was purchased by the New Jersey Railroad and Transportation Company in 1841. The PRR leased this small but busy line thirty years later. Over the next decade the docks, ships, and terminal buildings were enlarged into a sprawling patchwork that struggled to keep up with the growing

5.6. Map of Lower Manhattan shows principal ferry routes and terminals in 1886.

(Author's collection)

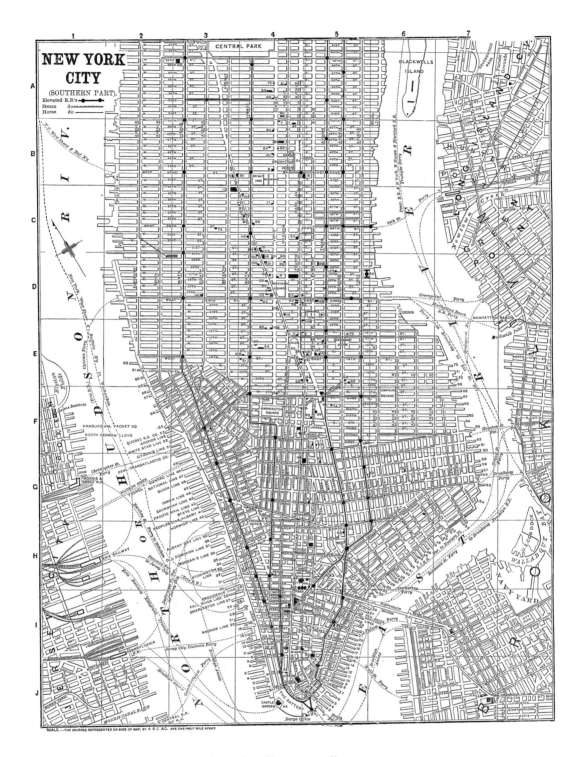

traffic. By 1875 this one terminal was handling 8.7 million passengers a year. Hundreds of trains a day arrived, some from as far away as Chicago and St. Louis. Although it was located in New Jersey, the Pennsylvania was the main station for New York City, because there was no way to deliver trains to Manhattan Island itself until a tunnel was built under the

5.7. A plan view of the 1882 *Baltimore*.

(J. E. Watkins, *History of the Pennsylvania Railroad*, 1896)

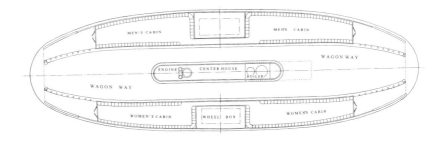

Hudson River, and that costly project was not even in the talking stage in the 1870s.

Meanwhile the PRR Jersey City ferry/rail station was running eight ferry lines from this one location. The most direct was across the river to Cortlandt Street. (The former World Trade Center towers stood about one block east of the old ferry terminal and displaced a portion of this very early street.) Just upriver were lines to Desbrosses, Thirteenth, Twenty-third, and Thirty-fourth Streets. Two lines went around the southern tip of Manhattan to Brooklyn. The eight lines went past Brooklyn and up the East River to Port Morris in the Bronx for a distance of about 12 miles. In May 1883 the PRR abandoned the Thirty-fourth Street line because of insufficient patronage, but elsewhere its traffic just kept growing, and by 1891 the PRR was handling 19 million ferry passengers and over 1 million vehicles a year. This required 162,110 trips. At the same time, a vast new terminal building that would be larger than Grand Central Station was under construction. It featured a mammoth train shed that measured 256 feet wide by 652 feet long and 115 feet high over the clerestory. The station would handle four hundred trains a day. Six ferry slips were arranged along the riverfront. To handle the crowd and speed, the loading and unloading, double-deck boats and ramps were installed. After four years of labor, the new terminal was ready in 1892.

The revenue generated by these busy lines allowed the PRR to purchase the best ferryboats available to serve the public. We will describe just two examples: the *Baltimore* and the *Cincinnati*. Built in 1882 by Harlan and Hollingsworth in Wilmington, Delaware, the *Baltimore* represents the old side-wheel design that had served travelers since almost the beginnings of steam navigation. The deck was 205 feet long and 65 feet wide. The wrought-iron hull was 13 feet, 9 inches deep and made from 7/16-inch-thick sheets (figs. 5.5, 5.7, and 5.8). She was painted a dull red externally. The cabin interiors were painted a robin's-egg green, and the floors were brick-red tiles. She made her trial trip on October 12, 1882, from Jersey City to Yonkers, New York, a distance of 17 miles, in one hour and twenty-five minutes. She ran for many years without incident until May 1906, when she sank after a collision with a lighter, or loading barge, near the Desbrosses terminal. All passengers were taken off safely,

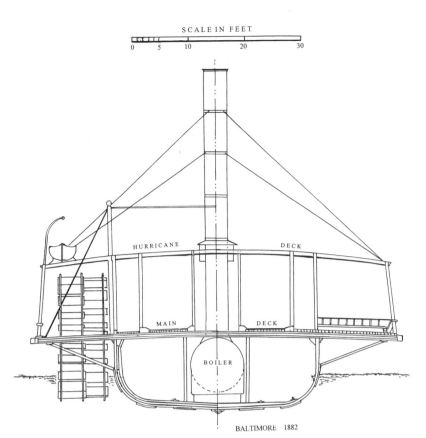

5.8. End elevation of the 1882 *Baltimore*.

(J. E. Watkins, *History of the Pennsylvania Railroad*, 1896)

and the *Baltimore* was repaired and returned to service. She remained in PRR service for another decade. Her new owner removed the engine and boiler and cut away the upper works. She was thus converted into a seagoing barge and worked out her last days in tow between Boston and Savannah.

Not many years after the *Baltimore* entered service, the Lackawanna Railroad introduced screw propulsion to New York ferryboat design. While screw propellers had become commonplace for oceangoing ships by the 1870s, ferryboat designers seemed content to stay with the old-fashioned paddle-wheel system. The *Bergen* entered service in 1888 and proved a success in every way (fig. 5.9). When the PRR was ready for a few new boats, it was decided to adopt the new form. The *Cincinnati* was launched in April 1891 at Elizabethport, New Jersey, and was a near duplicate of the *Baltimore* in size, but it had many new features other than screw propellers (fig. 5.10). Electric lighting and hot-air heating would please the passengers. Steam steering and an engine telegraph in place of the old manual steering and bell system helped the pilot. The twin-cylinder compound engine was rated at 1,000 hp, ample power for the twin-screw propulsion. Each screw was 8 feet, 9 inches in diameter. Considerable attention was paid to the boat's appearance; most ferries were finished in a plain, utilitarian manner, but not the *Cincinnati*.

5.9. Interior of the ladies' cabin of the Hoboken Ferry Company's *Bergen* of 1888. Most ferries were less elegant in décor.

(*Harper's Weekly*, January 5, 1889)

A top-ranking architect, Frank Furness (1839–1912) of Philadelphia, was hired to make sure the new vessel was as beautiful as it was technically advanced. An elaborate mahogany staircase led to the *Cincinnati*'s upper deck. An oval dome made of leaded glass offered natural lighting to the ground staircase. Mosaic floors and elegant carved embellishments added to the beauty of the interior space. This same attention to the exterior of the cabin brought the boat to the attention of the steamboat fraternity and the public. Seating was provided for 470 passengers. The wagon way could accommodate a dozen 5-ton wagons. The extra cost of the *Cincinnati*'s exceptional finish cannot be exactly documented, but the *Bergen,* a comparable vessel, cost $125,000. The *Cincinnati* was completed for $135,000; hence it seems likely that about $10,000 was expended on the grand stairway and other deluxe features of the boat. Was this wasted money? Perhaps so, but it is likely that officials of the railroad would contend it was good public relations. Some years later the upper cabin was removed and the *Cincinnati* was rebuilt to carry vehicles only. In 1929 the once beautiful vessel was sold for Delaware River service and was not retired until 1952. By this time both the great Jersey City train shed and the ferryboats were gone. The train shed was razed in 1941, and the last PRR boat ran in December 1949.

From about 1830 to 1950 New York Harbor was the busiest seaport in the United States. Despite its large size, traffic was dense with boats moving in every direction. Some two hundred steamship lines operated in these waters, ranging in size from ocean liners to small local craft. Dozens of Long Island Sound steamers, Hudson River boats, car floats,

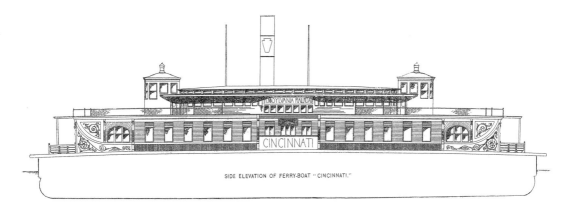

SIDE ELEVATION OF FERRY-BOAT "CINCINNATI."

5.10. The *Cincinnati*, Pennsylvania Railroad's double-deck ferry with embellishments, was designed by Frank Furness, a notable Philadelphia architect.

(*Engineering News*, November 7, 1891)

tugs, and coastal vessels competed for these waters. Collisions were commonplace, but most were minor in nature and rarely involved a sinking. Nevertheless, the ferryboat pilots had to be especially vigilant because they generally had to cut across traffic while going shore to shore. Pilots were forever ringing down to the engine room for more or less speed to avert ramming another boat in their path. Sometimes it was necessary to put the engines in reverse to avoid hitting another vessel. Whistles were constantly sounding as well, signaling, *We are passing on port or starboard side. We have the right-of-way; get out of my way, you damn fool!* It could be a testy and stressful business for the men at wheel as they picked their way through a sea of ships. An overly cautious pilot would always be late, so he had to be willing to take chances and hope he did not clip the stern off of another vessel as he passed just a bit too close. Close calls were standard practice in the waters around Manhattan.

The ferry collisions of record rarely resulted in a loss of life. Passengers might be frightened and literally shaken up, but few, if any, would perish. In March 1876 a large pilot boat rammed a Brooklyn ferryboat near the Fulton Street terminal. The ferryboat pilot whistled several times to warn the sailing vessel of the impending collision, but on they came, crashing into the rear of the men's cabin. Most of the passengers were at the other end of the boat, so only a few men were injured by flying glass and wood splinters. Although there were no serious injuries, the prow of the pilot boat was badly damaged and the ferry was out of service for a few days.

Late in 1887 an Erie Railway ferry was hit by a large steamer that knocked a sizable hole in the cabin, but the hull escaped intact. Three or four passengers were injured but not in a serious manner. A more serious collision happened in the summer of 1901 at the south end of Manhattan near the Whitehall Street terminal between a steel ferry, the *Mauch Chunk,* and a wooden ferry, the *Northfield.* The *Northfield* sank, but not before the passengers were removed. First reports indicated that everyone was safe, but the next day divers found five bodies aboard the sunken vessel. New York ferryboats would have an exemplary record in terms

5.11. The Jersey City ferry steams across the Hudson while passengers assume a casual, if unsafe, position on the forward deck.

(*Ballou's Pictorial*, January 30, 1858)

of low passenger fatalities except for one terrible accident – the worst in the history of New York ferries. July 30, 1871, was a very hot Sunday afternoon, and at the Whitehall ferry terminal the Staten Island boat the *Westfield* was ready to depart with 250 passengers on board. This vessel was powered with a low-pressure boiler (25 psi) and had been recently inspected. Even so, the boiler suddenly exploded with a terrific blast that destroyed much of the upper cabin and killed more than 85 passengers. The engine room crew and a defective piece of boiler plate were blamed for the tragedy. The *Westfield* was repaired and continued in service until 1905 without future incidents.

Most passenger injuries were self-induced. Many passengers were quite indifferent to their own safety and would jump off the boat before it landed to be the first off and on their way home or to work. So many succeeded that they continued to jump, thus encouraging other foolhardy folks to follow their bad example. Some commuters would jump aboard the boats as they departed, not wanting to wait ten minutes for the next ferry. Most presumably landed intact on the deck. Others ended up with

5.12. The fog bell at the Roosevelt Street ferry terminal on New York's East Side helped pilots find the slip.

(*Harper's Weekly*, Feb. 8, 1873)

a broken leg or some other injury. A few landed in the river. Some passengers felt it was right to sit on the edge of the deck with their legs over the side. An engraving of a Jersey City ferry published in *Ballou's Pictorial* for January 30, 1858, shows a large number of passengers seated this way as the boat steams ahead at full speed for the opposite shore; some of those so depicted are children (fig. 5.11). In time the operators of the boats placed gates on the ferries to hold passengers from occupying the forward sections of the deck.

Fog was a serious cause of delays to early ferryboat operations. A light fog would slow traffic, but a thick one could completely shut down operations, for when pilots cannot see other boats, they really cannot run freely or safely through congested waters. It was said that on a foggy day half of the New York workforce would be late to work. One of the worst fog days was reported on February 10, 1898; the fog settled in around 5:00 AM and did not lift until almost noon. The movement of oceangoing steamers was shut down and ferry operations were greatly hampered. Two of the Erie Railroad's ferries rammed each other near the New Jersey dock; a number of the standing passengers were knocked down and injured. Several other ferries collided or damaged the piers; others became lost. One of the South Brooklyn ferries ended up in the Hudson River and ran into a fireboat. The accident and delay reports were numerous. Fog bells were a standard feature at each ferry terminal (fig. 5.12). These were large bells that measured 4 or 5 feet in diameter. They were manned by a bell ringer whose duty was to ring a set signal so that the pilot could find his designated landing. The code for each landing is not recorded as far as we know, but each dock was assigned a specific number of rings. By the 1940s radar would solve the fog problem for navigation, but before that time ferryboat pilots depended on their compass and the song of the fog whistles and bells to guide them through the murky atmosphere.

Ice and fire were hazards faced by the ferrymen as well. New York Harbor was known to freeze every few years, but it normally did not last very long, because the tides were strong enough to break it up. In January 1867 the ice formed a bridge across the East River. It was so solid that no boat could move and the public began to walk across. When the tide turned it began to break up, and one man partway across was drowned. Fire was an enemy to all watercraft, and since so many ferries were of wood construction they were vulnerable to the flames. In late November 1866 a Brooklyn ferry named *Idaho* caught fire in the evening just after the rush hour was past. There were only about forty people on board rather than the usual six hundred to eight hundred. The boat had life preservers and a metal lifeboat, but all of this safety gear was on the top deck and the flames blocked access to this part of the ship. Passing boats pulled to and took off the freight and passengers. There were a few other such fires, but none managed to cause much destruction except for a ferry docked at the Lackawanna ferry terminal in Hoboken. Around eleven in the evening, flames from this boat put the torch to this venerable wooden structure on August 5, 1905. In a few hours, the Delaware, Lackawanna, and Western Railroad was in the market for a new terminal. Fortunately, most passengers and workers were at home in bed at the time, so the big blaze did not manage to claim any human victims.

The patrons of New York ferries were described by reporters of the past as an interesting cross-section of the great metropolis' population. It was a cosmopolitan crowd of the rich and poor, the educated and the unschooled, the fair and homely – in short, a cross-section of the entire inhabitants of the area. The greatest mix of classes was found on the Brooklyn ferry, where one could see laborers and millionaires, Chinese and Greeks, tramps and peddlers, and businessmen and farmers. On the other lines the classes were more separated and tended to come in waves. At sunrise the poorest class would arrive, consisting largely of grimy laborers, shop boys, early-duty clerks, and cashiers. Around 7:30 AM the office workers started toward the city; they were cleaner and better dressed. The big rush was over by about 9:00 AM when the professionals and managers made their way to the boats. Seats were now generally available, and passengers were middle-aged and more genteel. They seemed content and sat quietly reading their newspapers. Mixed in with the young clerks were a few beards; a few at fifty-five likely understood that their dreams of becoming a partner in business would not come true. There was a lull in traffic around 10:00 AM, but an hour later the wealthy classes came to the ferry landing. These were rich men, business owners, who arrived in

5.13. Ferryboats at night glide across the dark water. Most ferries ceased running by about 10:00 PM.

(Reverend Samuel Manning, *American Pictures Drawn with Pen and Pencil,* 1870)

silk top hats and fine overcoats. It was a privilege of the wealthy to lie in bed and have a late breakfast. The poorest traveled first and the richest could arrive late. The masters not only got to their desk past noon but also wandered off quickly for a rich lunch at Delmonico's.

The flow of travelers in the evening followed a similar routine. As the night sky took over New York Harbor, the river would be aglow from the lights of other vessels, the lamps along the shore, and perhaps a little moonlight (fig. 5.13). The passengers, weary from the long workday, tended to be subdued. The rumble of the machinery belowdecks could be heard, but little else. Occasionally a party of strolling musicians would enliven the scene. It might be a one-man band with a monkey passing around a tin cup or a group of young migrants putting heart and soul into a collection of battered brass horns. Once every few weeks came the call "Man overboard!" awakening the crowd. The boat would stop and use a searchlight to scan the water looking for a form in the waves. Was it a suicide or just a deckhand who had lost his footing? After a time, the search would be abandoned and the engines would pick up their labors, pushing the boat toward the far side. The late evening travelers, particularly after midnight, were usually a less respectable crowd, consisting of old and young sinners who were a little worse for the pool room or clubhouse. The bars so conveniently near the ferry station often encouraged a few more drinks before boarding the boat to home, making some of the travelers overly talkative or quarrelsome. Around 3:30 AM the newsboys started selling papers. As dawn began to brighten the mist over the river, the gardeners and farmers would bring wagonloads of produce to the ferry landings from outlying New Jersey and Long Island. Most were thrifty, plodding Germans hoping for a small profit at the big-city markets.

Today millions of commuters stream into and out of Manhattan. Most are now office workers since the factories and workshops are largely gone. Rather few travel by ferryboat, and those boats presently operating are small motorcraft very unlike the turtle-shaped steamers of the Victorian era. The decline of the system began with the opening of the Brooklyn Bridge in 1883 and advanced slowly at first as new bridges and river tunnels

5.14. The *Maryland* carried passengers across the lower Susquehanna River starting in 1854.

rendered the ferries obsolete. The last of the old steam fleet was the Erie/Lackawanna *Elmira,* which made its final run on November 22, 1967.

FERRIES ACROSS AMERICA

New York might have been the capital of ferryboat operations, but such vessels were hardly unique to this great city by the sea. They were introduced in settlements so small, they were hardly even villages. Wright's Ferry on the lower Susquehanna River is a good example of a backcountry ferry operation. In about 1730 a Quaker settler named John Wright was given a patent to operate an animal-powered ferry 40 miles upstream from the river's entry into Chesapeake Bay. The Susquehanna is very wide, shallow, and rocky at this place, midway between Lancaster and York, Pennsylvania. As the area developed, this crossing offered a direct path to the west and south. Wright's Ferry developed into the town of Columbia, Pennsylvania, and there was a serious effort to make it the seat of the federal government in the late 1780s, but southern politicians won the day by placing the U.S. capital farther north, on the Potomac River. In about 1812, soon after Columbia's ambitions had been smitten, a young Russian diplomat named Paul Svinin (1787–1839) made the crossing over the mile-wide river. To commemorate this part of his tour he created a charming watercolor, now in the Metropolitan Museum of Art, that shows a long, shallow raft carrying a two-wheel carriage, two horses, and several passengers. Two men seated facing the rear of the boat row mightily across the swift-moving current.

5.15. The *Solano* moved passenger trains in the San Francisco area between 1879 and 1930.

(*Railroad Gazette*, July 30, 1880)

Downstream the Susquehanna grows in width as it enters Chesapeake Bay, a shallow body of water that was once part of this same river before it sank to be engulfed by the salty tides of the Atlantic. On the south bank of the river was the hamlet of Havre de Grace. Louis Philippe, Duke of Orléans, while touring the United States in the late 1790s, attempted to take the ferry here, but the winds were so fierce that the ferrymen would not leave the dock. So this future king of France was obliged to seek shelter in a local inn. The weather was not much improved by the next day; yet even so, the ferry operators agreed to take the duke and his three companions across. Their horses were unsettled by the wind and the rattling sails and rigging. One fell into the water and was pulled back aboard with great difficulty. The strong headwinds pushed the boat back three times. At last they were able to land and proceed on toward Baltimore.

The perils and inconvenience of this broad river crossing were lessened some years later when the Philadelphia, Wilmington, and Baltimore Railroad completed its track between those three cities in 1838. The cost of a long bridge at Havre de Grace was simply too great for this pioneer coastal railway to undertake. A steam-powered ferryboat called the *Susquehanna* was built in Baltimore in 1837 to carry passengers and a limited number of baggage cars across the river. This may well have been the first steam-powered car ferry in the world. Passengers were obliged to walk down a path to board the boat with their hand luggage. The baggage and mail cars were pushed onto a single track mounted on the roof of boat's upper works. This structure was not strong enough to carry locomotives, and there was not enough room for the coaches. The boat crossed over in a few minutes. Passengers then proceeded up a path on the opposite bank to a waiting train. The baggage cars were pulled off the roof track and attached to the rear of the train, which then proceeded to the other end of the line. The whole process was reversed for trains heading in the opposite direction. The system worked fairly well; however, the *Susquehanna* was not powerful enough to break through ice, so service was suspended during severe cold spells. If the river froze solid enough, a temporary track was laid across the ice, and baggage sleds were pulled along by horses. Passengers could ride in a sleigh or walk as they preferred – most chose to walk. But as traffic between these major East Coast cities grew, the railroad sought ways to improve operation. There was talk of a giant bridge, but the cost was too great, so a new ferryboat was completed late in 1854. The *Maryland* was larger and better in all respects than her predecessor (fig. 5.14). Her iron hull and powerful engines meant she could push through all but the most solid ice. Three, rather than one, roof-level tracks could accommodate twenty cars, so the entire train, minus the locomotive, could be carried over. Passengers, however, were still obliged to leave their seats and walk aboard the boat to make the crossing in the boat's saloon. The system worked well until it was interrupted by the traffic emergency caused by the Civil War. Plans for a bridge were quickly revised, but the work was not rapidly advanced for a variety of reasons, which included tornado damage to the nearly completed structure. Finally in November 1866 the bridge was opened and the ferry was retired.

Large railroad car ferries were operated elsewhere in the United States at locations from New London, Connecticut, to San Francisco. The inland rivers had such vessels in service at Coal Grove, Ohio (across from Ashland, Kentucky); Cairo, Illinois; New Orleans; and elsewhere. In California the Central Pacific Railroad was seeking a faster route to Oakland and its ultimate western terminal, San Francisco. This could be done by crossing the Carquinez Straits. A bridge was too costly, so a large car ferry named the *Solano* was constructed in 1879 (fig. 5.15). This monster wooden side-wheeler was 424 feet long and proved capable of carrying an entire train, including the locomotive, across the deep waters leading into San Pablo Bay. The *Solano* worked on until 1930 when she was finally retired. A fine new steel bridge ended the labors of this elderly steamer.

We tend to think of ferryboats as a holdover from the Victorian era – and so they might seem to modern travelers – yet many soldier on today carrying millions of passengers who can find no alternate way to travel.

SUGGESTED READING

Bates, Alan L. et al. "Falls Cities Ferries: A Note." *Indiana Magazine of History* 95, no. 3 (1999): 255–83.

Baxter, Raymond J., and Arthur G. Adams. *Railroad Ferries of the Hudson River, and Stories of a Deckhand*. New York: Fordham University Press, 1999.

Blount, Jim. *On the Road: A History of Travel in Hamilton and Butler County, Ohio*. Hamilton Ohio: Past/Present/Press, 1996.

Condit, Carl W. *The Port of New York*. Chicago: University of Chicago Press, 1980.

Crisman, Kevin J., and Arthur B. Cohn.

When Horses Walked on Water: Horse-Powered Ferries in Nineteenth-Century America. Washington, D.C.: Smithsonian Institution Press, 1998.

Carmer, Carl L. *The Susquehanna*. Rivers of America series. New York: Rinehart, 1955.

Cudahy, Brian J. *Over and Back: The History of Ferryboats in New York Harbor*. New York: Fordham University Press, 1990.

"The Evolution of the Ferryboat." *Harper's Weekly*. January 5, 1889.

"Fleet of Ferry Boats." *New York Times*. January 29, 1882.

Harlan, George H. *San Francisco Bay Ferryboats*. Berkeley, Calif.: Howell-North, 1967.

Hilton, George W. *The Staten Island Ferry*. Berkeley, Calif.: Howell-North, 1964.

———. "The Steamer Maryland Route." *Steamboat Bill* 95 (1965): 87–93.

Krieger, Michael. *Where Rails Meet the Sea: America's Connections between Ships and Trains*. New York: MetroBooks, 1998.

Kline, Mary S. and G. A. Bayless. *Ferry Boats: A Legend on Puget Sound*. Seattle: Bayless Books, 1983.

McCabe, James Dabney. *New York by Sunlight and Gaslight*. Philadelphia: Douglass Bros., 1882.

Newell, Gordon. *Pacific Steamboats*. New York: Bonanza Books, 1958.

Perry, John. *American Ferryboats*. New York: Wilfred Funk, 1957.

Staunton, Samuel. *American Steam Vessels*. New York: Smith and Stanton, 1895.

Wallace, Agnes. "The Wiggins Ferry Monopoly." *Missouri Historical Review* 42 (October 1947): 1–19.

White, John H., Jr. "Let Us Cross over the River – Cincinnati's Ferryboats." *Timeline* 23, no. 1 (2006): 44–57.

Yarmolinsky, Avrahm. *Picturesque United States: A Memoir on Paul Svinin*. New York: W. E. Rudge, 1930.

6.1. A typical American canal boat of about 1830 from an engraving of the period. Notice the steersman's shelter at the rear of the boat and the three-horse team on the tow path.

(Author's collection)

Canals   № 6

The Low & Slow Way to Go

THE CANAL IS AN ANCIENT FORM OF OVERLAND TRANSPORTAtion. Examples can be found in Egypt at the time of the pharaohs and in Rome when Caesar was alive. In the Far East, China's Grand Canal was being enlarged while Europe slumbered in a dark age. The Renaissance brought forward an Italian engineer named Leon Batista Alberti, who built a lock to raise or lower canal boats. Jean Colbert, Louis XIV's minister of finance, began construction of a canal network for France. England caught up with the canal mania a century later and had an extensive system of artificial waterways by 1830.

Young America adopted the canal because it was a proven and time-tested technology that could move heavy loads over long distances with minimum power. It could be built and operated by unskilled labor. Since canals were man-made, they could be built in a direct line of commerce between major cities in relatively straight lines. Rivers run where gravity dictates. They twist and turn and are very long and indirect pathways. In addition, canals are pacific by nature while rivers are ungovernable. Canals have a uniform depth. They are derived of rocks, sandbars, sunken logs, and currents. The canal was a good fit for an agricultural nation such as the United States of 1800, because it was so low tech. It was little more than a trench dug in the earth, made watertight by a thin layer of clay. The locks were built of native stone; the lock gates and boats were made of local timber. Power was furnished by horses and mules, draft animals well known to both farmers and city folk of the time (fig. 6.1). The boat crews and maintenance gangs were ordinary yeomen. Canal promoters ignored the canal's several defects, notably its slow speed and high cost of construction. Hilly territory drove up construction costs considerably and slowed traffic because many locks were needed to overcome the changing elevations. Mountains made canals uneconomic, and dry terrain made canal operations difficult because they required a good water supply to replace water lost through leaks, breaches in embankments, and evaporation.

THE AMERICAN CANAL SYSTEM

Some of the earliest canals were in New England; most were short and not remarkably successful. It was a poor start for this mode of transit in the New World. The South Hadley Canal carried boats on the Connecticut River around a waterfall via a 2½ mile channel. An incline plane powered by two waterwheels carried loaded boats from one level to another. Construction was under way from 1792 to 1795. The South Hadley Canal and incline operated for almost fifty years. The Middlesex Canal was a more ambitious project chartered in 1793 to build a canal from the Merrimac River (near Lowell, Massachusetts) and Charleston Mill Pond (near Boston). The canal was only 28 miles long when completed in 1803, yet it was the longest in the nation. Even so, neither the Middlesex nor any other Yankee canals inspired much enthusiasm for this mode of transport. It was the well-known Erie Canal in New York State that set off a frenzy for waterways.

When the Erie opened in 1825 it became the longest canal in the world. It enjoyed good traffic even before being completed and created a false notion that canals built on the same plan were bound to succeed in spectacular fashion. New Yorkers went ahead to build a much longer system then was needed, and while the original Erie continued to prosper, the branches generally failed financially. Pennsylvania watched the progress of its neighbors and plunged into the canal business in a major way, building one of the largest canal systems in the nation. Its state-sponsored Western Division Canal, known as the Main Line, ran from Philadelphia to Pittsburgh. Long branches reached north and south, and a separate series of canals were built in the eastern part of the state to carry anthracite coal. Even before the Erie was completed, Ohio started two north-south canals to connect Lake Erie with the Ohio River. Indiana yearned for a commercial contact with the East Coast and began work on an L-shaped canal that would connect Lake Erie to the Ohio River. At 468 miles the Wabash was the nation's longest canal when it was finished in 1853, but it proved an economic failure and closed down in 1872. Illinois was more temperate and attempted only one canal along the Illinois River from Chicago. No canals were built to the west, unless one wishes to consider the Sault Ste. Marie that connected Lakes Huron and Superior. Maryland largely supported the Chesapeake and Ohio Canal that fell far short of reaching the Ohio River. Virginia's James River Canal struggled westward from Richmond only to die in the foothills of the Allegheny Mountains. The Old South was home to no canals other than two short ones in North and South Carolina. In summary, only 4,468 miles of canal were built in this country, which is a rather modest network for such a large landmass. The canal era was also a short one in our national history.

There was little new construction after 1845, largely because canals could not compete with railroads, which offered faster service and were more adept at running through hilly and mountainous territory. The canals shut down in wintertime in northern locations, while the trains could operate in all but the most severe weather.

One of the country's most important canals was – and still is – the Erie Canal, and here is how it came about. The Mohawk River Valley in the state of New York had been recognized since colonial times as the only water-level passage through the Allegheny Mountains. It was an animal and Indian trail for centuries before the white man landed on the eastern coast of what is now the United States, and it was an obvious route for a canal to connect the Great Lakes with the Atlantic Ocean via the Hudson River. The city of Albany stands on the Hudson about 150 miles north of New York City, which has a large deepwater harbor. Albany is also almost due east of Buffalo at the end of Lake Erie. Western farmers could produce wheat, corn, hogs, and cattle cheaply in the Midwest; however, there was no economic way to ship these goods to the larger East Coast cities or overseas to the markets of the world. Shipping goods overland was very expensive. In 1814 Robert Fulton claimed it cost $2 to send a barrel of flour 130 miles by highway, while that same barrel could be sent from Albany to New York City, 160 miles, by water for only 25 cents. Such savings alone would justify the cost of a canal across the top of the Empire State. Canal advocates were delighted when the brilliant secretary of the U.S. Treasury, Albert Gallatin, issued his comprehensive report on internal improvements in 1808, which recommended roads and canals to upgrade the internal transport system in the eastern half of the country. The Erie Canal was a key element in Gallatin's plan. The War of 1812 delayed action on this master plan, and of course Congress had its own difficulties in passing any funding bills to make it happen. In 1817 they finally presented President Madison with a bill that would use revenues received from the Second Bank of the United States to fund internal improvements. Madison vetoed the bill, saying the Constitution did not give Congress such specific powers.

The battle for the Erie Canal shifted to Albany. Since federal funding seemed uncertain, the partisans for the canal hoped to persuade the state legislature to provide the necessary money. The estimated sum required was a staggering $4.9 million, a vast sum in 1817, and opposition lined up quickly to oppose such lavish expenditure of the public purse. Fortunately, the friends of the canal had a strong leader, DeWitt Clinton, whose father had been a general in the American Revolution (fig. 6.2). Clinton had been a member of the state assembly, a U.S. senator, and mayor of New York City. He was elected governor of New York in 1817. His position of power helped, but Clinton was a determined and able politician

6.2. DeWitt Clinton, governor of New York State, was a key figure in the building of the Erie Canal.

(C. D. Colden, *Memoir of the New York Canal*, 1825)

who knew how to get things done in government circles. It was not an easy fight, but Clinton and his allies got the authorization laws enacted. A ground-breaking ceremony for the Erie Canal was held at Rome, New York, on July 4, 1817. Benjamin Wright was appointed as the project's chief engineer. Wright was trained as a lawyer but found engineering a more satisfactory occupation and proved himself very competent in his new trade. His major challenge was to determine a true level as each section of the canal was laid out. He handled this assignment with a precision rare for the time and went ahead to hire contractors to take over the actual construction.

A thousand men were at work by early 1818. This number would grow to two or three thousand over the next few years. Shovels and wheelbarrows were used in great numbers, but much of the earth moving was done with plows and horse-drawn scrappers. A machine using a screw and crank could topple trees without the use of a saw or ax. Another machine was devised to uproot tree stumps. It consisted of two 16-foot-high wheels and a third smaller wheel that was attached to teams of horses or oxen by

6.3. A large cut through a rocky ridge near Lockport, New York, was a challenge to the builders of the Erie Canal.

(C. D. Colden, *Memoir of the New York Canal*, 1825)

a chain. These teams turned the third wheel, which was attached to the axle. A chain firmly fastened to a stump was wrapped around the axle. The mighty stump puller could remove thirty to forty stumps a day.

There had never been such a large-scale construction project in America before, so it was difficult to estimate how quickly it would be completed. It involved 364 miles of canal, 83 locks, and 18 aqueducts. The removal of earth and rock equaled 11.4 million cubic yards. The locks were built of stone that had to be quarried, cut, and fitted (fig. 6.3). Some of the aqueducts were massive affairs built of stone and timber. One of these structures carried the canal across the Mohawk River. It was 1,200 feet long and rested on twenty-six stone piers. Despite the size of tasks, the work proceeded faster than expected. The middle section of the canal between the Mohawk and Seneca Rivers, about 94 miles, was completed by the summer of 1820. Work continued on the canal section by section. Because the operation of boats began as each section opened, the state of New York was earning revenue even before the project was fully complete.

On October 26, 1825, the canal was officially finished (fig. 6.4). A grand celebration was planned that featured the transportation of a barrel of water from Lake Erie to New York Harbor, where the barrel was emptied into the Atlantic Ocean. Governor Clinton was on board the first boat to share in the glory of this magnificent accomplishment. Well that he should, for he had a major role in its success. He died early in 1828 in his fifty-eighth year.

The Erie Canal was a busy and profitable waterway for many years and was one of the great success stories in American history. It paid for itself

6.4. The east end of the Erie Canal at Albany, New York, as it appeared in 1825. The canal packet S. Van Rensselaer is shown on the right, and a freight boat is depicted on the left side.

(C. D. Colden, *Memoir of the New York Canal*, 1825)

by 1837 and was rebuilt and enlarged several times. Its success inspired many other canal enthusiasts to assume their projects would be equally busy and profitable, but unfortunately this assumption was unfounded.

Every major seaport on the eastern seacoast had its own plan to capture the western trade. Baltimore hoped its railroad to the Ohio River would secure a hold on exports of the interior states. Charleston, South Carolina, had an identical dream. Other cities, such as Philadelphia, considered a canal to be the more prudent road to riches but lacked the natural gift of a Mohawk River Valley and so had to find a way over the Alleghenies. Engineers recommended following the Susquehanna and Juniata Rivers westward to Hollidaysburg. From Pittsburgh the route was along the Allegheny River to the Conemaugh River to Johnstown. The scheme for a Main Line of Public Works was taken over by the state of Pennsylvania. It was envisioned as a grand canal from Philadelphia to Pittsburgh. The Ohio River would offer a connection to the entire Ohio-Mississippi River network. After the usual political bickering the project passed the state legislature in early 1826.

Work began in July of that year at Harrisburg. It was planned as a combination railroad and canal. Tracks would run 82 miles from Philadelphia to Columbia, Pennsylvania, where a canal would proceed across most of the state to Hollidaysburg. A short railway of inclined planes and connecting rail lines would go over the mountains to Johnstown. A 104-mile canal carried boats into Pittsburgh. The total length of the system was 395 miles, but it involved 174 locks, 49 aqueducts, and 3 tunnels. It was more complex than the Erie Canal and would cost $5 million more than its New York rival. The need to reload freight from railroad to canal no less than three times delayed transit and drove up costs. It was annoying to passengers as well. There was no practical way to build a canal over the mountains of western Pennsylvania. The legislators were too conservative to make the Main Line a railroad, fearing the technology was as yet unproven, so they created a technical monstrosity that was part railroad and part canal.

Work proceeded with reasonable speed considering the hilly nature of most of the route. By 1829 portions of the canal were ready for service. Three years later the entire Juniata division was complete. The complex portage railroad ran a test train over the summit at Blair's Gap, 1,400 feet above Hollidaysburg, in November 1833. In March 1834 the entire Main Line of Public Works opened from Philadelphia to Pittsburgh. The parade of wagons heading west over the mountains, packed with settlers and their baggage and furniture, now shifted to the Main Line. The boats enjoyed good traffic at times but nothing in comparison to the Erie. By 1845 the Erie Canal was carrying about 350,000 tons of freight while the Main Line's revenues were too small to pay the interest on the bonds. The failure of the Pennsylvania canal system was made even greater by the construction of several long branch canals. The total cost of the system was $65 million. Comparisons of canals pointed to the large passenger traffic on the state works. It was impressive that in 1846 the number of passenger miles westbound was 953,000 and eastbound was 274,790. However, the fares were so low that the total revenue was modest, and most of that was kept by the private operators who ran the boats. The state received only a small toll fee.

The prospects of the Main Line of Public Works declined as more railroad mileage opened in Pennsylvania during the 1840s and 1850s. The Pennsylvania Railroad reached Pittsburgh in 1852, rending the canal largely obsolete. Five years later the Main Line was sold to the Pennsylvania Railroad and much of the old system was abandoned. The eastern section of the canal continued to operate with some services up until about 1875. A big flood in 1889 greatly damaged that portion of the system. By 1890 only 144 miles were still being used, and this was abandoned by 1903.

Just south of the Pennsylvania Main Line enthusiastic promoters proposed an even more unrealistic route for a canal to the west. It, too, would connect the Atlantic Coast to the Ohio River and tap the rich lands of the middle west. The route was slightly shorter than the Erie's or the Main Line's route, but it involved a very notable disadvantage: it would have to cross the Alleghenies through a more rugged mass of mountain than the Pennsylvania canal faced between Johnstown and Hollidaysburg. Short of the Rockies, this region of western Maryland and Virginia was about as unfriendly canal territory as one could hope to find. Yet optimism knows no bounds like that of the true believers who promoted the Chesapeake and Ohio (C&O) Canal (fig. 6.5). A charter was granted to this enterprise

6.5. Aqueduct of the Chesapeake and Ohio Canal over the Monocracy River was completed in 1833. It remains standing in a somewhat ruined state.

(*Harper's Weekly*, September 14, 1861)

in 1828, but it was only because of funding from the federal government and the state of Maryland that it was built. Private investors were reluctant to fund the enterprise despite a very low estimate of $4.5 million to produce a canal from Washington, D.C., to Cumberland, Maryland, in seven or eight years.

Work on the C&O Canal started in 1828 in Georgetown, a suburb of Washington. It reached Harper's Ferry, then part of Virginia, in 1834. That's only 55 miles in six years. Canal planners had intended to be almost to Cumberland by this time, but construction remained 130 miles to the west. Over the next five years the C&O reached Hancock, Maryland, with just 55 miles to go. By now they were well into the foothills of the Alleghenies and construction moved even slower. Having to drill a great tunnel at Paw Paw was one reason faster progress was not made. The bore was 3,118 feet long, and the tunneling took almost fourteen years to complete. To support the terminal roof 3,500,00 bricks were used to create a lining that was 13 inches thick. In 1850 the C&O reached Cumberland, 185 miles from Washington, but short of the Ohio River by over 150 miles. The way from the capital city was made easy by the Potomac River, but that expired at Cumberland. There were no rivers or convenient valleys through the heart of the mountains that lay just west of Cumberland.

This was the end of the road for the C&O Canal. There seemed little purpose to push on, because the Baltimore and Ohio Railroad that paralleled the canal along the Potomac River was now building on toward Wheeling, West Virginia, and the Ohio River. After having spent $14 million, the C&O was resigned to linger on the far side of the Eastern Continental Divide. It had cost about $60,000 a mile, while most canals were built for half that amount. It was clear that hilltop canals were costly by their nature. Beyond the Paw Paw tunnel the only other truly expensive element of the canal was the aqueduct over Monocracy River, which empties into the Potomac near Dickerson, Maryland. This elegant all-stone structure has seven arches and is 516 feet long. It stands today looking like a Roman ruin some 30 miles west of Washington, D.C.

Because the canal did not serve any large cities, passenger service on the C&O was never extensive. Washington remained a small community until the 1930s. By 1859 even this traffic was largely excursion runs rather than regular passengers. The coal trade, however, sustained the C&O for many decades; such traffic was one-way, however, going downstream to Washington. Canal traffic peaked in 1877 at almost 1 million tons, with five hundred boats active at the time. A year later a flood ravaged the canal. It was hit again by the angry waters of the Potomac in 1889. Traffic declined greatly soon after this flood. By 1910 there were only thirty boats in active service, and ten years later the number was down to fifteen. With so little activity moss tended to cover the now ancient waterway. In 1924 a flood did so much damage that the canal was abandoned. In more recent years most of the canal property was acquired by the U.S. Parks Service as a preserve for hikers, naturalists, and anyone interested in studying the slumbering remains of this once busy canal.

The canal movement was taken up enthusiastically by a few Midwestern states, especially Ohio and Indiana. For example, the Miami and Erie (M&E) Canal ran from Cincinnati to Toledo on a north-south line very close to the Ohio and Indiana border. It was a state-operated enterprise and was one of two north-south canals in Ohio. The Ohio and Erie Canal served the center of the Buckeye State, connecting Cleveland, on Lake Erie, and Portsmouth, on the Ohio River. Politics demanded that the western part of the state receive equal treatment, while the eastern segment was apparently too weak to rate a canal of its own. The M&E Canal was surveyed in 1822 as canal fever began to heat up. Typically, it follows a series of river valleys on its path northward from the Ohio River to Lake Erie. Mill Creek follows from the Ohio River, to the Great Miami River, to St. Mary's near the center of the state. The canal then follows the Maumee River to Toledo. Very near St. Mary's is the Loramie Summit, which at 512 feet above the Ohio River is the highest point between Lake Erie and the

Ohio River. A series of locks was needed here to get canal boats over this higher ground. As planning for the canal moved ahead, the engineers laid out 19 aqueducts, 103 locks, and 3 reservoirs. It would be 248 miles long and cost almost $8 million, about $1 million more than the cost of the Erie Canal. The Ohio State Assembly authorized construction in 1825 with financing to be funded by the sale of public lands and bonds.

Ground-breaking for the M&E Canal took place at Middletown, a small community about 35 miles north of Cincinnati. Governor Jeremiah Morrow, a strong advocate for internal improvements, officiated at the ground-breaking ceremony held on July 4, 1825. His special guest was DeWitt Clinton, governor of New York and champion of the almost-finished Erie Canal. There was hardly a larger celebrity in canal world than Clinton.

By October 1827 the canal advanced to the northern suburbs of Cincinnati. In early 1829 it reached Dayton, and 66 miles of the ditch were ready for service. Traffic on the canal developed quickly, and by 1832 it was carrying one thousand passengers a week. Most days, seventy freight boats moved between Dayton and Cincinnati carrying flour, corn, and salt pork.

Progress on the northern end of the M&E Canal stopped because the terrain grew more difficult and the money had run out. The panic of 1837 was efficient in drying up funds for large public projects such as this one. The federal government came forward with another land grant that furnished money to resume work on the Miami Extension Canal. In 1828 the federal government gave Ohio one half million acres of public land to help finance the extension. It worked its way slowly northward to the Ohio cities of Troy, Piqua, and Delphos. Meanwhile, Indiana's Wabash and Erie Canal cut across the northwest corner of Ohio to Toledo. A union was made at Defiance with the Wabash and Erie Canal, and the M&E reached Toledo in this manner by 1845. The cost of the M&E averaged $10,983 per mile. It was a trifle late because the railroad era was already under way, and within a decade the M&E was rendered largely obsolete by the newer form of transit (fig. 6.6). Proponents of the canal pointed out that the M&E remained vital to local transportation needs and that traffic peaked in 1851. Four hundred boats produced revenues of $351,000 per year. Their arguments seemed convincing until it was pointed out that the system had operated at a deficit most years and that the state was required to make up the losses. Canals required continuous maintenance. Each spring debris had to be removed by dredging. Breaks in embankments could be very costly, because not just the canal itself was damaged, but nearby property could be ruined as well. In April 1852 a large break in the M&E Canal sent a 12-foot wave of water that partially demolished the House of Refuge, a

MIAMA CANAL PACKET LINE.

A Packet Boat in the above Line will leave CINCINNATI

Every Morning at 10 o'clock,

For Hamilton, Middletown, Franklin, Miamisburgh, Dayton, Troy, Piqua, St. Mary's, and the Junction,
CONNECTING WITH A LINE THROUGH TO LAKE ERIE.

The Proprietors of this Line have within the last year built several splendid Packets, which for convenience and elegance of finish are not surpassed by any Packet Boats at the *East* or *West*. These Packets are commanded by experienced and gentlemanly Captains.

This Line, which connects with the Steamboat Line from Detroit to Buffalo, is now in full and successful operation, and persons travelling to or from the East, will find this route by the LAKES the most desirable, in point of comfort, speed and economy.

An OMNIBUS connected with this Line will carry passengers to and from the Boats without charge.

PACKET OFFICE in the MANSION HOUSE,

On Main Street, near the Canal,

CINCINNATI.

DOYLE & DICKEY,
Proprietors.

6.6. This advertisement for passenger service on the Miami Canal Packet Line appeared late in the canal era. Note that *Miami* is misspelled.

(J. F. Kimball, *Business Directory for Ohio, Kentucky and Indiana*, 1846)

children's home in Cincinnati. Fifty-four residents in the home narrowly escaped drowning.

In 1877 Ohio attempted to officially abandon the canal system. Leases dating back to the early 1860s reverted to the state in 1879. Water rights to mill operators who used wheels and turbines for power gave the canal system some extra income. Many factories in the city of Hamilton were powered in this manner. Maintenance was cut back to a minimum, but the fix and patch methods managed to keep an old system going so that sections were open until 1900. In 1899 an aqueduct collapse near the center of the M&E shut down that section of the canal, cutting the system in half. Even so, boats continued short hauls of ice, grain, and other bulk materials for local shippers. Boats were also rented to excursionists for picnic trips. The devastating flood of 1913 along the Great Miami River destroyed large sections of the southern end of the waterway. The last trip on the Cincinnati end of the canal, which was purely ceremonial, was made in July 1917. Since that time much of the right of way has been converted into highways.

CABIN LIFE

Fortunately several travelers recorded their experiences of canal journeys, which allows us to create a word picture of what life was like on early American waterways. As might be expected, the experience varied, but the general feeling was that canal travel was pleasant enough during the day but disagreeable at night. If the boat was full or nearly empty, the comfort level was also affected. Even the season had a pronounced bearing on how travelers perceived life along the waterway. Summer was not a good time of year to go by canal, because lower water problems were a problem. And on summer days the low-ceiling cabins became insufferably hot. Roof seating was no better, because the sun beat down on passengers seated there. Mosquitoes were particularly annoying and plentiful during the summer, too. Wintertime was rarely mentioned, because most canals were shut down by freezing temperatures.

The best way to understand what canal travel was like in the nineteenth century is to examine a typical boat of that time. They were long and narrow and almost always painted white with a band of color – orange, red, or blue – running the length of the hull well above the waterline. The stern was the most lavishly decorated part of the exterior of the vessel and sometimes featured elaborate carvings of scrolls or nautical subjects. And almost always the name of the boat was painted on in elegant lettering.

The hull had a snub-nosed bow and a rounded stern. The bottom was flat. There were small open decks at both ends; the front was manned by a deckhand when needed and the rear by a steersman whenever the boat was in motion. The cabin was low with a slightly arched roof and ran about three-quarters the length of the hull. Many small windows admitted light or air when opened. Shutters were in place and could be closed as desired by the crew or passengers. The cabin floor was laid just above the bottom of the hull, so passengers walked down a few steps to reach the floor. The

6.7. The interior of an Erie Canal boat at bedtime. A crew member assigns bunks to male passengers from a list. The ladies' compartment is behind the curtain. The height of the cabin is exaggerated in this engraving.

(*Marco Paul's Voyages and Travels*, 1852)

cabin was generally divided into spaces. The main compartment served as a sitting room by day. At mealtime several small tables were assembled in the center of the space to form one long table. At night the main cabin was the gentlemen's sleeping space. Berths were hung by ropes or light chains from the ceiling in tiers of three. A heavy curtain separated a small part of the main cabin for ladies (fig. 6.7). It would appear that ladies traveled in much smaller numbers than men. The small rear portion of the cabin was reserved for the kitchen. The very front end was sometimes partitioned off for the crew. Rarely more than seven men, the crew slept in the main cabin with the male passengers if no separate crew cabins were provided.

Boats on the Ohio canals had slightly different cabin arrangements. A separate ladies' cabin, limited to eight passengers, was at the front of the boat. The main cabin was toward the rear, just like the Erie boats, and the kitchen was also at the stern end of the cabin. The better beds were the side seats of the main cabin. This seating on both sides of the room had cushions. The men would sleep foot to foot on these settees. Hanging bunks were erected each night in the center of the cabin for the remaining male passengers.

Most of the boats were 80 feet long and 14 feet across. The ceiling inside the cabin was only about 7 feet high. The construction was almost entirely wooden, although a few iron boats were constructed. Boats weighed around 20 tons and drew 1 to 2 feet of water. Boats cost around $1,000.

6.8. The Miami and Erie Canal crossing over the Great Miami River. The *Experiment* was a special boat outfitted with a canopy-covered upper deck.

(*The Ladies' Repository*, December 1842)

Furnishings and accessories cost another $500. During the heyday of canal travel a well-managed boat could earn $6,000 in a nine-month season. Even boats that never earned a big profit carried stirring names such as *Truth, Courage,* and *Hope.* Others were named for towns along the river and for famous Americans such as *Washington, Franklin,* and *Madison.* There were surely a good many vessels named after DeWitt Clinton. There were few exceptions to the standard design of canal boats. The Miami and Erie had a boat named the *Experiment* that went into service around 1830. A newspaper advertisement for the boat appearing in the *Cincinnati Gazette* in October 1830 commented on its patented design that offered passengers a cool and pleasant ride. A line cut showed that the boat had a canopy roof above the roof deck so that the passengers were protected from the sun. An identical boat was pictured in the *Ladies Repository* for December 1842 (fig. 6.8). Just how the canopy was rigged to clear low bridges is uncertain. The patents for canal boats taken out by Cincinnatians named Bakewell and Brownswell in June and August of 1829 might explain how this necessity was achieved; however, the details of the patents were lost when the patent office burned in 1836.

When railroads began to attract more passengers in the 1840s, a few boat operators on the Erie Canal began to offer more deluxe boats in hope of winning back passenger patronage. Captain Daniel H. Bromley, of the Red Bird line, was a leader in this movement. His luxury liner, the *Niagara,* was completed in 1846 at Seth Jones's boatyard in Rochester, New York. She had a cedar hull and measured 100 feet long. There were separate men's and ladies' cabins. Large picture windows, a smoking room, a library and writing desks, and a bar and refreshment counter were provided. Best of all there was a washroom. The cabins were elegantly decorated, and the table was set with fine china and silver-plated eating utensils. But for all of her splendor, the *Niagara* could not travel any faster than the plainest boat in the system, and with our speed-obsessed society, all long-distance travel on the canal gave way to steam cars. Captain Bromley philosophically quit the canal a few years later and took a job as a railroad conductor. Still later he opened a hotel in Rochester before his death in 1876.

During the day, canal travel was a serene and lovely way to go as long as you were not in a hurry. It surely was superior to the rock and roll of the stagecoach. Nor was there the dust of summer or the bitter wind of winter. The canal boat moved along in a noiseless manner. The luggage was piled along the center line of the roof, but there was usually room for a chair on the remaining space. Some passengers sat on the luggage. However, the stillness was broken every few minutes by the steersman call of "Bridge!" Passengers knew to bend low as the boat glided below an overpass. If the pilot cried out "Low bridge" and emphasized "low," veteran canal travelers knew they must drop to the deck. The density of bridges depended on how active local residents were in erecting such structures over the canal. On the Erie Canal between Albany and Utica, roughly 90 miles, there were some three hundred bridges. Some passengers prepared to stay down below because of the bridge hazard, where they could read, write letters, or doze. If it was a hot day, however, most passengers would go up top to catch the breeze. If you were lucky you might make a friend with another passenger and would spend part of the slow journey in conversation.

Mealtime occupied part of the trip during the working hours. In general, the cook managed to prepare a good meal in his tiny kitchen that would satisfy both the patrons and, more importantly, the captain, who was the cook's boss. Charles Dickens recorded the food served on the Pennsylvania Main Line during his first visit to America between January and June of 1842. The evening meal consisted of tea, coffee, bread, butter, salmon, shad, liver, steak, potatoes, pickles, ham chops, black puddings, and sausages. He was amused when his neighbor at the table passed him a bowl containing potatoes, milk, and butter, saying, "Will you try some of these fixings?" Americans, Dickens noted, used the word *fix* or *fixings* for just about every human activity. The novelist noted with less humor that all of the meals were exactly the same, except that the dinner lacked tea or coffee. The cook was generally black and would function as a bartender or barber when not active in the kitchen.

The boat traveled twenty-four hours a day, so passengers were, in effect, inmates aboard this traveling prison. They could jump off briefly during the day while the boat stopped to pick up or drop off passengers or while it waited near a lock for its turn to pass through. Some restless passengers would jump off and walk the tow path for a while just to break the monotony but would then jump back on after a few miles. When darkness fell, however, this option was not a good idea, for you might get left behind.

Bedtime was the least happy part of the day, especially if the boat was full. Just imagine a compartment 12 feet wide and 40 feet long with forty men needing a berth. It was too many people in too little space. The beds were most unappealing. They were more like shelves than bunks. On some boats a thin straw mattress was provided, but on others beds were a wood frame with a canvas covering tightly attached. The sheets were sometimes the tablecloths used during the day. (Don't let a little gravy or relish ruin your sleep.) These bunks or shelves were attached to ropes or thin chains in layers of three that left very little room between each berth because the ceiling was so low. The heaviest man was normally put on the lowest level, but if there were too many portly gents on board, some of them were, by necessity, assigned to the upper bunks. A German visitor woke up late one night to find that the man above him, who happened to be very stout, had broken through the canvas stretcher and was now resting upon his chest. The weight was very uncomfortable, and every effort to wake the sleeping giant failed. The victim remembers his tie stickpin, which he put to good use and so aroused his tormentor.

Even when weighty hazards such as this one were not present, the average sleeper would toss and turn to some degree, so the hanging bunks would shake. Those who could not go through the night without relieving their bladder would clamber out of bed to awake their neighbors. In addition, the boat that seemed so quiet during the day became alive with noises in the night. Frogs along the canal bank choked out their annoying chorus. A baby in the ladies' compartment, just next door, might cry most of the night. The steersman's horn seemed to blare every few minutes because of an approaching boat or lock. When the boat attempted to enter the lock, it always seemed to bump into the gate or side wall hard enough to shake the boat, waking all but the soundest sleeper. As a sleeping chamber, the canal boat seemed more like a chamber of horrors. John Quincy Adams made his first canal trip in 1843 when he was in his mid-seventies. He said he hoped it would be his last voyage by waterway mostly because of an inability to get a decent night's rest. The lack of privacy was another of his complaints; the canal boat was a far too democratic conveyance for this former chief executive.

Even the getting-up process was disagreeable to many travelers of the time. If you were not out of your bunk promptly at 5:30 AM, the rude cabin boy would yell "Get out!" in your ear. You were then ushered through the kitchen and out onto the rear deck. There you would find a tin basin and dipper with a long handle. This was used to fetch water from the canal for your morning wash-up and shave. Fussy people would pick out the leaves and other debris as they filled the basin. Commodes were emptied into the canal whenever the cabin boy remembered to do so.

CANAL BOAT CREWS, SPEED, AND FARES

A fully manned passenger packet required a crew of ten to operate on a twenty-four-hour schedule. Smaller crews were possible if the boat stopped overnight. Included were a captain, a cook, a steward, and a cabin boy, who worked a single shift. Two steersmen, bowmen, and drivers were needed, because their work was divided into two twelve-hour shifts. The steersman had the most responsible job, because he steered the boat and called out the approaching bridges. He also navigated the boat in and out of locks and around approaching boats and thus had to master a coach horn well enough to clearly signal ahead to lock tenders and nearby boats as needed. The bowman, stationed at the front of the boat, had the job of making sure the tow rope did not get caught on passing boats or lock gates. If that did occur, he would cut the rope with a large knife.

The duties of the other crew members were fairly obvious from their titles. Some boats did not employ both a steward and a cabin boy and instead made one worker do the work of two. Boys were paid half wages, or about 50 cents a day. The drivers were generally boys, often homeless kids who were forced to accept any job that was available. They grew up without the benefit of schooling but managed to learn all of the world's vices before reaching maturity. They were described by Benjamin Taylor in his book of 1874, *The World on Wheels,* as looking like a bundle of old clothes that could walk. These ragged lads spent their day or night walking with the mules or horses along the tow path. Very often they rode bareback and, being such a light load, did little to slow the animals' pace. It was their job to keep the team moving steadily along the 10-foot-wide path. They would stop the team when other boats passed and at locks while waiting for the water to rise or fall. They could also be useful in preventing or stopping runaways. Horses were easily startled and might bolt off the tow path or into the canal itself. If the animals were frightened enough, however, there was no stopping them, and lads had to hold on tight until the horses were winded and came to a stop.

During normal operations fresh teams were put on every six hours or so, and the spent horses were stabled to rest until their next shift. The operation was very much like the system used by stagecoaches. On some canals, such as those in Ohio, an extra team was carried on the boat, usually in a cabin near the center of the boat. Fresh and spent teams were exchanged at some convenient stopping place. Mixed teams did not generally work well together, so it was prudent to segregate mules and horses. Slower boats normally used only two animals, but the fast packets used three and often had a rider for each horse. Teams were changed every 10 to 15 miles on express passenger boats that cruised along at 4 mph. By the

6.9. Advertisement for a packet line on the Pennsylvania Main Line from April 1837.

(*Catalogue of the Exhibit of the Pennsylvania Railroad Company at the World's Columbian Exposition, Chicago, 1893*)

early 1880s, long after the fast passenger boats were retired, Erie Canal boat owners seemed to prefer mules because they were more durable. A horse was worn out after a few seasons, but a mule could remain in service for eighteen to twenty years, or as long as most boats would last. Steam power was used on the Erie Canal with some success in the 1880s when some steamers were reported in operation.

Speed was never a strength of canal travel, a fact already alluded to earlier in this chapter. Why not higher speeds, and why did the faster boats not exceed 4 mph? That was about as fast as a horse could go for any reasonable distance. Of course, horses could run much faster, but only for short sprints and not when pulling a heavy load such as a canal boat. Why not use steam propulsion, which had come into commercial

Locks at Lockport, N. Y.

6.10. A stairway of five locks at Lockport, New York, dropped the Erie Canal 66 feet near the western end of the canal.

(Author's collection)

use by 1830? It was tried and worked reasonably well, except that steamers tended to exceed the maximum speed allowed on traditional canals. Thus the boats were still limited to 4 mph, because greater speed created wakes that would wash down the soft side walls. This caused the canal to fill up with silt and so required frequent and costly dredging. In addition, speeds above 4 mph pushed up the power requirements, which did not just double but quadrupled. Hence instead of three horses, a boat would need a dozen steeds to maintain a faster speed. The fastest boats on the Erie Canal made 80 miles in a twenty-four-hour day, which is only 3⅓ mph. Normal line boats made just 60 miles in the same time, or 2½ mph. Freight boats required ten days to make the run from Albany to Buffalo and averaged a little over 1 mph. On the Pennsylvania Main Line the Pioneer line claimed in 1836 to make the journey from Philadelphia to Pittsburgh in just four days but charged a premium fare of $10. The Leach line took six and a half days for the same trip but charged only $6. Meals were extra at 37½ cents. By April 1837 the Pioneer line advertised service across the state in three and a half days (fig. 6.9), which was possible only because part of the journey was made by railroad.

Travel speed could be affected negatively by other factors such as weather or traffic density. Whenever locks were present there was a good chance for traffic jams. The boats would line up waiting their turn. The actual passage through an individual lock required only a few minutes for

6.11. The tow rope from the northbound boat was dropped to the bottom of the canal so that the southbound boat could pass over it.

(Drawing by the author)

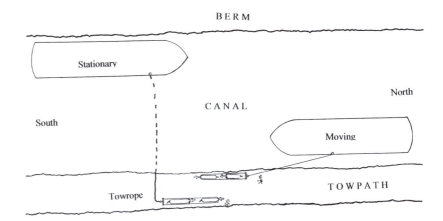

each boat, but if twenty or thirty boats were waiting, the wait might be considerable. The lock tenders grew weary and slowed down as the day wore on from pushing the heavy gates open and closed. A concentration of locks was another obvious time killer (fig. 6.10). At the Albany end of the Erie Canal, there were forty locks in 28 miles. Sixteen locks were required to drop the Erie in its last 3 miles downhill to the Hudson River, a passage that required five hours. Most passengers abandoned the canal at Schenectady and rode into Albany on a stagecoach. In 1831 a new railroad could make the trip in an hour. If an embankment failed, the canal was closed by temporary dams until the break was repaired. This could require a day or weeks, depending on the size of the break. Boats sometimes got turned across the canal and stuck in the mud of the canal's soft side. Boats also sank in inconvenient places that stopped all traffic. A boat on the Ohio and Erie Canal sank inside a lock. It was full of heavy whiskey barrels that had to be cleared before boats could pass.

The method used for boats to pass each other was another factor contributing to delays and hence the lowering of the average speed. The canal was wide enough for boats going in opposite directions to pass with ease. However, the tow path was on only one side of the canal (fig. 6.11). The towlines of boats going in the opposite direction would tangle if they both kept moving as they passed; hence one boat would stop and move its team to the far side of the tow path. The tow rope would go slack and be allowed to sink to the bottom of the canal. The moving boat (southbound) could pass over the towline and continue on its way. Once it passed, the waiting boat (northbound) would proceed until it met another southbound boat.

Delays were also caused by the captain, who might promise to sail in the morning and then wait for hours or even days until more passengers were found to make a full load. If the boat carried both cargo and passengers, the captain might delay his departure until more freight was on board. Such a vessel would stop along the way to pick up and drop off cargo. These small delays added to the already slow progress of the boat.

Another factor that affected canal speed, one that is generally overlooked, was the ever present, slow-moving cargo boats. The main business of canals was freight traffic such as lumber, grain, coal, and stone. If any of these commodities arrived a few days late, it hardly mattered. This parade of plodding freighters created a blockade that prevented the passenger packets from making better time. There always seemed to be another one up ahead. While the cargo boats ran night and day, it took them ten and a half days to go from Albany to Buffalo, a distance of 364 miles, making their average speed a little over 1 mph. The crewmen worked two six-hour shifts a day. In 1874 there were 7,000 boats; 28,000 men; and 16,000 horses and mules at work on the Erie Canal. Each boat could carry 8,000 bushels of grain, and the Erie moved about 3 million tons of freight a year.

Regardless of the imperfections of canal travel, it was generally seen as a good bargain. Part of this was likely due to the inherent cheapness of water transport, which was possible because of the low power requirements to move large loads through a fluid such as common H_2O. In 1836 fares on the Pennsylvania Main Line were as low as $6 for a 400-mile journey that took six and a half days. The fare jumped by $1 for a faster boat that made the trip in just five days. A premium fare of $10 was charged by the Pioneer line, which got passengers across the state in just four days. Meals were not included in these prices, but instead cost 75 cents each (3 shillings) and were considered a bargain.

The cost of transportation was more negotiable on the Erie. Passengers seeking a boat at Schenectady were approached by crew members who called upon travelers to ride with them. The fare was announced at 3½ cents a mile with meals for 2 shillings. Cheaper rates were offered by competing boats. One passenger obtained a low fare by booking with the Clinton line at 1¼ cents a mile and meals at 1 shilling. During the 1840s many business-class passengers abandoned the canal packets for faster railroad trains. But low fares kept poorer travelers loyal to the packets. Emigrants were especially good patrons, because they were the most thrift-minded travelers. Canal captains would take them and their considerable baggage the full length of the Erie Canal for just $2. No bed or meals were provided. By 1845 a series of small railroads paralleled the Erie and offered travelers through car service across New York State in just forty hours versus seventy-five hours via the canal. The big difference was the fare: $7.75 by canal or $13.50 by rail. Speed had its costs, so a certain number of travelers whose time was not particularly valuable went the water route. During the midwinter, these same thrifty folks would have to wait until the spring thaw for the next boat.

Was the American canal system a success or failure? As an investment most of the system was a failure. The Erie Canal was a notable exception to this judgment. It generated enough traffic and revenue to require two major rebuildings. It continues to operate today as a barge canal using diesel-powered towboats to propel a sizable fleet of cargo barges. The coal canals in eastern Pennsylvania provided economic fuel carriers for decades and so, too, were generally financial successes. It is difficult to make a case for any U.S. canal as a successful passenger carrier in economic terms. A few enjoyed fairly good passenger traffic until about 1850, but the revenues generated did little to justify the high cost of canal construction and maintenance. The carriage of goods was another matter, for in this area of commerce the canal system performed very well. This was especially true for bulk cargoes such as lumber, grain, and coal. None of these commodities were time-sensitive, so low-speed shipping was acceptable. At the same time, the cheap transport of cargo was essential to many industries. Ice and barley, for example, were as basic to beer making as salt was essential to meatpacking. The canal system benefited the general society by offering low-cost transportation.

If our forefathers only could have foreseen the rise of railways during the beginning of the canal mania, it is likely that fewer waterways would have been built. But who could foresee in 1825 that in just a few decades the iron horse would revolutionize land transport? Investors and promoters tend to support the success of the recent past and reject more recent technologies as visionary. Almost no one could foresee the rise of the automobile when it was introduced in the 1890s, so huge sums were invested in electric railways that were soon rendered redundant by the motor car. We are no better predictors of the future than our ancestors.

SUGGESTED READING

In addition to the sources listed above, Charles Dickens's *American Notes* 1842 is available in many modern reprints and contains a lively statement on canal travel. *Philip Hone's Diary* was edited by Allan Nevins in 1927. A German perspective of canal travel is offered by Dr. Albert Koch in an English translation by Ernest A. Stadler of a *Journey through a Part of the United States in the Years 1844 to 1846* (Carbondale, Ill.: Southern Illinois University Press, 1972). Warren S. Tryon has edited two volumes of travel accounts that explore canal travel: *My Native Land: My Life in America, 1790–1870* (Chicago, 1961) and *Mirror for Americans: Life and Manners in the United States, 1790–1870* (Chicago: University of Chicago Press, 1952).

Baer, Christopher T. *Canals and Railroads of the Mid-Atlantic States, 1800–1860.* Wilmington, Del.: Regional Economic History Research Center, 1981.

Drago, Harry. *Canal Days in America.* New York: C. N. Potter, 1972.

Fatout, Paul. *Indiana Canals.* West Lafayette, Ind. Purdue University Studies, 1972.

Goodrich, Carter. *Government Promotions of American Canals and Railroads.* New York: Columbia University Press, 1960.

Hadfield, Charles. *World Canals.* New York: Facts on File Publications, 1986.
———. *Canal Age.* Newton Abbot, U.K.: David and Charles, 1968.
Harlow, Alvin F. *Old Towpaths.* New York: D. Appleton and Co., 1926.
Rubin, Julius. *Canal or Railroad.* Philadelphia: American Philosophical Society, 1961.
Sanderlin, Walter S. *Great National Project: A History of the Chesapeake and Ohio Canal.* Baltimore: Johns Hopkins University Press, 1946.
Shaw, Ronald E. *Erie Water West.* Lexington: University Press of Kentucky, 1966.
———. *Canals for a Nation.* Lexington: University Press of Kentucky, 1990.
Taylor, Benjamin. *The World on Wheels.* Chicago: S. C. Griggs and Co., 1874.
Taylor, George Rogers. *The Transportation Revolution, 1815–1860.* New York: Rinehart and Co., 1951.

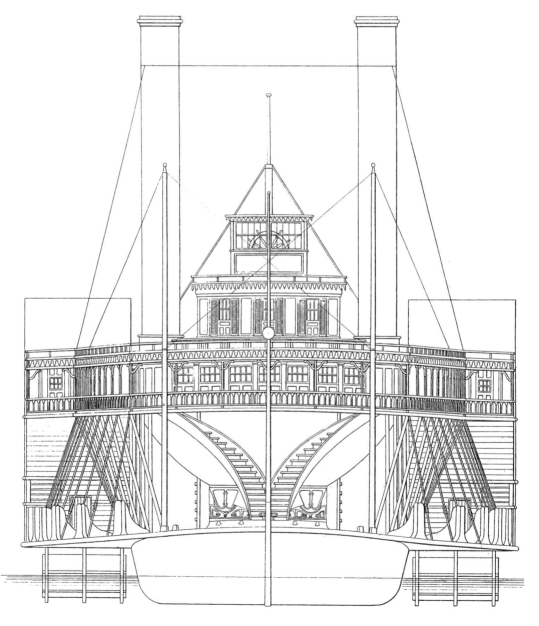

River Steamers № 7

White Swans on the Inland Rivers

EUROPEAN SETTLEMENTS WERE WELL ESTABLISHED ALONG THE Atlantic Coast by the beginning of the eighteenth century. The Allegheny Mountains discouraged migration to the west, except for traders, military men, explorers, and the eccentric. A few forts and trading posts were established by the French, which led to territorial disputes with Britain. A war erupted in 1756 between these European powers. Britain won the conflict and established its claim to most of North America. The British Colonial Office prohibited settlement in these territories as a way to end conflicts with the Native Americans who inhabited these vast lands. The peace was kept only temporarily; however, American independence reopened the settlement issue, and by the late 1780s land-hungry settlers began moving into the Ohio country. The only easy route to get there was the Ohio River, so the pioneers gathered at Pittsburgh and were carried down the river in flatboats piled high with people and their sundry possessions. The Ohio River was the east-west branch of two other major inland rivers: the Mississippi and the Missouri. There were also about fifty tributaries large enough to allow navigation by smaller boats, in some cases for several hundred miles. Nature also provided an excellent regional waterway – the Great Lakes. By 1850 the center of the nation was filling up with people. There were a dozen new states and about ten million residents. Pittsburgh, Cincinnati, and St. Louis were expanding. Most of this growth can be attributed to the rivers.

The rivers became the principal avenue of commerce for the western settlers. They adopted a variety of water crafts, including canoes, dugouts, flatboats, and keelboats. The latter were the most finished style of vessel on the river system; they had a cabin, a prow, and a stern and were intended for long-term service. Regular monthly keelboat service between Pittsburgh and Cincinnati began in January 1794. The 20-ton vessel was well armed with muskets and an ample supply of ammunition. Separate cabins for men and women were provided, as was food and liquor at reasonable prices, and onboard toilets eliminated the need to stop en route. Each

7.1. The bow-on view of the *Memphis* 1860 shows the size, grace, and elegance of the American packet boat. This vessel was designed for the cotton trade on the lower Mississippi River. Its main deck was an impressive 71 feet wide.

(E. J. Reed, ed., *Transactions of the Royal Institution of the Naval Architects*, 1861)

year about five thousand keelboats were powered by men using oars or poles; the river current carried the vessels downstream. Keelboats and flatboats drifted down the Ohio and Mississippi Rivers as far south as New Orleans. The trip normally required two months; poles, oars, and sails assisted in passage, but progress was extremely slow. The return trip was far slower and more difficult – so much so that flatboats were routinely broken up for their lumber, and crews walked home. A favored route was the Natchez Trace, a narrow path carved out by animals centuries before any humans lived in the area. It ended at Nashville, where travelers would follow other woodland trails homeward. Today the Natchez Trace is a paved parkway.

It should not be assumed that the inland rivers allowed navigation year round. Even the largest of these streams were problematic. The Mississippi River is interrupted by falls at St. Paul, Minnesota, and is encumbered by many twists and turns, some at right angles. The channel can shift in a few days and move a mile away. In 1876 the channel shifted 1½ miles below Vicksburg, isolating this important port from regular river services. Boats could land at Vicksburg only during times of high water. At the same time, the Mississippi is generally 3,000 feet wide most of the way from St. Paul to New Orleans. Its bends widen out to a mile or a mile and a half, allowing plenty of space for steering. The Mississippi generally has enough water volume to offer enough draft for navigation. This is especially true of the lower Mississippi, where the depth of the stream is considerable. The river divides into several branches below New Orleans to exit into the Gulf of Mexico. None of these branches were deep enough for easy navigation by seagoing ships, however, and in the 1870s jetties were built to scour out the South Pass Channel. The father of waters was like all American rivers; it had its share of snags, sandbars, and floods that hamper river traffic. It was subject to freezing at the northern end but rarely had this problem below Cairo, Illinois.

The Ohio and Missouri Rivers were more troublesome than the Mississippi. Their defects were more serious and were only partially corrected at considerable expense. The Ohio River begins at Pittsburgh and drifts in a southwesterly direction, 981 miles, to Cairo, where it joins the Mississippi. It suffers from low water and freezing that can shut down navigation for weeks or even months at a time. Typically summer and fall are the dry seasons. Around Thanksgiving the rains return and the river rises; floods commonly develop in January. Freezing is of shorter duration and rarely lasts more than a few weeks, but when the thaw comes the ice piles up in dams and advances southward, crushing everything in its path. Many riverboats met their end that way. It is also true that freezing was less common than low water, and a decade might pass without the river freezing solid. Boat operations relied on special low-water boats. The larger boats were tied up temporarily. The 1880s were bad years for low water. In August 1883 the Ohio River dropped to just 23 inches at Cincinnati. Nothing much larger than a rowboat could move. The drought returned the next May, and the boats that normally made ten trips to New Orleans during the year did well to make one to three trips. In times of especially low water, tiny steamers known as bat wings were put to work moving whatever freight and cargo their narrow decks could handle. The solution to the Ohio River's low-water problem was solved by a series of locks and dams financed by the federal government, which were completed between 1875 and 1929.

The Ohio River had a major obstacle near its center; the Falls of the Ohio, between Clarksville, Indiana, and Louisville, Kentucky, is actually more of a falling rapids. It drops just 22 feet in 2 miles. When the river was high, boats could run the falls in both directions, but this was true only periodically, so passengers and cargo were portaged around the rapids, thus adding to the slowness and expense of the trip. After much discussion, a canal was opened late in 1830 around the falls, but it was built on too small a scale and was enlarged in 1872. Large boats continued to shoot the falls for many years under the guidance of skillful pilots. Most such runs were successful, but enough boats were lost that a lifesaving station was established to oversee the dangerous operation.

Another danger already alluded to was the presence of snags and sawyers in the river. These were large submerged logs that came from trees growing along the shore. Trees need water and grow rapidly where it is plentiful. What better place to find it than on a riverbank? Very often the bank is weakened by the stream and at some point a tree topples into the river. The branches break off or fall away in time, but the trunk remains intact. It becomes waterlogged and sinks below the surface; this is the snag at its most dangerous, because it is so difficult to see. These very heavy logs could easily knock a hole in a wooden hull, especially if the boat was moving rapidly. Sinking occurred in a matter of minutes. The severity of the accident depended on the depth of the water and the timing of the collision. If it happened in a deep section of the river late at night while the passengers were asleep, the death toll could be significant.

Snags were the chief cause of steamboat accidents and accounted for 57 percent (about fourteen) sinkings a year. Fatalities were not inevitable, however, because some boats made it to shore before sinking or sank in water so shallow that the upper decks remained dry. Snag removal remained a leading concern of boat operators, and, once again, as much as they despised government interference in their private affairs, they seemed convinced that eradication of snags was a federal problem. The government did respond early, since the river system was seen as a national highway and necessary to the postal service. An effective snag removal program began in 1829 that greatly reduced this menace to navigation; however, political support for this program was inconsistent. The Whigs argued for funding; the Democrats remained opposed. By the end of the Civil War snag removal became a fixed line in the federal budget.

The Missouri River is a long, slender stream that joins the Mississippi River above St. Louis at St. Charles, Missouri, and crosses half a dozen states before ending in northwestern Montana. This 2,300-mile-long stream has been described as turbid and impetuous and frequently alters its channel. It was clearly not ideal for navigation, but because the river reached so far west, it was a logical route for travelers. Lewis and Clark followed it on their epic trip of exploration, and it served hunters and others seeking a way west equally well. Riverboats became plentiful on the eastern end of the Missouri as far as Council Bluffs, some 660 miles from the Mississippi. The upper reaches of the Missouri River required very light shallow-draft vessels. They were Spartan in nature and ran successfully on only 30 inches of water. Boats of this type ran as far as Fort Benton, Montana, and were largely used to service the fur trade. As with the Ohio and Mississippi Rivers, the Army Corps of Engineers has improved portions of the "Big Muddy" for navigation.

EVOLUTION OF THE INLAND RIVERBOAT

The early years of river navigation were largely a downstream business. There was no easy way to propel boats upstream against the current. Human power was sufficient only to power empty or lightly loaded vessels. Many inventors in the western nation designed steamboats to answer the need for a vessel powerful enough to overcome river currents. The British and French were active in such efforts, but Americans seemed especially attracted to steamboat experiments. Some of those tested were technically successful. For example, after many experiments John Fitch operated a steamboat on the Delaware River in the summer of 1790. The boat offered service between Philadelphia, and its suburbs Trenton and Burlington, New Jersey. It ran on a regular schedule at speed from 6 to 8 mph. The public was not ready for such an advanced mode of travel – steam engines were unfamiliar and viewed as dangerous. Another American, more artist than engineer, Robert Fulton reintroduced a steamboat on the Hudson River in 1807. He housed passengers inside an elegant cabin; the engine and boiler were out of sight. Fulton was smooth and gentlemanly – so unlike Fitch – and he was able to convince the traveling public that his low-pressure steam plant was as safe as a nursery. Fulton's principal backer, Robert Livingston, was the head of an elite New York family and a prominent diplomat. His endorsement was important in creating a positive reception for this new way of traveling.

The partners built more boats for service on the Hudson River, New York Harbor, and Long Island Sound and planned a monopoly to control steamboats on every American waterway. Livingston had enough political connections to receive such a grant from the state of New York and several parishes in Louisiana. However, although they were less successful elsewhere, in 1824 the U.S. Supreme Court declared that our national waterways were open to all citizens. Fulton and Livingston had died a decade earlier. In 1810 Fulton pushed ahead with plans for an inland riverboat. He established a yard in Pittsburgh and hired Nicholas Roosevelt to manage the project. The engine was built at Fulton's shop in Jersey City and was carried overland by wagons to Pittsburgh. The boat was similar to those Fulton had built for Hudson River service. It was narrow, long, and deep – a suitable shape for rivers like the Hudson, but very wrong for the shallow Ohio River. The boat, named the *New Orleans*, was finished but could not proceed because of insufficient draft. By late October 1811 the river rose and the *New Orleans* left on its epic voyage. No passengers could be convinced to join Roosevelt and his crew, as the strange and futuristic craft was viewed with suspicion. All went well, however, until the *New Orleans* reached Louisville. The water was not deep enough there to shoot the Falls of the Ohio, so the boat returned upstream to visit Cincinnati. Suspicion and indifference were instantly overcome – the little sawmill on a raft had proven herself. She had bucked the current and moved upstream without difficulty. The steamboat was a reality, one that would revolutionize river travel. The *New Orleans* continued its trip southward and reached New Orleans in December 1811. She was found to work well in the deep water of the lower Mississippi River and continued operations there until sinking in 1814. Fulton died a few months later, ending his dreams of fame and fortune from a steamboat empire.

Many others were ready to build and improve steamboats for the western rivers. A few, such as Henry Shreve, can be named, but most of the pioneers are largely anonymous or forgotten. What they did, however, is well recorded. Fulton's steamboat was radically altered between 1815 and 1830. The hull was made flat and wide rather than narrow and deep. This single change made it suitable for shallow-river travel. The boat would skim over the top of the water rather than plow through it, and the hull became a buoyancy chamber. The hulls were built from heavy oak or locust timber. The bottom planks were often 3 inches thick. The hull was heavy and strong to resist snags and rocks. To gain more room for cargo, the first deck was made to overhang the hull. The overhang was considerable so that a hull 20 feet wide would support a deck that was 35 feet wide. The section that overhung the hull was called the *guards*. The guards also served to protect the paddle wheels from colliding with passing boats or other obstructions. They added to the peculiar appearance of the American riverboat. It was also a feature that remained in favor until the end of the steamboat era. This feature is illustrated in figure 7.1.

The engines and boilers were placed on the first deck. Freight was placed on the same deck in any open space available. Emigrants and other deck passengers were housed on the main desk as well. First-class passengers were housed on the second, or boiler, deck in small cabins that surrounded a large central cabin. This chamber served as both a sitting and dining room. A smaller and much narrower cabin rested on top of the second-deck cabin. It was called the texas and was divided into small compartments for the crew. The pilothouse was placed on top of the texas. The steering wheel was inside the pilothouse. The upper works – that is, all of the cabin decks above the hull – were very lightly constructed in an effort to reduce the boat's weight so that more cargo could be carried. This part of the boat was weak and flammable. If the boat caught on fire, the cabins would burn quickly. If the boat sank, the upper works sometimes broke loose from the full and floated away or sank. The oversized upper works and undersized hull made the American riverboat a most unusual looking and unique vessel. On the water it appeared to be all cabins and looked like a hotel gone adrift. The American riverboat was described as a most un-navigable-looking craft. It was a huge structure of flimsy wooden pieces, windows, doors, railings, long verandas, and great chimneys. These smoke pipes were topped with decorative crowns that resembled the paper frills that adorn broiled lamb chops. Humorists said the boats looked like a floating sawmills except for the glory of the white paint and the elegant artwork on the wheel boxes. This general plan, for all of its peculiarities, proved very successful and was never greatly altered during the history of the riverboat.

To illustrate the development of inland riverboats we will offer several examples of such vessels during the nineteenth century. The *New Orleans II* is a well-documented vessel of 1815 described by German visitor J. G. Flugel during a visit to New Orleans in 1817. The vessel was built in Pittsburgh at Robert Fulton's yard, where the original *New Orleans* had been built in 1811. The 1815 *New Orleans* was 116 feet long and 20 feet wide. She carried no sails and was capable of running 3 to 4 miles an hour upstream and 9 to 10 mph downstream. The 30-foot-long ladies' cabin was at the stern below the top deck. It was elegantly furnished with white window curtains, sofas, chairs, looking glasses, and an ornamental carpet. There were twenty built-in beds enclosed with red curtains and mosquito netting. The men's cabin was on the top deck. It measured 28 by 42 feet and was described as a "round-house," which presumably means the ends were rounded. This space was divided into thirteen staterooms, each having two berths. Each berth had a window. The mattresses were stuffed with Spanish moss, easily found in the Louisiana woods. The bed linens were handsomely flowered. The furniture included settees, chairs, tables, and a large gilt-frame looking glass. Forward of the men's cabins was a bar room, managed by a most agreeable attendant. The captain's room was on the starboard side. Separate cabins were also provided for the chief engineer, the bar keeper, and the clerk. The kitchen was forward of the engine. A bedroom for the mate and pilot was located ahead of the kitchen. The deckhands and firemen had spaces in the forecastle for twelve berths, a table, and seats.

Flugel's description seems to mirror Fulton's general design for Hudson River boats. The *New Orleans II* consumed six cords of wood a day, which cost $2.50 per cord. Passengers could enjoy a view of the river from a roof deck on top of the men's cabin. It was surrounded by an iron railing. An awning protected passengers from the sun. The boat was fitted with a 4-pound swivel gun that was fired to signal arrivals and departures. The crew consisted of twenty-four people: a captain, mate, pilot, engineer, clerk, bar keeper, steward, assistant steward, cook, cook's mate, two firemen, eight deckhands, and four waiters. The total yearly salary paid to the crew was $9,720. The boat's route was limited to New Orleans and major towns as far as Natchez, some 314 miles upriver. The fare between New Orleans and Natchez was $30 upstream and $15 downstream. The captain claimed that net proceeds per trip were never less than $4,000.

Well to the north of Louisiana, a description was published in a Cincinnati newspaper of the *General Pike*, named in honor of pioneer military officer and explorer Zebulon Pike. The hull for the center-wheel steamer was launched in September 1818. It was outfitted as a deluxe passenger carrier. Its keel was 100 feet long and the beam measured 25 feet. According to an engraving published in 1873 she was no thing of beauty externally. Yet her interior was elegant and comfortable. The main cabin was 40 feet long and 25 feet wide. Marble columns, rich carpets, and mirrors gave the space "an air of elegance which borders on magnificence." There were twenty-four built-in berths in this space, each enclosed by crimson curtains. In addition six staterooms were at one end of the main cabin and another eight at the other end. Special settees designed for sleeping offered space for another sixty overnight guests. The *General Pike* ran upriver between Louisville and Cincinnati in thirty hours at an average of about 6 mph. By 1823 she was worn out and retired.

The *Tecumseh* of 1826 was in most respects a near duplicate of the *New Orleans II*. She operated on both the Ohio and Mississippi Rivers and is remembered for her speed. The hull was built by the Stephen Weeks yard located in the east end of Cincinnati. Weeks and his several sons were New York boat builders who relocated to Ohio around 1820. Their products reflected the style of boat they had built for service in New York waters. The passenger cabin was at the stern of the main deck. The ladies' compartment was below the main cabin in the hull. The vessel had a figurehead, a bowsprit, and a decorative panel on the stern transom. The keel measured 130 feet; the hull was 22 feet wide by 7 feet deep. A watertight compartment in the bow was designed to contain snags and prevent the boat from being sunk by predatory logs. Work started in the summer of 1825, and the hull was launched in February of the next year. She was fitted with a single-cylinder engine that featured a flywheel and clutches so that one paddle wheel might be disconnected to aid the boat in making quick turns. She drew 62 inches of water without cargo and consumed between 24 and 30 cords of wood a day.

The arrangements of the cabins and passenger spaces followed the eastern plan used for steamers in the Hudson River and Sound established by 1810. It was essentially the traditional plan used by sailing ships. The cabin was at the stern, the bunks were built in, and there were no staterooms. The top cabin was an open veranda covered only by canvas with a railing around the edges. The exterior of the boat was very plain, the only adornments being the figurehead and transom. When her first trip began on March 10, 1826, the river was high and the weather was wet and foggy. Somehow the pilot lost his way, and the *Tecumseh* veered out of the channel and over the bank, where she became wedged between two trees. The damage was minor, and once free from the trees she began service between Louisville and New Orleans. She could not compete with the larger boats in this service, however, and so took up cotton shipping on the Tennessee River. In 1827 the *Tecumseh* demonstrated her speed by running from New Orleans to Louisville in just nine days and five hours. The notoriety was sweet, but the boat was not a moneymaker. In 1829 she was retired. Her machinery was removed for a new boat in 1830, and the hull was burned in June 1831 to recover the spikes and other iron fittings. Five years was the average life for a riverboat at this time, so the *Tecumseh*'s demise was right on schedule.

Foreign travelers offered some of the best information available on early American life. Austrian engineer Franz von Gerstner explained Ohio River steamers of 1839 in considerable detail in just a few pages. Rather than generalize, he used specific examples. By the time of his visits, the distinctive flat-bottom boat with two decks had replaced the eastern, or Fulton-style, vessel previously described. Boats were built in sizes ranging between 100 and 600 tons. Smaller vessels had single-cylinder engines with flywheels 10 to 15 feet in diameter. Larger boats had two-cylinder engines, one for each paddle wheel. Steam pressure was normally 70 to 120 psi and in a few cases 150 psi. Some boats recouped their purchase price in one year of operation. They were lightly built and rarely remained in service more than five years. Depreciation was generally figured at 25 percent per year.

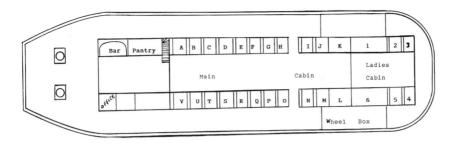

7.2. The boiler or second deck of the *Homer* of 1832 shows the general plan long in favor for river steamers. Small sleeping rooms called staterooms surrounded a large, open cabin used as a combination dining room and parlor space.

(After a drawing made by Karl Bodmer in January 1833; *Karl Bodmer's America*, 1984)

Gerstner offered the following particulars on *Diana,* a packet built in Louisville in 1838 for service to New Orleans. The *Diana* was a first-class boat built at a cost of $40,000. She was 170 feet long; 23 feet wide; and 7 feet, 2 inches deep. She drew 4½ feet empty and 6½ when loaded. Her normal time to New Orleans was four and a half days downstream and six and a half days upstream. She had seventy sleeping berths and charged passengers $40 downstream and $50 upstream. Deck passengers paid only $8 but received no meals or sleeping berths. They could travel for $5 if they assisted in taking on wood for fuel. The *Diana*'s gross receipts for the 2,900-mile round trip between New Orleans and Louisville were on average $5,100 for first-class passengers; $650 for deck passengers; $1,937.50 for freight; and $240 for mail, for a total of $7,927.50. Expenditures for the round trip were $4,000; $1050 of this amount was for fuel. Monthly wages for thirty-eight crew members equaled $1,785. The boat made twelve round trips a year. The year's net income for *Diana,* including depreciation, came to $37,130, or very nearly the original cost of the vessel. The deck plan in figure 7.2 is for the *Homer,* a vessel very similar in size and date to the *Diana*. The *Homer* was built in 1832 in New Albany, Indiana, across the river from Louisville. The exterior of a generic boat of this period is reproduced in figure 7.3. This engraving shows a typical western riverboat of the late 1830s. The engraving is likely a reasonably accurate depiction of the *Diana* described by Gerstner during his 1839 inspection of such vessels. Boats of the period were plain and utilitarian in appearance. They were almost entirely devoid of exterior ornamentation. There were no jigsaw scrolls, no gingerbread, nor even fancy smokestack tops. The excesses of steamboat gothic became fashionable after 1860 and continued into the 1880s and 1890s.

By 1850 larger boats were running between major cities such as Pittsburgh and Cincinnati. Considerable details on the *Buckeye State* were recorded in the 1851 edition of Thomas Tredgold's book on steam navigation published in London. This roomy yet plain steamer was 260 feet long and 54 feet wide. The hull was 29 feet; 4 inches wide; and 6 feet, 6 inches deep. This sizable vessel drew only 4 feet of water loaded and ready for service. The main passenger cabin was as long as many steamers running in the 1830s; it was 192 feet long and 15 feet wide. A separate ladies' cabin,

7.3. This Ohio River steamer was sketched by the Scottish engineer David Stevenson in 1838 to represent a typical boat of that time.

(David Stevenson, *Sketch of the Civil Engineering in North America*, 1838)

to the rear on the second deck, added another 40 feet to the main cabin. There were small cabins at the front end of the main cabin for the bar and excess baggage. Fifty-four sleeping cabins surrounded the main or central cabin. Each of these 6-foot-square compartments, or staterooms, contained a bunk bed and little else. The ladies' washroom and toilet were on the starboard side of the second deck behind the paddle wheel house. The men's room was on the opposite side of the vessel. In April 1850, just a few months after entering service, the *Buckeye State* made an upriver trip to Pittsburgh from Cincinnati in fifty-four hours. This included sixty-two landings to pick up or drop off passengers and cargo. One hour of the 465-mile journey was lost due to fog. Fifty-four hours was considered good time on the river in 1850. The downriver trip normally took thirty hours. The *Buckeye State* was part of the Pittsburgh and Cincinnati line, which offered daily service between these river locations for a one-way fare of $6.

Size and decorative excess were combined in the *Great Republic* completed at Pittsburgh in 1867. This large, handsome vessel measured 335 feet in length yet drew only 4½ feet of water when loaded. She had fifty-four staterooms, each 8 feet square, and a palatial main cabin that measured 267 feet by 28 feet. The interior was steamboat gothic in all of its excesses and magnificence. Every surface was ornamented in white and gold. The carpet was English velvet rich in roses and scrolls. Adorning the walls were sixty-six oil paintings depicting river scenes around the nation. The silverware and table china were made especially for the boat. The *Great Republic*'s stained glass was rivaled by that of other boats, such as the *J. M. White* of 1878. They were chaste in execution but had a bust of statuary in the center of each light. The glass was a pearl gray or a blue background enclosed by a wreath of ivy. The borders were made in purple and gold shades. The *Natchez* of 1879, the seventh boat of that name, had twenty-two stained-glass clerestory windows, each with an etched portrait of a Natchez Indian. They were rendered in soft tones of tan, russet, and brown. The sunlight coming through these stained-glass windows created a kaleidoscope of color. Artificial light reflected off them at night

as it did off the mirrors and cut-glass prisms attached to the chandeliers. A few boats had interior statues; the *Eclipse* of 1852 had a gilt statue of Andrew Jackson in the main cabin and one of Henry Clay in the ladies' cabin. Many boats had large silver-plated water coolers at one end of the main cabin (fig. 7.4). These containers sat on a tall wooden pedestal and were almost 6 feet tall. Silver cups attached by a light chain were available to all who cared to drink. Silver cake stands, cream-and-sugar sets, and cut-glass bowls added to the glitter of the dining room. A fifteen-room nursery was located below the ladies' cabin. It included its own washroom and ironing facility. The boat cost an estimated $350,000.

The *Great Republic* left Pittsburgh on her maiden voyage on March 14, 1867, making stops downriver so that visitors might have a firsthand look at this incredible example of marine architecture. The boat was bound for service on the Mississippi River, so everyone along the Ohio River knew they would have only one chance to see the river giant. During her brief stop in Cincinnati 25,000–30,000 people came to visit the *Great Republic*. Louisville was next, and because the boat was too wide for the canal, she was run over the falls. She did this in a fine style, in part because of high water and in part because of expert piloting. By March 29 she was at Memphis and her working career on the lower Mississippi had begun. Being big and beautiful did not guarantee success. In less than two years the Queen of the River had rendered her owners bankrupt. New investors

7.4. A silver-plated water cooler stood at one end of the main cabin on board the Anchor line's *City of Providence*. Silver cups were attached to the cooler by small chains and were used by anyone desiring a drink.

(*Harper's Monthly*, January 1893)

put her back in service but with no better result. In 1876 the *Great Republic* was rebuilt and renamed the *Grand Republic.* In May of that year she carried Emperor Dom Pedro II of Brazil from St. Louis to New Orleans. More trips followed, often with huge cargoes, yet a steady profit seemed to elude the *Grand Republic.* During a dormant interlude when she was laid up at St. Louis for a time, she caught on fire early in September 1877 and was reduced to ashes.

Readers should not assume that the *Great Republic* failed because the riverboat industry was in trouble. The popular belief that railroads stole traffic away from the rivers soon after the Civil War is somewhat erroneous. They did begin to take over long-distance passenger travel to a large degree as well as time-urgent cargo shipments. However, river traffic remained strong until the 1880s. At the same time, new passenger boats were being built. Some were of a good size and quality, such as those made for the Anchor line that offered service between St. Louis and New Orleans. One of the largest and most elegant vessels to serve on the inland rivers, the *J. M. White,* entered service in 1878. It was just slightly smaller than the *Great Republic* but was no less grand or costly. It was noted for its fine stained-glass windows and excellent food. It also featured large staterooms, some measured 9 by 14 feet. The boat made money because it was managed by an experienced river man. The *White* grossed $15,000 a trip and paid for itself over and over during its brief service life.

River steamers of the post–Civil War era were proving more reliable than their prewar ancestors. This is true in part because of more consistent snag removal, federal inspection of boilers and hulls, as well as the testing of key employees like pilots and engineers. In October 1879 the *Louis A. Sherley* had completed 26,920 miles and 946 trips between Cincinnati and Louisville in three years and two months. The *Fleetwood* of 1880 was another steady performer. During 1888 she ran every day and never missed a trip. Water levels that year were good on the Ohio River, allowing this big boat to perform steadily. At the same time, some boats continued to be very profitable. A Missouri River boat, the *Waverly,* paid for herself ($50,000) on its first round trip to Fort Benton in 1866. In June of the following year she returned to St. Louis loaded with bales of buffalo, wolf, deer, and antelope skins. In 1896 the *Virginia,* an Ohio River stern wheeler, earned enough to repay her owners their investment in one season.

Our final example of a Victorian-era river steamer, the *Queen City,* was completed in June 1897 for Ohio River service between Cincinnati and Pittsburgh. This was a well-made boat but not a deluxe or extravagantly finished vessel. She was of a more modest size than giants such as the *J. M. White* or the *Great Republic.* The hull was 235 feet by 44 feet and was a wooden structure in keeping with western riverboat tradition. The main justification for choosing wood over steel was that the cost was greatly reduced. The general arrangement was equally old-fashioned; the arrangement of cabins and machinery was unchanged from boats built sixty years earlier. Mounted on the front deck was a landing stage that could be lowered to the riverbank to load passengers and cargo. This feature dates back to almost the beginning of the western steamboat, because landings were made anywhere along the riverbank, not just in towns where wharf boats were available. A farmer might want to send some sheep upriver to market. He would wave a white flag in the daytime to an approaching boat and hope it would pull over. If the boat ignored his signal, he would try the next boat. At night he would build a fire on the bank. The same signaling method was employed to fetch a steamer to take family members up or down the river. Most passengers were seeking transport to a nearby river town. Going by boat was often about as fast as going by train, because trains often had to take a more indirect route. However, for long-distance travel the train would be faster, and the routing, unless unusually complicated, was of less importance.

There were features about the *Queen City* that set her apart from her ancestors. Electric lighting was a relatively new invention. Power steering was another fairly new system on riverboats. Folding chimneys were introduced soon after the Wheeling Bridge opened in 1849, but they became more of a necessary as an increasing number of bridges crossed the Ohio River. In times of high water, boats lowered their smokestacks to pass under the bridges. That the *Queen City* was a stern wheeler set her apart from earlier packets, which were largely side-wheelers. The fact that the wheel shaft was nickel steel was surely an improvement over the wrought-iron shafts formerly used.

At the time the *Queen City* entered service on the Ohio River, boat operators could still boast of an investment of $8.5 million in their various vessels. They were carrying 7 million tons of freight and 1.5 million passengers a year. As to the boat itself, she proved durable, especially for a wooden-hulled vessel, and remained in service until 1933. Her hull was used as a wharf boat in Pittsburgh for another seven years.

RIVER TRAVEL: COMFORTS AND DISCOMFORTS

Riverboats were considered one of the nicer ways to get around in the Victorian era. They were roomy with interior space to move around inside. Those seeking fresh air could stride around the verandas or climb up to the hurricane deck or the pilothouse. On fair days a chair or bench on the veranda offered seating with an enjoyable river view. The tree-lined banks, the towns, farms, and passing steamers were all of interest. Flatboats were still plentiful until around 1880. The food was generally good and plentiful. It was served on time and at regular intervals. Toilets, wash

7.5. A view of the interior of the ladies' compartment of the steamer *Planter* in 1860 shows that even smaller packets had well-appointed spaces for cabin-class passengers.

(Author's collection)

basins, and clean towels were available at all times on the better boats. The bathrooms were large facilities intended for the first-class passengers, much like those found in any public facility such as an airport or school. Separate rooms were provided for men and women. Stoves kept the main cabin, which was illuminated in the evening, tolerably warm during the winter. Pioneers would remember their first river trip on a flatboat with only a tent for shelter. They could hardly believe the luxury and comforts commonly provided on the most average steamer. Some even had gaslights and hot-water baths. Other travelers would compare the riverboat to the stagecoach or walking through the forest mile after mile. Nothing available at the time could compare except the railroad; long-distance travel west of the Alleghenies by rail was not possible much before about 1855. Modern travelers, however, would find riverboats of the nineteenth century intolerable. The tiny sleeping cabins had no running water, heat, or toilets. The mattress and bedding would be unacceptable. Where were the TV, the Internet, the electric lights, and the air conditioning? The only way to educate contemporary travelers about the merits of river travel would be to have them spend several hundred miles traveling by stagecoach. Citizens of the twenty-first century have no conception of how soft modern travel is in comparison to what it was in the past.

7.6. The *Washington* was completed in 1825. The figurehead and bowsprit were old features, but the passenger cabin on the second deck was an advanced feature. The boat lacked a pilothouse. It was 130 feet long.

(Frederick Way collection)

Firsthand accounts are a rich source for what it was like to travel in early America. Some appear in books like Charles Dickens's published record of his visit to the United States in 1842. Others were published as articles in magazines of the time, while still others were handwritten and printed many years later by historical societies. Yale University Press published the journals of well-known architect Benjamin H. Latrobe (1764–1820) in 1977. In one of these volumes, Latrobe describes moving his family to New Orleans in the winter of 1820. Latrobe's family began the trip by road. They reached Washington, Pennsylvania, going by wagon and sleigh, in late January. The weather was so frigid, they stayed at an inn awaiting a thaw. They crossed on the National Road to Wheeling and boarded the *Columbus,* which was bound for New Orleans. The nearly new vessel was one of the largest in service. The trip should have taken only about eight days, but the *Columbus* was subject to breakdown. They laid over at Marietta, Ohio, for three days to replace a broken paddle-wheel shaft. The boiler required attention at Maysville, Kentucky. One of the paddle-wheel shafts cracked, resulting in another stopover. More stops were needed to fix other minor mechanical problems. The *Columbus* finally reached the Mississippi River late in March. The boat settled down and better progress was made. They finally reached New Orleans on April 3 or 4 (the record is unclear) after a trip that had required almost five weeks.

In April 1827 William Bullock, a British traveler, rode the *George Washington* from New Orleans to Louisville (fig. 7.6). In contrast to many of his countrymen, Bullock found the boat and the journey excellent. The accommodations were perfect and the cabins were furnished in the most superb manner. The veranda extended all around the boat on the upper level and was sheltered from the rain and sun. It offered a fine view of the surrounding scenery. The food was excellent as well and was served in a superior style. The ladies had a separate cabin with female attendants and a laundress. There was a library and smoking and drinking rooms for the men. The boat stopped twice a day for wood; fresh milk and other necessities were procured at this time, and passengers could go ashore for a brief visit. The trip upriver took only eleven days (1,500 miles) and cost about $40. Bullock was amazed as the boat passed impossible wilderness and unsettled lands without the least hazard or discomfort. The scenery on the lower Mississippi was flat, but it was lined with pretty homes, plantations, gardens, and sugarhouses. Sugar cane, rice, and orange groves made the land rich and productive. Unlike so many of his countrymen, Bullock found his American passengers to be pleasant, intelligent, attentive, and obliging. They were proud of their country and its democratic government and believed others should come and see what they had accomplished.

Bullock offered no details on the *George Washington,* but Captain Fred Way prepared such an account in more recent years based on original records. The boat was 130 feet long; 30 feet, 6 inches wide; and 8 feet, 6 inches deep. She entered service in 1825 and cost $31,982. The ladies' cabin was at the rear of the second deck. The decorations included a large mirror and oil paintings of Daniel Boone and Washington's farewell to his troops. Staterooms and beds were provided for sixty passengers. Forward of the main cabin was an open cabin with 101 hammocks for deck passengers. Normally deck passengers slept wherever space could be found on the first or main deck. No bedding of any kind was provided.

Basil Hall, a former British naval officer, traveled extensively in the United States in 1827–1828 with his wife and young daughter in tow. In general he recorded a favorable opinion on American riverboats, finding them comfortable and inexpensive. When he was ready to return to England by the summer of 1828, part of the journey was by river steamer from Cincinnati to Pittsburgh. It happened to be a hot and humid part of the summer. Everyone on the boat was suffering but no one more so than Hall's daughter. The Halls were concerned that she had contracted malaria. She became so ill that her parents began to despair that she might not survive their journey. Upon reaching Pittsburgh they quickly boarded a stagecoach for the East Coast. As the coach pulled uphill into the clear, cool air of the Alleghenies, their darling child began to show signs of recovering and her improvement continued. Hall's three-volume report on his American visit remains a testimonial to the positive features of American river travel. His excellent account became a standard reference in our young republic.

Other travelers in the 1820s present a less flattering verbal picture of river travel. In 1828 a Methodist minister named Peter Cartwright boarded the *Velocipede* at St. Louis bound for Pittsburgh. She was a small vessel and very crowded. The passengers were described as a "mixed multitude" and seemed largely composed of profane swearers, drunkards, gamblers, fiddlers, and dancers. Cartwright was a strong, charismatic man who worked to turn these fallen people away from their card playing to the merits of Christianity. Some boats of this time had no staterooms, but berths folded down from the sidewalls of the cabin for a bed. The ladies' cabin was separated by a curtain. There were so few beds that a lottery was held each night to see who would win a bed and who would win a chair, bench, or table.

The dangers of river travel were recalled by a pilot on the *Patriot*, a first-class packet built in 1824. She was, however, built with secondhand machinery. By 1830 the elderly boilers were showing signs of distress. The boat was on its way to New Orleans and was nearing the end of the Ohio River. A passenger wanted off at the town of Trinity, Illinois. At the same time, the pilot was warned that water was very low in the boilers and that the engineer would pump them up to a proper level once the boat stopped at Trinity. But just before the landing was made, the forward end of the far-left boiler burst open like a cannon. The chimney on that side popped up into the air and crashed down on the pilothouse. The guy rods supporting the chimney became entangled with the steering wheel, and the pilot had to struggle through the wreckage to steer the boat to shore. The front deck was covered with debris and four wounded men. The forward deck was also on fire. The captain managed to quench the fire. Although three of the injured crew members died, none of the passengers were harmed. Normally after such a mishap the trip would be abandoned. However, Captain Levi James and his crew made temporary repairs and went on to New Orleans with one smokestack and five, rather than six, boilers. The *Patriot* continued running for another year.

Most river travelers made their journeys for conventional reasons of business or pleasure. Some, however, traveled for science and art. A few made trips that were bound to be dangerous and uncomfortable because steamboats went to inaccessible places, such as the upper reaches of the Missouri River. The American Fur Company began sending boats into these remote and unsettled areas in 1831. They carried trading goods, ammunition, and a grisly crowd of trappers, hunters, and other frontiersmen to this outpost beyond civilization. No ordinary citizen would think about booking passage on one of these boats. However, Prince Alexander Philipp Maximilian of the small Germanic state of Wied-Neuwied was eager to make the trip and did so in 1833. He was intent on documenting the American Indian tribes of the region before they are contaminated by civilization. A self-taught American artist, George Catlin, traveled by steamer up the Missouri River at the same time as the prince. He lived with the tribes, who came to trust him. He made hundreds of paintings showing all phases of Indian life. His portraits preserved a likeness of their leaders and their ordinary people. Prince Maximilian kept a careful journal of his trip but depended on a Swiss artist to prepare illustrations to document Indian life. Much of this material now resides in the Joslyn Art Museum of Omaha.

In 1843 John James Audubon would retrace the journey of Catlin and the prince to paint four-legged creatures of the forest rather than American Indians. He would travel on a new American Fur Company boat, the *Omega*. The ladies' compartment was reserved for Audubon and his several associates. The artist had his own room and made this area complete with a double bed and a stove. The boat was well stocked with food, including six thousand eggs and plentiful boxes of wine and whiskey. They shared the boat with a large number of frontiersmen who were drunk or half drunk, with almost none in the crowd who could be registered as completely sober. They would sing and howl like madmen or fire their guns to break the silence of the Missouri River valley. The boat fought its way over sandbars much of the way upstream. Audubon would leave the boat to search for birds and quadrupeds. He brought dead specimens back to his cabin for examination and sketching. The *Omega* reached Fort Union, Missouri, just above the mouth of the Yellowstone River, on June 13, 1843, after fifty days of travel. The material gathered along the Missouri River resulted in the publication of three volumes with 150 folio plates. Art and science were thus assisted by the humble riverboat.

The average riverboat patron rarely encountered a vulgar crowd like those associated with Missouri River packets. He would expect, however, a mixture of people. American sailor and fur trader Joseph Ingraham observed what he called a strange medley of people on his boat heading upriver to Natchez in 1835. There were merchants and planters in the main cabin and a few sporting gentlemen who won handily at the card tables. The men played cards to pass the time and seemed ready to lose a goodly sum. There was an important-looking French gentleman who bore the title of general. The cotton planters wore broad-brimmed white fur hats but were otherwise clothed in a careless half sailor-like and half gentleman-like attire. In contrast was a Yankee lawyer in a plain black coat, closely buttoned, a narrow hat, and gloves. A minister sat alone by the stove reading a small book. In the place of black he wore a bottle-green coat, a fancy vest, and white pantaloons. There were two or three fat men in gray and blue, several Germans, a sharp-nosed New York speculator, and four elderly French Jews with noble foreheads. The most interesting woman was an intelligent young lady from Vermont. She possessed a cultivated mind and a full share of Yankee inquisitiveness. Ingraham's ruminations were suddenly interrupted by the loud report of the boat's cannon, which made the boat tremble through every beam. The boat was about to land at Natchez.

Dr. T. L. Nichols recalled a trip down the Ohio River in 1845 that was a delightful adventure. He described the river as charming and grandly beautiful. It was broad and splendid in great reaches, with graceful curves and picturesque banks. The crewmen sang merrily as they stoked the furnaces. The boat got stuck on a sandbar but floated off the next morning. The clear sunlight glittered on the river and lit up the forest in a golden radiance. Blue sky and cool air added to the scene. When the boat stopped for wood on the lower Mississippi, Nichols jumped to the shore. The air was soft and delicious. The gardens were filled with flowers, the rose bushes were blooming, the oranges had turned from green to gold, and the figs were ripening in the sun.

A few years earlier Charles Dickens toured America, traveling down the Ohio River to Cincinnati on the steamer *Messenger*, but he found it a cheerless journey. Meals were eaten in silence, and after dinner the men would stand around the stove, spitting without uttering a word. A few days later the English novelist was on a second boat going downstream. On his way west he happened upon a Choctaw chief who was cultivated and engaging, and the two struck up a lively conversation. Dickens was pleased that the chief had read several of his books. He invited his new friend to visit England. The chief responded that the Englishman should come to Arkansas for a buffalo hunt. Dickens later reflected that the only really engaging person he had met during his travels was an American Indian, which most U.S. citizens dismissed as savages.

Another English novelist, one even more prolific than Dickens, came to America in 1862. Anthony Trollope found steamboating when it was in a most distressing slump. Most of the boats at Pittsburgh were tied up, because the Confederates had stopped navigation at Vicksburg. Later in his tour Trollope found boats running on the upper Mississippi and cruised the river from La Crosse, Wisconsin, to Dubuque, Iowa. He was on the boat for four days but found his fellow passengers strangely silent. If he asked a question, they would answer him in a civil fashion, but there it ended. None seemed inclined to converse. The men on the boat would sit together for hours, hardly speaking a word. He found the women equally taciturn. They seemed hard, dry, and melancholy. He was also astounded by their general indifference to the splendid scenery around him, declaring that the Rhine River did not compare to the bluffs of the upper Mississippi. Added to the bluffs were the woodlands, Lake Pepin, and the color of the scenery. Trollope went away wondering about the unresponsiveness of Americans to the joy of life and the beauty of nature.

Walt Whitman was another literary figure who traveled by riverboat and made a record of his journey. In February 1848 he was on his way to New Orleans to become editor of a newspaper. This was a new experience, for he had never been west of the Hudson River and was about to visit unfamiliar regions of America's interior. He boarded the packet *St. Cloud* at Wheeling, West Virginia, for a twelve-day sojourn down the inland rivers. The scenery was dismal during the winter, and, except for a few large towns, most stops were made at villages or dismal wood yards populated by loafers and dirty children. The boat itself impressed this romantic young man as splendid and comfortable. He was especially pleased by the food and admitted he loved eating. Breakfast consisted of ham, eggs, steak, sausage, hot cakes, and plenty of good bread. Dinner offered roast beef, mutton, veal, turkey, goose, plus pies and puddings. Shooting the falls at Louisville was less pleasant; it was an ugly part of the river, he thought, and boats went wildly down the boiling chute. Other passengers, however, were excited by the wild ride.

About two years after Whitman's trip, a German visitor to America, Moritz Busch, recorded his dining experience on an Ohio River steamer. The tables were covered with dishes of fruit, vegetables, jelly molds, meats, cakes, biscuits, and breads. The men stood behind their chairs. The main course, generally a large roast of beef, was placed before the captain, who would preside as host to the passengers. The bell was sounded for the ladies to enter and take their seats. The meal was a bountiful and even a noble experience although no one in the cabin was an aristocrat. In fact, not long before the meal was served, most of the passengers were demanding that the captain race the boat running ahead of theirs. The captain at first ignored these insane demands, but finally ordered the engineers to make all speed possible. Bets were set up, and the fireman worked furiously to make more steam. After an hour the steamer was just behind its rival. Shouts and cries went up, but as Busch's steamer passed the other boat, it proved to be another vessel, not the one named in the bet. Too often racing ended in an explosion; fortunately, this one resulted only in a few red faces.

In 1846 Sir Charles Lyell, professor of geology at Kings College, toured America. He started his journey in New Orleans on board the steamer *Rainbow* but switched to the *Magnolia* at Natchez. The *Magnolia* was a large boat built for the lower Mississippi. She was a fashionable vessel and a favorite with society ladies and bridal parties. The captain was French and was fond of rich food, especially roast duck. Professor Lyell noted that the menu was sumptuous and included soup, two kinds of fish, a chain of entrees, and desserts. The claret was excellent, but Lyell was puzzled why some guests quaffed down river water. It was cloudy and full of tiny particles and silt, yet those consuming it declared it was healthy and drank it as a physic. Other travelers spoke of other boats where the food was well cooked and carefully served. The waiters stood by like bronze statues. A few boats kept a cow on board for fresh milk.

STR. "ED. RICHARDSON."

DINNER.

For _____ 1879

SOUP.

FISH.
Broiled Red Fish, au maitre d'hote.

BOILED.
Leg of Mutton, Caper Sauce		Corned Beef and Cabbage
Chicken, Egg Sauce	Ham	Fulton Market Beef

ROAST.
Loin of Beef	Pork	Chicken
Saddle of Mutton		Turkey

VEGETABLES.
Mashed Potatoes	Rice	Cabbage	Hominy
Turnips	Snap Beans	Green Corn	

RELISHES.
Crosse & Blackwell's Pickles

Gherkins	Currant Jelly		Cheese
Tomato Catsup	Walnut Catsup		Chow-Chow
Piccalilli	English Onions		Mushroom Catsup
The Lea & Perrin Sauces	Spanish Olives		Cold Slaugh
Maunsel White	Lettuce		John Bull's Sauce
Horse Radish			French Mustard

ENTREES.
Calves'-feet a la Puceline	Pieds de Veau a la Puceline
Filets of Chicken with Truffes	Filets de Poulets aux Truffes
Braised Brisket of Lamb with Green Peas	
Poitrine d'Agneau au Brasier avec Pois Verts	

GAME.

COLD DISHES.
Corned Beef	Tongue	Ham	Salad

PASTRY AND DESSERT.

PUDDINGS.
White Raisin, a la Windsor, Vanilla Sauce

PASTRY.
Lemon Pie	Green Apple Pie
Petite Puit d'Amour	Fachennottes, a la Flour de Orange

CAKES.
Pound	Fruit	Almond	Jelly Cake
Lady Fingers		Cocoanut Plarine	

CREAMS AND JELLIES.
Jelly de Macedonia	Maraschino Jelly
Meringue aux Peche	Cream a la Roman
Belle Fritters	

FRUITS.
Pecans	Figs		Almonds
Pine Apples			Raisins
Brazilian Nuts			Filberts
English Walnuts			Fresh Dates
Oranges	Bananas	Apples	Prunes

——COFFEE.——

☞ Any want of attention on the part of attendants, please report to the
STEWARD.

Seymour & Stevens, Print, 96 Common St.

Many had a henhouse on an upper roof. All stopped to pick up fresh food en route. Some boats offered a third seating to deck passengers who were willing to pay for a meal. Printed menus were common on the better boats (fig. 7.7). Special meals were prepared for visiting dignitaries. The menu for a breakfast served to General Ulysses S. Grant on September 3, 1865, included soft-shell crab, lamb chops, and prairie chicken. One of the notable and unusual characteristics of riverboat menus was the absence of prices. This is because meals were served "free" to first-class passengers. At least no money was collected at mealtime, but of course the cost was buried in the overall fare. Gerstner estimated the costs were about $1 a day, so if the trip lasted six days, the steamboat operators add $6 to the fare.

Most of the profit in the steamboat business came from the freight carried on the main deck; however, boat operators added to their revenue by carrying second-class passengers on the same deck. While a very few boats offered rustic wooden bunks, none included mattresses or bedding. In most cases, deck passengers looked for an empty place among the barrels and boxes. Emigrants, flatboat men heading home, farmers, and any poor person needing a cheap ride went as deck passengers. One such traveler was Andrew Carnegie's father, a hand weaver whose dyeing trade paid so poorly he could not afford a cabin. Andrew and his father

7.7. This menu was used on the *Ed Richardson*, a large Mississippi packet built at the Howard Yard in Jeffersonville, Indiana, in 1878.

(G. L. Eskew, *Pageant of the Packets*, 1929)

RIVER STEAMERS 199

traveled on the same boat, but only the younger Carnegie could afford a first-class ticket.

The lower deck was a scene of filth and wretchedness, but the fare was cheap, just $1 to go from Pittsburgh to Cincinnati. At less than a penny a mile, the riverboat was about the cheapest way to travel anywhere in the world. There might be 150 passengers on the deck, making sleeping space scarce. Dinner would consist of items taken on board by the travelers, such as sausage, dried herring, cheese, bread, and whiskey. A few boats sold food to deck passengers, but at 25 cents most would decline the offer. Sleeping on the freight deck could be dangerous. Cattle, sheep, and hogs were loaded and unloaded at stops along the way, which could include early morning hours. Sleepers might get trampled by the exiting animals. It was possible to roll over and drop off the deck into the river. Some passengers simply lost their balance and dropped over the side to drown in the muddy water. Some travelers were in good spirits despite the primitive accommodations. They were traveling to a new home in the west, where rich soil and cheap acreage promised them a better life in the new world.

Not all river travel was made on the three major branches of the inland rivers. Travelers patronized smaller boats that plied the Cumberland, Arkansas, and Illinois Rivers and dozens of other tributary streams. A college student named Theodore Hibbett was returning to his home in Nashville in June 1852. His previous experiences with stagecoach travel prompted him to try a river trip. For $10 he could go from Cincinnati to Nashville. The *Jenny Lind* was scheduled to follow the Ohio River to the mouth of the Cumberland River, which is about a dozen miles east of Paducah, Kentucky. There was only one boat a week between the two cities. Steamboats had been following this winding river 193 miles to Nashville since 1818. It was never an easy passage, especially in the dry season. By the fourth day the *Jenny Lind* started up the Cumberland River. There had been delays all along the Ohio River due to fog, sandbars, and a broken pump. As they proceeded, the water level dropped to 18 inches. The captain stopped and ordered the removal of cargo to lighten the vessel. Late that night they started up the Cumberland again, but by 10:00 the next morning, the boat was hung up on a sandbar. The captain resolved to return to Cincinnati. Once free of the sandbar, Hibbett got off rather than backtrack. He hoped to take a stagecoach or another boat to Nashville. A very small boat appeared at 1:00 AM and tied up because of fog. Hibbett bought a ticket as a deck passenger, because all the cabins were full, and sat up for the rest of the night.

The *Jenny Lind* proceeded at sunrise, rarely going faster than 2 mph and stopping to pick up more passengers for this already crowded boat. Even more passengers were added from a stranded boat. It was extremely hot, and there was only river water to drink. The cabin smelled so vile

7.8. The *Benton* was a typical Missouri River mountain boat designed for light draft service. It was built in 1875 for T. C. Power and Brother's "P" line of steamers. Notice the spars attached to derricks at the bow. These sturdy wood poles were used for grasshoppering across sand or mud bars on the Upper Missouri River.

(*James Rees and Sons Company Illustrated Catalog,* 1913)

that Hibbett could not think of eating. The mosquitoes were as thick as a swarm of bees. This day was pure torment, and the following night was the longest he could remember. Five days out from Cincinnati, they had reached Clarksville, Tennessee, and were still more than 50 miles from Nashville. The boat continued to battle its way over shoals. After two or three tries, the deckhands would wade up the river to pull the boat by ropes. By early afternoon of the sixth day, they were within sight of Nashville, but it took almost three hours to get the boat around an island. What an exhausting and uncomfortable journey! Hibbett must have wondered if steamboating was so superior to stagecoach travel after all.

A few years after Hibbett's misadventure, Frederick L. Olmsted traveled as a correspondent for the *New York Times.* He was on his way to Texas and wrote a series of articles about his journey. Olmsted retraced the exact path that Hibbert's boat had taken. Low water was again the problem, but matters went more smoothly for Olmsted. The captain of the *D. A. Tomkins* promised to reach Nashville in a day, but the trip took about four days. The boat had hardly started on its way before a snag damaged the paddle wheel. After the repair was completed, a fog settled in, so they did not proceed. The following day they passed another boat abandoned on a sandbar. Upstream several other large boats were unable to move because of the low water. The *D. A. Tomkins* was a little vessel with a small draft. When a low place was encountered, the freight was transferred to barges tied onto either side of the mother boat. This lightened her load enough to go forward. In other places, spars were planted in the river bottom at the boat's bow. She was lifted upward a few inches by a windlass, on these timbers that acted as crutches. The paddle wheel, working at top speed, would propel the boat forward and over the sandbar. This method was much used on the Missouri River and was called grasshoppering or walking the boat (fig. 7.8). It had been in use since the 1820s. On the nearby Tennessee River, boats were helped upstream by large shore-mounted capstans. The manually powered capstan ropes attached to the boat and pulled the vessel upstream.

In general, Olmsted found traveling the Cumberland River more boring than unpleasant. The scenery remained monotonous, with a steady line of drooping tree branches and uncleared land. The boat engine's exhaust kept up a steady *choosh, choosh, choosh* that could be heard for miles. This, too, Olmsted found to be tiresome. He was happy to return to the Ohio River and continue his travels on a full-size, mainline river. The Cumberland River was much improved by the early twentieth century with locks and dams, canalization, and deepening the shoals. Light draft boats, at 30 inches deep or less, could reach Nashville year round, but larger steamers drawing no more than 36 inches could operate for only six to eight months. Eventually navigation was opened to Burnside, Kentucky, 518 miles upstream from the river's mouth on the Ohio River.

The headwaters of the Monongahela River are in southeastern West Virginia. The narrow stream winds its way northward into Pennsylvania and joins the Allegheny River at Pittsburgh to form the Ohio River. Steamboat navigation began in 1825 between Pittsburgh and Brownsville, Pennsylvania, a distance of 35 miles. However, service could be maintained only when the water level was sufficiently high. A private corporation was organized to improve the river so that boat service could be maintained year round. Rather than beg for public funding, the Monongahela Navigation Company was established to do the job. Instead of wasting years hoping for state or federal subsidies, this company went to work. By 1844 several locks and dams were completed, creating a series of pools or lakes and allowed year-round steamboat service. The Baltimore and Ohio Railroad had reached the Cumberland by this time. A stagecoach line connected Cumberland, Maryland, to Brownsville. This part of the trip was just 73 miles. The entire journey from Baltimore to Pittsburgh required just thirty hours, which was considered a very fast time in 1844. Passengers arriving in Pittsburgh had a choice of numerous steamers leaving for ports as far away as New Orleans. This multi-mode route to the West proved popular for about eight years; the northern end of the Monongahela teemed with passenger traffic. In 1847 the local packet line carried 445,825 through passengers and 39,777 way passengers; even more were transported during the next year. By 1852 the Pennsylvania Railroad opened its line to Pittsburgh. Riverboat passenger traffic fell off dramatically that year. It was quickly reduced to local or way passengers.

Freight traffic on the Monongahela continued to grow. Millions of bushels of coal went to market on this small tributary river. More dams and locks extended commercial navigation to Morgantown, West Virginia, in 1904. Many other secondary steamers in the inland river system also offered steamboat service during the Victorian era.

MORE DANGEROUS THAN A SHIP AT SEA

In 1851 the *Irish Emigrant's Guide to the United States* claimed that steamboats were "more dangerous than a ship at sea," and in January 1864 the *American Railroad Journal* offered transportation statistics for the years 1853–1863. Steamboat accidents were responsible for 3,545 deaths compared to 1,699 deaths on railroads. The exactness of these statistics might be challenged, but it is a fact that the riverboat industry had a poor safety record and thus was perceived by the public as a dangerous means of travel. The U.S. Congress reacted to public complaints in 1838 by enacting a steamboat safety act. It proved to be little more than a gesture, however, because little funding was appropriated to enforce the law. In 1852 a second bill was passed that included money for inspection and enforcement. A list of riverboat accidents was compiled in that year. It was a historic survey covering the years 1811 to 1851. The data was gleaned from available sources – notably, newspaper accounts – and is likely incomplete, yet the total of 995 accidents remains alarming. The greatest cause of accidents was snags at 57.5 percent. Boiler explosions were a poor second at 21 percent, and the remaining 21.5 percent was divided between fires and collision. The number of lives lost from all causes was just a little over 7,000.

Snags were the great sinkers of riverboats. In terms of property damage, they proved the greatest hazard, particularly before a systematic removal service was established. Relatively few passengers died in the resultant vessel loss, because the boat was often beached on the riverbank before the sinking occurred. At times of low water only the first deck was submerged and the passenger deck remained above the river. In such cases it was safe for the travelers to remain abroad until rescued. Boats could go down quickly, especially if the snag was large and hit the bow. This happened to the *Arabia* in September 1856 on the Missouri River near Kansas City. The snag was a large walnut tree that was both heavy and tough. The *Arabia* sank in just ten minutes, but the only fatality was a mule. In 1988 work began at the wreck site to recover the cargo and parts of the boat for display in a museum in Kansas City.

Not all sinkings resulted in tragedy; some were harmless and even somewhat amusing as this story about the *Messenger* illustrates. She was a nearly new side-wheeler on her third trip to New Orleans from Cincinnati. It was around suppertime on August 13, 1866, and the boat was moving along the Mississippi River with a barge attached on either side. It was proceeding below Island Number 26 and was about 55 miles north of Memphis when the bow struck a submerged tree stump. A good-size hole was made and the boat sank in ten minutes. One of the loaded barges broke loose from its lines and floated downstream. The second barge was empty. It stayed alongside and the passengers and crew climbed aboard it as a precaution. The stump, firmly implanted in the riverbed, supported the front end of the *Messenger* while the rear of the boat sank in shallow water. The main deck was flooded by just 6 feet. Seeing that all was safe, everyone climbed back on board. Dinner was served and proceeded normally until the limber structure of the vessel began to settle into the soft mud at the river's bottom. Just an inch or two of settlement caused the hull and cabin to pop and crack. These sounds so unnerved one young man that he jumped up on the dining table to escape what he perceived was a sudden danger. He collided with an overhead lamp and broke the glass shades and chimneys. The broken glass hit the table, setting off alarm among the diners. When it was explained that these cracks and pops were normal sounds that were sure to continue, the dinner proceeded. The passengers returned to their sleeping cabins. The next morning another boat stopped by and took aboard all who wanted to go upstream. Later, a second boat rescued those wanting to go downstream. The boat was raised, repaired, and continued in service until 1875.

A snag could also result in a tragedy, however, as was true of the *Belle Zane* one cold January night in 1845. She struck a snag on the Mississippi River below the mouth of the White River in east central Arkansas. The collision was so violent that the boat rolled over. The passengers were in bed, and only about fifty of those on board managed to escape from their berths. Of these, only sixteen survived that bitterly cold night. Some of the bodies were buried along the riverbank.

Fire was far more lethal because of the flimsy nature of the upper cabins and the boat's inflammable nature. Smoking, open-flame lamps, and heating stoves all contributed to the fire risk. Boats burned individually or in groups. There was a mass burning of steamers along the Cincinnati Public Landing in the early morning of May 12, 1869. The fire is believed to have started in the nursery of the steamer *Clifton*. By 2:00 AM it had spread to five other vessels, sending flames 100 feet into the sky. Fortunately, the passengers had departed some hours earlier and only the death of one employee was reported. Two other boats escaped by backing out into the river and out of harm's way. A second major fire occurred in the same place in 1922. Once again, several steamers were destroyed as the flames spread from one boat to the next. The origin of the fire was a large container of roofing tar being heated on a galley stove. A much larger riverfront fire started in St. Louis innocently enough in May 1849. Chamber maids had put bedding out to air. Sparks set it on fire around 10:00 PM. The flames spread to other boats and nearby buildings. In all, twenty-three steamers were destroyed as well as many blocks of the warehouse district.

Fire accidents on riverboats sometimes involved the loss of human life. The *Ben Sherrod* was on her way to Louisville when she began to overtake another boat upstream. It was 1:00 AM on May 8, 1837, and most passengers were fast asleep in their cabins. The crew decided it would be fun to stage a race. They provided the fireman with a barrel of whiskey as a reward to stoke the fireboxes full of wood, pine knots, and rosin. The boilers supplied steam in ever-increasing amounts to push the vessel faster against the current. The cord wood was stacked next to the overheated boilers and caught on fire. The smoke began to wake the passengers, but it was too late for an orderly evacuation. Many jumped into the river; a lucky few found a barrel or some driftwood to sustain them. Two passing boats drew alongside to rescue some of the passengers. Of the three hundred on board only about half survived.

A much less deadly fire consumed a stern wheeler named the *Iron Queen* near the small town of Antiquity, Ohio, in the spring of 1895. If everyone on board had followed the captain's orders, the blaze would have claimed no one. Passengers had gathered in the cabin for breakfast. Roustabouts were loading cargo on the lower deck when one of them accidently knocked over a lantern. It fell behind some crates and smashed on the floor, starting a small fire. No one noticed the flames until the fire had grown too strong to extinguish. Everyone was ordered off the boat. A chambermaid named Mattie Mosby could not bear the thought of being seen in public without her hat and impulsively ran back on board to retrieve this precious item. Once on the burning boat, however, she was unable to make it back to shore. Trapped by the flames, she jumped into the river and drowned. It was a sad and unnecessary death.

Riverboats were considered floating volcanoes that were likely to self ignite. The *Pacific* proved the validity of this saying while taking on coal at Uniontown, Kentucky, in November 1860. The pine-knot basket torches were the common form of lighting used to illuminate the first deck during any nighttime loading event. One of these medieval torches set the boat on fire – she burned to the waterline and killed eight people.

Collisions were another hazard that destroyed boats and their human cargo. The *Thomas Sherlock* was leaving for New Orleans in February 1891. It was early evening but the sun had already set. The boat backed into the river and made ready to swing around and head south. The current was very strong that evening – it carried the boat downstream faster than usual, and before the pilot could swing her around, the boat ran into a bridge pier with a mighty crash. The smokestacks collapsed and the upper works separated from the hull. The cabin floated downstream with thirty passengers and some of the crew. The wreckage traveled 10 miles before another boat could push it back to shore. Only two people died in this extraordinary accident, which indicates that the upper works or cabins could hold together well enough to carry all but two safely downriver.

Collisions between boats were common enough and often involved only minor damage. The collision of the *United States* and the *America* on the evening of December 4, 1868, was of a more serious nature. Both vessels were owned by the U.S. Mail line that offered overnight service between Louisville and Cincinnati. Both were large, deluxe packets of recent construction. The night was windy but clear, and the boats met near their normal passing place, two miles below Warsaw, Kentucky. On this night, however, a substitute pilot was at the wheel of the *America*. The regular pilot kept toward the Kentucky shore when going upriver while the down boat stayed toward the Indiana shore. In violation of custom, the substitute man decided to cross over to the Indiana shore. He signaled his intention to do so, but the pilot on the down riverboat, the *United States,* responded so quickly to the signal that he drowned out the sound of the second whistle blast. The *America* cut across the stream and slammed the *United States* amidships. The collision knocked down many passengers and toppled over a cargo of oil barrels. Fire broke out on both boats. Passengers and crew members scrambled to get off both vessels, which were burning and sinking at the same time. Estimates varied between 63 and 170 deaths. Many were injured. The *America* was a total loss, and the *United States* was heavily damaged. This terrible accident was the result of a misunderstanding of the whistle signal, demonstrating that small mistakes can result in tragic consequences.

Boiler explosions were a leading cause of deaths for riverboat travelers (fig. 7.9). In 1852 it was estimated that one-half of steamboat deaths were the result of such explosions. Higher steam pressures resulted in greater power but at the price of safety. Racing led to over-firing that taxed the wrought-iron boilers of the time; this, too, resulted in explosions. Careless and reckless management on the part of the engineering crews also led to failures. A fireman on a Mississippi steamer was quoted by a traveler in 1844 as saying, "But I tell you, stranger, it takes a man to ride one of these half alligator boats, head on a snag, high pressure, valve soldered down, 600 souls on board and in danger of going to the devil." Many innocent travelers were blown to the devil by such men. In April 1838 the new steamer *Moselle* was ready for her second trip to Louisville. Her captain ordered the engineer to produce the maximum amount of steam so that his fine new boat would make a speedy pass along the Cincinnati riverfront and impress everyone who saw her leave port. The safety-valve levers were laden with extra weights. The boat was packed with passengers, including a large number of German immigrants. Before her wheels

7.9. The steamer *Magnolia* blew up and burned on the Ohio River several miles above Cincinnati on March 18, 1868. It was not a major disaster, yet thirty-five lives were lost.

(*Harper's Weekly*, April 4, 1868)

had made a single turn, there was a tremendous roar and the boat disappeared from view in a cloud of steam and smoke. Pieces of wood and iron fell from the sky into the river and on the nearby shore. Bodies and parts of bodies rained down as well. Of the estimated 280 on board, around 150 were dead or missing. Only a week earlier, the *Oronoko* had blown up on the Mississippi River, resulting in about 100 deaths.

The U.S. Congress passed a steamboat inspection law in 1838 that temporarily quieted the public alarm over the issue of riverboat safety. However, the bill was far too general in its wording; it did not provide for meaningful inspections and was largely ineffective. In 1852 a much more specific federal act was passed, which included detailed provisions for boiler and hull inspections. Engineers and pilots would now be tested and licensed. Meaningful results were soon evident. Between 1848 and 1852 there were 50 major accidents and 416 boiler explosions, resulting in the loss of 1,155 lives. Between 1854 and 1858 there were 20 accidents, 214 boiler explosions, and the loss of 224 lives. Despite this general improvement in safety, the accident rate increased during the Civil War years, because boats and men were being worked very hard and maintenance tended to be neglected because of the war emergency.

There was also the matter of greed. The war was over in April 1865, and thousands of troops started for home. Boats were being loaded well above their legal limits, which seemed to be a necessity since there were too few boats, and captains were happy to collect the extra fares. The *Sultana* was a big boat with wide decks; her legal passenger limit was 376, but 2,000 troops were put on board when she docked at Vicksburg. They were a lean and sickly collection of young men. Most were just released

Table 7.1. Annual Salary for Crew of *New Orleans II*, 1817

Captain	$2,500	Assistant Steward	$360
Mate	$600	Cook	$360
Pilot	$600	Cook's Mate	$240
Engineer	$600	2 Firemen	$480
Clerk	$500	8 Sailors (deck hands)	$1,920
Barkeeper	$360	4 Waiters	$840
Steward	$360	**Total:**	**$9,720**

Source: *Louisiana Historical Society Quarterly* 7, no. 3 (1924).

from Confederate prisons and knew the meaning of hunger and harsh conditions. The boat was less than two years old, but she was already experiencing boiler trouble. Repairs were made at Vicksburg, but she stopped at Memphis for additional work. The *Sultana* left late that evening and was just a few miles above Memphis when her boilers exploded. It was dark and cold, and the river was in flood stage. Many were killed or blown into the river by the explosion. The boat began burning at the same time, prompting more passengers to jump into the cold water. Other passing boats attempted to rescue those still on the *Sultana* or visible in the dark water. About 600 people were recovered, but about one-third of these died. The official death toll was over 1,500, making it the worst accident on the inland rivers, as great a loss of life as was suffered in the sinking of the *Titanic* in 1912.

It is obvious that ships at sea can be damaged by high winds. The same is true for river craft, because their large upper cabins act as a sail. River steamers could be blown off course and damaged by windstorms and tornadoes. In Minnesota pilots also experienced problems with the wind on Lake Pepin, where the Mississippi River widens below St. Paul, forming a lake about 3 miles wide and 25 miles long. Steamers were routinely pushed across this broad body of water by strong winds. In the 1860s the side-wheeler *C. T. Dumont* was struck by a tornado that demolished her cabin and pushed the boat across the Ohio River to the Kentucky shore. There were some injuries, but no one was killed. The boat was repaired and ran until 1872. A much stronger tornado struck Natchez in May 1840. The steamer *Hinds* was blown out into the river, where it sank, and fifty-one died. Another packet, the *Prairie,* was also lost with all of her passengers. Of the 120 flatboats tied up at the Natchez landing, only 4 survived the storm. Two hundred flatboat men were killed. Another powerful tornado ripped through St. Louis in May 1896 and damaged scores of boats docked at the public landing. Twenty-five steamers were blown across the river or sunk. Many had their upper works torn off. Others were blown downriver or capsized. There was wreckage everywhere, and the property damage was estimated at $12 million. Some 255 people died in this catastrophe.

Table 7.2. Salary Figures for Crew of Steamer *Diana*, 1839

Captain	Annual $1,800	8 Deckhands	Monthly each $25
Clerk	Annual $1,200	2 Cooks	Monthly $50 and $30
2 Mates	Monthly $40 and $75	1 Steward	Monthly $50
2 Engineers	Monthly $75 and $125	8 Waiters	Monthly $30 and $15
Carpenter	Monthly $60	Chambermaid	Monthly $25
12 Firemen	Monthly each $30		

Source: Franz Anton Ritter von Gerstner, Internal Communication of the United States as reprinted in *Early American Railroads*, 1997.

Statistics offered in Louis Hunter's seminal study of the riverboat reveal that the actual number of accidents by the vessel was less than is often assumed by historians. He reports, for example, that between 1811 and 1851 there were only 995 accidents reported, or an average of 24.8 from all causes such as collision, fire, boiler explosions, etc. In tables for the years 1860–1889 Hunter lists a total of 1,235 accidents. He adds that a total of 8,783 lives were lost during this twenty-nine-year period. When we consider the riverboats' average loss per year, the number is far less than fatalities on record for modern automobiles. Boiler explosions that were killing a large portion of the population according to popular accounts of the period were in fact relatively rare. For the years 1811–1851 they average just 5 a year; for the years 1860–1889 there were 3.4 a year. These numbers also suggest that federal steamboat inspection did rather little to improve the safety of these vessels.

MEN AND WOMEN OF THE RIVER

A variety of workers was needed to operate riverboats. These ranged from managers to laundresses. In 1817 an account of the *New Orleans II*, mentioned earlier in this chapter, included a list of staff together with their yearly salaries (table 7.1). The total staff was twenty-four.

By the time of Franz von Gerstner's investigation of American travel in 1839, crew size and wages had changed somewhat. The data given in table 7.2 is for the *Diana*.

The barber received no salary but presumably was given room and board and kept tips from his customers. The bartender worked as a concessioner, paying the boat owners a monthly fee of $50. He was also required to provide the crew with hard liquor at no cost; hence his income came from his patrons. The crew of the *Diana* consisted of thirty-eight, and the monthly salary total came to $1,785.

Eleven years later the Ohio River packet *Buckeye State* had a crew of fifty-seven. No salaries were included in the published description of the boat. Most of the increase in number of employees was in the hotel or

Table 7.3. Crew and Wages for a Typical 500-Ton Packet Boat

	Monthly Wages	Total
1 master	$125	$125
1 mate	80	80
1 second mate	50	50
3 clerks:		
One	100–150	
One	50–80	220
One	25–35	
1 watchman	30	30
2 pilots	125	250
1 engineer	85	85
1 second engineer	50	50
1 striker	30	30
2 steersmen*		
1 steward	60	60
1 second steward	20	20
1 carpenter	60	60
10 cabin crew	15	150
2 (cook and assistant)	135	135
2 chambermaids	30	60
2 deck hands	30	60
1 sweeper	10	10
6 firemen and ashmen	30	180
30 roustabouts	25	750
70 Total		**$2,405**

*Steersmen generally received no payment other than meals. The nature of their job is uncertain.

Source: *U.S. Census*, 1880.

service side of the crew. There were four cooks rather than two, as on the *Diana,* ten deckhands rather than eight, twelve waiters rather than three, and two chambermaids rather than one. The *Buckeye State* was 90 feet longer than the *Diana,* which would account in part for the larger crew. Crew size was also affected by the business of the boat. If freight was an important source of revenue, a large deck crew would be needed, as might an extra clerk to record the cargoes and make sure they were put off at the correct place. If speed was a priority, more firemen would be needed. If passenger service was a major issue, more waiters and chambermaids would be hired. If cost cutting was deemed imperative, then a reduction in force would eliminate all but the most important workers.

The U.S. census of 1880 included a report on steam navigation. It included a table listing the crew and wages for a typical 500-ton packet boat. Table 7.3 lists positions not found in earlier lists, such as a striker (an apprentice engine-room worker), a third clerk, and a sweeper. Note that only 2 deckhands were listed but 30 roustabouts were required. Now that coal was the fuel, ash men were needed to dispose of the ashes and clinkers. With such a large crew, monthly wages had increased to just over

7.10. The *Jacob Strader* was a large and deluxe packet built for the U.S. Mail line in 1853. The boat was 347 feet long and had space for 310 first-class passengers. She had gas lighting and a large nursery for children.

(Frederick Brent Read, *Up the Heights of Fame and Fortune*, 1873)

$2,400. In all, 7,090 were employed on the Ohio River steamers. The exact number of roustabouts could not be determined but was estimated to be about 2,000.

As master of the boat, the captain was required to be a leader and make quick and accurate decisions. He must be a good judge of character and hire able men to serve him. He must also be a good businessman and produce a profit. The captain might own the boat, or at least a share of it, and so generally had a direct interest in earning good profits. Some captains became managers of steamship lines and spent most of their time in an office. They were seldom seen on the boats. Jacob Strader entered steamboat service in 1819 as a young man. He began as a clerk but was quickly promoted to captain. Very soon he became a boat owner and by 1831 was too busy and rich to remain in river service. By 1847 he decided riverboating was too competitive, because periodic rate wars ruined any chance of dependable profits. Strader sold out and spent his remaining years as a banker and railroad promoter. Many captains would never consider leaving the river trade no matter how troublesome it became. Captain Thomas P. Leathers was a river loyalist who owned and operated seven boats named *Natchez*. By the end of the Civil War he was penniless, but he recovered by 1869 to build a new boat. He raced the *Robert E. Lee* in 1870 and lost, but would not retire until the early 1890s. He was proud to have a son who also loved the river deeply and became a riverboat captain.

The pilot operated the boat by steering the vessel and controlling its speed. He was required to know the river in all of its details, habits, and landmarks. The location of sandbars, islands, curves, and channels required a specific and up-to-date knowledge, since these features were constantly changing. How deep was the water along this segment of the stream? Were there any rocks? How fast was the current? What was the shape of the riverbed? Few men could learn so many specifics for more than a few hundred miles, so a series of pilots were generally needed for long trips. After the federal law governing steamboat safety was created,

7.11. The interior of a pilothouse shows the pilot at the steering wheel and several visitors. The front window directly ahead of the pilot was unglazed – wooden shutters could be lowered to partially cover the opening. The two rings hanging from the ceiling were attached to the whistle rope. Mouthpieces for the speaking tubes to the engine room can be seen at the right side above the head of the bearded man.

(*Frank Leslie's Illustrated Newspaper*, November 10, 1883)

pilots were tested and licensed. There was not much science to navigating the inland rivers; it was so unlike the charts and positions in ocean navigation. On the river it was all instinct and experience. Pilots watched the color and motion of the water. They had an understanding of the river's habits and moods. It helped them find their way safely.

Steering was managed by the huge wooden wheel inside the pilothouse on the forward end of the upper cabin. Ropes connected the wheel with the rudder at the stern. Rope was subject to damage by fire or rats, and wire cable was substituted starting around 1850. When rounding a sharp curve, the pilot would use both hands and one foot to spin the wheel until the rudder was hard over. If the vessel was a side-wheeler, the pilot could signal the engineer to speed up one of the wheels to steer the boat round a curve. The signaling was done by a set of four or more bells in the engine room connected to the pilothouse by thin wires. The stopping bell was the largest, the backing bell was a little smaller, third in size was the gong, and the smallest was the jingle bell. Most signals – such as *go ahead, slow,* and *fast* – were made by a combination of these bells. The bell system was not perfect and occasionally was the cause of a mishap, so the pilot and engineer also communicated through speaking tubes (fig. 7.11).

Pilots also needed to communicate with other boats. The early boats depended on a large bell mounted on the roof near the front of the boat. It was about the size of a church bell and could be heard for a good distance. Other boats were advised by its ringing to watch out, another boat was approaching, was passing on the port or starboard, or needed assistance. Whistles, which seem so much a part of steamboats, were rather late in being adopted. The first vessel with a whistle on the Ohio River was the

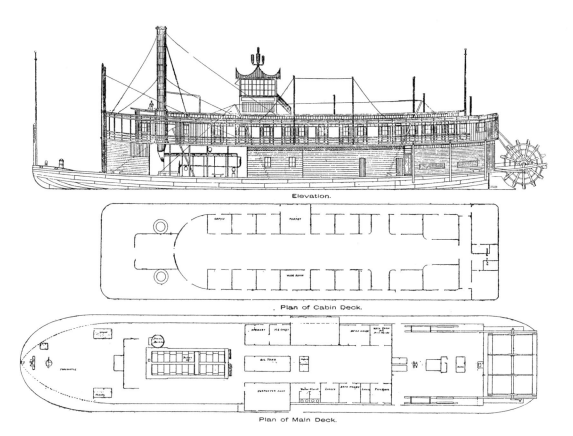

Revenue in 1844. The *General Warren* on the Green River (Kentucky) was so equipped at about the same time. Sir Charles Lyell mentioned that in 1846 the *Clipper* had such a device that gave a wild and harsh scream when blown. The *Dr. Franklin* in 1847 is reported as the earliest boat on the upper Mississippi River with a whistle. Whistles became more melodious when three and even five chimes were used in place of a single tube. These improved models could play chords that echoed along miles of river valleys. Riverboat whistles heard late at night often sounded deep and melancholy, as if they were mourning the passing of some long-departed spirit.

Nighttime travel on the rivers was considered dangerous, and cautious captains would tie up for the evening. Moonlight excursions were considered reasonably safe. For boats offering overnight service between cities, night running was a requirement and an accepted hazard by the crews and passengers. Navigation lights were installed as early as 1869 on the lower Ohio River. These lamps, called beacons, were mounted inside boxes on tall posts driven into the riverbank. These kerosene lamps were too feeble to illuminate the river, but they offered a viable target that helped the pilot find his way along the darkened stream. Pilots were able to steer safely along the river, meandering the course from one light to the next. Local farm women were hired to light and extinguish the lamps. They also refueled and trimmed the wicks. By 1882 the federal government

7.12. The *Goldenrod* was a small stern wheeler that served as a beacon light tender, but she was built on the standard packet boat plan. The boat was 150 feet long. It was built at Jeffersonville, Indiana, in 1888.

(John Fehrenbatch, *Library of Steam Engineering*, 1895)

7.13. The scene is Memphis in about 1870. Riverboat transport remains important to the local economy. About thirty boats a day arrived making connections with St. Louis, St. Paul, New Orleans, and other cities and hamlets along the inland river system.

(Author's collection)

managed the system. It included 324 lights on the Ohio and 480 on the Missouri and Mississippi Rivers.

The pilothouse was meant to be a solitary place where nothing would distract the steersman from his important duties. It also happened to be a great place to view the river. Other river men traveling on the boat would drop in for a visit. They would occupy a bench at the rear of the house to enjoy the splendid view and exchange gossip and stories. Few pilots could resist joining the conversation. Passengers were brought up by the captain for a special visit. Before long they might return, hoping not to bother the pilot, but just to see the scenery go by or listen to stories. Pilots were supposed to discourage such visitors, but some liked the company and could not resist explaining their wonderful knowledge of the Mississippi or a half dozen other rivers. A young woman passenger confessed she would regularly escape to the pilothouse as a way to avoid the dozens of unruly children racing around the boat. It was such a pleasant and adult retreat, high above the noise and confusion below.

THE LAST HURRAH

Mark Twain declared the steamboat dead in his 1883 volume *Life on the Mississippi*. He contended that the St. Louis levee was now home to six lifeless boats while he remembered a solid line of them. There were more optimistic reports from business sources. The Cincinnati board of trade report for 1881 noted daily service between Pittsburgh, Pennsylvania; Wheeling, West Virginia; and Pomeroy, Portsmouth, and New Richmond, Ohio. Weekly service on the Kanawha River in West Virginia and triweekly boats ran to Portsmouth, Ohio, and Maysville, Kentucky. From

THE MEMPHIS AND CINCINNATI Packet Company.

REGULAR TRI-WEEKLY LINE

Leaving Cincinnati for Memphis and Intermediate Ports on

TUESDAYS, THURSDAYS, AND SATURDAYS, OF EACH WEEK.

This Line now comprises the following New Side Wheel Steamers, viz:

ALICE DEAN,	Captain Frank Stein.
SILVER MOON,	" C. D. Conway.
ROBERT BURNS,	" W. B. Miller.
DARLING,	" F. T. Batchelor.
GOLDEN EAGLE,	" Lewis Kates.

Passengers and Shippers may rely upon the regularity of these Boats.

THEO. COOK, PRES'T.
GEO. D. HOOPLE, GEN'L SUP'T.

7.14. This advertisement for the Memphis and Cincinnati Packet Company appeared in the 1865 Cincinnati City Directory.

Cincinnati three boats a week ran to New Orleans and Memphis. The daily line to Louisville was established in 1819. All of these boats were fully and profitably employed. In addition, flatboats and rafts ran in large numbers to carry coal, salt, clay, bricks, and lumber. A few years later Cincinnati was home to ten riverboat lines, for a total of thirty-eight boats in regular service. Tramp steamers augmented the fleet as did a regular parade of towboats and coal barges. *Harper's Weekly* in July 1883 reported boats tied up two and three deep at the Cincinnati Public Landing. The

Table 7.4. Number of Boats on Inland Rivers

Year	Packets	Towboats
1811	1	
1817	17	
1820	69	
1825	73	
1830	187	
1840	536	
1845	557	
1850	740	
1855	727	
1860	735	
1870	435	325
1880	490	362
1890	637	284
1900	596	304
1910	232	471

Source: Louis C. Hunter, *Steamboats on Western Rivers*, Cambridge: Harvard University Press, 1949.

British magazine *Engineering* in August 1890 reported the following service out of Cincinnati: 11 boats to New Orleans, 6 to Memphis, 4 to Louisville, 3 to Pomeroy, 2 to Huntington, 1 to the Kanawha Valley, and 3 for the Tennessee River.

The true state of the riverboat industry likely rested somewhere beyond Mark Twain's pessimism and the board of trade's optimism. The number of boats in service remained high, as indicated in table 7.4. Long-distance passenger traffic had declined, but local travel was healthy; the 1890 census listed the number of inland river passengers as 10.8 million. Cargo accounted for most of the profit.

What changed was the quality of the passenger service. Some lines continued to operate clean and well-maintained boats, but in general, because the clientele was less affluent and more interested in cheap fares rather than deluxe accommodations, many boats were seedy and ill kept. A *New York Times* correspondent took an extended river trip in 1883. His description of the boats, passengers, and food creates a picture of a general decline. The correspondent signed his article as W. D. His journey began in Pittsburgh in November 1883. The view of the river from a hotel bedroom window was remarkable. Immediately below was the broad, sloping levee – the wide space of blackness was the river, which reflected the orange glare of the ironworks on the opposite shore. Streetlights and lamps strung along the bridges stood out like tiny beacons. The white gleam of a searchlight swept across the scene as a steamer picked out a landing. The deep, discordant boom of her whistle echoed from the hills as the boat pushed its flat bow against the bank. The scene was less romantic in daylight. The boats looked like dirty white houses set on flat scows only a

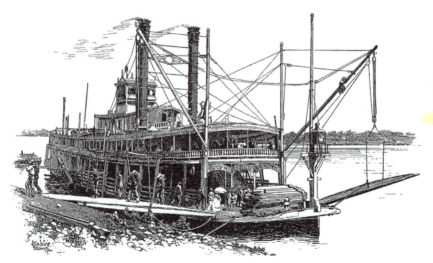

7.15. In July 1889 *Century Magazine* printed this engraving of a typical packet steamer that carried both cargo and passengers on American inland rivers. The vessel shown is a stern wheeler.

few inches above the water. Where were the bright paint and graceful lines of the earlier floating palaces? The grace and beauty of the side-wheelers was replaced by more utilitarian stern wheelers. Only the tall smokestacks were reminiscent of the older side-wheel clippers. W. D. booked passage on a small steamer bound for Wheeling, where passengers would board other boats for service to Cincinnati and beyond. The fare was only $2. The river was low, even in November, and the gossip among the other passengers predicted a slow trip and the likelihood of spending hours stuck on sandbars. The cabin smelled of coal smoke and kerosene. Soon after the boat departed Pittsburgh, the dinner bell was sounded. There were only fifteen cabin passengers who rushed to the table. Once seated they were intent on eating. There was no conversation, and no one showed any sign of recovering from their sullen manner. The meal consisted of cornbread squares, very tough beefsteak, and boiled and sweetened water that was served as coffee. The group that sat around the table was poorly dressed, and only two of the men wore shirt collars. Because conversation was so scarce, there was little else to do but go to bed early. W. D. walked back to his stateroom, but upon opening the door he thought he had mistakenly stepped into a pantry. Before him were two wooden shelves and a pile of napkins. The shelves were actually bunks, and the napkins were sheets and bedding. The compartment was otherwise empty. There was no washstand or chair. Our New York dandy adopted a frontier mind-set and went to bed, making do with the chamber as it was. Around midnight he woke up. The engines were barely running, and a deckhand was out on the forward deck taking soundings. They were in low water; the sounding registered just 30 inches. The hull then caught on a mud bar, but she managed to pull over it. Forward progress was very slow as the boat stopped, backed up, and then moved ahead once again. The morning arrival was delayed until 11:00 A.M. W. D. asked about going on to Cincinnati but was

RIVER STEAMERS   217

told the river was falling and all the big packets were tied up. He could go ahead by switching from one small boat to another, but that would likely take a week. W. D. walked uptown and took a train that arrived in Cincinnati in twelve hours.

Once in the Queen City W. D. felt he was duty bound to continue his river journey. An overly helpful runner directed him to the steamer *Paris C. Brown.* The runner insisted that the *Brown* was an excellent packet in every way and was scheduled to leave that afternoon at 5:00 AM for New Orleans. W. D. was eager to get on with his trip and did not want to spend another day in Cincinnati, so he bought a ticket to Memphis for $12. He had high hopes for the *Brown,* having been told she was one of the best on the river. He expected to find the legendary splendors of the inland river steamboats, but discovered her to be rather sad and dingy. His eyes watered, not from joy, but from sadness and disappointed hopes. She was large, but the only decoration was a large photographic portrait of her namesake near the front of the main cabin. Otherwise the *Paris C. Brown* was like a large barge with a big paddle wheel at one end. The staterooms were grossly misnamed and were just large enough for a thin man to turn around in. There was a bunk bed and a mirror but nothing else, not even a stool. The chamber was dark and unwholesome, and the bedding was unclean. W. D. explored the upper decks some 50 feet above the water. The hurricane deck was actually the roof of the main cabin, and it had an uncomfortable way of yielding under foot. However, sometime later a farm wagon and some five hundred empty oil barrels were loaded onto the same roof, and it was clear that this springy structure was capable of sustaining a great weight.

The passengers ambled on board dressed in old suits, flannel shirts, slouch hats, and muddy boots. None had enough money to go by train. Some were good folks, surely, though not affluent. First-class passengers no longer went by river except for short excursions. There were about thirty woodcutters taken on board. They and their kin were heading to the Red River to cut timber in the swamps. They were known up and down the river as swampers. Once the boat was under way the swampers would sit on the upper decks and fire revolvers at ducks and other objects along the shore. This annoying sport continued as long as there was enough light to see a target.

Mealtime found everyone in the main cabin. This included a sizable number of children who were described as an ill-bred, dirty, and unmannerly lot of brats as had ever been collected together. They ate with the adults and were enough to take away one's appetite – that is, if the sodden and greasy appearance of the food were not enough to suppress one's hunger. Since the parents ignored their offspring, the waiters took time from their normal serving duties to cut up the meat and mash the potatoes for these little cherubs. Red napkins were used, because they were less likely to show the effects of a week of usage.

W. D. was alarmed at the amount of freight taken on board before the departure. Cargo was piled high everywhere on the vessel, including the roof. Barges were lashed onto either side of the boat and they were full. The captain advised W. D. that more freight would be picked up all the way to Memphis. True to his word, the captain stopped at towns and landings every few miles. The roustabouts rested between the stops, but the men never had time for any real sleep. The stage was dropped and men moved boxes and barrels off and on the boat. The bell would ring, followed by two or three blasts from the whistle, and the boat was soon back in the middle of the river. Her progress was recorded by clouds of black coal smoke.

The *Paris C. Brown* reached Louisville about sixteen hours after leaving Cincinnati, which was good time considering the number of cargo stops. The two barges were removed and the *Brown* would have to go over the falls, because the canal was undergoing repairs. A special pilot was hired to steer the boat through the rapids and crooked channel that ran near the Indiana side of the river. The passengers gathered on the roof for a better view of this exciting "scoot." The water raced and boiled over the rocks as the boat slid along and tilted down toward her bow. All went well during the first part of the scoot. Many passengers went below thinking the fun was over. And then there was a grinding sound from the bottom of the hull, followed by four sharp bumps. The boat continued ahead, but within seconds a deckhand shouted, "She's full of holes!" Those passengers still on the roof went below. At the same time, several roustabouts ran up to the main cabin and began pulling mattresses, quilts, and pillows to stuff into the holes in the hull. This would stop the leaks temporarily.

The captain and crew kept their heads and remained at their duty posts. The pilot guided the boat through the rapids into calmer water at the base of the falls. The clerks tried to calm the passengers and to get women and children into life preservers. One heroic man who was down inside the hull stuffing bedding into the holes stayed until the water was up to his neck before climbing out. The pilot guided the boat toward the Kentucky shore. There the *Paris C. Brown* sank in 5 or 6 feet of water. The main or lower deck was dry, and everyone was safe. Four other steamers came alongside and hooked up hoses to pump water out of the stricken vessel's hull.

The pumps worked their magic by ten o'clock that evening. The hold was dry enough to fasten planks over the holes that were clustered in only one part of the hull. A large wooden box was built around the patches and filled with mud. By Sunday morning, and fourteen hours after the accident, the *Brown* was steaming down the river. W. D. had nothing but praise for the crew and their calm and efficient handling of this emergency. These simple men were responsible for saving everyone on board and seemed to consider their actions a normal part of working on the inland waterways.

A decade after the *New York Times* article on the decadence of river passenger service, another reporter, Julian Ralph (1853–1903) prepared a sketch about Mississippi riverboating for *Harper's Monthly*. Ralph wrote many articles about his travels, and his sketches were often published by *Harper's*. It was a nostalgic piece titled the "Old Way to Dixie." It featured the Anchor line of St. Louis, which had been running boats to New Orleans since the 1860s. It maintained a high level of quality service until the end of its operations in 1898 and had a fleet of large, handsome steamers that truly harkened back to the golden age of river travel. Ralph rode the *City of Providence*; a well-appointed and costly vessel built in 1880. He found everything aboard to be first class, from the décor to the passengers. His stateroom had a double bed with room for another bed of equal size. It included a chair, a marble-top washstand, carpeting, and curtains. It was the largest stateroom he had seen on any steamboat. The main cabin was a great chamber, all in cream-white with highlights in gold. The ceiling ribs were supported by ornate columns hung with gilded pendants. At the forward end of the cabin, tables were set for male passengers, while at the other end stood the captain's table, with space for married ladies, girls, and such men who traveled with them. The chairs, tablecloths, walls, and aprons of the waiters were all white. The food was well prepared and nicely served. The men stayed at their end of the cabin, next to a well-kept bar, and the captain and the ladies kept to their end as if they were on a separate boat. The interior of the boat was quiet; landings were made with a deathlike stillness. The whistle sounded only when they were approaching a landing to notify the roustabouts to be ready. They would back off of mud when departing with no whistle signal, and only the long-drawn gasps of the engine's exhaust steam could be heard. The pilots felt there was no need to disturb the neighbors. This trip was a delight for Ralph, who found it to be a pleasant week of rest uninterrupted by the telephone or the rush and bustle of life as it had become by the 1890s.

Baedeker's 1893 guide to the United States was published in the same year as Julian Ralph's trip. It advised tourists that steamer service was available on the Mississippi River from St. Paul to New Orleans for those seeking a leisurely trip. The Diamond Jo line ran boats twice a week in the summer from St. Paul to St. Louis for a fare of just $16. It required four and a half days of travel. The Anchor line offered once-a-week service from St. Louis to New Orleans for $20. The trip required seven days. Few passengers, according to the guide, opted for such a lengthy excursion, but a day or two on the river was a nice change from the dusty railways. Combination rail and river tickets were available for the use of both modes, partway, with liberal stopover privileges. This advisory underscores the obsolescence of river travel for ordinary transportation needs. It was, indeed, the old way to Dixie.

During these twilight years of the packet steamer, boat owners searched for ways to find passengers. River excursions had been popular for short-term vacations, especially for city dwellers looking for a way to escape the summer heat. The boats moved just fast enough to create a breeze as well as a change of scene. Large boats were often marooned during the summer because of low water, yet they could carry a good load of passengers and navigate to nearby destinations. *Harper's Weekly* for June 18, 1881, reported on cheap excursions on the Ohio River. A round-trip fare of 50 cents took passengers on an excursion lasting from morning until midnight. A big boat, such as the *Thomas Sherlock,* could carry from fifteen hundred to three thousand persons. Sundays and holidays, especially the Fourth of July, were bonny days for riverboat men. No liquor was served, but beer and soft drinks were offered. Music was furnished by a band or passengers who brought their own instruments.

The number of passengers was subject to limits imposed by the steamboat inspectors, but these rulings were not rigorously enforced. Some boats were surely overloaded and, considering the possibility of boiler explosions, fires, or collision, were a hazard to all of those on board. Yet no serious accidents were reported. One of the largest crowds handled was fifty thousand attendees to a German singing society that gathered at Cincinnati in 1870. Ten boats were used to carry the crowd to Parlor Grove, about 12 miles south of the city. Each of the boats made two or three trips. Excursion boats remained popular well into the twentieth century, keeping the inland river open to the public as a playground. Fares were cheap, meaning all but the very poorest citizen could enjoy a ride. Some boats had ballrooms and live music. The Streckus line of St. Louis was a family-run enterprise that operated excursion boats for almost a century.

Riverboat passenger travel lingered on into the twentieth century, but on a descending scale. A few new packet boats were built in the 1920s, but the overnight service between Louisville and Cincinnati ended in 1931. Very small operators, such as the Greene line, continued for a few more years, but by 1936 their passenger trade was limited to excursion cruises. Today diesel towboats move millions of tons of coal and other bulk cargoes efficiently along the inland river system. Pleasure boats remain popular on these waters, but at this writing no overnight excursion boats are in service. It is a pity that the scenic beauty of American rivers is no longer available to citizens of the twenty-first century.

SUGGESTED READING

Baedeker, Karl. *Baedeker's United States 1893, with an Excursion into Mexico: A Handbook for Travellers.* Leipzig: Karl Baedeker, 1893.

Banta, Richard E. *The Ohio.* New York: Holt, Rinehart, and Winston, 1949.

Bates, Alan L. *The Western Rivers Steam Cyclopoedium.* Leonia, N.J.: Hustle Press, 1968.

Chittenden, Hiram H. *History of Early Steamboat Navigation on the Missouri River.* New York: Harper, 1903.

Dayton, Fred E. *Steamboat Days.* New York: Frederick A. Stokes, 1925.

Eskew, Garnett L. *The Pageant of the Packets.* New York: H. Holt and Company, 1929.

Ferris, Ruth. *St. Louis and the Mighty Mississippi in the Steamboat Age.* St. Louis: Mercantile Library, 1993.

Gillespie, Michael. *Wild River, Wooden Boats: True Stories of Steamboating and the Missouri River.* Stoddard, Wisc.: Heritage, 2000.

Gould, Emerson W. *Fifty Years on the Mississippi.* St. Louis: Nixon-Jones Printing Company, 1899.

Grayson, Frank Y. *Thrills of the Historic Ohio River.* Cincinnati: Allied Printing [1929].

Hunter, Louis C. *Steamboats on the Western Rivers.* Cambridge: Harvard University Press, 1949.

Havighurst, Walter. *Voices on the River.* New York: Macmillan, 1964.

Jackson, Donald. *Voyages of the Steamboat Yellow Stone.* New York: Ticknor and Fields, 1985.

Kane, Adam I. *The Western Steamboat.* College Station: Texas A&M University, 2003.

Lloyd, James T. *Lloyd's Steamboat Directory and Disasters on the Western Rivers.* Cincinnati: J. T. Lloyd & Co., 1856.

Olmsted, Frederick L. *A Journey through Texas, or, a Saddle-trip through the Southwestern Frontier.* New York: Dix, Edwards Company, 1857.

Peterson, William J. *Steamboating on the Upper Mississippi.* Iowa City, Iowa: State Historical Society, 1937.

Read, Frederick B. *Up the Heights of Fame and Fortune.* Cincinnati: W. H. Moore, 1873.

Stevenson, David. *Sketch of the Civil Engineering of North America; Comprising Remarks on the Harbours, River and Lake Navigation, Lighthouses, Steam-navigation, Water-works, Canals, Roads, Railways, Bridges, and Other Works in that Country.* London: J. Weale, 1838.

Tredgold, Thomas. *The Principles and Practices and Explanations of the Machinery Used in Steam Navigation.* London: J. Weale, 1851.

Twain, Mark. *Life on the Mississippi.* Boston: J. R. Osgood, 1883.

Watson, Ken. *Paddle Steamers: an Illustrated History of Steamboats on the Mississippi and Its Tributaries.* New York: Norton, 1985.

Way, Frederick, Jr. *Way's Packet Directory, 1848–1994: Passenger Steamboats of the Mississippi River System since the Advent of Photography in Mid-continent America.* Athens: Ohio University, 1994.

Lake Steamers № 8

On the Inland Sea

NATURE KINDLY DUG FIVE LARGE LAKES ALONG THE NORTHERN border of the United States about twelve thousand years ago. Humans have used these convenient waterways as a means to get around the region since the ice age finally released its frigid grip on North America. The Great Lakes are the largest reservoir of fresh water in the world. They measure from east to west about 1,500 miles long (fig. 8.1). They rank in size, starting with the largest, from Lake Superior to Huron, Michigan, Erie, and Ontario. Superior has places that are 1,000 feet deep; Ontario's mean depth is 400 feet, while Erie's mean depth is only 90 feet. Erie's shallow waters are more easily disturbed by winds, making it stormier than its sisters. She is considered treacherous and dangerous to navigate and so is disliked by sailors. The other lakes can swell up in a grand fury, though they are somewhat more pacific than the Erie. All of the lakes are graveyards of sunken ships and lost seamen.

Even on a calm day, sailing on the Great Lakes can be dangerous. Fog is a common problem, and when you can't see what is ahead, accidents are a certainty. Icebergs are never seen, but thick ice is common after about mid-November. It can get 30 feet thick in places. Hence, navigation shuts down for the winter and doesn't resume until mid-April, except for car ferries and a few other vessels. The shipping season is generally figured at between 225 and 240 days. Tides on the Great Lakes are minimal; Superior has the largest, with a rise of about 3 inches.

As a navigation system, this chain of lakes has a few weak links. Although they are all connected, differences in their elevation cause problems for shipping. Superior is 20 feet above Huron, while Erie is some 325 feet above Ontario. There is also a large descent from Ontario along the St. Lawrence River into the Atlantic Ocean. Man-made improvements in the form of locks and channels have smoothed the way for navigation, but such projects are costly and require years to construct. (More will be said on this subject later in this chapter.)

8.1. The Great Lakes form a giant avenue for travel across middle America.

In pre-Columbian times canoes were skillfully fabricated from animal skins and light wooden framing by the Indian tribes who lived along the shores of the Great Lakes. By the time of the fur traders, some canoes were 30 or 40 feet in length and could carry 3 or 4 tons of goods. Eight men could paddle such vessels 40 miles a day. The first large vessel was built by the French explorer Robert LaSalle in 1679 on the Niagara River in New York. Named the *Griffin,* she sailed as far west as Green Bay, Wisconsin, but disappeared on the return trip and was presumed sunk by a storm. The next large boat did not appear until 1755, and it was a mere sloop. It was built by the British and named the *Oswego.* More European-style boats began to appear after the end of the French and Indian War. John Jacob Astor, a German immigrant who settled in New York City, came to dominate the fur trade. In 1817 he established a trading post on Mackinac Island, Michigan, where Lakes Michigan and Huron meet. At the time, Lake Superior was remote and unsettled. Vessels of any size were not seen on its waters until a schooner named after Astor appeared in 1835. The trading post gave way to a federal fort, and later in the nineteenth century Mackinac became a summer resort visited by yachters and excursion steamers.

As the lands west of the Alleghenies were opened to settlers after the American Revolution, settlements began to appear along the shores of the Great Lakes. Buffalo was an old French settlement that grew into New York's second-largest city. Cleveland was laid out in 1796 by Moses Cleaveland and grew to a thousand inhabitants within twenty years. Detroit was another French settlement started in 1701 that became a busy lake port and, until recent times, the motor capital of the world. As more and more towns were established around the lakes, the need for more boats became apparent. It was found that fully rigged ships with three masts were too labor intensive for lake travel. Barks, or barques, were square rigged but had only two masts and required smaller crews. Two-masted brigs also worked well in moving people and cargo around the lakes, but schooners were soon the most popular style of commercial sailboat on the Great Lakes. A big schooner could be handled by just six men. None of the sailboats could compete with a steamer for swiftness and did well to operate at half the speed of a propeller or a side-wheeler. But where cost was more important than speed, the schooners had no competition.

Grains, lumber, stone, and salt were low-value products that were in no hurry to reach their destination. If they were weeks in transit, rather than days, it made little difference. In 1870 sailboats outnumbered steamboats by four to one. There were 214 barks; 159 brigs; and 1,737 schooners running on the lakes that year. This golden age of sail did not continue for long, however. By 1890 few commercial sailboats were built. The old veterans in the fleet continued working into the 1920s and even the 1930s. Steam then ruled the waves for a few more decades.

THE BEGINNING OF THE STEAMBOAT ERA

The steam era, in terms of a commercial success, began on the Hudson River in 1807. Robert Fulton's North River steamboat was not the first successful vessel of this type but the first that the public accepted as a safe and convenient form of transportation. Fulton's effort to monopolize steamboat operations failed, but it did delay the spread of similar inventions for a time. The Great Lakes did not have one until 1816 when the *Frontenac* appeared on Lake Ontario; she was built at Kingston on the Canadian side of the lake. Next came the *Ontario* in the spring of 1817; she operated across the lake from Oswego to York and Niagara in Canada.

The first steamer launched in Lake Erie was the *Walk-in-the-Water*, named for a friendly Wyandotte chief; it was completed in August 1818 on the Niagara River. She was 136 feet long and carried a good deal of sail to supplement her rather small A-frame engine. The hull was built by Noah Brown, a New York City boat builder who fabricated a fleet for Commodore Perry on the shores of Lake Erie in 1813. He returned to build the steamer five years later. The engine was built in Manhattan by Robert McQueen. It was very much in the style of the engine perfected by Fulton for Hudson River service. The engine was disassembled and hauled in wagons from Albany to Buffalo. The trip required almost a month and

8.2. The *Charles Townsend* was built at Buffalo in 1835 and was retired fourteen years later.

an unknown number of horses. Once completed, the *Walk-in-the-Water* proved a steady, if not very fast, steamer. She ran weekly from Buffalo to Detroit returning via Sandusky and Cleveland. The round trip took five days. The cabin- or first-class fare was $18 dollars; deck passengers could travel for $7. Samuel F. B. Morse traveled on the boat as a young man. In the summer of 1821 *Walk-in-the-Water* carried two hundred passengers as far as Green Bay. The 1,200-mile journey was made in thirteen days. During her last voyage of that year, she was hit by a sudden gale while leaving Buffalo. Her seams began to open, but before she could sink the boat was blown to the beach. The passengers and crew escaped, but the gallant little steamer was a wreck. The engine was soon salvaged and placed in three other lake steamers. It served for some years aboard the *Charles Townsend* (fig. 8.2).

The opening of the Erie Canal in 1825 greatly stimulated traffic on the Great Lakes. Products of the field and forest could now travel from the interior of the nation directly to the port of New York and so up and down the coast of the United States. Grain and salt pork could travel to the Atlantic Ocean and on to European markets. This trade helped towns like Cleveland and Chicago to grow, and in turn encouraged greater passenger traffic. Yet by 1833 there were only eleven steamers on the Great Lakes. Sailboats were too slow and deemed old-fashioned for passengers in a society that considered itself a "go ahead" nation. In 1837 David Stevenson, a Scottish engineer who traveled in North America to study technical subjects, said there were forty to fifty steamers a day in and out of Buffalo during the peak season from spring to early fall. Stevenson also noted that lighthouses, beacons, and buoys had improved the safety of navigation. The Welland Canal and improvements to the rapids near Montreal on the St. Lawrence River had facilitated the movement of boats around the inland seas.

By the time of Stevenson's visit, the problem was too many boats. It would appear that boat builders were very busy after 1833, because rate wars within the next few years led to a cartel whereby boat owners formed an association to control fares and thus guarantee a profit. The first association agreement collapsed in 1836. Fares dropped to a little over 1 cent a mile, and while travelers enjoyed cheap transportation, the boat operators were going broke. A new association, popularly called the Combination, was organized in June 1839. Shares were based on the size and value of the boat. Gross revenues were pooled and 15 percent of this was set aside to run the association. The remaining money was divided up at the end of each month, with the largest share going to the largest and most valuable vessels. It was established that seventeen boats could handle the traffic, meaning the other thirteen boats in the group stood idle unless there was an unexpected rise in traffic. The monopoly was never complete, and none of the schooners would join the cartel. It was generally effective in controlling fares, and most members seemed happy with the agreement because even the idle boats received a share of the profits.

By 1841 the Combination increased its membership to forty-eight boats, which together carried one thousand immigrants a week to Milwaukee. Cabin fares were $20, and deck or steerage passengers went for half that amount to Chicago. Yet enough non-association boats were running that fares were gradually forced down. By 1844 cabin class to Chicago was $14 and steerage just $7. Two years later fares fell again to $12 and $6. In 1847 the People's line ran in opposition to the monopoly and dropped first-class fare to $8 dollars and steerage to $3. The association was dead by June 1848. New shipping was increasing by 25 percent a year in terms of tonnage at this time, and it was very different for the cartel to prevail with so many new boats entering service.

Austrian engineer Franz von Gerstner visited the United States between 1838 and 1840 to gather information on internal transportation. His report, published posthumously in 1842 and 1843, contains a section on lake travel. His comments on the steamer *Erie* give an exact account of the operation of this vessel. The 176-foot-long side-wheeler was built in Erie, Pennsylvania, for the Buffalo-to-Detroit trade. She made the 360-mile run in thirty-seven hours and made six to eight stops along the way. Her running speed was 14 mph. The gentlemen's cabin was 50 feet long. It had fifty three-tier berths. The ladies' cabin was on the deck above but had staterooms instead of the curtain berths. A third sleeping cabin was located on the foredeck. Some freight was carried on the main deck, but none was placed below. During her eight-month season the *Erie* made forty trips and traveled 28,000 miles each season. There were thirty-four members in the crew, which included officers, engineers, firemen, deckhands, porters, stewards, chambermaids, and cooks. Their annual salaries equaled $7,670. A cord of wood powered the *Erie* for 4 miles, and she consumed 180 cords per trip at a cost of $315. Fuel, labor, and other incidental costs came to $700 per trip. The boat itself cost $80,000 and was fully depreciated over ten years. Cabin fares were $8, and deck-class passage cost $3. The gross receipts per trip were $1,200. The boat earned $12,000 a year, which equaled a return of 15 percent.

Thomas L. Nichols recalled the maiden voyage of the *Erie* in the summer of 1839 in his book *Forty Years of American Life*. He offers none of the facts and figures that so occupied Gerstner, but speaks of a jolly cruise involving chats, singing, excellent dinners accompanied with the captain's wine, and beautiful scenery as they made a circle of all five of the Great Lakes. He was a guest of Captain T. J. Titus, who entertained with a generous and hearty hospitality. They stopped at Erie, spent a few hours in Cleveland, visited the picturesque bay of Sandusky, and steamed along the wooded banks of the Detroit River. Nichols commented on the change from the dark blue of Lake Erie to the crystal-clear water of Lake Huron, which became black in its depths. Green Bay was still a military port, Mackinac was a missionary station, and Milwaukee had no harbor. It had a store on the creek and five or six cottages on the bluff. Chicago was a town of perhaps five thousand, and old Fort Dearborn was well remembered by local residents.

The *Erie* remained in service for two more years with Captain Titus still in command. Memories of the happy first cruise were still fresh, but less happy times were ahead. The boat left Buffalo on August 16, 1841. On board were six painters bound for Erie. Their baggage included several large demijohns of turpentine and varnish. The containers were placed on the second deck directly over the boiler. The boat was just 33 miles out in Lake Erie when passengers on the top deck heard a muffled explosion and then a column of black smoke rose above the promenade deck. The smoke cleared and the bemused passengers were assured that all was well; however, red flames soon appeared. The painter's demijohn had started a fire between decks. The boat kept moving ahead, fanning the flames that grew in her innards. Many women and Swiss immigrant passengers were trapped in the decks below. Captain Titus ordered the engines to stop, but the boat kept moving. Three lifeboats were lowered but capsized upon reaching the water. A few passengers tore up bench seating on the upper deck and jumped overboard with enough wood slats to stay afloat for two hours until another steamer, the *DeWitt Clinton,* arrived to pick them up. Captain Titus survived but was seriously burned. Of the approximately 240 on board, only about 50 survived the burning of the *Erie*.

The 1840s was a forward-moving decade on the Great Lakes. The economy had recovered from the lingering effects of the 1837 panic. Some boat owners earned 70 to 80 percent of the cost of their vessel in just one year of operation. Larger and more luxurious passenger vessels were coming into service. These wooden side-wheelers were closely patterned on the Hudson River and Long Island Sound boats. The *Empire*, built in Cleveland in 1844, was one of these splendid boats. She was 254 feet long and was said to be the largest steamboat in the world at the time. Steam whistles began to appear on lake boats at this time. Before their adoption, large bells were the only signaling devices available. The *Empire* was soon outclassed by three deluxe steamers; the *Mayflower, Atlantic,* and *Ocean* were built for the Michigan Central Railroad in the late 1840s. The boats left from Buffalo on alternate evenings at 8:00, Sundays excepted.

Isabella Bird, a British traveler, rode on the *Mayflower* between Detroit and Buffalo in about 1850. She claimed it was the most splendid boat she had encountered and that it was grander than the palaces of England. The main cabin, or saloon, was 300 feet long. The ceiling rose up in a gothic arcade festooned with gilded grapes and vines, panels, and rich moldings. It had eighty-five staterooms that offered space to 300 first-class patrons. Space was provided for 350 immigrants. The engine rose up through the main cabin and, rather than being hidden from view by solid panels, was surrounded by large plate-glass windows so that its elegant molded décor might be seen and its polished steel and bronze parts might be watched while in motion. The great engine was made by the West Point Foundry in Cold Springs, New York. Comfortable sofas were placed nearby so that curious or scientific travelers might sit and watch the steady, powerful strokes of the machinery. The floor of the great cabin was covered in velvet pile carpet decorated with brilliant flowers. The walnut furniture was covered in green velvet. A handsome piano, eight chandeliers, and huge mirrors at the ends of the space completed the décor.

Ms. Bird had expected such a glorious space to be peopled with equally elegant ladies and gentlemen, but instead she observed mostly rustic men in palmetto hats and great boots lounging casually about on the furnishings, which were unsuitable for their support. The area was garnished with porcelain spittoons. These bespattered containers were even found in the ladies' saloon. Ms. Bird found almost no one aboard who was a suitable companion except for one tall lady who was in mourning. Fortunately the sleeping arrangements were more hospitable. She roomed in a separate cabin on a lower deck with several southern ladies. One of the women traveled with her two servants; a second lady traveled with four former slaves she had purchased in order to free them. The beautiful *Mayflower* was lost in November 1854. The fog was thick at the western end

8.3. The *Badger State* (1862) was a wooden-hulled propeller, one of the most popular boat types on the lakes. The arch truss or hog frame near the center of the vessel stiffened the hull.

(Samuel Stanton, *American Steam Vessels*, 1895)

of Lake Erie, and the boat ventured too close to the shore and wrecked on Canada's Point Pelee. Many boats were lost at this place near Leamington, Ontario.

Late in 1841 a new style of boat was introduced on the Great Lakes. It was not grand or elegant like the *Mayflower,* but it would evolve into a distinctive style of boat design not found elsewhere in the maritime world. The *Vandalia* was the first propeller boat on the lakes. She was built at Oswego, New York, with the engine and boiler at the very rear of the vessel. At just 90 feet long she was small enough to pass through the Welland Canal. She had a long and low cabin. A single mast up toward the bow was sloop-rigged. There was no great beauty in the layout of the *Vandalia,* but she cost only $12,500 and proved cheap to operate, with a cruising speed of about 10 mph. The most remarkable feature of this plain little boat was its propulsion by twin screw propellers. Each was $4\frac{1}{2}$ feet in diameter, and they were constructed on the plan of a Swedish-American inventor named John Ericson. The propeller was not a new idea, but Ericson was energetic in advocating its virtues over paddle wheels. Wheels tended to break off these paddlers in heavy ice, while the propeller was generally below the ice and so was not damaged.

More propeller boats began to appear over the next few years, such as the *Samson*. She had a gentlemen's cabin with ten staterooms with paintings and other decoration equal to the best side-wheelers in service. The propeller boats grew in length and soon were built with two decks and a pilothouse at the forward end of the cabin. An arched hog frame stiffened the hull but did little for the beauty of the boat. An engraving of the *Badger State* shows the features of the propeller design (fig. 8.3).

8.4. The *Western World* was built for the Michigan Central Railroad in 1854. The large and elegant vessel operated for only three years.

(*Frank Leslie's Illustrated Newspaper*, June 7, 1856)

Propeller boats were cheaper to operate than side-wheelers. They consumed ten cords of wood a day at a cost of $17, while most side-wheelers used two cords an hour for a daily cost of $80. The typical big side-wheeler ran thirty to thirty-five round trips a season and consumed about five thousand cords of wood a year. Fueling boats would service vessels in motion, so they did not have to stop for wood. By 1860 propeller boats were the most common style of vessel on the Great Lakes. Thirty years later they offered the cheapest freight rates in the nation. They could haul a ton for 1 mile at less than 1½ mills. A ton of coal could be carried for 1,000 miles for just 30 cents. Low tariffs made possible the movement of iron ore over long distances. Low fares kept travelers loyal to lake boats, assuming speed was not an important issue. In 1853 a British traveler named Alexander Majoribanks reported a combination rail-and-lake boat ticket that carried him from Buffalo to Cincinnati for just $10. Meals were included on the boat portion of the trip from Buffalo to Sandusky. A decade later advertisements appeared for pleasure excursions of 2,000 miles and a duration of nine or ten days from Detroit to Cleveland to Lake Superior. Side trips to iron and copper mines of the region were part of the package. The price from Detroit was $22. Meals, berths, and staterooms were included. Servants and children (from three to twelve) went at half price.

The age of the side-wheelers continued until the end of steam navigation on the lakes. Propeller boats may have dominated the inland seas, but their rule was never complete. The Michigan Central Railroad brought out two worthy successors to the elegant *Mayflower* in 1854: the *Western World* (fig. 8.4) and the *Plymouth Rock*. These vessels were designed by Isaac Newton of New York City, the dean of steamboat designs in his day. Newton had made plans for the finest steamers on the Hudson River, which looked nothing like the flat-bottom boats on the inland rivers. The Hudson River craft had deep-water hulls and could race along at speeds never attempted on the Ohio or Mississippi Rivers. The *Western World* and her sister were also built in the same yard that produced a fleet of vessels for the Hudson River and Long Island Sound, the John Englis yard at Greenpoint, Long Island, above Brooklyn. The 1,500 hp beam engine was made by the Allaire Iron Works, on the other side of the East River in New York City. The vessel and its machinery were disassembled and transported in pieces for reassembly at a boatyard in Buffalo.

The *Western World* was 348 feet long and 72½ feet wide over the main deck; the hull was 15 feet deep. There were 150 staterooms and many other spaces, for a total capacity of 1,500 passengers. Two bridal chambers were accessible to newlyweds for an extra change of $5. The décor was described as being regal with white satin bed coverings and cupids suspended from the ceiling. The walls were covered in beautiful floral designs. A sink with hot and cold running water was a novelty in a time when a washbasin and pitcher were normal. The sink had valves with ivory handles. Immigrants were confined to far less handsome quarters on a lower deck. Cabin-class passengers could relax in a giant main cabin with a high ceiling decorated with Gothic, Ionic, and Doric arches and columns. Stained-glass dormers let in filtered light from above. There were fountains with splashing water, satin and lace curtains, rosewood furniture, and splendid mirrors to make the space appear even larger. The dining room seated 200 guests and had a specially made silver service costing $15,000. On the more practical side, the hull had four watertight compartments. Six lifeboats and one thousand life preservers were in place should the vessel founder. The boat cost $250,000 and completed her first trip to Detroit on July 7, 1854. The *New York Times* reported a large and jubilant crowd on the dock as she departed from Buffalo. Passengers commented on the excellent design of the cabins, which allowed a through draft to cool the interior spaces during the summer heat.

During the winter shutdown of 1854–1855, the boilers on the *Western World* were altered to provide more steam and hence greater speed. She now made the cruise from Buffalo to Detroit in just fourteen hours. Railroads in the area were making better time as well, and in 1857 the Michigan Southern and Northern Indiana Railroad built a new direct line between Toledo and Chicago. This new trackage was direct, flat, and fast. Passengers abandoned the big side-wheelers for the new speedway. In the same year, the Michigan Central Railroad lost $50,000 on its marine operations, and big steamers like the *Western World* were put in storage. None were suitable for carrying cargo and thus stood forlornly at the docks until 1863. The engines were removed and returned to New York, where they were installed in new vessels. The hulls of the former railroad

8.5. The *Christopher Columbus* was the only whaleback passenger-carrying vessel built. It operated from 1893 to 1930.

(*The Engineer*, June 16, 1893)

lake fleet were rebuilt as barges or sailing vessels. The *Western World* was converted into a floating drydock.

Iron hulls appeared on the Great Lakes during the decade of the American Civil War. Actually, the U.S. Navy acquired a patrol boat made of iron in 1844. The *U.S.S. Michigan* was built in Pittsburgh by an ironworks firm and sent in pieces by wagon overland to Lake Erie. It was a fair-sized vessel, being 163 feet long. She was renamed *Wolverine* in 1905 and remained in service until 1923 when her engine failed. Efforts to preserve her as a relic failed, and the old veteran was cut up in 1949. The *Merchant*, built by David Bell in Buffalo in 1862, was the first propeller boat built of iron. It was 192 feet long and cost $90,000. It required no hog frame, so it had a less cluttered look than its wooden counterparts.

Some people believed iron boats were noncombustible and unsinkable. Yet the *Merchant* sunk after hitting a reef near Racine, Wisconsin, in 1875, and many a metal vessel burned furiously, as was true of the *Northwest* when she burned at a Buffalo pier and sank in 1911. Iron boats were durable if not indestructible. They were more costly than wooden ships, but a certain percentage of the iron vessels' initial cost was recovered when they were scrapped. Wooden boats had almost no salvage value, and many were worn out after fifteen years of service, yet a few lasted much longer. By 1890 steel was replacing wrought iron for many purposes, including shipbuilding. One of the more curious new steel passenger vessels to appear anywhere in the world was the *Christopher Columbus,* completed in 1893 (fig. 8.5). It was built on the unique whaleboat plan of Alexander McDougall.

The top and bottom of the hull were flat, but the sides were rounded. The bow was described in a British technical journal of the time, *The Engineer*, as "porcine shaped." The large white boat was designed for daytime cruising and had no staterooms or sleeping accommodations, save perhaps a few for the crew. She carried visitors from downtown Chicago a short way down the lake to Jackson Park and the World's Fair grounds. The *Christopher Columbus* could carry five thousand passengers and did a fine trade in carrying passengers during the World's Fair. *The Engineer* described the *Christopher Columbus* as being elliptical in cross-section. The vessel was 362 feet long, 42 feet wide, and 24 feet deep. The hull had a double bottom for water ballast. This greatly stabilized her movement in water, and the ballast could be varied as required by the roughness of the lake. Her maximum speed was 20 mph.

PORTS AND NAVIGATION ON THE GREAT LAKES

Although nature was generous in creating the Great Lakes, it was not at all good about providing harbors, so most lake towns had to build their own. About the only really good natural harbor is that found at Erie, Pennsylvania, yet, curiously, Erie never became a major port. Sandusky, Ohio, and Superior, Wisconsin, also had good harbors, but everywhere else harbors were created by widening rivers and dredging and building breakwaters, which was slow and costly work. In 1833 Chicago was described as a little mushroom of a town that sits on the edge of an empty prairie. Its river formed no harbor, and vessels had to anchor in the open lake. Even after it was improved, Chicago's harbor remained crowded and subject to traffic jams.

Milwaukee was required to perform considerable work on its two small rivers to make room for lake commerce. It cut a new channel to provide a more direct access into the harbor. Cleveland widened the Cuyahoga River for more dock space and became home to a large shipbuilding industry that included the Globe Iron Works. Yet the business of the harbor could be exciting as well, with bells ringing, runners crying out short messages in praise of their boat, steam escapes from vent pipes, brass bands playing on the deck hoping to attract passengers. The water would be covered with graceful yachts, puffing tugboats, four-masters, bulky propeller boats, and excursion boats. The confusion or beauty of the scene would intensify at night as colored lights glowed against the dark sky and steamers whistled their departure signals.

Connecting the Great Lakes so that passage was possible between all of them was the most fundamental improvement possible. Lakes Erie, Ontario, Superior, and Huron were connected by rivers that were not

CLEVELAND, DETROIT, AND LAKE SUPERIOR LINE.

1863. 1863.

The First-Class Low Pressure Steamers **NORTHERN LIGHT** and **CITY OF CLEVELAND** will leave Cleveland for Lake Superior, regularly, on the days named below:

NORTHERN LIGHT, JOHN SPALDING, Commander.		CITY OF CLEVELAND, BENJAMIN WILKINS, Commander.	
Monday, at 8 P. M.	July 6	Friday, at 8 P. M.	July 10
Friday, "	" 17	Wednesday, "	" 22
Wednesday, "	" 29	Tuesday, "	Aug. 4
Tuesday, "	Aug. 11	Monday, "	" 17
Monday, "	" 24	Friday, "	" 28
Friday, "	Sept. 4	Wednesday, "	Sept. 9
Wednesday, "	" 16	Tuesday, "	" 22
Tuesday, "	" 29	Monday, "	Oct. 5
Monday, "	Oct. 12		

These Steamers will leave Detroit on the day following, at 10 A. M.

During the months of July and August, the above Steamers will make

GRAND PLEASURE EXCURSIONS,

Leaving Cleveland on their regular days. On these trips they will carry good BRASS AND STRING BANDS, and every effort will be made to secure the comfort and convenience of passengers. Each point of interest on the route will be visited, giving pleasure-seekers an opportunity to fully enjoy the finest, most healthy, and instructive trip on the Continent.

☞ Passengers will find their advantage in embarking for the trip at Cleveland, in having the first selection of rooms.

For further information, regarding Freight and Passage, address

WILLIAMS & CO., Agents Northern Light.
S. P. BRADY & CO., Agents City of Cleveland.
ROBERT HANNA & CO., Agents, Cleveland, Ohio.

8.6. An advertisement for the Cleveland, Detroit, and Lake Superior line.

(John Disturnell, *The Great Lakes, or Inland Seas of America*, 1863)

navigable. Overland portages offered a temporary but not very economical connection in both cases. In 1825 work started on the Welland Canal, which would parallel the Niagara River and unite Lakes Erie and Ontario. It was completed in 1829 but was large enough only for small ships. This canal had to overcome a difference in elevation of 326 feet in 27.6 miles. As built, it had too many locks and was in general too small. Because it was entirely within Canada, which was, at the time, a large but poor nation, funding was not available for a better canal. A private company took on the job with limited capital. When the Welland Canal opened in November 1829 there were forty locks. Four years later the lock size was increased to 110 feet by 22 feet by 8 feet deep. In 1841 the government of Upper Canada purchased the canal and began a program of improvements. The number of locks was reduced to twenty-seven and the canal could now handle boats drawing 9 feet of water. By 1887 the canal was deepened again, this time to 14 feet, but it was still too shallow for many boats. The year 1870 saw 2,884 U.S. vessels and 3,856 Canadian vessels pass through the Welland Canal. Just three years earlier Canada had consolidated and achieved dominion status. It was on its way to independence from the British Empire. It constructed a transcontinental railway and found funding to construct a completely new Welland Canal between 1913 and 1932.

The St. Lawrence River flows from the east end of Lake Ontario to the northeast, passing the cities of Ogdensburg, Montreal, and Quebec on its way to the Gulf of St. Lawrence and into the Atlantic Ocean. For most of its 1,000-mile length the river is navigable; however, the western end is a broken series of lakes and rapids. If these obstacles to navigation could be reworked or improved, ships could enter and leave the lakes and sail the oceans of the world. The potential for trade encouraged by cheap water transport was enormous. The cost of taming the rapids with locks and canals was significant, and the work proceeded slowly as a result. Among the more troublesome of the rapids were those at the Long Sault (French for "leap"), about 75 miles above Montreal, and the Lachine Rapids above Montreal. Work was finished at Lachine in 1825 on a small canal that was large enough for boats of only 4½ feet draft. In the 1840s its depth capacity was doubled. The capacity was later increased to boats with a 14-foot draft. The Long Sault underwent improvements between 1834 and 1843, and it, too, was enlarged in 1885 for larger vessels.

Passage to the Atlantic Ocean via the St. Lawrence River was improved. Sailboats began to carry wheat to England in 1844. Five years later the *Eureka* left Cleveland for San Francisco. This required sailing around South America, a journey that took months to complete. International travel was never robust, because the canals and locks were big enough for only the smaller commercial vessels. In 1898 a report stated that lake traffic following the St. Lawrence River was largely limited to Canadian boats that carried cargo to Montreal and the Canadian seacoast. The tonnage was hardly worth reporting. The big shipments were transferred from lake boats to the Erie Canal and the railroads that served Buffalo. The St. Lawrence route remained little more than a grand promise until the St. Lawrence Seaway, a system of canals, channels, and locks on the river, was opened in 1959, and even then it soon proved too small for the ships of succeeding decades.

Boats of moderate size had little trouble descending the rapids as long as the water was reasonably high. Even after the rocks were cleared from

8.7. Running the rapids along the Upper St. Lawrence River was an exciting experience for tourists. Regular shipping used the canal and locks built along the side of the river.

(*Harper's Monthly*, September 1881)

the north side of the Lachine Rapids, some passenger steamers continued to shoot the rapids as a tourist attraction. It was a thrilling ride that caused some white-knuckle moments, but in reality it was as safe as most amusement park rides (fig. 8.7). Passengers stood on deck clinging to the rail, where they would shout with enthusiasm or hold their breath in fear, depending on the state of their nerves. The boat would sway, shiver, and careen as the water boiled up in waves up to 12 feet high. It was like being at sea in a violent storm – the boat would charge ahead in water moving at 40 mph. The engines would be shut down, and four men would stand at the wheel in the pilothouse to make sure the boat ran straight ahead and did not turn in the slightest degree sideways in raging water. Four more men would be back at the rudder post, which had an iron tiller attached in case the rudder chains should break. And then the mad journey was over as the steamer glided into smooth waters again and soon passed under the giant iron bulk of the Victoria Railroad Bridge.

In June 1857 *Ballou's Pictorial Magazine* ran a feature on shooting the rapids on the Long Sault. Nine miles of continuous rapids were divided in the middle by an island. Passengers gained an extra measure of confidence when the well-known Indian pilot Batiste stepped aboard to man the wheel (fig. 8.8). This well-muscled fellow with his somber but confident appearance was a man of considerable nerve and skill and so was well equipped for this dangerous mission.

A canal was needed at the western end of the lakes to connect Huron and Superior at Sault Ste. Marie, Michigan. The waters of Lake Superior flowed down the St. Mary's River into Huron, but the fall was 20 feet and no boat of any major size could pass. A portage road carried goods and

8.8. Batiste was a skilled pilot who steered excursion boats through the rapids of the St. Lawrence River.

(*Ballou's Pictorial Drawing Room Champion*, June 6, 1857)

passengers between the lakes. The traffic was comparatively light, because there was so little settlement in the region. After Michigan became a state in 1837 there was more interest in building a canal around the falls of the St. Mary's River. There was talk and visiting contractors, but no progress was made. In 1844 copper was discovered on the Keweenaw Peninsula. A mountain of iron was found in the Marquette Range at about the same time. Shipping was needed to exploit these mineral deposits. President Polk vetoed a bill that would have helped finance a canal. In 1852 President Fillmore signed legislation that gave 750,000 acres of government land to finance the project. Charles T. Harvey (1829–1912) was put in charge.

Ground for the Sault Sainte Marie Canal was broken on June 4, 1853, with Harvey moving the first wheelbarrow of dirt. He imported labor from Detroit, because local men were opposed to the canal, feeling it would end their jobs in portaging cargoes. Harvey soon had two thousand men at work. He pushed and cajoled them to work faster, and his energy and good planning got the job ready before its deadline. The canal was only a little more than a mile long, but it was built on a generous scale,

8.9. One of the locks at Sault Ste. Marie as it appeared in 1891.

(*The Engineer*, November 27, 1891)

unlike the Welland Canal. It was 115 feet wide and 12 feet deep. The locks were 350 feet long and 70 feet wide. It opened in June 1855 and made travel possible between the upper and lower Great Lakes. Larger locks were opened in 1881. Eighteen thousand boats passed through canal in 1897. A few years later traffic in terms of tonnage through the Sault Ste. Marie Canal (commonly known as the Soo) was several times larger than that passing through the Suez Canal (fig. 8.9).

ACCIDENTS ON THE LAKES

We have already mentioned several accidents in this chapter, enough to advise the reader that the travel on the Great Lakes was no safer than other forms of travel. No exact record has been established for the loss of vessels on the lakes, but the estimates range from five thousand to ten thousand, and this does not include pleasure craft. The bottom of Lake Erie is littered with remains of sunken vessels. Storms were the cause of many losses, but human error was surely a reason for disasters as well. Some losses stemmed from the lack of good harbors; from 1834 to 1842 about ten boats a year sank, because they could find no safe haven to escape storms. Yet even in mild weather years, such as 1860, a total of 377 wrecks and the loss of 594 lives were recorded. In November 1869 a four-day squall blew in early in the month, starting at the Soo and blowing across Lakes Huron, Erie, and Ontario, and then out to sea. Estimates of ship loss range from 97 to 138, but no one attempted to calculate the loss of lives for this big blow. Another giant storm, in November 1913, began as just another early winter storm but picked up speed on the second day. Winds were up to 80 mph, and waves were reported as high as three stories. It proved to be the most powerful storm on record up to that time, pulverizing not only ships but docks, too, and much else along the shoreline. Chicago's newly made Jackson Park, site of the 1893 World's Fair, was washed away. Milwaukee's massive breakwater was pounded to rubble by Lake Michigan. Even the lightship at the entrance to Buffalo's harbor was destroyed.

Boats went down even in calm seas. In September 1860 the elegant side-wheeler *Lady Elgin,* named for the wife of the governor general of Canada, was on her way back to Milwaukee with a special excursion party. The passengers were mostly Irish supporters of Stephen A. Douglas who had gone to Chicago to support their presidential aspirant. The night was dark and foggy. The *Lady Elgin* was aglow with lights. A heavily laden schooner named the *Augusta,* running under full sail but showing no lights, was on a collision course with the *Lady Elgin.* The *Augusta* hit its target squarely amidships. The captain of the *Elgin* assumed the damage was minor and signaled the schooner to sail on. It was 2:00 AM and the Irishmen and their ladies were very much awake, dancing and partying as if nothing had happened. The steamer was taking in water rapidly and began to sink bow first. She went under in twenty minutes, before any of the lifeboats could get under way. Of the 398 people aboard only 98 survived. If only the *Augusta* had stood by, most of the crew and passengers might have been saved.

Ironically, the greatest loss of life on the Great Lakes was experienced with a boat at dock. There was no fire, explosion, collision, or storm involved in the sinking of the *Eastland* at Chicago on July 24, 1915. The *Eastland* was completed at Port Huron, Michigan, in 1903 as a four-deck, twin-screw passenger vessel intended for express service. She looked like a small ocean liner but proved too slow to be an express boat. She was demoted to excursion work and ran between Cleveland and Cedar Point Amusement Park near Sandusky, Ohio. In 1913 she returned to Lake Michigan to run between Chicago and St. Joseph, Michigan. Her new owners were not aware of her stability problems or that she had come close to capsizing during her first years of operation. Ballast tanks were added to correct this deficiency, but, like most lake boats, the *Eastland* had a flat bottom and a small keel.

The sinking of the *Titanic* in April 1912 had created much public excitement over issues of safety at sea. The U.S. Congress indicated its interest in the matter by passing the LaFollette Seamen's Act in March 1915. The law was also applicable to passenger ships on the Great Lakes, so the *Eastland*'s owners added a considerable number of lifeboats to the top deck. At about the same time, they poured a layer of concrete on the dining room floor and the main deck. All of these well-intended improvements added greatly to the boat's top-heaviness. The additional lifeboats allowed the steamboat inspectors to certify that the vessel was safe for twenty-five hundred passengers. Yet the federal law had inadvertently turned the *Eastland* into a death trap, because she was now more unstable than ever before.

She ran several trips lightly loaded that summer. On July 24, 1915, she was booked for a maximum load consisting primarily of employees from Western Electric Company, mostly young employees and their children. Boarding began at 6:40 in the morning at the dock on the Chicago River (now Wacker Drive) between LaSalle and Clark Streets in the very heart of downtown Chicago. As people came aboard, the ship would list to port (left) or starboard (right). The engineer pumped water to and from the ballast tanks to correct the tilt, but he was unaware that so much weight had been added to the upper decks earlier that year. The gangplank was pulled up at 7:18 with 2,573 on board. The boat was to depart in twelve minutes, and some of the lines had already been cast off. The tilt was now decidedly to port and the boat was leaning away from the dock. The engineer's efforts to bring her up to an upright position failed, and at 7:28 AM she began a slow fall onto her side and into the Chicago River. Half of the boat was now underwater. Anyone inside was thrown into the submerged side of the vessel, furniture and other articles piled on top of them. Those on the high side of the boat scrambled to get off, assuming they were not thrown into the water.

The surface of the river was covered with people, some swimming, others holding on to the few bits of wreckage. Those who could not swim went quickly to the bottom. Small boats appeared to rescue those within reach. Bystanders on either side of the river threw in boxes, crates, and lines trying to save the victims. A few heroic men jumped in to pull out anyone needing help. Police, firemen, and the Red Cross were soon on the scene, and a more organized rescue effort got under way. Ambulance crews carried the wounded to hospitals, but it was already too late for many; some passengers were dead within minutes of the capsizing. A temporary morgue was set up in the basement of a nearby building. Around ten o'clock, firemen used torches to cut a hole in the side of the vessel and pulled out forty people.

The Cook County coroner put the death toll at 812, but the *Chicago Tribune* and later historians, such as George W. Hilton, claimed it was 844. The legal action following the tragedy was prolonged and unsettling. The steamboat operators were absolved of any criminal intent, and the crew was not convicted of negligence or any other crimes. The suits over wrongful deaths went on for more than twenty years, but according to naval law the claims were limited to the salvage value of the vessel, which in this case was only $46,000. The survivors of the victims never collected anything. The *Eastland* was not seriously damaged by the accident. She rested in storage for some time and was sold to the U.S. Navy in 1918 for conversion into the light gunboat renamed the *Wilmette*. Her upper decks were cut down, and in this new profile she would serve the navy for many years. She returned to Chicago and was stationed at a Randolph Street slip. No one could imagine this navy vessel was the former *Eastland,* a boat that had suffered the worst disaster in Great Lakes history. She was retired in 1945 and cut up two years later.

THE END OF LAKE PASSENGER SERVICE

Commercial travelers, including immigrants, had largely abandoned lake boats by 1860. The speed of railway travel captured the first-class trade quickly while cheap, special rail fares won over the immigrants. Even so, the passenger lake steamer continued running but on a much smaller scale. They survived by offering a more relaxed way to go and were in fact more of an excursion service rather than a bona fide transportation carrier. In pre–air conditioning days, train travel was hot and dusty. Passengers might get to their destination much quicker but often arrived exhausted and ill-tempered. The boats offered a breezy deck, a private cabin, good food, and a beautiful natural scene over the freshwater seas.

One of the early lines to survive into the twentieth century by adopting to the travel realities of the time was the Detroit and Cleveland (D&C) Steam Navigation Company. It started in 1850 with a single boat but by 1869 was large enough to incorporate. They offered overnight service between Detroit and Cleveland and extended regular operations to Chicago. The D&C was profitable enough to attract a takeover by James McMillan and several of his associates in 1878. As a railroad president, a railroad car builder, and a U.S. senator, McMillan was wealthy and influential. Soon after acquiring the D&C line he established the Detroit Dry Dock Company, which, naturally enough, built boats for his steamship line. Frank E. Kirby designed boats for McMillan that were not only large but also equaled the most famous Long Island Sound boats of the time. Kirby was a gifted designer and planned vessels that were reliable, stable, and attractive. The *City of Detroit II* (1889) was 300 feet long and 72 feet wide. She carried twenty-five hundred passengers and 800 tons of freight. Her 2,700 hp engines drove her at an average speed of more than 18 mph. The boat was lighted by electricity and steered by steam-powered rudder. The grand saloon was finished in mahogany and stamped leather, and the boat cost $350,000. Passage on a special four-and-a-half-day excursion to Mackinac was $7 round trip. Meals cost 50 cents, an upper berth was $4, and a lower berth cost $6. Room accommodation for two was $9. Kirby's *City of Cleveland III* (1907) was a large vessel that continued in service until June 1950. Two simplified sectional drawings of the boat are reproduced in figure 8.10. The exceptionally decorative Grand Stairway of this floating palace may be seen today at the Dossin Great Lakes Museum in Detroit.

The D&C did well financially through the 1920s, but its revenues were reduced by three-quarters during the depression of the next decade.

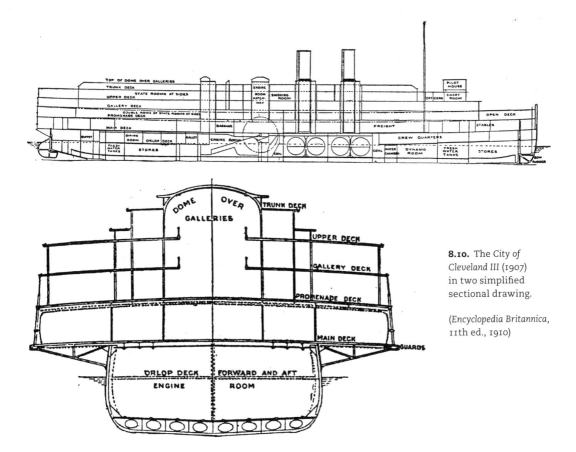

8.10. The City of Cleveland III (1907) in two simplified sectional drawing.

(Encyclopedia Britannica, 11th ed., 1910)

Service to Chicago was ended in 1938, and the line's larger boats were put into storage. By the end of World War II traffic showed signs of a revival. The McMillan family decided it was a good time to sell the line, and new owners took over in 1947. In June 1950 a collision put the *City of Cleveland III* out of service. The D&C suspended operations in 1951. Travelers were now wedded to the automobile and efforts to revive the line were unsuccessful.

A few other Great Lakes steamship lines should be noted before concluding this chapter. The first of these operations was established in 1892 by T. F. Newman, the general agent for the D&C line. Newman suggested that D&C open an overnight line to Buffalo, but when his plan was rejected he found other entrepreneurs to back him. Service on the 189-mile route began in April 1893 with two secondhand steamers. Within a few years the Cleveland and Buffalo line was prosperous enough to order a new vessel. Good times continued, for the new line was grossing over $.5 million a year by 1911. The company commissioned Frank Kirby to design a new, large side-wheeler with seven decks. With four smokestacks she was large and impressive, if not notably handsome. Her 510 staterooms could accommodate fifteen hundred passengers, but she could handle thirty-three hundred day passengers. The $2 million vessel was ready for

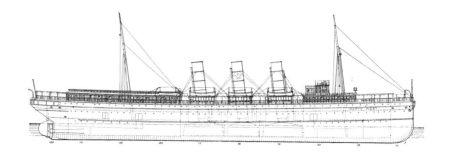

8.11. The *Northwest* was built in 1894 for a subsidiary of the Great Northern Railway to offer fast services from Buffalo to Duluth.

(*The Engineer*, Feb. 8, 1895)

service in June 1913. The winning name in a name-the-boat contest for her was the *Seeandbee*.

The big boat's appearance was ill timed, because the *Eastland* disaster had reduced enthusiasm for lake excursions. The LaFollette Seamen's Act required such large crews that the *Seeandbee* could be run at a profit only during the warm weather season. The Cleveland and Buffalo line operated through the prosperous 1920s without difficulty, but traffic declined quickly in the hard times of the next decade, and the company was bankrupt by the spring of 1937. It was reorganized and resumed operations briefly but collapsed in 1939. A Chicago investor bought the *Seeandbee* in 1941 for $135,000. This proved to be an excellent investment, because the entry of the United States into World War II created a demand for reusable vessels. The U.S. Navy purchased the *Seeandbee* for $750,000 and promptly rebuilt her as an aircraft carrier. Renamed the *Wolverine,* the boat remained on the Great Lakes as a training vessel. She was retired in 1946 and cut up for scrap the following year.

James J. Hill was seeking a way to attract more passengers to travel over his Great Northern Railway in the early 1890s. There were so many transcontinental lines radiating from Chicago and St. Louis that the Great Northern had no special advantage to offer travelers in terms of speed or comfort. Hill felt that direct, fast steamer service from Buffalo, New York, to Duluth, Minnesota, might entice travelers to choose the Great Northern for the remainder of the trip to the West Coast. By terminating at Duluth, travelers could avoid all the hassle of changing trains in Chicago, which involved a slow and vexing transfer between stations. Duluth was a small place, and the train would be waiting at the dock to pick up through passengers as they walked off the boat. The Northern Steamship Company was organized for this purpose. Two ocean-style boats were built in Cleveland for the 1,100-mile, sixty-hour trip. Between Buffalo and Duluth, stops were made at Cleveland, Detroit, and Sault Ste. Marie. Two engines per boat produced 7,000 hp and an average speed of 20 mph. The interiors were outfitted to be equal to the best hotels. Accommodations were "en suite" and very elegant, with several rooms together like a small apartment. Brass bed stands and elegant parlors and baths were decorated

8.12. The *Chicago* was built in 1874 as a wooden-hull side-wheeler. It served the Goodrich line until 1915.

(Fred I. Dayton, *Steamboat Days*, 1928)

in perfect taste. Meals were prepared by high-priced chefs. Passengers could see beautiful scenery along the shore or on passing islands and enjoy all the pleasures of an ocean voyage for a low price. In an advertisement in the June 1898 *Harper's Monthly* magazine, travelers were assured they would find no Spanish cruisers on America's inland seas, a reference to the war then under way.

The *Northwest* was the first of the Northern Steamship Company line to enter service (fig 8.11). She made her first trip in June 1894 and looked perfect with an all-white hull. Her sister, the *Northland,* began running soon afterward. In 1911 the *Northwest* burned at her pier in Buffalo and sank. She was not raised until 1918 when a shortage of ships promoted her rebuilding. The locks of the Welland Canal were too short for the hull, so it was cut in two. The halves were being towed across Lake Ontario when the forward section sank. It was salvaged and towed to Lauzon, Quebec, where the two sections were reunited and given a new bow. The reconstituted boat operated until 1940 when it was rebuilt for ocean service. In February of the following year it was torpedoed and sunk off the coast of Ireland.

A few major lines were started by individuals such as Albert E. Goodrich (1826–1883). He started in lake service at the bottom, as a clerk on a small steamer in 1847. In just nine years he was a director of the Clement Steamboat Line. Later in 1856 Goodrich decided to establish his own business, and by 1860 he had several boats in operation. The operations grew so quickly that he incorporated his business in 1868. By this time Goodrich had expanded his service all around Lake Michigan. The focus was in connecting towns large and small along the lake's shore, so one boat would stop at Whitehall, Michigan, and make one small loop after another to stop at each community along the way to St. Joseph. From this eastern shore settlement, the vessel would cross Lake Michigan to Chicago.

The service on the Goodrich line was slow, but it satisfied many commuters who depended on it. It could be as fast as rail service, which was often indirect. Goodrich offered direct service from Michigan City, Indiana, to and from Chicago. The longest line went north from Chicago along the western bank of Lake Michigan to Racine, Milwaukee, and other towns, and on to the top of the lake at Escanaba, Michigan. It then proceeded to St. Ignace and Mackinac Island. Most service on the Goodrich line was the unglamorous business of moving ordinary people and freight. The boats tended to be plain and economic without grand stairways, fancy cabins, or superior food. An example of Goodrich's fleet is shown in figure 8.12, a reproduction of the side-wheeler *Chicago*. This wood-hulled vessel enjoyed a busy service life from 1874 to 1915. The goal was affordable transportation. However, Goodrich did venture into the excursion business. In 1898 his company acquired the whaleback *Christopher Columbus* for daytime service between Chicago and Milwaukee. It proved very popular and did a fine business for a $1 excursion fare. A third deck was added in 1899 to offer more space for merrymakers. But hard times finally caught up to the whaleback; she was laid up at the end of the 1930 season, and after six years in storage the *Christopher Columbus* was cut up.

Time was running out for the Goodrich line itself by the late 1920s. The automobile had replaced it as a local carrier. Efforts to salvage the company failed, and in November 1930 it was in receivership. As the economic depression worsened, Goodrich slipped into insolvency. All operations ended in July 1933.

Freight service continues today on the Great Lakes at a reasonably high level, but passenger service has all but disappeared. A few tour boats can be found around the larger harbors, and car ferries still handle passengers, but the great days of lake travel have disappeared.

SUGGESTED READING

Barry, James P. *Ships of the Great Lakes: 300 Years of Navigation.* Berkeley, Calif.: Howell-North, 1973.

Dayton, Fred E. *Steamboat Days.* New York: Stokes, 1928.

Elliott, James L. *Red Stacks over the Horizon: The Story of the Goodrich Steamboat Line.* Grand Rapids, Mich.: Eerdmans, 1967.

Disturnell, John. *The Great Lakes, or Inland Seas of America.* New York: Scribner, 1863.

Gerstner, Franz Anton von. *Die innern communicationen der Vereinigten Staaten von Nordamerica, 1842–1843.* Reprinted and translated as *Early American Railroads.* Stanford, Calif.: Stanford University Press, 1997.

Hilton, George W. *The Great Lake Car Ferries.* Berkeley, Calif.: Hilton, 1962.

———. *The Night Boat.* Berkeley, Calif.: Howell-North, 1968.

———. *Lake Michigan Passenger Steamers.* Stanford, Calif.: Stanford University, 2002.

———. *Eastland Legacy of the Titanic.* Stanford, Calif.: Stanford University, 1995.

Havighurst, Walter. *Great Lakes Reader.* New York: Macmillan, 1966.

———. *Long Ships Passing.* New York: Macmillan, 1975.

Inches, H. C. *Great Lakes Wooden Shipbuilding Era.* Vermilion, Ohio: H. C. Inches, 1962.

Kuttruff, K., R. E. Lee, and D. T. Glinka. *Ships of the Great Lakes.* Detroit: Wayne State University, 1976.

Lane, Carl D. *American Paddle Steamboats.* New York: Coward-McCann, 1943.

Mansfield, John B. *History of the Great Lakes.* Chicago: Beers, 1899.

Morrison, John H. *History of American Steam Navigation.* New York: Sametz, 1903.

Nichols, Thomas L. *Forty Years of American Life.* 1864. New York: Stackpole and Sons, 1937.

Read, Frederick B. *Up the Heights of Fame and Fortune.* Cincinnati: Moore, 1873.

Smith, Maurice D. *Steamboats on the Lakes.* Toronto: Lorimer, 2005.

Stanton, Samuel W. *American Steam Vessels.* New York: Smith and Stanton, 1895.

Van Der Linden, Peter J. *Great Lakes Ships We Remember.* Cleveland: Freshwater, 1979.

———. *Great Lakes Ships We Remember II.* Cleveland: Freshwater, 1984.

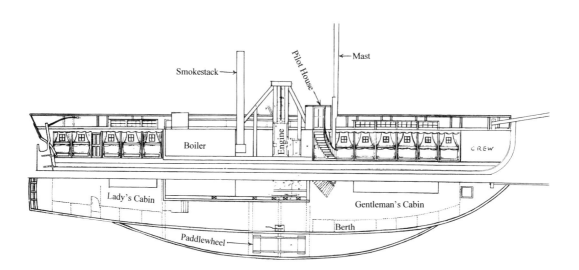

9.1. The *Fulton* was completed in 1813 to the design of Robert Fulton. Because of the War of 1812 it did not enter Long Island Sound service until 1815.

(Jean-Baptiste Marestier, *Marestier's Report on American Steam Boats*, 1824)

Coastal & Sound Steamers   № 9

Close to Shore

THE ATLANTIC SEACOAST WAS THE GREAT HIGHWAY OF COLOnial America. Small ships sailed over these waters from Maine to Florida, stopping at dozens of ports or inlets. The sinking eastern coasts of North America formed numerous natural harbors, inlets, sounds, and bays, all of which encouraged maritime travel. Some boats ventured no more than 100 miles from home while others sailed the length of the coast to New Orleans. Even more adventuresome sailors would circumnavigate South America and head for San Francisco. Such ambitious sojourners covered 14,000 miles in 180 days. Yet most coasters were content with more modest travels and engaged in transfer trade. They would stop at several small ports to gather shipments for oceangoing vessels. The coaster would transfer goods to larger ports where the cargo would be loaded upon a ship heading for Europe or the Far East. In the same way, they would distribute goods or passengers, dropping them off at large ports by the sea to hamlets on the coast. A typical merchantman would take six to ten days to sail from New York to Charleston, a distance of approximately 650 miles. Small sloops were faster, but they could carry only limited cargoes and so were more often used for shorter commuter trips. Steam power offered both speed and capacity, and by the 1830s it began to offer passage between Charleston and New York in three days. Travelers to New Orleans could expect more than a dozen days at sea, often leaving New York by steamer. Such a journey could be pleasant as long as the sea was reasonably calm.

Sailing close to shore meant the ship could seek protection in a harbor, bay, sound, or river. The eastern seacoast offers many such harbors. On the other hand, being so close to the shoreline meant a storm could drive ships onto a reef or rocky point that would send it to the bottom. Locals along the coast made their living by salvaging wrecked ships, and it seemed that every few weeks nature landed a pile of treasure near their front yards. The wrecked ships and their cargo were a rich store of building material, food, and trade goods, so salvagers were opposed to lighthouses

Table 9.1. U. S. Steam Navigation, 1851

Region	Number of Ships	Crew Members	Passengers Carried
Atlantic States	385	6,318	33,144,000
Gulf States	109	3,347	148,000
Pacific States	50	1,418	79,000
Long Island Sound	N.A.	N.A.	382,000

Source: Treasury Report to U.S. Senate, January 1852.

and other navigation safeguards that would end their trade. The best sailing season along the coast was April to November, but there was always the danger of a storm blowing in; these events were almost always a surprise, because there was no weather forecast available. Sea captains kept an eye on the sky to seek some indication of what might be developing.

Pirates were yet another danger along the North American coast because of so many well-laden vessels traveling along this busy trade route. It was said that a person could stand at the coast and see as many as six boats passing at a time. The British navy did a poor job of defending the merchantmen, because they had too many assignments elsewhere in the world. The empire was growing, and His Majesty's service was well engaged elsewhere. During the Revolution and the War of 1812, American shipping became prey to the British fleet. Once these hostilities were concluded, the pirates returned and were not subdued by the U.S. Navy until the 1830s.

Traffic along the coast was stimulated by the growth of population in eastern cities and the expansion of industry in young America. Manufacturing was discouraged under colonial rule. America was to supply raw material to the mother country and import her manufactured goods, but since independence all of that had changed. Industrial towns such as Paterson, New Jersey, were established as early as the 1790s. A cotton mill was set up in Pawtucket, Rhode Island. This meant cotton was transported from the north for New England's textile mills. Molasses came in great drums from Havana and the sugar islands to be processed into sugar and rum. Shipping lines were being established on Long Island Sound; Chesapeake Bay; and the James, Potomac, Delaware, and Hudson Rivers, which fed more travelers and cargo to the coastal ships. In 1888 John Ringwalt estimated that one-half to three-quarters of all American shipping was coastal. Because Britain so clearly dominated world shipping, America concentrated on the coastal trade; however, the country's transatlantic lines tended to be short-lived or feeble. In 1817 the U.S. Congress passed legislation that closed coastal shipping to foreign ships. This protective law would create a nursery for seamen and thus strengthen one branch of the country's marine industry. In 1845 Congress acted again by offering mail subsidies for maritime carriers. The payments were not generous

Table 9.2. U. S. Steam Navigation, 1880

Region	Number of Ships	Crew Members	Passengers Carried
New England	463	N.A.	15,474,000 (of these, 12,629,000 were ferry pass.)
Middle States	1,459	N.A.	135,653,000 (of these, 128,040,000 were ferry pass. and 103,000 were ocean)
South Atlantic	266	N.A.	1,787,000 (of these, 1,502,000 were ferry pass.)
Gulf States	126	N.A.	79,000
Pacific States	319	N.A.	6,604,000 (of these, 6,303,000 were ferry pass.)
Long Island Sound	N.A.	N.A.	937,338

Note: In 1880 there were 56,811 crew members plus 1,032 roustabouts in Western river service. The value of all vessels combined equaled $112 million.
Source: U.S. Census 1880, vol. 8.

but large enough to encourage the expansion of shipping lines by river, lakes, and seas. The effect was to support new steamer lines to Charleston, Savannah, Norfolk, New Orleans, Havana, and elsewhere.

Statistical information on U.S. shipping is difficult to assemble other than data on freight tonnage. However, tables 9.1. and 9.2 provide some idea of steamship activity for 1851 and 1880. (Data for lakes and inland rivers are reported elsewhere in this book.)

LONG ISLAND SOUND

Daniel Webster once referred to Long Island Sound as the "Mediterranean of the western hemisphere." It was the busiest corridor for passenger vessels along the East Coast. Although it generally appears placid and is protected by Long Island from the Atlantic Ocean, the sound is part of the ocean and is just as salty and treacherous. It is about 100 miles long and as wide as 30 miles. It has many fine harbors and inlets with a dozen mid-sized towns. Of more importance, it connects New York with Boston. It would do so directly were it not for Cape Cod. The way around this barrier is an overland portage from one of the coastal cities, such as Fall River. Such travel was initially made possible by stagecoach connections, and by the late 1830s by a series of railroads radiating from Boston.

Nature created a few more defects to travel through the sound. The entrance from the East River at the New York end is hampered by the connecting channel, purposely named Hell Gate, which is short but narrow and rocky. Worse yet, it has two tides – one from Long Island Sound, the other from Sandy Hook. The tides collide at Hell Gate and create whirlpools that pitch small ships around and over the rocks and reefs. It was said in those days that for every fifty ships passing through Hell Gate, one was seriously damaged. In 1851 work was started to remove some of the rocks; more work was done over the next several decades, and by 1885 Hell Gate had lost much of its bite. The channel was 26 feet deep and 200 feet wide at its narrowest place. At the other end of the sound is Point Judith, standing at the lower tip of Rhode Island and the entrance of Narragansett Bay. The problem here is not rocks so much as the confused currents that come together from the sound, ocean, and the bay to produce a swirling merry-go-round that can drive ships against the point. A Stonington Steamship Line advertisement referred to Point Judith as a "dangerous promontory" where waves rose in a fearful violence, making passage, if not always dangerous, at least unpleasant to persons unaccustomed to life at sea.

Sloops carried passengers and household goods along fish-shaped Long Island in colonial times. Large and slower vessels carried the freight. British patrols during the War of 1812 delayed the testing of steam vessels for a few years, but Robert Fulton built an elegant little steamer especially for such service in 1813. She ran on the Hudson River until the British withdrew. Figure 9.1 shows a cutaway drawing of this vessel, named the *Fulton*. She measured about 134 feet long and had the boiler and engine in the center of the vessel. Two-tier bunk beds were built in the cabin. Draw curtains made them into a private compartment. A small cabin at the stern was reserved for ladies. Both cabins had a skylight. The crew slept in the forecastle. She made a trip to New Haven in March 1815; this 75-mile trip took eleven hours. Later she ran to Hartford and Norwich, Connecticut. Her normal running speed was 6½ mph, and her cost was $87,000.

Fulton built a similar boat for service in Russia in 1816, and when the promoters of this venture failed, the vessel was renamed the *Connecticut* and put into operation with the *Fulton*. The little *Firefly* had been tried a year later on a run between New York and Newport, Rhode Island. She was much too slow to win many admirers, taking twenty-eight hours to finish the trip. The packet sloops could outrun her with a favorable wind. They also dropped their fare to 25 cents and sent the *Firefly* into an early retirement. Fulton's reputation was vindicated several years later by the performance of his last ship, the *Chancellor Livingston*. This vessel was completed nearly two years after the designer's death in 1814. She provided good service on the Hudson River by running at 8½ mph and consuming 1½ cords of wood per hour. She was rebuilt with new machinery in 1827 and put into sound service. There she ran three round trips a week between New York and Providence. In 1832 the *Livingston* began the Providence-to-Boston run. Two years later the aging vessel was running between Boston and Portland, Maine.

Meanwhile Fulton's steamboat monopoly had been overruled by the U.S. Supreme Court as an unconstitutional violation of interstate commerce. Only New York and part of Louisiana had agreed to the Fulton and Livingston monopoly. Elsewhere steamboats were operating freely and could run at will through all of Long Island Sound. Many independent operators were contemplating a monopoly of their own by setting up powerful lines of steamers owned by wealthy partners or corporations. Cornelius Vanderbilt was one such operator. Vanderbilt had already made a small fortune from Hudson River boats, so an expansion into sound steamers was only natural. He was not a gentleman in manner or speech, but he was smart, bold, and cunning. He also liked to win. In 1835 Vanderbilt decided to build a sound boat that would win greater traffic for his operations and put his rivals to shame.

The *Lexington* was the commodore's pride. He had personally supervised her construction. She was framed with the best white oak for strength. At 205 feet, she was long and elegant like a racer. In June 1835 she began service between New York and Providence and made the round trip in twelve hours and twenty-eight minutes. Her average speed was over 12 mph, which was a record. A New York newspaper declared her the fastest steamboat in the world. Vanderbilt was happy, and when she hit a reef sometime later at 16 mph and revealed no damage, he was even happier. The *Lexington* performed well in regular service, making three trips a week. The fare was $4, with meals available at an extra charge. The *Lexington* was sold to the Stonington line in part because they offered a good price, and Vanderbilt was always ready to build a new and faster boat. However, the *Lexington* did not go quietly in the night.

The *Lexington* operated on the Stonington line without apparent incident until early 1840. She left New York at 3:00 PM on January 13 of that year bound for Stonington, Connecticut. The line called itself the Great Inside Route because Stonington was just to the east of Point Judith, and passengers could relax knowing they would be spared that hazard. The Providence and Stonington Railroad opened a 93-mile-long rail connection to Boston in 1837 that ranked next to the Fall River line in popularity. The *Lexington* steamed ahead in what promised to be another routine trip. At almost 7:00 PM flames were seen near the smokestacks. Some of the cotton bales stacked all around the boat were on fire. Captain George Child seized the wheel and headed for shore. They were 3 or 4 miles below Eaton's Neck, Long Island, or roughly opposite Norwalk, Connecticut. A fresh wind fanned the flames. Soon the tiller rope was burned in half. The lifeboats were either swamped by overcrowding or were smashed by the paddle wheels. About 150 people on board were killed by the fire or the frigid water of the sound. Four saved themselves by clinging to cotton bales. One of the swimmers floated in this uncomfortable position for two days. The *New York Sun* heralded this major news story by issuing an EXTRA with a lithograph on the front page depicting the horrific scene

9.2. The *Cleopatra* was built in 1836 for Cornelius Vanderbilt and was used on Long Island Sound. Her two boilers were made of copper.

(Samuel Stanton, *American Steam Vessels*, 1895)

of flames and death. Nathaniel Currier, an obscure printmaker, furnished the lithograph and continued to sell it for another eleven years. No longer obscure, Currier would become more famous in later years as a partner of James Ives.

Not all of Vanderbilt's sound steamers met a violent end. The *Cleopatra* had a long and peaceful life. She entered service in 1836 on the New-York-to-Hartford run. Her long and low look was typical for most of the early sound steamers (fig. 9.2). After a few seasons she was assigned to the Providence, Norwich, and New York run. In 1845 Vanderbilt opened a railroad to the end of Long Island at Greenpoint, New York. A dock was built, and steamers such as the *Cleopatra* carried travelers to Providence and other sound ports serviced by the Vanderbilt lines. Travel time was reduced and those passengers in a hurry patronized the Greenpoint line. The *Cleopatra*, unlike her ancient namesake, went out quietly. She never wrecked, burned, or blew up but worked out her last day as an excursion boat in New York Harbor.

George T. Strong (1820–1875) recorded a diary account of his trip on the sound steamer *Massachusetts* dated May 5–7, 1836. Strong was a student at Columbia and was taking a trip to Boston with his father. He booked two berths at the dock and then walked uptown to St. John's Park, where he sat on the grass and visited with a classmate. The next day he left school and went directly to the dock. The *Massachusetts* was a new boat and much like the *Lexington* in size. She had space for 142 berths. Strong estimated there were one hundred people on board. She made her first trip to Providence in thirteen hours and thirty-two minutes. The cabin was in the hold, as was typical of the time, and well fitted out, she cost over $100,000. The trip had not been under way long when they came up to another steamer, the *President*, which was unable to move because of a broken paddle wheel. The *Massachusetts* stopped and took on some of the stranded passengers, which took almost an hour.

Strong got a cup of coffee, walked forward, watched the sound, then went below to read, and at nine he adjourned to his berth. It was narrow but better than the temporary beds set up for the *President*'s passengers. He found sleep difficult – perhaps too much coffee, the motion of the boat, or the serenade of snoring around on all sides kept him awake. At five the next morning he was summoned by his father to go up on deck to witness the specter of Point Judith. For all of its terrible reputation, it looked very placid through the fog. They passed Newport, which Strong described as mean and contemptible looking, then sped up Narragansett Sound, where our young traveler judged the great city of Providence as worse in appearance than Newport. They arrived at a little after 8:00 AM and proceeded directly to the railroad. Strong had never ridden before on a "decent railroad" and wondered about the effects of a fast ride. They were now clicking along at 25 mph, which was very rapid traveling for 1836, yet our cavalier New Yorker perceived no danger or fear. They arrived in Boston at 10:15 AM in perfect condition except for a copious sprinkling of dust. And here our firsthand account of travel in 1836 ends.

Several boat lines were operating on the sound by the 1830s. There were also many independent boats in service, so Long Island Sound was a busy waterway filled with steamers and sailing vessels moving in all directions and patterns, yet taking care never to collide. In 1847 another new line would start up to make the busy waterway more crowded. It began as the Bay State Steamboat Company but would evolve into the famous and long-lived old Fall River line. In 1869 it was merged into the Narragansett Steamship Company by James C. Fisk, the Wall Street speculator. After Fisk's murder in 1872, it was reorganized as the Old Colony Steamboat Company, a subsidiary of the Old Colony Railroad. When that railroad was absorbed by the New Haven Railroad in 1893, its steamboat properties were added to New Haven's New England Navigation Company. This last combination was part of an ambitious scheme by J. P. Morgan to assemble all of New England's public transportation into one company. It would be efficient and would benefit both stockholders and the public. Morgan was a brilliant and able man, but this proved to be one of his mistakes. The Fall River line would remain part of the New Haven Railroad's empire until its final days of operation.

The Fall River line began with just two boats, the *Bay State* and the *Empire State*. The *Bay State* was 317 feet long and 82 feet wide. Her wheels were 38 feet in diameter and 10 feet, 3 inches wide. She made a run from New York to Fall River, including a stop at Newport, in eight hours and forty-two minutes and became known as a sound flyer. Two boilers sat on the guards on either side of the hull. These low-pressure vessels burned 6,500 pounds of hard coal an hour. This hot-burning fuel produced very little smoke. A correspondent for the *Illustrated London News* reported on a visit to the Fall River dock in April 1852, saying that the interior of

9.3A & 9.3B. The *Old Colony* dating from 1865 experienced an unfortunate engine failure in 1878 when one end of the walking beam fractured and crashed through the vessel's cabin. There were no injuries to crew or passengers.

(*Scientific American*, May 25, 1878)

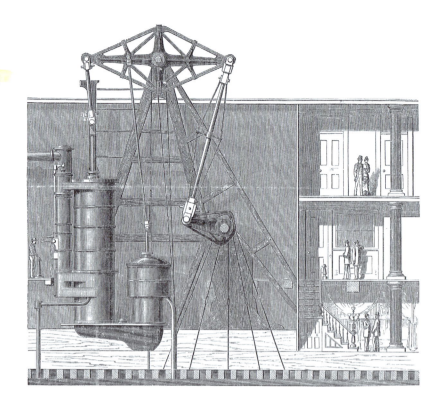

the *Bay State* offered every comfort and luxury a passenger could hope for – rich décor, damask curtains, excellent food, a fine upper deck to view the scenery, and a saloon and cabins that approached splendor. But upon examination of the lower deck the reporter found a large open warehouse suitable for rough cargoes. It was here the immigrants were sent to find a place among the boxes and barrels or perhaps a soft plank in the floor. It was a picture of misery. The reporter noticed that at the end of the trip the hot coals and cinders were raked out of the boiler's firebox directly into the river. A huge flag at the stern of the boat at least 30 feet long read, "*Bay State*."

The *Empire State* was somewhat newer than the *Bay State* and was equally elegant. An English woman traveler, Marianne Finch, recorded a tea aboard this big side-wheeler in 1848. It was held in the main cabin on a long table covered with everything beautiful and edible. There were pineapples, butter, tea cakes, pies, tongue, ham, and all kinds of delicacies served by waiters in white linen uniforms. At the end of the banquet a waiter whispered in passengers' ears "half a dollar." A coin was produced and silently disappeared, not a clink was heard. For all of its refinement of service, the *Empire State* was not a particularly lucky ship. She suffered a boiler explosion, a fire, and two serious groundings in her twenty-three years of service. The *Bay State* was better behaved than the *Empire State*

and ran until 1864 with no major problems. She was lengthened in 1854 to 352 feet. Her engine was removed and placed in a successor named the *Old Colony*. These old beam engines were hard to wear out, so reuse was commonplace. The old engine performed well for many years in the second boat until one day in 1878 the walking beam, the top of which was about 45 feet above the keel, cracked in half. This massive piece of iron, together with the connecting rod, crashed through a partition and stairway, landing on the keel; fortunately, no one was injured. The fact that the beam did not break through the keel saved the boat. A defective forging was likely the cause of the rupture. The good luck of the old *Bay State* had apparently carried over, for the accident could have caused a disaster (figs. 9.3a and 9.3b).

Sound boats of the 1850s continued to grow in elegance and comfort. The *Commonwealth* of 1854 cost $250,000 and was the standard-bearer for a time in terms of style and finish. After just eleven years of service she burned at Groton, Connecticut, and was deemed a total loss. The *Metropolis* combined beauty with speed, and in June 1855 she made a trip from Fall River to New York in eight hours and fifty minutes, averaging 20 mph. She steamed on until 1879. American steamers of the time were seen as splendid and glittering, all white and gold on the outside and grand and elegant on the inside. As more decks were added to make them taller,

9.4. The *Bristol* of 1867 was one of the largest and most decorative sound steamers of her time. She was 375 feet long and had 1,200 berths.

(Asher and Adam's *New Columbian Railroad Atlas*, 1887)

steamers took on a regal yet top-heavy look. But make no mistake, they could cut through the water like a swordfish.

James Fisk Jr., also known as Admiral Fisk or "Jubilee Jim," had been involved in Wall Street investments for many years, but he found steamboats an attractive business, a way to both emulate and annoy Commodore Vanderbilt. In 1865 he purchased two large sound steamers: the *Bristol* and the *Providence*. They were designed and built by celebrated naval architect William H. Webb. The boats were outfitted with rosewood doors, a mahogany stairway, velvet pile carpets, gas lighting, and steam heat (figs. 9.4 and 9.5). At a cost of $1.25 million each, one would expect some luxuries. Fisk added his own touches, too, such as a lavender trim to the paddle boxes, deep yellow for the smokestacks, and 250 gilded birdcages complete with yellow canaries. He dressed the ships' officers in overly elaborate uniforms, with the most ostentatious admiral's uniform for himself. He and his paramour, Josie Mansfield, would stand at the gangplank welcoming passengers aboard. All of this buffoonish behavior seemed to amuse New York society, which only encouraged Fish into great acts of questionable taste. In 1867 he took hold of the old Fall River line, and the *Bristol* and the *Providence* became part of its fleet. The old-fashioned placement of the boiler on the guards was ignored, and the boilers were placed inside the hull. Rather than the usual fan pattern, the paddle-box fronts were rendered in what might be described as the Capitol Dome pattern. The *Bristol* burned at the Newport dock on December 30, 1888, just after completing a trip. The *Providence* was retired about two years later but was kept in reserve until around 1896.

Not long after the *Bristol* entered service, the Norwich line introduced the *City of Lawrence,* which boasted an iron hull. A few of the lines had talked about such improvements, but it was not until 1881 that the New London line put the iron-hulled *City of Worcester* in service. She had

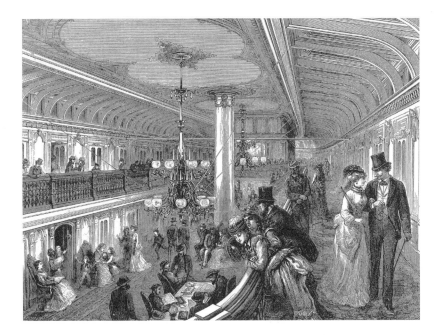

9.5. The main cabin of the *Bristol* is shown in this engraving to be as grand as any palace hotel in the world.

(Jim Harter collection)

electric lighting, which was an innovation in steamboating. In 1898 she sank at Cormorant Reef, Rhode Island, but only went down to her upper decks. The boat was raised and remained running until 1915.

In May 1877 steamer service to Providence was revived by a new line. One of its new boats, the *Massachusetts,* had two hundred rooms and several family-size compartments. The dining room was on the main deck rather than below as was customary. Aft of the dining room were staterooms and berths set aside exclusively for ladies. Almost an hour before departure, an orchestra would begin playing in the main saloon and continue to do so as the boat began its trip. Most of the sound lines had docks on the Hudson River, along West Street. The *Massachusetts* left from Pier 29 and headed south to the Battery and Castle Garden, where she passed around the southern tip of Manhattan. She would then bend to the north and pass the great line of large sailing ships along South Street. There were wharves on both sides of the East River crowded with ships. The boat would pass Brooklyn and the navy yard, continuing on a northern course past the shipyards at Greenpoint. All the while legions of boats would pass by as ferries darted back and forth in front of and behind the *Massachusetts*.

The boat would then steam alongside the long, slender Blackwell's Island, square in the middle of the upper East River, moving slowly because of the traffic of ships. It would then turn eastward and thread its way through the narrow Hell Gate, past Ward's Island and Randall's Island, until it entered the sound. It would pass Riker's Island, Flushing Bay, and enter a narrow channel at Throgg's Neck. Down below, the orchestra would temporarily stop playing when dinner was served. Some passengers chose to sup later and stay on deck to catch a few more sights of the boat's entrance into Long Island Sound proper. To the right was King's Point, and up ahead, Pelham Bay. As the *Massachusetts* moved along, the towns grew smaller, especially on Long Island. There were cottage villages, green fields, rocky bluffs, and an occasional lighthouse. Passengers would go below to be in time for the last leavings of a beautiful meal. The musicians reassembled at 8:00 PM and offered two more hours of beautiful melodies. Then passengers would go to bed, to rest awhile, before an early morning landing. In Providence, passengers boarded a boat train that would reach Boston in one hour and fifteen minutes. Holiday passengers could go on by rail to Cape Cod, or the White Mountains, or as far north as Bar Harbor for the summer.

Later in the nineteenth century the service varied by the season. Most of the sound lines carried seventy to seventy-five passengers a day, even in the winter months. However, during the summer peak each boat might carry up to a thousand. The Fall River line, for example, ran its smaller boats in the winter and offered a fare reduction of 25 percent. During the warm weather months they ran four boats a day. The basic fare was $4, with an extra charge of $1–$2 for a stateroom, depending on its size.

There was much to praise about the sound boats. They were large, comfortable, reasonably fast, and safe. The crews were helpful. The officers were gentlemen and as polite and refined sailors as are likely to be found. A popular writer of the day, J. D. McCabe, was offended by the number of ladies of ill fame who made the boats their home and plied their infamous trade in the most shameless manner. He said that a trip on these deluxe boats was an experience never to be forgotten. Perhaps that was true because of the ladies he so disparaged, but the average passenger was more likely bothered by the difficulty encountered in getting on and off the boat at the dock.

Runners were hired to persuade travelers to ride on "their" boat and to avoid the inferior vessel operated by competing lines. These impertinent and aggressive salesmen were paid a fee for every passenger they could deliver to the ticket booth. They would block passengers from buying a ticket while degrading the vessel nearby, saying she was unsafe and had a hole in her bilge large enough to crawl through, the captain was a drunk, the boilers blew up regularly, the food was like fodder, or she would get stuck on a sandbar every trip for three hours. At the same time, two or three other hucksters shouted the merits of their particular vessel and the defects of the competitors. They held on to your coat or tried to grab your bag and move you away from the dock to one down the street. Each of them offered a cheaper fare or a free meal if you would only sail on their boat. A strong traveler would pull away from these rascals but not with ease. Otherwise, one could only hope a policeman would appear to handle the situation.

Getting off a boat could be as great an ordeal, because passengers leaving the vessel faced a gauntlet of cab drivers, porters, and expressmen, all seeking their business. They shouted, yelled, and grabbed in a wild and aggressive manner. The hackmen wanted your taxi fare, while the porters and expressmen wanted your baggage. In the Victorian era, upper-class travelers needed many changes of clothes in that dressed-up age when appearances were important. This called for a large wardrobe and hence many bags and trunks. A *New York Times* reporter recorded a scene at the Fall River dock late in August 1882. It looked and sounded like a mini riot, he said, and the three policemen assigned to keep order were overwhelmed. They did what they could to keep a path open for the passengers. The weak and timid were literally grabbed by a burley cab driver and pulled over to his vehicle and pushed inside. The young, fleet, and strong might escape, but they faced a second lineup of hackmen and porters on West Street, where the hectoring began all over. A certain number of older gents with a military bearing, head held high, would hold out their walking stick as if to say, "Get out of my face or get a taste of this stick." They alone might be allowed to pass through unmolested.

Despite the building of more railroads, New Englanders seemed determined to go by boat when traveling to Manhattan. It was fashionable and more dignified and it became a tradition. Grandfather had always taken the boat train to Fall River and continued on by steamer to Gotham. His son would do the same, and the grandson, not one to upset the status quo, would do likewise. They knew the schedule by heart. The boat train left Park Square station at 6:00 PM and arrived at the Fall River wharf at 7:25. The steamer left just ten minutes later and arrived at Pier 28 in New York City at 7:30 the next morning.

Maintaining the loyalty of its traditional patrons prompted the Fall River management to purchase a series of new vessels starting in 1883. The *Pilgrim* was the first of this iron hull generation. It was a double hull with 90 watertight compartments and 6 watertight bulkheads that extended to the top of the hull. She was 385 feet long and had 219 staterooms and 10 parlor bedrooms. There were 695 berths on board, including 93 for compartments. The *Pilgrim* would carry 540 passengers and 200 crew members. The interior of the boat was similar to earlier steamers such as the *Bristol*. There was no effort to update this aspect of the vessel design. Figure 9.6 shows the *Pilgrim* as she appeared when first entering service in June 1883. The *Puritan* followed in 1889 and was somewhat longer than her predecessor. The hull was steel in place of iron. She carried 800 passengers and had a compound engine for greater fuel economy.

9.6. The *Pilgrim* became the flagship of the Fall River line when she entered service in 1883. The several interior views show the attention to passenger comfort, including electric lighting.

(*Leslie's Weekly*, June 30, 1883)

But the *Puritan* was to have a different and more sophisticated look about her. She was in no way modest or puritanical in dress. Traditional steamboat interiors were fabricated and designed by ship carpenters whose idea of beauty was anything that could be cut with a scroll saw. The *Puritan* was to be artistic as well as seaworthy. The interior followed the Italian Renaissance plan for ornamentation. Care was taken that the gilding was not too heavy. Dark varnished woods and bright accent colors were less often used. Boston native Frank Hill Smith (1842–1904) directed the work. He had been educated in France, specializing in interior decorating, and favored classical designs. Smith and his artists used white or pale colors and decorations molded in low relief. Walls were divided into panels by fluted pilasters. Dignified figures – often half-draped females – filled in the panels. The ornamental ironwork was graceful and not gilded. The hardware was ornamental but cast in dark bronze (figs. 9.7 and 9.8). Other boats in the Fall River's new fleet were the *Plymouth, Priscilla, Providence,* and the mighty *Commonwealth* of 1908, all of which proved to be excellent boats.

Train service improved between Boston and New York after the opening of the New Haven shoreline in 1889. Completion of the Hell Gate Bridge in 1917 brought the New Haven trains directly into Pennsylvania

9.7. The *Puritan* entered sound service in 1889. She was a giant at 420 feet. Her paddle wheels weighed 100 tons. She was also beautiful as can be seen by this engraving of her grand staircase.

(*Century Magazine*, July 1889)

Station. This was the beginning of direct passenger service from downtown Boston into the heart of Manhattan. But no matter, the old ways continued to a degree and conservative Yankees preferred the sound steamers. Passenger service on the Fall River line actually peaked in 1906 at 444,500 and stayed near that number during much of the 1920s. However, by 1928 the line was losing money. The Depression cut patronage so that by 1936 traffic was down to about 127,000. Yet the Fall River line took pride in its good safety record, which recorded only one passenger fatality in its history. This meant little to workers, who wanted a wage increase in the summer of 1937. The line's management reacted to the workers' demands by ending operations. A judge granted the Fall River line permission to shut down on July 27, 1937. And so ended the strike and a glamorous chapter in coastal steamer history.

NEW ENGLAND COASTAL TRAVEL

New England has always been associated with the sea. Most of its population continues to live along the Atlantic Coast. This section of the nation was devoted to shipbuilding, fishing, the China trade, and seafaring in general. Today the area's most fashionable seaside summer resorts are at

9.8. A squadron of stokers shoveled vigorously to feed her furnaces to produce enough steam to drive the *Puritan* along at 20-plus mph.

(*Century Magazine*, July 1889)

Bar Harbor, Cape Cod, Martha's Vineyard, and Nantucket. Yachting is more than a pastime for those Yankees who love the sea and wind.

Colonial New England was a maritime economy. Many worked their farms during the spring and summer but cut timber or built ships during the other seasons. Some fished or converted logs into boards. Large tracts of virgin timber furnished excellent lumber for ship hulls, masts, and spars. The tall trees found in Maine were ready-made for masts. The plentiful supply of wood reduced American shipbuilding costs, compared to European yards, by 60 percent, and America built many vessels for the British merchant fleet. Large vessels were being built at Salem, Massachusetts, as early as 1641. The schooner was introduced by Yankee shipwrights in 1716 and grew in popularity over the next century because it required such a small crew to handle the sails. Schooners grew in size and remained economic into the twentieth century.

New England's reputation for fine sailing ships was greatly enhanced by the clipper ships built by Donald McKay (1810–1880) at his East Boston boatyard. McKay was a native of Nova Scotia but came to New York as a teenager to become an apprentice ship's carpenter. After mastering the trade he opened his own yard near Boston in 1845. The *Stag Hound* was his first clipper, completed in 1850. She was long and narrow and intended for speed rather than maximum cargoes. Such ships were described as "knives with sails." The plentiful sails towered almost 200 feet above the deck. It was McKay's hope that a line of such fast vessels might capture the cotton trade between New Orleans, Savannah, and Boston; however, this scheme did not succeed. At the same time, British builders introduced composite hulls with iron frames and wooden planking, which produced a stronger and cheaper vessel than the American all-wooden hulls. The panic of 1857 forced McKay to close his yard. He attempted iron ships but failed to make a profit and so retired in 1869.

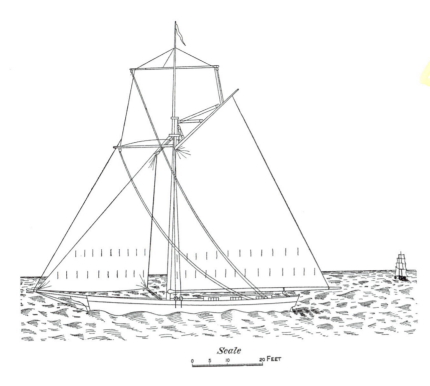

9.9. Sloops were popular along the Atlantic Coast from New England to Florida. They carried passengers and freight between small ports. This vessel was about 60 feet long and featured a topsail.

(1880 U.S. Census, Vol. 8)

Clipper ships sold for about $90,000 and routinely set speed records that exceeded those of steamers of the period. A clipper named the *Northern Light* dashed from San Francisco to Boston in just seventy-six days and six hours. By 1883 there were 270 clippers in service. The great American historian Samuel Eliot Morison wrote this eloquent description of a proud clipper ship's entry into Boston Harbor during the age of sail.

> After the long voyage she is in the pink of condition. Paintwork is spotless, decks holystoned cream white, shrouds freshly tarred, ratlines square. Viewed through a powerful glass, her seizings, flemish-eyes, splices, and pointings are the perfection of the old-time art of rigging. The chafing-gear line has just been removed, leaving spars and shrouds immaculate. The boys touched up her skysail poles with white paint, as she crossed the Bay. Boom-ending her studdingsails and hauling a few points on the wind to shoot the Narrows, between Georges and Gallups and Lovells Islands, she pays off again through President Road, and comes booming up the stream, a sight so beautiful that even the lounging soldiers at the Castle, persistent baiters of passing crews, are dumb with wonder and admiration.

The coastal trade began with the earliest settlers around the Massachusetts Bay Colony. The only convenient way to travel between Plymouth and Boston was by boat. Small sloops and ketches were soon venturing along the coast (fig. 9.9). These small boats had only a single mast, and there were no cabins and few comforts or protections from the weather. They could move quickly with a good breeze, but at the first sign of a storm these little craft would seek a safe harbor. Boats that didn't head to shore soon enough would be blown out to sea. Fishermen were the most subject to such misadventures and were blown out to the Grand Banks off of Newfoundland. One New England crew found itself far to the south after a gale blew them east of Bermuda. What happened to fishing boats happened to the largest sailing vessels as well.

A lively trade developed between ports along the Atlantic seaboard. Coastal ships carried lumber, stone, fish, and lime to the south. Bangor, Maine, became the lumber capital of New England after 1820. During its peak year of 1872 it shipped out more than 240 million board feet. Excellent granite was found on the mainland, as well as on some of the islands off the northeastern coast, and would be carried south to Boston, Philadelphia, and other ports by ship. Some blocks weighed as much as 650 tons. Firewood went from Maine to Boston by coasters. These same vessels would carry coal back east. Perhaps the most remarkable fact about the Yankee seaman was the beginning of trade with the West Indies in about 1640. A schooner could expect to reach Philadelphia from Portland, Maine (about 450 miles), in about five days with favorable winds. It could require almost three times longer if the winds were contrary.

One of the most important changes that occurred to coastal shipping before the advent of steam power was the establishment of ship lines that worked on common carriers. Traditionally the ship's captain carried his own goods or that of his partners. He sailed when and where he pleased. The ship lines ran on a fixed schedule over a fixed route. For example, the Red line sent out a ship between New York and Charleston every Wednesday. This vessel was open to all shippers at a uniform charge. Many small shipments put together added up to a full or nearly full load. The idea became so popular that by 1815 there were boat lines between every major port on the East Coast. Some lines even serviced Richmond, Virginia, by using smaller vessels to navigate the James River.

The steamboat appeared in northern waters about a decade after Fulton convinced American travelers that such vessels were both safe and convenient. A small open boat named the *Tom Thumb* was built in Boston in 1818. It was only 30 feet long and had paddle wheels. Initially it was used on the Kennebec River between Bath and Augusta. Despite its small size, it was used along the Maine coast and ran as far east as Rockland. A larger boat appeared in 1824 intended for service between Portland and Boston. It was built in New York and was named the *Patent*. The vessel was 80 feet long and had a proper cabin for passengers, plus a separate ladies' cabin. Finished at a cost of $20,000, it exceeded the humble *Tom Thumb* in every particular. It operated at 10 knots. The fare was $5, meals included. The *Patent* ran on its intended route for six years and then was transferred to the Penobscot River for another five years. After that assignment was concluded, she was sold down south. Another interesting pioneer was the *Eagle,* which was set to work between Boston and Hingham, Massachusetts, in 1818. This route, just 11 miles long, cut across Boston Bay and offered local citizens a quick way to commute. By 1832 the route was taken over by the Boston-Hingham Steam Boat Company. Half a century later this line became part of the Nantucket Beach Steam Boat Company. It was more into the excursion trade than commuter business and was especially busy in the summer season.

In 1835 Cornelius Vanderbilt tried to take over the Boston-to-Portland route. Why Vanderbilt desired such a line is unclear, because the traffic between the cities was not sufficient to generate a large profit. Boston was a major city, true enough, but Portland at the time had only about thirteen thousand residents. Although Vanderbilt normally employed the very best vessels, he now proceeded in an uncharacteristic manner by entering two well-used vessels to win the competition for the route. The *Chancellor Livingston* of 1816 was the last boat designed by Robert Fulton. When new it was possibly the best steamboat afloat. She was designed for Hudson River service but operated successfully on Long Island Sound. She had been re-engined in recent years but even so remained an obsolete boat. Her companion was another Fulton boat, which had been built for Russia but never delivered and was subsequently renamed the *Connecticut.* She was smaller than the *Livingston* but was completed in the same year. The established line he had hoped to defeat held fast, and Vanderbilt was forced to retire. He returned, however, in 1838, hoping to unseat the local operators on the Boston-to-Portland route. Fares were cut to $1, and Vanderbilt had a fine boat to represent him this time. But the local vessel outran Vanderbilt's best and made the run to Boston in a record nine hours and ten minutes. The commodore did not accept defeat easily, but in this case he decided to give New England a long rest.

The Boston and Bangor Steamship Company was established in 1833 by a group of Boston investors. A new boat named the *Bangor* was built in New York for the company. It burned twenty-five cords of wood on each trip. In 1842 the vessel was sent to Turkey for service on the Mediterranean Sea. There was a second *Bangor* built for the Boston-to-Bangor service by Betts, Harlan, and Hollingsworth of Wilmington, Delaware. This was an iron-hull vessel driven by screw propellers and was very advanced for its time when completed in August 1845. On her second trip a fire broke out in the boiler room. It was decided to run the *Bangor* ashore near Castine, Maine. Passengers and crew were taken off without any injuries, but the boat was seriously damaged. She was rebuilt and returned to service. Late in 1846 the *Bangor* was sold to the U.S. Navy and refitted as a gunboat for service in the Mexican War.

A more typical steamer for the time also served the Bangor route. This was the *Penobscot,* built by James Cunningham of New York in 1844. She had a wooden hull, side wheels, and a walking beam engine. Samuel Stanton produced an attractive ink drawing of this vessel. The *Penobscot* was renamed the *Norfolk* and sent south where she was lost off the coast of Delaware on September 12, 1857, in the same storm that sank the *Central America.* This boat gained considerable notoriety in more recent years when its cargo of gold was recovered from the frigid depths of the Atlantic Ocean.

Miss Isabella Bird, mentioned earlier, was an English lady who toured Canada and the United States in the early 1850s and published a book about her travels in 1856. After landing in Halifax and touring Nova Scotia, she departed from St. John, New Brunswick, for Portland, Maine. It was a bright day in August when she stepped aboard the *Ornevorg,* a former Long Island Sound side-wheeler now being used in this short international run. Miss Bird entered through a side door on a lower deck into what looked like a large hall. It had a ticket office and a curtain that separated the ladies' compartment. Behind the curtain she found sofas, rocking chairs, and tables. This otherwise comfortable space was too airy for Miss Bird. Berths were built in on both sides of the room. The drapes were satin damask while the curtains were of muslin with rose-colored binding. On the deck above was a large saloon for the male passengers, with 170 berths. The large beam engine propelled the boat along at 15 mph. A stop was made at Eastport, Maine, where the midday meal was served, because dining was much more pleasant when the boat was stationary. The ladies were seated first, but the men made a rush for the food when they were brought in. There was an abundance of food for everyone. The table was piled high with pork roasts, leg of mutton, broiled chicken, turkey, roast duck, beef steaks, yams, tomatoes, squash, and endless breads and pastries. While Miss Bird was finishing her soup, the others were eating their dessert. A waiter asked her for a dinner ticket or 50 cents.

The sea began to pick up with a fresh breeze. The boat was too low in the water and had so little free board that water came rushing into the passenger deck. A wave came down the companionway into the ladies' compartment and upset the tea table, scattering its contents around the deck. The boat was now rocking, groaning, and straining heavily as a gale blew in. A lamp fell from the ceiling, rendering the cabin dark. Furniture continued to be knocked around, and enough water was in the lower decks to put out the fire under the boilers. The boat was now at the mercy of the sea. The men pumped and bailed. Miss Bird was thrown against a bulkhead and was stunned insensible for three hours. By morning the storm began to moderate. Another boat pulled alongside and gave the stricken vessel a tow into Portland, arriving at 1:00 PM, damaged but afloat. The passengers were simply happy to still be alive.

Many towns along the New England coast did not have harbors or docks for larger boats. Some of these vessels would stop as close to such towns as they could, and small boats could shuttle back and forth with passengers and cargo. It was an inexpensive, if not notably efficient, way for a hamlet to have access to good transportation. In other areas, local lines would use small boats that could land in shallow harbors. There were some steamboat operations that specialized in local service. Cosco Bay lies offshore from Portland and is dotted with islands. The Cosco Bay Steam Boat Company offered service to these islands with four miniature side-wheelers. It was claimed there were 365 islands in the bay. Daily mail service was offered, and the boats were especially busy during the summer resort season. The Harpswell Steam Boat Company, also based in Portland, was another "island hopper." The Portland Packet Company took vacationers directly from Boston to Bar Harbor, a rich man's summer haven after it was discovered by the Rockefellers. In the early 1890s boats left Boston's India Wharf every evening at 7:00 except Sundays. After Mount Desert Island was partially converted into a national park, more ordinary tourists began to visit Bar Harbor.

Steamboating was not damaged by the spread of railroads in coastal New England, as the boats managed to compete fairly well. It was the automobile that destroyed passenger service by both rail and sea. While the automobile was the rich man's toy, an ambitious businessman named Charles W. Morse attempted to consolidate the northeastern coastal lines as far north as the Canadian Maritimes. In 1901 he created the Eastern Steamship Company. Several lines were combined, some of them very old, such as the Boston and Bangor and the International Steamship Company. Morse had previously made a fortune in the ice business and other enterprises. He controlled a number of banks that proved useful in financing his steamboat adventure. He was counting on the good economic times continuing but did not foresee the panic of 1907. Morse was ruined and lost control of the Eastern Steamship Company, which was forced into receivership. It recovered and continued to do well until 1914, when it once again failed. However, this was only a temporary setback, and good times were ahead. In 1916 the Cape Cod Canal opened, which offered a direct water route to Boston. The Eastern Steamship Company purchased the Boston-to-Yarmouth, Nova Scotia, ferry line. This service started in 1855 and proved successful because it was more direct than the overland routes. Service continues today, but it now runs from Portland to Yarmouth. Two new boats were built in 1924 for the Eastern Steamship Company, and traffic remained strong, especially in the vacation trade, until 1930. The effects of the Great Depression meant an end to many businesses, and the Eastern Steamship Company was no exception. The lines from Boston to Portland closed in 1932, and the Bangor service was gone three years later. The New-York-to-Boston boat ran as late as 1941. The Yarmouth line was closed during World War II. It was restored after the war but ran only until 1954, when the Canadian government took over the operations as a public service.

SOUTHERN COASTAL TRAVEL

Most modern Americans go south in the winter to find sunshine, warm beaches, and orange blossoms. In the antebellum era southerners headed north in summer to escape the heat and tropical diseases of Dixieland. The most comfortable place for southerners was Newport, Rhode Island. Here was a seaside town in the heart of New England that contained almost no abolitionists. It started as a seaport and working place for traders, fishermen, and shipbuilders. It had no ambition to be a fancy resort catering to wealthy southerners, but that is how it evolved by about 1730. Prosperous sea captains built handsome homes and patronized excellent schools. Art and music flourished to a degree, and all of this superficial refinement appealed to the upper-class southerners. The wealth of Newport was built on the rum and slave trade. Ships carrying rum distilled in Newport sailed to the west coast of Africa and traded rum for slaves. The slaves were brought back to the West Indies and traded for molasses that was carried north to Newport, where it was converted into rum or sugar. This exchange was one of the most lucrative trades for American seamen. Ships had full cargoes on all three legs of the triangular trade and profited each mile of the way. The final section of the voyage followed the eastern U.S. coast from Florida to Rhode Island. Because almost everyone in Newport was supported by the slave trade to some degree, abolitionist sentiments were subdued at best. Southerners might go there with their house servants and never have to be confronted with the issue of slavery. Newport became such a popular resort for the Old South, many referred to it as the Carolina Hospital. Boats heading north from late spring to early fall were well patronized.

During the American Revolution the British occupied Newport, putting an end to its glory days as a seaport. It fell into a general decline after the war but retained its resort trade. By the 1840s rich northerners were beginning to assemble there as an escape from the overheated cities of the northeast. Anthony Trollope reported it as still busy in September during his visit in the early 1860s. Southerners were no longer present at this time because of the war. Wealthy New Yorkers made it a summer retreat for the top four hundred in the American society. Great mansions, called cottages, were built by the Astors and the Vanderbilts. But high society is fickle, and by 1920 the magic of Newport had worn off and the four hundred withdrew to newer and more fashionable locations. Today tourists come to see what remains of the great houses and wonder how this sleepy place could have once been the largest seaport in colonial America.

Southern merchants also headed north in the summer on yearly buying trips to restock their shelves with bonnets, shoes, perfumes, and other fancy goods best found in New York City. Some was of local manufacture, but much was imported from England, France, and other overseas suppliers. The businessmen were also happy to have a good excuse to leave the heat behind them, and some would linger on until September. The best way to reach Manhattan was by packet boat, the same vessels that carried so much cotton northbound. These same vessels returned to the south laden with fancy goods that were high-value cargoes. When the sailing packet *Louisa Matilda* wrecked just north of Hatteras, North Carolina, in August 1827, her cargo's estimated value was between $300,000 and $400,000. New York was a fine place to find entertainment and diversion. In 1825 it was estimated that ten thousand southerners sailed from various southern ports to New York City. No breakdown was included to distinguish just how many of this total were merchants or vacationers.

Sail prevailed longer on the southern routes than it did along the northern coastline. Steam was championed by New York–based coastal lines, but it took longer to take hold. One of the first steamers to head south was the *Robert Fulton*, launched at New York in 1819. In April of the next year it ran to Cuba, some 1,300 miles, in seven days. Part of the trip was made through a storm, and the *Fulton* proved seaworthy. The boat ran successfully on this route for five years but could not maintain a regular schedule as a single vessel. Profits were not enough to justify a second boat, so the service was suspended.

Robert Albion, in his seminal study of square riggers, contends that marine historians have generally ignored coastal history in favor of more glamorous deepwater trans-ocean subjects. He contends that American coastal routes were universally long and were as great a challenge as crossing the Atlantic Ocean. Good ships and skillful crews were needed to get coastal cargoes and passengers to their destinations. Expert seamanship was required as well, of course, in order to average 100 miles a day whether the sailing ship was on the edge or at the center of the sea. At this speed, Charleston was 6.6 days from New York, Mobile was 17.7 days, and New Orleans was 18 days. Adverse weather and contrary winds could adversely affect sailing schedules. One of the slowest trips between New York and Charleston took 23 days. Being blown off course or out to sea made timely travel by sea impossible. Pirates were active in the Gulf of Mexico into the 1830s, not only interrupting schedules but sometimes murdering or

9.10. The *Home* (1838) was a pioneer in the New-York-to-Charleston trade. She sank on her third trip to the south at Cape Hatteras, North Carolina.

(S.A. Howland, *Steamboat Disasters*, 1846.)

torturing ship crews. Those merchantmen carrying specie shipments were generally well armed.

Perhaps the most important fact concerning southern coastal trade was its control by New York shipping interests. These shrewd and aggressive agents controlled the cotton trade by about 1835. This meant cotton sold to New England and British mills went via New York. It involved hundreds of thousands of bales a year and thus amounted to huge transportation fees. Southern cotton growers contended that for every dollar received for their crop, 40 cents went to New York. Charles Morgan was among the largest of the New York shippers to benefit from the southern coastal trade.

Charles Morgan (1795–1878) came to New York City in 1809 to make his fortune. Over the next several decades he did so, mainly in southern shipping and railroads. In 1819 he invested in a sailing packet working the New York, Charleston, New Orleans trade. He later joined James Allaire, a marine engine builder, in starting a steam packet line to service the same ports. The two men began with a line to Charleston in 1832. Four years later service was extended to Havana, Key West, and New Orleans. In 1837 Morgan pushed the operations to Galveston, Texas. This was the pioneer southern steam packet operation, but it was a troubled business. Several boats were lost and passengers lost confidence in it.

The sinking of the line's *Home* was featured in a sensational book of the time by S. A. Howland called *Steamboat Disasters and Railroad Accidents in the United States*. The boat owned by Morgan and Allaire had made a fast trip to Charleston, South Carolina, in just sixty-four hours. Good publicity helped sell tickets, but the next voyage, on October 7, 1838, was to be her last. It started poorly when the *Home* became stuck on a shoal before leaving New York Harbor. A rising tide set her free after a few hours, but once into the Atlantic Ocean the *Home* was overwhelmed by a

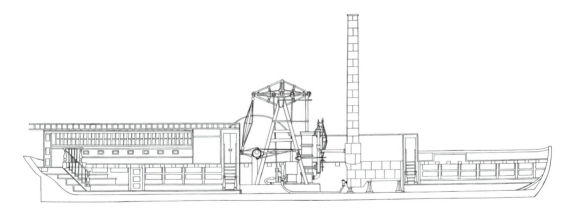

9.11. The North Carolina ran between Wilmington, North Carolina, and Charleston, South Carolina, in the years 1838 through 1840. It was built in New York City.

(Thomas Tredgold, *The Steam Engine*, 1838)

stubborn gale. As they headed south the boilers failed, the hull began to leak, and the sails, now the only means of power, were torn to pieces. She made it as far south as Cape Hatteras when the captain decided to drive the vessel onto the beach and end the trip before she came apart at sea. It was a desperate measure, and the boat came to pieces in the surf before landfall. Ninety-five lives were lost near the beach at Ocracoke, North Carolina. Forty people managed to reach shore, but many children and women were among those lost (fig. 9.10). The unfavorable publicity from this tragedy prompted Morgan and Allaire to abandon their operation. But Morgan was only temporarily stalled in his effort to build a coastal shipping business.

Morgan refocused on his operations in Texas, and before others reorganized the business opportunities in this remote part of Mexico, Morgan monopolized the Texas trade. He built a railroad east from Texas that ended opposite New Orleans on the Mississippi River. After Texas became a republic and then a state, Morgan's transport empire flourished. After his death, the Southern Pacific Railroad took over his transport business that stretched from New York to Texas.

The internal plan of a cotton state coastal steamer, the *North Carolina*, was printed in Thomas Tredgold's folio volume *The Steam Engine* (fig. 9.11). It was constructed in 1838 for a coastal line serving Wilmington, North Carolina, and Charleston, South Carolina. Wilmington was 30 miles up the Fear River; the remaining 130 miles to Charleston was along the Atlantic Coast. The *North Carolina* was almost 160 feet long with a beam of 24 feet. She had side wheels and a single-cylinder low-pressure engine 40 inches in diameter with a 10-foot stroke. The engine was rated at 100 hp. Copper boilers were used because they were more durable than iron ones, since seawater was used to make the steam. Two cabins had beds for 72 passengers, and another 28 temporary beds could be set up in the main cabin. The coastal line had four boats, three built in New York, under the direction of Cornelius Vanderbilt, and a fourth made by Watchman and Bratt of Baltimore. Operations were done at night, so the vessel ran slowly as a precaution. The journey took 14 hours at an average speed of 11 mph. Fourteen cords of wood were consumed during each trip. Passenger loads averaged only 18 per trip, and some of the travelers rode only partway, resulting in a rather disappointing gross income of $1 per rider. Operating expenses, wages, fuel, repairs, and so forth came to a little over $30,000 for a nine-month season. It was hoped that revenues would rise as the rivers became better established. However, there was more trouble ahead for this small coastal line. Late in July 1840 the *North Carolina* was struck by the steamer *Governor Dudley*. They were at sea about 20 to 30 miles northeast of Georgetown, South Carolina. The accident happened at about 1:00 A M, and both captains had just gone to bed. The *North Carolina* sank almost immediately, yet no lives were lost. Most of the luggage was lost, however, and because some of the passengers were congressmen returning home, a great deal of money was lost as well.

Meanwhile, on the eastern seacoast, the age of sail continued south of Philadelphia. Large ports such as Savannah were served by six packet lines consisting of thirty-eight barks and brigs (fig. 9.12). They sailed alternate days to divide up the business. Finally in 1846 the U.S. Post Office awarded mail contracts that were large enough to encourage a new steamboat line between New York and Charleston. A fine new steamer named the *Southerner* made its first trip to Charleston in September 1846 and completed the journey in two days and eleven hours. Other mail contracts encouraged steamer lines from New York to Key West and Havana.

The most convenient place to see U.S. coastal trade in action was New York Harbor. Boats lined up in close ranks along the Hudson and East River docks. Boats left daily for dozens of ports along the East Coast and the Caribbean Islands. One of the biggest coastal lines in the 1890s was the Clyde Steamship Company located at Pier 29 on the East River at the foot of Roosevelt Street. It was easy to find, because the pier was below the Brooklyn Bridge. This company was founded in the 1840s by Thomas Clyde, who immigrated to Chester, Pennsylvania, from Scotland in 1820. Clyde worked with John Ericson in perfecting the screw propeller. In 1844 he built a vessel named the *John S. McKim,* said to be the first screw propeller used in the coastal trade. The *McKim* ran between New York and Charleston.

Over the following years the Clyde line expanded its operations to include Boston; Philadelphia; Washington; Norfolk, Virginia; New Berne, North Carolina; Georgetown, South Carolina; and Jacksonville, Florida. Its boats ran up the St. John's River in Florida for 195 miles, landing at Green Cove Springs, Palatka, Astor, Blue Springs, and other Florida landings. A subsidiary line to the West Indies left from Pier 15 of the East River for Turk's Island, Haiti; Puerto Plata, in the Dominican Republic; and Samna, Sanchez, and San Domingo City, in the Republic of San Domingo.

9.12. Brigs were well suited to coastal service and were a common type of sailing vessel in that trade before the advent of steamships.

(*Merchant Vessels of the United States*, 1892)

Thomas Clyde's son William played an active part in the steamboat business. In 1873 he became president of the Pacific Mail Steamship Company. He managed the Panama Railroad and for a time the Richmond and Danville Railroad as well.

The Savannah line operated by the Ocean Steamship Company was acquired by the South Carolina Railroad in 1872 (fig. 9.13). This line served both Boston and New York and thus did much to strengthen the Port of Savannah. In 1890 it ran four boats a week from Pier 35 on the Hudson River. Time to Savannah was fifty-five hours, and the cabin fare was $20. Vacationers took the Savannah line to Bermuda for a quiet rest; it was only two days from New York. Visitors found a restful beach warmed by the Gulf Stream. It was a balmy and relaxing place to visit, and it had a fine hotel. William Dean Howells, Mark Twain, and Woodrow Wilson were all guests at the Princess Hotel.

The Old Dominion Steamship Company ran boats from Pier 26 on the Hudson River four times a week to Norfolk and Newport News, Virginia, in just twenty-four hours. The fare was $8 and included all meals. Old Point Comfort offered a resort hotel. The Cromwell line was established in 1855 by H. B. Cromwell and Company. By 1860 it had ten screw propeller steamers running to Charleston and Savannah. It was building more boats to connect Boston and Charleston. By 1890 it offered service every Wednesday and Saturday from Pier 9 directly to New Orleans. A special vacation cruise of sixteen days with a four-day layover in the Big Easy was offered for $60. The *New York Times* carried a story about the southern coastal trade out of the Port of New York in January 18, 1860. The

COASTAL & SOUND STEAMERS

9.13. The Savannah line was a railroad-operated steamship company that continued running into the 1940s.

(*Official Guide of the Railway*, 1893)

business was flourishing, according to this report, and went far beyond passenger travel. The Harden Express line had been in southern trade for eight years and never experienced such a good business with large and small shipments. The Adams Express Company reported handling sixteen hundred packages for the south during the week before Christmas.

The Ward line started running between New York and Cuba in 1840 with a small fleet of schooners. James O. Ward, formerly of Roxbury, Massachusetts, started the operation and passed it on to his son, James E. Ward, in about 1856. The younger Ward soon had schooners landing in many West Indies ports. The New York and Cuba Mail Steamship

Company, as the company was also called, acquired its first steamer in 1866. By 1877 it had faster steamers, which made the trip to Havana in four days and one hour. The return trip was faster yet, three days and nine hours, because of the Gulf Stream. By 1892 the Ward line had ten steamers servicing Cuba, Mexico, and Nassau.

Although most citizens could only dream of taking a steamer to the Caribbean Islands or the ports of old Spanish Main, even the poorest New Yorker could have a small sample of coastal sea travel for just 25 cents. This modest fare purchased a round trip to and from Coney Island. The 12-mile excursion started at Pier One at the Battery or southern tip of Manhattan Island and headed down the upper bay past the Statue of Liberty and out to sea at Sandy Hook. Here the boat entered into the lower bay of New York Harbor. The steamer then turned north and continued along the eastern coast of Long Island to Coney Island (fig. 9.14). Some trips continued north to Manhattan or Rockaway Beach. With a round trip lasting about two hours, the passenger was at sea and gained brief exposure to coastal travel. Some passengers stayed aboard just to enjoy the sights of the busy maritime scene, the sun and fresh air, and some time away from the congested city. Excursion boats had started service to Coney Island in about 1845, but the trade was taken over by the Iron Boat Company, which built seven new steamers in the early 1880s. This firm adopted the motto "cannot burn, cannot sink" to assure timid travelers about the Iron Boat line's safety. But accidents do happen. In July 1894 two of the line's boats collided, and a third, the *Pegasus,* hit a cattle boat one day later. With three boats out of service at peak season, the Iron Boat line had difficulty

9.14. Passengers enjoy a concert on the rear deck of this small steamer heading for Coney Island on the Atlantic Coast just outside of New York Harbor.

(*Harper's Weekly,* August 6, 1881)

handling its traffic of ten thousand passengers a day or in providing a boat every thirty minutes. These delightful, if abbreviated, sea excursions continued until about 1932.

New York was the dominant eastern coastal port and so prevailed over the Atlantic coastal trade. There were competitors elsewhere attempting to break the Empire City's monopoly, such as the Merchant and Miners Transportation Company of Baltimore. The firm was incorporated in April 1852 but was slow in getting under way. Service started in December 1854 with a seventy-six-hour trip between Baltimore and Boston with a big side-wheeler named the *Joseph Whitney.* When two more boats were acquired in 1859, service was expanded to Savannah and Providence. Two years later the Civil War created an emergency and the line's boats were seized by the federal government, but by 1864 the line was able to resume operations on a limited basis, and three years later they could offer service to Boston and Norfolk. In 1873 the line to Providence was restored. A Savannah line was purchased in 1876, allowing the company to resume its southern connection. By 1890 Merchants and Miners had eleven steamers, all with iron or steel hulls. In 1907 the line was taken over by the New Haven Railroad, but this arrangement was terminated seven years later because of the railroad's financial problems. During World War I the federal government took over the fleet as part of the war emergency. By 1921 Merchant and Miners had recovered and went on to rebuild its fleet to eighteen vessels. The Great Depression created another test for all transportation companies. The Merchant and Miners line was again taken over by federal action early in 1942 for the duration of World War II. Private ownership was not restored until 1948, but the shareholders decided to dissolve the corporation rather than resume operations, thus ending Baltimore's coastal shipping line.

Southern coastal lines were controlled largely by northern businessmen. One of the more dominant of these was Henry B. Plant (1819–1899), a Connecticut Yankee who spent most of his adult life in the south. He had declined the offer of a college education and went to work at the age of eighteen as a deckhand with the New Haven Steamboat Company. He soon found work with the Adams Express Company. In 1854 he was sent to Augusta, Georgia, to manage the company's business in the southern states. A few years after the Civil War began, Plant reorganized the business as the Southern Express Company and worked to cultivate good relations with Confederate leaders. But he felt compelled to leave the south in 1863 because he felt so unwelcome. He returned after the war and revived the express business. By the late 1870s he saw better opportunities in the railroad business and purchased the Atlantic and Gulf Railroad. As he added new railroad properties, he saw the need for steamboat connections to Central and South America. Florida fascinated him, and he correctly saw it as a great winter vacation area. Tampa became the center of his new world. He had visited Florida years before with an ailing wife and came to see that it was neither a water wilderness nor a land of swamps, alligators, and mosquitoes, as so many northerners assumed. Meanwhile, his railroad empire expanded into a 1,000-mile system and he expanded steamship operations to Cuba. Plant decided a deluxe hotel was needed to bring more affluent tourists to his sunshine resort and built the lavish Tampa Bay Hotel in 1891. The Hotel Seminole was next constructed in Winter Park, also on Florida's west coast. After his death in 1899 Plant's steamboat lines were merged into Henry Flagler's Peninsula and Occidental Steamship Company. Plant's railroads became part of the Atlantic Coast line.

Henry M. Flagler (1830–1913) was another northerner who became impressed with Florida's warm winter climate. Like Plant, Flagler believed better hotels and transportation could draw wealthy tourists from the northern states. He, too, first visited with an ailing wife, in 1878. They found the ancient city of St. Augustine (1565) quaint but run-down. His attachment to the Sunshine State grew during a visit with his second wife in 1883. Development of the area became his new passion, and raising capital to do so was not a problem. Flagler was a wealthy man, having been a close associate of J. D. Rockefeller and vice president of the Standard Oil Company for many years. He purchased the local railway and put it into first-class order. At the same time, he built a large hotel in St. Augustine, the Ponce de Leon, which became a marvel of its day because of its concrete construction. When it opened early in 1888 it was seen as the beginning of the winter season for America's first families. As the bitter memories of the Civil War gradually began to fade, northerners felt comfortable in going south for part of the winter season.

Flagler began to extend his railroad south along Florida's east coast. In 1889 it reached Daytona Beach, and within five years it entered West Palm Beach. More hotels followed the railroad's steady progress. Those seeking a little sun in January were soon heading south to patronize Flagler's domain. Briefly Flagler felt he had ventured as far south as necessary, but an unusually cold winter in 1894–1895 prompted him to consider an extension to Miami, which at the time was a forlorn fishing village. In 1880 there were only 257 residences in most of South Florida. The magic of Flagler's money soon transformed Miami into the pride of Biscayne Bay.

Meanwhile, Flagler started operation of the Florida East Coast Steamship Company and like his counterpart, Henry Plant, was engaged in coastal shipping. Boats ran to Key West, the most southern island in the United States; other lines served Nassau, Cuba, and Savannah. By 1904 Flagler was feeling his years but decided to make one last, grand extension of the Deep South transportation empire. He would build a railway to Key

West, which in effect meant laying a track over the sea. Much of the line was built on concrete bridges as the railroad hopped from one island to the next. It was a daring and expensive project that required seven years to complete and cost upward of $20 million. The line opened on January 12, 1912. Flagler died in May of the following year feeling that his life's mission had been completed. The Florida East Coast Railway operated ferry boats directly to Havana from Key West, making travel from East Coast cities like New York an almost effortless experience. However, a powerful hurricane in 1935 put an end to the overseas railway; the damage was so severe that the line was abandoned. It was soon rebuilt into a highway that extended Route U.S. 1 to Key West. In more recent years new, wider bridges were built to improve the highway, but many of the original railway bridges still stand to one side of the new roadway.

PANAMA PACIFIC TRAVEL

Europeans began to explore the Pacific Ocean and the western coast of the Americas in the early sixteenth century. Magellan's men cruised along the Mexican coast in 1521. Francis Drake explored the coast of California fifty-some years later. It was not until 1776 that Spanish clergy opened a mission in San Francisco. Two years later Captain Cook discovered the Sandwich Islands, which are today the state of Hawaii. At the end of the American Revolution the British Navigation Acts no longer hampered American sailors, who began to search the globe for new markets. In 1783 a sloop from Hingham, Massachusetts, visited Canton, China, and a few years later there were fifteen U.S. vessels in the China trade whose cargoes of tea, silk, spices, and sandalwood made a few American merchants wealthy. As the waters of the Pacific became more familiar, whalers ventured around the south end of South America to hunt the oil-rich giants of the sea. Long before the United States claimed any land on the West Coast, John J. Astor opened a fur-trading post on the Columbia River in 1811. By the 1840s America was fussing with Britain over Oregon and with Mexico over California, winning both land disputes without major warfare, if the brief war with Mexico can be forgotten.

 By early 1848 America owned what we now call the lower forty-eight and became a vast nation that stretched from the Atlantic to the Pacific. However, most of the land west of the Mississippi River was thinly populated. There were no large cities, and the towns already settled were very small. San Francisco, San Diego, and Los Angeles were small villages. There was no mail service to the east, and the telegraph did not arrive until 1861. Few settlers seemed attracted to this beautiful but remote region. Richard Henry Dana was one of the few Yankees to visit the Golden State before the gold rush. He sailed around the horn of South America to California on the brig *Pilgrim* in 1833 and wrote about the hardships of being a sailor in *Two Years before the Mast*. His book was complimentary to California, but it hardly encouraged a rush to the West Coast. Early in 1848 a nugget of gold was discovered in a branch of the American River not far from Sacramento. News traveled slowly from this isolated area, and few Americans knew about it for almost another year when President Polk mentioned the golden nugget in his State of the Union address. In a matter of days every able-bodied man in the nation wanted to be in California. Where there had been no demand for transportation to the West, there was now a desperate demand for ships. There were no existing boat lines to that part of the world. Boats came and went on an as-needed basis, to haul lumber or hides in slow-moving (non-naval, non-troopship) merchantmen or to carry the more profitable high-class goods from China. They were not set up for passengers, and most of the captains did not want passengers on board their vessels no matter what the demand.

The crowds at the dock were handled in a disorganized manner by more speculative owners who saw this unexpected enthusiasm for westward migration as an opportunity for quick profit. Any available ship was pressed into service, whether she was ready for such an extended voyage or not. The first to leave is said to be the *J. W. Coffin,* a bark that left Boston on December 7, 1848. She was followed by another 774 vessels, both sail and steamer, that had been pressed into service to meet the sudden demand. In all, nearly 100,000 people headed to the gold fields. Few had a pleasant or safe journey, but these men were possessed by a gold fever that had affected their judgment.

The story of one such voyager was published many years later in the *Century Magazine* of April 1891. The story was written by Julius H. Pratt, a New Englander, who otherwise did not reveal much about himself. He claimed his story was typical and suggested that most of the adventurers would have been better off in every way if they had stayed at home and never gone to California. Pratt relates that in 1849 he was twenty-seven, in robust health, fond of adventure, and temporarily out of work. News of gold had men of all ages and professions in a wild excitement to go to California. It was common for twenty men to form a company and seek sponsors to put up money to fund the expedition. At the end of two years, the money would be equally divided among the participants and the investors. Each of them put up $10,000, a fair-size sum at the time, but since everyone was from the same village, and some were related, there was no question of trust. Baggage was limited to 75 pounds per man and included tools, clothes, bedding, some food, plus a carbine and a pistol. The Panama route was selected. This meant sailing from the United States to the east side of Panama, crossing over to the west side, and then boarding a second boat to carry them to California. It was a 5,700-mile trip.

Pratt's company sailed out of New York on the brig *Mayflower* for Chagres, Panama, on March 22, 1849, but just as they entered the Atlantic Ocean, a gale blew in that lasted for two days. The storm blew down the main mast and topsails, which crashed through the main cabin. The damage was severe enough that the captain planned to interrupt the trip for repairs, but Pratt convinced the captain to allow his men to make the repairs as they sailed on. There were enough good carpenters in the group that this was easily done. They landed in Chagres on April 13 after three weeks at sea.

Now, to find a way across Panama, it's only about 50 miles, but there is a jungle and mountains to overcome. Pratt's party rented ten boats and hired thirty local boatmen. The latter were a sullen lot who chanted monotonous songs as the boat progressed up the Chagres River. The boatmen mutinied and got ugly, but a show of guns soon settled the dispute. They reached the dismal village of Gorgona, 28 miles upriver from the Atlantic. The gossip was that matters were worse in Panama City. There were no accommodations but only crowds awaiting the next ship and much illness. Pratt and his men decided to wait in Gorgona for another three weeks. Growing impatient, they rode a mule train down the mountain trail and camped outside of Panama City, finding food by hunting in the forest. Finally they were able to make passage on the *Humboldt* at a combined fare of $200, but the number of passengers was limited to four hundred. They set off making almost no progress, because the winds had died and the currents were against the ship's progress. They were on this rotten ship for forty-eight days and found it miserable beyond belief.

Finally Pratt's company reached Acapulco, Mexico, on July 7 but had to remain aboard the *Humboldt* awaiting permission to come ashore. They all resolved to stay on land for a time to recover and restore their health. A house was rented, servants hired, and good meals enjoyed. After three weeks of resuscitation they were ready to move on. The steamer *Panama* pulled into the harbor. When they attempted to board, soldiers at the wharf prevented their leaving the dock – just why is unclear. Pratt bought some canoes for his men, but they were once again stopped. Some of the men stole a small boat, but it leaked so badly they returned to shore. The *Panama* left without them. A month passed before another boat stopped, but it was so overcrowded it refused to take on any more passengers. The *California* stopped, but she was heading south to Panama City; however, her captain agreed to stop on his return trip in about a month. The captain kept his word, but the boat was so full he refused Pratt's pleas for accommodations. Finally the captain agreed to take Pratt's party if his men would eat sailor's fare and sleep on deck. The passengers on board agreed to this arrangement. The deal was made, but Pratt made a private deal with one of the stewards for a room at the rear of the vessel, hidden away from most of the passengers. They were careful to stay out of sight but smuggled a good quantity of food aboard during a stop in San Diego. The boat passed into San Francisco Harbor on October 1, 1849, after seven months at sea.

Pratt and his men sailed up the river to Sacramento to look for lost members of their group. At last they were in the gold fields but found the best claims were long gone. Their mission was to find gold and make money for their sponsors and family. After three months of intense work they agreed it was a futile game; they, like thousands of others, had found a little gold but not enough to equal their wages as ordinary workingmen back home. They closed down and sold off their tools, tents, and equipment. The total amounted to about 60 percent of the $10,000 invested in their foolish adventure. They headed home; travel was far easier heading east, and they experienced few delays returning. Pratt lost his trunk in Panama by trusting a dishonest porter. It contained his clothes, a gold watch, and $600 in gold. He returned to New York with little more than his shabby clothes, corduroy pants, a soiled shirt, and a brown coat. He had learned a great lesson about life and the fatal allure of gold.

There were several ways to reach California in 1849, but none of them were quick or easy. The shortest in terms of mileage was overland through the western United States, which was wild and unsettled territory. There were a few trails and forts but little else to help the greenhorn traveler. The second shortest was the route across Nicaragua, which had a few advantages over Panama in that the jungle was less intense, the overall distance a little less, and the land more level. This route was used but to no great extent. The Panama route that Pratt and his men took was much improved over the next few years. The fourth alternative was the very long voyage around South America to the Pacific Ocean and a long sail along the coast of South America to San Francisco. Despite the mileage and the hazards of rounding the southern tip of South America, it was a popular way to go in the early days of the gold rush, because it was a dependable and hassle-free way to go, as long as you could accept up to eight months of travel.

The federal government was seeking ways to connect its new far western territories to the more settled eastern half of the country. At that time, California, Texas, and the other western territories were being annexed from Mexico. It would be years before a railroad or telegraph would reach the Pacific Coast. The first stage line did not open until 1858. Mail service via Panama appeared to be the easiest way to open a communications link to California. Late in 1847 the U.S. Postal Service was ready to award contracts for this new service. Two contractors would split the trip; the first leg would run from New York to Chagres (now Colón) on the east coast of Panama, then over that narrow land to its west coast. This route was given to George Law (1806–1881) and his U.S. Mail Steamship Company.

Law made his fortune as a contractor. The High Bridge over the Harlem River was his most notable achievement, and he went on to pile up more money in banking and shipping.

The West Coast portion of the trip would be handled by the Pacific Mail line, headed by another wealthy New Yorker, William Aspinwall (1807–1875). Aspinwall came from a prosperous mercantile family but proved himself to be a skillful businessman and died as one of the richest men in America. Both lines received a substantial government subsidy and agreed to build a small fleet of side-wheel steamers. Aspinwall's line got under way when its first boat, the *California,* left New York on October 6, 1848, with only seven passengers aboard. News of gold at Sutter's Mill was as yet unknown to most Americans. The only way to get vessels to the Pacific Ocean was around South America, for the Panama Canal did not open until 1914. By the time the *California* reached Panama City in January 1849, a large crowd of 1,500 men was waiting, because news of California gold had become common knowledge. The captain could accept only 375 passengers, as the ship's normal capacity was 200. Coal ran out during the trip, and furniture and any wood onboard, such as spare masts, were burned. On February 28, 1848, the *California* entered San Francisco Harbor, 144 days after leaving New York. She was the first steamship to reach San Francisco.

Service from New York to Panama was disorganized but plentiful. George Law could not control the service, and many independent ship operators were ready to run in opposition. The demand for service was large and high fares were charged. By 1854 Law was disenchanted and sold his interest in the U.S. Mail line.

In 1849 Aspinwall was desperately trying to improve service on the West Coast. His three-boat fleet would have been adequate in normal times, but under the traffic crisis created by the gold rush, he needed more boats quickly. The first relief came when he chartered the *Unicorn* from the Cunard line in 1849. He bought a larger vessel, the *Tennessee,* from the New York and Savannah line in 1850. By the following year the Pacific Mail line had fourteen boats in operation (fig. 9.15). Fares remained high: $315 for cabin class and $200 for steerage. The food had improved greatly as well. First-class passengers found the food abundant and well prepared. Steerage passengers had to make do with the common sailor's fare of salt pork; pudding made from flour, suet, and dried fruit; coffee; and soup. Coaling stations had been established en route to ensure an adequate fuel supply. Oceangoing steamers of the period consumed 60 or 70 tons of coal a day, hence stocking the coaling stations was a major expense. Each ton delivered to these remote stations cost the U.S. Mail line about $50 a ton, whereas a ton of coal in the United States fetched only about $3.

9.15. The *Golden Gate* was a wooden side-wheeler completed for the Pacific Mail line in 1851. She burned off the coast of Mexico in July 1862 with a loss of life totaling 223.

(C. B. Stuart, *Naval and Mail Steamer of the United States*, 1853)

The route across Panama was being improved as well. Small steamers on the Chagres River replaced the native boats and crews. The mule trail over the mountains was somewhat rebuilt to speed passengers across to Panama City. The greatest improvement was a new railroad financed by Aspinwall and his partners for $6.5 million. This was an enormous cost for a 50-mile railroad, four times the cost per mile of a railroad in the United States. This route was not only mountainous but also passed through a tropical jungle. Some of the extra cost was attributed to the first several miles being built upon pilings from the Atlantic end. Work began in 1850, and as the track progressed it was opened to passenger service. The crest of the mountains was reached in January 1854, and the last rail was laid one year later. Passengers could go across Panama in four hours, a journey that had previously required four or five days via small boats and mule trains. The comforts of riding the steam cars came at a considerable cost. Someone had to pay for this big investment, and it was not going to be the stockholders. The adult passengers paid $25, or about 50 cents a mile, whereas the common fare in the States was 3 cents a mile. Lesser fares were offered to children, but how many toddlers were heading off to the gold fields? Why did a railroad operating in a province of Columbia have a charter issued by the New York state legislature, and why was its headquarters at Nassau Street, New York? The locals may also have wondered why Chagres was renamed Aspinwall in 1850. It was renamed Colón in 1890 in honor of Christopher Columbus.

The experience of riding the Panama Railroad was a unique opportunity to examine tropical flora and fauna from the comfort of a coach seat.

All the fruits of the jungle could be seen up close. Bananas, pineapples, and mangoes were exotic to most North Americans of the 1850s; there were also lordly palm trees, giant flowering creepers, and sturdy groves of cane. Many of the grasses were matted, but they managed to show off their gorgeous colors. Troops of monkeys kept up a constant chatter in the trees, and other strange creatures offered fleeting glances as they moved behind the thicket of vegetation. Since at that time there were no zoos in the United States, the Panama Railroad offered its patrons their first glimpse of jungle wildlife. Transit time was now greatly reduced between New York and San Francisco to just twenty-eight days. Total passenger count over the Panama Route 1848–1869 was 808,769.

Ironically the gold rush was ebbing now that transport was so improved, for most Americans became convinced that the stories of El Dorado for the common man were a fable. It is true that gold production in California averaged about $70 million a year until 1853 when it began dropping. Little of this filtered down to the common man who panned the stream for gold dust. Traffic held up on the Panama route well enough that the railroad earned its cost and remained valuable enough to be sold to the French Panama Canal Company in 1880 for a good price. The railroad returned to U.S. ownership in the early twentieth century when the United States began construction of the Panama Canal. Today the line benefits from the container revolution in freight service. It also continues to operate a limited number of passenger trains.

The most comfortable way to reach California, especially in the first years of the gold rush, was around Cape Horn. It was the traditional way to reach the Pacific Ocean and the only route open to ships of the time. Most of the journey was made in calm water. The eastern coast of the United States could be stormy, and the Straits of Magellan and Cape Horn could be dreadful, yet the straits and cape were both mercifully short. The 14,000-mile trip could take up to eight months on a merchantman, but if you could find passage on a clipper ship it was much faster. These long, slim-hulled greyhounds of the sea were driven by an abundance of sail that reached so high above the sea they were called sky-scrapers. Most clippers made the trip in 100 to 130 days. Some steamers made the trip in about 60 days during times of fair weather. In 1853 fares were about the same as going via Panama; first class ranged from $250 to $350 and steerage was from $150 to $200.

A resident of Frankfort, Maine, J. Lamason, published an account of his 1853 trip to California on the sailing ship *James W. Paige* twenty-six years later. The *Paige* was a bark that had been refitted for passengers late in 1852. The work was not well done, for water leaked into the cabins, making the berths wet. The main cabin was below the main deck. It had

9.16. Passengers on the *Edward Everett* are heading to California around Cape Horn during the gold rush. The view is from the front of the boat looking toward the stern.

(Ernest Ingersoll, *Book of the Ocean*, 1898)

twenty-eight double berths that slept fifty-two passengers, meaning just four were single occupancy. A smaller after-cabin was provided for the lady passengers. A deckhouse over the main cabin provided fourteen more berths plus a stateroom for the captain. A second deckhouse offered space for the mate and four or five other passengers. The galley was in a small house on the top deck near the center of the ship. The crew slept, as usual, in the forecastle. Lamason does not mention the sailing date but recounts that by April 18, 1853, they had reached the Cape Verde Islands, some 400 miles west of Senegal, Africa, which was approximately 3,000 miles from Maine. The ship would then head for the South American coast. By late June they were rounding Cape Horn. The progress was slow because of strong headwinds, but they managed to sail around the cape in less than two days.

Yet greater trouble was found within the ship and its contentious human company. It began even as the ship left the dock. The lady passengers were in a huff because a minister had been given a berth in their cabin. Man of the cloth or not, what was a male doing in the ladies' cabin? Some people simply took a dislike to each other, and being so confined these ill feelings tended to only grow worse as the trip progressed. Near the end of the trip a fight broke out that was so large it took hours to restore order. There were smaller battles between individuals that resulted in bruises or cuts with a small knife. If such behavior was typical or not is uncertain, but in the case of this good ship it seems it was common enough. This account surely upsets the view of our Victorian ancestors as prim and proper genteel folk who would never resort to violence.

According to Lamason's account, passengers on the *Paige* were united on the topic of food: it was terrible. The cook was inept and personally dirty and disgusting. Beans and pork were served three or four times a week. The bread was dreadful. There was no butter or molasses for the biscuits. Sometime applesauce was provided for a spread, but in such small amounts that most diners were denied even a taste. Appeals to the mate brought no results. The captain was no more responsive. His job seemed to be making the largest profit for the ship owners, and one way to achieve that was to cut back on the quantity and quality of the food. He and some of the ladies enjoyed, in secret, such treats as fried mince pies. No one was ready to take on the captain, who was a giant of a man, vulgar and profane in speech, and surely no gentle giant. Both the bad food and the in-fighting continued until the end of the voyage. A prayer meeting a few days before the final landing failed to restore good feelings between the various combatants. The *Paige* entered San Francisco on September 7, 1853 – 158 days after leaving Frankfort, Maine.

Most forty-niners were new to the sea, and most succumbed to seasickness on the first day out of port. The ship was never still; it rolled and dipped in an unpredictable fashion, even on a fairly calm day. The less cargo or ballast on board, the worse she rolled. During a storm even experienced seamen had difficulty in keeping their balance, or their stomachs, in check. But normally after a few days many new sailors got their sea legs and could walk the deck at an acute angle. Their stomachs became somewhat accustomed to the constant motion. There were always a few who could not make the adjustment, however, and the long journey was pure hell for them.

Provisioning a ship for such a long trip required planning and storage room. It was possible to pick up fresh water and provisions along the way, but better to be prepared for an emergency when you had a big crew and passenger load. One captain left port with sixty barrels of salt pork and beef, thirty hogsheads of molasses, fifty bags of coffee, twenty hogsheads of sugar, a good supply of spirits, and several large barrels of fresh water. He would take a lesser amount of beans, rice, and tinned meat as provisions for the officers and first-class passengers. Other than eating, passengers would amuse themselves by reading, talking, or drinking. It was a once-in-a-lifetime vacation for most working-class men. Even so, much of the trip was spent in idle hours and profound boredom. However, few were bored during the passage through the Straits of Magellan or when going around Cape Horn.

The cape is the one of the most fearsome and most dangerous nautical passages in the world. It has bad weather for 200 days of the year as well as another 130 days of high winds and strong waves. On a stormy day the waves can be 65 feet high. They can batter the hull, smash deckhouses and lifeboats, and wash men overboard. The winds can reduce sails to rags. The Straits of Magellan are somewhat calmer but remain a challenge to navigation. This is one reason patronage of the route slackened off by 1850. This and the improvement in Panama helped shift passengers to this short route. The carriage of heavy freight continued to go around South America until the transcontinental railroad opened in 1869.

The Nicaragua route was the least used way to California, not because it was inherently inferior but because it was the least developed. It was 750 miles shorter than the Panama route and comparatively level. In addition it had a river and lake that offered a water route for all but 13 miles. The San Juan River runs 79 miles to Lake Nicaragua. The river passage is broken at Castilian by rapids, but otherwise it was suitable for light draft steamers. Passengers were portaged around the rapids. Lake Nicaragua was a sizable body of water that was also suitable for small steamers. The far western land link was improved by a plank road suitable for wagons and carriages. The jungle and insect life were minor compared to that of Panama. A suitable port, Greytown, already existed on the east coast. The overland crossing was about 135 miles and could be completed in forty hours.

Cornelius Vanderbilt believed the Nicaragua route was the best way to California, because it would save one or two days of travel just by its shortness and likely could save much more time if improved. Vanderbilt began running steamers to Nicaragua in 1850 and made a personal inspection of operations at that time. He became convinced that a deepwater canal could be built allowing ocean steamers to pass between the Atlantic and Pacific Oceans. Meanwhile he offered cut-rate fare to draw passengers away from Panama and looked for partners to help him develop the Nicaragua crossing. He formed a partnership with two other men who were active in the shipping business: Charles Morgan, mentioned earlier in this chapter, and C. K. Garrison. They formed the Accessory Transit Company, with Vanderbilt as president. Improvements were made as promised, and traffic picked up but never exceeded about 60 percent of the Panama route's patronage. Vanderbilt resigned as president of the company in September 1852 and went on an extended vacation to Europe several months later, assuring his partners that during his absence he would manage the company for his benefit as well as theirs. While in England, Vanderbilt hoped to raise money to build a great canal across Central America. The scheme received a favorable reaction at first, and Vanderbilt believed if it were completed he might be remembered as an international hero. However, the cost of the project rather quickly ended all serious plans for financial arrangements, and Vanderbilt returned to New York a disappointed man.

His mood quickly changed when he discovered his partners had taken over the transit company during his absence. He swore to ruin them and set out running an opposition line to kill their business. Morgan and Garrison responded in a dramatic fashion by supporting the invasion of Nicaragua by William Walker and his small army, who hoped to open it to slavery. Walker landed in June 1855 and briefly established a dictatorship. By the time he was ousted in 1857, almost no one was using the Nicaraguan route. Between the war and the opening of the Panama Railroad two years earlier, few found the transit company an attractive way to go. Vanderbilt then began offering cut-rate service to Panama. The Pacific Mail line began paying him a bribe of $40,000–$65,000 a month for not doing so. This arrangement went on until 1859.

The gold rush clearly was responsible for establishing new and faster ways to reach the Pacific Coast and can be credited with long-term changes in American travel history. These avenues of travel did not die in 1856 when the rush to California expired. The Pacific Mail steamed on for another seventy years. In the early 1890s it ran a boat from Pier 34 at the foot of Canal Street in New York to Colón every ten days. Once across the isthmus, passengers went to San Francisco on a connecting boat. The travel time was twenty-five days. The fare was $90, but forward cabins were available for $40. The Dollar Steamship lines continued this service after the demise of the Pacific Mail in 1926. The federal government organized the American President lines, which continued limited passenger service on some of the former Dollar lines until 1973.

TRANS-PACIFIC TRAVEL

Perhaps the most curious consequence of the interest in travel to the western United States was the beginning of regular passage to Asia by American liners. Trade with Asian ports had been going on since the first days of our nation, as already noted, but the carriage of mail and passengers did not happen until almost a century later. Then again, this is understandable considering the weaknesses of the American merchant marine in the Victorian era, when the British dominated world shipping. Most Westerners heading to the Orient left from England on a Peninsular and Oriental Steam Navigation liner that, after 1869, would pass through the Suez Canal on its way to India and Hong Kong. Passengers were delivered by the P&O in forty-four days to that island city port. The U.S. Postal Service decided in 1864 that mail and passengers should be able to go directly to the Far East aboard an American ship. A generous mail subsidy

9.17. A Pacific Mail advertisement.

(*Railroad Gazetteer*, June 1881)

of $.5 million was offered to stimulate interest in starting such operations. Only the Pacific Mail Steamship Company responded to this tender (fig. 9.17). Pacific Mail remodeled one of its newer side-wheelers, the *Colorado*, for this service. A number of passenger cabins were removed to provide more room for coal. The first trip was not made until January 1867. The *Colorado* reached Japan in just under twenty-two days, and a week later she landed in Hong Kong. The mail contract called for monthly service, but the Pacific Mail line had difficulty meeting the schedule during the first year. New boats were purchased, the schedule was improved, and the *Colorado* was returned to coastal operations between Panama and San Francisco.

9.18. The *City of Tokio*, 1874, is shown in San Francisco Harbor carrying General Ulysses S. Grant on the final segment of his around-the-world tour. The vessel operated between the United States and Asia.

(*Harper's Weekly*, October 25, 1879)

The Pacific Mail line added Singapore to its ports of call. It is one of the most important seaports in the world and one of the most international, for every race and almost every nation is represented here. Hot and humid, it is surprisingly busy and fast moving as cargoes and passengers are exchanged daily between hundreds of vessels. It is about 1,500 miles south of Hong Kong and midway between India and China, so it serves as a major fueling station for steamers. In 1874 the Pacific Mail ordered two large vessels to speed up service to this faraway port. They were named the *City of Peking* and the *City of Tokio* (using the old spelling for Tokyo) and built with iron hulls and screw propellers. Gone were the old-fashioned wood hulls and side paddle wheels that the Pacific Mail line had so long favored. Both vessels were made by John Roach's yard in Chester, Pennsylvania. At 409 feet they were the largest passenger vessels built in the United States up to that time. Their 4,000 hp engines could push the boats along comfortably at 15 knots. In general appearance they were very similar to the White Star line's *Brittanic,* the last word in luxury and speed. At a cost of $1.4 million each, one would expect them to be splendidly fitted out.

The *City of Peking* was launched March 18, 1874, and twenty-five thousand people attended the event. President Grant and his cabinet were on hand for *Peking's* trial run. Several years later Grant would return to the U.S. aboard the sister ship *City of Tokio* from an around-the-world tour (fig. 9.18). Before these two giants entered service the normal schedule from Yokohama took seventeen days. They could make a roughly 5,000-mile trip in twelve days. One of the notable passengers on the *City of Peking* was Rudyard Kipling, who sailed on her from Yokohama to San Francisco in 1889. The sea was rough during the crossing, and Kipling declared she was a "daisy at rolling." Trunks were in constant motion and could be heard hitting the bulkheads. If you were thrown out of your berth, you could join the sliding trunks. The *Tokio* was wrecked near the entrance to Yokohama in June 1885, but her sister ran on until retirement in 1904.

Pacific Mail reduced its rates in 1873 to boost traffic by taking passengers away from the transcontinental railway. The railroad responded by starting its own steamship line, the Occidental and Oriental Steamship Company. The operations were managed by the British White Star line; they leased nine boats and managed to take back most of the trade. Curiously, the railway had been credited with helping the Pacific Mail line's Far East traffic. Now the competitors came together to divide the traffic in 1875. Eighteen years later C. P. Huntington, president of the Southern Pacific Railway, bought the Pacific Mail line. It became independent again in 1915 but remained in operation for only about a decade.

The business traveler is normally the mainstay of public transport lines, but the tourist must be their number-two patron. People travel to restore their health, see family or the old homestead, or visit some new exotic place that is nothing like their home country. They travel to get away from the routine of life or perhaps even a failed romance. Sailing along the route of the gold rush era, travelers passed by many picturesque ports that were worthy of a very long and slow sea journey. Such a trip will close this chapter. It is based on an article in *Leslie's Weekly* from March 1878 and *Scribner's Magazine* from September 1891.

✳ ✳ ✳

Although trips to Europe were common in the Victorian era, more experienced travelers would advise the ill to go a gentler way. The Atlantic Ocean is the most violent of seas; go south or west to the Pacific. There you will find soft breezes, saline air, and the warmth of a perpetual summer to cure you. The bosom of the broad Pacific was made to restore the invalid. The Pacific Mail will carry you from San Francisco along the coast of

California, Mexico, and the Central American republics to Panama City. In 1878 it was 3,200 miles of charming scenery much unchanged since the Spanish invasion. The pace is leisurely; it takes fifteen to twenty days depending on how much cargo is picked up or dropped off. The schedule was not designed to please high-energy types.

After departing from San Diego, we cruise along the narrow and brown Baja Peninsula. There are no large ports in this part of Mexico, so we sail around the tip and visit Mazatlan, on the western coast of Mexico. It's a cosmopolitan city that some visitors have named the Paris of the Pacific. The next port is Manzanillo, which is something less than a Paris. Most of the ports along this cruise are best viewed from the boat. Too close an inspection only reveals how unattractive and dirty they are. Acapulco is an obvious exception, for both the harbor and town are handsome and well kept. We pass by the former western port of the old Nicaragua route, San Juan Del Sur, largely unused since 1856, but we drop anchor at both San José de Guatemala and La Libertad, Salvador.

At last we pull into the large harbor of Panama City. The city was rebuilt on the present site after the original town was destroyed by British buccaneers in 1671. On one side stands the massive fortress built by the Spanish during colonial times. The grand cathedral in the center city has a roof that shines like mother of pearl in the bright tropical sun. Many travelers leave the ship to ride the railroad across Panama and go directly by ship to New York. They will be home in a week and a day, but we prefer to follow the old route around South America and continue our restorative cruise. We have hurried all of our lives and have come to like this slower-paced way of life.

We book passage aboard a Pacific Steam Navigation (PSN) boat. We are told it is a British line but that it was founded in 1840 by an American named William Wheelwright, a native of Newburyport, Massachusetts. He came to South America as a cabin boy and made it his home. He was successful and saw the need for a steamship line for the western coast of South America. He could not find financial backers in the United States, so he went to England. There he succeeded and returned to Chile with two fine steamers. He managed the PSN until 1852 when he resigned to spend more time on a railway, the second in South America, which he built to service the copper mines at Copiapó, Chile. The PSN continued under British management for many years and prospered as a cargo carrier. Passengers were never plentiful, and most were South Americans with a few adventuresome foreigners mixed in. The officers were all British, and the crew were native-born sailors.

The boat stops at twenty-five ports during its 3,100-mile journey from Panama to Valparaiso, Chile. Most are forlorn provincial places, including Peru's major port of Callao. Even so, some passengers leave the boat because the capital city is only a few miles away. If passengers find Lima not that enchanting, they can board a train for the top of the Andes Mountains some 15,000 feet above sea level. This incredible piece of engineering arose from the efforts of American railway builder Henry Meiggs (1811–1877). We return from Lima to see the preserved bones of Francisco Pizarro in the cathedral before heading for the steamer. It is then another eleven days at sea before reaching Valparaiso in southern Chile. This busy town was built on hills surrounding a harbor full of ships. The Andes tower in the background of this attractive town. The streets are clean and the architecture is pleasing to the eye.

We switch steamers at Valparaiso to continue our trip around South America. The sea has been long and smooth, but as we proceed southward it grows rougher and colder. As we near the inside passage it becomes thick and unsettled, and there is the prospect of a foul gale. When the storm breaks, it comes with a tremendous blast. Nowhere else does the wind blow as hard or the sea rise higher. Curiously, as we swing into the Straits of Magellan, we leave the mad sea behind and the waters become reasonably calm. We move between high walls of bare stone and high bluffs. Blue glaciers can be seen in the distance. We exit the straits at Cape Virgins and head north for Montevideo up the east coast of Argentina. Moving northward we reach Rio de Janeiro with its large and beautiful harbor. At Rio we have a choice of a dozen lines to European ports and three lines to the United States. The United States and Brazil Mail lines run once a month to New York, making many stops along the way, including Barbados in the Windward Islands. St. Thomas is just one day's sail and 300 miles. From here it's 1,450 miles to New York, a journey of six days.

To recap our leisurely sea journey from San Francisco to New York we traveled 16,500 miles in one hundred days. This journey cost $1,000 for the cheapest accommodations. The price for first-class service was $2,000. The cost, even at the lower rate, was more than an average person earned in a year. What working person could afford to take off from work for one hundred days? Travel in the late Victorian era was possible only for the upper classes.

SUGGESTED READING

Albion, Robert G. *Square-Riggers on Schedule.* Princeton, N.J.: Princeton University Press, 1938.

Bauer, K. Jack. *A Maritime History of the United States: The Role of America's Seas and Waterways.* Columbia: University of South Carolina Press, 1988.

Baughman, James P. *Charles Morgan and the Development of Southern Transportation.* Nashville, Tenn.: Vanderbilt University Press, 1968.

Berthold, Victor M. *The Pioneer Steamer California, 1848–1849.* Boston: Houghton Mifflin, 1932.

Braden, Susan R. *The Architecture of Leisure: The Florida Resort Hotels of Henry Flagler and Henry Plant.* Gainesville: University Press of Florida, 2002.

Chadwick, F. E. et al. *Ocean Steamships.* New York: Scribner, 1891.

Cudahy, Brian J. *How We Got to Coney Island: The Development of Mass Transportation in Brooklyn and Kings County.* New York: Fordham University Press, 2002.

Dana, Richard Henry. *Two Years before the Mast.* 1869. New York: Westvaco, 1992.

Dayton, Fred Erving. *Steamboat Days.* New York: Frederick A. Stokes Co., 1925

Delgado, James P. *To California by Sea: A Maritime History of the California Gold Rush.* Columbia: University of South Carolina Press, 1990

Dunbaugh, Edwin. *The New England Steamship Company: Long Island Sound Night Boats in the Twentieth Century.* Gainesville: University Press of Florida, 2005

Duncan, Roger F. *Coastal Maine: A Maritime History.* New York: W. W. Norton, 1992.

Hill, Ralph Nading. *Sidewheeler Saga: A Chronicle of Steamboating.* New York: Rinehard and Co., 1953.

Hilton, George W. *The Night Boat.* Berkeley, Calif.: Howell-North, 1968.

Howland, S. A. *Steamboat Disasters and Railroad Accidents in the United States. To Which is Appended Accounts of Recent Shipwrecks, Fires at Sea, Thrilling Incidents, etc.* Worcester, Mass.; W. Lazell, 1846.

Kemble, John H. *A Hundred Years of the Pacific Mail.* Newport News, Va.: Mariners' Museum, 1950.

———. *Panama Route, 1848–1969.* Berkeley: University of California Press, 1943.

King, Moses. *King's Handbook of New York City: An Outline History and Description of the American Metropolis.* Boston: Moses King, 1892.

Lane, Wheaton Joshua. *Commodore Vanderbilt: An Epic of the Steam Age.* New York: Alfred A. Knopf, 1942.

Leavitt, John F. *Wake of the Coasters.* Middletown, Conn.: Wesleyan University Press, 1970.

Marestier, M. (Jean-Baptiste). *Memoir on Steamboats of the United States of America (Memoire Sur Les Bateaux A Vapeur Des Etats-Unis D'Amerique [1824]).* Mystic, Conn.: Marine Historical Association, 1957.

McAdam, Roger W. *The Old Fall River Line.* New York: Stephen Daye Press, 1955.

Mencken, August. *First-Class Passenger.* New York: Alfred A. Knopf, 1938.

Morison, Samuel Eliot. *The Maritime History of Massachusetts, 1783–1860.* Boston: Houghton Mifflin, 1921.

Morris, Paul C. *American Sailing Coasters of the North Atlantic.* Chardon, Ohio: Block and Osborn, 1973.

Nevins, Allen, and Milton Halsey Thomas, eds. *The Diary of George Templeton Strong.* New York: Macmillan, 1952.

Otis, Fessenden N. *Illustrated History of the Panama Railroad; Together with a Traveler's Guide and Business Man's Hand Book for the Panama Railroad and Its Connections with Europe, the United States, the North and South Atlantic and Pacific Coasts, China, Australia, and Japan, by Sail and Steam.* New York: Harper, 1862.

Smith, Eugene W. *Passenger Ships of the World, Past and Present.* Boston: George H. Dean Co., 1963.

Somerville, Duncan S. *The Aspinwall Empire.* Mystic, Conn.: Mystic Seaport Museum, 1983.

Stanton, Samuel W. *American Steam Vessels.* New York: Smith and Stanton, 1895.

Stick, David. *The Outer Banks of North Carolina, 1584–1958.* Chapel Hill: University of North Carolina Press, 1958.

Stuart, Charles B. *Naval and Mail Steamers of the United States.* New York: Charles B. Norton, 1853.

Ocean Sail № 10

At the Mercy of the Wind

TRAVEL BY SEA WAS ESPECIALLY DIFFICULT FOR FIRST-TIME travelers. Almost no one was prepared for the constant motion of the ship, for even in a relatively calm sea it rolls and dips. The floors, always called decks, are on an angle. The vessel makes strange sounds as the rigging and sails rattle and sing. The timbers deep in the hull groan and creak. When you go outside, the scenery is not pastures and fields or streets and buildings but a vast expanse of water that heaves and rolls to a distant horizon. This is a bizarre and different world that frightens and disorients the average person. Yet there is no getting off. Once the ship leaves port, you are its prisoner, and no matter how unhappy, you are condemned to ride on until land is once again at hand.

Finding the way across the sea is an art known only to seafarers. Some of it is intuitive – you follow the winds and currents. Sailors from Columbus's time knew that the winds from North America blow in a westerly direction. The Gulf Stream flows north and then west to Europe. This made sailing to England and France simple as long as you followed the wind and current. It was fast and was called the downhill trip. Most sailing ships could go from New York to England in about twenty to thirty days. Typically they would follow the North American coast to the southwest tip of Newfoundland (Cape Race) then head out into the Atlantic Ocean and follow a curving path that led to Ireland. Some navigators preferred a more northerly course, claiming the sea was calmer away from the Gulf Stream. Coming back from Europe was slower, because both the wind and the currents were against the ship. This was the uphill trip. It took much longer to go westward. The time was generally reckoned at about thirty-nine days. The only fast western way across the Atlantic was offered by the trade winds. It was necessary to go along the African coast to the Canary Islands, where the trade winds would blow the ship westward at a good speed to the Caribbean. Columbus made use of these winds in 1492 but also knew enough to return to Spain by going north to take the westerly trade winds home.

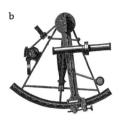

10.1. (a) Man at the wheel. (Thomas A. Croal, *A Book about Traveling: Past and Present*) (b) Sextant, 1870. (*Nautical Illustrations by Jim Harter.*) (c) Anchor. (Desmond, *Wood Ship-Building*) (d) Capstan.

(Charles G. Davis, *Ships of the Past*, 1929)

Another mystery of ocean travel was finding the location of a ship in the great sea, where there were no landmarks, road signs, or settlements to mark even an approximate location. Much early navigation was done by guess and by God; the ship's master depended on his experience and estimation as to the approximate location of the ship. He knew the boat was traveling at almost 5 knots, hence in twenty-four hours they had gone about 130 statute miles. A sailor in ancient times also followed a particular star that was directly over his home port; it would guide him back on the return trip. The morning star, Venus, comes up in the East. Mars is the red star, so it is easy to recognize. The North Star is better, because it is in a fixed position over the North Pole. Mariners in the northern hemisphere can measure the altitude or angle of the polestar to determine the latitude of the ship. Printed manuals were published in the 1790s that gave the position of various stars and planets throughout the year and allowed unskilled navigators to make more precise sightings. The sextant, introduced in 1757, when used with the manuals, could give an exact location of the ships. One of the captain's duties was to appear on deck a few minutes before noon and "shoot" the sun through his sextant. Three celestial bodies were sighted and the exact location of the ship was recorded as 12:00 noon in the ship's log. High noon is also the beginning of the nautical day (fig. 10.1).

Sailing ships are so foreign to people of the present century that a brief discussion of their construction and general arrangement seems necessary. Sailing ships belong to an age that had no plastic or aluminum and

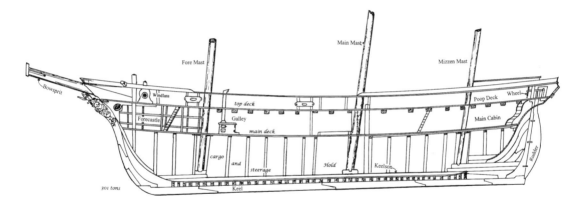

10.2. Longitudinal cross-section of a typical wooden sailing vessel of the nineteenth century.

(Author's collection)

very little steel. Even the largest naval ships were almost entirely wooden. Small amounts of iron, copper, and brass were used for certain fittings. Seagoing ships consisted of a massive wooden hull surmounted by masts and riggings. The front of the ships housed the crew. The rear portion was reserved for officers and first-class passengers. The large, hollow central section housed cargoes and third-class passengers, such as immigrants.

The keel was the ship's backbone and was generally made of elm. For a 1,000-ton vessel of 140 feet, the keel would measure 14 inches wide and 15 inches deep. It would of course be built up from many pieces that were spliced together. The bow timbers were made from the best wood available. The sternpost was in one piece and had to be made from the best-quality white oak in the yard. The frames were riblike in shape and were spliced together out of several pieces. White oak was preferred for all framing members. But when oak became scarce, live oak, from the new territory of Florida, purchased in 1819 from Spain, proved a good substitute. Yellow pine also proved a fine material for ship construction, and the United States was fortunate to have huge forests of this sturdy timber growing along its southern seacoast. Yellow pine was also used for planking the "skin" of the hull. It was cut in thicknesses of 3 to 6 inches. Manually powered pit saws produced the lumber used into the 1860s, as documented by an article in *Harper's Monthly* for April 1862. The broadaxes and adze also continued in everyday use to shape certain parts, such as the knees and other curving pieces. By the mid-nineteenth century wrought- and cast-iron knees were used. The wooden members were fastened together by long wooden dowels called, variously, treenails or trunnels. Sometimes large copper bolts were used. After the planking was in place, workmen filled every crack and crevice with a soft but waterproof rope called oakum. It was driven into place with a blunt chisel-like tool. Once the caulking was finished, the hull and decks would be watertight. Oakum is made from hemp fiber salvaged from old rope that was then mixed with tar. Boys were employed to tear the old bits of rope apart.

OCEAN SAIL 299

The hull was launched as soon as possible to make way for the construction of another ship. Christening was always a grand and joyous occasion. Gorgeous banners, flags, and streamers were attached to every available port of the finished vessel. A large crowd stood hushed and expectant. The crash of the wine bottle on the bow brought hurrahs from the crowd. As the 3,000-ton hull slid down into the water, all wished her a long career as she sailed the oceans of the world.

The hull was covered with sheet copper below the waterline. This could be done in a dry dock or by pulling the hull over on its side at a dock. The sheets were 14 by 48 inches and weighed about 20–28 ounces per square foot. Copper nails were generally used. About five thousand sheets of copper, about 15 tons, were used. Coppering the bottoms was a costly but necessary precaution to prevent sea worms from eating into the bottom planks of the hull. They could devour a wooden hull in a matter of weeks. The copper was also effective in discouraging seaweeds, grasses, and barnacles from attaching to the ship's bottom. This meant less frequent cleanings of the subaqueous portions of the vessel. Copper bottoms were introduced by the British navy in 1761 and were adapted for merchant vessels by the early nineteenth century.

The rigging, masts, and spars were made and installed by a separate contractor once the copper work was finished. Setting the masts was a tricky and specialized task. They were made in three or four pieces, each piece becoming smaller in diameter as it reached the top. The bottom of the main or center mast was about 30 inches in diameter. Canadian fir was used because it was straight, uniform, and strong. The bottom of the mast was set into the keelson in the lower part of the hull. A 100-foot-tall main mast was common. They could be up to twice that height on a clipper ship. The mast was braced and supported by a complex web of heavy rope called stays, backstays, and shrouds. The latter doubled as rope ladders that allowed the men to get up into the rigging. Even a small ship required 3 miles of rope for the rigging. The bowsprit projected out from the bow and was in effect a fourth mast. It carried several small jib sails and was strongly stiffened by stays.

The sails were made by another specialist or subcontractor. The typical ship had three masts and was square rigged – that is, the main sails were set across the hull to better catch the wind from behind. They could be turned to the right or left by some degree, because the wind was not always behind the ship. Most square-riggers had a few fore and aft sails that were set parallel to the centerline of the hull. These were the jibs at the front of the vessel and the mizzen or spanker sail attached aft of the rear-most mast. For centuries sails were made from linen, which tended to be soft and rather loose in weave and hence did not hold the wind all that well. By the second decade of the nineteenth century, cotton was mixed

10.3. Sail diagram of an American ship. Some sailing ships carried forty sails.

(Richard Henry Dana, *The Sailor's Friend*, 1851)

with flax thread, thus producing a better grade of canvas. Machine weaving produced a closer weave that was harder, more durable, and more uniform in texture. Much of it was manufactured in Kentucky. *Godey's Lady's Magazine* published an article on shipbuilding in 1854 that stated the best sailcloth was made from Russian hemp. It came in rolls 24 inches wide by 120 feet long. The best grade weighed 44 pounds per roll. A normal packet boat of the 1850s required forty sails, which equaled 9,000 yards of canvas. Note that the schematic in fig. 10.3 is a later style of sailing ship that used just twenty-seven sails. An extra set of new sails was carried aboard any well-equipped ship.

Although a ship's sails were functional in purpose, they also added greatly to its appearance. They gave the ship a majestic appearance as they billowed out in their whiteness. James Cooper, himself a navy veteran, wrote in his novel of 1823 titled *The Pilot*, "The vessel glided over the water with a grace and facility that seemed magical to the beholder." Richard Dana had the opportunity to see these grand "wind muscles" in action. He was on deck one night, and as he looked up into the rigging the sails stood out in a steady breeze that created no ripples or quivering. They looked like sculptured marble, he thought, and he noted how quietly they did their work.

TRANSATLANTIC PASSENGER TRAVEL

The North Atlantic is a little over 3,000 miles wide and about 2 miles deep. Its salt content is approximately 3.5 percent. All of the world's oceans have storms and spells of violent weather, but the North Atlantic is the stormiest of all the seas. It experiences winds of 75 miles an hour and waves 100 feet high. Bad weather is a regular thing on the most dangerous sea of all. Ironically it became the busiest in terms of shipping because of the concentration of the world trade war between Europe and North America. The parade of ships started about fifty years after Columbus's epic voyage and continues to the present day.

In the beginning, ships tended to be general carriers. Their primary business was the carriage of cargoes. Passengers were secondary, almost an afterthought, put back in a few cabins near the captain's quarters at the ship's stern. Human cargo was seen as offering a little extra revenue but not taking up too much space. When large numbers of people wanted to cross the ocean – and this trade did not become particularly significant until around 1800 – more specialized ships were developed. The poorest travelers were handled like so much bulk grain or lumber and were placed in the cargo hold with no special accommodations. First-class passengers, who were willing to pay the freight, received greatly refined and more costly accommodations aboard ships especially designed to cater to their needs. This specialization grew apace until ships devoted to passengers were built and the ocean liner was born.

Passengers traveling at the beginning of the transatlantic era could only dream of luxury liners, for the vessels of the time were surely elementary in just about every detail from heating to lighting to toilets. It must be remembered that amenities we take for granted were not available even to the elite in the sixteenth century. Hence when a traveler boarded a ship and found no flush toilets or automatic central heating, he was hardly nonplussed; in fact, he would have been very puzzled and perhaps even frightened if he found any modern conveniences aboard the boat. Passengers would find most ships in service between the years of roughly 1500 and 1800 remarkably spartan affairs. The hull, or body, was largely an open cavity, roofed over by the main deck. A second, lower deck offered a more or less flat space to support cargo, which was lowered down through a large central hatch, or opening, in the main deck. Toward the bow was a small cabin called the forecastle that offered shelter to the crew. To the rear or stern was another cabin or set of cabins for the captain, the mates, and a few passengers. Even these cabins were fairly plain and sparsely furnished. A few bunks, tables, chests, and chairs, but not much else was placed here. There would be a chamber pot or two plus some washbasins, but running water was unheard of. About the only complicated things on the ship were the masts, spars, sails, and the tangle of rigging. The whole plan was to keep the ship as simple as possible so that it could carry itself and its cargo from one shore to another, but no more than that.

Ship size was rather stagnant during most of the colonial period. Vessels typically were 90 feet long and 25 feet wide whether built in 1600 or

1750. After 1800, however, larger ships came into favor; length grew to 120 feet, and tonnage[1] ratings doubled from about 200 tons to 400 tons. By the 1850s 1,000-ton ratings were becoming common. As hull size expanded, ceiling heights began to increase so that tall passengers no longer had to duck in passageways, cabins, or doorways. By the early 1850s clipper ships were ushering in a new age of very large wooden sailing vessels. Some measured 220 feet long with a tonnage rating of 2,000.

Passengers could hope to book passage on either a tramp or a regular trader. The tramp was a transient ship that followed no fixed route and kept to no schedule. It roamed the seven seas in search of cargo. It would leave its home port and wander from harbor to harbor, from one land to another, and be gone two or three years before returning home. Passengers did not find tramps well suited to their needs. If the ship was loaded and ready to go to Charleston, your port of destination, fine, but often as not the needs of the passenger and the tramp did not match. Passengers found regular traders far more agreeable. Such vessels shuttled back and forth between a predetermined number of ports. Many a trader was shipper-owned and carried the owner's goods between, say, Bristol and Boston. Travelers going between these two ports knew that one or more of John Hancock's ships regularly plied those waters. Traders tended to sail between the larger ports. They also tended to be larger and better ships than the tramps, making them more attractive to travelers.

Because of their regular routings, traders' captains were asked to carry packets of letters to and from their destinations. In time, these semi-official mail boats became known as packets. In time this designation was applied to almost any vessel that carried both passengers and cargo, including river steamers. The packets performed well for most passengers, but they had one major failing: no fixed departure date. The ship did not leave the dock until the cargo hold was full or full enough to make a paying load. Captains and owners were inclined to sit at the dock for weeks at a time waiting for cargoes. Conversely, passengers were ready to go now, or at the least to go at some fixed or definite time. The uncertainty of a departure was a particular irritant characteristic of early sea travel. About the only ships following a fixed schedule were the British Mail brigs that began operations in the eighteenth century. Most carried passengers, but their indirect routing, with stops at many ports, resulted in a slow schedule, so they were not particularly popular as passenger carriers.

All of this changed on January 15, 1818, at 10:00 AM when the Black Ball line inaugurated regular service between New York and Liverpool, the most heavily traveled water route between the New and the Old World. This was a new concept in ocean travel. Several boats would shuttle back and forth over a fixed route and with a fixed departure time. When one boat left Liverpool, a sister boat would leave New York a few days later – they would pass each other in mid-ocean. The boats would leave full or not full and in good weather or foul. To prove this promise, when the first Black Baller left port she had only eight cabin passengers, with room for twenty more, and only a small freight cargo. In addition, it was snowing. No regular trader would have left the dock under those conditions, but the Black Ball line sailed on schedule. At first there was only one boat each way per month. After four years of running, however, three packet lines offered a weekly boat, and by the 1840s scheduled service was offered to London; Le Havre, France; Antwerp, Belgium; as well as Liverpool. By this time so many scheduled ships were tied up at New York's South Street that it was called Packet Row.

The English architect and engineer Benjamin H. Latrobe (1764–1820) left behind an excellent record of what sea travel was like before regular packet lines started. He had inherited some land from his mother in Pennsylvania and decided to emigrate to America in 1795. He recorded this experience in a journal that was published in 1977. Latrobe took passage on an American vessel named the *Eliza,* bound for Norfolk, Virginia. She left from Gravesend, about 15 miles east of London on the Thames estuary, on November 15 with thirteen passengers and a crew of sixteen. It was not to be a happy trip. There was in fact nothing that Latrobe found to his liking. The ship's captain, Captain Noble, was boorish and inept. He could not navigate and had no idea how to get the ship out of the English Channel. Fortunately, the first mate was a reasonably competent seaman or they might have never made port. As it was, the trip lasted 105 days rather than the usual 40 days required for a westward crossing.

There was a great deal of bad weather, which again is the norm for a wintertime crossing – January is generally the worst month. On December 12 an unusually strong gale stripped away the sails; the masts seemed ready to go as well, according to Latrobe. The captain had no idea what to do, and the first mate and one of the passengers who happened to be an expert seaman saved the ship. There was only one spare sail rather than a full set. Nor was there any canvas on board other than scraps of old odds and ends. The crew mended what they could. The lack of sails explained their slow progress.

Matters on the *Eliza* were no better belowdecks. The main cabin that housed all of the passengers measured 14 by 22 feet. Berths were built in along both sides, and two more berths were placed across the lockers. The cabin and everything in it were unspeakably dirty. The tablecloth was a filthy piece of old sailcloth. The pewter was black, never having been polished. The glasses and silverware were never washed, but only wiped off for reuse. There were so few glasses that they had to be shared among the passengers. The same kettle was used to make both tea and coffee and so affected the taste of both. The stove could not be used, because it smoked badly, so the cabin was always cold. Much of the slovenliness of the passenger quarters could be blamed on the cabin boy, Dick. He was short, thick, lame, and, needless to say, personally very unkempt. He served the meals and cleared the tables. After everyone had finished, he would sit on the floor at the cabin door and eat the leftovers.

Latrobe left a fine record of the not-always-so-fine food served aboard the *Eliza*. He and a few other passengers took the precautions of bringing aboard a supply of cabbages, parsnips, and other foods to supplement the ship's stores. Typically the ship carried some livestock for fresh meat. There were four sheep, four pigs, and a dozen chickens. The sheep alone seemed to thrive aboard ship. The pigs did poorly, and the one killed was in such poor condition that the meat was thrown overboard. The chickens soon became too thin and tough to eat. The salt beef held up well but was too salty for most tastes. The biscuits were good, but the butter was only tolerable. Water was in very limited supply. The crew was allowed only ½ gallon a day. There is no record of the passengers' allotment. Wine and porter's beer were consumed instead. There is no mention of desserts or sweets in Latrobe's account. The edibles seemed to have agreed with him; he never complained of seasickness, but there were times when he did not eat. The ship rolled more than it might because of too little ballast or cargo. Surely all aboard were happy when the *Eliza* entered Hampton Roads, Virginia, on March 8, 1796. The 105-day journey had ended at last.

LIFE ABOARD THE PACKETS

The beginning of packet ship service was surely a new and wonderful day in transatlantic travel. The contrast in the travel experience between Latrobe's dismal trip to Norfolk and lines running out of New York and Liverpool could hardly be more pronounced. The captains were first-rate. They were competent, concerned, and reliable – experts, in fact, in managing ships in a safe and efficient manner. Many were also charming and personable. The ships were excellent, too. They were heavy, strong, and yet fast. The interiors were beautiful and clean. Passengers had a small sleeping cabin, limited only by double-occupancy requirements. The food was excellent, fresh, well-prepared and elegantly served. The dishes and tableware were top quality and were often made for that particular ship. Everything was first class. Fares were high, as might be expected, because someone had to pay for the deluxe service.

The founders of the Black Ball line were merchants who were active in the shipping trade. They needed to cross the Atlantic Ocean in connection with their business, so they dealt with merchants and salesmen who traveled over the same waters regularly. All knew the shortcomings of seagoing ships and understood that there were many people who would

10.4. The *Isaac Webb* of 1850 was named for W. H. Webb's father, a pioneer shipbuilder in the New York City area. It was operated by the Black Ball line until 1878.

(*Gleason's Pictorial,* May 17, 1851)

pay for a better class of service. The Treaty of Ghent ended the War of 1812 and opened the seas to peaceful trade and travel. It was a good time to reform ocean travel and make it a fit way for gentle folk to get around the world in a civilized manner.

The chief partner in the Black Ball enterprise was an English Quaker, Isaac Wright, who came to New York to establish a dry goods business. He dealt in quality goods such as fine imported British woolens. For all of his commitment to the simple life, Wright and his partners understood the need for fine accommodations to attract first-class travelers. One of their first ships, the *James Monroe,* had an elegant main cabin done up in the Egyptian style. Doorway arches were supported by white marble columns; paneling was in satinwood; furniture was in the latest fashion, with upholstery in shiny black horsehair. The mahogany dining table was long and elegant. Hair mattresses were used instead of the more common straw-filled variety. Chamber pots were decorated with gilt and flowers. How different from the *Eliza*'s gritty appearance. The decorating became increasingly elaborate with the passage of years. The ladies' cabin on the *Victoria* of the Black X line (1843) was painted in the French-style white and gold with graceful carved panels. Circular sofas in green and gold brocade and giant gold-framed mirrors were soon the fashion.

At the same time, our caring Quaker manager made sure the hold of these floating palaces were filled with high-paying cargoes. Specie was transported in the packets because they were fast. The Bank of England sent several large shipments of gold coins to bolster the financial health of the United States after the panic of 1837. Most came in $.5 million installments. In April the Black Ball's *Mediator* arrived with $1.25 million in British coins. No one at the time wanted paper money. Cotton was a more common cargo and was one of America's leading exports. Apples, flour in barrels, and naval stores were other commodities sent by packets. While many merchant ships jockeyed for the immigrant trade as a good return cargo, the packets ignored them until the steamships began to draw away more and more first-class passengers.

The most common activity on first-class transatlantic ships was eating. Four meals a day were served: breakfast, luncheon, dinner, and tea at around 8:00 PM. Dinner usually lasted one and a half hours. During the three courses, wine, hock (Rhine wine), claret, Madeira, and port were offered freely. Champagne was served three or four times a week. Holland's grog was offered as a nightcap. The meals were large and of long duration, but they served a useful purpose. They kept the passengers busy and happy. They would sleep contentedly after a long, rich meal, thus giving cabin attendants a few hours of peace. The various packet lines that developed in the first half of the nineteenth century put great emphasis on food, its preparation, and serving. To ensure freshness, animals were carried aboard the packets. This was not a new idea, but the way it was handled was surely better than the offhanded manner demonstrated aboard the *Eliza*. Animals were fed and looked after carefully. There were ducks and pigeons in addition to chickens. Eggs were collected.

Most animals were kept on the main deck around the long boats that served as a partial shelter. But in high seas the chicken coop might be swept overboard. When a sheep met its end this way, the passengers were cheated of a ration of mutton. An onboard cow provided milk and cream. French boats often carried small hand-operated flour mills to make fresh flour each day and thus avoid vermin. Canned goods had been available since Napoleonic times; this allowed the serving of peaches or green beans in the middle of the raging Atlantic in midwinter or, for that matter, in any season. In an emergency some captains might organize a hunt for fresh meat – young sea lion was said to be very tasty. Polar bear meat was much like beef. Whale was also something like beef. Sea cow and manatee meat had their admirers. The meat of fur seals on the table smelled as strong as an old goat, so those animals were generally left in peace.

During the year, special dinners were served to first-class passengers, who were accustomed to gracious and festive dining. The captain of the *Cortez* happened to be a Scot, and as November 30, 1822, approached he planned a grand feast in honor of Scotland's patron saint, Andrew. The meal began with real turtle soup, then a fine salmon and a tasty array of vegetables and starches. It ended with a rich cake, puddings, tarts, preserves, fruits, and nuts. Choice white and red wines and champagne were served during the evening. There was much good humor, amusing toasts, and hilarity during the long banquet. Many years later a passenger

10.5. This deck scene dates from 1831. The artist was at the very rear of the top deck looking forward. This illustration was redrawn from a watercolor drawing in the collection of the New York Historical Society.

(Drawing by Rebekah Powers)

recorded a Christmas dinner aboard the Red Swallowtail line's *Cornelius Grinnel*. The feast started at 2:30 with soup, and then came entrees of boiled codfish and potatoes, roast turkey, stewed chicken, and macaroni pie. Diners might also choose from roasted and boiled potatoes, mashed turnips, French bread, sea biscuits, pickles, and other such fixings. Plum pudding and champagne ended the meal.

The galley, or kitchen, was placed on the top deck in a cabin or just below the deck in a hatchway near or against the foremast. It was kept out of the hull as a fire precaution measure. Its forward placement kept the cooking odors and smoke away from the main cabin that was at the stern. Separate galleys were usually kept for the seamen and officers and first-class passengers.

Fares were high aboard the packets because of the elaborate cabins and fine foods and wines offered. When Black Ball started service in January 1818 the first-class fare to cross the Atlantic Ocean was 40 guineas ($186). By 1823 enough packet lines were running that fares dropped to $140. Passengers who did not drink wine were given a discount of $20. Once competition with steamers began in a serious fashion by 1843, the fare dropped to $80 and then to $75.

A private stateroom was available at double fare. It gave you a small cabin about 8 feet square with a bunk bed. Joseph Bonaparte (1768–1844), one-time king of Spain and a brother of Napoleon, resided in exile for a number of years in Bordentown, New Jersey. Joseph would book an entire packet for him and his retinue for occasional European visits. The cost of such a trip is not recorded, but it is known that he tipped the crew generously. Payment was made in gold or specie; paper money was not accepted except at a discount.

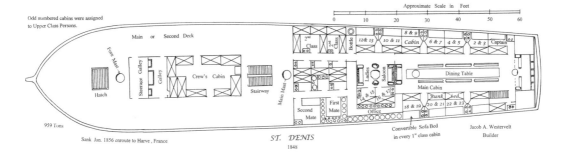

10.6. The St. Denis was built in 1848 by Jacob A. Westervelt for the New-York-to-Havre packet line. The second or main deck is shown in this plan drawing.

(Redrawn from Charles G. Davis, *Ships of the Past*, 1929)

The transatlantic traffic was not that great, as the average load was only ten to twenty passengers per trip. It was rarely more than twenty-five, and by the 1830s many packets had room for fifty to sixty cabin passengers. Robert Albion estimated in his book *Square Riggers* that from 1818 to 1857 the U.S. packet lines serving Liverpool, London, and Le Havre carried eighty thousand passengers. Yet the service was clearly profitable, because the owners and managers of the lines became wealthy. The high-priced freight carried in the hold is likely the source of the ship's earnings. The federal government in its early years collected almost all of its revenue from duties collected at seaports. There was no income tax at the time. In 1828 the duties collection from New York Harbor paid for the entire expenses of the central government.

While the packets were considered fast for their day, the trip eastbound took generally twenty-five days and the westbound took about forty days. This was a lot of time to be confined in a small cabin. In the winter it was not safe or pleasant to spend much time on the deck, and when the weather was bad, passengers were confined to the cabin, lest they be washed overboard or injured by a falling piece of rigging. Most travelers, from Alexis de Tocqueville to Ralph Waldo Emerson, found life aboard ship very confining and crowded. The cabins were so small that it was necessary to step out into the main cabin to dress. The lack of space was annoying – so many people talking or just breathing – that it irritated sensitive persons who wanted more privacy. Longfellow hoped to do some writing but found it impossible to concentrate because of the noise of passengers and the ship itself, which seemed to creak, groan, or pop every few seconds. The cold and constant wetness bothered others. Some women needed to be held and consoled when a storm blew up – they were so frightened. Many just drank to relieve the boredom or annoyances of the long journey.

Wives would share a stateroom with their husbands when traveling together, but women traveling alone or in pairs were assigned separate cabins. These compartments were generally separated from the men's quarters. There was also a separate main cabin set aside for the ladies' daytime use. Men and women would dine together in the main cabin. The

OCEAN SAIL 309

deck plan for the New-York-to-Le-Havre packet ship *St. Denis* offers more details on these arrangements (fig. 10.6). In general women were offered separate space whether traveling by ferry boat, riverboat, or railroad coach during the Victorian era.

Seasickness was a common misery. It was normal for a large number of passengers to stay in bed the first few days out to sea. The dining table was a lonely place, especially if the sea was running high. After about a week, many passengers had gotten their stomachs under control and did fairly well until the end of the trip unless a gale got the ship rocking greatly. Seasick remedies of the day were bogus concoctions that offered no relief. Sucking lemons was a standard cure that rarely worked. Passengers would recline on a sofa in their silent agony, their pale, hollow faces looking most pitiful. Others would rush to the deck and stand at the lee rail, paying tribute to old Neptune. Some ships had a surgeon on board, but he was often a surgeon in name only. His one effective remedy was laudanum, a tincture of opium that could become a lifetime habit. It was not until the mid-twentieth century that effective drugs for seasickness were introduced.

SAFETY AT SEA

The sea is not a safe place, and the Atlantic Ocean is the least safe of all the seven seas. Ironically, however, it was the busiest in terms of passenger travel during the Victorian era. Storms are epidemic in this angry, dark gray ocean. Sailors have a weather eye, watching the sky and the wind direction. The first sign of trouble can be a shift in the wind. Next is the appearance of dark purple clouds topped by a copper-colored formation. They move rapidly across the sky and bring lightning. The sea picks up, and then comes torrents of rain. The men scramble up rope ladders to save the topsails before they are blown away by the storms. An alert captain and a responsive crew can usually save the ship, but there were some who could not.

During the packet era, 1818–1858, about ninety seagoing American ships were lost each year. However, only twenty-two packets were lost during this forty-year period. Their safety record was extremely good. Packet passenger mortality was only six per every one hundred thousand persons carried. Travelers could hardly hope for better odds. The Black Ball line had a perfect safety record during its first four years. On April 1, 1822, the Black Ball liner *Albion* left New York for England with fifty-four on board, counting passengers and crew. By the twenty-first they sighted the southwest tip of Ireland. A sudden storm blew up and grew more violent until around nine o' clock that evening a great wave hit the ship. The main mast, the compass, the steering wheel, and much of the rigging

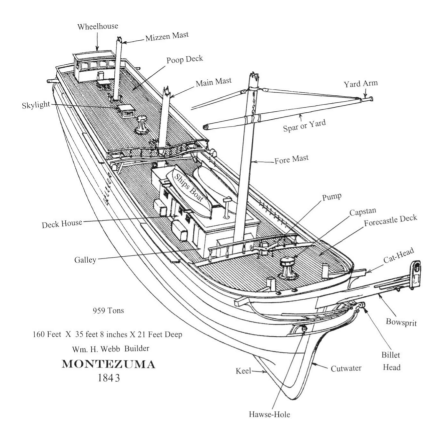

10.7. The *Montezuma* was built for the Black Ball line in 1843 by William H. Webb. It was lost on Jones's Beach, Long Island, in May 1854.

(Modified from a drawing in Charles G. Davis, *Ships of the Past*, 1929)

were swept overboard, along with several sailors and one passenger. The hatches were torn open and the cabins filled with water. As the crewmen worked the pumps, the captain remained calm and directed the work in the best manner. The ship was helpless with so little sail, and the wheel was gone, so the *Albion* was at the mercy of the wind. At about 3:00 that night she hit the rocks near Kinsale, Ireland. A few passengers on the forecastle deck were crushed by the anchor, which had broken loose. The captain and several others were swept out to sea and never seen again. As the dawn's first light appeared the ship broke apart. Only eight survived the disaster.

Three months after the loss of the *Albion* another Black Ball liner, the *Liverpool*, was making her maiden voyage to England. Partway across she encountered some fog and her sails were taken in, but once in the clear again, the sails were reset. She came upon more fog but kept moving ahead hoping to make up lost time. This was not to be, for she hit an iceberg head-on, which stove in the ship's bow. The *Liverpool* went down quickly, but all aboard got into the longboats safely. They made their way back to St. John's, Newfoundland, in about a week. In May 1854 the Black Ball lost another packet, the *Montezuma*, when it was driven ashore at Jones Beach, Long Island, New York. The storm continued to pound away at the stranded vessel, but before she broke up, all of those aboard were safely

OCEAN SAIL   311

10.8. The *Tornado* was partly dismasted by a whirlwind in 1852 but was jury-rigged well enough to return safely to her home port of New York.

(*Gleason's Pictorial*, January 29, 1853)

escorted away from the shore, including nearly five hundred immigrants (fig. 10.7).

Wind can wreck a ship, but it doesn't have to spell her doom. A resourceful captain aided by a good crew can save their ship and themselves with a little hard work. In September 1852 a whirlwind ripped off the bowsprit and foremast of the *Tornado*. The boat was at the mercy of the sea for about two weeks as Captain O. R. Mumford and his men attempted to mend her. They jury-rigged a temporary mast and restored lost sails and rigging into a workable arrangement that got them back to New York in just sixty-five days (fig. 10.8).

Wooden hulls could develop leaks in a stormy sea, and seams would open up, letting in seawater. No captain or crew could ignore a rising bilge. In his novel *Lord Jim* Joseph Conrad wrote about a ship coming apart at sea; she was working herself loose and leaking badly. The bulwarks went, the stanchions were torn out, the ventilators smashed, the cabin doors were busted in, and there was not a dry spot in the ship. The sea churned white like a cauldron of boiling milk, and the infuriated waves would not settle down. The crew kept pumping – it seemed for all eternity. And pump they must, for to stop meant to be drowned. Self-preservation was a mighty motivation to pump (fig. 10.9).

Fire at sea might not seem likely, because a ship is surrounded by water; nevertheless, they tended to burn quite easily once ablaze. Cooking fires were a source of such disasters, and for this reason the galley was shut down temporarily during very heavy weather. It has been claimed that immigrants started a severe fire aboard the *Ocean Monarch* in 1845 by attempting to prepare a meal in a ventilation shaft; however, passengers smoking may have been the actual cause. Four hundred lives were lost because of this stupid mistake. Dropped lanterns and candles set a certain

10.9. A crew pumps desperately, hoping to save their ship in this drawing based on Henry S. Tuke's painting of 1888–1889.

(Drawing by Rebekah Powers)

number of ships on fire. Lightning caused the *Poland*, a New-York-to-Le-Havre packet, to go up in smoke on May 11, 1840. The ship was passing through a thunderstorm when a flash of lightning found its way down the foremast and into the hold and struck a cargo of cotton. The crew could not get to the cotton, because so much other cargo was in the way. Efforts to suffocate the flames failed. The fire continued for about two days. Fortunately another ship came by, and the *Poland* was abandoned to her fate when the crew and passengers were taken aboard the other vessel. The single loss of life was the ship's unfortunate cow. The vessel was worth about $40,000, only part of which was covered by insurance.

Perhaps the saddest of all ship losses were the vessels that simply disappeared. They left a port on a certain date but failed to appear at their destination. Sometimes they might have been sighted partway across by another vessel. Weeks would go by and no ship would be seen. Family waited pensively for word about the fate of their loved ones. Wives, mothers, fathers, and children grew depressed as they waited, but the wait was not always in vain, because sometimes a vessel was late only because there was no wind or a storm had blown it off course. There was no radio to explain the reason, no surveillance planes to find the lost ship. Then again, months might go by and there would still be no word. The ship was presumed lost and the families were left to speculate on what might have happened to their now vanished friends or relations.

THE CAPTAIN AND HIS CREW

The captain of a ship was at the apex of the floating world. Aboard ship he was the master, and his word was literally the law. Anyone who contradicted him or disobeyed an order – and this included passengers – could be punished. Any behavior that undermined his authority might endanger the ship. Punishment might be half rations, bread and water, confinement to a cabin, time in the brig, or being put in irons. At the same time, the captain was solely responsible for the ship and what happened to her, the cargo, and the passengers. If anything went wrong, he was accountable and had better have a very good explanation for whatever transpired. He needed good technical skills to navigate the ship. He had to be strong enough to bully the crew and yet charming enough to engage the passengers. He sat at the head table with passengers who often bored or annoyed him, yet he would smile and pretend to be enjoying the meal. At the same time, his was a solitary life. He would be away from his wife and family for weeks or months at a time. He was friendly only with the first mate but distant and reserved around the rest of the crew. He spent long hours in his cabin going over logbook entries, charts, and shipping manifests. He stood no regular watches, but was on call every hour of the day. If anything unusual happened, the crew knew they must go and wake up the Old Man. A good captain never undressed, but kept on his trousers and shirt. He could get up, slip on some shoes, and be on deck in a matter of seconds. Captains were often called "Skipper," a word of Dutch origin, by the crew but not to his face unless it was a very small and informal vessel. A naval captain is a rank given by commission, but smaller naval ships had captains of a lower rank. William Bligh, for example, was only a lieutenant when he served as captain on the *Bounty* in 1788.

One of the more successful captains was Edward Knight Collins (1802–1878). His father was a captain and his mother's uncle was a British admiral. At the age of twenty he became a supercargo on a West Indies trader, meaning he was in charge of the sale and purchase of the ship's cargo. During his five years in the Caribbean he escaped from pirates and survived two shipwrecks. In 1825 he joined his father's shipping firm on South Street in New York City. Giant sailing ships sat at the dock outside of their office. Following a tip on rising cotton prices, Collins chartered a pilot boat for a quick trip to Charleston, where he hoped to buy cotton before the price went up. He sailed the yacht-like boat close to shore to take advantage of the tides, currents, and land breezes. His saucy little craft got him south in time to buy cotton before prices escalated. He soon had capital enough to buy more ships for runs to Vera Cruz and Tampico. In 1833 he had built a 750-ton vessel, the *Mississippi,* which was considered very large for the time. She could carry twenty-six hundred bales of cotton. In 1836 Collins started a packet line from New York to Liverpool. It became known as the Dramatic line, because all of its ships were named for famous playwrights or actors. The *Shakespeare* was the first vessel. In 1838 the *Roscius* entered service; it was a giant for the time at 1,030 tons and measuring 167 feet long. By 1843 the Dramatic line had twenty vessels in service, some of them costing as much as $80,000. Collins was ranked as one of the most able men in the American Merchant Marine.

Other captains were destined to die while trying to save their ship. Captain Ira Bursley (1798–1850) was in command of the Liverpool New line packet *Hottinguer* when she wrecked early in 1850 on Blackwater Bank, located at the southeastern tip of Ireland. The passengers and most of the crew were rescued, but Bursley and a few of his men stayed on board hoping to save the ship. The storm became more intense that night, and all of the ship's brave seamen perished.

Samuel Samuels (1823–1908) was another brave captain who managed to survive many a bad situation at sea (fig. 10.10). He also lived long enough to write his autobiography, *From Forecastle to the Cabin,* published in 1887. He was best known as the captain of the *Dreadnought,* a vessel built especially for him in 1853 at Newburyport, Massachusetts, by backers who believed in his seamanship. She looked like a clipper but was actually too wide and heavy to fit that description. Even so, she proved remarkably fast, though she was a little sluggish on calm days and ran best in heavy weather. Samuels was one of those kick-'em-in-the-pants sort of sailors who would leave all the sails up to see how much speed he could get out of her. If the sails blew away he would put up new ones. Cautious, he was not. She became part of the St. George's Cross line, which ran the New-York-to-Liverpool route. There was a large red cross on her fore topsail (fig. 10.11). She was rated at 1,400 tons and measured 200 feet long. Her first round trip to Liverpool was made in fifty-eight days, better than a Cunard line steamer, and netted $40,000. She made seventy-five trips across the North Atlantic. Samuels drove the *Dreadnought* so hard that she kept breaking her own record, and she ran best in winter when wind

10.10. Captain Samuel Samuels (1823–1908) was notable for his fast sailing speeds.

(*Harper's Weekly*, January 19, 1867)

was howling wildly. Early in 1859 she made a record run to Liverpool: 3,018 miles in just thirteen days and eight hours. Samuels was capable of other feats beyond fast sailing. He took his red-cross beauty through Hell Gate at night, a feat no other full-rigged ship dared to attempt. In 1862 after a storm removed the rudder, he sailed the *Dreadnought* backward for 280 miles, where she landed for repairs. Time was running out for Samuel's ship; she was lost on rocks while attempting to go around Tierra del Fuego in 1869. All fourteen crew members escaped in a lifeboat and were picked up fourteen days later.

Even the most driven captain could not always make a fast voyage, no matter how much extra sail was put up. A still wind moved no ships, but beyond that obvious fact there were often delays in to the dock, including at New York Harbor. The entrance was partially blocked by a long sandbar called Sandy Hook. The service of a pilot was required to get ships safely across it, even at high tide. The provincial government of New York enacted a law in 1694 requiring the service of pilots to enter the harbor. These canny gents always knew just where a boat of a particular size could pass

10.11. The *Dreadnought*, a modified clipper built in 1853 at Newburyport, Massachusetts. She ran on the St. George's Cross line, New York to Liverpool, for many years. Samuel Samuels was her captain.

(*Harper's Monthly*, January 1884)

over the sandbar. When traffic was heavy there was a wait – sometimes for days – because the number of pilots was limited. Crews and passengers might fret and fume, but it did no good, for the ship would not move until the pilot stepped off the small boat that came next to the waiting ship. He would clamber up the ladder that had been let down for him. He knew the depth at low tide was 23 feet and just 5 feet more at high tide, and he knew the tricky shoals and strong currents. He would stay with the ship until she was docked. The pilot would stand by the wheelman, guiding him carefully along the 25-mile route through the lower bay and the Verrazano Narrows, into the upper bay and around Governor's Island to Manhattan. Before landing, the ship would be visited by health inspectors and customs officers. The health inspectors would ask the captain if any sick persons were aboard and take only a quick look around the ship if the captain asserted that no one was ill. If a sick person was noticed, a more careful examination of everyone on board was undertaken. If a contagious disease was found, the ship was quarantined and all aboard were transferred to a special hospital established on Staten Island in 1799.

The customs men were looking for any goods, especially jewelry, fur coats, designer clothes, or other luxury goods. Even ordinary clothing purchased abroad was subject to a federal tax. If the traveler failed to declare it, the item or items would be confiscated. The revenue raised from this tax generated 50 percent of the national government's revenue. (There was no income tax until 1913.) Baggage and even one's person were subject to a detailed examination. The customs searches were normally

OCEAN SAIL

made after the ship had docked. Diplomats, U.S. government officials, ministers, and invalids and their companions were exempted from custom inspections. Passports were not required in the Victorian era except during the Civil War. This requirement was reinstated in 1918 and made permanent in 1921. First- and second-class passengers were free to leave after they cleared customs, but immigrants were subject to a little more scrutiny.

Most seamen were poorly paid, but not so the captain, who could usually retire young and wealthy. His salary might only be $50 a month, but he also received 5 percent of the cargo earnings, 25 percent of the passenger fares, and all of the money for carrying the mail. This gave him an annual salary of $5,000. One could live very comfortably on such an income in the Victorian era.

The officers served directly under the captain and transmitted his orders to the crew. The captain rarely spoke to the crew directly. On a larger sailing ship there was usually a first and second mate; they were also called first and second officers. The first mate was, in effect, a vice president who would take over command should the captain die or become incapacitated. The first mate could navigate and get the ship safely to port. The first mate sometimes worked as a substitute captain, especially in the winter months, when shipping was less active. His wage was a modest $1 per day. He rarely went aloft, and on some ships he would dine with the captain. The second mate was more of a workaday person. He was in charge of the second watch and was directly responsible for the masts, yards, sails, and rigging. If the ship was too small to afford a sailmaker, he made the repairs himself. He did not eat at the captain's table but ate the leftovers. (Food served at the captain's table would be the best available aboard ship, so even the leftovers were very good. Hence the sail maker was a lucky fellow.) He went aloft to the very top sails. Second mates were as young as nineteen and were more likely to be lost overboard because of their aloft duties.

Most ships of any size would also employ a cook, a carpenter, a sailmaker, and a cabin boy or two. A packet ship would have a steward or stewardess to attend the first-class passengers. The duties of the cook are obvious. He had one peculiar distinction among his workmates. He alone was permitted to whistle aboard ship. Most sailors believed whistling would whistle up a storm. However, if the cook whistled, it only proved he was not eating up the crew's food. The carpenter made repairs around the ship. This would include replacing an upper mast, yards, railings, cabin doors, panels, and beams in the hull. If there was nothing else requiring his attention, he would mend buckets and barrels. The sailmaker usually had plenty of work, especially if the captain was a speed advocate or if the trip was particularly stormy. Even new sails would rip or unravel. None of this trio stood regular watches. They worked all day, ten to twelve hours, and slept at night like regular folks. They lived in the cargo section of the hull, not in the forecastle with the crew. Any of them might be an older sailor who was too infirm for regular duties or a former sailor who had lost an arm or a leg.

The size of the regular crew varied with the size of the ship and its budget. A vessel with a great number of sails (such as a clipper) would require a larger number of men. The *Eliza* (1795), mentioned earlier in this chapter, had only sixteen sailors on board. She was a comparatively small vessel. Packets employed from twenty-four to thirty-six. They were broken down into two teams for the starboard and port watches. The first mate managed the port watch and the second mate handled the starboard. The seven watches were broken up into shifts – four hours on and four hours off – so when one team was working the other was resting. The "dog watches" were from 4:00 PM to 8:00 PM. There were two two-hour watches called the "first dog" and "last dog" watches. In the event of an emergency, such as a storm blowing in, the off-duty watch was called back to duty. It was an urgent call into the forecastle: "All hands! Tumble up, here; don't stop for your clothes. Aloft, men!" They knew to scramble up the shrouds in bare feet to the topsails and take them in before the winds blew them away. The entire crew was on deck when the boat left the harbor. It took a lot of muscle to get the anchor up. Here again the mates urged the men to "Heave-oh, boys, o-o-o-oh!" Once up and out of the mud, the anchors were lifted over the bow and lashed down to the forecastle deck. When aloft, the men would loosen the furled sails with nimble fingers and see them unfurl in a winglike fashion. The mate would shout commands such as, "Clew up the royals. Sky sails, men, aloft. Lively there, boys. Let go your top gallant halyards." This would go on until the sails were all adjusted in a perfect manner.

The seamen were ranked into three classes. Green hands, those with no experience or skills, were called "boys" regardless of age or size. Ordinary seamen were a step above the boys but lacked the experience or strength to handle the job well. They were not required to go to the end of the yards or above the tops when furling the sails. It would take about four years to train them fully. The able seaman could do all normal duties. In addition to dealing with the sails, he could steer the vessel and keep her on a specific course. He could make repairs to the rigging and was an expert at knots. He knew to go up the shrouds on the weather side so that the wind would blow him into the rigging and not overboard.

On calm days the crew kept busy with repairs or cleaning. Painted surfaces were scraped and repainted. The bell, the top of the capstan,

10.12. A young crew aloft "reefing," or taking in, the sails in this illustration from the 1890s.

(J. D. Jerrold Kelley, *The Ship's Company*, 1898)

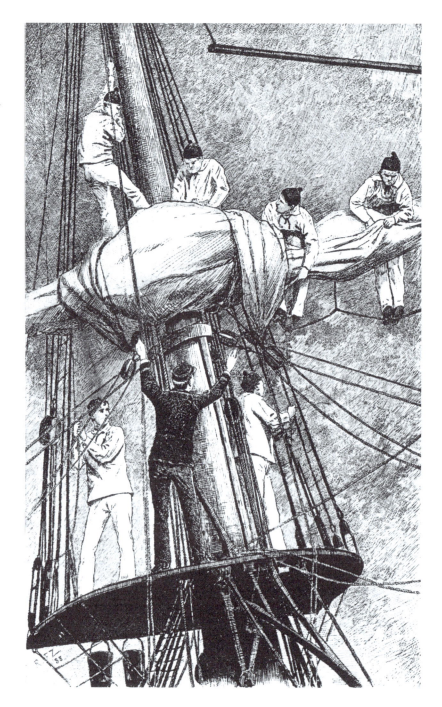

was polished until it gleamed like gold. The decks were scrubbed with holystones (so called because they were about the size of a Bible) and sand until the bare wood was smooth and white. It was important to keep the men busy, as idle hands only encouraged trouble. There was no talking while on duty. The second mate kept order, and when a harsh verbal command failed he used his fists or a belaying pin to convey the message.

10.13. Men taking in sail from a precarious perch on the bowsprit in this nineteenth-century engraving.

(*Nautical Illustrations by Jim Harter*, 2003)

Captain Samuels, who spent a lifetime working with sailors, said the Liverpool sailors had no idea of morality, honesty, or gratitude. They were the toughest class of men, who could stand the worst weather, food, and abuse and get by on less sleep and more rum than any other laborer in the world.

Indeed the living space and food were bad. The forecastle was a foul, suffocating abode. It was wet and nasty and it stank. So many men in this small space, none of them neat, tidy, or very clean. Here they sat, slept, and ate in their time off. It was unbearably hot when the ship was in the tropics and colder than Siberia when near the Arctic Sea. No fire of any type was allowed in this part of the ship. From time to time someone would fumigate it with a burning sulfur torch. The deck was washed with vinegar, which only added to the odors of wet canvas, tar, stagnant seawater, and rotting timber.

The food for the crew was plain but reasonably plentiful on a good ship. Breakfast would consist of coffee, sea biscuits, and salt pork. The biscuits, or hard tack, were a staple made from flour, salt, and a little water, baked very hard in 4-by-4 squares ½ inch thick. They were so hard that no insect would bother them, but it required some soaking to make them edible. Beans, rice, salt beef, and duff, which was a steamed flour pudding that might contain some dried fruit, were also served. Oranges and lemons were provided to stave off scurvy.

The sailor's pay was less than that of a store clerk. At the beginning of the nineteenth century it was about $15 a month, but by 1845 it was up to $21. However, each man received room and board while on duty. Neither might have been superior in quality, but it was there at no charge and may

10.14. This cross-section drawing of a late-model wooden hull shows that old techniques continued into the early twentieth century. The hull is about 35 feet wide.

(Charles Desmond, *Wooden Ship-Building*, 1919)

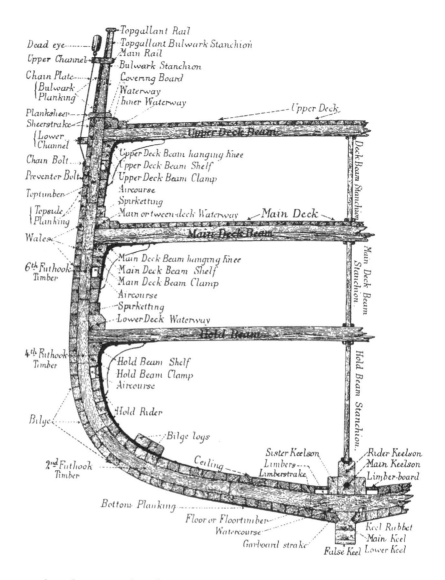

not have been greatly inferior to that available to other common laborers of the time. Ordinary seamen received $12 and boys just $8 a month. Some ships used a profit-sharing scheme where the owners and the captain got the lion's share; the first mate would get $1/27$, the second mate $1/36$, and each able seaman $1/50$, ordinary seaman $1/75$ and boys or green hands $1/100$ or $1/200$. However, if the voyage was not profitable no one received payment.

The Victorian era was notable for its charities, and sailors were among those singled out for special attention. Many were single men who had no family to help them through illness and old age. A home called Sailors'snug Harbor was established at New Brighton, Staten Island, in 1801 to care for aged and infirm seamen. By the 1890s this 180-acre, self-supporting facility cared for one thousand men. Separate homes were established elsewhere in the New York City area for the dependents and children of deceased seamen. The federal government operated a network of marine

Table 10.1. Decline in American Shipping, 1820–1900

Year	Ship Tonnage	Exports & Imports Carried in U.S. Ships
1820	583,000	89.5%
1840	527,000	82.9%
1860	2,379,000	66.5%
1880	1,314,000	17.6%
1900	816,000	9.3%

Source: Winthrop L. Marvin, *American Merchant Marine*, 1902.

hospitals across the nation. (One was located in my hometown of Cincinnati, because riverboat men were considered part of the Merchant Marine during wartime.)

At the end of a long sea journey the men might go ashore cursing the captain or the mates, but they usually left with a feeling of camaraderie. While at sea they would curse the ship, curse the job, and complain all the time, but by the end of the trip they had developed a feeling of communion with the ship, although they would not admit it. The ship had the power to demand great effort and to create a feeling of oneness among the crew.

THE END OF THE SAILING SHIP ERA

Simply stated, steam supplanted sail, but it was not quite that simple. American ship owners remained stubbornly loyal to sailing ships long after steam proved practical. The British seized the new technology and pressed ahead improving steamers to make them more reliable and efficient, while American packet line operators, such as Charles H. Marshall (1792–1865), head of Black Ball, ordered new sailing packets of a traditional design. The last of the Black Ball's fleet was the *Charles H. Marshall*, completed in 1869. Marshall and his successors would likely defend their preference on practical grounds by arguing that sailing vessels were cheaper and just as fast as steam. This was true, at least for speed, in the early years of steam, but not after about the early 1840s. Old-line seafarers would also contend that a sailing ship would last indefinitely if properly maintained. Typically, however, a wood hull was considered beyond its prime after just twelve years of service; after that they no longer could be insured as a first-class vessel, even though some did sail on for a very long period.

The Swallowtail line's *Independence* of 1829 is an example of long-term service. She made 116 round-trip crossings of the Atlantic Ocean in her twenty-nine years of packet service and never lost a seaman, sail, or spar. She carried about thirty thousand passengers and witnessed the birth of around fifteen hundred babies and two hundred marriages. She was retired to coastal service in 1863. Another long-in-service vessel was

10.15. South Street on the East River in New York City in the late 1870s. Sailboats remained in service but largely as freight rather than passenger carriers.

(*Harper's Weekly*, April 20, 1878)

the *Maria* of New Bedford. Built in 1782, she worked for many years as a whaler and ended her sailing days in Vancouver in 1872 at the age of ninety. The old packet lines gradually shut down, and some were gone by the end of the Civil War. The pioneering Black Ball line was out of the passenger business by 1878, and the Swallowtail's last packet landed at New York on May 18, 1881.

There were larger changes in international maritime shipping. Britain had replaced America as the leading maritime power. The decline of American shipping can be seen in table 10.1.

From 1800 to mid century the United States dominated transatlantic passenger travel and cargo shipping. There were no Cunard, French, or German lines for most of this half century. If you wanted fast, deluxe service it was necessary to patronize an American line. By the late 1840s Europeans began to subsidize lines through postal subsidies. The Civil War destroyed many U.S. ships. Many were pressed into military service. America's boatyards built largely for the U.S. Navy and remained devoted largely to wooden vessels; only a few took a serious interest in iron construction. Investors turned to railroads as a better investment; by 1880 $4.7 billion had been invested in the American railway system and only $100 million in ocean shipping. The most surprising fact about the American fleet was revealed by the Bureau of Navigation Statistics in 1898. U.S. ocean shipping was 49.6 percent sail powered. Much of this was in the coastal trade that carried coal, lumber, and lime rather than passengers. America's fleet was surely old-fashioned. Wooden hulls were replaced by iron or steel – in fact, the country's first steel-hulled sailing vessel was the *Dirigo,* a four-masted ship. American shipbuilders were enthusiastic about metal-hulled sailing ships and produced a considerable number of them. Downeasters, introduced in about 1860 and used largely in the coastal trade, were modified clippers and were an important part of the American Merchant Marine fleet until about 1900. Windjammers were iron- or steel-hulled sailing ships, most with three masts. These heavy types of boats were slow but economical, and a few were in commercial service until the 1950s.

Britain would dominate transatlantic travel in the steam age. The United States played a minor role in this epic of passenger travel, and Americans going overseas were obliged to travel mainly in foreign bottoms. National pride aside, it remains a fascinating story.

NOTE

1. A note on tonnage – what does it mean? References to a ship of 300 or 3,000 tons does not mean the ship weighs 300 or 3,000 tons, nor does it mean she can carry that much cargo. It is not a designation of weight, but rather a rough measure of cubic cargo space. There are many formulas for calculating tonnage, but the simplest method is 1 ton = 100 cubic feet.

SUGGESTED READING

Abbot, Willis J. *American Merchant Ships and Sailors.* New York: Dodd Mead, 1908.

Albion, Robert G. *Naval and Maritime History: An Annotated Bibliography.* Mystic, Conn.: Munson Institute of American Maritime History, 1972.

———. *Square Riggers on Schedule.* Princeton, N.J.: Princeton University Press, 1938.

Allen, Oliver E. *Windjammers.* Alexandria, Va.: Time-Life, 1978.

Bathe, Basil W. *Seven Centuries of Sea Travel: From the Crusades to the Cruises.* New York: Tudor, 1973.

———. *Visual Encyclopedia of Nautical Terms under Sail.* New York: Crown, 1978.

Bowen, Frank. C. *A Century of Atlantic Travel, 1830–1930.* London: Low Marston, 1932.

Braynard, Frank O. *Famous American Ships.* New York: Hastings House, 1978.

Bunker, John G. *Harbor and Haven: An Illustrated History of the Port of New York.* Woodland Hills, Calif.: Windsor, 1979.

Carter, Edward C. *Virginia Journal of Benjamin H. Latrobe, 1795–1798.* New Haven, Conn.: Yale University Press, 1977.

Chapelle, Howard I. *The Search for Speed under Sail, 1700–1855.* New York: Norton, 1967.

Chatterton, E. Keble. *Sailing Ships and Their Story.* London: Sidgwick and Jackson, 1923.

Cornwall-Jones, R. J. *British Merchant Service.* London: Low Marston, 1898.

Dana, Richard Henry. *Seaman's Friend.* Boston: Eliot, 1817.

Davis, Charles G. *Ships of the Past.* Salem, Mass.: Marine Research Society, 1929.

Desmond, Charles. *Wooden Ship-Building.* 1919. New York: Vestal Press, 1984.

Fairburn, William A. *Merchant Sail.* Center Lovell, Me.: Fairburn Marine Educational Foundation, 1945–1955.

Gardiner, Robert. *Heyday of Sail: The Merchant Sailing Ship, 1650–1830.* London: Conway Maritime, 1995.

Giambarba, Paul. *Surfmen and Lifesavers: Including Heroes of the Lifesaving Service.* Centerville, Mass.: Scrimshaw, 1985.

Greenhill, Basil. *Traveling by Sea in the Nineteenth Century: Interior Design in Victorian Passenger Ships.* 1972. New York: Hastings House, 1974.

Harter, Jim. *Nautical Illustrations.* Mineola, N.Y.: Dover, 2003.

Hutchins, John G. B. *American Maritime Industry and Public Policy, 1789–1914.* Cambridge: Harvard University Press, 1941.

Ingersoll, Ernest. *Book of the Ocean.* New York: Century, 1898.

Kelley, J. D. Jerrold. *Ship's Company and Other Sea People.* New York: Harper, 1897.

Kemp, Peter. *Oxford Companion to Ships and the Sea.* Oxford: Oxford University Press, 1992.

Kennedy, Ludovic. *Book of Sea Journeys.* New York: Rawson Wade, 1981.

Laing, Alexander. *American Sail: A Pictorial History.* New York: Dutton, 1961.

———. *American Ships.* New York: American Heritage, 1971.

Lindsay, W. S. *History of Merchant Shipping and Ancient Commerce.* 1874. New York: AMS, 1965.

Macgregor, David R. *Merchant Sailing Ships: Supremacy of Sail.* London: Conway, 1984.

Marvin, Winthrop L. *American Merchant Marine, Its History and Romance, 1620–1902.* New York: Scribner, 1902.

Miller, Byron S. *Sail, Steam, and Splendour: A Picture History of Life aboard the Transatlantic Liners.* New York: Times Books, 1977.

Morton, Harry. *Wind Commands: Sailors and Sailing Ships in the Pacific.* Middletown, Conn.: Wesleyan University Press, 1975.

Nevins, Allan. *Sail On: The Story of the American Merchant Marine.* New York: United States Lines, 1946.

Paine, Lincoln P. *Ships of the World: An Historical Encyclopedia.* Boston: Houghton Mifflin, 1997.

Rogers, Stanley R. H. *The Atlantic.* New York: Crowell, 1930.

Samuels, Samuel. *From Forecastle to the Cabin.* New York: Harper, 1887.

Spears, John R. *Story of the American Merchant Marine.* New York: Macmillan, 1910.

Thomas, R. *Interesting and Authentic Narratives of the Most Remarkable Shipwrecks, Fires, Famines, Calamities, Providential Deliverances, and Lamentable Disasters on the Seas, in Most Parts of the World.* 1835. Freeport, N.Y.: Books for Libraries, 1970.

Volo, Dorothy D. *Daily Life in the Age of Sail.* Westport, Conn.: Greenwood, 2002.

Ocean Steam №11

The Triumph of Technology

THIS CHAPTER IS ONCE AGAIN ABOUT PASSENGER TRANSIT across the North Atlantic, the most heavily traveled sea lane during the Victorian era. The motive power was now steam, and Britain would replace the United States as sovereign of the sea. Steam power was readily accepted for river and lake travel in the United States after Fulton's North River boat proved herself in 1807. The Hudson River had a sizable steamer fleet by 1825. Steamers appeared on the Ohio River in 1811, and others were soon running on Lake Champlain, the Delaware River, and the Great Lakes. A congressional report on steam engines published in December 1838 stated that some eight hundred steam vessels were in operation on U.S. waterways. It would seem natural that ocean shipping would be part of this fleet, yet there was not a single vessel in such service. America's pioneer ocean steamer, the *Savannah,* crossed the Atlantic in 1817, but most of the trip was made by sail. It is true that the Dutch sent a small steamer to the island of Curacao off the coast of South America in 1827. Two years earlier the *Enterprise* steamed from London to Calcutta in 113 days. The trip was made partway by sail. Even so, popular opinion was that no steamship could possibly carry enough fuel for a 3,000-mile journey. In late 1835 an eminent technical authority of the time, Dr. Dionysius Lardner, declared in a public lecture in Liverpool that a steamship might as well attempt a voyage to the moon. An American expatriate living in England at the time of this lecture hoped to prove the learned doctor wrong.

Junius Smith (1781–1853) went to England in 1805 to represent his brother's import/export business. He became heavily involved in trade and shipping and came to understand that quickness is the life of business and delay is its death. Sailing vessels could never hope to answer this need, for they required from three to eight weeks to make a westward passage. Some superior type of vessel was an absolute necessity. After years of frustrating delays, Smith found enough backing to organize the British and American Steam Navigation Company in 1836. Smith hoped

to have his first vessel ready by 1837 or 1838, but the bankruptcy of one of the company's suppliers delayed the *British Queen* by over a year.

Meanwhile the Great Western Railway decided to extend its transportation service from Bristol to New York by offering transatlantic steamer service. Isambard Kingdom Brunel, a British engineer of considerable talent and originality, had no experience in ship design but felt confident he could produce a superior vessel. He had performed admirably in building the Great Western Railway, so the commission was given to him. Brunel's plan was rather conservative, given his penchant for innovative and odd designs.

The *Great Western,* as Brunel's ship was named, featured a wooden hull and side-wheel propulsion. She was 212 feet long and registered at 1,340 tons (fig. 11.1). The hull was launched at Bristol in July 1837. She was not ready for the engines until March of the next year, and a serious fire delayed her completion until the following month. Meanwhile Junius Smith had leased a small coastal steamer named the *Sirus* to make sure the *Great Western* did not eclipse his efforts to be the pioneer operator of transatlantic steam. The *Sirus* was hastily refitted for long-distance travel and set off for New York just as Brunel's ship was nearing completion. The *Great Western* left England on April 8, 1838, with only seven passengers (she had room for 240). Nevertheless the race was on and the *Sirus* had left four days earlier.

An American newspaperman, W. A. Foster, was a passenger on the *Great Western*. He recorded that the reason for the delayed departure was because of difficulties in raising anchor. A strong headwind and a hard sea slowed them down more. Six days out the engines were stopped so that the paddle wheels might be thoroughly examined. All the sails were set and the ship moved nobly on. On April 21 a squall plastered the sails, masts, and deck with 2 inches of snow. A snowball fight ensued to the merriment of all on board. Two days later they picked up a New York pilot at Sandy Hook; at 3:00 PM they passed through the Narrows into New York Harbor with sails furled and the engines going at full speed. What a proud sight she made. Other boats gathered around with flags flying, people cheering, and salute guns firing. It was an exciting moment, a moment of triumph. Their time across the Atlantic Ocean was fifteen days and ten hours, less than half the typical sailing ship time of forty days. She had burned 450 tons of coal and had 200 tons in reserve, proving that Dr. Lardner's calculations were totally false.

The *Sirus* had won the race by several hours, but she limped into port completely out of fuel and was forced to burn some of her furniture and woodwork to make it to dockage. The *Great Western* continued crossing the Atlantic for sixty-four more passages. Her best time was twelve days and eighteen hours. It's uncertain, however, if she recovered her original

11.1. The *Great Western* was the first steamer built specifically for transatlantic service. She entered service in 1838.

(Ithiel Town, *Atlantic Steamships*, 1838)

cost of $300,000. She was retired in 1843 but returned to service four years later by the West India Mail line and ran for about another ten years. Brunel had proven himself as a talented marine architect; his first boat was seaworthy if not notably profitable.

In 1842 the Great Western Railway decided to build a larger second vessel and again engaged Brunel to prepare the drawings. His first designs were for another conventional wood-hull side-wheeler, except this one would be much larger than the *Great Western*. However, Brunel grew dissatisfied and started over with a more radical plan for an iron hull, an idea tested so far only for small ships. This would be a giant for its time, at 289 feet long and 50 percent larger than any ship in the Royal Navy. Some of the hull plates were ⅞ inch thick, and more than 1,000 tons of wrought iron was used in the hull. As the hull design was being completed, Brunel decided paddle wheels would never do and substituted a screw propeller, a device that most mariners considered unproven. She would have six masts for auxiliary sails supported by wire ropes. The hull was built in Bristol at the Great Western Railway dock. Prince Albert was present at the launching in July 1843. The hull could not be moved beyond the dock, leading to much embarrassment for all involved, and it was some time before the mighty *Great Britain*, as she was christened, could be moved out into the harbor for completion. The interior was outfitted in a chaste and elegant style with white and gilt columns, and panels ornamented with birds and flowers in the Chinese style. The bulkheads were painted a delicate lemon, relieved with blue, white, and gold. There were 26 single rooms and 113 double cabins, each with single beds. The main cabin measured 98 by 30 feet and seated 360.

The *Great Britain*'s maiden voyage was made in July 1845 two years after the launching. She made the trip from Bristol to New York in fourteen days and twenty-one hours, about the same speed as her predecessor.

American packet managers were unimpressed by the speed of the early ocean liners, saying they had sailing packets built twenty years ago that could do that well. However, they neglected to add that because the winds were rarely that favorable, especially on the westbound trip, the average speed of sailing packets was not equal to pioneer steamers. In addition, steamships could maintain their speed with no help from the wind. Mechanical problems on the *Great Britain* were soon evident; the giant single propeller began losing blades, and the engines and chain drive required rebuilding. On her fifth trip the *Great Britain* went aground south of Belfast on the Irish coast. Everyone aboard was removed safely, but the ship remained where she landed for almost a year. The $.5 million ship never operated again for Great Western and was sold at a large discount for Australian service. It was converted to sail in 1882 and became a derelict in the Falkland Islands several years later. Its durable iron hull was returned to Bristol for restoration in 1970. It may be seen today in that port city in a much rejuvenated condition as the only sizable relic remaining from the first generation of ocean steamers.

Who would make a success of transatlantic steam? The Great Western Railway had failed. Junius Smith had given up after his deluxe liner the *President* disappeared, never to be seen again, on her third trip in March 1841. A most unexpected and unknown figure would emerge from the obscure port of Halifax, Nova Scotia, to become the king of merchant shipping. Samuel Cunard (1787–1865) was a small-time ship operator of no particular distinction, wealth, or experience. He was not even English but descended from German and Irish stock. But his family, at least, was of Tory loyalties and had fled Philadelphia at the close of the American Revolution to resettle in Nova Scotia. Cunard learned about the British Admiralty's mail subsidy from a newspaper notice. The $400,000 annual subsidy for hauling the Royal Mail from England to Canada excited his attention, not that he was a very excitable person. In his manner and habit, he was shrewd, careful, and conservative – in short, a good businessman. He went to England and through a series of fortuitous introductions managed to meet all the right people. Two of these new acquaintances were critical to the success of the new venture. They were George Burns and David MacIver, experienced ship operators and men of wealth with good banking connections. At fifty-two Cunard was successful but hardly rich, and he needed help in securing the $13.5 million to float the British and North American Royal Mail Steam Packet Company.

An officer of the East India Company introduced Cunard to Robert Napier, an important engine builder in Glasgow. Napier seemed to be built very much in the same mold as Cunard and his partners. He was a true Scot, being cautious, practical, and thrifty. Napier was given a contract to build four identical wooden side-wheelers. Cunard made it clear

that they should be safe and reliable vessels that operated at moderate speeds and were not ostentatious or experimental in any particular. Both the purchaser and the builder agreed that maximum economy was a moral imperative and that to create an ornate ship only increased human pride and tempted providence. The vessels as built were actually graceful in appearance and included some decorative elements on the clipper bow, the wheel boxes, and the stern. The interior was pleasant, if not elegant, while the individual cabins were small and spartan. Charles Dickens traveled on the first Cunard liner, the *Britannia,* early in her career and described

11.2. The *Britannia*, 1840, was the first Cunard liner; she had three identical sisters. The several deck plans are the best record available for a packet steamer of this period.

(Maginnis, *The Atlantic Ferry,* 1892)

OCEAN STEAM 331

the main cabin as a "gigantic hearse" with a "melancholy stove" at one end. He found his cabin "utterly impractical, thoroughly hopeless and a profoundly preposterous box." For the return trip, he chose a Black Ball sailing packet.

The *Britannia* was not ready for service until early July 1840, so Cunard borrowed a coastal steamer from George Burns to make the first crossing in May of that year. The *Britannia*'s maiden trip was uneventful. She crossed from Liverpool to Halifax in eleven days and went on to Boston, making the entire journey in fourteen days and eight hours. Her running speed was a steady 8½ knots. She measured 228 feet long and had space for 115 first-class passengers. (No second-class or steerage passengers were carried by Cunard until 1862.) The fare was 38 guineas (about $170), wine and liquors were extra; there was a steward fee of 1 guinea, and dogs were carried for £5 each. The diagram drawings in figure 11.2 show the ship's internal arrangement clearly.

The other three sister ships were soon in service, and the Cunard line was off to a fine start. Travelers came to find it safe, steady, and predictable, exactly as Cunard had planned. He had no competitors worthy of mention. The British government was an enthusiastic supporter, and his partners were as solid as the Rock of Gibraltar. Cunard moved to England and bought a fine residence in the west end of London. Some years later he was elevated to the peerage and became a baronet, the highest rank possible for a commoner. The only blemish recorded during these early years of the line was the loss of the steamer *Columbia* in July 1843 near Halifax; however, everyone aboard was rescued, so Cunard's record for perfect safety was maintained.

Unfortunately, trouble was ahead. The Americans were very unhappy that Britain was taking over the transatlantic passenger trade and was making plans to challenge the notion that Britannia ruled the waves. Captain E. K. Collins began to champion for an American line of fast deluxe liners to give Cunard a run for his money. Collins was a convert to the new age of steam. He was ready to follow Commander Vanderbilt's wholehearted espousal of "bilers and injines." To create a first-class American line would be expensive, and there was only one logical source for such funding: the American taxpayer. Such talk in an age of private capital and free enterprise seemed alien to a society committed to the doctrines of Herbert Spencer. Collins's efforts to obtain a federal subsidy in 1838 were flatly rejected by President Van Buren.

Several years later Collins found friends in Senator King of Georgia and President Polk. In 1847 he signed a contract with the U.S. Postal Service for a mail service of twenty round trips a year with a subsidy of $385,000. Early the next year he organized the U.S. Mail Steamship Company. An agreement for four 2,800-ton wooden side-wheelers was completed with

11.3. This scene on the *Arabia*, 1856, shows passengers airing out on the top deck. The small arch-roof structure on the left side covers the stairway leading down to the cabin and staterooms. The *Arabia* was a large side-wheeler with two funnels and auxiliary sails.

(*Ballou's Pictorial*, Feb. 26, 1859)

W. H. Brown of New York. They were named for major oceans – the *Arctic*, *Atlantic*, *Baltic*, and *Pacific* – and cost more than $700,000 each. Some of the cost was attributed to the ships' lavish interiors, which were oriental in their magnificence. The paneling was made from rare woods such as rose, satin, and olive. For table tops nothing would do other than Brocatelli marble. There were so many mirrors that the Halls of Versailles looked empty by comparison. The spittoons were a special sea green cast in a shell shape. Steam heat was one of the more practical features of the new ships. While Cunard served wholesome meals, they were considered pedestrian by gourmets, who found satisfaction in Collins's liners green turtle soup, made from a Delmonico's recipe, and the turkey in oyster sauce or the red current tartlets.

The *Atlantic* was the first of the quartet to enter service. She left New York for Liverpool on April 27, 1850. National pride sailed with her, as many Americans hoped to win this international contest between the New and Old World players. Cunard held steady in making no changes in his philosophy or the details of everyday operations. The British government stood by their contractor and raised the subsidy to over $700,000 in 1848. Cunard began serving New York late in the previous year with pierage in Jersey City, but the boats were as slow and plain as ever. Collins was showing a real gain over his rival; in 1852 his ships carried 4,306 passengers compared to Cunard's 2,969. Some claimed Collins actually had 70 percent of the business.

The managers of Cunard realized that the time had come to react more directly to Collins's challenge. They ordered a side-wheeler named the *Arabia,* designed specifically for better speed, that would offer greater space and more commodious appointments, despite the managing director's misgivings concerning such matters. The food might be notched up a few degrees with less old mutton and finer cuts of beef. The *Arabia* was 285 feet long, or just 5 feet longer than the Collins liners, but she had the largest marine engines yet built. The cylinders were 103 inches in diameter with a stroke of 108 inches. This monster rated at 938 hp nominal or 3,000 indicated hp, and pushed the boat along at 15 knots in smooth water, but under normal sea conditions she did well to make 13 knots and generally cruised along at an even slower pace. She entered service on New Year's Day 1853. In May of that year she made the eastern crossing in ten days, a record that beat Collins's best time by four hours. The *Arabia* traveled 342 miles in one day. The Brits were jubilant and repeatedly fired their salute cannon on entering Liverpool Harbor. A *New York Times* reporter of the day was more taken with the ship's interior design than the triumph of her speed. The main saloon seated 160. It was paneled in bird's-eye maple, and the ceiling's oak leaves were rendered in green, gold, and white. The furniture was upholstered in crimson. The sofas were covered in Utrecht velvet and the floors with tapestry carpet. The stern cabin windows were stained glass with scenes of camels and other Near Eastern subjects. The figurehead was of an Arab chieftain. Two large reddish-orange smokestacks loomed over her sturdy black hull. The *Arabia* was impressive and fast, but her engines were too powerful for the wooden hull, so she generally cruised along at 11 knots. She was also a notorious fuel consumer and at 120 tons of coal a day was deemed too uneconomic for long service. She was sold in 1864 and converted to sail. Figure 11.3 is an illustration of the *Arabia*'s top deck.

It was one thing to capture most of the trade and another to realize a profit from it. Collins's ships were pushed hard to outpace the British ships, which they generally did by a small margin. This was done by driving the vessels at their top speed. The engines showed the strain of such service by requiring costly repairs at the end of each trip. The engine foundations were coming loose and racking the hull, which reduced the service life of the vessel. Fuel consumption was also very high, averaging about 85 tons a day. Collins admitted he was losing almost $17,000 on each trip and needed a larger government subsidy. This was granted, but the amount was only enough to reduce the size of the loss. In addition, the Collins line carried a heavy debt that was payable at 7 percent interest a year.

All of these numbers did not indicate much of a victory. But such matters were soon overshadowed by the sinking of the *Arctic* on October 27, 1854. The Collins liner was hit in the bow by an iron French steamer moving at 11 knots near Halifax. At first it appeared the small French vessel had suffered the greatest damage, and after a brief discussion she pulled

11.4. These two interior views show the rear of the ladies' cabin (top) and the main cabin and dining tables and benches (bottom) of the Collins line's last vessel, the *Adriatic* of 1856.

(*Leslie's Weekly*, November 28, 1857)

around and headed for port. On closer examination, however, it was found the *Arctic* had been mortally damaged. The captain was starting to organize an evacuation when most of the crew mutinied and began deserting the ship. They took off in several of the lifeboats and abandoned those aboard to the mercy of the sea. A raft was put together by the captain, the third mate, and a few passengers. Seventy-two climbed aboard the makeshift craft. Thirty-two others climbed into the one remaining lifeboat. Captain James Luce remained on board until the ship began her final roll. He jumped off, holding his small son in his arms, but lost the boy in the water. He found some wreckage and floated for two days in the frigid water until he was picked up by a passing boat. Only one person survived on the raft. Everyone in the lifeboat survived. Out of the 400 on board, 322 were lost. These included the wife, son, and daughter of E. K. Collins.

The news of the tragedy hardly prompted travelers to choose the American line over the stodgy but safe British company. Cunard's record indeed was perfect. Between 1840 and 1854 Cunard had made seven thousand trips across the Atlantic and carried around one hundred thousand passengers without losing a single passenger or letter.

Worse news was to come. Fifteen months after the *Arctic* misadventure, the *Pacific* left Liverpool on January 25, 1856, with 145 passengers and 190 crew. She headed down St. George's Channel, past Tuskar Light, then into the freezing Atlantic Ocean and was never seen again. Collins's reputation was again badly damaged. His company was down to two ships and could not maintain service, according to the government contract. Because of this, the subsidy was cut in July 1856. Collins's dream had become a nightmare. A new boat was on order, but the handsome *Adriatic* would not be ready until November 1857 (fig. 11.4). She went into service with space for 300 first-class and 60 second-class passengers. Her designer, the brilliant George Steers, had put his best into this excellent vessel. Steers died before the ship's maiden voyage on November 23, 1857. The *Adriatic* made only a few trips before creditors foreclosed on the Collins line in a grim April Fool's Day action in 1858. The three remaining ships – the *Atlantic, Baltic,* and *Adriatic* – were sold for a meager total of $50,000. Some historians claimed Collins was ruined and died a pauper, but this is an exaggeration. He surely lost much of his wealth and reputation because of this failure, but he started over in another business and died in the comfort of his Madison Avenue townhouse on January 22, 1878.

The failure of the Collins line is a long forgotten incident in business history, but its effect was long term. It marked the end of the United States as a leading player in the Merchant Marine. Travelers no longer saw an American flag on a transatlantic steamer. Britain came to control this trade and by late in the Victorian era was the dominant power in the maritime world. In the 1870s the United States made a weak reentry into the transatlantic passenger trade, but it was so minor as to go unnoticed.

BRITANNIA RULES THE WAVES

Samuel Cunard lived long enough to see this victory achieved and also long enough to witness more competitors attempt to take over a piece of what surely belonged to the official British steamboat line. At least most of these pesky rivals had the decency to be British. Cunard's monopoly was challenged from 1850 by a series of upstart operators. Some, like Collins, would expire after a few troublesome years, but others, like Inman and White Star, would develop into formidable rivals. There were also foreign

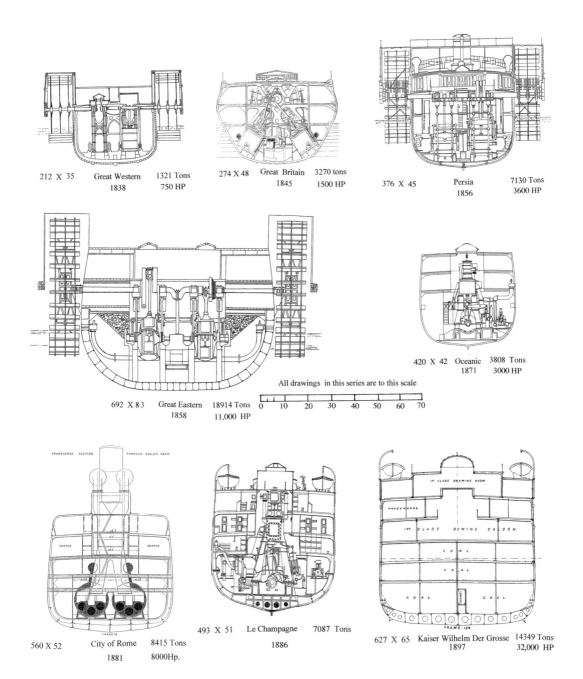

11.5. This series of cross-section drawings shows the development of transatlantic steamers during the Victorian era. Are all drawn to one scale.

(Author's drawing)

lines vying for a piece of a very small market. Emigrants were a massive trade, but first-class passengers were comparatively few in number, so any and all new lines were viewed with suspicion and contempt by the managers of Cunard.

One of the earliest of the new British lines was started by William Inman (1825–1881) late in 1850. Inman was born in the Midlands far from the sea, but at the age of thirteen his family moved to Liverpool. He attended school for a few more years but dropped out to become an apprentice with a firm of wholesale grocers. He was now working at the docks of the busiest seaport in western Britain. Ships, sailors, and cargoes were ever present, most of them coming or going to the Americas. Inman soon took another job with Richardson Brothers and Co., a firm that dealt in linens and provisions. He was put to work in the company's shipping department and dealt directly with provisioning ships. Much of the firm's business was in Philadelphia, and Inman went to that distant port regularly. His love for the sea and ships grew stronger. He was able, energetic, and was soon made a junior partner by the Richardsons. Inman soon found he cared more for transport than linens or canned goods. He had watched the progress of a new iron steamer built at a local yard. The *City of Glasgow* performed very well and was a good prototype for the screw propeller, which had proved more efficient than the standard side-wheeler and was favored by Cunard and the British navy. He talked with his senior partners and persuaded them to help him organize the Liverpool and Philadelphia Steamship Company late in 1850. The *City of Glasgow* was their first boat.

The *City of Glasgow* steamed off for Philadelphia on December 17 of that year. Her departure went largely unnoticed; no one could imagine just how successful Inman would become and how large his new line would expand over the next few decades. Inman was a skilled manager; he did not overspend and under-deliver as Collins did. He watched his costs and prospered, growing quietly into a formidable rival while his noisy American competitor raced ahead into bankruptcy. During her first year the *City of Glasgow* made a profit of 40 percent. Inman had the interior remodeled for more emigrant space and began landing at Queenstown to save his poorer clients the inconvenience and cost of coming to him in Liverpool. In 1851 he bought a larger second ship, the *City of Manchester*. The line was doing well by concentrating on emigrants and high-value cargoes. More ships were acquired, but a crisis developed in 1854 when the British government pressured Inman to lease several ships to carry troops and munitions to Crimea. England and France were at war with Russia. The Richardson brothers were Quakers and pacifists and thus strongly opposed this contract. But the government officials insisted, so the Richardsons reluctantly sold their interest in this profitable business rather than become complicit in a military action. Inman was now the virtual owner of this new and growing enterprise.

Inman promoted traffic by offering cheaper fares; his boats were a little slower and smaller than Cunard's, and most travelers headed for New York rather than Philadelphia. First-class fares were set by the number of occupants and the placement of the cabins within the ship. With two to a cabin the fare was 21 guineas (about $98); three to a cabin, 17 guineas (about $89); and cabins in the forward end of the ship, 15 guineas (about $79). The fare included food, wine, and the steward's fee. Dogs were carried for 3 pounds sterling each (about $15). Late in 1856 Inman's boats were

11.6. A ship stops to send a lifeboat to search for survivors as another sailing ship sinks. Passengers stand on deck to witness the dramatic scene. Note the women weeping near the rail. The ship and incident are unknown.

(*Scribner's Magazine*, April 1891)

delayed because the Delaware River was frozen; this prompted him to shift from Philadelphia to New York. During 1856–1857 he carried 85,000 passengers. It was mostly one-way traffic of emigrants to New York, but it helped keep the cash drawer full.

In 1858 Inman picked up the U.S. mail contract for service to Britain. When Cunard stopped serving Halifax, the British mail was given to Inman as well. Inman seemed to miss nothing that might generate a little more income. By 1860 he was offering weekly service to and from New York. Three years later service was increased to three trips every two weeks. By 1866 two boats a week were operated. Four years later Cunard had a strong rival for first-class passengers: Inman carried 3,635 first-class and 40,635 third-class passengers, while Cunard carried 7,638 first-class and 16,871 third-class passengers. Cunard had reason to be upset, for here was a rival that kept gaining traffic and did not conveniently self-destruct the way the Collins line had done in 1858.

It might appear that Inman's progress was a trouble-free sequence of expansion and profits; however, there was much pain and death in the rise of this enterprise. Operations were hardly begun when the liner's premiere ship disappeared without a trace. There were 480 on board; all vanished somewhere in the great ocean in March 1854. In September of that year the *City of Philadelphia* went aground at Newfoundland on her maiden trip; fortunately everyone on board was saved. In late March 1864 the *City of New York* wrecked near Queenstown and was lost, but once again everyone was saved. On January 28, 1879, the *City of Boston* left Halifax and headed for Liverpool. Did she hit an iceberg? Was she swept under by a rogue wave? No one could explain her disappearance with 177 on board. No wreckage or survivors were ever found. William Inman could not admit she was lost until June. Three years later the *City of Washington* hit the rocks at Cape Sable, Nova Scotia, and everyone on board was rescued. There were many additional fires at sea and collisions to other Inman liners, proving that indeed Atlantic crossings were risky business. The sea was ever ready to destroy anything and anyone that dare float upon its waters (fig. 11.6).

The rivalry between Cunard and Inman had grown intense by the early 1870s. Inman owned thirty ships and had carried one-half million passengers across the Atlantic Ocean since 1850. Both lines built new vessels hoping to outdo each other in terms of comfort, luxury, or speed. Being too conservative or parsimonious could allow the competition to gain an advantage. It was an expensive and exhausting game, and it became more complex and troublesome as more steamship lines came into operation. They seemed to appear out of nowhere and for no reason. The Guion and White Star lines were good examples of this phenomenon.

Stephen B. Guion (1820–1885) was born in New York City. Little is recorded about his early years, but by 1843, while he was still a young man, he formed a partnership with John S. Williams to run a line of sailing packets between New York and Liverpool. They carried a thousand steerage passengers a week during the peak summer months of the travel season. Guion moved to Liverpool to manage that end of the business in 1851. By the early 1860s most emigrants were traveling on Inman and other lines that offered faster steamer service at cheap fares. Williams and Guion were forced to abandon their fleet of aging packets. Guion worked

11.7. These two interiors show a stateroom (top) and the captain's cabin aboard the Guion line's *Minnesota*, 1867. Captain James Price, age fifty, is shown marking a navigation chart.

(*Harper's Monthly*, July 1870)

for both Cunard and the National line in rounding up emigrants for passage. He preferred being his own boss and rejoined his former partner to establish the Liverpool and Great Western Steamship Company in 1866.

They started with the *Manhattan*, a fair-sized iron-hulled vessel capable of running at the moderate speed of 10 knots. She was not fancy or grand. Space for first-class passengers was limited to 72, but the emigrant decks accommodated 800. The *Manhattan* had three sisters: the *Chicago, Colorado,* and *Minnesota*, all built by Palmer's Shipbuilding and Iron Company in Newcastle, England (fig. 11.7). In the early 1870s the *Idaho, Nevada, Wyoming, Dakota,* and *Montana* were added to the fleet. An advertisement in 1875 listed cabins at from 12 to 20 guineas depending on size and location. A guinea equaled £1 and 1 shilling, or about $5.10. Children under twelve traveled at half fare. Second-class cabins cost £8 and 8 shillings. Steerage was £5. All fares included food and bedding. An experienced surgeon was stationed on all ships. Ships left Pier 46 on the Hudson River every Tuesday and Friday. The operation had expanded, but it presented no threat to the big players in the transatlantic game. Cunard and Inman did well to ignore minor operatives such as Guion, who seemed content to coast along and not create a fuss. Williams died in about 1876, but Guion's American backers held firm. Nothing changed much, although a few new ships were acquired, all bearing American names. Then in about 1878 Guion met with William Pearce (1833–1888), the managing partner in the John Elder and Co., later the Fairfield Ship Building Company of Glasgow. Pearce knew shipbuilding from the bottom up and in his younger days was considered the prince of marine architects. Now he was top man at the yard, a Member of Parliament, and a man with good banking connections.

Pearce made Guion a proposition: if Guion could raise a certain sum, Pearce would find the rest of the capital and build the Guion line, a spectacularly fast ocean liner that would race across the stormy North Atlantic like a greyhound. The traveling public wanted speed and more speed. Plugging along at 12 knots might be economical, but it attracted few first-class passengers. In this way Guion could become a leader in the high-price end of passenger trade and leave stodgy old Cunard and Inman behind in the salt spray. There was big money to be made, and think of the prestige of taking the Blue Riband away from Cunard. (The Blue Riband was an unofficial award given to the passenger liner that crossed the Atlantic Ocean in regular service with the highest speed.) The deal was made and Pearce set to work on the *Arizona*. It came out in 1879 and at 450 feet long – and surely the quickest – was the largest steamer built at any of the yards on the River Clyde. In her trials she ran at 17.3 knots, but fully burdened her speed dropped to a little over 16 knots, still fast enough to win the Blue Riband. Inman reacted by ordering the *City of Rome* while

Cunard had the *Servia* built. Pearce built the *Alaska* to keep the Blue Riband for Guion. In September 1882 the *Alaska* made the westward crossing from Queenstown to New York in six days and eighteen hours. It took Cunard almost three years to create a ship capable of winning the coveted Blue Riband back from Guion.

Guion's brief moment in the sun had already passed. When Williams's estate was finally settled in 1883, the Guion line could not pay his heir's claim. The company cut back operations and some boats were put up for sale. The new *Oregon* was sold to Cunard in June 1884. Guion's death in December 1885 hastened the end of the line, but operations continued on a limited basis until the spring of 1894. The line carried more than 237,000 passengers between 1881 and 1891. Regrettably, no figures are available from its earlier years of operation.

The firm Pilkington and Wilson established a sailing ship line in 1843 that took emigrants from Liverpool to Australia. They traded under the name of the White Star line and were a minor house in the shipping world. In 1863 they bought a steamer to modernize their fleet, but the vessel hit an iceberg on the return of her maiden voyage to Melbourne. Her loss meant bankruptcy for Pilkington and Wilson. At the sale of their meager assets Thomas H. Ismay (1837–1899) bought their trade name and goodwill for a small sum. He was the son of a shipbuilder from Maryport, England, on the Solway Firth. He became an apprentice to a ship broker and succeeded in that trade so well that he was made a director of the National Steamship line, a minor competitor of Inman and Cunard, established in 1863.

Ismay was ambitious and hoped his own steamship line – the White Star – would shake the ocean lines' trade to the depths of the ocean's floor. He found a German banker, Gustave Schwabe, living in Liverpool who would help him; however, Schwabe had a condition for his support: Ismay must promise to patronize a shipbuilding firm in Belfast. Schwabe's nephew, Gustav W. Wolff, was a junior partner in the firm of Harland and Wolff, which had opened about ten years earlier. They built good ships, but like all such fabricators, they needed more business. Ismay agreed and never regretted his decision; Harland and Wolff served him well. At the same time, Ismay took in an old friend, William Imrie, as his partner in a newly formed oceanic steamship company. Ismay, Imrie and Co. was established in 1868 with a capital limit of £750,000. They ordered four ships from Harland and Wolff that were to be luxurious and fast. Some months later Wolff, who was in charge of the drafting office, presented Ismay and Imrie with some startling general arrangement drawings. The cabin arrangement was totally new. The main cabin was the full width of the hull and was above, not below, the main deck and in the very center of the ship. Sunlight could enter through portholes directly into this grand space, because the staterooms and cabins were placed at either end of the main

11.8. *Above:* The *Oceanic* was the first vessel of the White Star line. She had a revolutionary cabin plan that featured a main cabin on the top of the deck at full width of the hull. She was completed by Harlan and Wolff of Belfast, Ireland, in 1871. *Below:* The main cabin shown at the bottom is likely from the *City of Paris*, 1889. The arch roof stood 20 feet tall and was fitted with stained-glass windows.

(Author's collection; *Scribner's Magazine,* April 1891)

saloon. There were no wooden cabins built on the top deck, nor skylight, in an arrangement that went back to sailing ship days. The design of ocean liners was forever changed.

The first of the Ismay, Imrie and Co. quartet, the *Oceanic,* was launched in August 1870 and made her maiden voyage in March of the following year. She measured 420 feet long and was registered at 3,808 tons. A 4-cylinder compound engine, 3,000 indicated hp, drove her along at 14½ knots (fig. 11.8a). She was the largest ship to arrive in New York since the *Great Eastern*'s visit a decade earlier. One writer of the time said her arrival burst upon New York like a meteor. Large crowds visited

Table 11.1. Early Blue Riband Speed Records (Eastbound Trips)

Ship's Name	Date	Line	From/To	TIME Days	TIME Hours	Speed in Knots
Great Western	May 1838	GWR	NY to Bristol	14	15	9
Britannia	Aug 1840	Cunard	Halifax to Liverpool	9	21	10
Canada	July 1849	Cunard	Halifax to Liverpool	8	12	12
Persia	Aug 1856	Cunard	NY to Liverpool	8	23	14
City of Brussels	Dec 1869	Inman	NY to Queenstown	7	20	14
Germanic	Feb 1876	White Star	NY to Queenstown	7	15	15
Alaska	Sept 1882	Guion	NY to Queenstown	6	18	17
Oregon	July 1884	Cunard	NY to Queenstown	6	12	18
Etruria	July 1888	Cunard	NY to Queenstown	6	4	19
City of New York	Aug 1892	Inman	NY to Queenstown	5	19	20
Kaiser Wilhelm per Grosse	Nov 1897	North Germanic Lloyd	NY to The Needles*	5	17	22

*The Needles is the western tip of the Isle of Wight.

her at her Jersey City dock. The main cabin was the major attraction. It was 41 feet wide, 82 feet long – big enough for a grand ball. Press officers emphasized that it was placed at the middle of the ship, where motion was least felt. Waves were greatest at the ends of the hull, and the vibration of the propeller was felt more at the stern. Other notable features were steam steering and an elevator. Space was provided for 166 first-class passengers and 1,000 in steerage. Staterooms cost $80, payable in gold; the steerage fare was $30, payable in paper currency.

With such a strong beginning the White Star line continued to grow under the strong leadership of Thomas Ismay. He pressed Harland and Wolff for a faster ship to beat the competition. Cunard had continued its founder's belief in economy by staying with moderate speed to conserve fuel. Even Inman, who catered to the emigrants, a clientele that valued cheap fare over a fast trip, was tempted by the Blue Riband. It was a battle between the various lines with the prize passed around between the big three. Cunard held on between 1852 and 1869 to lose it to Inman's *City of Brussels*, which made the eastward crossing in seven days and twenty hours. Ismay won by besting Inman in 1873 with the *Baltic*, which won by just a few minutes – really not much of a victory. White Star's *Germanic* made the trip in seven days and fifteen hours in February 1876 and wrested the Blue Riband back from Inman. Her reputation was somewhat diminished some years later when she capsized in New York Harbor during a blizzard. The accumulation of ice and snow made her top-heavy.

Table 11.1 shows some of the eastbound travel speed records in the battle for the Blue Riband.

This is only a sample history of some of the winners. There was actually no Blue Riband or Cup. The records are those provided by the ship's captain, and his word was accepted by the maritime community. The physical prize was entirely notional.

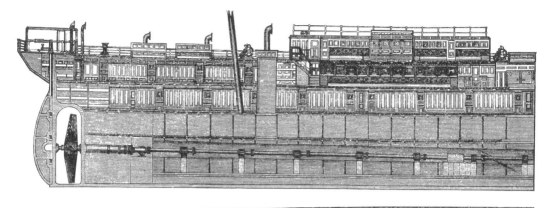
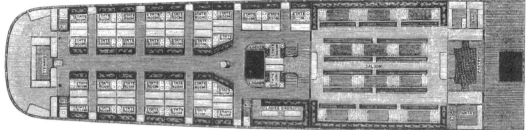

11.9. A sectional and deck-plan view of the Cunard line's *Bothnia* and *Scythia* of 1874. These iron-hulled vessels were driven by a single screw propeller. They had a capacity for 300 first-class and 548 third-class passengers.

(*Lindsay's History of Merchant Shipping*, Vol. 4, 1874)

THEN CAME THE GERMANS, FRENCH, AND AMERICANS

British seafarers worried about foreign competitions to a degree, but Germany was not considered much of a threat. It was not even a country but, rather, a collection of city-states or tiny principalities, except Prussia. The people still dressed in quaint medieval costumes and spoke a language suitable for music hall comedians. There was certainly nothing to fear from that quarter of the world. This was an accurate judgment at the beginning of the Victorian era and one that would continue for several decades, but by the 1860s Germany was uniting under the leadership of Prince Otto von Bismarck. Alfred Krupp was quietly developing a giant steel plant in Essen, while other industrialists were converting Germany into a remarkable economic powerhouse. By 1890 the world, including Britain, would come to understand the strength of this central European kingdom. Queen Victoria's least favorite grandchild, Wilhelm II, sought respect for the *Deutsch Volk*. Two small North German shipping companies would play a role in the emperor's grand scheme for Germanic supremacy: the Hamburg America line and the North German Lloyd line.

Hamburg America started operations in October 1848 as a sailing ship line to connect the port of Hamburg to Asia, Africa, and the Americas. It was a low-cost sailing ship line. By 1851 the company owned six vessels. Five years later they acquired their first steamers: the *Hammonia* and the *Borussia*. Both had a single-screw propulsion and iron hulls. They were built in Scotland, as were most German ocean liners up to about 1890. The first trip was made in June 1856 from Hamburg to New York.

In 1857 Hamburg America bought two more steamers from British builders: the *Austria* and the *Saxonia*. The North Atlantic section of their fleet expanded to five by the next year. By 1871 nine Hamburg America ships served New York and Baltimore, but other vessels in their growing fleet ran to South America, Africa, and Asia.

The New York–bound ships began stopping at Southampton. By 1891 they owned forty-two vessels, almost all of which were built in Britain, because the Brits could produce a first-class iron ship cheaper than any other industrial nation. This was true because British iron was so cheap. They outproduced and undersold everyone until the 1880s. They mined more coal than the United States until 1898. How did little England do it? In part because they started so early, coal mining was under way in Elizabethan times, and iron making was very advanced by the late eighteenth century. In time the United States and Germany caught up and in some cases surpassed Britain's lead. The German lines began buying steamers from the Vulkan Works in Stettin in 1890. This North Sea manufacturing plant built some of the largest steel passenger steamers in the world, such as the *Kaiser Wilhelm der Grosse* (1897) and the *Deutschland* (1899). Hamburg America became the largest steamship company in the world, and by 1901 it owned 202 ships, 40 of which were over 1,000 tons.

By 1875 Hamburg America had taken over several German competitors and become the largest of all the continental steamship lines. Albert Ballin (1857–1918) had been employed by one of the absorbed lines and was now working for the Hamburg America. He was a native of Hamburg, a graduate of a local business school, and as a young man had been much attracted to the marvelous parade of seagoing ships that visited the great port of Hamburg. He went to England soon after graduation, specifically to work in the merchant marine and see how the British handled the details of that business. He spent several years in England and became fluent in the language. He was bright, enthusiastic, and full of energy. On returning to Germany Ballin found work with a shipping company. Once inside the Hamburg America offices, he proved himself to be an effective manager. In 1886 he was made director of passenger traffic. He became a micro-manager and personally checked, adjusted, and reformed every detail of the operation from menus to steam plants, to lighting, bedding, and advertising. He proved himself to be a genius; the stockholders received good dividends, the customers wonderful service, and workers a pension fund. In 1885 he worked out a price fixing deal with his major competitor, the North German Lloyd line of Bremen. There would be no more fare wars between them; prices would be fixed that did not discourage travel yet yielded a reasonable profit. In 1899 Ballin was named director general of the Hamburg America Steamship Company. He was soon a confidant of Chancellor Bismarck and Kaiser Wilhelm II.

The North German Lloyd line started up about the same time as the Hamburg America line. Its early years were more stressful financially than the Hamburg America, but it was healthier by the late 1860s and began to expand operations to Central and South America. In 1881 the North German Lloyd line received an express ship named the *Elbe* built in Glasgow by John Elder and Co. She was 418 feet long with a fine lined hull and large compound engines built for speed. Two sister ships were to follow from the same yard. The Germans were now into the Blue Riband race. The *Elbe* and her sisters were not fast enough, but in 1897 the North German Lloyd had a much larger express boat built by Vulkan. The *Kaiser Wilhelm der Grosse* took the Blue Riband from the Cunard line on her maiden voyage. The fact that she had four funnels seemed to upset the British public more than her speedy crossing, the four stacks suggesting a power that the British had lost. The North German Lloyd also had almost captured a quarter of the transatlantic trade, a trade once exclusive to the British lines. It would be ten years before Cunard won back the Blue Riband and then only because of a massive government loan.

The French were hoping for a little attention from the Atlantic shipping community, but established shipping lines were too busy to notice their small but high-quality efforts on the high seas. A French line was established in 1855 by Emile and Isaac Péreire that ran to Algeria and expanded to the United States and Mexico by 1861. Emperor Napoleon III urged the brothers to enter the transatlantic trade so that France would be represented with the other great nations of the world. He promised generous government support. The first boat of the Compagnie Générale Transatlantique was the *Washington*, an iron-hulled side-wheeler built in Greenock, Scotland, in 1864. She made her first trip from Le Havre to New York in June of that year. More ships followed and weekly service was eventually started. The *Washington* was rebuilt with twin screws in 1868, which is thought to be a first application of the double screw. By 1885 the French line was considered a strong operation and noted for its good service. It owned no really large vessel until 1912 and continued to operate until the end of the transatlantic era. The *France* of 1961 was one of the last transatlantic steamers to enter service.

America had been gone from the transatlantic race for so long, they were almost forgotten. Only a few embers glowed in the firebox of American shipping when it came to the Atlantic trade. The United States was strong in South American and Pacific trade, but the prestige was in the Atlantic. There was some hope when the Pennsylvania Railroad organized the American line in 1873. No established line wanted to serve Philadelphia, so the Pennsylvania Railroad would create its own by holding 60 percent of the stock and guaranteeing the bonds. Four ships were built at yards of William Cramp and Sons in Philadelphia. Each ship was 355 feet

11.10. The *City of New York* was an express steamer built for the Inman and International line in 1888. Its clipper bow and slim hull made it look like a giant yacht. It is recognized as one of the most beautiful ocean liners in history. Her main cabin was a near duplicate of the *City of Paris* shown in fig. 11.8b.

(*Harper's Weekly*, March 30, 1889)

long and had space for one hundred first-class and eight hundred steerage passengers. It would have been cheaper to build them in Scotland, but the U.S. government would register them only if they were built in America. The Guion line, which was financed mostly by American money, registered its ships in England for this reason. The American lines became associated with the International line by the early 1880s. International gained control of the Red Star and Inman lines at the same time. Red Star operated under the Belgium flag, and many of its captains and crew were Belgian citizens. Many of its ships were old Cunards: the *Waistland* was the old *Russia* (1967), the *Lava* became the *Zeeland,* and so on. Red Star served Antwerp and Jersey City. The docks at the latter place were cheaper than those on Manhattan. Red Star had the support of King Leopold, who helped finance it in 1873. Its boats were not glamorous or fast – the trip to Antwerp took from ten to fourteen days. It was a cheap way to go and put its passengers off on the continent not that far from Paris, so it was a good way for poor artists to get to the City of Light.

The old Inman line fell upon hard times after the death of its founder in July 1881. None of his twelve children were able or ready to take on the burden of management. The line continued as a private stock company and built several remarkably beautiful vessels; its *City of Rome* (1881) was said to be the most beautiful ocean steamer ever constructed. It had a long, slim hull; three funnels that leaned back at a rakish angle; and a clipper bow. The firm attempted to raise capital to build two sister ships but failed in that effort. In 1886 the International Navigation Company, a successor to the Red Star line and an American corporation, purchased Inman and reorganized as the Inman and International Company Limited. Inman was failing financially because the company had too many lines and too few passengers. Costs had to be cut, and offices were merged or closed. The Inman pier burned in 1885 and no funds were available to rebuild it, so they now shared piers in Jersey City with Red Star boats. There were rumors that the Anchor line had purchased the Inman boats, which proved false. Times improved and Inman and International went ahead with the sister ships the *City of New York* (1888) and the *City of Paris* (1889). These ships were more successful than the *City of Rome,* which failed to meet her speed requirements and was returned to the builder and resold to the Anchor line in 1882. The *City of New York* reached 20 knots during her sea trials and went on to become a greyhound of the sea (fig. 11.10). J. P. Morgan took over the International line in 1893, but was too engaged in other matters to do more than hold on to the shares until a more opportune time.

Morgan was the most powerful banker in the world. He managed big deals in business but also financed a giant loan to the U.S. Treasury in 1896 to restore its gold reserves. In 1907 he ended a Wall Street panic that was threatening to become a national recession, and in 1901 he created the first billion-dollar corporation, U.S. Steel. Morgan was also busy assembling New England railroads into a single system and in creating the International Harvester Company, but he found time to rationalize the transatlantic steamer trade. There were too many lines, too many price wars, and far too little profit to justify these costly operations. The public might enjoy good service, but the shareholders suffered from poor dividends. Investors were not earning a fair return on their shares; this was of paramount importance to the king of Wall Street. Shareholders assumed real risk by investing, and they needed protection or capitalism would fail. By consolidating all the major lines, Morgan hoped to reduce operating costs by eliminating redundant service, overlapping schedules, and excessive speeds. He would stabilize fares and make the business lean and efficient.

In September 1902 Morgan organized the International Mercantile Marine (IMM) Company with a capital limit of $120 million to take over all transatlantic service. The Inman and International was first in line to become part of IMM, since it was already a Morgan property. The American and Red Star lines were included in this package. The Dominion and Leyman lines were then acquired. The White Star could not refuse Morgan's generous offer of $25 million in gold. He never quibbled over price, be it an old master or a steamship line. Thomas Ismay's playboy son, J. Bruce Ismay, was soon president of the IMM. Morgan told him to order some first-class liners and he, Morgan, would attend their launching. The results of this suggestion were the *Olympia,* the *Titanic,* and the *Britannic.* The two German lines did not want to sell, but they agreed to otherwise cooperate and finally to sell Morgan's 51 percent of the shares if they could maintain nominal control of the line's day-to-day operations. Hamburg America's Albert Ballin presented a detailed contract to the kaiser, who read it line by line and demanded an explanation of its many provisions. At last he was satisfied and Ballin was free to join the monopoly.

Table 11.2. The World Fleet of Ocean Steamers (in Millions of Tons)

	1870		1886		1899	
British	2,426 ships	1.65	4,852 ships	6.40	7,837 ships	7.1
United States	597 ships	.51	355 ships	.54	605 ships	.51
Germany	127 ships	.10	509 ships	.56	1,133 ships	1.21
France	288 ships	.21	505 ships	.75	639 ships	.51
All others*	640 ships	.60	2200 ships	2.80	6,500 ships	.60

*Estimated

There were a few holdouts. The French line flat out refused to sign on; their generous government subsidy made it possible for them to ignore Morgan's offer. The Anchor line also declined, but neither of these operations were big enough to cause much trouble. Cunard played a clever game of acceptance and rejection while stirring up public objections to the prospect of an American takeover. The British government, led by Arthur Balfour, was under pressure to keep Cunard going as a British enterprise. White Star had already sold out, so the dear old Cunard, then the oldest steamer line still operating, had to be preserved. After lengthy negotiations the British government offered Cunard a loan of £2.6 million at a low interest rate to build new ships and receive a £150,000 subsidy each year. In turn, Cunard promised to remain British. In 1901 the Atlantic steamer traffic was divided roughly into thirds: IMM with 64,738 passengers; German lines with 66,838; and the Cunard, Anchor, and French lines with a combined total of 59,506. However, Morgan's plan failed because no one was in control of the North Atlantic passenger traffic. Despite all of his money and power, there were some things even J. P. Morgan could not control. No one man could hope to control the Atlantic Ocean. The White Star line eventually returned to British control, and Morgan's marine empire faded away a decade or so after his death in 1913.

PASSENGER TRAVEL; OR, DAILY LIFE ON THE HIGH SEAS

An ocean steamer was like a city gone to sea. It had streets, shops, and a great community center. The streets were passageways, some so narrow only one person could pass at a time, much like an alley. There was a butcher shop, a bakery, a pastry shop, a confectioner, a tavern, and a bar. The main cabin was the community center; it served as a grand saloon, a parlor, a drawing room, a dining room, and as a chamber for invalids. On the better ships the main cabin was baronial, with gilt mirrors, Axminster rugs, polished lamps, oil paintings, and elegant furniture. Meals were served in silver-plated covered dishes, and the china and glasses sparkled in the sun from a skylight high overhead. Such luxury could only be found in the best hotels or palaces.

Two travelers on the Cunard line in the 1850s prepared excellent accounts on what it was like to cross the ocean in the mid-Victorian era. Isabella Bird, the English travel writer mentioned earlier, took the *Canada* in the summer of 1854 to Boston. William Chambers, publisher of the *Edinburgh Journal,* took the *America* to Boston the previous September. Both also stopped at Halifax and left from Liverpool. The experiences and observations of the two travelers were similar, so they are combined in the paraphrased account below.

❋ ❋ ❋

The ships are anchored in the center of the estuary of the Mersey River that forms Liverpool's harbor. Passengers and luggage are ferried out to the ship from the dock by a small side-wheel steamer called a tender. Cabin space is limited, so many passengers stand on the open deck near the luggage and mail bags. Several tenders are generally needed to handle the passengers and their visitors. The night before, the ship leaves the dock after provisioning and the loading of coal are completed. The boat is empty except for the crew. Steam is up; they are ready to leave. Most lines are already cast off, the officers on the bridge are alert, and the engine room crew watches the big dial of the telegraph. Then the captain nods, there is a sharp order from the bridge, slow astern, and the answer is a high-pitched repeat of the order. The big side wheels begin to turn, with the rudder hard to starboard. The giant ship backs up and swings to clear the pens end – "All clear, sir," calls the bo'sn. The final line is tossed to the deck. The signal bells ring back and forth between the engine room and the bridge as the ship is turned and stopped. Once she is lined up properly, the bridge orders, "Slow ahead," and the engines throb, the boat vibrates, and then quiets down as she majestically heads out into the middle of the Mersey, leaving the gray and clammy docks behind in the shadows. The engines are stopped, the anchors are dropped, the fires banked, lamps belowdecks extinguished, and much of the crew heads to their bunks. The passengers will board in the morning; sailing time is 12:00 NOON. *The fog and rain move in as the ship sleeps.*

Passengers file aboard the tender; it's still foggy, and there is a small mountain of baggage and two loads of mail. The helmsman can't see and bumps into a passing steamer; some of the luggage goes overboard and is lost. Many passengers are knocked down, but none are seriously injured. The steamer does not stop, and in recovering passengers begin to jeer the helmsman. They reach the ship a few minutes later. Everyone climbs aboard, to be welcomed by the officer of the watch. Like all Cunard crews, he is dressed in a splendid blue uniform. The Royal Mail, some two tons of it, is stashed with considerable dispatch, into the mailroom. Most passengers are disappointed by the size of their tiny cabin. The steward reminds passengers that the main cabin is very spacious and that there is a separate smoking room for men and a ladies' parlor for

11.11. A steamer ready to leave the wharf in New York. Last-minute passengers hurry up the gangplank while visitors, on the left side, exit the ship. It is an exciting moment, spirits are high, and there is much shouting and waving from the crowd.

(*Scribner's Magazine*, April 1891)

the women. Passengers assigned to the forward cabins have more to complain about, because the bow of the ship rides worse than the rear and takes on the most water. In a storm the forward cabins generally have wet floors.

The confusion of boarding has calmed down. The visitors are now gone, and the last hugs and tears and good-byes are over (fig. 11.11). Steam is sputtering from the escape pipes; the captain and his men are at their duty stations. It's a few minutes before noon, and the captain quietly orders the anchor raised. Passengers notice that the officers give orders calmly; there is no bluster and certainly no profanity – the crew responds promptly – everything is executed in a sharp, fast, military manner. The capstan clatters as the anchor chain comes up – the anchor is made fast. The salute cannon fires a farewell – the whistle gives a long, mournful call to announce that the ship is under way at exactly 12:00 NOON. Cunard likes to be exactly on time. As the boat moves steadily down the channel, we pass dozens of merchant ships at anchor. There is a timber ship from Quebec; a high-sterned Dutch galliot; nearby is a black-hulled Black Ball liner, the Marco Polo; and near the end is a troop ship bound for the Crimea. We pass Birkenhead and cross over the harbor bar. We proceed at half speed to the lighthouse at Holyhead. The pilot is discharged. Lookouts remain at their stations watching for other ships as we pass into St. George's Channel and proceed along the southern Irish coast. Captain N. Shannon remains on the bridge until the ship is out to sea. He is a Scot who is agreeable in manner but will not engage in long or personal conversation. This would distract him from his first duty, and that is the safety of the ship, its passengers, and cargo. He is a particularly careful commander who gives his orders in writing to avoid the misunderstanding of a purely verbal command.

※ ※ ※

Most passengers were seasick for the first two days, despite relatively calm seas. Most recover and begin to attend meals and mix with the other passengers gathered in the main cabin. Ms. Bird was impressed by the mixture of nationalities. Of the 168 first-class passengers, only 20 were English; the rest were Canadians, Americans, Dutch, Germans, French, Spanish, and Bavarians. There was a young woman looking for a husband, an old gentleman with a pretty woman – *Are they father and daughter, or husband and wife? Who is the silent woman who knits all day? Is she as calm and introspective as she appears? What about that pompous fellow who enters the room with such an air? Is he a mighty general, or only a clerk with pretensions?* The steward is willing to share what he knows. He says if the man is attentive to the lady, they are engaged; if she is attentive to the man, they are newly married; but if they tend to ignore each other, they are long married.

Seating at the dining table consumed a considerable part of the day. Seatmates become companions, and the mix could be awkward: Ms. Bird noticed that a duchess was seated next to a cook, and a Jew seated beside a pork merchant. Care was taken, however, to put officials of the Cunard line and pretty single women at the captain's table. Those who traveled alone took a chance when it came to roommates. Ms. Bird had the misfortune to share space with a lady alcoholic who kept bottles of gin, brandy, and beer in her berth. The woman was frequently intoxicated, and the more she drank the more foul her language became. Ms. Bird endured this person for more than ten days.

According to Chambers, dining aboard the *America* was equal to any served by the best hotels. Breakfast was served at 8:00 AM, exactly, and all the meals began upon the minute. The menu included Irish stew, cold meats, ham, mutton chops, fish, eggs, tea, coffee, and hot rolls. Luncheon was the most popular meal. Passengers, 160 in number, would rush in to take their seats. Each table had a large silver soup tureen. When the

Sports on deck - a Boys' Obstacle Race

11.12. Games were organized for boys to let off steam, much to the merriment of the adult passengers and crew. The ship was identified as a Trans-Atlantic Express liner but no name was given.

(Leslie's Weekly, June 30, 1888)

captain entered and was seated at the first table on the left, the stewards would uncover the tureens and the meal would begin. A dozen stewards in smart blue uniforms worked quietly and silently. Printed menus were on the table, and diners would order from a great variety of dishes. The elegance and bounty of the meals was amazing and ranged from game fowl to roast beef. Side dishes were prepared in the French style, and the pastry was fresh and delicious. Ice water was served in abundance; those wanting wine presented a card and settled this account at the end of the voyage. There were always a few passengers who never attended meals because they were chronically seasick and subsisted on a small ration of tea and biscuits. They would remain silent and miserable in their cabin for most of the journey. When the weather picked up and the ship began to roll and dip, many others would take to their beds and forgo the rich fare offered in the saloon.

Cabin attendants were busy throughout the trip sweeping and cleaning the public spaces. They also handled a considerable amount of linens that needed washing and airing out. The Cunard liner *Persia* (1855), for example, carried 1,200 blankets; 1,600 sheets; 800 pillowcases; 4,000 napkins; and 400 tablecloths according to a report in the *New York Times* of February 11, 1856.

Both Ms. Bird and William Chambers were good sailors and rarely missed a meal nor hid away in their cabins during rough seas. Ms. Bird donned an oilskin coat and cap to walk the wet and sooty main deck as waves broke over the bulwarks. She considered it a fine promenade. Chambers liked to sit on the roof of the wheelhouse at the stern and look over the broad, drab, green sea and the long wake left by the ship. Most passengers, however, stayed inside the main cabin unless the weather was fair. They would read, gossip, write letters home or in their diaries, or play cards or chess. Parlor games were another way to fill the long hours at sea. On stormy days passengers were confined to the cabin; it simply was too

11.13. On a calm day at sea a mother and child enjoy the salt air. Mother knits while an officer standing above the main deck explains the bridge and wonders of navigation to a lady passenger.

(*Century Magazine*, September 1882)

dangerous to have them on deck. Even during normal seas the ship could take sudden nose dives, so passengers were prohibited from walking on the forecastle deck.

When the sun was out and the sea was more languid, almost everyone went topside. Mothers would sit with their children. Men would stroll up and down, smoking or debating how far they would go today. Would it be 225 or 260 miles? They might ask a passing officer, "How fast is she going? His reply would always be about 1 or 2 knots faster than the actual speed. Children and adults would play deck games or hide and seek. Invalids would sit in deck chairs well bundled up. Even the seasick folks would step out for some air. Life seemed very good (figs. 11.12 and 11.13).

Because the Victorian era was a time when appearances were extremely important, almost everyone on board would attend the Sunday morning service in the main cabin, even if their faith was questionable. On British ships it was always an Anglican service. The captain read from the *Book of Common Prayer*. He normally chose the short service. If there was a piano or organ on board, a few hymns were sung. The captain's reading usually had a more military than ecclesiastical tone about it. Occasionally the captain might make an appeal to passengers at the end of the service for donations to a charity such as the Home for Children of Sailors Lost at Sea.

Outing magazine, a journal devoted to hunting, fishing, and travel, offered an account of a trip on the North German Lloyd liner *Elbe* (1881) in its September 1887 issue. The *Elbe* was an express steamer and so attracted first-class passengers seeking a fast way to get from Southampton

11.14. North German Lloyd's *Elbe*, 1881, the first express liner built for a German line. She sank in 1895 with a large loss of life.

(W. T. Knox, *Life of Robert Fulton*, 1886)

or Bremen to New York (fig. 11.14). The author of this brief account may have been a journalist, since he had access to the engine room and the bridge. He describes the ship leaving New York with great clouds of black coal smoke rolling out of her funnels in calm air. There was the ever-present throbbing of engines, which was an indication of their tireless power and perfect rhythm. They ran at 60 rpm, which pushed the ship ahead 30 feet every minute. On the first day there were many empty seats at the dining table; the promenade and deck chairs were empty as well, telling a mute story of seasickness. On this lonely day our scribe visited the wheelhouse on the stern. The helmsman stood before a small wheel with his attention fixed on a dimly lit compass. A much larger manual wheel was nearby, used only when the power steering failed. It was very quiet until the stern raised up out of the water; the propeller raced and the ship began to vibrate gingerly. When the ship fell back into the water the propeller slowed to a soft throbbing. The only other noise, beside the wind, was the dumping of ashes over the side. These were brought up from the fire room in large buckets. There was much dust and rattling involved with this work. The *Elbe* was making 375 miles in a day, which was good time. At this speed the ship would soon be in the "roaring forties," an unusually stormy part of the Atlantic between 40 and 50 degrees of latitude, about midway in the North Atlantic.

❋ ❋ ❋

Our narrator visits the bridge in the company of the captain. It is located on top of the forward cabin ahead of the second mast. At center is a compass and speaking tubes connected to the wheelhouse and the engine room telegraph. A heavy iron railing 4½ feet high, covered by a thick tarpaulin, protects them from the sea. The captain relates that during last winter's great storm, a monster wave smashed one end of the bridge into pieces and he fell under the wreckage. He was lucky to escape with his life. Some water from this same wave drowned out the furnaces on one side of the ship. The Alaska lost her rudder

OCEAN STEAM

in the same storm. Some storms will literally stop a powerful ship like the Elbe *if they hit her head-on – she will tremble, stop, and then regain her hold on the sea and proceed. On the eighth day the* Elbe *anchors in Southampton Harbor. A tender pulls up – first to leave the* Elbe *are bags of silver ingots, then the baggage, a mixed collection of the new and spotless along with battered veterans covered with travel tickets. There are leather and canvas bags plus a few baskets. Then the passengers are allowed to depart, our scribe among them. It will take the* Elbe *another 30 hours to reach Bremen.*

✳ ✳ ✳

The *Elbe* continued in service for several years and was making a routine crossing on the North Sea when she was hit amidships by a British steamer on January 30, 1895. It was dark and foggy, a normal condition for this season and location. Were the watches doing their duty? Were they looking intently? Or had they drifted off into a daydream rather than search for a red or green lamp or a white forecast light? Had they left their duty post for a nap? Had the officers checked on the men? We will never know, because almost all of the crew was killed. Two compartments were breached; the crew fled but neglected to close the bulkhead doors, and the ship went down in about twenty minutes. There was no time to get the passengers off; 350 were lost and only 20 survived. It was a major disaster and an unnecessary one, for if the crew had done their duty, most on board could have been rescued. Such are the ways of men, and such are the risks of sea travel.

The last example of steamer life takes place late in the Victorian era as described in *McClure's Magazine* of March 1895. The ship is an ocean flyer, the *Furst Bismarck* (Prince Bismarck) built five years earlier for the Hamburg America line. This great liner is 504 feet long with space for 420 first-class, 127 second-class, and 700 third-class passengers (fig. 11.15). Her large upper structure is surmounted by three immense funnels, painted an orangish tan color. At midnight before the departure day, fires are lit under the nine boilers – yellow smoke rises lazily from the funnels. By dawn steam is nudging the needle of the steam gauges. As early as 6:00 AM a few passengers appear at the Hamburg dock. Boarding does not begin until 8:00. Passengers are welcomed while suspicious persons are turned away by the inspectors. There is much noise and confusion as people, baggage, and cargo are put on board. The dock is very crowded. At 10:00 no visitors are admitted except messengers with packages or flowers for passengers. Visitors are escorted politely but firmly down the gangplank. At precisely 10:30 the captain signals the engine room and the great twin propellers begin to turn. Hundreds of handkerchiefs flutter, and the crowd on the pier shout good-byes; some cry, some laugh. It's

11.15. The *Prince Bismark* was a North German Lloyd liner of 1890. Note that she still employs auxiliary sails.

(Jim Harter collection)

an emotional moment, as if a great national hero were exiting for the last time. The *Bismarck* is visible for some time as she slowly passes through the harbor, but few remain long to watch her disappear over the horizon. The passengers begin to learn their way around this huge floating hotel. With its many floors, stairways, cabins, and public spaces, it's easy to get lost, and not a few must ask for help to find their deck or cabin. Ocean liners of the future will be even larger and more confusing, growing to two times the size of the *Bismarck*.

The food service was made complicated by three galleys, one each for the three classes of passengers. Each had a head chef, several assistant chefs, and a battalion of carvers and scullions. Steerage was well fed, considering the fare of $18 and seven days of travel over 3,000 miles as part of that modest sum. The food in second class was better, as good as could be found in a moderately priced hotel. First-class meals involved seven to ten courses and were fit for an emperor. The wines and ales were excellent and priced 40 percent cheaper than in New York. A special feature was offered to first-class patrons who preferred to dine in a deck chair: an elegant tray of food made to order could be served at no extra cost. Inside the main cabin, stewards wore neat uniforms and white gloves. They would march in and out of the main cabin keeping time with the music and provided a floor show just by serving dinner. A few hours later a tea was served. One hour later a band concert was given in the second-class saloon, but many first-class passengers would attend as well. Dainty sandwiches were served along with beer as the band performed. These musical groups were famous around the world and would perform again late the next morning. On Sundays they played sacred music most of the day; no one would forget the sound of "Nearer My God to Thee" as played by one of these groups. Even the most seasick person would feel better hearing the sound of a good German band.

Cabin-class passengers were pampered, as the larger staterooms had private toilets – no more walking down the hall. Their shoes would be polished every night by an attendant known as "Boots." Those who desired a bath were escorted down the hall by a steward to a large bathroom with two giant marble tubs, one hot and one cold.

The men on board who were most in need of a good bath would never see the inside of this fancy bathroom, however. They worked at the bottom of the hull, feeding coal into the hungry furnaces, making steam to push the *Bismarck* along at 12 knots. At this speed she burned 90 tons of coal a day; passengers wanting the speed notched up by a few knots did not understand that fuel consumption is cubed as speed increases. Hence to run at 16 knots would require 180 tons of coal, and to go 20 knots would require 300 tons a day. As it was, the ocean expresses were considered uneconomic because of their high operating costs. White Star was very content to run at lower speeds and hold down fuel consumption. Visitors to the engine room were shown the steam-powered compartment doors that could be closed in one minute and were tested twice a day. The huge 16,000 hp engines were impressive. So, too, the propeller shafts, which measured 2 feet in diameter, weighed 1 ton per foot, and revolved at 75 rpm.

Near the end of the trip a special farewell dinner was served. The cabin was decorated with bunting and flags, and a few speeches were offered. The French line outdid the German and British lines by making it the captain's dinner with a champagne toast offered in tribute to the passengers for their patronage. The *Bismarck* was a fine ship but so costly to operate that Hamburg America sold her to a Russian firm in 1904, and she went on to several other owners before being scrapped in 1924.

"FOR THOSE IN PERIL ON THE SEA"
(U.S. NAVY HYMN 1860)

The beauty of the sea is undeniable, but, ironically, it is equally deadly. It would be difficult to make an exact count of the ships lost at sea during the Victorian era. However, according to *Lloyd's List*, between 1793 and 1829 the number of British merchant vessels lost each year was 557, which equaled 2/40 of the fleet. The loss of life among passengers and crew members was likely around 1,000 per year. The *Engineer,* a British journal, offers a general account for British steamers in May 1863, claiming about thirty packets had been lost since the beginning of steam navigation, some twenty years before. Upward of 2,000 people died, and $15 million worth of property was lost. The British system alone covered some three million miles and carried about two million passengers a year. In a report of the

Table 11.3. Steamships of the Victorian Era

Name	Line	Year	Hull	Length	Speed/ knots	Gross Tonnage	Propulsion	Steam Pressure	Indicated Horse power	Remarks
Great Western	GWR	1838	Wood	212	8.5	1,340	Paddles	15	750	Space for 148 first-class only. Scrapped in 1857.
Britannia	Cunard	1840	Wood	207	8.5	1,150	Paddles	12	740	Sunk as a target ship in 1880. Space for 115 first-class only.
Great Britain	GWR	1845	Iron	270	11	3,270	Screw	25	1,500	On exhibit in Bristol, England. 252 first-class only.
Arctic	Collins	1850	Wood	282	12.5	2,860	Paddles	17	2,000	Sank in 1854. 250 first-class only.
Persia	Cunard	1856	Iron	360	12.5	3,300	Paddles	20	3,600	Scrapped in 1872. 200 first-class. 50 second-class.
Great Eastern	G.E. S.S. Co.	1858	Iron	680	13	18,915	Paddles + Screw	30	11,000	Scrapped in 1891. 800 first-class; 2000 second-class; 1,200 third-class.
Russia	Cunard	1867	Iron	358	13.5	2,959	Screw	25	2,500	Sold to Red Star line in 1881. 235 first-class.
City of Brussels	Inman	1869	Iron	390	14.5	3,081	Screw	65	3,000	Sank in 1887.
Oceanic	White Star	1871	Iron	420	14.7	3,707	Screw	70	4,000	Scrapped in 1896. 166 first-class. 1,000 third-class.
Arizona	Guion	1879	Iron	450	16.2	5,147	Screw	90	6,300	Scrapped in 1926. 140 first-class. 70 second-class. 140 third-class.
City of Rome	Inman	1881	Iron	560	17.5	8,144	Screw	90	11,500	Sold to Anchor line in 1882. Scrapped in 1902. 520 first-class. 810 third-class.
Oregon	Guion & Cunard	1883	Iron	501	19	7,375	Screw	110	13,000	Sold to Cunard in 1884. Sank in 1886.
Etruria	Cunard	1885	Steel	501	19.5	8,120	Screw	110	14,500	Scrapped in 1909 . 550 first-class. 800 third-class.
City of New York	Inman	1888	Steel	528	20	10,499	Twin Screw	N.A.	N.A.	Scrapped in 1923. 540 first-class. 200 second-class. 1,000 third-class.
Furst Bismark	Hamburg American	1890	Steel	502	19.5	8,874	Twin Screw	160	17,000	Scrapped in 1924. 420 first-class. 172 second-class. 700 third-class.
Campania	Cunard	1893	Steel	598	22	12,950	Twin Screw	165	30,000	Converted to aircraft carrier in 1914. Sank in 1918. 600 first-class. 400 second-class. 1,000 third-class.
Kaiser Wilhelm der Grosse	North German Lloyd	1897	Steel	625	23	14,350	Twin Screw	178	32,000	Destroyed by British cruiser in 1914. 332 first-class. 343 second-class. 1,074 third-class.
Oceanic II	White Star	1899	Steel	685	21.5	17,274	Twin Screw	192	29,000	Wrecked in 1914. 410 first-class. 300 second-class. 1,000 third-class.

Note: 10 knots = 11.5 mph, 15 knots = 17.2 mph, 20 knots = 23 mph, 25 knots = 28.7 mph.

Source: This table is based on E. W. Smith's *Passenger Ships of the World* and *The Encyclopedia Britannica*, vol. 24, 1910.

Royal Commission on Unseaworthy Ships, 1873–1874, it was reported that between 1847 and 1873 a total of 22,000 ships left British ports carrying 6.2 million passengers and crew. Of these, 103 ships and 6,129 lives were lost. The percentage of loss was less than 1 percent. *Harper's Book of Facts* (1895) reported that the U.S. Merchant fleet's average number of wrecks per year between 1879 and 1889 was 1,919; the loss of life per year was estimated at 535. This same source stated that the larger British merchant fleet had 664 wrecks per year and experienced a loss of 1,913 lives during this same ten-year span.

Many improvements appeared in following decades, such as iron hulls, power steering, double bottoms, steel hulls, watertight compartments, twin screws, and separate sea-lanes for ships traveling east and west. More and more lighthouses, buoys, fog bells, and channel markers were installed. The British established a life-saving service in 1824 to rescue passengers from ships wrecked along the shore. Sturdy lifeboats went through the surf to pick up stranded crews and passengers and bring them back to the beach. Over the years thousands of lives were saved by the heroic work of the surfmen. The U.S. government began such operations in 1848. Many great advances came in the twentieth century, including the wireless telegraph, radar, sonar, and celestial positioning. Yet none of these remarkable improvements have ended disasters at sea or the loss of ships and men.

We have already mentioned shipwrecks, including the loss of the *Arctic, Pacific, Elbe,* and other liners. We have not, however, considered fire at sea. One of the greatest disasters on the Atlantic Ocean occurred on September 13, 1858, aboard the iron-hulled Hamburg America ship the *Austria*. She had stopped at Southampton and was heading for New York with a human cargo of 608 on board. The boatswain's mate was ordered to fumigate the cabins with a flaming bucket of tar. The noxious smoke would presumably kill the vermin hiding in the mattresses and bedding. When the mate dropped the bucket, the flaming tar became a liquid and quickly spread across the wooden deck, setting fire to the bunks, furniture, bedding and all else in its incendiary path. Within five minutes the middle of the ship was on fire. Some of the passengers began to panic.

The captain should have organized his men to quench the fire and remove the passengers in lifeboats. However, he panicked and lost control of himself. He suffered serious burns dashing around the top deck and either fell or jumped overboard and drowned. The other officers were unable to organize the crew. Only one lifeboat was successfully launched and it capsized several times. Twenty-three people managed to stay aboard, but all the others were lost. Meanwhile the *Austria* was steaming ahead with the engine room crew trapped belowdecks; all had perished, and there was no one to shut down the machinery. While some passengers were

11.16. The burning of the *Austria* in 1858 was a major disaster at sea, resulting in a large loss of life.

(R. M. Deems, *Our First Century*, 1878)

not able to reach the top deck, those who had done so huddled at the bow or stern trying to avoid the flames. However, the sails and rigging caught on fire and rained down on the helpless passengers, setting their clothes or hair ablaze. Some were soon in the nude as they tore off their flaming garments. The masts and spars fell one by one, adding to the inferno, but the iron hull was not greatly affected by the heat. This entire time people were dropping off the ship in ones or twos. Most of them drowned. Only a lucky few found bits of driftwood to sustain them. Finally a French sailing vessel appeared, but her progress toward the *Austria* was slow because the wind had died. At last she was near enough to begin a rescue. Only 67 people survived that terrible fire aboard the *Austria* (fig. 11.16).

There was another major accident in 1873 that can be blamed on a negligent captain. It, too, resulted in a large loss of life and would have been easily avoidable if the crew and officers had acted in a more professional manner. The White Star liner *Atlantic* was heading for New York late in March. A strong westerly gale slowed the vessel's progress, and she was consuming coal at a high rate to maintain even a minimal speed. While still 460 miles east of New York she had only 127 tons of coal left. Captain James Williams decided to alter course and make a run for Halifax to refuel. There were 942 on board, which included the crew. Williams plotted a course intended to take the ship directly to the Halifax harbor entrance. At midnight he went to bed. The ship steamed on, but Williams's course was in error; he had seriously miscalculated. At about 3:00 AM on April 1, she slammed into Marr's Rock, about 15 miles southwest of Halifax. It was a tremendous crash that likely woke up everyone on board, but many of those on the lower decks were drowned before they could escape. Williams led a rescue effort, but before much could be done the *Atlantic* rolled over on one side, the hull broke in half, and the rear section sank under the waves. Only the forward part of the hull and the rigging were above the waves. Those who could climbed into the rigging and held on for hours, but the cold, wind, and exhaustion were too much for them – they began to drop off into the icy waves. A line to shore was rigged up and about two hundred people managed to climb over the rocks to shore and safety.

A few fishermen discovered the wreck before sunup and did what they could to pick up survivors. Word was sent to Halifax, and the first rescue ship arrived at 6:00 AM. At the same time, scavengers came out in small boats to pull bodies out of the water, search for valuables, and drop the corpses back into the sea. They picked up floating luggage for the same purpose. In all about 480 died; of these, 350 were women and children. Only one child survived the disaster. Testimony against the captain claimed discipline on the boat was lax, the crew was unruly, and the officers seemed more interested in cards and whiskey than in running the ship. The ship had been sailing through shallow waters, yet no soundings were taken by lead lines nor were special watches posted to look for obvious hazards, such as riffs or rocks. All agreed, however, that the captain behaved in a heroic manner after the sinking and saved many lives. His punishment seemed very mild, considering the loss of a nearly new vessel and so many lives. His license was suspended for two years.

The history of accidents tends to dwell on the catastrophic that involve a large loss of life, but many mishaps were just as remarkable because no one was killed or even injured. A fast, elegant steamer, the Cunard line's *Oregon* (1884) was steaming toward the Fire Island lighthouse in March 1886 when a heavily laden coal schooner rammed into her side, knocking a good-size hole in her hull. The order to close the bulkhead doors proved of little use. Coal dust and bits were packed so tightly in the sills that many doors could not be moved. Water began to spread slowly into many compartments. Fortunately a North German steamer came by, and all 852 on board the *Oregon* were transferred to the *Fulda*. Several hours later the *Oregon* sank into the Atlantic 10 miles off of Long Island. Her remains are still there in just 120 feet of water (fig. 11.17).

The Cunard line had lost several other ships before the *Oregon*. The *Columbia* was lost in 1843 at Cape Sable; in 1872 the *Tripoli* went down at Tuskar Rocks on the Irish coast near Queenstown. No one died. Cunard could boast that they had never lost a passenger. Was it just luck, or did they have an immunity to disasters? The reason was more likely Cunard's insistence on good seamanship and caution. No Captain Williams would remain in Cunard's employ very long. One Cunard captain traveled 630,000 miles, carrying 26,000 first-class passengers without a

11.17. The *Oregon* was a Cunard liner that sank off the Long Island coast in 1886 with no loss of life. The captain is shown at his duty station, the bridge.

(*Century Magazine*, August 1886)

single accident. The reason, as with all Cunard commanders, was strict discipline, good and faithful lookouts, care with lamps, only the best men at the wheel, slowing down during fog or snowstorms, and the constant use of lead lines in shallow waters.

There were non-fatal accidents that would have resulted in a large loss of life except for lucky circumstances. The Inman liner *City of Paris* was a grand ship and surely one of the most beautiful to cross the Atlantic. She had been in service for only a year when the piston rod of a starboard engine's low-pressure cylinder came loose. This was a freak accident, but it destroyed the engine, then running at high speed. Chunks of the engine flew around the engine room. One knocked a hole in the hull 20 feet below the waterline. Another punched a hole in the bulkhead of the port engine. Seawater rushed in, and the crew abandoned the space before all the bulkheads were closed. Both engines soon were flooded. There was no power or lighting, because all such apparatus was in the engine rooms. The power steering was knocked out as well. The great ship was at the mercy of the sea and rolled and turned helplessly. More water found its way into the hull through leaks in the propeller shaft tunnels. The ship was settling down in the stern. Given enough time she would have sunk. She was in this condition for several days. A rescue ship finally appeared and 900 people were taken off the *Paris*. The stricken vessel, now settled deep in the water, was towed back to Queenstown for repairs.

Icebergs were a problem since the beginning of transatlantic travel. They were great hunks of ice that broke off glaciers that advanced to the end of the Arctic Ocean. The smaller pieces were not very dangerous, but some were of a prodigious size. The largest ranged up to 1,000 feet long and 200 feet high. Hitting one of these was like running into a mountain. Most bergs came from the west side of Greenland; thousands were adrift each year, but only a small number came as far south as the steamers' normal track. Only a tiny percentage got as far south as Florida. They were most prevalent in shipping lanes in May and least present in December. Ship captains reported sightings of bergs to the Canadian Hydrographic Service, which issued updated charts to shipping companies so that vessels would be appraised of the icebergs' most recent positions. They were moved by wind and ocean currents and lasted for about two years.

It is assumed that many of the ships that left the harbor and were never seen again were victims of iceberg collisions, but there is no way to prove such an assumption. It is a matter of record that the Cunard line's *Persia* hit an iceberg, cutting the ice in two, on its maiden voyage in early 1856. This vessel was Cunard's first iron-hulled ship. The hull withstood the accident well, but one of the paddle wheels was destroyed. An Allan line steamer hit a berg in the Straits of Belle Isle, off the coast of Labrador, in June 1861 with 35 lives lost. A Dominion liner, the *Vicksburg*, went down in June 1875 off the coast of Newfoundland after striking a berg, and 47 perished. The *City of Berlin* smacked head-on into a berg in May 1886; fortunately, she was going slowly. There was considerable damage, but Captain Francis S. Land managed to get her home safely. In gratitude the 1,281 passengers presented him with a watch for "being cooler than the iceberg."

The Guion express steamer the *Arizona* had an exciting encounter with an iceberg 240 miles east of Newfoundland that ended happily. The ship was making good time on the fourth day out from New York. S. B. Guion and some of his family were on board, and the captain was inclined to run fast to impress his boss. The sky was overcast but reasonably clear. Lookouts were posted on the bow and crow's nest of the foremast. At 9:00 PM Captain Jones retired after a long day on the bridge. There were about 300 on board, including the passengers and crew. It was a fairly light load because the summer travel season was long past. First-class passengers were having a gay old time in the main cabin; a small group of singers were entertaining their fellow passengers with a sentimental song of the day, "See Our Oars with Feathered Spray." And then came a sudden and startling crash: the ship abruptly stopped dead, recoiled, and crashed a second time. Passengers were thrown to the floor; one lady flew across the cabin and was injured. The men in the smoking room were thrown into a heap at the forward end of the cabin. One brave fellow got to his feet and said, "Steady, gentlemen, steady."

After a few minutes the passengers began to file out on to the deck to see what had happened to their now very still greyhound. Captain Jones had raced up to the bridge and shouted, "My God, men, where were your eyes!" The front end of the ship had collapsed like a cardboard box; most

11.18. The *Arizona* smashed in her bow by hitting an iceberg head on. By a miracle there were no deaths or serious injuries. The ship is shown here at dock in St. John's Newfoundland.

(*The Engineer*, November 28, 1879)

of the bow was now a crumpled tangle of broken iron plates. Twenty-six feet of the forecastle was smashed back against the front bulkhead. The *Arizona* was listing to one side, with the bow down in the water. The crew thought she was sinking and began to lower the lifeboats. Their panic increased when several off-duty members of the crew appeared on deck, bleeding and shaken. They had been asleep in the forecastle when the ship hit the iceberg. The crew was ordered to calm down. A careful inspection of the damage commenced; passengers were assured that all was well and were asked to return to the cabin. The inspection team could find nothing untoward. The passengers said a prayer and sung a hymn with considerable feeling for their deliverance. The ship headed back to St. Johns for repairs, but when she arrived Saturday evening they found the port shut down. A pilot appeared the next morning and the *Arizona* was soon at the dock. The townspeople were astonished at her appearance – a ship with no front end but still afloat (fig. 11.18).

THE TRIUMPH OF STEAM

The progress of steam navigation is well recorded in terms of cargo tonnage, but reports on passenger traffic are far less complete and can be found only in fragmentary accounts. The earliest statistics for Cunard came from John Hutchins's book, which states that between 1841 and 1846 the average yearly passage between Liverpool and Boston was 1,428 first-class passengers. The return trip came to 1,276. Such a small amount of traffic surely required a subsidy. The report to the U.S. Senate on Steam Marine Affairs for the year ending July 1, 1851, reported that U.S. ships carried over 33 million passengers but offered no breakdown between river,

Table 11.4. Numbers of U.S. Steamers and Passengers, 1880

	Number of Steamers	Number of Passengers Carried
New England group	463	15,474,710
Northern lakes	947	1,356,010
Upper Mississippi River	366	1,299,553
Ohio River	473	3,961,798
Middle states [NY/NJ/PA/etc.]	1,459	136,653,282
Lower Mississippi River	315	1,385,357
Gulf of Mexico [AL/MS/LA/TX]	126	79,260
South Atlantic Coast [VA/SC/NC/GA]	266	1,787,065
Pacific Coast	319	6,604,712
Upper Missouri River	44	81,359
Total	**4,778**	**167,683,106**

Source: U.S. Census 1880.

lake, coastal, and transatlantic travel. There were 1,390 steamers in service; about half of these were riverboats. The report to the U.S. House for 1838 stated that of the 800 steamboats operated by American owners, only a few were seagoing vessels and none were in transatlantic service. The *New York Tribune* for August 1, 1865, was more helpful in reporting that the Cunard line had eight to ten ships, the Inman line had thirteen vessels and twice-weekly service, the National line had eight ships, the French line ran monthly service, and the two German lines offered twice-weekly service. There were in all about fifty steamers in transatlantic service. A Cincinnati newspaper offered statistics for the travel year June 3, 1877, to June 3, 1878, as 30,974 first-class and 77,360 third-class passengers to the United States from Europe and 36,555 first-class and 50,344 third-class passengers in the opposite direction. There were now about ten lines with more than one hundred steamers. The 1880 census published the figures summarized in table 11.4. Some of the numbers are very large because they include ferry statistics, and there is no separate data offered for transatlantic travelers.

The data in table 11.5 was given in Henry Fry's book of 1896.

The number of transatlantic travelers has grown greatly since the 1840s in part because so many more Americans can now afford to travel. In 1840 industrialization was only beginning to make millionaires. This, a growing population, and the exploitation of natural resources, together with the discovery of gold in California, created a Gilded Age upper class who could afford to travel. By the 1890s about 80 percent of transatlantic travelers were Americans. About 85 percent of the ships landed in New York, while Boston, Philadelphia, and Baltimore watched on with envy and frustration.

Many of the operators issued no public reports, because their stock was controlled by just a small clique of owners. Cunard had many shareholders and so issued a report and often made no profit but would issue

Table 11.5. Number of First-Class Passengers on Transatlantic Lines, 1881–1893

All Transatlantic Lines Landing in New York	First-Class Passengers
1881	51,229
1886	68,742
1889	96,686
1890	99,189
1893	121,824

Source: Henry Fry, *The History of North Atlantic Steam Navigation: With Some Account of Early Ships and Shipowners*, London, 1896.

a 2 percent dividend from its reserve funds. White Star offered a more concrete example in 1893. Its *Tentonic* (1889) averaged 1,400 passengers in all three classes and made seven round trips a year. The passenger fares yielded about $53,750 per trip. Its operating costs were about $20,000, for a gross profit of $32,750. However, when depreciation, insurance, maintenance, and other costs were deducted, the profit was surely less generous. The ship cost about $2 million, but we cannot even estimate the other costs.

World War I put an end to luxury liners for a few years, but by 1920 the industry had started up again with larger and more luxurious ships going into service every few years. A few of us can remember when the *Queen Mary,* the *Normandie,* and the *Queen Elizabeth II* were new liners. The appearance of the jet aircraft in 1958 began to cut into the transatlantic trade. At first, according to the common wisdom, there would always be service to Europe by ship, because so many people enjoyed the experience or were afraid to fly. However, such wishful thinking could not counter the fact that a jet could cross the ocean in a few hours rather than a few days. By 1976 the *Queen Elizabeth II* was the only superliner in transatlantic service. She survived until 2008 only by becoming a cruise ship. A glorious era in the history of travel had ended.

SUGGESTED READING

Abbot, Willis J. *American Merchant Ships and Sailors.* New York: Dodd, Mead, 1902.

Armstrong, Warren. *Atlantic Highway.* New York: Day, 1961.

Bathe, Basil W. *Seven Centuries of Sea Travel: From the Crusades to the Cruises.* New York: Tudor, 1973.

Beard, John, comp. *Blue Water Views of Old New York, Including Long Island and the Jersey Shore.* Centerville, Mass.: Scrimshaw, 1970.

Benstead, C. R. *Atlantic Ferry.* London: Methuen, 1936.

Bird, Isabella L. *The Englishwoman in America.* London: John Murray, 1856.

Bonsor, N. R. P. *North Atlantic Seaway: An Illustrated History of the Passenger Services Linking the Old World with the New.* Prescot, Lancashire: T. Stephenson, 1955.

Brinnin, John M. *The Sway of the Grand Saloon: A Social History of the North Atlantic.* New York: Delacorte Press, 1971.

Bunker, John G. *Harbor and Haven: An Illustrated History of the Port of New York.* Woodland Hills, Calif.: Windsor, 1979.

Chadwick F. E. *Ocean Steamships: A Popular Account of Their Construction, Development, Management, and Appliances.* New York: C. Scribner's Sons, 1891.

Chambers, William. *Things as They Are in America.* London: W. and R. Chambers, 1854.

Coleman, Terry. *The Liners: A History of the North Atlantic Crossing.* 1976. New York: Putnam, 1977.

Cornwall-Jones, R. J. *The British Merchant Service: Being a History of the British Mercantile Marine from the Earliest Times to the Present Day.* London: S. Low, Marston and Co., 1898.

Devens, R. M. *Our First Century.* Springfield, Mass.: Nichols, 1878.

Dodman, Frank E. *Ships of the Cunard Line.* London: Coles, 1955.

Fraser-Macdonald, A. *Our Ocean Railways; or, The Rise, Progress, and Development of Ocean Steam Navigation.* London: Chapman and Hall, 1893.

Fry, Henry. *History of North Atlantic Steam Navigation with Some Account of Early Ships and Shipowners.* New York: C. Scribner's, 1896.

Griffiths, Denis. *Brunel's Ships.* London: Chatham, 1999.

Hansen, Clas B. *Passenger Liners from Germany, 1816–1990.* West Chester, Pa.: Schiffer, 1991.

Helmuth, William T. *A Steamer Book: A Picturesque Account of a City on the Sea.* New York: G. W. Carleton, 1880.

Hutchins, John G. B. *American Maritime Industries and Public Policy, 1789–1914: An Economic History.* Cambridge, Mass.: Harvard University Press, 1941.

Ingersoll, Ernest. *Book of the Ocean.* New York: Century, 1898.

Johnston, Paul F. *Steam and the Sea.* Salem, Mass.: Peabody Museum of Salem, 1983.

Kelley, J. D. Jerrold. *The Ship's Company and Other Sea People.* New York: Harper, 1897.

Kemp, Peter, ed. *Oxford Companion to Ships and the Sea.* London: Oxford University, 1976.

Kludas, Arnold. *Record Breakers of the North Atlantic: Blue Riband Liners, 1838–1952.* 1999. Washington, D.C.: Brassey's, 2000.

Knox, T. W. *The Life of Robert Fulton and a History of Steam Navigation.* New York: G. P. Putnam, 1886.

Lindsay, W. S. *History of Merchant Shipping and Ancient Commerce.* Vol. 4. London: S. Low, Marston, Low, and Searle, 1874.

Macpherson, Arthur et al. *Mail and Passenger Steamships of the Nineteenth Century, the Macpherson Collection.* Philadelphia: J. B. Lippincott, 1929.

Maddocks, Melvin. *The Atlantic Crossing.* Alexandria, Va.: Time-Life, 1981.

Maginnis, Arthur J. *The Atlantic Ferry: Its Ships, Men, and Working.* London: Whittaker, 1892.

Mencken, August. *First-Class Passenger: Life at Sea as Experienced and Recorded by Landlubbers of the Past.* New York: A. A. Knopf, 1938.

Paine, Lincoln P. *Ships of the World: An Historical Encyclopedia.* Boston: Houghton Mifflin, 1997.

Ringwalt, J. Luther. *Development of Transportation Systems in the United States.* Philadelphia: Railway World, 1888.

Rogers, Stanley R. H. *The Atlantic.* New York: Crowell, 1930.

Russell, W. Clark. *The Ship, Her Story.* New York: F. A. Stokes, 1899.

Smith, Eugene W. *Passenger Ships of the World, Past and Present.* Boston: Dean, 1963.

Spears, John R. *The Story of the American Merchant Marine.* New York: Macmillan, 1910.

Talbot, Frederick A. *Steamship Conquest of the World.* Philadelphia: J. B. Lippincott, 1912.

Town, Ithiel. *Atlantic Steamships: Some Ideas and Statements, the Result of Considerable Reflection on the Subject of Navigating the Atlantic Ocean.* New York: Wiley and Putnam, 1838.

Tute, Warren. *Atlantic Conquest: The Men and Ships of the Glorious Age of Steam.* Boston: Little, Brown, 1962.

Writers' Program/WPA New York. *Maritime History of New York.* Garden City, N.Y.: Doubleday, 1941.

Emigrant Travel № 12

A Nation of Nations

EMIGRATION IS AS NATURAL TO MANKIND AS THE PATH OF THE earth revolving around the sun. Our ancestors have been wandering around the planet since their eviction from the Garden of Eden. They traveled incredible distances on foot or by log rafts. Curiosity drove some to move on just to see what lay beyond the next hill. Hunger was another obvious motivation that drove ancient peoples to explore foreign territory. The emigration to the New World was motivated for similar reasons but also by the desire for personal and religious freedom and a better standard of living. By the Victorian era Europe was becoming overpopulated, and America had a comparatively small population for its land mass. In 1860 the U.S. population was 31 million, or one-tenth of the present population. By 1880 Europe was home to over 300 million people, while the U.S. population was at only 50 million. Table 12.1 shows that many came. Such a table does not demonstrate that only a few were chosen to succeed to any great measure. A number returned to their native land defeated and poorer than when they began their American adventure.

During the eighteenth century only about 4,500 people arrived each year on America's shores. A goodly portion were Scots who had been resettled in Ireland as part of Oliver Cromwell's plan to dilute the Catholic majority in that beleaguered land. The Scots began to leave Ireland for America after the 1716 crop failure. The British Parliament added to the flow with the Transportation Act of 1717, which punished felons by sending them to the colonies rather than imprisoning or hanging them. Britain shed other undesirables, such as paupers, vagrants, orphans, and prisoners of war, by sending them to America as well. By 1815 the European population had grown to such levels that restrictions on emigration were eased to reduce the surplus numbers. Industrialization reduced the need for manual labor, and there were fewer reasons to discourage workers from moving abroad.

The breakdown of newcomers by nationality evolved over the decades. The majority of early emigrants were largely from the British Isles.

Table 12.1. Immigration to the United States, 1820–1910

1820	8,000	1861–1870	2,314,000
1821–1830	143,000	1871–1880	2,812,000
1831–1840	399,000	1881–1890	5,246,000
1841–1850	1,713,000	1891–1900	3,687,000
1851–1860	2,548,000	1901–1910	8,795,000

Note: Immigration numbers are rounded to the nearest 1,000.
Source: Philip A. M. Taylor, The *Distant Magnet: European Emigration to the U.S.A.* New York: Harper and Row, 1972.

The flow from Britain remained strong until almost 1880. The potato crop failure in 1845 set off a massive exodus from Ireland, and by 1854 about one-quarter of the Irish had left their homeland. That number grew to 3.5 million by 1880. Many clustered in East Coast cities such as Philadelphia and Boston. Others went west to build canals and railroads. They proved adept at politics and became powerful in New York's Tammany Hall and the Boston political machine under such leaders as boss James M. Curley. They also gave rise to the Know-Nothing Party, which opposed the entry of more immigrants into the United States in the 1840s. The New York draft riot of July 1863 raged on for three days. The mob was made up mostly of underemployed Irish men who burned and pillaged freely. Upward of 1,200 died in this siege that required federal army troops to restore order. Yet the Irish proved themselves to be good citizens, and in less than one hundred years the president of the United States, John Fitzgerald Kennedy, was of Irish heritage.

The Germans began to settle on these shores early in the colonial period. William Penn visited the Rhineland in 1677 to encourage some of the locals to relocate into what is now eastern Pennsylvania. Germantown was one of their settlements. About sixty years later a German religious group, the Moravians, came to Georgia. A political revolution in 1848 sparked a large-scale emigration to the United States that lasted for several decades. These people had a reputation for hard work, thoroughness, and thrift. Their children had ruddy, healthy faces and attire that looked like it was from the Middle Ages. About four million Germans came to the United States between 1840 and 1890. They were the largest single group to come to this country. In 1990 the persons of German ancestry equaled 23 percent of the population. A breakdown by national origin was given in Osgood's *Handbook for Travellers in the Middle States* (1847). For the years 1847–1870 the numbers of foreign-born people in the United States were as follows: 1,664,009 Irish; 1,636,254 German; 539,668 English; 111,238 Scotch; 77,200 French; 66,607 Swiss; 64,538 Swedish; 28,347 Dutch; 23,834 Welsh; and 19,757 Norwegian.

The composition of immigrant arrivals began to change in about 1880. More and more came from southern and Eastern Europe. Hungarians,

Serbs, Russian Jews, Spaniards, and Italians got off the boat as confused and hopeful as all of their predecessors. By 1900 they constituted 90 percent of the new immigrants. The concept of the Melting Pot, now much disputed, came into being not long afterward. It was introduced in a four-act play of that name written by an English Jew, Israel Zangwill. Teddy Roosevelt insisted the play was a work of genius, so the term *melting pot* was introduced into American popular culture, where it remained until relatively recent times. Most of these southern and eastern Europeans were seeking a better life, but many Italians came seeking better nutrition. Less than 25 percent of Italy was flat or fertile. It was one of the most populous nations in Europe, hence food was both scarce and expensive. By the 1890s 300,000 Italians came to North and South America in search of good farmland. Among those who ended up in California was Louis M. Martini. He was a pioneer vintner in the western part of the United States and helped establish California's wine industry.

It is common to think of the immigrant as uneducated and dirt poor. As with every generalization, however, there are always some notable exceptions; three of them are mentioned here. John Jacob Astor (1763–1848) was mentioned in a previous chapter in connection with the fur trade. He was born in the Grand Duchy of Baden as the son of a poor butcher. He left his south German home for England at the age of seventeen to work with a brother living in Britain. His real plan was to emigrate to the United States, which he did soon after the Treaty of Paris was signed in 1783. He traveled by steerage to Baltimore but was soon working in New York City for a fur dealer. He walked the western woodlands trading trinkets to the Indians for furs. In time he established his own business and invested $2 million in New York real estate. This tidy sum grew to $20 million, making Astor one of the richest men in America.

Carl Schurz (1829–1906) was another German emigrant seeking a new life in the United States, but he was less interested in making a fortune. He was a political liberal who supported causes that ranged from civil rights to anti-imperialism. Schurz was a newspaper editor but also served as a U.S. Army general and secretary of the interior. His wife, Margarethe, established the first kindergarten in the country.

One of the most remarkable emigrants was Andrew Carnegie (1835–1919). He was a small man whose appearance belied his energy and ambition. This son of Scotland came to America as a teenager without benefit of an education or a trade. He was put to work in a cotton mill by his impoverished parents. He later learned telegraphy and quickly advanced himself in the business world, first as a railroad manager. By the end of the Civil War Carnegie got into iron and steel making. He came to dominate that industry by the 1890s and became the richest man in America. His last years were devoted to philanthropy and the cause of world peace.

THE TRIP: A NEW EXPERIENCE IN MISERY

Most emigrants were poor folks who understood hardships and hunger. In their home countries they often lived in unheated huts made from mud and straw. They ate a monotonous diet of potatoes or oatmeal and cooked over an open fire. Their toilet was at the bottom of the garden. They had a single set of clothing that was replaced only when it was beyond mending. They never saw a doctor. Their lives were generally short and brutal. But going to sea for six weeks was a new and often terrifying experience. Few had seen the ocean and certainly were not prepared for the terror of a storm at sea or the long-term misery of seasickness. Some indeed did not survive the trip. Their bodies were thrown overboard with little ceremony or tenderness. The ship proceeded as if nothing had happened.

During the age of sail, ship masters showed little concern for their steerage passengers. There were some kind captains and crew members who tried to assist their third-class passengers, but in the main the general view was that they were like so much cargo, a package or bundle of old cloth to be stowed in the hold where they could survive without the benefit of much air, light, food, or water. If they were delivered all in one piece, that was good enough. Special care was not required. They were just filling space, because there wasn't much cargo heading west. Emigrants provided a little extra revenue. Civil-minded people protested the uncivilized treatment of the poor in transit, and news items appeared on the subject. Governments on both sides of the ocean enacted very specific laws meant to regulate the traffic in emigrants, although a lack of inspectors and lax enforcement of these laws rendered them largely ineffective. However, reforms did begin in 1850 when ship operators, motivated in part by paternalism, also realized that humane service was good business. This business became more competitive as the century closed and shipping lines offered more and better services to gain a larger share of the steerage trade. As the volume increased, steerage became a very lucrative business.

Guidebooks were written for steerage passengers. Some were only pot boilers written for the market, but others were honest attempts to assist the travelers. An English doctor by the name of Robert Holditch published pocket-size guidebooks of 123 pages in 1818. He promised to explain the climate, price of land, and the population of North America. Very brief descriptions of states, cities, and everyday manners were included. The governments of the United States and Canada were explained. Property laws were outlined as were elections and newspapers. Holditch made a serious effort to condense a large amount of information into this small book. Much of the data came from the published accounts of travelers such as John Palmer and Captain Basil Hall. Holditch urged his more adventuresome readers to make a beeline for the Northwest Territory. Here settlers would find a virgin forest and rich soil such as they had never seen before. Immigrants were advised to buy a wagon and head to Pittsburgh, which stood at the head of the Ohio River. The men were advised to walk behind the wagon to lessen the horse's load. All members of the party should sleep in or under the wagon to save money. A flatboat could be purchased at Pittsburgh for $75. These simple vessels generally measured 14 by 50 feet. The river's current would carry them downstream at about 4 mph. Oars, sails, and poles could be used to increase the speed. One of these boats was actually big enough for three or four families as long as they did not attempt to carry too much in the way of tools, furniture, and supplies.

A larger guidebook was the *Emigrant's Friend,* written many years later by Evan R. Jones, the U.S. consul at Newcastle, England. He included a section on what to take as well as what to do after arriving in the United States. Rule number one was to not take too much; it would only be a burden during and after the voyage. A limited wardrobe should be supplemented by bed linens and towels. A soft hat was fine; you would not be suspected of being a Communist or revolutionary in the United States. *Be careful not to hide lace, jewelry, perfumes, or other luxury goods inside your luggage. If you are suspected of smuggling, the customs officer will seize all of your baggage. They tend to be liberal with emigrants, so don't try their patience. Take on board a plate, a mug, knife, fork, spoon, and a water can. Each steerage passenger is allotted 10 cubic feet of space to store extra luggage. If you need more, it is available at a charge of one shilling per cubic foot. Once on board don't expect too much from the steward or the ship's company – they have no time for excessive politeness. You are only paying $30 for a 3,000-mile trip that includes room and board. Each child over eight years will have his own berth. Married couples and their children are kept together. Single men and women are placed in separate compartments. Try to find a berth amidships if possible, as the light and ventilation will be better. Seasickness is normal for a day or two. Stay on deck as much as you can, the air will help to settle your upset stomach. Keep something in your stomach even though you do not want to eat. Some have advised soda crackers; Lord Byron recommends beef steak. When you feel better, let go and enjoy a dance to the pipes of Caledonia or the fiddle of Erin.* Mr. Jones's advice ended with the reassuring thought that doctors recommend sea trips for good health.

Before the nineteenth century, emigrants were often placed within the hull at the very stern of the ship, just below the wheel. This cramped area was called steerage, since the helmsman stood just above it. It had nothing to do with cattle or steers as some people incorrectly assume. Emigrant space began to expand into almost any part of the lower decks as the traffic increased. The term *steerage* lost its original meaning quickly and became a more general term for any space allotted to the emigrant

12.1. Sailing packet leaving Liverpool in 1850. Emigrants are on the forecastle deck as the ship is towed down the Mersey River to the sea.

(*Illustrated London News*, July 6, 1850)

passengers. In ships designed for such service, steerage could occupy two full decks. Emigrants were given space on the top deck to sun and air out, a pleasure not offered in earlier times. They were not allowed, however, to mix with the first-class passengers.

Bunks were built into the spaces that were more like pens than beds. Each bunk was long enough for several people, generally four to six. Passengers were required to supply bedding and a mattress. Bags filled with straw provided a cheap, if not very comfortable, mattress. Some passengers were too poor to afford a blanket. One such person slept on deck next to a funnel to keep warm; he would have been heated on only one side at a time. At least he was not trapped belowdecks in a dark, airless hole. During rough seas the hatches were tightly closed, which cut off both ventilation and light. There were no portholes in sailing ship times, and an open flame belowdecks was generally prohibited. Even the Cunard line enforced a curfew on first-class passengers at an early hour to reduce the fire hazard.

Ship owners provided no food to emigrants. They were expected to bring their own. This was a most difficult requirement for a trip that would last forty days. The sheer bulk of what would be needed for a family for that length of time made it nearly impossible. Since there was no refrigeration at this time, fresh food was impossible beyond a few days' supply. Only smoked or salted meats could be kept for any duration of time. If the trip's progress was delayed by bad weather or a lack of wind, the food problem grew worse. A law was passed in Britain in 1815 requiring passenger ships to supply food to all passengers. In 1842 the act was replaced by a more

12.2. Cabin of a sailing ship heading to California in 1849 shows typical emigrant bunk beds and dining tables.

(*L'Illustration*, Feb. 10, 1849)

specific law that required 7 pounds of provisions per week, half of which was to be in bread or biscuits, the other half in potatoes. In 1846 flour, rice, tea, sugar, molasses, beef, and pork were added to the requirement. All of this legal action was commendable, but its enforcement remained lax, and passengers, especially children, continued to die from malnutrition.

A sailor by the name of Denis Kearney wrote a reminiscence of conditions on the Black Ball liner *Isaac Webb* in the 1850s. It was one of the largest and best sailing packets of its day, but even so the emigrants were poorly fed and housed. The main food ration was cornmeal, which the women would bake into bread. They took the meal to the galley on the top deck toward the front of the ship. This meant carrying the meal up several stairways to the top deck and going forward to the deckhouse, which contained the galley. It would not be a difficult journey on a calm day, but the cruise Kearney wrote about was during stormy weather. The ship rocked and dipped, making walking difficult. Big waves crashed over the bulwarks with enough force to knock down all but the strongest man. Kearney witnessed women being thrown to the deck while their cornbread scattered across the wet deck. Some of it washed through the scuppers and into the sea. Other pieces were picked up by alert seagulls. The sailors helped the ladies up and led them back to the hatch and down the stairway to the steerage bunk cabin. The poor women were wet, cold, and miserable. They and their companions had little to eat other than plain cornmeal, which was at least edible if not very nutritious. After six weeks at sea the once youthful and handsome emigrants were a woebegone and dirty group, who had spent the trip as seasick or hungry. Kearney stated in his narrative that he and some of his shipmates shared their own meager rations with those unfortunate passengers.

The lack of food aboard the *Isaac Webb* was relieved to a degree by a kindly crew, yet even this small mercy was not present on all ships. There is a report in the British Parliamentary Paper for 1851 describing a trip on the American steamer *Washington* that reads like a trip to hell. It was based on an account written by one of the cabin passengers, Vere Foster, an Irish philanthropist who took an interest in emigrant affairs. He not only observed the handling of steerage passengers on the ship but also volunteered as a cook and helped prepare their meals. Foster began his account with praise for the *Washington*. She was nearly new and was designed specifically to carry emigrants. She was solid and dry with two high-ceiling decks, thus offering a fine space for the nine hundred emigrants on board. She was likely the best emigrant ship serving New York, Liverpool, and Bremen. The berths were shelflike structures built the length of the ship. Each berth had space for four to six people. There were also a dozen cabins with from two to six berths; each berth held two people. The standard fare was £5, with a few spaces going as cheaply as £3 and fifteen shillings, or about eighteen dollars.

If only the crew had been up to the standard of the ship, it might have been a pleasant voyage; however, they seemed better suited to handling prisoners. From the officers down, they were rude and violent in their treatment of steerage passengers. The abuse began with loading the passengers. Men and women were pulled, pushed, and kicked on board. Foster, who boarded with the emigrants, was knocked to the deck. Before he could get up, another man was thrown on top of him. All the while the sailors and officers were shouting, cursing, and using filthy language to urge the hapless emigrants to move faster. After everyone was on board the first allowance of water was given out. Normally this would be done with patience, order, and, most of all, a system. But there was none of that on the *Washington*; instead it was a free-for-all with much punching, hitting, and verbal abuse. Most of the water was spilled on deck and wasted. The service did not improve much during the trip, and even after the passengers learned to line up and wait their turn, the bullying and abuse continued. No food was distributed for five days. Apparently some passengers had brought a few provisions on board, but many others went hungry. Even after rations were offered, the supply was erratic. Some emigrants began to bribe the cook for an extra share. Foster went to the captain hoping to remedy the more serious problems. The captain listened for a few minutes and then called Foster a pirate. He threatened to put him in irons if he did not end his complaining. One of the mates threatened Foster with a good beating if he did not stop interfering with the crew and their management of the ship.

The *Star of the West* left Liverpool for New York in 1850, and as she left the dock several late arrivals appeared. They threw their bags onto the deck – a few went into the water. The dock was high, so some of the latecomers jumped into the rigging and climbed down to the deck. One lady became entangled in ropes; somehow she slipped upside down, exposing her legs to the crowd. This amused the onlookers greatly and increased the volume of the farewells and laughter. The remainder of the trip was a good deal less humorous. Some four hundred passengers were crammed together in the dark and poorly ventilated hold that soon became a place of filth and squalor. Conditions were surely worse on the Canadian lumber boats that headed home empty. To raise some income they offered a low emigrant fare of about $7.50. That amount did not buy much comfort. Even poorer accommodations were offered by the Welsh slate boats heading to the New World. They had a good cargo but also made space for steerage by putting down a layer of sawdust over the slates.

Water on ships was often bad or in short supply. On the American packet *Toronto,* adults received just ½ gallon and children 1 quart per day. Washing became a luxury on such rations. Even when the supply was more plentiful, the water might smell, taste foul, or be germ-laden. This was true because the barrels used to store it were often secondhand whiskey, cider, or turpentine containers. Impure water is associated with cholera and typhus. The latter disease was so common that it was called the "ships' fever." It was highly contagious and often fatal. In tightly packed steerage spaces it would travel through the passengers quickly. In 1847 nearly 5,300 emigrants died in transit and another 10,000 expired after landing. Because ships were often overloaded with 250 more passengers than their legal limits, contagious diseases took their toll on the poorest citizens. The National line's steamer *Egypt* landed in 1873 with a record load of 1,767 emigrants. Such crowding only multiplied the suffering on such ships. Yet reform was under way and emigrant travel would soon improve.

STEERAGE GOES UPSCALE

Regulation of emigrant traffic was attempted through a series of laws passed by the United States, Britain, and various European nations. It was well intended but largely ineffective, because there was there was so little funding for inspection or enforcement. Greater success in improving the transportation of emigrants came from inside the shipping industry. One of the pioneers in this movement was William Inman, mentioned in the preceding chapter. When most shipping lines looked only to revenue and profits, Inman and his wife, Anne, took a personal interest in the welfare of their poorest customers. These ragged patrons were their family and were all good people. They were just poor, but even so they deserved a safe and pleasant trip. Inman himself went to Ireland to watch the emigrants boarding. He had his ships land at Queenstown so that these folks did not have to make a trip to Liverpool. Mrs. Inman disguised herself as one of the poor and traveled incognito to obtain an inside picture of what it was like to go steerage. Was the food acceptable and plentiful? Were soap, hot

12.3. Inman line steerage ticket of the 1870s.

(Author's collection)

water, and clean towels available? Her husband had already made a major improvement by providing steamers for the trade in 1850. Heretofore emigrants went by sailing ships and endured a forty-day voyage. The steamer trip might be ten or twelve days at this time, but every day eliminated was a great bonus in terms of comfort and health. The fare was $30, or a penny a mile.

By 1857 Inman had captured one-third of the transatlantic traffic. Three meals a day were served. It was not gourmet dining, but the meals were filling and nutritious. Oatmeal and porridge, arrowroot in sugar and milk and molasses were regular fare at breakfast. Dinner would include fresh beef and mess beef (barreled salt beef). Supper was tea and gruel. In time, Inman's competition would copy his methods and try to improve on them. Food was soon being served home style, so passengers could help themselves to as much of any dish as they wanted. Figure 12.4 is an illustration of such a meal on a French liner in 1890. Note that the food was ladled out directly from the cooking pots. The captain not only inspected steerage each day, but at least one skipper had his noon meal served from the steerage galley to check on its quality.

Much greater improvements would come toward the end of the Victorian era. The tide had turned in the humble emigrants' favor. In 1861 Cunard began carrying steerage passengers. At first it was just one ship, the *China*, and soon more Cunard lines were handling steerage passengers. In time Cunard created an emigrant village in Liverpool with a capacity of two thousand persons. Those too ill to travel were treated in the hospital. The dormitories had steam heat, electric lights, clean beds, and good food. The Hamburg American line created a suburban village outside Hamburg that had room for four thousand emigrants. It featured hotels, shops, restaurants, and churches. There was also a band concert every afternoon.

12.4. Dinner is served in a French line emigrant cabin.

(*Harper's Weekly*, November 22, 1890, as redrawn by Jim Harter)

Emigrant travel had improved so greatly that skilled workers began to commute between the United States and England. Carpenters, bricklayers, and plasterers would go over to the States in spring as the construction season opened. Wages were more than double what they could receive in England. Some would return late in fall or just before Christmas. They had made enough to live through the winter even if there was no work at home. Then, like the swallows, they would head off for the United States again about the time the tulips appeared. Others who were seeking travel bargains began to use third class as well. College students and teachers in the States would head to Europe for the summer. Some of the more adventurous went to South America, Africa, or China if they could find a boat offering third-class fares.

One such wanderer was James Ricalton, a schoolteacher in Maplewood, New Jersey. He went off in summer 1886 on Cunard's *Aurania*, which took him from New York to Liverpool in seven days for just $23. When Ricalton arrived at Cunard's New York terminal at the foot of Clarkson Street, black clouds of smoke were rolling out of the *Aurania*'s funnels. The approaches to the pier were lined with vendors peddling wash basins, tin plates, pillows, and other wares aimed at third-class passengers. The steerage passengers were already assembled but were made to wait until the first-class passengers were on board. When permission was finally granted, there was a noisy stampede of people heading up the gangplank, bedding under their arm, and a clatter of their tableware erupted as the crowd raced to claim a berth on the lower deck. The mail was the last thing put on board.

The middle-age teacher secured a berth by placing his baggage on one of them, and then he raced up to the top deck to witness the departure.

12.5. (a) Emigrants race for the best bunks. (b) Mealtime in the emigrants' cabin.

(Both engravings from *Outing*, May 1887)

The departure bell was rung rapidly. A few minutes later the heavy vessel swung gently away from the pier. On his return to the cavernous lower cabin, Ricalton found that his berth had been taken over by a stranger. An argument ensued, but the steward settled the matter in Ricalton's favor. Because the berth had a canvas bottom, Ricalton made himself comfortable without a mattress. He found that a pillow, lap robe, and blanket were enough for a good bed. The 150 steerage passengers made considerable commotion coming and going to move or set up their considerable bundles and baskets. There was much noise and excitement and very little privacy. While most of the crowd snacked and talked happily, others sat sadly wondering if they were ready for seven days of such intense commotion. Actually the number of steerage passengers was comparatively small, as was typical for the eastbound trip. On the westbound trips, the same ship often carried 700 emigrants.

Ricalton was stationed in the men's section, since he was traveling alone. His main complaint was the volume of snoring at night. Some restless sleepers added various sounds that rose and fell. Their flabby windpipes produced wheezes, gurgles, sniffing, and raucous intonations that drowned out the sound of the sea and the engines. Ventilation was another problem in the steerage compartments that was difficult to correct. There were portholes at this level, but because they were so close to the waterline they were permanently closed. In heavy weather the main deck hatches were closed, which greatly reduced the flow of air to the lower decks. Washing was another difficulty on most ships in emigrant service. Basins would be placed between the berths on the floor or placed on the bed itself, and the bather would partially undress and wash himself as best he could in the space available. The *Auramin* had a washroom on the main deck set aside for steerage passengers, which illustrated Cunard's concern for emigrant sanitation.

The food service was showing improvement as well. The quantity of food served exceeded the legal requirements, and passengers could have as much as they cared to eat. Breakfast was served at 8:00 AM and consisted of French bread, biscuits, butter, oatmeal, and coffee. Irish stew was served as a part of a meal every other day. Lunch came at 1:00 PM and included potatoes, boiled salt beef, and pork. On Sunday a pudding called plum duff was served for dessert. Supper was offered at 5:00 and consisted of biscuits, butter, and tea. Gruel was sometimes added. Tasty dishes were offered when the first-class galley had made too much and there was a surplus. In Ricalton's opinion, the bread was uniformly good, the soup excellent. The potatoes and meat were only fair, the butter acceptable, but the coffee was bad and the tea was worse than the coffee. Passengers were permitted to make their own coffee or tea, and hot water was freely given out in the galley. The galley was on the top deck, and stewards delivered food in large tin pails. Dippers were used for serving most food, but baked potatoes were distributed by hand. The servers would dig into the pails and pass out the spuds by the handful. Seating was limited, and some patrons would call and wave their tin plates at the servers from the berths surrounding the tables. The good-natured stewards would toss biscuits to them as they might throw scraps to a pet dog.

The steerage decks were scrubbed every day and then sprinkled with sawdust. The ship's doctor would make his inspection after this cleaning was finished. He or one of the stewards would distribute medicines as needed without charge. There was a room set aside as a hospital, but it was not equipped for that purpose, nor did the doctor offer much attention to the needs of the steerage passengers beyond his daily visits. *If an emigrant dies during the voyage, the body will be kept for about thirty-six hours. Should this occur near the end of the trip, the body will then be consigned to the family or the police. Otherwise, the remains are placed in a wood box and weighted with iron (furnace grates were often used). Holes are drilled in the box to ensure its sinking.* On sailing ships, a canvas bag was used instead of a box. The Anglican burial service was read, because the *Aurania* was an English ship. If a crew member died at sea, his body was lowered into the water by ropes or slid off a plank into the deep. The ship's engines would be stopped and the burial service read by the ship's captain before the body went over the side. Ricalton wrote several small books about his travels elsewhere in the world. He continued to travel on the cheap until old age forced him to retire in the late 1920s. His story about the *Aurania* appeared in the magazine *Outing* in May 1887.

Another personal account of emigrant travel was recorded in a series of letters by Karl S. Puffe late in 1892. Puffe was heading to the United States to establish himself before the rest of the family would cross over from what is now the Czech Republic. At the time of Puffe's trip, his homeland was part of the Austro-Hungarian Empire. Puffe went by train to Bremerhaven, Germany, and boarded a ship bound for New York. There were 2,258 on board, most of them emigrants. The weather was good at the beginning of the trip, and most passengers sang, danced, and enjoyed the salt air. A few were already seasick, however. Puffe said the meals were awful. The white bread was good, but the black bread, which he preferred, was terrible. Food was plentiful – one meal consisted of meat, sauerkraut, and potatoes. One evening plums were served. Everyone had to wash their own dishes. The boat was crowded, as there were too many people on board.

The trip went downhill quickly. On the third day it became stormy. The waves were so huge, the whole mighty ocean was in an uproar. Everyone was seasick. Puffe was dizzy, his tooth hurt, he couldn't eat, and there was no coffee – the one thing he wanted most. The storm grew even worse the next day. Luggage, benches, and boxes slid and crashed together. No one could walk. The waves now washed over the top of the ship. Puffe was so sick. He missed his wife and children. His tooth was hurting again, and he had broken his bottle of medicine. On the sixth day the sea was calmer. He felt much better. He did not vomit despite all the rocking of the ship. He ate an apple and a few pretzels. *A woman and child died last* night. Almost everyone was feeling better. *The children do not seem to be so much affected by seasickness as the adults. The children were given extra milk twice today. We have to fix our own meal, which is difficult because the space is wall-to-wall people. I want news from home, to take them all in my arms again.*

When the sea finally calmed, Puffe felt better, and his shipmates were well and happy. *It's getting colder. There is such a mix of people here, and they cannot understand one another. This life is tiring. Yesterday was so nice, but now we have sorrow.* The mood changed again on the twelfth day; they would be in New York soon. The people were happy. Everyone was cleaning up and putting their belongings together. They were advised to wear clean clothes. Many were dressed in their best outfits. On the thirteenth day the immigration doctor came to look over everyone on board. After fourteen days aboard the ship, they were transferred to the temporary immigration station next to the Castle Garden. Two years later Puffe was united with his wife and children at Ellis Island.

In the summer of 1897 H. Phelps Whitmarsh of Oxford, England, booked passage as a steerage passenger to gather material for *Century Magazine* on how the "other half" traveled. The steamship line replied with a questionnaire that had to be filled out before it would issue a ticket. This was a requirement of the U.S. Immigration Bureau, and the document asked some pointed questions. Just how much money did the traveler possess? Was it more or less than $30? Had the traveler ever been in prison, the poorhouse, or been supported by a charity? Was he a polygamist? Was he deformed or crippled, and if so, what was the nature and cause of these deformities? The bureau also wanted details on his physical and mental health. Whitmarsh apparently answered to the satisfaction of the steamship line's staff, and a ticket was issued. The ship would head for New York from Liverpool; however, steerage passengers boarded at Birkenhead, which was located nearby.

The steerage office was in the basement of a large stone building near the dock. Whitmarsh found forty of his fellow travelers sitting in the dimly lit waiting room, all of them wearing a weary, resigned look. Long waits were common when going by steerage. Eventually they were led to a landing stage and put aboard a tender for transfer up the Mersey River to the ocean liner that lay at anchor. The crowd had now grown to three hundred. Nearby was a Welsh family that included five small children, none over eight years of age. All had pretty eyes, but they were so dirty. A high-water mark was visible on their necks. Not far away was a Finnish family with the typical high cheekbones, white hair, and cleanliness. The emigrants sat stiff and silent, looking blankly across the cabin.

Within half an hour the tender reached the steamer. A bugle sounded and the stewards lined up to receive the small segment of the world's tired and poor. The emigrants climbed aboard and were directed along a

12.6. A side-wheel tender is shown in the foreground of this 1874 engraving as emigrants climb a stairway to the main deck of an ocean steamer. Both vessels are standing in the Elba River downstream from Hamburg, Germany.

(Walter Havighurst Special Collections, Miami University Libraries, Ohio)

narrow passageway on the main deck to a steep stairway. Single English-speaking males were sent to the number 1 cabin. It had space for 118 occupants and contained row upon row of iron bunk beds all running fore and aft in double banks. The bunks contained five beds in each tier. There were also narrow wooden tables and benches in the space. Non-English-speaking single males were placed in cabin number 2, which was located a deck below. Two decks down was the married or family cabin. Single females were stowed in rooms along both sides of the ship. Each room held from four to fourteen persons. The ladies had a separate dining room. Whitmarsh was put in number 1 cabin. He found a straw mattress and a cheap blanket on his bunk together with a full emigrant's kit provided by the steamship company. It included a tin plate and cup plus a knife, fork, and spoon. The plate was battered but serviceable and saved each passenger the cost and trouble of providing his own kit. The quarters were spotlessly clean, yet there was a sour, disagreeable smell to the place that never went away.

Whitmarsh managed to obtain a breakdown of the emigrants on board. By the time of departure the number had grown to 403. The breakdown by nationality is listed in table 12.2.

Two-thirds of the group were men, who were generally over thirty years of age. The remainder were women and children. Most of the Scandinavians were going to the western states, but the others were booked for

Table 12.2. Nationality of Emigrants on a Single Steamship Trip (Summer 1897)

American	59	Irish	113
Bohemian	1	Norwegian	25
English	51	Russian	1
Finn	43	Scotch	4
German	7	Swedish	77
French	1	Welsh	21

Source: H. Phelps Whitmarsh, *Century Magazine*, February 1898.

eastern cities. A goodly portion of the Irish passengers were young women heading for jobs as house servants.

While the steerage passengers were settling in and arranging their considerable luggage, the ship began moving downstream to a landing stage to pick up the first- and second-class passengers. This was done with reasonable dispatch, and the big liner moved down the murky river into the bay. She was soon into the Irish Channel. By ten that evening they were out to sea. Already most of the passengers were seasick. Many had armed themselves with various cures such as apples, lime drops, or raw onions. The much advertised patent medicines made specifically for this purpose were no more effective. The cause of the cabin's sour smell soon became evident. Whitmarsh noticed that most of the sleepers in his compartment went to bed in their street clothes. They failed to remove their overcoats, shoes, or hats. Henceforth, Whitmarsh slept on the deck.

At four the next morning they landed at Queenstown. Seventy more steerage passengers came on board. They were in a festive mood, and despite the early hour the girls began to dance and sing to the accompaniment of an accordion. Other musicians woke up and joined the merrymakers, and soon a tin whistle and flute reinforced the accordion. The travelers made friends, and the coolness of the first day gave way to warm feelings, conversation, and a sharing of drink and tobacco. The partylike atmosphere died down quickly, however, whenever the wind picked up and the sea began to rise and fall in great rolling waves. When the sea settled down, the passengers would again look for diversions.

The emigrants were very curious about the accommodations of the cabin passengers. Were they as grand as homes of the nobles? Such speculation finally encouraged six members of steerage to steal a look. They waited until ten in the evening; then they climbed up a ladder that led them up from an after hatch to the second-class deck. They slipped past a barrier into the first-class quarters. Here they observed comfortable apartments, luxurious furnishings, and artwork fit for a palace. There was the sound of a piano and a woman's voice in the distance. The air smelled sweet; there was even a whiff of a good cigar. Seconds later they were discovered and hustled back to the lower decks. But the brief look at the upper-class world had been fun.

12.7. Emigrants on deck when land is sighted. Their long journey is nearly over.

(*Harper's Weekly*, June 3, 1871)

On the seventh day, passengers could detect the scent of land, and the water took on a greenish cast that indicated Sandy Hook was not far off. Several hours later the ship was tied up to her dock in the Hudson River. The first- and second-class passengers made their exit, but the emigrants remained below. The steamship company could not afford to let one escape, or it would be subject to a heavy fine by the U.S. immigration agency. The delay continued not just for a few hours but until the next morning. It was hot and uncomfortable belowdecks. *Too bad, you are just a miserable emigrant.* There was no relief in the morning, more delays; at last they were let out on the deck. It was eleven o'clock. Customs now examined their baggage for another two hours on the baking-hot deck. Then they were put on board a barge and towed to Ellis Island.

The passengers in steerage began to feel like criminals as they were once again questioned and examined. But with so many people seeking citizenship it was believed that the rigorous procedure was necessary. The group was actually processed quickly and then dropped off at the Battery by five o'clock that evening. Heartfelt farewells were made as the emigrants headed off for a new life in America. Whitmarsh felt the trip was a good experience. These humble folks had welcomed him and made him a brother, asking for little in return. Best of all, it knocked some of the conceit out of him.

THE ARRIVAL: CASTLE GARDEN AND ELLIS ISLAND

In colonial times incoming ships were free to drop passengers and cargo freely at almost any dock. This was an unfortunate practice because dozens of petty crooks made a living by preying on the newcomers. They were known as runners, because they ran to the docks when a ship was about to land. They were cunning devils, all smiles and grins and so clever in effecting a cheerful welcome to America. Some even spoke a little Gallic or German so as to convey the notion they were there to assist a fellow countryman. They would recommend a boardinghouse, sure to be a den of criminals, or a porter to take away the luggage. All of the bags would disappear and be sold after the contents were searched for valuables by the porter, who was actually a confederate of the runner. After a friendship was established, the runner would ask for a loan – he would pay it back quickly – on his honor. If he discovered the immigrants were traveling west, he would produce discount tickets, which were likely counterfeit, out of date, or otherwise worthless. If there was an attractive wife or daughter in the group, the runner would try to find a way to get her alone and in private. The new arrivals were easy targets for these unscrupulous villains. They came off the boats exhausted, hungry, confused, or ill. The first friendly person to approach them was likely to be a runner. His only interest was in fleecing these poor folks as they stepped ashore in a new land. It happened to thousands each year and was the subject of comments in travel accounts and newspaper articles of the time.

About the only laws effecting immigrants before 1847 were the quarantine and poor laws. Incoming ships were inspected for typhus, cholera, and other infectious diseases. This was done rigorously at the time of epidemics. If the crew and passengers were infected, the ship was put under quarantine until the illness had subsided. It could not land and discharge anyone on board. Originally ships were anchored off of Fire Island. In 1797 a marine hospital was established on Staten Island. The ships were then anchored in the harbor and the most seriously ill were transferred to the hospital. A larger hospital was built for this purpose some years later on Ward's Island, at the north end of the East River near Hell Gate. The city and state poorhouses would handle indigent immigrants as well as such imperfect institutions could deal with the problems of the poor. Several immigrant groups organized volunteer aid groups to welcome and help settle newcomers. The Irish and German immigrant aid societies were especially active in making the arrival of their fellow countrymen more secure and comfortable. They would drive off the runners as much as possible and direct newcomers to honest boardinghouses and porters. They could help their brethren in finding jobs or passage to the West. Even so, reformers called for an official public service to receive and process immigrants upon arrival in this country.

Since so many immigrants landed in New York the state government debated on how to handle the problem. Before 1860 about 60 percent landed in New York City. The number kept growing, and by the 1890s it was 80 percent. The remainder of the immigrant arrivals were divided between Boston, Baltimore, Philadelphia, and New Orleans. The effort to establish a public agency at New York Harbor was being talked to death by the legislature in Albany. Was it the right solution, and was it affordable? Thurlow Weed, a powerful member of the Whig Party, made it his cause and pushed his fellow legislators until a bill was passed in May 1847. Finding a large site at a convenient location on the harbor slowed the work of the immigrant commission. They worked out of temporary locations but finally secured Castle Garden on the south end of Manhattan. The giant brown sandstone fort, completed in 1811, stood just offshore at the west side of the Battery. A short wooden bridge connected it to the Battery. In 1824 it was decommissioned and given to the city. Work began to convert it into a theater named Castle Garden. By about 1870 a landfill made it part of the Battery.

The Garden stood at the lower end of Broadway and loomed above nearby buildings. There was a fine view of Staten Island, Governor's Island, and the New Jersey shore. It was a breezy point, making the old fort one of the best ventilated buildings in the city. The remains of the old fort are preserved today by the National Park Service. It was opened to immigrants on August 1, 1855. After oceangoing ships discharged their first-class passengers at their own docks (large lines such as Cunard and Hamburg American had their own piers), the immigrants and their baggage were transferred by a harbor steamer to Castle Garden, where they entered the building in single file. Upon entering the great rotunda, which was 300 feet in diameter and 75 feet high, the line of newcomers was separated. English speakers went in one direction and non-English speakers, mainly Germans, went the opposite way. They soon came to a desk where a clerk entered their name, birthplace, and destination into a huge register book. (These books are a mine of information to present-day genealogists.) The line moved slowly because of the confusion in languages or the lapse of memory in some of the more fatigued travelers. Most of the younger Irish spoke English, which helped the line to move along (fig. 12.8).

Next to the booking station was the ticket desk, where a clerk helped travelers secure railway tickets for travel beyond New York City. In this way the immigrant was assured of getting the correct ticket at the cheapest

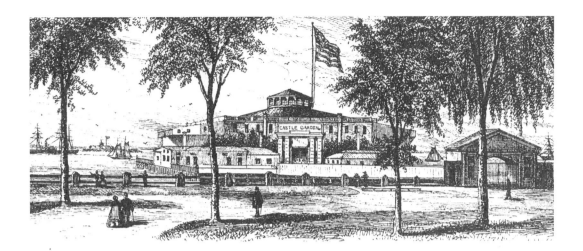

12.8. Castle Garden served as emigrant processing terminal from 1855 to 1890. It was located on the Battery on the south end of Manhattan Island.

(Author's collection)

price. The railroads offered very low rates to immigrants. They also offered ferry service directly from Castle Garden to their New York depots. The big Pennsylvania Railroad station was at Jersey City, and the Erie Railway depot was several blocks north of the Pennsylvania station. The Erie's ferry was a large barge with a cabin that was towed by a small steamer lashed to one side of the barge. Because tickets were paid for in U.S. currency, many immigrants were required to step to a nearby currency exchange. Here again, travelers were guaranteed to receive a fair exchange and not be robbed as they would likely be by a runner. The public and runners, except for a few certified ones, were excluded from Castle Garden. A high wooden fence, gates, and the presence of policemen inside and outside of Castle Garden would ensure this exclusion. The ticket agents were required to know the many languages spoken well enough to assist the travelers. Even so there was some confusion each day. An 1871 article in *Harper's Monthly* mentions a befuddled Swedish man who could remember only that he was heading for Farmington. The clerk did his best to help but explained there were twenty-one Farmingtons listed in the railway guide. Finally the Swede recalled that there was something about a "D" or maybe a "DA." Finally, he searched through one of his bags to recover a note – it was Dakota County in Minnesota. And within minutes he was on his way, ticket in hand.

The next station inside Castle Garden was the baggage check-out. Here the immigrants' baggage would be weighed and checked through to its destination. The newcomers were not rushed or hurried. They could stop and write a letter back to the old country. The postage was free. If they wished to send a telegram, however, this was done at cost. There was a restaurant inside the rotunda that served simple food such as bread, sausage, pie, and coffee. There was a washroom near the exit with a good supply of clean water, soap, and towels. For those needing to rest for a time, there were benches set aside for that purpose. Most immigrants

12.9. (a) The interior of Castle Garden as it appeared in the 1870s. (b) Each emigrant registered his or her name, country of origin, and other vital information upon entering the United States.

(Both from *Harper's Monthly*, March 1871)

spent only about four to six hours inside the Castle Garden. The sick and helpless were sent to Ward's Island, as were immigrants awaiting contact from relatives.

After departing the rotunda the immigrants went to customs for baggage inspection. Their person was subject to inspection as well, but this was rather occasional. A labor exchange was established in 1867. It was housed in a separate building within the fenced confines of the facility. It was a busy office where many found jobs as housekeepers, cooks, laborers, and mechanics. The typical rate was 700 to 800 newcomers was per week.

On leaving the grounds many would head for a nearby boardinghouse on Greenwich or Washington Streets that was certified to be honest and reasonably clean. The boardinghouses charged $1.00–$1.50 a day. Immigrants were strongly advised to ignore the aforementioned runners, who stood in wait just outside the gates and would lead them to lodgings where they would likely be cheated and ill treated. They were told to keep an eye on their children, because some of the more aggressive runners would grab a small child or even a baby and run off with it, knowing the family would follow them. In this way the runner hoped to draw them inside one of the disreputable boardinghouses.

In 1866 Castle Garden was processing about 650 immigrants a day (fig. 12.9). The clerk of the immigrant commission reported 649 ships landed at New York in 1867 delivering 238,708 immigrants. Two hundred fifty of the ships came from Liverpool and 146 were from Bremen. Capacity was generally given as 2,000 a day, but in 1882 it was claimed that 7,000 went through the facility in a day. The total number of people processed by Castle Garden during its thirty-four years of operation is about eight million.

For all of its good work, the reputation of the Garden began to decline about a decade after it opened. When Tammany Hall took an interest in the immigrant station, it became more political and corrupt. Contractors were expected to give kickbacks. Accounts were doctored. Most of these indiscretions were likely of a petty nature, but it was enough to arouse the interest of the federal government. The U.S. Congress began investigating the operations. The Supreme Court declared the head tax used to fund the operations as unconstitutional. The Congress increasingly viewed the regulation of immigrants as a national and not a state concern. Castle Garden was declared too small and antiquated for such a big job. In February 1890 the U.S. secretary of the treasury informed the New York Immigrant Commission they had sixty days to turn the operation over to the federal government. New York retaliated by refusing to rent Castle Garden to the government. A temporary facility was opened at the nearby U.S. Barge Office. Plans were under way to build a new facility on Ellis Island.

This uninspiring dot of land was located a little over a mile from Castle Garden. It was just over 3 acres and was too small for the planned facility. Yet it was conveniently located and could be enlarged as a landfill. Eventually it grew to 27½ acres. After the landfill had progressed to a suitable extent, a large wooden building was erected (fig. 12.10).

The Ellis Island immigrant station was opened on New Year's Day 1892. The once uninhabited island was soon crowded with people (fig. 12.11). On some days as many as 15,000 people came though the facility in single file. Everyone wore a large cardboard name tag. The medical examination was now much more detailed. Doctors now looked for indications

12.10. Ellis Island as it appeared in 1891. The building shown here burned in 1897 and was replaced by a brick structure that stands to the present time.

(*Harper's Weekly*, October 24, 1891)

of imbecility or insanity. Once the medical examination was over, the newcomers were integrated by examiners looking for indications of any undesirable traits. Paupers, criminals, prostitutes, anarchists, and the very ill were sent back to their homelands at the expense of the steamship line that had brought them over. The wire cages, iron railings, and ID tags gave the place the feel of a prison. The inspectors and guards seemed rigid, stern, and heartless. It could take three days to be processed, not just a few hours as was the case at Castle Garden. Much of the time was spent in waiting. People became depressed and anxious. They wondered, *Will I pass or will I be sent back?* In 1902 the following numbers were reported: 4,479 paupers; 274 contract laborers; 711 very sick persons. For all the trauma associated with passing through Ellis Island, the great majority were accepted. Those rejected could appeal and hope the review board would reverse the ruling of the inspectors. Many were saved by a relative who would volunteer to take in the immigrant and be responsible for his maintenance. Some called it Heartbreak Island, but most visitors came to understand on reflection that it was an island of hope and fulfillment.

The main wooden building burned in June 1897, and it was nearly three years before a new brick structure was ready. Increased traffic through the new facility made the processing of new arrivals slower and more difficult. By 1914 there was a dramatic drop in arrivals because of the Great War in Europe. In 1921 a quota law was put into effect and new arrivals dropped to 300,000 a year. The economic depression that followed the stock market crash of 1929 discouraged the flow of immigrants, because unemployment in the United States rose to about 25 percent, and by the 1930s the arrivals had dropped dramatically. In 1943 Ellis Island was closed to new arrivals but continued to be used as a holding station for deportees for another decade. It was then abandoned and gradually decayed and became an unsightly ruin. In more recent times it was restored and declared a national park. Thousands of visitors come each year to see where their ancestors first stepped onto American soil.

12.11. (a) A Mother and her son from Holland have just disembarked at Ellis Island. (b) An English boy traveling alone to America.

(Both from *Harper's Weekly*, October 24, 1891)

INTO THE PROMISED LAND

Many immigrants got off the boat and remained in New York or one of the other port cities along the East Coast. Many of their descendants can still be found nearby. They have left the old ethnic neighborhoods and melted into the suburbs. In some cases their names have been altered to sound more English or to simplify the spelling; Von Poppen became Poppen, Poppe, or even Pope. The older neighborhoods were generally recycled as homes for more recent immigrants. The giant Irish shanty town along upper Fifth Avenue stood for years in contrast to beautiful mansions at the lower end of that grand avenue. The area was leveled to make way for brick apartment buildings by the early twentieth century.

Many new arrivals wanted nothing of the city or tenements or shanty towns. They craved land and a chance to become farmers. Few such opportunities existed in the old country, but America offered millions of acres of unoccupied land. Homesteading was encouraged by the federal government and western railroads, which were eager for settlement in the empty plains and woodlands west of the Alleghenies. The rivers and animal trails offered access to those with the will and energy to become pioneers. In 1790 settlers would go by coastal ship from New York to Philadelphia. They would walk or ride partway by wagon to Pittsburgh and continue by flatboat to Cincinnati in about sixty days. An experienced pioneer, Gilbert Imlay, recalled an immigrant move to Ohio in 1793. A good wagon could be purchased on the East Coast for about $50. Horses adequate for the journey sold for about $60 each. Most families would sleep inside the wagon, but some with a bit of extra cash would stay at a wayside inn. Horse feed, hay and corn, came to about 25 cents a day. The cheapest vitals were those cooked in a kettle over a wood fire. Once Pittsburgh was reached, it was possible to proceed downriver on a flatboat. By 1800 there were 55,000 settlers living in the Ohio Territory. Ten years later Cincinnati had grown from a cluster of huts and cabins into a village of 2,800, but the trip from New York still required about two months. In the fall of 1811, just one year later, the first steamboat appeared on the Ohio River. It easily outran the flatboats by traveling at more than twice their speed. The Erie Canal brought immigrants to the eastern end of Lake Erie by 1825. It was possible to transfer to sailing or steamships and reach Cleveland or Chicago in a few days. Eight years later the Ohio and Erie Canal picked up travelers in Cleveland and dropped them off at Portsmouth, Ohio, where steamers were available to complete the journey to Cincinnati or St. Louis. Other boats would take immigrants to St. Paul or up the Missouri River to points west. The travel was neither comfortable nor fast by modern standards, but by 1840 travelers could go 800 miles in two or three weeks, not two months.

The biggest change in land travel began in the 1830s as railroads began to reach from the East Coast into the interior of the United States. By the late 1850s it was possible to go directly from the seaboard to both St. Louis and Chicago. Immigrants benefited from this transit improvement, and the industry wanted their business. The accommodations were surely spartan, even rustic, but the fares were very low. Most of the freight traffic was west to east, but the cars had to be returned to the West for new shipments. Most returned empty, so it made sense to fill some of them with immigrants and their belongings.

The Austrian engineer Franz Anton von Gerstner reported briefly on immigrant railroad traffic in an 1842 report on American transportation. The data gathered reflects the state of American railroading in the previous decade. The Utica and Schenectady (U&S) Railroad acquired special cars for immigrant travel sometime after its opening in 1836. The fare was a little less than 2 cents a mile, but only about 2,000 immigrants a year traveled over the U&S and the service was abandoned in 1839. An early line, the Mohawk and Hudson (M&H) Railroad, carried immigrants in freight cars, seeing no need to purchase more specialized equipment for such poor-paying patrons. In 1838 they reported carrying 39,838 immigrants at one-half the first-class fares. By 1843 the several small railroads stretching across northern New York were offering through service between Albany and Buffalo. The U&S and M&H were part of the 326-mile network that within a decade would be reorganized as the New York Central Railroad. The express train required twenty-five hours to make the journey, resulting in an average speed of 13 mph. Immigrants were carried by special contract on slower-moving trains.

As the railroad network expanded into the western states, the immigrant traffic began to grow. In June 1854 the Lake Shore and Michigan Southern Railroad delivered eight hundred immigrants to Chicago on four trains in one day. The Pennsylvania Railroad reported carrying 11,880 immigrants in 1862. An Aurora, Illinois, newspaper reported the daily increase of immigrant travel in the spring of 1879. Many freight trains included six or more cars filled immigrating families and their property heading west over the Chicago, Burlington, and Quincy Railroad. These foreign pioneers were seen on station platforms and were notable by their old-fashioned and ill-fitting clothing; some had overcoats made from old blankets. They found cheap food and lodging in Omaha in an immigrants hotel operated by the Union Pacific Railroad where meals were just 25 cents. An outfitters shop, also operated by the railroad, sold tools and household goods designed to meet the needs of the immigrant settler. A farm wagon with horses was available for just $250; a plow and implements cost only $100. The settlers would live in a sod house to cut expenses. That way they set up an 80-acre farm for about $800.

There were millions of acres of land available in the West. The railroads acquired 132 million acres in land grants. The government retained alternate sections, and when the railroad opened, the land became valuable because transportation was available. So both the railroad and the government benefited from the scheme. There was little purpose in farming without an economic way to send the crops to market. Immigrants were among the thousands who came west to homestead, and the railroads were eager to accommodate them. Farmers were shippers, and the railroad needed traffic. The Illinois Central Railroad was involved in real estate development in a large way in 1855. They offered land at from $5 to $25 an acre depending on the quality of the soil, its location, and its distance from the track. No farmland would be more than 15 miles from the railroad. Stations would be about 10 miles apart. Buyers received a five-year credit, the first payment was not due for two years, and the interest on the loan was 2 percent.

The majority of immigrants were unfamiliar with this new land. Did they want a farm in Iowa or Indiana? Was this cheap land, so gloriously described in the railroad's advertisements, truly rich and fertile, or was it all rocks and clay? Such skepticism was understandable. The industry responded by offering land-exploring tickets and free rooms. *Come out to Burlington or North Platte. Bring the entire family. Look around. You can move on and inspect several locations. If you buy from us within thirty days, the cost of the tickets will be refunded. Even if you decline to do so, the tickets are cheap, so you will not be out very much.* Adults traveled for one-half regular coach fare, children from four to twelve traveled at one-quarter fare, and children under four years of age traveled free. Some railroad colonial offices would advise immigrants of cheaper ways to travel west. During the summer, eastern railroad fares generally dropped. The immigrant fare from New York to Chicago dropped from $11 to $9. If you took a steamer to Albany and had a through ticket by rail, you spent only $7 to reach Chicago; however, this special fare was offered only in the summer.

Immigrant fares were a subject of some debate in the press and the commission that managed Castle Garden. Three major railroads serving New York City – the Erie, the New York Central, and the Pennsylvania – were allowed to sell tickets inside of Castle Garden. This was intended primarily as a convenience for the immigrants. It was understood that this poorest class of society should travel at a discount. For a time the rate to Chicago stayed at $7.50. During one of the periodic rate wars it dropped to $1.00, but by 1888 it was back up to $13.00. This seemed much too high when compared to the ocean steamer fare of $22.00 for a trip of 3,000 miles. The steamer fare also included a berth and food, while the railroad offered nothing but a seat for a trip of just under 1,000 miles.

The business was far more complex than the fare structure. By 1886 no less than eleven railroads were involved in the immigrant clearinghouse. It was no longer just the main lines that were directly involved in moving immigrants out of New York but more distant railroads such as the Grand Trunk, the Boston and Lowell, and the Vermont Central as well. The industry began pooling traffic that involved more complex formulas for dividing up the traffic and the revenues it produced. In October 1880 the *New York Tribune* outlined the Byzantine scheme that was then in operation. It started with the Erie Railway, which made a secret agreement with the North German Lloyd line for all of its immigrants rather than sharing this trade with their partners. The New York Central and Pennsylvania Railroads then wanted separate pieces of the traffic. The New York Central would carry the North German immigrants on alternate weeks. It also got all of the State line's immigrants. The Erie Railway was to receive all of Inman's and Guion's traffic, except for the Mormon immigrants. The Mormons and Scandinavians went to the Pennsylvania Railroad, which also received the immigrants of the National and Red Star lines. Pooling arrangements such as this one were made illegal with the establishment of the Interstate Commerce Commission in 1887.

HOW THE IMMIGRANTS WERE CARRIED

Typically the immigrants were carried in elderly day coaches that had been downgraded for this particular class of passenger. The upholstery might be well worn. The lamps and paneling had lost much of their former brightness. The real failing, however, was that even a railroad's best day coach was a miserable conveyance for nighttime travel. The seats made an extremely poor bed. If the car was crowded, almost everyone was required to sit in an upright position. The low seat back was an impossible headrest. Only a midget or a child could lie flat on the seat cushion, should a full seat be available. Such cars had a toilet at either end, but running water was a rarity. Drinking water was generally dispensed by a train boy who carried a water can through the train. Cooking was out of the question.

The Illinois Central Railroad experimented with a special style of box car in 1855 – end doors and a few windows were provided. The seats were removable so that the cars could be used as ordinary boxcars on the eastbound trip. The Michigan Central copied the idea, but the plan was apparently considered too expensive even for immigrants. The Grand Trunk Railway continued to employ ordinary boxcars into the late 1860s. A large party of German immigrants was packed into ten cars without the benefit of seats, food, or water. After three days of misery the train stopped at Guelph, Ontario, where a newsman witnessed several pails of water being passed up to the thirsty immigrants. The reporter said it was the most inhumane scene he had witnessed. These wretched people had many more days of travel ahead as the train pulled out for western Canada.

The need for better accommodations was obvious, and it is interesting to note that reform was forthcoming from an official inside the railroad industry. Alban N. Towne, general superintendent of the Central Pacific Railroad, decided it was time to develop a comfortable car for the humble immigrant. It would not be a fancy or elegant palace car, as luxury was not needed, but reasonable comfort and economy surely were a necessity. The railroad's Sacramento shops were put to work in April 1879 converting twenty-five second-class coaches into immigrant sleepers. By the end of the year the Central Pacific had sixty-eight such cars in operation. The berths followed the general plan of the Pullman open section car. The bottom berth was made by laying a mattress over the seats. The upper berth was hinged and could be opened and lowered for sleeping purposes. In figure 12.12 some of the upper berths are open and occupied, but the lower berths are being used for daytime seating. There are no curtains as would be found in a Pullman sleeper of the period. The interior is plain and unadorned. The floor had no carpeting, the lamp is simple, but the car was neat and utilitarian. No bedding was provided, and some berths were

12.12. Immigrant sleeping car used on the Santa Fe route in 1884. They would leave Kansas City on both morning and evening trains.

(Author's collection)

upholstered in black leather for cleaning and sanitary reasons. There were, of course, no porters or attendants other than the regular train's crew. However, a stove and sink were at one end of the car for cooking. Passengers took turns in preparing their meals, and space was large enough for several people to work in the kitchen at one time.

A description of a passenger in such a car appeared in *Harper's Weekly* on November 13, 1886. It reads, in part, as follows:

> Most of the berths are turned up for the day, and the passengers of various nationalities and conditions of life, are seated in the sections, gazing out of the windows at the strange landscape, or occupied at some task or amusement. Right in front of us, her baby at her breast, sits a comely German woman, knitting complacently at some blue worsted work, and keeping her eye on a flaxen-haired youngster, who, seated on the floor of the car at our feet, is discussing a not over-savory mess from the tin dish before him. Parcels and boxes are stowed under the seat, a bird-cage and some clothing hang suspended from pegs, while behind the woman, in the next section looking down from the upper berth, the father, frowzy-haired and with matted, unkempt beard, lies stretched at full length, smoking his porcelain pipe in calm indifference to the olfactory nerves of his fellow passengers.
>
> A respectable, neat old Englishman, in corduroy clothes and a billycock hat, sits with folded hands in the opposite section, while a delicate, pretty girl in a black dress gazes – leaning her elbow on the sill and her chin on her hand – dreamily out of the window at his side. Back in the car, up the long perspective of the aisle, various groups are gathered together, according to their nationality or dispositions, talking and laughing, or moving on about different errands, while one little knot of men, from their physiognomy and dress evidently subjects of "her Majesty," are listening with intent faces to some yarn from one of the train-men.

Other western railroads followed the Central Pacific Railroad's example, but not all did so quickly. These immigrant sleepers were called colonist cars in Canada, an interior of a Canadian Pacific Railway sleeper is shown in figure 12.13. This style of car evolved into the tourist sleeper designed for families wishing to travel at cheaper rates and ready to forgo the niceties of Pullman service.

Robert Louis Stevenson left behind a firsthand account of a trip on board an immigrant sleeper. Stevenson made a trip from Scotland to San Francisco in August 1879 to see a sweetheart he had met in France a few

12.13. The interior of an immigrant sleeping car on the Canadian Pacific Railway in 1888.

(*Illustrated London News*, December 15, 1888)

years earlier. It was an arduous trip for this sick and frail young man. He was a poor and largely unknown writer at the time. He became a famous literary figure in the following decade. It was necessary for Stevenson to travel cheaply, because his father would not bankroll the trip. He went by steamer from Glasgow to New York and then by railroad to the West Coast. He booked passage on the Anchor liner *Devonia* (1877) as a second-class passenger, but from his description, the travel experience was little better than that offered in steerage. The fare was 8 guineas (about $42) – steerage was 6 guineas (about $31.50). Table 12.3 outlines his trip – the numbers are estimates based mainly on the author's text.

The railroad portion of the trip began early on Monday morning at the Cortlandt Street ferry boat station. Several hundred immigrants from four ships stood in the rain waiting for the boat to carry them across the Hudson River to the Pennsylvania Railroad's depot in Jersey City. The loading process was difficult with so many people and so much baggage to move. But disembarking turned into a stampede: the crowd pushed and elbowed one another; children fell down and were pulled up while others ran ahead; and all of this uproar was for nothing. The train was not ready. The car doors were locked. There was no waiting room available nor a restaurant nor even a lunch counter. The soggy crowd stood on the platform while the rain blew in to make them wetter yet. The doors were unlocked after a long wait, and in time the train pulled out for Philadelphia. An accident up the line slowed their progress. Bypassing Philadelphia they headed over the main for Pittsburgh. The few stops for food were too short for any but the very strong to reach the counter and be served. The

Table 12.3. Robert Louis Stevenson's Trip from Scotland to San Francisco (August 1879)

Mode of Travel	Miles	Days	mph
Steamship (Glasgow to New York)	3,000	10	12½
Pennsylvania RR (Jersey City to Chicago)	1,000	3	12
Chicago, Burlington & Quincy RR (Chicago to Council Bluffs)	500	1½	14
Union Pacific RR (Omaha to Ogden)	1,000	3½	11
Central Pacific RR (Ogden to Oakland)	900	3	10

Note: All numbers are approximate.
Source: Author's various data files.

remainder of the immigrants were at the mercy of the newsboy, who sold fruit or snacks at inflated prices. After nearly thirty hours they reached Pittsburgh, where they changed trains for Chicago. There was a long enough break to eat a proper meal. The next morning they were rolling across Ohio, which Stevenson described as being as flat as Holland yet far from dull because of the graceful trees, the green fields, and the tall corn.

They reached Chicago in the evening, and Stevenson went by omnibus to the Burlington station for the next leg of his trip across the United States. A long, crowded train stood next to the platform. He found an empty seat but was warned to watch his valuables because a pickpocket was at work. The next morning the train was at Burlington, Iowa, after crossing the Mississippi River. Time was allowed for a quick breakfast.

The train rolled slowly to the southwest, stopping at most stations. Immigrants traveled on the slow trains, and the frequent stops made the trains even slower. They waited on a siding to allow superior trains to pass. But if you were poor, you learned to accept not just inferior accommodations but slower service as well. At one station an intoxicated man got on board and made enough of a disturbance that the conductor heaved him off the train. Fortunately for the drunk, the train was moving at a leisurely pace. That evening a little before nine o'clock they pulled into Council Bluffs. Most of the immigrants headed for a cheap hotel run by the railroad, but Stevenson needed a break from this life of poverty and booked into a first-class establishment for the night.

The next afternoon he resumed his humble life among the one hundred immigrants lined up at the Pacific transfer station. An officious conductor insisted on breaking the group into three categories: married couples and their children, single men, and Chinese travelers. After everyone was on board, the passengers largely ignored this division and mixed as they pleased in the three cars assigned. With considerable dismay Stevenson noted the prejudiced voice against the Asians as he went more toward the West Coast. Just why Americans felt this way was not apparent to the Scottish traveler. The train's cars were assembled and put in order – baggage and mail cars up front, then coaches, and at the rear the sleeping cars – as the immigrants, typically, sat passively waiting for the trainmen to finish assembling the cars. It was pulled slowly across the great iron bridge that spans the Missouri River and on to the Union Pacific main line bound for Ogden, Utah.

The Union Pacific, like most western railroads, was a lightly built, single-track line with two-way traffic. The rail was light and the ties were widely spaced. Hence the trains moved slower than on the better eastern lines. It must have struck Stevenson how different America's railroads were from those in Britain. Back home every main line was double-tracked, there were few grade crossings, and signals and fencing were common. Trains flew along at 50 or 60 mph. But here in the American West they crept along at 15 or 20 mph. No wonder it took days to get anywhere.

Stevenson had worked out a routine on this slow train. He slept on the floor using a straw mattress. Since space was so limited, he must have curled up between the seats. There was no sleeping in the center aisle because of the traffic; at night passengers moved around to a degree and the train crew needed the aisle to be open. He made friends with two other male passengers. They looked out for one another and agreed on a system for their morning wash-up. Stevenson had a tin wash basin that he shared with his companions; they had soap and a towel. The drill in the morning was to share these belongings. They would take turns filling up the basin from the water tank at one end of the car, step out onto the open platform at one end of the car, and then wash up as best they could. At meal stops the immigrants learned to keep one eye on the train. The crew made a point of not alerting them that the train was about to leave and would start up without a sound, meaning to leave the miserable immigrants behind at some lonely depot. This hostility was apparent when every one of the immigrants asked a question or needed assistance of some sort. Just why the conductor and his fellow crew members were so uncivil toward their down-and-out charges was not apparent to Stevenson.

Even the newsboy was a dark, insolent scoundrel. One day a few of the male passengers had had enough of his attitude and put him in his place for the remainder of the trip. There were other, more agreeable newsboys mentioned in Stevenson's narrative, including one who had been initially rude but became concerned about Stevenson's ill health. The boy gave Stevenson a pear one day and began to sit with the Scottish traveler trying to cheer him up. A third newsboy proved to be a fine fellow. He knew the train's schedule and would share this information with the travelers. He would tell them when a meal stop was coming up and how long the train would remain at that particular station. Because the immigrants were so unaccustomed to being treated in a kind or friendly fashion by any railway employees, this lad became a favorite among them.

A change of trains took place in Ogden, Utah, where the Union and Central Pacific railroads exchanged passengers. The Central Pacific treated its immigrants to sleeping cars, which represented an upgrade from the dismal coaches normally provided. Travelers could stretch out and lie flat rather than curl up on a seat or on the floor. Stevenson remarked on the cars' high ceilings, brightly varnished interiors, and upper and lower berths, but otherwise limited his remarks to towns, scenery, and people along the way. A few of his fellow passengers seemed to think it humorous to call out "All aboard!" and watch the crowd run for the cars. Much of the fun subsided as the train passed across the alkali and sand desert of Nevada. It was a hot, dusty ride. Once in the Sierra Nevada Mountains the trains plunged through several short tunnels and a longer series of wooden snowsheds that blocked out the natural light. As they rolled down the grade through the old mining towns of Alta and Dutch Flat, California, they neared Sacramento. Stevenson's long pilgrimage was coming to its end. At dawn of the next morning they arrived in Oakland. A ferry boat took them to San Francisco.

It was some months before Stevenson and his sweetheart were married. Meanwhile Stevenson's father reconsidered and gave his son an annual allowance. The newlyweds went by Pullman car to New York and booked first-class tickets on the Inman line to Britain. Later in life Stevenson recorded his excursion to America in two small publications, *The Amateur Emigrant* and *Across the Plains*.

There were other poor folks who, while not technically immigrants, traveled in much the same way. They, too, were seeking a new home and a better life. These were the orphans who were sent west by train in search of foster parents. Charles L. Brace devoted his life to homeless children. In 1853 he organized the Children's Aid Society in New York City. Its primary purpose was to house, feed, and educate street children. It was equally important to find homes for the orphans. When too few New Yorkers volunteered to take them in, the process of outplacement was mobilized. In September 1854 the first orphan train left New York for the West. The children were cleaned up, given new clothing, and sent off to seek a family. The railroads cooperated by offering group fares at greatly reduced rates. When the train would stop, the children stepped down to the platform for inspection by prospective parents and their kin. Those not selected climbed back on board and rode on until someone took them in. Many a happy home was found by this process, but there were failures as well. Children were abused or treated like indentured servants. Some were sent away after taking in the harvest. For all of its good intentions, the orphan train was increasingly viewed as a flawed institution. The last orphan train rolled to a stop at Sulphur Springs, Texas, on May 31, 1929.

SUGGESTED READING

Berger, Max. *British Traveller in America, 1836–1860.* New York: Columbia University Press, 1943.

Bunker, John G. *Harbor and Haven: An Illustrated History of the Port of New York.* Woodland Hills, Calif.: Windsor Publications, 1979.

Burrows, Edwin G. *Gotham.* New York: Oxford University Press, 1999.

Coleman, Terry. *Going to America.* Garden City, N.Y.: Anchor/Doubleday, 1973.

Cowan, Helen I. *British Emigration to British North America, 1783–1837.* Toronto: University of Toronto Library, 1928.

Erickson, Charlotte. *Emigrants from Europe, 1815–1914.* London: A and C Black, 1976.

Gates, Paul Wallace. *The Illinois Central Railroad and Its Colonization Work.* Cambridge: Harvard University Press, 1934.

Guillet, Edwin C. *The Great Migration: The Atlantic Crossing by Sailship since 1770.* Toronto: University of Toronto Press, 1963.

Handlin, Oscar. *A Pictorial History of Immigration.* New York: Crown, 1972.

Hansen, Marcus. *The Atlantic Migration, 1607–1860: A History of the Continuing Settlement of the United States.* Cambridge: Harvard University Press, 1940.

Holt, Marilyn I. *The Orphan Trains: Placing Out in America.* Lincoln: University of Nebraska, 1992.

Jones, Evan R. *The Emigrants' Friend Containing Information and Advice for Persons Intending to Emigrate to the U.S..* London: Tyne, 1881.

Jones, Maldwyn A. *Destination America.* London: Weidenfeld and Nicolson, 1976.

Marzio, Peter. *A Nation of Nations: The People Who Came to America as Seen through Objects and Documents Exhibited at the Smithsonian Institution.* New York: Harper and Row, 1976.

Overton, Richard. *Burlington West: A Colonization History of the Burlington Railroad.* Cambridge: Harvard University Press, 1941.

Stevenson, Robert Louis, et al. *From Scotland to Silverado.* Cambridge: Belknap Press of Harvard University Press, 1966.

Taylor, Philip A. *Distant Magnet: European Emigration to the U.S.A.* New York: Harper and Row, 1972.

Wittke, Carl. *We Who Built America: The Saga of the Immigrant.* Cleveland: Western Reserve University Press, 1964.

Wyman, Mark. *Round Trip to America: The Immigrants Return to Europe, 1880–1930.* Ithaca, N.Y.: Cornell University Press, 1993.

Passenger Trains №13

Coach Class

THE RAILWAY WAS ENGLAND'S GIFT TO THE WORLD. PRIMITIVE tramways were used to carry coal to coastal ports since Elizabethan times. They gradually evolved into carriers for both passengers and cargo by 1825. Iron rails and wheels provided a low-friction means of transport that remains economical today. The introduction of the railway was an epic improvement in an epic time. It revolutionized travel as well as our concept of time and space. It required a massive investment and was an unprecedented enterprise in terms of management and employment. Ralph Waldo Emerson once wrote, "Railroad iron is a magician's rod, in its power to evoke the sleeping energies of the land and water." Even Henry Thoreau, no friend of industry, was impressed by the iron horse. Its snort sounded like thunder, he said, and its feet shook the land "as if the earth had a race now worthy to inhabit it." Many writers have observed that railroads bound our nation together by pumping commerce across the vast continent. An explosion of industrial power followed the creation of a national rail network. The United States was transformed from underdeveloped pastoral land into a leading producer of iron, coal, lumber, and steel. The country's population doubled and its exports tripled as America became the world's wealthiest nation. Trains raced over the mountains and prairies, their mournful whistles and rhythmic rumble awakening generations of Americans. The countryside grew quiet again as the train passed and disappeared. The iron steed never rested as train followed train. The cars merrily followed along, clicking and grinding over the iron rails. They were, as Walt Whitman put it, the "emblem of motion and power, pulse of the continent."

The railroad also profoundly affected ordinary citizens. A New Englander named Christopher Baldwin, after first seeing a train in 1835, exclaimed, "What an object of wonder." It seemed like a dream to Baldwin. Some of his contemporaries were more skeptical, however, and considered the talk of travel at 15 mph nonsense. Until we had bones of brass or iron it was foolish to speculate on rapid travel, yet in a few decades speeds of

13.1. Passengers, rich and poor, passed through iron gates by the millions each day to board humble locals or deluxe express trains. Railroads dominated passenger travel for almost a century starting in about 1855. This is Broad Street Station, Philadephia, in 1888. It was one of the largest depots in the nation.

(*Scribner's Monthly*, September 1888)

40 mph were common. Indeed the railway would greatly change how we lived and traveled. Charles Francis Adams, writing in 1880, claimed that 1835 was a historic dividing line because of the introduction of railways. Before that time little had changed for centuries. Sailing ships, horse-powered vehicles, and small business enterprises were the norm. But after 1835 the railway made Boston a metropolis (fig. 13.1). Large businesses created a new capitalist class of great wealth. Much of the population lived in the suburbs and commuted by railroad. Long-distance travel was no longer figured in weeks or days but in hours and minutes.

The first American railways were inspired by British prototypes. Some were directly copied by American engineers who visited the motherland of railways. Erskine Hazard went to England in 1826 to collect data for a narrow-gauge mule-powered railroad in eastern Pennsylvania at Mauch Chunk. Its primary purpose was to carry coal from a mountaintop mine to a canal at the base for trans-shipment to Philadelphia. Passengers were carried on a daily basis, so the line was more than an industrial railway. William Strickland, a Philadelphia architect, was sent to England during the same year as Hazard's visit. Based on his observations he produced a book about British canals and railways, explaining the details of their design and construction, as a guide to help others build a canal and railroad across Pennsylvania. By 1830 more railroad projects in the planning or construction phase could be found in every region of the nation, except for the far West. Almost all had some form of governmental support. The federal government avoided direct monetary aid but was willing to lend army engineers to several inaugural lines, because America had so few engineers at the time. Enthusiasm was high, but investment capital was scarce. Cheaper construction methods were adopted, notably in track construction, where wooden rails with thin iron straps took the place of solid iron rails. Wood trestles were constructed in place of more expansive stone or iron bridges. Stations, signals, and track-side fencing were seen as luxuries. Double tracks were also considered unnecessary. A single track with occasional passing sidings was adopted for two-way traffic. These economies permitted a fair amount of mileage to be built. By 1837 almost 1,500 miles of railroad were in place, and America was clearly the most enthusiastic nation outside of England in creating new railroads. Although the financial panic late in 1837 slowed progress to some degree, mileage continued to advance despite the hard times. Promoters began to seek investors in Europe, where bonds were sold with considerable success to finance America's growing system.

By the 1840s a few long railroads were in operation and more mileage was being added on a daily basis. The South Carolina Railroad stretched for 136 miles between Charleston and Hamburg and would finish a 60-mile branch line to Columbia, South Carolina, in November 1840. The

Wilmington and Weldon Railroad (North Carolina) completed 160 miles in March 1840 and was the longest railroad in the nation. The Baltimore and Ohio Railroad pushed its main line 161 miles to Cumberland by late 1842, and its branch line to Washington, D.C., opened in August 1835. Elsewhere matters were less positive. Indiana's public works program of 1836 had nearly bankrupted the state government, and Michigan was in serious financial trouble as well. Good times would return by the mid-1840s, and California's gold did much to revive America's national economy later in the decade.

The 1850s was a time for coming together for the American railroad system. In April 1851 the New York and Erie Railroad reached Dunkirk, New York, 469 miles north of New York City and thus united Lake Erie with the Atlantic Ocean. In February of the next year the Lake Shore and Michigan Southern Railroad entered Chicago. In January 1853 it was possible to travel by rail from New York to Chicago. Another long-distance route was finished at the same time when the Baltimore and Ohio (B&O) reached Wheeling, West Virginia, 379 miles west of Baltimore. The Atlantic Ocean and the Ohio River were now connected by a rail link. In the spring of 1857 the B&O and its western connections offered through rail connections from Baltimore to St. Louis via Cincinnati. This linked the Atlantic Ocean with the Mississippi River. A year earlier the Rock Island Railroad had completed a bridge over the Mississippi at Davenport, Iowa. In February 1859 the Hannibal and St. Joseph Railroad reached the Missouri River, making the American West part of the growing rail network.

13.2. The typical local station was far removed from the grand monuments that served most major cities. They were plain and simple wooden structures with few comforts. The better ones had a separate waiting room for ladies. No matter how humble, they were often a beehive of activity, gossip, and the news that arrived over the telegraph.

(*Scribner's Monthly*, November 1888)

For all of the growth, America's railway network was provisional in nature at mid-century. It was done on the cheap. At many stops there were shabby and rude stations; indeed at some stops there was no station at all (fig. 13.2). There were no fences to keep cattle off the tracks or crossing gates to keep vehicles and pedestrians safe from the locomotives. Some contended that this primitive style of railroad was well adapted to our new nation. An article in 1867 in *Atlantic Monthly* disagreed. America was too swift in building new public works that were at a low level of technical excellence, it said. The country was also careless in the management of these projects.

Because some railroad lines were so large, it was necessary to devise a more efficient system of management. By 1855 there were twenty railroads in the United States that were 250 miles long. Ten were capitalized at more than $10 million each, while five had a capital value over twice that amount. The New York Central, organized in July 1853, had gross revenue of $6 million and a bonded indebtedness of $14 million (fig. 13.3). The Erie was twice the size of the Central and had forty-seven hundred employees. It needed a central control, an accounting system, and communications and information systems to efficiently manage such a large enterprise. The railroad's plan was modeled on the military, where a chain of command was established from the president down to the most humble worker through a series of managers and assistant managers. A large bureaucracy resulted that included clerks, station agents, car cleaners, repairmen, and accountants, as well as engineers, conductors, and other trainmen. The largest segment of railroad workers maintained the track, bridges, cars, and locomotives. The railroad was broken down into divisions, usually 100 miles in length; the divisions were broken down into sections, usually 5 to 7 miles long depending on the traffic.

Every employee received a rule book to memorize, some containing up to four hundred rules. Failure to know or observe the rules could lead to dismissal. The railroad industry was large and bureaucratic by the 1850s. According to Professor Alfred D. Chandler Jr., it was also the nation's first big business. Everything about it was growing to gigantic dimensions – mileage, traffic, employment, and investment.

The political and economic influence of its leaders was also growing. The British diplomat James Bryce wrote the following about American railroad presidents in his 1888 study, *The American Commonwealth*:

> The railway kings are among the greatest men, perhaps I may say are the greatest men in America.... They have power, more power ... than any one in political life, except the President and the Speaker, who after all hold theirs only for four years and two years, while the railroad monarch may keep his for life. When the master of one of the greatest Western lines travels toward the Pacific on his palace car, his journey is like a royal progress. Governors of States bow before

13.3. Ten small railroads offer joint service between Albany and Buffalo at a leisurely pace in 1843. By the 1850s improved track and connections reduced the travel time to fourteen hours. These companies united in 1853 as the New York Central Railroad.

(*Scribner's Magazine*, September 1888)

him; legislatures receive him in solemn session; cities seek to propitiate him, for has he not the means for making or marring a city's fortunes?

This power was useful in creating a marvelous transportation system that transformed America into an industrial giant that employed millions of workers and created wealth for investors, as well as cheap travel for the public and economical carriage for shippers. Some railroad titans used their power to undo all of the positive aspects of American railroading. The chief villains in American business history include railroad executives such as Jay Gould, Jim Fink, and Daniel Drew.

By the 1860s the railroads began to dominate U.S. transportation, especially passenger transport, because of their comparative advantages in speed and price. The Civil War drove up the price of iron goods considerably, and inflation became a problem. Yet the growth in mileage continued. Work on the transcontinental railroad to link California and the western territories to the eastern states started at the end of the Civil War. The task was finished ahead of schedule on May 10, 1869. At this time the national rail system was valued at approximately $2 billion. Yet in many ways it remained a provisional system. Most of it remained a single track. The bridges, cars, and stations were mainly wooden. The locomotives were largely wood-burning. Manual brakes and link-and-pin couplers prevailed. There were major river crossings, such as the Susquehanna and Hudson Rivers, without bridges. Passengers were required to transfer by ferries. There was only one railroad bridge over the Ohio River. Long-distance passengers were required to cross through major cities by omnibus or taxi, because there were so few union stations. Train speeds remained at about 25 to 30 mph; even on express trains average speeds were much lower. While most northern lines were built to a standard gauge of 4 feet, 8½ inches, those in New Jersey and Ohio had an odd gauge of 4 feet, 10 inches. Some lines, such as the Erie, and the Delaware, Lackawanna, and Western were broad gauge. The southern lines were uniformly 5-foot gauge except for those in North Carolina, so the interchange of cars was possible south of the Mason-Dixon Line. Sleeping cars were becoming popular by this decade, but diners and parlor cars remained rare. Coach passengers made do with a coach, infamous for their low-back seats, hand-fired stoves, and poor lighting.

For all of the imperfections of the American rail system, it did provide cheap and dependable transportation and so became a model for railways elsewhere in the world. The British and European railways were better in about almost every way, but they were also far more expensive than America's lines. Fares in Britain were twice as much as in the United States. Where long distances and light traffic prevailed, the American system was copied. Railways in South America, Africa, and Asia were largely built on the American plan. In time, as the population and the traffic grew, the rickety bridges, tracks, and rolling stock were improved and a more sophisticated railway was created.

In 1884 it was estimated that the United States had just over 50 percent of the world's railways, and yet they cost only one-third of the railways elsewhere. American engineers would agree, however, that our railways were more costly to operate and maintain because they were constructed on a low standard and tended to devour themselves so quickly. Our huge network of steel was built with no master plan – no national agency planned what and what not to build. It simply grew like a blanket of mushrooms in a rain forest, and many redundant lines were constructed, but in general the overall plan made sense because it was produced by hardheaded business leaders who wanted to make money. This could only be done by adding mileage that would find enough traffic to make a profit. Most new lines were built to serve an area or cities requiring more service. Stronger systems absorbed weaker railroads.

For all the complaints about safety, the American railway grew up in many admirable ways. America was a leader in providing deluxe cars for first-class travel. Pullman and his competitors introduced palace sleeping cars in the 1860s, and they were commonplace by the next decade. Dining cars were another American innovation that appeared in 1868 and were common on the better trains by the 1880s. Steel rail was a standard by the same decade and did much to lower maintenance costs and upgrade safety. The air brake, introduced in 1869, was in wide use on passenger trains by about 1880. Railroads were slower to adopt this excellent invention for freight trains. A train traveling at 30 mph could be stopped by hand brakes in 1,600 feet. There was usually one brakeman for every two cars. A few domestic lines adopted double tracks as early as 1834. This increased the capacity and safety of the line and made faster speed possible. The New York Central Railroad was all double tracks except for 15 miles by 1866 and rebuilt part of its system with four tracks during the same decade. The Pennsylvania Railroad completed double-tracking its main line in 1877. Track elevation in dense traffic areas was a costly but effective way to eliminate grade crossings. Many railroads undertook such projects around major cities later in the nineteenth century. The New York Central dug a trench through the center of Manhattan Island to Grand Central Station at Forty-second Street. It was covered over in later years to become Park Avenue, making it a fashionable part of the city.

Large, successful enterprises have their admirers, but they seem to generate a considerable number of enemies as well. Many people hated the railroads because they believed they were too large and profitable. Many lines paid dividends of 8 percent year after year. They came to control one-sixth of the nation's wealth. Their annual income was four times that of the federal government. One in every sixty-two citizens was a railroad employee. They carried 98 percent of the intercity passengers and 77 percent of the freight. The railroad system was divided between elite families or individuals with surnames such as Gould, Harriman, Vanderbilt, and Morgan. Another convenient way to group the major lines was this regional scheme:

New England	Boston and Maine/New Haven/Maine Central
Trunk Lines	Pennsylvania/New York Central/Baltimore and Ohio

Anthracite Roads	Central of New Jersey/Lackawanna/Reading/Delaware and Hudson
Pocahontas Lines	Norfolk and Western/Chesapeake and Ohio
Bridge Lines	Wabash/Nickel Plate (New York, Chicago, and St. Louis)
Southern Roads	Louisville and Nashville/Southern/Seaboard Air line/Atlantic Coast line
Granger Roads	Rock Island/Chicago, Burlington, and Quincy/Chicago and North Western/Chicago, Milwaukee, St. Paul, and Pacific
Transcontinental	Union Pacific/Southern Pacific/Northern Pacific/Great Northern

Trunk lines referred to those with major traffic and income. Anthracite is hard coal; the main traffic on Pocahontas lines was soft coal. Bridge lines connected trunk lines. Granger roads ran through the grange or Midwest, where much grain is grown. The transcontinental railroad actually went only from the Mississippi River west to the Pacific Ocean.

Just how to control these giants was a puzzle that was never solved. It began with state railroad commissions that were intended to regulate rates, safety, and other matters of public concern. Massachusetts and New York created such bodies in the mid-nineteenth century. The farmers' Granger movement in the 1890s pressured midwestern states to do likewise. The farmers contended that unfair freight rates were bankrupting them. No one would contend that the railroads were blameless, but in truth both freight and passenger rates in the United States were the lowest in the world. The agitations were strong enough that the federal government created the Interstate Commerce Commission in 1887. Its powers were gradually broadened over succeeding decades until this federal agency was overseeing about every detail of railway operations. One could debate the benefits derived from the agency's operation. The Interstate Commerce Commission faded away during the deregulation era of the 1980s, and its remaining responsibilities were transferred to the U.S. Department of Transportation.

Despite an almost complete monopoly of passenger travel, by 1900 that part of the business was not particularly profitable. It was not a large income producer. Freight service produced 70 percent of the gross revenue and almost all of the profit. Passenger operations brought in about 20 percent of the revenue. Mail, express, and other miscellaneous sources brought in the remaining 10 percent. Passenger rates were 3 or more cents a mile until about 1865 when it began to decline. By 1916 it was down to 2 cents a mile.

Table 13.1. United States Railroad Statistics, 1830–1890

Year	Miles	Passengers Carried	Passenger Cars	Locomotives	Employees	Value of the System	U.S. Population
1830	23	?	?	?	?	?	12 M
1840	2,800	?	900*	475*	5,000*	$75 M	17 M
1850	9,000	?	3,000*	3,000*	18,000*	$310 M	23 M
1860	30,000	?	10,000	8,500	80,000	$1.1 B	31 M
1870	53,000	?	13,000	12,500	163,000	$2.5 B	38 M
1880	93,000	280 M	17,000	17,900	418,000	$5.4 B	50 M
1890	166,000	520 M	32,400	31,800	749,000	$10.0 B	62 M
1900	193,000	600 M	34,000	37,600	1,018,000	$11.8 B	76 M

* = estimate;
M = million

Note: Most numbers are rounded off. Passenger cars include baggage, express, and mail. "Locomotives" and "Employees" columns include all in service and not those used only for passenger traffic.

Source: *Historical Statistics of the United States* (Washington, D.C.: U.S. Census Bureau, 1960); Poor's *Manual of Railroads* (New York: H. V. and H. W. Poor, various years); Albert Fishlow, *American Railroads and the Transformation of the AnteBellum Economy* (Cambridge: Harvard University Press, 1965).

Edwin A. Pratt toured the United States starting late in 1902 to write a series of articles about American railroads for the *London Times*. He was amazed to hear railway managers report that the passenger business did not pay and that it was more an expense than a revenue source. It was a given among industry leaders that most of the income and almost all of the benefit came from the freight business. Even so the industry regarded passenger transport as a necessary public service and one not easily closed down. They justified it for its advertising value; it was the showy side of the business. The newspapers largely ignored freight operations but would print long accounts of a new express train, the lavish décor of a palace car, the delicacies served in the diner, or dashing performances of a high-wheel passenger engine. If a shipper was happy with the passenger service, he would likely ship over the same line and become a business patron as well as a traveler. At the time of Pratt's visit railroads were a substantial business in terms of employees. The system had, in round numbers, 11,000 conductors; 25,000 trainmen; 70,000 station agents and helpers; and 10,000 telegraphers. The Pullman Palace Car Company employed 18,000 to operate and maintain its 4,000 cars; thousands more worked in repair shops or in track and bridge maintenance. That passenger trains were popular was evident from a visit to one of the great city terminals. In its first year, 1881, Broad Street Station in Philadelphia handled 200 trains a day. Within seven years that number grew to 300. In 1888 there were 1,672 trains a day running out of New York, not including excursion and race track specials. There were stations in Manhattan along the New Jersey waterfront, Queens, and Brooklyn. Seven to eight thousand cars were in daily service moving about 40 million passengers a year in and out of greater New York. Yet a large business is not always a profitable one, especially when the great numbers are short-haul commuters.

During his tour of America in 1882, Oscar Wilde was greatly impressed with the popularity of railway travel. He quipped that the major occupation of Americans was catching trains. Table 13.1 summarizes railroad passenger operations from 1830 to 1900.

THE OPERATION OF TRAINS

No train could operate on the main line without the permission of the railroad dispatcher. There was no "free will" on an American railway. Each train had a number and was scheduled to leave and arrive at a specific time. It got off the main line to allow superior trains to pass, and it passed inferior trains. The lower the train number, the more important the train. Trains number 1 and 2 were generally the fast mail or top express. Trains with a high number – the 221, for example – were locals of little prestige or importance. They spent considerable time on a side track so that their superiors might pass. On a single-track railroad the direction of travel could determine who made way. Generally, even numbers were assigned to east- or northbound trains while the west- and southbound trains had the odd numbers. The trains with even numbers had preference over odd-numbered trains of equal rank. The inferior train had to pull into the siding five to ten minutes in advance of the superior train's scheduled arrival. By 1880 many major railroads operated one hundred or more trains a day. The dispatcher was a busy man as he played chicken with these 200-ton giants. It took a cool head and steady nerves to keep the trains running in a steady fashion with no collisions or slowdowns. At this time there were no – or at best few – signals. The dispatcher contacted crews by sending telegraphs to station agents and tower operators along the line, who were to pass written instructions or orders to the crews as the trains passed by. Considering the elementary nature of the system and the number of trains in operation, it is a wonder there were not more accidents.

A typical passenger train of the 1880s would consist of one or two baggage cars and four or five coaches. The baggage or head-end cars carried parcels, mail, newspapers, and express items in addition to the larger pieces of baggage. Small bags and personal items were stowed in racks mounted above the coach seats. Passenger cars would seat sixty people in double seats on either side of a center aisle. These wooden cars would be 60 feet long, 10 feet wide, and about 14 feet high. Such a car would weigh about 25 tons and cost $5,000. More deluxe cars, such as sleepers, ran only on the better trains and required payment of a higher fee. The locomotive would be a common eight-wheeler weighing about 30 tons and costing about $10,000. The tender, a most necessary auxiliary, carried water and fuel. Such a train would weigh around 200 tons altogether and travel along at 35 mph. Because frequent stops were common for coach trains, the average speed would be 25 mph, perhaps less, depending on traffic density, weather conditions, accidents, trade conditions, as well as the condition of the rolling stock. An elderly or poorly maintained engine could affect the schedule greatly. Average mileage for a coach of this era was from 40,000 to 60,000 miles a year. The locomotive could be expected to run about the same mileage. According to the 1880 census, a typical passenger traveled only 27 miles while few main-line trains ran less than one division, or 100 miles, and many operated over much greater distances. According to the same source, the trains ran nearly empty, averaging only 45 passengers at a time during the run. There was clearly much getting on and off.

Some specifics on traffic for the Erie Railway's Delaware Division were reported in *Engineering News* in January 1896. This section of the line was double track, 104 miles long between Port Jervis and Susquehanna, New York. It was a busy trunk line, but less busy than the Pennsylvania or New York Central Railroads. In the summer it handled twenty-four passenger trains and forty freights per day. In winter passenger trains fell to twenty and freights rose to sixty per day. This does not include work trains, specials, or second sections. Some trains were so long that they were divided up into sections. All of the sections operated under one train number and followed one another by about ten minutes. Hence, the first section of train 23 would arrive in Buffalo at 12:05, the second section at 12:15, the third at 12:23, and so on, assuming there were more than three sections. Yet all were counted as one train.

TRAIN CREWS

The operation of passenger trains was labor-intensive. Crews ranged in size from five to seven men and even larger on longer trains. This was especially true before air brakes were common, because one brakeman was required for every two cars. The conductor was captain of the train and supervised the action of the other crew members, including the locomotive engineer (fig. 13.4a-d). Only at his signal did the train start or stop. His actions were, of course, under the general management of the dispatcher. The brakemen were called to man the brake wheels, mounted on the end of cars, by signaling with the locomotive whistle. One short whistle meant "Stop" or "Apply brakes." Two shorts meant "Go ahead" or "Release brakes." The whistle was also used to signal many other matters and actions. The brakemen also worked as the conductor's assistants on board the cars. In addition to tending the brakes, they helped passengers on and off the cars at station stops, tended the heating stoves, and helped the conductor deal with unruly passengers. This included ejecting such individuals in extreme cases, which usually involved intoxication. The brakemen would also tend to the car lamps by adding kerosene and adjusting and trimming the wicks as needed.

13.4. (a) The brakeman turns the brake wheel while standing on the open end platform of the car. (b) The interior of the locomotive's cab is shown from the tender deck. (c) The fireman stokes the firebox while the engineer sits to the right with his hand upon the throttle. (d) The conductor checks his watch and raises his hand to signal "Go ahead" to the engineer.

(All from *Harper's Monthly*, August 1874)

Another duty of the brakeman was to act as flagman if the train stopped for any reason along the main line. One brakeman would walk to the rear of the train for a half mile, while a second brakeman did the same for the front of the train. In daylight they held a red flag, which was useful in warning an approaching train to stop. At night lanterns with red globes were used. Flares and torpedoes were employed to warn approaching trains that another train was just ahead. The torpedo was a small explosive cap strapped to the top of the rail that would blow up with a loud bang when run over by a locomotive. When the tie-up was cleared, the locomotive whistle would signal the flagmen to return to the train. They had best hurry, for the conductor was ready to roll. Most flagmen knew from experience to sprint back or be left behind. This was mainly a young man's job. Competent flagmen were generally promoted to a conductor position after a few years of experience.

The engine crew stayed with the train for one division. At the end of divisions the engine and crew switched off. The engine was cleaned, inspected, lubricated, and turned around to take another train back home at the opposite end of the division. It could operate in this back-and-forth manner for most of its career. The crews worked in the same fashion. They would work their way home on a train heading back to the original terminal. The conductor and his assistants generally worked to the end of the train run, assuming it did not greatly exceed ten to twelve hours, which was the normal working day at the time. The normal work week was six days, and many railroads offered only limited service on Sundays. Yet other lines considered railroading a seven-days-a-week enterprise. They used excuses such as the need to move mail or cattle trains in response to complaints about breaking the observance of the Sabbath. Railroads in New England and the south began as strict observers of the Lord's day. The Boston and Maine Railroad operated a few trains on the Sabbath but required passengers to sign a pledge that they were traveling only to attend services. By the 1880s most railroads, including those in New England, had ended the moratorium on Sunday operations. However, Samuel Sloan, president of the Delaware, Lackawanna, and Western Railroad, was adamant about keeping the policy of no Sunday service for thirty years. It was only when Sloan retired as president of the line that Sunday service was instituted in March 1899. Railroad workers generally supported the curfew on Sunday service, because it gave them one day of rest.

The train conductor was a very important person, because he dealt so directly with the traveling public. Few passengers saw, much less interacted with, railroad officials. If the cars were dirty, the train was late, or the fares were too high, almost the only railroad employee to hear about it was the conductor. Since he was in charge of the train, he was also likely responsible for everything else related to railway operations. He had to deal with all questions and complaints in a dignified yet sympathetic manner. He was at the front line of the industry's public relations. His real responsibility was the train's safety and the collection of tickets and cash fares. Yet he was often asked about connecting trains, tomorrow's weather, how to find a good but cheap hotel, or how late was the train running and would the lost time be made up before reaching Columbus. He watched over children traveling alone and elderly or ill travelers who needed special attention (fig. 13.5). At the same time, he had to admonish passengers not to stick their heads out the car windows nor ride on the open platforms at either end of the coach, lest they become injured. In a time of heavy tobacco use, he had to enforce the unpopular no-smoking rule. Gentlemen

13.5. Passengers cluster around the conductor, all having concerns that require his undivided attention. He stoically deals with them one at a time. The lady seated beside him watches intently as he punches her interline ticket.

(*Scribner's Magazine*, November 1888)

were reminded to keep their boots off the seats. Ladies were told they could not keep their pet dog in the car; the animal, no matter how small or how precious it might be, must ride ahead in the baggage car.

Some conductors showed considerable determination to get their passengers to their destination. One such man was Andrew Quintin of the Camden and Amboy Railroad. In January 1841 his train was stopped by a flood near Trenton, New Jersey. Quintin found several rowboats to ferry his patrons down the line, where a second train got them as far as a bridge over Rancocas Creek. The floodwaters damaged the bridge, so the train could not pass over it, but the gallant conductor walked his flock over the structure. He then garnered several farm wagons and proceeded toward Burlington, but they were once again stopped by rising waters. Local farmers took in the soggy travelers for the night. The next morning Quintin and the farmers fashioned several rafts from barn doors. The travelers and train crew poled their way to the next depot, where a train took them to the end of the line at Camden. Quintin continued to work as a conductor until almost his last day. There were few retirement plans for ordinary working-class people at this time.

Some less-scrupulous conductors had their own retirement plan under way. The collecting of cash fares tempted some to pocket a goodly part of the company's money. Since the conductors were responsible for accounting for what was collected, there was no effective way to document what they reported. The conductors were paid a better-than-average wage in the Victorian era of from $3 to $4 dollars a day, yet some seemed to enjoy homes and lifestyles well beyond that wage. Railroad managers believed embezzlement was a common crime and employed detectives or spotters to check on the conductors' work habits. When enough evidence was in hand, the men were dismissed. The Concord Railroad fired all of its conductors in 1865 to clean out such swindlers. Some years later the Philadelphia and Reading claimed its conductors kept 32 percent of the cash fares collected. The problem was never completely solved, but many conductors were totally honest men. It is also true that passengers and ticket scalpers devised elaborate schemes to defraud the railroad industry of its revenue. Counterfeit tickets were common during this time. The Victorian era was no more honest than the present one.

The popular notion of a railroad conductor is a figure in a dark blue uniform with bright gold buttons. Such was not the case for the first generation of conductors. They strongly resisted the regimentation of a uniform. They dressed as businessmen of the time in a dark suit and a top hat, although they might wear a badge denoting their position. Uniforms were fine for the military but were not sought by train captains. The Erie Railroad required train crews to wear uniforms in 1855. This requirement was not popular, but conductors wishing to hold their positions were forced to do as ordered. The editor of *American Railroad Journal* saw the imposition of uniforms as akin to European nobility love of showy dress for their servants and as such was alien to our democratic ideas about dress. By the late 1860s the uniform was accepted, in part because the public wanted a way to identify the train crew more easily. Within a few years the uniform was an industry-wide standard on major railroads.

Child labor was quite common during the nineteenth century in just about every industry. Railroads employed boys for a special purpose on trains. A railroad boy was called by many names: *train boy, news butcher, the butch,* or *the news agent* were common. Most passengers found these persistent lads a nuisance and referred to them as *little devils, imps of Satan,* or *apprentice hoodlums*. They were usually poor boys off the streets with little education, few manners, and fewer scruples. They also were generally aggressive, rude, and annoying as they passed through cars offering a variety of goods for sale. Newspapers, magazines, and cheap books were pushed eagerly. Apples, candy, coffee, and even ice cream were also offered. The Union News Company also employed the boys and contracted with major railroads to run the service.

It was the repeated appearance of the boys that was so tiresome. And not all of the boys were so nasty; some could be charming and decent. Those who were tended to sell more and make friends with the passengers. A few became well known later in life. Thomas Edison is likely the most famous example. A clever newsboy could make as much as $20 a week, which was far more than that of an adult day laborer, who generally earned $6 a week. The job began to disappear by the beginning of the twentieth century. Station newsstands were established to serve the passengers.

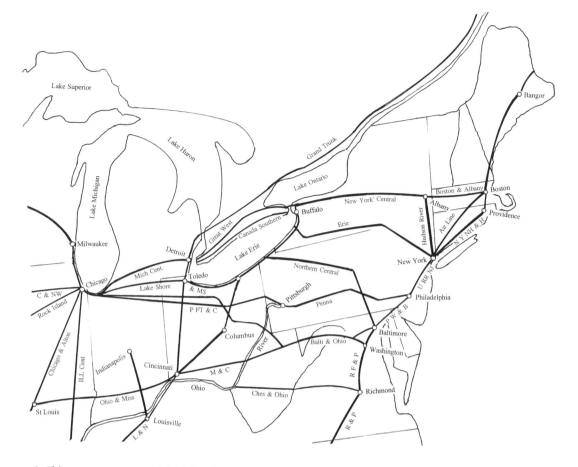

13.6. This map shows some of the major trunk lines in the eastern half of the United States in about 1880. A map of the complete system would be too dense in this small scale to label the individual lines.

(Author's collection)

Child labor laws and enforcement of school truancy did much to end the employment of younger workers. The train boy has been gone from the American scene for so long that his history is mostly unknown today.

PIONEER RAILROADS

Railroad fever was epidemic in America by 1830, with dozens of railroads chartered or under way. New England's first public railroad, the Boston and Lowell, was a gilt-edged property financed by Patrick T. Jackson and some of his wealthy associates. It began operations in May 1835, built a long bridge into Boston, and by 1838 was operating 1,711 passenger trains a year. By the late 1880s the Boston and Lowell was almost 900 miles long and carried more than seven million passengers a year. New England was covered with a dense railway network by this time. Much of the mileage was consolidated into three systems: the Boston and Maine; the New York, New Haven, and Hartford; and the Maine Central (fig. 13.6).

The Middle Atlantic states were ahead of New England in getting started in building railroads. The Baltimore and Ohio Railroad was chartered in 1827 to build a long and expensive line across the Alleghenies to

Table 13.2. Passenger Service on the Big Three Railroads, 1855–1895

Year	Baltimore and Ohio		New York Central		Pennsylvania (Main Line Only)	
	Passengers Carried	Passenger Revenue	Passengers Carried	Passenger Revenue	Passengers Carried	Passenger Revenue
1855	599,000 B	$911,000	X	$3.14 M	798,000	1.25 M
1865	NP	$3.99 M	5,851,000	$6.62 M	2,861,000	$5.45 M
1875	NP	$1.73 M	9,422,000	$7.27 M	5,609,000	$3.77 M
1885	NP	$1.83 M	12,747,000	$6.21 M	12,341,000	$5.49 M
1895	8,207,000	$5.04 M	24,135,900	$13.0 M	21,402,000	$9.18 M

the Ohio River. The first train began services in May 1830 with horses rather than steam power. Finding the capital to complete such an ambitious project was the major obstacle faced by the B&O. It did not reach Wheeling until Christmas Eve of 1852. Meanwhile its rivals were already working on connections to Chicago. The Erie Railway opened to Dunkirk, New York, on Lake Erie in 1851. The first predecessor of the New York Central Railroad ran its inaugural train between Albany and Schenectady on August 9, 1831. A locomotive named ironically for the canal champion DeWitt Clinton pulled the train. It was a slender, light machine that resembled a racehorse; however, despite its fleet appearance it was a poor performer and was retired after only a few years. Yet it performed well enough on the opening trip of the Mohawk and Hudson Railroad. The crowd was large, so five or six flatcars fitted with temporary bench seats were added to the three stagecoach-style coaches. The asthmatic DeWitt Clinton propelled its long train surprisingly well at speeds up to 30 mph. However, the only way to maintain steam was to feed pitch-pine logs into the firebox. A torrent of sparks and burning embers blew out of the smokestacks. Some passengers raised their umbrellas to fend off the sparks but threw them away after they burst into flames. The sparks continued to rain down, igniting hats, hair, and clothing. Fortunately the trip was only 17 miles, and excellent refreshments awaited the excursionists at the end of their incendiary journey.

The New York Central grew into one of the giant rail systems of America. After Cornelius Vanderbilt became president in 1867, the railroad gained control of major western links such as the Michigan Central; the Lake Shore and Michigan Southern; and the Cleveland, Cincinnati, Chicago, and St. Louis Railroads. The Pennsylvania Railroad finished its main line between Philadelphia and Pittsburgh in 1854 but raced ahead with considerable energy to rival the Vanderbilt lines in traffic, mileage, and income. Table 13.2 explains how the Big Three evolved over the years in terms of passenger traffic.

The division of passenger traffic by region was by no means equal. The eastern half of the country carried the bulk of the passengers, yet

M = million

NP = Not Published

X = In 1858 the New York Central carried 2.25 M passengers; only 7 percent were through travelers.

B = More than half were carried over the 40-mile Washington Branch.

Source: *Poor's Manual of Railroads* (New York: H. V. and H. W. Poor, various years); *American Railroad Journal*.

Table 13.3. Division of U.S. Railroad Passengers by Region in 1893

Region	Passengers Carried	Mileage of Railroad	Areas Served
New England States	32.4 M	7,139	Maine, Vermont, Connecticut, etc.
Middle States	87.1 M	30,413	New York, New Jersey, Pennsylvania, etc.
Central Northern	111.1 M	53,582	Ohio, Michigan, Illinois, etc.
South Atlantic	22.3 M	18,171	Virginia, Florida, South Carolina, etc.
Gulf & Mississippi Valley	16.6 M	11,134	Alabama, Tennessee, Kentucky, etc.
Southwestern	30.7 M	30,777	Missouri, Texas, Arkansas
Northwestern	24.3 M	21,882	Iowa, Nebraska, Montana, etc.
Pacific States	22.5 M	10,273	California, Nevada, Oregon, etc.

M = million

Source: *Poor's Manual of Railroads* (New York: H. V. and H. W. Poor, 1894).

this generated no envy on the part of the western lines. They were content to be largely freight carriers, because a boxcar full of grain created more profit and far fewer management problems than a coach full of passengers. The division of passengers by region in 1893 is outlined in table 13.3.

The Old South showed surprising energy in moving into railroading. The South Carolina Canal and Railroad Company began operations in December 1830 with a small American-made locomotive. It was named the Best Friend of Charleston. This small engine weighed just 3¾ tons yet proved capable of pulling four cars filled with passengers at an average speed of 12 mph, and running alone it raced along at 30 mph. Sadly, the Best Friend blew up in June of the following year. No passengers were harmed, but to reassure its future travelers the railroad placed a barricade of cotton bales on a flatcar between the locomotive and passenger cars. The 136-mile-long railroad was completed with considerable speed and reached Hamburg, Georgia, by October 1833. The pace of southern railroad construction did not, however, keep up with this pioneering effort. The Confederate states in general had less mileage than their northern counterparts. By 1860 the South had a system of just 9,000 miles when the North could boast of 21,000 miles.

Railroad lines west of the Alleghenies were projected early but often got off to a slow, if not uncertain, start. Kentucky's pioneer railroad, the Lexington and Ohio, began to run cars over a short length of track in the summer of 1832, yet the railroad remained incomplete until 1852. The Erie and Kalamazoo Railroad connected Toledo, Ohio, and Adrian, Michigan, in 1836 and prospered for a few years. By late 1841, however, its trains could not always complete a trip on one run. The engines ran out of fuel and water, and passengers were forced to walk the final 4 miles. Yet matters would greatly improve over the next decade as the Midwest was covered by one of the densest networks of railroad iron in the world. Chicago had

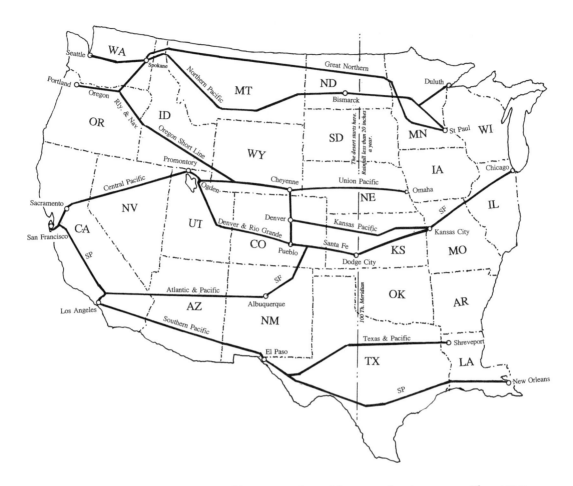

13.7. The western railroad network was much less complete than the eastern systems but served the under-populated region adequately. This map represents the West at the end of the frontier in 1890.

(Author's collection)

become the American railroad capital by 1860 and would grow to be the country's second largest city. On the eve of the Civil War eleven railroads entered Chicago; long-distance travelers could not go east or west without changing trains there. By 1900 the city had grown to 1.7 million and had five downtown stations serving twenty-three railroads and about eleven hundred passenger trains a day.

Lines west of the Mississippi River began to appear in the 1850s. The Pacific Railroad started construction at St. Louis in 1851 and made only slow progress in its march toward the state capital of Jefferson City. Construction of the Hannibal and St. Joseph line got under way in the spring of 1853 but did not reach St. Joseph, some 207 miles west of the Mississippi River, until six years later. It served as the western terminal for stagecoaches to the Pacific Coast until serious work began on the transcontinental railroad at the close of the Civil War. The pioneer railroad in the far West was the Sacramento Valley line, chartered in August 1852. It was not an ambitious project, but it was a beginning of America's Pacific Coast rail network. It would remain a much less dense system than the network in the eastern half of the nation. The small population and lack of major settlements in the West required a sparse system with great open spaces

Table 13.4. Rail Passengers and Revenue in the Western United States, 1870–1900

	Atchinson, Topeka & Santa Fe		Union Pacific		Northern Pacific	
Year	Passengers Carried	Passenger Revenue	Passengers Carried	Passenger Revenue	Passengers Carried	Passenger Revenue
1870	X	NA	142,600	$3.81 M	73,000 (1871)	NA
1880	381,000	$1.78 M	807,000 (1881)	$5.13 M	178,000 (1881)	$668,000
1890	1.29 M	$1.29 M	1.47 M	$4.22 M	2.21 M	$6.16 M
1900	4.81 M	$9.33 M	1.76 M	$4.03 M	2.34 M	$6.21 M

M = million
X = Atlantic & Pacific carried 86,000 passengers in 1871–Predecessor of AT & SF
Source: *Poor's Manual of Railroads* (New York: H. V. and H. W. Poor, various years); *American Railroad Journal*.

separating the Union Pacific and the Northern Pacific from other trunk lines in the region (fig. 13.7).

A MAJOR TRAVEL CORRIDOR

The heaviest travel routes tend to run between cities, and when they are found in a string, such is true along the Atlantic Coast, we have a travel corridor. Boston and New York are at the north end of this chain, and travel by stagecoach and coastal ships was well established along this route a century before the appearance of the iron horse. A popular route ran west from Boston to Springfield, Massachusetts, and then east along the Connecticut River through New Haven, Connecticut, and finally south to New York. It was about 230 miles long. An all-rail route along the path developed slowly during the 1830s and 1840s. By October 1839 the Western Railroad reached Springfield. The New Haven and Hartford Railroad opened seven months later and eventually promoted a second line to Springfield that began operations late in 1844. It was another four years before New York and New Haven met the New York and Harlem Railroad at Williams Bridge, just six miles north of Manhattan Island. The Harlem line allowed its Yankee neighbor to use its tracks and depot to enter New York City for a hefty annual fee. These several railroads formed a continuous rail line between Boston and New York. The system was completed by December 1848. The Harlem line's new Grand Central Station was shared with the New Haven line in 1872. By the middle 1880s the fastest train ran in just six hours. Other expresses required over nine hours for the Boston-to-New-York trip. The daily passenger load was about a thousand a day, but that was divided among four different lines. Typically the travel season traffic was greater in the summer than in the winter.

A second direct line between these two cities was assembled in the same fashion eleven years later. It became known as the Shore line and followed Long Island Sound from New Haven through the town of Old Saybrook at the mouth of the Connecticut River, on to New London at

the mouth of the Thames River, and on to Providence and into Boston (fig. 13.8). The mileage was identical to the Springfield line; however, the route had a few disadvantages, notably the two wide river crossings at Old Saybrook and New London. Bridges were considered too costly, so car ferries were employed to move the trains. This was annoying to the passengers, because each crossing represented another delay. In 1870 a bridge was completed over the Connecticut River, but the New London span was not finished until 1889. By this time the New York, New Haven, and Hartford Railroad had consolidated most of the lines in southern New England. Today the Shore line is part of Amtrak's high-speed Northeast Corridor. Few modern travelers are aware of the ancient origins of this high-speed rail line.

The southern end of the Northeast Corridor was by far the busier portion. It connected New York with Washington, 220 miles, and passed through Trenton, Philadelphia, Wilmington, and Baltimore along the way. It was a flat and uninspiring landscape but perfect for railroad building. Five railroads formed links in this chain, but none were built with the intention of doing so; hence there were serious defects in the line for through service. First in line was the Camden and Amboy (C&A) Railroad, which offered a land and sea connection between New York and Philadelphia. It was a makeshift connection that involved a 23-mile

13.8. Railroads tended to build along rivers. It was an easy way to find a comparatively level grade. This image dates from the 1870s and shows a Springfield, Athol and North Eastern train standing alongside the Swift River about 25 miles south of Athol, Massachusetts. This track is now submerged below the Quabbin Reservoir.

(Author's collection)

steamship ride from South Ferry in New York around Staten Island to South Amboy, New Jersey. A railroad carried passengers for 63 miles to Camden, where a ferry took them across the Delaware River to Philadelphia. Service began early in 1834. The C&A devised a better all-land route five years later between Trenton and New Brunswick that connected to the New Jersey Railroad and Transportation Company at Jersey City. The New Jersey line began in Jersey City and had a ferry connection across the Hudson River to New York City. A few years earlier the C&A had purchased the Philadelphia and Trenton Railroad and thus could offer an all-rail route between the two largest cities in the nation. This line was soon carrying one thousand passengers a day. However, there was a gap at Philadelphia of 2½ miles between the Philadelphia and Trenton station and that of the southern connection, the Philadelphia, Wilmington, and Baltimore Railroad. Travelers complained because the omnibus drivers waited to fill every seat, and this delayed those wanting to proceed. The trip across town was slow and rough. This part of the journey between New York and Washington was considered the most tedious and disagreeable. Yet it was not corrected until 1863.

Once aboard the Philadelphia, Wilmington, and Baltimore, all proceeded smoothly until the train approached the Susquehanna River, about 60 miles south of Philadelphia. There was no bridge, because the river widened out to become Chesapeake Bay, so at the point of crossing the waterway was a mile wide. A bridge of this size was too costly, so a ferry boat took passengers across. Travelers were asked to leave their seats and walk down a gravel trail to the boat. The vessel had a rooftop track so that the baggage cars could be ferried across the estuary. Meals were served aboard the ferry. On reaching the opposite shore, the passengers climbed a gravel path uphill to an awaiting train. The baggage cars were pulled off the boat and connected to the rear of the train. Off it went, racing along the west bank of the Chesapeake Bay toward Baltimore, where another hiatus was encountered. The train stopped at the President Street station on the north side of Baltimore. The Baltimore and Ohio station was one mile to the southwest. Passengers bound for Washington were advised to remain in their seats. The cars were uncoupled and moved one by one by powerful teams of horses through the street of the city on tracks buried in the pavement. A driver stood on the platform at one end of the car as the team trotted along. An English traveler named Alfred Pairpoint wrote that the driver called to the horses, "Get up, Miss Nancy," "Get up, Massa Pete," as the car rolled ahead. After reaching the B&O station the cars were coupled to the waiting train, and after the baggage was put on board, the train left for Washington.

Horace Greeley once quipped that "the chief miseries of travelling are changing cars and crossing ferries." Modern readers can better understand

Greeley's sentiments after reading this account of the Northeast Corridor. It should be understood that changing cars was routine in early railroad travel, because through cars were a rarity. Conductors would explain, "You must move to the last three cars; those are the through cars to Washington. This car will be switched off at Baltimore for York." Or he might explain to a hungry passenger, "Sorry, the diner was dropped off last night at Trenton."

For all the complications and frustrations of travel, matters did improve along the corridor. In June 1846 the *American Railroad Journal* reported the trip from Jersey City to Washington required sixteen and a half hours. By 1860 the fastest train made the journey in almost eleven hours. By 1885 the best train was down to just six hours. The Civil War created a traffic crisis, especially on the lower end of the corridor from Baltimore to Washington. The B&O opened this 40-mile segment in 1835 and made few improvements, because they enjoyed a monopoly. The time was cut by thirty minutes from two hours in 1854. Traffic there was over three hundred thousand – more passengers than were carried on the main line to Wheeling. But it remained a single track, and as traffic escalated during the war years this branch line was overwhelmed. Double tracking was completed in 1864, but only after Congress, with considerable public approval, threatened to seize the line. At the same time, the Camden and Amboy Railroad rebuilt its line belatedly. Double track and the elimination of many curves improved it greatly. After much talk about a bridge over the Susquehanna, the Philadelphia, Wilmington, and Baltimore Railroad finally finished the structure late in 1866. A temporary loop was hooked up in 1863 to take trains around Philadelphia, which ended the hellish omnibus ride. A more direct line that went by the Zoo Junction was opened in 1867 and remains in use today. The B&O finally abandoned the transfer of cars through downtown Baltimore in 1880. It lost its monopoly of serving Washington, D.C., in 1872 when the Pennsylvania Railroad built its own line into the nation's capital and placed a station on the mall where the National Gallery of Art now stands. That station was removed when Washington's Union Station was completed in 1907.

Travelers heading south of Washington along the Atlantic Coast found only a fragmentary series of railroads ready for service in the antebellum era. In a region devoted to fox hunting and genteel living, railroads seemed less necessary. Even so, southern merchants and some state governments showed energy in promoting the iron horse. By the middle 1840s part of the journey was made by railroad, but to go beyond Wilmington, North Carolina, coastal vessels became a necessity. At this time through tickets were not available, so at each transfer place it was necessary to buy tickets and transfer luggage. Paper money was accepted only at a discount, and few travelers carried enough gold coinage, because it was scarce. Porters were also hard to find, so passengers were required to carry their own luggage. Those missing a connection would likely have to lay over a day. In short, train travel was not easy or convenient. Interline or coupon tickets were introduced in the 1850s that permitted passengers to travel over several railroads, thus ending the tedious task of re-ticketing at the depot of each new railroad.

The trip from Washington began by steamer. Travelers left from the Seventh Street wharf about eight blocks south of the capitol. This was a pleasant three-hour trip on the Potomac River. The boat passed Mt. Vernon on the 55-mile journey to Acquia Creek. Passengers then gathered together their luggage and children and walked uphill to a waiting Richmond, Fredericksburg, and Potomac Railroad train. On reaching the Virginia capital, travelers rode across town by omnibus to the Petersburg Railroad depot. Before leaving Richmond experienced travelers knew to purchase a lunch basket for the trip ahead. Another transfer was made at Weldon, North Carolina. The Wilmington and Weldon was the longest railroad in the nation when it was completed in 1840. On reaching Wilmington the traveler was 380 miles south of Washington, D.C. Those heading to Charleston could proceed by stagecoach or coastal steamer. Most travelers wisely chose the steamer for greater comfort and better food. The journey could be made in three and a half days from New York if all connections were made and the weather was cooperative, but four days was a more realistic timetable. Going on to New Orleans required a little over seven days from New York. Some travelers used a shortcut – the Florida Railroad – that cut across the state from Fernandina on the Atlantic Coast of the state to Cedar Key on the Gulf Coast. Steamers at either end made the connections. The Mobile and New Orleans Mail Route advised travelers to avoid the Florida shortcut because of the swamps, illness, and hazards of Indian attacks.

Travelers could also go the long way around to reach New Orleans. By 1842 the B&O Railroad carried southbound travelers to Cumberland, Maryland. A stage ride to Brownsville, Pennsylvania, connected with steamboats on the Monongahela River to Pittsburgh. There was an abundance of river steamers heading south at the headwaters of the Ohio River. The time from Baltimore to Pittsburgh was about thirty-four hours. The river journey to New Orleans was almost eleven days. The total time for this 2,000-mile journey would be twelve days and ten hours. The cost – an estimated $45. It was a slow but comfortable and inexpensive way to go a great distance.

As the southern railroads filled in, the speed of travel increased. *Railway Age* in July 1880 proudly explained that modern travelers could go to New Orleans from New York in sixty hours and forty-five minutes with only one change of cars. In 1866 the same trip had required five days and nine changes.

FARES AND SPEED

The basic rule for figuring American railroad fare in the Victorian era was 3 cents a mile. As is true with simple rules, however, there are exceptions. Southern and western fares tended to be higher because the amount of traffic was smaller, so there were fewer customers to share in the costs. In 1839 the Western and Atlantic Railroad raised its fare from 5 cents to 7½ cents. The Petersburg Railroad charged 8 cents a mile in 1840. What likely was the highest coach fare in the United States was charged by Colorado's Silverton Railroad; in 1889 the fare was 20 cents a mile on this mountainous short line.

In general, U.S. coach fares declined because there were so many special deals. The 1880 census gives the average fare as 1.71 cents per mile. Consider that children between five and twelve years old were charged half fare and those under five rode free. Commuters were offered substantial discounts by buying seasonal passes or booklets of tickets. Many rode for less than ½ cent a mile. Excursion tickets were sold at this extraordinarily low rate to groups, religious, fraternal orders, veterans, and so on, by railroad ticket agents eager to fill up empty seats. The Grand Army of the Republic was a good traffic generator for the nation's railroads. This Civil War veterans group had more than four hundred thousand members by 1890, and its annual meetings attracted thousands of them. It was only one such organization that helped swell passenger travel. Most railroads reported low average train loads, often only enough to fill one car. While fares much below 3 cents a mile were less than operating costs, any and all revenue was welcome. There were one-day excursion tickets available to an individual, but they were good only for the date specified or on the train number specified. Single travelers could also avail themselves of a 1,000-mile ticket. Coupons attached were removed by the conductor, and the traveler could keep going when and where he pleased until the final mileage had been traveled.

Some railroads offered a discount if you paid in gold. The Central Pacific Railroad offered a $27.50 discount on a $150.00 Sacramento-to-New-York fare, an example of what low esteem greenbacks were held in the western states. Another way to render a discount was to create classes. European lines did this routinely and offered first-, second-, and third-class accommodations. In the United States regular coaches were considered first class. However, a few railroads went the class route. In 1865 the Camden and Amboy Railroad offered first-class coach fares from New

York to Philadelphia at $3.00, accommodation at $2.25, second class at $1.75, and immigrant at $1.50. A higher fare meant newer cars, more space per passenger, better seating, and a more deluxe car. To travel by Pullman the coach fare was collected by the railroad, and an extra charge, usually $1.00 or $2.00, was collected by the Pullman Company for a berth or parlor car seat. Drawing rooms were available at an extra charge as well. The Pullman Company would furnish a private car, complete with attendants, for $85 a day. In 1881 the Pennsylvania Railroad began running a fast-moving "limited" train between New York and Chicago. In April of the following year they added a surcharge of $4.00 to the first-class fare because of high operating costs. Since the train was patronized largely by wealthy travelers, it was accepted and helped guarantee that only the elite would ride upon its velvet cushions.

The free pass was one of the great ironies of railway travel; it allowed the rich and powerful to ride at no cost while the poorer classes generally paid full fare. The pass was an elegant printed piece of cardboard given out routinely to railroad officials, members of Congress and state legislators, judges, bankers, and other fat cats who might be of service should a railroad need help. They were good for one year, although some were marked for shorter periods of time. Half-fare passes were also given to clergymen, although just why these men of God were considered less worthy than a banker or politician was never explained. There was much newsprint on the evils of the pass systems. It was outlawed during the Progressive Era in 1906 by the Hepburn Act, which greatly expanded the power of the Interstate Commerce Commission.

The public enjoyed bargain fares during one of the rate wars that seemed to erupt every few years. In 1855 the Erie and New York Central Railroads engaged in such combat. The New-York-to-Buffalo fare dropped to $6.50. The rivals finally agreed to end this ruinous practice, but it started all over again two years later. The Centennial Exposition of 1876 prompted a rate war over fares between New York and Chicago. They fell to $18 and then to $13 before the battle subsided. The practice of ticket scalping was alive and well before professional sports became established. Dealers in secondhand tickets maintained offices in every city and had confederates stationed in all large depots. Less-scrupulous dealers sold counterfeit tickets or used tickets that were artfully reconstructed so as to look like new.

When railways were introduced, the public wanted to know, How fast will it go? The human race is fascinated with speed; poets of the day were inspired by King Steam's prospect of "Rattling over ridges / Shooting under the arches, rumbling over bridges / Whizzing through the mountains, buzzing o'er the vale, – / Bless me! this is pleasant, riding on the rail!"

13.9. The ornamental ticket was issued by the Boston and Worcester Railroad in about 1837.

(*Scribner's Magazine*, September, 1888)

Railroad managers, however, were considerably less whimsical when it came to speed. They believed the important question was, How fast *should* it go? In their view, operating costs and safety were the main issues to consider. In his 1861 book on railway management John B. Jervis, a prominent Victorian civil engineer, explained that cost increases as speed increases. The cost of running a train is doubled by running it at 30 mph instead of 20. It's more than just fuel. The wear and tear on the rolling stock, track, and bridges are also costly. Put another way, a 20 percent increase in speed requires a 50 percent increase in horsepower. Many northern railroads reduced running speeds during the winter because rails, axles, and wheels tended to break more readily in frigid temperatures. It was necessary to cut back schedules because frozen roadbeds made the track so rigid and unyielding that locomotive-driving wheel spokes were breaking. So many engines were out of service, it was necessary to borrow locomotives from connecting lines.

Stopping the train was another safety issue exacerbated by high operating speeds. An alert crew could stop a train traveling at 30 mph in 450 feet. Not all crews were alert, or were distracted by other matters, and might not get to the brake wheels as the whistle signaled "Down brakes." A slow-moving brakeman could increase the braking distance to 1,600 feet. Air brakes were introduced in 1869 that stopped trains going 30 mph in 380 feet. Some railroads, such as the Pennsylvania, had all passenger cars equipped with Westinghouse's brake by 1879. Other railroads moved more slowly. Freight trains were not fully equipped with this improvement until the early twentieth century.

Costs and safety be hanged, the public wanted speed. Oliver Evans, the early millwright and engine builder, speculated in 1813 that steam power would carry passengers "almost as fast as birds fly, fifteen or twenty miles an hour." Evans continued in his dream of the future, where travelers would breakfast in Baltimore and take dinner in New York all in the same day. It happened sooner than most of Evans's contemporaries could imagine. The steam locomotive showed its capacity for speed since its first appearance in America. Mention has already been made of the Best Friend and DeWitt Clinton running at 30 mph in 1830 and 1831. Two years later M. W. Baldwin's first locomotive, Old Ironsides, was timed at 62 mph by Professor Robert M. Patterson of the University of Virginia. The Experiment, of 1832, as rebuilt during 1833, ran 13 miles over the Mohawk and Hudson Railroad in fourteen minutes, including one stop for water. It was timed at 45 seconds for 1 mile of this extraordinary test. Other first-generation American locomotives demonstrated their ability to run fast. So why not fast trains? The track was not up to the fast running on a day-to-day basis. With few exceptions, tracks were cheaply built and intended for slow-speed operation. The cost and stopping problems were not eliminated just because the engine could be run at a mile a minute.

America's pioneer lines ran at very modest speeds. In 1841 Gerstner concluded after observing every railroad in the nation that most lines were content with 15 mph. In 1843 the ten little railways connecting Albany and Buffalo worked out a through-service scheme to speed passengers across the Empire State. The fastest train required twenty-five hours to complete the 326-mile journey, making the average speed a little over 12 mph. The main reason for such a tortoiselike pace was the strap-rail trackage. All-iron T rail (named for its shape) was installed by 1850, and running speed was increased to 30 mph. Elsewhere in New York, the Hudson River Railroad opened in 1851 specifically as a fast line. It had to be so in order to compete with the fleet Hudson River Steamer, which offered passengers comfort and cheap fares as well. The Hudson River Railroad was built with heavy rail, deep ballast, and used express locomotives. The express trains averaged 35 mph and made only a limited number of stops.

Long-distance trains, however, tended to average little better than 20 to 25 mph. In the 1870s both the New York Central and Pennsylvania Railroad's fastest New-York-to-Chicago trip required thirty-six hours. Frequent stops were one cause for slow time. Stopping for meals never took less than twenty minutes and often consumed thirty minutes. It was also necessary to slow down when going through a city or a railroad yard, or for a signal, a train ahead, pedestrians or cattle on the track, and many other reasons. By the 1880s the New York Central speeded up its best New-York-to-Chicago trains to twenty-four hours by eliminating all meal stops and limiting stations stops to eight. Just those eight stops consumed fifty-five minutes. Slowing down cost another three hours. Changing engines every 100 miles and refueling and taking water added to the slowdown. Nine engine changes were reduced to six, and track pans were installed so that water could be picked up on the fly. This latter idea was first used in England in 1860 and came to this country about a decade later. It is important to remember that coach passengers rode on secondary trains that ran at slower speeds because they stopped more often and were not prestigious-name trains, hence no one expected first-class service. Speed was costly, so only those willing and able to pay could afford extra-fare trains such as the Twentieth Century Limited (1902), which reached Chicago in twenty hours and made only one stop between Manhattan and Chicago.

During the Victorian period western trains demonstrated little get up and go. When the transcontinental railroad opened in 1868, no one expected a fast ride on a new railroad. It would take time for the track and roadbed to settle. Westbound from Omaha to Promontory, Utah, required fifty-four hours; the eastbound journey was six hours longer. It took one hundred hours to reach Sacramento from Omaha, a distance of 1,776 miles. The Central Pacific portion of the line was slower than the Union Pacific because of the mountains. A special Pullman train was put on in December 1869 that cut nineteen hours from the schedule, because there was a change of cars at Promontory and no meal stops, since hotel cars with onboard food services were used. The train was poorly patronized and was discontinued after one year. Travel from New York to San Francisco took a little over six days.

In 1876 Jarrett and Palmer, a New York theatrical company, hired a special train to carry them to San Francisco as fast as possible. Several railroads, including the Pennsylvania and Union Pacific, agreed to do their best. A bold plan was developed that would reduce the time by almost half. The train left on June 1 from Jersey City to see what the small locomotive and wooden cars of the time could accomplish. A single engine pulled the train from Jersey City to Pittsburgh in ten hours and five minutes, averaging 43.4 mph. On and on the little three-car train raced. The Pittsburgh, Ft. Wayne, and Chicago and the Chicago and North Western Railroads maintained an average speed of just over 40 mph. The Union Pacific took over at Omaha and, to the astonishment of some railroad men, kept up with its eastern competitors. At Ogden the Central Pacific would run the final leg of the trip to Oakland. A single locomotive, the Black Fox, made the entire 876-mile trip. It was a tour de force at 83 hours and 32 minutes coast to coast, compared to the normal time of 151 hours. From that time forward the question was repeated, Why can't we have a fast train to the West Coast? Railroaders would explain that the Jarrett and Palmer trip was a stunt only, possible by an extraordinary effort and not possible on a day-to-day basis.

Note: As the fares by railway are consistently varying and time-tables vary widely by different trains, the mail time and passenger fares above are given to be taken as approximately correct.

Compiled from the War Department Table of Distances and the Time Tables and Tariffs of the various railways.

Source: *American Almanac and Repository of Useful Knowledge* (Boston: Gray and Bowen; New York: G. C. and H. Carvill, 1881).

Table 13.5. Railroad Travel Data 1881 between New York City and Other Major U.S. Cities

Cities	Time when it is 12 noon in N.Y.	Distance by rail from N.Y. in miles	Mail time from N.Y. in hours	Fares from N.Y. in dollars/cents
Albany, N.Y.	12:01 PM	145	4.15	3.10
Atlanta, Ga.	11:18 AM	881	52.15	25.50
Baltimore, Md.	11:50 AM	188	6.0	6.20
Boston, Mass	12:12 PM	233	8.0	6.00
Buffalo, N.Y.	11:40 AM	424	14.0	9.25
Charleston, S.C.	11:36 AM	801	33.0	24.00
Chicago, Ill.	11:05 AM	913	35.0	20.00
Cincinnati, O.	11:18 AM	758	28.0	18.00
Denver, Col.	9:57 AM	1,982	92.0	59.75
De Moines, Iowa	10:42 AM	1,270	51.10	31.20
Detroit, Mich.	11:24 AM	776	24.0	15.00
Fort Wayne, Ind.	11:15 AM	765	29.0	16.75
Memphis, Tenn.	10:55 AM	1,245	50.0	32.00
Milwaukee, Wisc.	11:05 AM	9,98	40.0	23.00
Nashville, Tenn.	11:09 AM	1,053	43.0	29.45
New Orleans, La.	10:56 AM	1,377	58.0	12.75
Omaha, Neb.	10:32 AM	1,406	56.20	36.00
Philadelphia, Pa.	11:55 AM	89	2.0	2.50
Pittsburg, Pa.	11:36 AM	445	15.0	12.50
Portland, Me.	12:15 PM	341	14.0	9.00
Richmond, Va.	11:46 AM	343	13.0	12.85
St. Louis, Mo.	10:55 AM	1,066	38.0	24.25
St. Paul, Minn.	10:44 AM	1,322	54.0	31.35
Salt Lake City, Utah	9:28 AM	2,476	120.0	115.50
San Antonio, Tex.	10:23 AM	1,952	104.0	67.05
San Francisco, Cal.	8:46 AM	3,273	151.0	136.00
Washington, D.C.	11:48 AM	228	8.0	7.50

Schedules remained frozen for another decade. On November 13, 1887, the Union Pacific Railroad put in service the Overland Flyer trains number 3 and 4. The Central Pacific carried the same cars on to Oakland. The schedule was seventy-eight hours from Omaha to Oakland, or thirty-one hours slower than the Jarrett and Palmer train, but still an improvement over the standard schedule. The scheduled time might be better, but the actual time was a disappointment, for numbers 3 and 4 were rarely on time. In October 1899 a critical western newspaper printed humorous stories about the Overland Flyer that failed to fly. The ordinary slow pace of the train was made worse by being consistently late. Thirty minutes was acceptable, but five to nine hours late, even in fair weather, was shameful. In 1903 E. H. Harriman, president of the Union Pacific Railroad, talked boldly about an eighty-four-hour coast-to-coast train, but for all of his management skills, he failed to deliver this promise before his death in 1909.

13.10. Four-wheel cars were common on the first American railroads. The stagecoach style is shown, and the omnibus style is at the end of the train. Baggage was placed on the roof, and if the train was crowded, passengers occupied the roof seats. The locomotive would not go far without a tender for fuel and water. Not including the tender in this drawing was the printer's mistake. (Author's collection)

Table 13.5, condensed from the 1881 *American Almanac*, offers an overview of speeds, time, and fares between New York and other U.S. cities.

CARS AND CONSISTS

It was natural to go to coach and carriage builders for the first railroad passenger cars. James Goold and Richard Imlay produced cars based on stagecoaches of the time. Imlay's B&O cars seated twelve inside and another eighteen passenger on the roof seats. These cars were just 13 feet long and weighed 1.75 tons. Other coach builders, such as John Stephenson, built cars based on the city omnibus, but altered the design to include three compartments with side doors for each compartment. The pioneers were all mounted on four wheels and tended to gallop along the tracks like a frisky horse (fig. 13.10). The B&O began experimenting with longer, eight-wheel cars in 1831. They rode more smoothly and would go around fairly short curves, because the wheels were attached to independent underframes called trucks that could swivel or turn. By 1835 the B&O had refined this design for use on the Washington branch. The cars were 37 feet long, seated forty-four passengers in high-back seats, and weighed just 6 tons.

The eight-wheel car was quickly adapted by railroads in all regions of the United States (fig. 13.11). They looked very strange to British visitors, who described them as a long greenhouse on wheels. Dickens, in a contemptuous moment, referred to them as shabby omnibuses, only longer. Many of these vehicles were hardly shabby but were elegantly furnished inside and out. Imlay built large eight-wheelers that had drop-center floors and separate end compartments that featured a ladies' room and toilet at one end and a refreshment bar at the opposite end. The central compartment had a continuous oval seat so that passengers sat in a semicircle facing the center of the car. The paint scheme of one car is recorded by a contemporaries' model: The center body was a bright yellow highlighted with gold leaf and black bands. Fine brown and black lines outlined the gilt bands and window posts. Heraldry was executed in gilt, red, and green. The roof was dark green. The car seated sixty passengers and cost $2,000. Color and ornamental painting remained popular for many years.

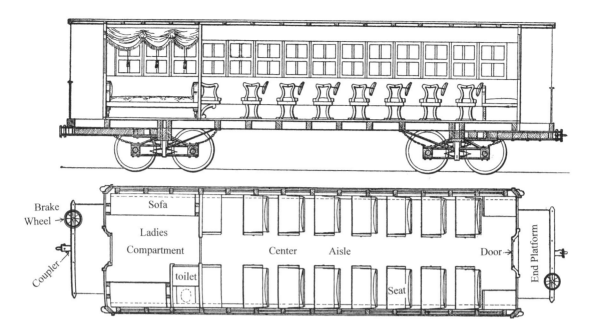

13.11. By the late 1830s the eight-wheel or double-truck car became the standard for passenger cars. Its long body carried more people, and it rode better than the four-wheel cars. This car was built in Cambridgeport, Massachusetts, in the 1840s. The car seated about 37.

(*American Railroad Journal*, August 7, 1845)

A car made by James and Cummins of Jersey City was described by the Jersey City *Daily Sentinel* of February 8, 1849, which said the exterior was claret in color with panels showing the coats-of-arms of New York and Connecticut. The corner of the body was painted to represent a furled American flag with a golden eagle at the top. It was one of a few cars made for the New York and New Haven Railroad.

Imlay's design had merit, but it had too many levels and carved panels to suit railroad managers. They wanted a simple rectangular box, and this is what the standard design became. A fine example is shown in figure 13.11 as built by Davenport and Bridges of Cambridgeport, Massachusetts. This car featured reversible seat backs and a ladies' compartment at one end. It cost $1,700. Notice the toilet off the ladies' compartment. It has a dry hopper, meaning that feces and urine would adhere to the side walls of the hopper. There was no water rinse to clean it, so the toilet soon was as pungent as an outhouse. The interior of a similar car is shown in figure 13.12. It is plain inside and has few decorative elements. The only lighting comes from lamps in one of the end windows at either end of the body. The ceiling height was exaggerated by the artist and was not much over six feet.

Passenger cars took on a new look around 1860 with the introduction of the clerestory roof. By raising the center part of the roof it was possible to add a row of small windows for both light and ventilation over the length of the car (fig. 13.13). It greatly changed the appearance of the car, giving it a lofty and more architectural look. There was also more space in the interior, which allowed center lamps to be installed. Car bodies were expanded during the next several decades, making interiors more roomy and boosting seating capacity. The Chicago and Alton Railroad

13.12. This is the best depiction available for the interior of a mid-century American passenger coach. Its simple and open appearance documents the notion that railway travel was a democratic experience. The artist has exaggerated the ceiling height considerably, however, as it normally would have been just over 6 feet.

(*Illustrated London News*, April 10, 1852)

introduced a large coach in 1870 that was 58 feet long and 10 feet, 3 inches wide with seating for sixty passengers. This ponderous vehicle weighed almost as much as a locomotive of the time. The Pennsylvania Railroad settled on a standard coach design in 1867 that remained in favor for a dozen years (fig. 13.13). It was about 5 feet shorter than the Chicago and Alton coach but featured modern devices such as air brakes, a stove at each end of the car, and gaslights. The *Railroad Gazette* praised the restraint of the interior décor as being "solid, square and honest" without the costly wood veneers or rare imported cabinet woods (fig. 13.14). The only imported product used was the French polished plate glass for the windows. The exterior was covered by sixteen layers of filler, undercoat, color, and varnish. The car weighed 21 tons, seated fifty-two, and cost $5,500. The Altoona shops required forty days to assemble one car of this design.

The wooden car kept growing in size, weight, and complexity into the late Victorian era. One of the largest such coaches was built for the New York Central Railroad in 1893. This giant was 80 feet long and required an elaborate wood truss inside the lower panel and heavy steel truss rods under the floor sills to support its considerable length. The car seated eighty-four, weighed 47½ tons, and cost $8,720.

The number and style of cars in a typical train of the nineteenth century is largely undocumented. It was composed of baggage, mail, express, and passenger cars in accordance with the job of the train. A small local train might consist of a single baggage car and one or two coaches. Locals were referred to as "accommodation" or "way" trains because they accommodated the needs of the great majority of travelers and stopped at all or most stations along the railroad (fig. 13.15). If the train regularly picked up milk cans at most stations, it might need an extra baggage car. If it also

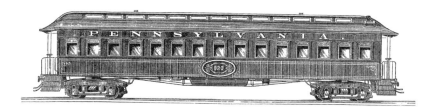

13.13. Around 1860 the appearance of passenger cars was altered by the clerestory roof, which remained a standard feature until the 1930s. This car dates from 1875 and was one of a thousand built at the Pennsylvania Railroad's Altoona shops. The car seated fifty-two.

(William B. Sipes, *The Pennsylvania Railroad*, 1875)

delivered newspapers, this, too, would require another head-end car. The number of coaches depended on how heavy the passenger load was along the line. It could depend on the clientele; if a fair number of passengers were bankers or upper-level management persons, a parlor car would be needed to satisfy such patrons. Farmers, miners, or lumberjacks might be satisfied with an old coach. A well-patronized through train would consist of a mixed variety of cars that would include baggage, mail, coaches, parlor, and sleeping cars. Through trains were for long-distance travelers. They made fewer stops and would bypass small stations. The makeup, or consist, would often change as the train moved along. The diner car would be dropped off at some convenient place after the evening meal was finished. Certain sleeper cars would go partway and then be dropped off one by one for different destinations. One would go to Cincinnati, another to Cleveland, while the main train continued ahead to Chicago. Cars would be picked up and added to the same train as it returned in the opposite direction. Most passengers would not notice these maneuvers.

Information on very large trains was newsworthy, and in 1838 an eighteen-car train on the Utica and Schenectady Railroad consisted of four baggage cars, one mail car, one wood car (next to the locomotive's tender), and twelve coaches. Such large trains were run in warm-weather months during the day. At night the train was reduced to ten cars, and in the winter it was only five or six. In September 1849 the same railroad ran a twenty-two-car train consisting of five baggage cars, one mail car, two immigrant cars, and fourteen coaches. Not to be outdone, the Michigan Southern and Northern Indiana Railroad ran a thirty-eight-car train carrying 2,200 passengers as reported in a La Porte newspaper in April 1855. About twenty years later the New York Central Railroad had difficulty with a train that was ten cars shy of this record length. When it reached Grand Central Station it was necessary to cut the train into three sections so that it could be switched inside the train shed. In June 1894 the Kansas City, Fort Scott, and Memphis Railroad ran a twenty-three-car train that carried 2,365 passengers. *Railway Age* reported that it was likely the largest passenger load reported up to that time.

Americans liked to boast about their long, open passenger cars as being democratic because everyone, rich and poor, sat together in harmony and peace. This idealistic notion was fine in theory but was not one that generally lasted long after the departure. Those sitting near the stove were

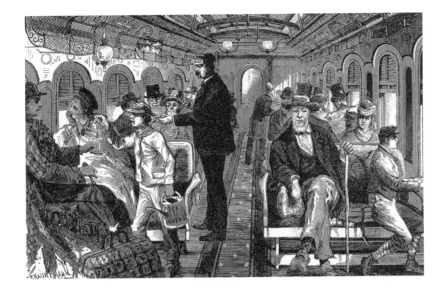

13.14. The interior of a Pennsylvania car in the style of the late 1860s is shown here. In the left foreground a lady accepts a glass of water from the trainboy. He will wipe the rim of the glass before serving the next passenger. The conductor stands behind the trainboy.

(*L'Illustration*, September 2, 1876)

soon too hot as the energetic brakeman kept stoking the fire – he was labeled the fire fiend. Some would get up to look for seats away from the stove. Solitary passengers soon had a seatmate, who might be congenial or not. Some travelers were very talkative, such as the overly friendly salesman who offered endless jokes and banal chatter; learning how to escape him became a necessity.

Even more irritating was the public reader. Such a person would read aloud from the newspaper stories he felt were of general interest and usually found a few devoted listeners who encouraged him to continue while the rest of the car's occupants sat fuming. He would go on about sporting events, murder trials, or political issues. He generally read poorly, stumbling over difficult words or mispronouncing them terribly. Stopping this fool became the wish of every sane person on the car. Short of throwing him under the wheels there seemed to be no sure way to restore quiet. Daniel Gooch, an official of Britain's Great Western Railway, was traveling in the United States in 1860 and found the lack of privacy in American cars troublesome. He was reading a book quietly when after a time he noticed a man behind him was leaning over the seat back to read along with him. But Gooch was reading too fast for this fellow, who complained that Gooch was turning the pages too fast. Gooch handed the book over the seat back and told the man to keep it.

The seat hog was another hazard of coach travel. There were often large, loutish fellows who would sprawl all over a seat. He would put his feet up on the seat or eat onions to discourage others from sitting beside him. This fellow was well fed but ill bred. The female seat hog was of a snappish nature and would pile bundles and bags to occupy an otherwise empty seat. It took a forceful conductor to deal with the seat hog. Ms. Isabella Bird mentioned one such man in her 1856 travel book on the

13.15. This handsome photograph shows a local train on the New Haven, Connecticut, shoreline in about 1890. The locomotive is old (1868) and its cars are of an age as well, but it is a typical train used for short trips.

(Alfred F. Bishop photo)

Illinois Central Railroad. When the conductor called out, "A seat for a lady," several men volunteered their seats quickly, but one fellow refused to move. After a short but heated discussion he was forcibly retired to an immigrant car.

Seats were used for more than sitting or napping. A young woman was riding on the Northern Pacific Railroad in the fall of 1877 to meet her husband. She was in the last stages of pregnancy, and as the train rolled along between Aldrich and Motley, Minnesota, the baby was born. The car was crowded, yet there were only three other women on board. They did what they could to help the new mother. A tea salesman had his sample case and managed to find hot water for a cup of tea. The conductor offered a berth in the sleeping car, but the lady declined and was content to hold the child close to her in a borrowed shawl. The youngster would make "music" occasionally as the train rocked along for another one hundred miles to his new home. The railroad was a universal carrier in the Victorian era. It carried everything from people to pig iron. Babies might ride free and so begin a lifetime of railroad travel. And at the end of life a special ticket was required for the coffin to ride in the baggage car (fig. 13.16). The American railroad literally offered cradle-to-grave transportation.

13.16. A ticket was required for the transportation of coffins. No one rode for free except for very young children or pass holders.

(Lionel Wiener, *Passenger Tickets*, 1940)

When passengers were not being annoyed by other travelers, they must be ready to contend with the sparks and smoke sent back along the train from the locomotive. The sparks were like fireflies that sometimes floated past the window or would find an opening and land in your eye. Clothing, hats, and luggage were other targets for these burning embers. Most were small and easy to extinguish, but some were the size of a hickory nut and were capable of setting the car itself on fire. Locomotive spark arresters worked to some degree but never well enough to eliminate the problem. A few railroads installed dust collectors in the roof of the car to draw air inside and clean it with water filtration and screens. They worked fairly well but were costly to install and maintain. Other railroads, such as the Stonington line, used track sprinklers to keep the dust from wafting up from the roadbed. *Merchant's Magazine* in December 1848 reported that the system worked very well in keeping the cars clean but also had the salutary effect of reducing hot boxes, cooling the train's axle bearings when they became overheated. While most travelers were content to keep the windows closed, a few would brave the sparks and dust for a blast of fresh air. Here again there was a cause for disagreement. The conductor was summoned to force this person to shut the window. An argument would break out. In one case a passenger stubbornly refused to obey, and only after being told he would be expelled from the train did he comply.

However, he did so by slamming the sash shut with such force that the glass shattered.

The cars were fairly noisy even when most of the occupants were silent. The noise of the wheels grinding over the rails, the brake rods and safety chains clanking, the locomotive chuffing up ahead or sounding its bell and whistle, created a heavy cacophony of sounds that never stopped until the train came to rest. Crying babies did their part to add to the discomfort level as did the trainmen who paraded back and forth through the cars. They could not, it seemed, close a door without slamming it. Or they would bawl out loudly: "The next station stop be Xteīnone-Oklis." What did he say? No one, except the trainman himself could understand the station's name. Yet any student could observe that democracy was noisy and imperfect, and coach travel was a good mirror of life in the American republic.

SUGGESTED READING

Alvarez, Eugene. *Travel on Southern Antebellum Railroads*. Montgomery: University of Alabama Press, 1974.

Appleton's General Guide to the United States and Canada. New York: D. Appleton & Co., 1881.

Baedeker, Karl. *The United States with an Excursion into Mexico: Handbook for Travelers*. Leipsic: Karl Baedeker, 1893.

Black, Robert C. *Railroads of the Confederacy*. Chapel Hill: University of North Carolina Press, 1952.

Bryce, James. *The American Commonwealth*. London: Macmillan and Co., 1888.

Chandler, Alfred D. *Henry Varnum Poor: Editor, Analyst, Reformer*. Cambridge: Harvard University Press, 1956.

Dilts, James D. *The Great Road: The Building of the Baltimore and Ohio, the Nation's First Railroad, 1828–1853*. Stanford, Calif.: Stanford University Press, 1993.

Drury, George H. *Historical Guide to North American Railroads*. Milwaukee: Kalmbach, 1985.

Fishlow, Albert. *American Railroads and Transformation of the Ante-Bellum Economy*. Cambridge: Harvard University Press, 1965.

Flint, Henry M. *The Railroads of the United States: Their History and Statistics, Comprising the Progress and Present of the Various Lines with Their Earnings and Expenses. To Which Are Added a Synopsis of the Railroad Laws of the United States, and an Article on the Comparative Merits of Iron and Steel Rails*. Philadelphia: John E. Potter and Co., 1868.

Frey, Robert L. *Railroads in the Nineteenth Century*. New York: Facts on File, 1988.

Gamst, Frederick, ed. *Early American Railroads: Franz Anton Ritter von Gerstner's Die innern Communicationen (1842–1843)* by Franz Anton Ritter von Gerstner; edited by Frederick C. Gamst; translated by David J. Diephouse and John C. Decker. Stanford, Calif.: Stanford University Press, 1997.

Gibbs, Montgomery. *The Englishman's Guide Book to the United States and Canada; with an Appendix of the Shooting and Fishing Resorts of North America*. London: E. Stanford, 1883.

Grant, Roger, ed. *We Took the Train*. DeKalb; Northern Illinois University Press, 1990.

Harlow, Alvin F. *Steelways of New England*. New York: Creative Age Press, 1946.

Jervis, John B. *Railway Property: A Treatise on the Construction and Management of Railways*. New York: Phinney, Blakeman, and Mason, 1861.

Johnson, Emery R. *American Railway Transportation*. New York: D. Appleton and Co., 1910.

Kirkman, Marshall M. *Science of Railways,* vol. 4, *Passenger Business.* New York: World Railway Publishing Co., 1895.

Middleton, William D., ed. *Encyclopedia of North American Railroads.* Bloomington: University of Indiana Press, 2007.

Poor, Henry V. *Poor's Manual of Railroads.* New York: H. V. and H. W. Poor, 1868–1924.

Pratt, Edwin A. *American Railways.* London: Macmillan and Co., 1903.

Ringwalt, J. Luther. *Development of Transportation Systems in the United States, Comprising a Comprehensive Description of the Leading Features of Advancement, from the Colonial Era to the Present Time, in Water Channels, Roads, Turnpikes, Canals, Railways, Vessels, Vehicles, Cars and Locomotives.* Philadelphia: J. Luther Ringwalt, 1888.

Sears, A.T., and Effie Webster. *American Railroad Guide from the Pacific to the Atlantic, 1878–1879.* Madison, Wisc.: Roger H. Hunt, 1985.

Shaw, Robert B. *A History of Railroad Accidents, Safety Precaution,s and Operating Practices.* Potsdam, N.Y.: Northern Press, 1978.

Stover, John F. *American Railroads.* Chicago: University of Chicago Press, 1961.

Sweetser, Moses F. *The Middle States: A Handbook for Travellers. A Guide to the Chief Cities and Popular Resorts of the Middle States, and to Their Scenery and Historic Attractions; with the Northern Frontier from Niagara Falls to Montreal; also, Baltimore, Washington, and Northern Virginia.* Boston: J. R. Osgood and Co., 1875.

Trollope, Anthony. *North America,* 2 vols. Philadelphia: J. B. Lippincott and Co., 1862.

Wellington, Arthur M. *The Economic Theory of the Location of Railways: An Analysis of the Conditions Controlling the Laying out of Railways to Effect the Most Judicious Expenditure of Capital.* New York: John Wiley and Sons. 1887.

White, John H. *The American Railroad Passenger Car.* Baltimore: Johns Hopkins University Press, 1978.

Wiener, Lionel. *Passenger Tickets.* London: Railway Gazette, 1940.

14.1. Woodruff sleeping cars were introduced on the New York Central Railroad in the late 1850s with considerable success. The berths were folded up, and the lower berth was converted into seats for daytime travel.

(Frank *Leslie's Illustrated Weekly*, April 30, 1859)

Passenger Trains

№ 14

First Class

HISTORICALLY, TRAVEL HAS BEEN TEDIOUS, UNCOMFORTABLE, and slow. At times it is also dangerous. How to temper or reverse these negatives has been a dilemma for transport professionals since ancient times. The top level of society could generally find a comfortable way to get around; for them, cost was not a problem. However, the problem of making quality travel affordable for the masses remains largely unsolved. Yet for those able and willing to pay, a smooth and pleasant trip was possible in Victorian times, as it is today.

Our ancestors were tough realists, but they were also given to idealist notions about "democratic" travel. We needed no first- or second-class cars in America, because, rich or poor, every native son was a gentleman. Nabobism belongs to the Old World. The British and European railways might have three or even four classes. Democratic travel was largely a canard in America. A few years after the first passenger trains began rolling across American soil, first- and second-class cars had been adopted by a majority of American lines. Von Gerstner reported many instances of dual class operations in his voluminous report of 1842. The *Niles Register* was talking about palace cars a decade earlier. The talk of democratic travel persisted. Anthony Trollope was more than a little annoyed by this false belief, saying it confused social and political equality. We should be equals before the law, but as individuals we are very different in terms of intelligence, physical strength, health, and much more. He also noted in an 1862 book on North American travel that we accept first-class houses, meals and horses, so why not a first-class railway car?

Some years earlier Samuel Breck, then a resident of Boston, recorded in his diary of July 22, 1835, a most undemocratic opinion about togetherness. He was taking the morning train to Providence, Rhode Island. The cars were crowded and became more so. Breck was squeezed into a corner by two workmen who smelled much like salt fish, tar, and molasses. Just before departure time a dozen bouncing factory girls came looking for a seat. The conductor ordered the men in Breck's car to jump up to the roof seats in order to make room for the ladies, but no one would move, including the sixty-four-year-old Breck. The ladies were then pushed into Breck's compartment, finding space where there was none. They cheerfully began sucking on lemons and eating green apples. Breck declared, "The rich and poor, the educated and the ignorant, the polite and the vulgar, all herd together in this modern improvement in travelling."

River, ferry, and canal boats had segregated men and women for some time. The precedent was already established. Cars or compartments were set aside for women. Ladies' cars were introduced in the 1830s as a courtesy or protective measure because women were considered fragile and delicate creatures. Male travelers were rude fellows given to heavy tobacco use, whiskey flasks, and indelicate speech. By offering separate waiting rooms at the depot and separate cars, women might travel in peace. Husbands were admitted to the ladies' car if the occupants agreed and if they promised not to chew or smoke. The conductor made sure no single males found a seat in those dedicated cars. They were in use in all parts of the United States, but it has been suggested they were especially prevalent in the Old South. They were often ordinary coaches, no better or worse than any other car in the train. They were often the last car and so offered a better view of the scenery.

The first sleeping car had a small compartment for ladies. This pioneering vehicle ran on the Cumberland Valley Railroad in south central Pennsylvania starting in February 1838. Later that year the Philadelphia, Wilmington, and Baltimore Railroad put on a sleeper with a commodious ladies' compartment and a female attendant. This style of conveyance came in and out of fashion. In September 1856 the New York Central abandoned ladies' cars, saying they were poorly patronized. The *Railroad Gazette* printed an editorial fifteen years later declaring the ladies' car out of date and unnecessary if the conductor could enforce the no smoking or spitting rules. Obsolete or not, the ladies' cars rolled on; however, the notion that ladies were safer in these special carriages was disproven by their involvement in accidents. The Richmond and Danville Railroad lost one of its ladies' cars in June 1866 near Coalfield, Virginia. The car flew over an embankment and rolled over three times before smashing below the track. A Mrs. Trotter was killed and thirteen other women were injured. Wrecks and editorials could not kill the ladies' car, however; railroads persisted with new ones being produced into the next century. In 1898 the B&O Railroad acquired three deluxe cars with ladies' rooms outfitted with settees, dressers, and bookcases. In 1911 the Chicago, Burlington, and Quincy Railroad acquired two special parlor cars with compartments set aside exclusively for women. To be fair, the men received a smoking lounge in the same cars.

There was much to praise in the first-class palace car. They were masterpieces of luxury created by the combined talents of the investor, car builder, upholsterer, artist, and decorator. Passengers sped along inside in a warm and richly furnished chamber, lounging on a soft seat as fine as that found in the best home or hotel. This space offered a degree of privacy, for instead of sixty to seventy passengers crowded into a coach, the first-class car rarely carried more than twenty-four in a car of the same size. It was neat, clean, refined, convenient, and so agreeable. An English author, Fredrick S. Williams, offered his impression of an American sleeping car in 1888. *In the midst of a dirty, noisy and wicked city, we step aboard a palace car to find a bed of perfect neatness. How fresh and cool the linens look. We hardly expect to find such domesticity or motherly provenance. How springy the mattress and soft the pillow. Surely this will be the happiest way to bridge the 200 odd miles between New York and Boston. How good it feels to escape all contact with the wretched newsboys and that foul depot at New Haven.*

THE SLEEPING CAR

The sleeper was the first palace car to gain popularity and a wide-scale use. It was introduced in the late 1830s as already noted, and many more were built in the next two decades. Most were rather modest vehicles and cannot properly be classed as palace cars, but they became increasingly elaborate after 1860. The basic plan involved converting the seats into a bed at night. An upper berth was made by a hinged bed that was lowered down to a level position. Mattresses, pillows, and bedding were stored in the upper berth in its closed or folded-up position. This scheme was used by the Cumberland Valley and Philadelphia, Wilmington, and Baltimore Railroads in 1838, yet its invention has been generally credited to George M. Pullman some twenty years later. Pullman, in fact, has been declared the father of luxury railroad travel. Although he was an excellent manager and organizer and did much to promote and improve sleeping car service and deluxe cars, he was not their inventor. A few other sleeping car pioneers should be mentioned in fairness to those whose efforts have been so eclipsed by the champions of Pullman.

Theodore T. Woodruff had become intrigued with sleeping cars while managing a railroad car repair facility in Illinois. In 1856 he obtained two patents and raised enough capital to have a demonstration car built the next year. The car's fine appearance and ingenious design prompted several railroads to adopt Woodruff's sleeping car (fig. 14.1). By 1858 he had twenty-one cars in service. Both the New York Central and Pennsylvania Railroads were among his customers, and his success seemed certain. Edward C. Knight, a wealthy sugar refiner, invested in T. T. Woodruff and

14.2. This elegant drawing room car dates from about 1875 and was operated by Webster Wagner, George Pullman's chief rival. It had parlor car seats for first-class passengers. Note the large windows.

(Asher and Adams, *Pictorial Album of American Industry*, 1879)

Company to help to reorganize it as the Central Transportation Company in 1862. Four years later the firm had eight sleepers in operation. They were very elegant cars that were valued at $8,000 each.

Meanwhile, Webster Wagner, a failed carriage builder, was a station agent for the New York Central Railroad and seemed to have few prospects for success. In 1858 he decided to take over the management of four Woodruff sleepers on the New York Central. From this small beginning Wagner nurtured his new enterprise. With care and good fortune he expanded, somehow becoming an associate of Cornelius Vanderbilt, who had abandoned steamboats for steam cars. In 1866 the New York Central Sleeping Car Company was organized with Wagner as president and Vanderbilt's money paying the bills. As Vanderbilt expanded his rail empire, Wagner's cars were soon found on the Lake Shore, the Michigan Central, and the Boston and Albany lines.

Pullman was furious to see a rival firm succeeding because of the commodore's patronage and hoped to throttle this troublesome competitor with a patent suit. However, the legal action was long and costly, and its mission failed. Even Wagner's death in an 1882 train wreck aboard one of his own cars did nothing to slow the progress of this New York Central–sponsored gadfly. A Vanderbilt son-in-law, Walter S. Webb, took over the management of the sleeping and parlor car concession. Webb spent lavishly and hired Louis Tiffany to handle interior design of some of the better cars in the fleet. By 1892 Wagner's old company was operating six hundred deluxe cars over 20,000 route miles with three thousand employees. Yet Webb had spent with too free a hand and in so doing had created a large debt. Profits were falling. By late 1899 the shareholders agreed to sell their assets to the Pullman Company, but since George Pullman had died two years earlier, he was cheated from witnessing the downfall of his longtime enemy.

Unlike Woodruff and Wagner, Pullman had no early connection with railroading. He had learned the cabinet maker's trade at his brother's workshop, but the craftsman's life held little appeal for this bright, ambitious young man. He became a contractor in moving buildings for the expansion of the Erie Canal. This profitable trade took him to Chicago in 1856. The city was elevating buildings and streets to stand above the

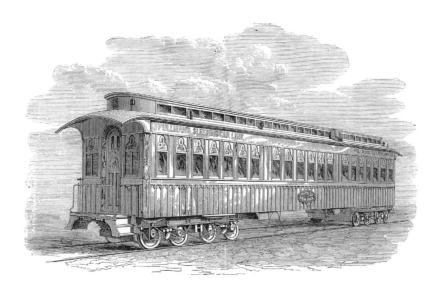

14.3. The City of New York was a deluxe Pullman sleeping car built by the Chicago, Burlington, and Quincy Railroad shops at Aurora, Illinois, in 1866.

(Illustrated London News, October 2, 1869)

lapping waters of Lake Michigan. The work paid well, but Pullman was looking for a bigger challenge. He sought fame and fortune and an outlet for his considerable energy. He explored Colorado and became richer as a trader and merchant. He returned to Chicago in 1863 in an unsettled state. Several years earlier he had dabbled in running Woodruff cars and remodeling a few coaches into sleepers for the Chicago and Alton line. He was comparatively poor then, but he had grown wealthy in the intervening years and now wanted very much to grow richer yet. Long-distance railroad travel was growing as the national rail network expanded. Pullman envisioned a developing market for sleeping car service and decided this business was the route to a greater fortune. In the summer of 1863 he purchased a deluxe sleeper from the Wason Car Company for service on the Chicago and Alton Railroad. He began contracting with railroad repair shops for a series of new palace car sleepers as he signed on more railroads for sleeping car services. By late 1866 he had more than forty cars on seven lines (fig. 14.3). Pullman served as the contract operator of the company's cars by providing porters, bedding, and the car itself. The revenue was shared between the contracting railroad and Pullman. In February 1867 he incorporated the Pullman Palace Car Company with the backing of Chicago money barons such as Marshall Field, who believed Pullman was a clear-headed industrialist with a genius for organization and finance.

Andrew Carnegie was another early champion of Pullman, declaring that Pullman was one of the ablest men of affairs he had ever known. Carnegie's investment in sleeping car stock was the beginning of his fortune. The future steel tycoon was so impressed with Pullman that he convinced the officers of the Central Transportation Company to lease their business to him. There were half a dozen smaller sleeping car operators in the country, but Pullman was able to take them over or drive them out of business. Only Wagner remained independent because of the backing of the Vanderbilts. Pullman had a virtual monopoly by 1880. He was operating seven hundred cars over about 60,000 route miles and carrying two million passengers a year. Profits were so large that dividends of 8 to 12 percent were common, and the company generated so much surplus cash, it was put into government bonds. Carnegie was right: Pullman was the ultimate capitalist and his touch was golden. Carnegie benefited from this golden touch and was given to saying, "Blessed be the man who invented sleep."

The Pullman empire kept growing. He established a sleeping car company in Britain and announced plans for a transatlantic steamship line. In 1881, south of Chicago, he completed construction of the largest railroad car–building plant in the world. It featured a model village where workers might rent homes, send their children to a company-supported school, shop in company stores, and attend a company-built church. It was a beautiful facility, carefully planned and built on a grand and generous scale. Yet its residents felt oppressed in this controlled and artificial town. Its puritanical rules meant that anyone wanting a glass of beer was required to go elsewhere. The model town exploded in 1894. When a reduction in wages prompted a strike, Pullman handled it badly and could not understand why his workers would revolt after all he had done for them. He became rigid and would not negotiate. The press and public opinion turned against him – Jane Addams likened him to King Lear – and he died a puzzled and embittered man in 1897.

The sleeping car company created in 1867 continued to flourish after its founder's death. Robert Todd Lincoln, firstborn son of Abraham Lincoln, succeeded Pullman as president of the firm. Between 1900 and 1910 its traffic tripled and revenues were so great that three extra dividends were paid, ranging from 20 to 50 percent of the stock's value. Through good times and bad the Pullman Company remained a dependable cash cow. The Great Depression of the 1930s was the end of this golden age. Matters only got worse in the following decades. The U.S. Justice Department took Pullman to court declaring the company was a monopoly. The government won its case and Pullman was ordered to separate its sleeping car service from its manufacturing division. In June 1947, after a long legal battle, the sleeping car business was sold to an alliance of fifty-seven railroads for a little over $40 million. Six thousand cars and thirty thousand employees were involved in this transfer. For a few years all went well, but the sleeping car and railroad travel had become obsolete as the public turned increasingly to highway and airline transport.

In 1968 Pullman operations were suspended, and the remaining sleepers were turned over to the individual railroads still offering that service. The Pullman enterprises had survived for one century and one year.

Today even the memory of this once grand company is disappearing into the dustbin of history. No one much under the age of fifty can remember the name or greatness of this long-expired enterprise. The public reaction to the sleeping cars was mixed. Some could not say enough in praise of this innovation, while others found them a total failure. Light sleepers and persons of a delicate nature had difficulty enough trying to get a good night's sleep in their own bed. Hence, no one could design a car good enough for these patrons. Yet the average person could surely get a few hours rest on all but the worse-kept sleeper. Being able to lie flat in a private space was surely better than toughing it out upright in a coach seat.

One of the earliest accounts in praise of sleepers appeared in the *New York Tribune* on December 31, 1858, regarding sleeping cars on the New York Central Railroad. The correspondent found them to be a marvelous answer to the misery of night travel by rail, and he heartily recommended them to all. His only complaint was being awakened too early in the morning for breakfast. About a year later a lady passenger wrote a glowing letter to the Michigan Central Railroad about their sleeping cars. She awoke refreshed in the morning after resting in a "huge cradle" that lulled her through the night. She wished to thank the designers of the car in the name of mothers, who now found it possible to travel by night with little children, saying, "If a mother likes it, it must be a good thing."

A more mixed report appeared a few years later in the *Western Railroad Gazette* concerning sleeper service on the Philadelphia, Wilmington, and Baltimore Railroad between Philadelphia and Washington. Traffic was heavy that evening, and passengers with only a single-berth ticket were forced to share their berth – a double ticket could guarantee single occupancy. Experienced passengers did not remove their topcoats or boots but bundled in as they were. After the train started, an argument broke out among the travelers over the proper temperature – it was too hot or too cool for some. The talking went on for some time among the passengers, thus making sleep nearly impossible. After a time all was quiet and it seemed as if everyone in the car was dead, but, no, they were just sleeping. A few hours later the train reached the Susquehanna River, and when the cars slowly rumbled aboard a giant ferry boat, one traveler woke up and shouted, "Suppose we slide off into this infernal water?" But of course the crossing was made safely dozens of time every day, and soon they were steaming toward Baltimore.

Talking was but one problem for light sleepers. The motion of the train was exaggerated for those consigned to an upper berth, as being higher above the track the effects of leverage were at work. David Joy, a British mechanical engineer, was traveling in an upper berth on an American train in 1882 and said he thought he was going to be tossed through the roof. Most travelers found the upper berth objectionable because it was so high off the floor, making it difficult to enter or exit (fig. 14.4). At bedtime the porter was there with a small ladder, which made egress easy for all but the infirm or elderly. In the middle of the night, should the traveler need to exit his bed for any reason, it was difficult to summon the porter, so the exit was often carried out in a rather clumsy manner. In addition, many travelers were bothered by the low ceiling and absence of a window, making this little chamber behind a heavy curtain claustrophobic. Joy makes no mention of these drawbacks, but he does go on about the locomotive's bell, which was audible inside his car. It rang whenever the train started or stopped and was at its worst when two trains passed each other. Joy wrote, "The clangor rises rapidly in pitch, 'til it shrieks and the two bells mingle their clangs in an inharmonious roar, and then, parting, die away into a moaning, melancholy dirge." One can only assume that Joy was happy to return to England, where locomotives have no bells.

It was another English writer who came to the defense of the sleeping car as an ingenious improvement to travel that was a great glory to American inventiveness. This was the great novelist, and one of the most prolific authors of the age, Anthony Trollope. Trollope wrote a two-volume study of his trip through the United States during the second year of the Civil War. He was frank and candid but was always fair and never resorted to the waspish outbursts of his mother's account of America. Trollope made frequent use of America's sleeping cars years before they appeared in Europe. He found them a blessing, but he discovered that many upper-class Americans would not travel on them because of the noise and dirt. He agreed that some were dirty, but no dirtier than the coaches. As to the noise, he found no problem in sleeping; one must tune out the noise and simply go to sleep. If noise and dirt were so offensive, then no one should ever travel. Had Americans gone soft? Where was their pioneer spirit? It seems odd that this well-educated Englishman found it necessary to give our ancestors a lecture on acting like grownups and accepting some discomforts as the price of travel.

The railroad car builders were busy in the first years of sleeping car service to create an even more luxurious vehicle. The description below from the September 1860 *American Railroad Journal* described a new sleeper built at the New York and Erie Railroad repair shop by H. J. Sweetser. This broad-gauge car cost $8,000, at a time when a standard coach cost about $2,000.

> The entire length of the car, including the platform is 65 feet, and it is 11 feet wide, and 8 feet high. It has seats for sixty passengers, which can be readily changed into double or single berths to accommodate fifty-two sleepers. The wood work of the seats is St. Domingo mahogany; the back and cushions of the seats are covered with royal purple plush, and the berths are inclosed [sic] with

satin damask curtains falling to the floor. The aisle between the seats is covered with Brussels carpet, and the lamps, upholstery, &c., are in keeping with the general fitting up of the car. At each end of the car are wash-rooms, supplied with marble basins, and every necessary convenience for the toilet.

Near these rooms heaters are placed, which, by a patented arrangement, throw the heat equally over the car and through a window into the washrooms, keeping the water from freezing in the coldest weather. The ventilating apparatus is of the most perfect character. A body of water under the car is forced up on either side into a recess where it breaks like the spray of a fountain, falling back into the reservoir. The air entering the car passes through this water, being cooled and purified from all dust and fumes its entrance through ventilators along the aisles between the seats. This creates a current from the center outward, which prevents the entrance of dust, cinders, or smoke, through the open windows and doors.

14.4. Passengers tumble out of their berths and dress inside a sleeping car in 1871.

(*Every Saturday*, April 29, 1871)

Rare cabinet woods became a hallmark of the nineteenth-century palace sleeper. Dealers searched the world for decorative and exotic varieties of cabinet-grade lumber. English oak, San Domingo and Spanish mahogany, ebony, satinwood, French walnut (for veneer), and rosewood were all imported by top-ranking car builders. Gilt and black highlights added to the richness of the interiors as did an abundance of mirrors, painted ceilings, and tasteful rugs and curtains.

The decorative treatment never stopped aboard a palace car. The entire surface was decorated with ornament, be it a wood carving of a Grecian face, a velvet plush seat covering in Gobelin blue, or a glorious center

14.5. One of Chicago's great stations was the Lake Shore and Michigan Southern depot on Van Buren Street. The giant train shed stood behind the head house. One of the Lake Shore's fancy drawing room cars stands just behind the baggage car. The station opened in 1867 and was destroyed by the fire of 1871. It was rebuilt immediately.

(*Appleton's Magazine*, April 2, 1870)

lamp in ormolu, a copper, tin, or zinc alloy. In 1866 Jonah Woodruff, the older brother of T. T. Woodruff, introduced the Silver Palace Sleeping Car. All of the interior hardware, including a row of thin metal columns on either side of the center aisle, was silver plated. All of this bright metal created a dazzling effect of great richness. Most of the hardware beneath its bright silver surface was made from a cheap white metal called pinchbeck. On closer examination much else about the palace car was a cheap sham. Some of the carving was in fact cast iron painted to look like wood. All of the gold ornaments were covered with a thin layer of ormolu. The Central Pacific Railroad, wanting no part of George Pullman, adopted Silver Palace cars for its own use and seemed to be unconcerned about what was genuine and what was spurious.

In 1869 the Lake Shore line completed an improved sleeper named the Elkhorn at its Adrian, Michigan, repair shop that exhibited the progress of the car builder's art. Gaslights were coming into fashion for the better cars as were staterooms. The Elkhorn, of course, had both. At each end of the car there were staterooms that included three berths and a tiny toilet. The center of the car had regular sleeping berths. The interior was paneled in mahogany and maple with gilt highlights. A cherry-colored Wilton carpet was on the floor. The seats were upholstered in matching cherry-colored moquette. Side lamps encouraged reading. The curtains were made of brown terry with velvet borders. The magnificent car cost a

little less than $20,000, or almost twice the cost of a new locomotive. An exterior of this car or one of its sisters is shown in figure 14.5.

Staterooms became a standard feature on many sleeping cars by the 1870s. They proved perfect for a couple or small family who wanted extra privacy and the convenience of their own toilet. But such comforts came at an extra price. While a lower berth might cost only $1 per night, a drawing room cost $2 extra. This small fee could add up on long trips – Chicago-to-San-Francisco trains had a room fee of $53. During the day the berths were folded closed to become small sofas. On some trains it was possible to receive a light meal from the lounge car.

First-class passengers were the first to receive hot-water heat in place of the much despised wood or coal stoves that were still common in the coaches. The new type of heating was more uniform throughout the car and was more easily regulated. Electric call bells were common in sleepers and parlor cars by 1890. The power requirements were modest, and a small battery was sufficient. Electric lighting demanded a greater power source, which meant a boiler, engine, and a generator in the baggage car. Only the best first-class train warranted this expense. Electric lighting gradually gained favor on the western railways after 1920. Electrical gadgets such as ticker tape machines were found on board certain premiere trains by 1890 to dispense the latest national and financial news. A more practical improvement was the double-sash window that kept out cinders

14.6. *Above left*, Bruce Price, a prominent architect of the time, designed the interior of the Boston and Albany drawing room car in a rich and dark Byzantine style. It was manufactured by the Wason Car Company of Springfield, Massachusetts, in 1887.

Above right, The parlor car interior shown here was exhibited at the U.S. Centennial Exhibition in Philadelphia in 1876.

(*Harper's Weekly*, August 25, 1888)

and smoke. These were in use by 1876 and were very similar to modern-day storm windows.

First-class travelers expected first-class trains – especially extra-fare trains, such as the Black Diamond Express – to be like traveling hotels. This expectation was soon realized for the sleeping car. It was only the beginning for the Pullman Company, and the wealthy trunk line railroads were ready to make these cars available to the traveling public. Parlor cars, lounge or club cars, and diner cars were introduced in fairly rapid succession (fig. 14.6). Travelers were to be made to feel they were guests. If they were tired, there was a berth to stretch out in or an easy chair where one might nap. Need a cup of tea or gin? It was ready at all hours in the lounge. Should you want a book or magazine, the lounge car was there for you. If you needed to dictate a letter, an alert secretary would take your dictation and type up a copy, all at no charge. When mealtime arrived, dinner was at your service.

The lounge car grew out of the smoking car. Such vehicles were introduced in 1846 on the Eastern Counties Railway in England. The elegant little six-wheeler featured side seats and a long table down its center. The idea became so popular that Parliament passed a bill in 1868 requiring a smoking car on each train and in all three classes of travel. The idea was not tried in the United States for a dozen years after they were first seen in England. The Pennsylvania Railroad put a special car on all through or express trains in July 1858. The New York Central upgraded the idea the following summer by outfitting special cars with swivel seats and an oilcloth floor. The outstanding feature of these cars was a small chamber at each end of the car wherein stood a boy offering cigars for sale. On most railroads the arrangement was much less formal. Smoking was prohibited in coaches, but some conductors did not enforce the rule or told the smoker to go to the baggage car, where he might smoke in peace and watch the scenery go by through an open side door. *Just take care not to set the car on fire.* There is also the story of the conductor who was astonished to find a refined lady smoking a pipe in a palace car. "Madame," he said, "we don't ever allow men to smoke in this car!" "That is an excellent rule," she coolly replied. "If I see a man smoking in here, I will inform you at once."

Standing was tolerable for a time, but the only seating would be a collection of suitcases, trunks, or boxes – the baggage car offered few comforts. On regular trains an old coach would be reserved for smokers, but on the better trains a drawing room would be set aside. By the early 1880s railroads began building cars in matched sets for their premiere trains. The Pennsylvania Railroad was a pioneer in operating such trains because of their forward-thinking chief passenger agent, James R. Wood. In October 1881 he convinced his employer to begin operation of a high-speed train between New York and Chicago. It would be all first class and

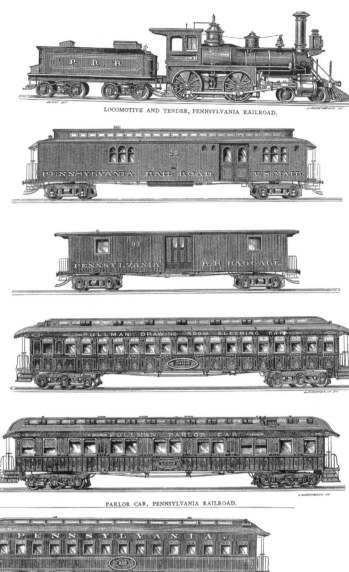

14.7. A Pennsylvania Railroad passenger train of 1875.

(Drawings from W. B. Sipes, *The Pennsylvania Railroad*)

featured a combination baggage and lounge/smoking car. The smoking compartment was first class in all ways and featured comfortable chairs, writing desks, and a small library with popular works of fiction. The train left Jersey City at 8:55 AM and stopped only at Philadelphia, Harrisburg, Altoona, and Pittsburgh. The western portion of the run was handled by the Ft. Wayne line and made only four stops en route to Chicago. This train was first called the Chicago Limited and was later renamed the Pennsylvania Limited; however, it is best remembered by its 1912 name, the Broadway Limited.

Figure 14.8, an illustration from 1893, shows the interior of a smoking car. The attendant served coffee, tea, and alcoholic drinks. He kept the

14.8. This is the first-class smoking compartment of the Chicago Limited. Here gentlemen sat and enjoyed the ambiance of a fine men's club while traveling the twenty-four-hour flyer to and from Chicago. A barber shop was in the next compartment.

(*Harper's Weekly*, April 29, 1893)

smoking lounge tidy, swept the floor, and emptied the ashtrays. This was said to be the fullest car on the train, as the smoky atmosphere seemed to relax the occupants and stimulate conversation. The conductor would sometimes take a seat and join in the clublike atmosphere. In 1898 the Pennsylvania Limited received a new set of cars. One of the baggage/library cars was named the Romulus. It had rattan chairs and a sofa for twenty-two occupants. The interior was furnished in vermilion wood and parquetry, and the ceiling was decorated in a Moorish design. The exterior was an unusually flashy combination of two-tone green and rich cream, leading the train to be nicknamed the Yellow Kid. The library offered a selection of popular fiction. A small barber shop offered haircuts at 50 cents and a shave for 25 cents. A bathtub was placed behind the barber shop and could be used for 75 cents.

The Romulus was a long wooden car, 78 feet and 3 inches, and weighed just under 60 tons. In 1898 the seven-car Pennsylvania Limited weighed just over 368 tons, excluding the locomotive, tender, and passengers. A single locomotive could handle the train over all of the main line except for the Altoona curve. It was there that the Pennsylvania Railroad climbed over the Alleghenies on a 1.61 percent grade. Since 1854, travelers were impressed by the procession of trains moving up the long, curving grade. The locomotives belched up great clouds of black smoke as they labored up the slope, demonstrating human might and enterprise warring against the difficult barrier of the Alleghenies. In April 1897 the British magazine *The Locomotive* described the scene:

> Leaving Altoona we have 1,000 ft. to ascend in a little over 10 miles, with sharp reverse curves very prevalent, consequently our "Limited" starts away with three engines ahead, each one of which is backed on singly at the station, or the shock of the three massive engines striking the cars to couple automatically

would probably lead to complaint from passengers, if not absolutely causing injury to the train. As the firemen give the last touch to the already heavy fires, the time gong sounds and the conductor, to give the starting signal, pulls the air signal cord, causing the little whistle in the cab of the rear engine to sound. Upon hearing this all three drivers open their regulators, and after a few strokes in full gear "notch up" their engines with the reverse levers to about 50% cut off, not much less, and at this the engines work to the summit of the Alleghanies [sic] at Gallitzin.

The train was all first-class and all Pullman. As such, a high fare of $29 was charged for a trip from New York to Chicago. This included the $4 extra fare and a $5 berth fee. The high fare was designed to offset the extra cost of a high-speed train with a limited passenger capacity. It had the secondary effect of discouraging less-affluent passengers from using the train. In fact, the only poor folks who regularly rode the Limited were the crew.

Fancy and fast-sounding-name trains appeared elsewhere soon after the Pennsylvania Railroad's Chicago Express inauguration. New England had its White Train, Boat Train, and Merchants Limited. In the south, the Fast Flying Virginian was a parody on the first families of Virginia. In the far west the Overland Limited and Sunset Limited became legends throughout the nation. The New-York-to-Boston express known as the White or Ghost Train captured the attention of Americans because it was so unusual. It started running in November 1884 at a time when brown, dark green, and Tuscan red were considered proper colors for passenger trains. These dark shades were adept at hiding the layer of coal dust they acquired every day. The word *White* was adopted by the New York and New England Railroad to demonstrate the clean-burning quality of their fuel. The engineer and fireman wore white coveralls and caps. Only the locomotive was black. The train was first named the New England Limited and ran along the Airline Railroad between Boston and New Haven via Willimantic, Connecticut. Its colors were conventional until March 1891 when the white paint scheme was introduced. The train's new color created a sensation even among dour New Englanders. Rudyard Kipling was so taken with its appearance that he wrote the short story ".007" about it. The railroad was doing poorly despite all of this good publicity and filed for bankruptcy in 1893. The White Train was discontinued in October 1893, ending this curious and beautiful express train.

For many years the New York Central Railroad had been content with a thirty-six-hour train between New York and Chicago. Even its Pacific Express rambled along at this leisurely rate. Its route was 68 miles longer than the Pennsylvania Railroad, but there were no mountains to cross on its route, so matching the speed of its chief rival was no problem. Whenever the Pennsylvania Railroad trimmed a few hours off its schedule, the Central would do likewise. Within days of the startup of the Pennsylvania

Railroad's Chicago Limited in the fall of 1881, the New York Central introduced a fast train to Chicago that would arrive in twenty-four hours, or two hours earlier than the Chicago Limited. But newspapers of the day reported that the Central was in the habit of being late. As to scenery, the owners of the Central believed the grandeur of the Hudson River Valley was a match for anything the Alleghenies could offer. Both lines had ample resources to buy the best equipment available, and few travelers could see much difference between a Pullman and a Wagner car.

The New York Central was very competitive and introduced an extra-fast express in May 1893 that would run for the duration of the Columbian Exposition. The express New York Central Flyer made the run to Chicago in just twenty hours. A firsthand account of the train appeared in *McClure's Magazine* of January 1894, written from the perspective of the engine crew and paraphrased in italics here. Passengers didn't think much about the locomotive or the men operating it unless it broke down. How well that machine was managed very much affected the train's schedule and the safety of everyone on board the cars. Engine running was not a simple task. It required skill, experience, and a special talent for coaxing all the power and speed that an engine could produce – much the way truly great musicians can make an ordinary violin sound like a Stradivarius. *The engineer would take the curves at just the right speed; he would open her up whenever possible to stay on schedule, yet make smooth stops every time. In short, he handles the locomotive as if he was a part of the machinery.*

Only the most talented and steady engineers were allowed to handle trains like the New York Central Flyer. He would arrive at the roundhouse well before departure time to inspect his engine, oiling and going over every part of the machine to see that all was right.

The engine is then backed at slow speed to Grand Central, where it couples onto the baggage car. The engine stands just outside the train shed so that none of the smoke blows back toward the boarding passengers. The fireman adds coal and adjusts his fire. He and the engineer fidget as they wait for the go-ahead signal. When it comes, the engineer gives one short blow of the whistle; at the same time, he puts the reverse lever all the way forward to achieve maximum starting power and opens the cylinder cocks. Within seconds he carefully opens the throttle. Nothing happens at first, so he gives a slight jerk on the throttle lever and the engine rolls forward. There is a deep chuff from the smokestack and then another and another – more quickly now as the speed increases. The fireman, meanwhile, rings the bell to warn one and all – we are under way. The engineer gently pulls the reverse lever back, and the exhaust becomes more rapid. He might open the sander to sprinkle a little dry sand under the driving wheels to keep them from slipping. The engine rides roughly over the switches, and the noise level inside the cab grows louder as the speed increases. Soon it's so noisy you must shout to be heard. The crew rely more on gestures and hand signals to communicate. The great iron machine rolls and sways; the exhaust becomes much quicker and higher pitched as the speed increases. It's hard to keep your balance on the deck plate, but the fireman stands easily and swings in a graceful and regular manner as he adds shovel after shovel of coal into the hungry firebox. He will shovel about seven ton of coal before we reach Albany and take on a new engine and crew.

We are running in a deep open ditch, four tracks wide for the first few miles. The ditch will eventually be covered over to become Park Avenue on the upper half of Manhattan Island. We cruise to the end of the ditch and are soon on the surface. The railroad crosses Spuyten Duyvil Creek, and we swing onto the tracks of the Hudson River Railroad, moving along the east bank of the river. On the west side of the river are the rocky steps of the Palisades. It is the most romantic and scenic part of the trip. We pass Yonkers, Dobbs Ferry, and Irvington – once the home of Washington Irvington – without stopping. The engine crew ignores these points of interest. The engineer is tense; he peers ahead at the track, at the signals and switches, hoping no one has forgotten to line up the switches good and proper. The fireman will join in with the engineer's visual, calling out the signals for a while and then back to his shovel if the pressure-gauge needle drops ever so slightly. The train rushes past Poughkeepsie, the largest town before Albany and home to Vassar College, but we stop nowhere, because the schedule will not allow it. To reach Chicago in twenty hours the train must pound along at between 60 and 75 miles an hour. We stop on this long trip only to change engines, and that is done in a few minutes.

The engineer and fireman know the railroad like their mother's face; every line and mole is familiar. They are now gesturing; we are just fifty minutes out of Grand Central. The engineer slackens the speed somewhat. The locomotive needs a drink; she evaporates about 60 gallons a minute. We are approaching a track pan; the fireman works a lever to drop a scoop under the tender, and water is picked up in a minute. The scoop is pulled up, the throttle is open, and we are quickly back up to speed. The tender has enough fuel capacity that we have sufficient coal to reach Albany.

The engineer stands rather than sits most of the time – he is too tense to relax. He occasionally sniffs the air; it's his way of telling if a bearing surface is running hot, as hot oil has a distinctive odor. No, nothing – all is well. He then turns to look back along the train just in case something is dragging or overheated. The train is actually running very steady for this speed; none of the cars are swaying more than 2 inches. Out West if the cars stay between the fences, the engineer and his crew are happy. We are approaching Albany and slow down upon reaching the yard limits; we sweep across a curving bridge that carries us across the Hudson River.

The engineer relaxes and actually smiles. We are on time – 140 miles in two hours and forty-five minutes. If the train were five minutes late, this intelligence and the cause of the delay would be telegraphed to the superintendent of the railroad.

A total of eight engines and crews were required to move the New York Central Flyer to Chicago. The extreme schedule lasted for the life of the Columbian Exposition, and in November the Flyer returned to a more reasonable schedule of twenty-four hours. While it lasted, it was the fastest long-distance train in the world.

Out West there were no fast trains. They had trains called expresses, but that was more in name than fact. These lines beyond the Mississippi River were not built for fast or heavy traffic. They were built lightly for low-volume use at an acceptable, but not high, level of engineering. They would be improved and upgraded when traffic developed to warrant such expenditures. Meanwhile there was something pleasant about the leisurely pace of a train gently rolling through this great empty landscape. The earliest through service over the Union Pacific Railroad began in 1869. One passenger train a day operated between Omaha, Nebraska, and Promontory, Utah, each way. The westbound trains made the journey in fifty-four hours; the eastbound required an extra six hours. The average speed was about nineteen miles an hour. It was a new railroad and the track was unsettled, so slow running was a necessity. A typical train consisted of seven cars – two sleepers, two coaches, one smoking car, one baggage car, and one mail car. There was room for about 110 passengers on each train. Passengers were required to transfer at Promontory to a Central Pacific train to go to Sacramento. This transfer place moved eastward to the city of Ogden.

First-class travel in the West was popular at first. Americans were curious to see the great, wide-open spaces if they could do so from the comfort of a car window. In October 1869 the Pullman Company began running a train of hotel cars direct from Omaha to San Francisco. The food stops and transfer between the Union Pacific and the Central Pacific Railroads were eliminated, thus allowing an eighty-one-hour schedule. However, in June 1870 the Central Pacific withdrew from the agreement. It was said the heavy palace cars were destroying the track, but it is also likely that the Central Pacific management just did not like having an outlander such as Pullman on their tracks. They ran their own Silver Palace Sleeping Cars and wanted no competitor operating so near at hand. It would be many years before through service was restored. The exchange of passengers at Ogden would continue for some time.

In the spring of 1877 New York publisher Frank Leslie traveled on both the Union Pacific and Central Pacific with his wife and several associates for a western tour. They came in their own hotel car, the

President, a splendid vehicle lent to Leslie for the trip and with the expectation of some mention of the Pullman Palace Car Company in the pages of *Leslie's Illustrated Newspaper*. Additional publicity was provided by Leslie's artists, who prepared engravings of the President, George Pullman inspecting its wheels and cars, and staff preparing meals and making up the berths. It showed how anyone blessed with an adequate bank account could see the Wild West and do so aboard a luxurious hotel car.

Mrs. Leslie wrote her own impressions of a ride across the Overland Route for a national readership. She wrote that most of the scenery was rather dull or repetitive, being vistas of the great savannah that was the western plains. The scene was enlivened occasionally by prairie dog villages, an antelope herd, a reluctant coyote or elk. Once past the one hundredth meridian the rainfall was less than 20 inches a year and tall grass gave way to Buffalo grass. The plains were dry, brown, and monotonous. The view grew more interesting at the western end of the Union Pacific; there was Castle Rock at Green River, a few tunnels and the rapids of the Weber River, and the narrow chasm formed by Echo Canyon was an impressive sight.

Once beyond Ogden, the Central Pacific exhibited the beauty and hazards of the Rocky Mountains. Miles of snowsheds blocked the view of the snow-clad peaks. These sturdy wooden structures were a necessity in the Sierras. There were 25 miles of them near Donner Pass. The area had an average of 31 feet of snow a year and at times received up to 65 feet. Before reaching the mountains, the Leslie party endured mile after mile of the Utah and Nevada alkali desert. About the only inhabitants in this forlorn district were track workers who lived near the small sheds placed every 5 miles or so to house the handcar and track tools.

As part of her daily routine Mrs. Leslie liked to stand on the President's rear platform and watch the countryside pass by. Theirs was the last car on the train, so their view was unobstructed. She would spend a few minutes with the amiable cook in his small kitchen (fig. 14.9). At nine o'clock Howells, the steward, would fasten a small table to the wall and cover it with a white cloth. Breakfast was hearty; it began with fish, then beef steak, hot rolls, cornbread, broiled chicken on toast, potatoes fried Saratoga style, and milk that was half cream, or tea and coffee. No wonder our Victorian ancestors tended to be portly. After the meal it was time to again stand on the rear platform to look for game, such as deer or prairie dogs; to spot other trains; and to watch the scenery. From time to time a Chinese track gang would hitch a ride by attaching a rope to the end of the handrail of the President. Mrs. Leslie was astonished at their rough looks and shabby clothing. She concluded they were of the lower classes. Was she expecting China to send over the ruling members of the

14.9. Frank Leslie, his wife, and a few associates rode the Pullman Hotel car *President* from Chicago to California on an extended tour from July 1877 until late in 1878. This is the car's kitchen and its portly cook.

(Frank *Leslie's Illustrated Weekly*, August 25, 1877)

Manchu dynasty, dressed in their finest silk, to rake ballast and replace ties and fishplates? Others in her company wrote in a diary, scribbled a few postcards, opened a darning bag, or studied French. The men napped or smoked in a tiny room at the far end of the car.

Not long after breakfast a table in the parlor was filled with platters of sandwiches, salad, biscuits, and fruit. There was no lack of food on the train. When it stopped at a station for food, the occupants of the parlor car never ventured near the dining hall but walked briskly up and down the station platform. Inside the station a train load of people pushed against the counter, hoping to grab something edible before the train pulled out. They had only twenty to thirty minutes, depending on the schedule. The food was tolerable, but the main complaint was the lack of variety. Breakfast, lunch, and dinner, it was always buffalo steak, ham and eggs, boiled corn, sweet potatoes, and hoe cakes with syrup. A few stations might offer antelope chops, the worst-prepared prairie dog stew, mule steaks, sagebrush tea, and coffee made from dried peas or beans. When they were hungry and out in the frontier, travelers would eat almost anything.

14.10. Many trains carried no diner, and poorer travelers in general depended on food prepared and sold by vendors at busy junctions such as this one at Gordonsville, Virginia. Coffee, fried chicken, and hot cakes could be purchased through the car windows.

(*Scribner's Magazine*, December 1872)

The Leslie party would leave their luxurious car occasionally to walk through the rest of the train. It rolled and swayed gently at 20 mph, making these sojourns easy and pleasant. In a seven-car train one would expect a variety of passengers from the old and ill to the young and vigorous, with just about every social and economic level represented. Children ran down the aisles shouting or laughing. A consumptive man was doubled over in a seat coughing. He hoped to recover in sunny California. Newlyweds sat very close to engage in each other to notice the scene around them. A few seats ahead a middle-aged man struggled to arrange himself on the coach seat for a nap.

The center of activity was inside the drawing room of the sleeper Palmyra (fig. 14.11). Pullman had designed this car as a chamber for Sunday services. It had an open compartment at the center with an expensive eight-stop double-manual pipe organ. The *London Illustrated News* depicted it in use as Pullman envisioned it: as dignified old gents sit at the keyboard – perhaps music teachers or church organists – a collection of angelic-faced young people stand or sit to solemnly sing praise to our merciful Lord. However, this is not what the Leslies encountered during their brief time aboard the Palmyra. Instead they found a lively party belting out a rendition of "Hold the Fort." Perhaps a few drinks had energized their performance; anyway it wasn't Sunday morning. Others who had berths on the car found the merrymaking annoying because of amateur organists and off-key singing. In June 1878 a British traveler named Marshall had a go at the Palmyra's organ as the train proceeded some miles

PASSENGER TRAINS: FIRST CLASS   467

14.11. The Palmyra was a Pullman sleeping car with a central parlor and a reed organ. Here a Sunday service is being conducted; however, rowdier gatherings were perhaps just as common. The car was built by the Hannibal and St. Joseph Railroad in 1868 and became part of the Pullman fleet in 1871.

(*Illustrated London News*, March 20, 1875)

west of Laramie. He played for two hours. The conductor, being musical, would stop during his turn through the train to join in the singing. Marshall noted that only one of the manuals worked, because the porter had packed the upper manual with pillowcases and blankets.

In the spring of 1882 Horace R. Hobart, assistant editor of *Railway Age* magazine, headed west to examine the local railroad operations. He was an old hand and could remember travel in the area in 1860 when Ben Holladay ran stagecoaches between Omaha and Denver. The fare was $175, and travel time between the two cities was seventy-two hours. Much had changed in the past twenty-two years. A coach ticket on the Union Pacific was $25 and time just twenty-four hours. Omaha had grown from a town of no consequence to a city of more than thirty thousand. The frontier days were about over, and eastern dandies could travel through these once dangerous traces with little fear of molestation. The train remained slow, and the best train carried only one sleeping car and no diner. There was normally a long wait at Council Bluffs, Iowa, because the Union Pacific operated only one through train a day. With five connections it was a rare day when they all arrived on time. Hence, travelers had an hour or two to tour the town or just sit and stew. The track had improved considerably in recent years. It was smooth, and steel had replaced most of the old wrought-iron rail. The speed level remained conservative and ranged between 20 and 25 mph.

Stops were made for meals at station dining rooms. Contractors leased and operated the food service for the railroad. As happens, some were good and some were very bad. The evening meal at Grand Island and breakfast at Sidney, Nebraska, were acceptable, but dinner the next day at Cheyenne was terrible. Now, Cheyenne proclaimed itself as the Magic City of Plains, and indeed it was the capital of Wyoming Territory, but there surely was no magic performed in that station's kitchen. The service and staff were lousy as well. The train pulled into Ogden on the third day at 6:15 PM. The switch of cars continued – the needless disruption and annoyance for the passengers. Why couldn't the two Pacific railroads work out through car service for the convenience of their customers?

Before they pulled out, Hobart noticed that on the end platforms of the baggage car a number of Indian passengers were setting, all well bundled up. It would be a cold ride, as the train gained altitude just ahead. No regular passengers would have been allowed to ride in this manner, but it was a long-standing rule that the Indians could ride in this way at no charge. No trainman would bother them. Most would silently hop off down the line a way and disappear into the night. Hobart was also interested to see the mixture of races working in the station dining rooms along the Central Pacific: Indian, African, Chinese, and Caucasian. They worked together in harmony. Hobart was certain this was because of the opening of the railroad, an institution that was surely responsible for all the good things in life, including better race relations.

On the morning of the fifth day, the train reached Sacramento. Time was allowed for breakfast, and then the train continued to Port Costa, where a giant ferry boat waited for the locomotive and its cars to board. The fine vessel built at the Central Pacific shipyard carried everyone to Oakland. Those heading to San Francisco boarded a smaller, more conventional ferry for the City on the Bay. Reflecting back on his journey, Hobart believed the Union Pacific track and equipment could easily handle a faster schedule, but this was not done, because the management didn't really consider it important. The physical plant of the Central Pacific would require some expensive betterments that its management didn't feel were warranted, and slow service remained a given on the Overland Route for the present.

14.12. The Golden Gate Special was an all-Pullman train operated over the Union Pacific Railroad between 1888 and 1889. It offered separate bathing and barbering services for men and women. The barber chair was in the baggage car, while the ladies' tub was in the observation car at the end of the train.

(Southern Pacific Railroad)

The Pullman Company had never given up its hope of running a truly fine train over this route. By late 1888 the company produced a set of cars specifically for that purpose. It was to be called the Golden Gate Special (fig. 14.12) and was designed to take the fatigue out of long-distance travel. There would be a crew of twenty to care for the travelers. A chambermaid would watch over the ladies and children. The men would find a barber shop and bathtub in the rear half of the baggage car. The ladies would find equal facilities next to the observation room on the last car. Two sleepers and a full diner eliminated three stops a day and the hazards of lunch-counter cuisine. The fare was set as a bargain to lure passengers aboard. A $100 ticket from Chicago to San Francisco included all costs and fees except for use of the berth and barber shop. The tickets were good for six months. The regular fare by sleeper was $226. Just why the Union Pacific management agreed to operate this train is puzzling, since they had put on their own fast train in November 1887 named the Overland Flyer. It appeared they were competing against themselves. Pullman's deluxe train moved along at 30 mph, which was fast for a western train. Yet its speed and luxury were not enough. That coupled with once-a-week service doomed the Golden Gate Special and it was abandoned. About a year after entering service, the Overland Flyer was upgraded in terms of rolling stock and speed over the years. In 1895 it was renamed the Overland Limited and became America's most distinguished western train.

In September 1896 a correspondent for *Engineering News* reported that the Union Pacific was now running twelve- to sixteen-car passenger trains at running speeds of 50 to 60 mph. They were powered by heavy ten-wheelers that were painted brown with gold striping. These engines had an old-fashioned look because of their diamond smokestacks, a necessity because of the lignite, or brown coal, fuel that was light and friable. They were modern and fast, making the run between Omaha and Ogden in twenty-nine and a half hours at an average speed of 35 mph. Seventy-pound rail and stone ballast provided a solid track and a smooth ride. The frontier was receding into the past as the western states came of age. Omaha was now a large city of 150,000 people. It would host an international fair in 1898, the Trans Mississippi and International Exposition, and was planning a fine new railroad terminal as part of that celebration.

Transportation had greatly improved since the days of stagecoach kings, but for all of the investment and high-quality engineering, the railway did not always run like a twenty-one-jewel Elgin watch. A British correspondent for the *London Times,* Edwin Pratt, wrote about his trip to Denver in the winter of 1903. He was riding the Rock Island line on his first adventure west of Chicago. They came to a stop at the little town of Kanorado, which straddles the Kansas and Colorado border 180 miles east of Denver. A freight train had derailed, blocking the single-track main line. In addition, the locomotive on his train had broken down. A relief engine was on the way, but it promised to be a long wait. Pratt walked uptown seeking breakfast. There was a hotel, a few stores, and a wooden sidewalk. The estimated population was around fifty. The hotel was family operated; the owner's wife and daughter cooked meals and served the guests. Major employment in the region was cattle feeding; the cows were transported to Chicago when ready for packing. The town was surrounded by miles of flat prairie that was lonely, cold, and completely empty. There were no trees nor a house nor shed in sight. How different it was from the English countryside.

The relief engine arrived, the track was cleared, and Pratt's train steamed off toward the Mile-High City. At midday they came to Limon, Colorado, 89 miles east of Denver. Everyone on the train headed for the station's lunchroom. Once again Pratt noticed the temporary mixing of the classes. On the train it was largely segregated – the coach passengers in their car, the first class in the sleeper, and the crew at their duty posts. Because there was no dining car (generally attached only to the best trains), everyone – rich and poor, educated and ignorant, black and white, the lame and the able – would all dine together. The meal was typical station fare: cold chicken, hard-boiled eggs, a variety of pies, and coffee. At this depot the coffee was genuine and very palatable.

Limon was at the junction of Chicago, Rock Island, and Pacific Railroad and the Union Pacific's Denver-to-Cheyenne branch, the former Denver Pacific Railroad. Some of the Rock Island cars would be attached to a regular Union Pacific train when it arrived. Pratt wandered around the station and tower during this interlude. Being so late, they had missed the scheduled connection. There was a notice posted to a telegraph pole offering choice lots of land for sale at $25 to $50 each. A herd of cattle was quietly grazing on one side of the station. Pike's Peak could be seen in the distance. Finally the train left for Denver on a single-track line; the northbound train had precedence over the southbound, so Pratt's train sat on a siding at several places. But once back on the main track they would put on a little speed, although it was nothing like the Rock Island, where the train would get up to 65 mph at times. Pratt would count the telegraph poles and use the second hand on his watch to estimate the speed. They reached Denver nearly ten hours late on a journey that had started in Chicago, 1,083 miles to the east. But no one had been injured or killed, so the railway was guilty of inconvenience but not murder. Actually most railroad managers would be much happier to carry nothing but coal or grain, because nonhuman cargo never complained about the heat, the food, the seats, or the lighting, or grumbled about being late.

PROMOTING TRAVEL

All railroad presidents understood the need for good passenger service. True, it consumed most of their time and generated endless vexation and very little direct profit. But service was the façade of the industry and the only side of the business that touched the public directly. If it was performed badly, the newspaper would hammer the railroads without mercy. *The Flyer was nine hours late, true enough, but allow us to explain all of the reasons. Another railroad accident – when will the Shore line stop murdering its patrons? Fares are much too high, commuters demand relief.* The railroads had an enormous job in responding to all of the bad news. Its press agents and chief passenger director were constantly trying to placate their critics. The newsmen could smell blood. *If it bleeds, it leads.* The industry responded by enforcement of their own safety rules, employee training, electric signals, air brakes, steel cars, all of which helped but could not make railway travel completely safe.

How to generate goodwill and a positive perception of railroading engaged some of the best minds in the industry. The Vanderbilts were clever; they made a public relations man president of their railroad. Chauncey M. DePew was a lawyer and Yale graduate. He was active in politics and served in the U.S. Senate, but he was best known as a wit and an after-dinner speaker and raconteur. He was dignified, smart, and very likeable. In 1865 he became a lobbyist for Cornelius Vanderbilt, just when the commander was getting serious about railroads. Vanderbilt was blunt, outspoken, and much in need of the services of a man like DePew, who could tactfully explain away the failings and misdeeds of New York

14.13. One of the first high-speed, long-distance trains in the United States was the New York Central Exposition Flyer that ran from New York to Chicago in twenty hours. The average speed was about 50 mph. The train ran only from May to November 1893 but was replaced several years later by another fast train that was soon renamed the 20th Century Limited.

(*McClure's Magazine*, January 1894)

Central in a convincing manner. He was made vice president and then, in 1885, president. His door was open to the press, the public, and even his employees. DePew's reputation grew so large, Benjamin Harrison offered to make him secretary of state. After retiring as president of the New York Central, he remained chairman of the board until his death in 1928.

Few other railroads were fortunate to find a chief with so great a talent. They tried to gain public favor with general passenger agents who also acted as press agents. One of the best was George H. Daniels (1842–1908), who was also employed by the New York Central. He was born in northern Illinois and entered railway service at the age of fifteen as a rodman for a survey team. By 1872 he was general traffic agent for the Chicago and Pacific Railroad. He worked for a number of western traffic associations before being appointed as the New York Central's general passenger agent in 1889. He proved to be a bold and imaginative promoter and an expert at grabbing headlines. Edward Hungerford claimed Daniels was the Prince Charming of the railroad industry. He understood America's love of speed and convinced the executive and operating departments to back his scheme for fast trains and high-stepping locomotives. In October 1891 the Central introduced the Empire State Express, a New York to Buffalo train, at an average speed of 50¾ mph. It made only four stops and was limited to four cars; the train's total weight was 270 tons, including the locomotive and tender. When in motion, the train traveled over 60 mph. The public, especially the male segment, was thrilled and wanted more. Daniels, eager to oblige, lobbied for the Exposition Flyer, which we have already discussed (fig. 14.13). For the Columbian Exposition itself, the New York Central created a high-wheel express locomotive, the 999, a steam-powered hot rod of its day. During a test that was staged and timed by the railroad's motive power staff, the engine recorded a speed of 112½ mph. Just how accurate this official speed was remains a question, but the

PASSENGER TRAINS: FIRST CLASS 473

stunt was a press agent's dream and is commonly recorded in reference works to the present day.

Daniels remained on the New York Central's staff long enough to see the 20th Century Limited installed in 1902 as their premier New-York-to-Chicago train with a running time of twenty hours. In other areas of his trade, which was not above considerable exaggeration, Daniels invented the slogan "America's Greatest Railroad." But the fact that the train followed a relatively straight water-level route was a more important point and Central's real selling argument. Travelers on the B&O Railroad, for example, were tossed from one side of the berth to the other as the train twisted and turned on the curving track, whereas travelers on the New York Central were much more comfortable because of the straight route. After a time Daniels's slogan was altered to read "The Water-Level Route – You Can Sleep." Daniels and his staff were active in publishing leaflets, brochures, and a house magazine called *Four Track News*. He published a directory describing the reports and places of interest on America's Greatest Railroad; the 1896 edition contained 532 pages. Daniels also spoke at professional meetings and was sure to flatter his audiences – for example, when he spoke in Chicago he likened that city to Florence, the economic and artistic powerhouse of Renaissance Italy. He might be best remembered for introducing redcap service to America (fig. 14.14). Porters were commonly found at British railway stations, where they helped with baggage and children. They would lead travelers to the front door, where they might find a streetcar or taxi. The service began at New York's Grand Central Station in March 1895 with a dozen men wearing conspicuous uniforms and a red turban cap. The redcaps were salaried employees and were ordered to refuse all tips or attempts of payment. (This tradition was eventually broken and the redcaps came to depend on tips for a living.)

The Baltimore and Ohio Railroad was into advertising and promotion from its beginning. Small newspaper notices provided information on schedules and fares. Broadsides were printed and posted to promote business. A freelance writer named Eli Bowen was hired in the mid-1850s to prepare a volume titled *Rambles in the Path of the Steam-Horse*. It featured a lively text intended to be cute and amusing. Dozens of line engravings showed scenes along the B&O line. It is almost certain the volume was sponsored by the railroad. A more formal account was published in 1858, *The Book of the Great Railway Celebrations of 1857*, which offered some history, an account of the formal opening of the line to St. Louis, and a transcript of the many speakers associated with that event. The volume of around 450 pages was prepared by the B&O's superintendent, William Prescott Smith. It, too, was well illustrated with engravings. A condensed version appeared in *Harper's Monthly* for April 1857 using many of the

14.14. Redcap service was introduced in Grand Central Station in March 1895 as one of George Daniels's many schemes to win patronage for his employer, the New York Central Railroad.

(Frank Leslie's Illustrated Weekly, June 26, 1896)

same line drawings. Smith was the likely promoter of the "artists special" excursion train that ran from Baltimore to Wheeling in June 1858. The story of this trip was also recorded in pages of *Harper's Monthly* about a year later. In 1880 the railroad hired a newspaperman to take over its advertising and promotions.

Joseph G. Pangborn was no match for George Daniels, and he found a greater challenge in representing the B&O in a fiercely competitive battle for passenger traffic. Both the New York Central and Pennsylvania Railroads had great resources as well as the advantage of better routes. The B&O main line was encumbered by a long, slow track through the West

14.15. An affluent group of diners enjoy a fine meal on a Baltimore and Ohio dining car at 40 mph.

(J. G. Pangborn, *Picturesque Baltimore & Ohio*, 1883)

Virginia mountains. Pangborn could not claim that the B&O trains were faster, offered a smoother ride, or were more luxurious. However, the scenery was better, and the B&O was one of the first eastern trunk lines to adopt dining cars (fig. 14.15). Pangborn's hook was history: the B&O was historic. He claimed it was the nation's first railroad, the Tom Thumb was the first locomotive, the Baltimore line was the pioneer mail carrier, and so on. Accuracy did not matter, but it was all more or less true.

As an ex-newspaperman, Pangborn could prepare copy that was certain to catch the attention of an editor. *Our trains roll through historic Harper's Ferry, site of John Brown's notorious raid and a place much liked by George Washington. We connect the historic nation's capital to the nation.* A circular trademark or logo was adopted by the B&O that showed the Capitol dome in its center and read around the border "All Trains Run Via Washington." Soon every railroad in the country had its own logo. All were eye-catching and were used with a promotional slogan such as "The Main Street of America" or the "Big Four Route." In 1883 Pangborn produced a sizable book called *Picturesque B&O: Historic and Descriptive* that was part travel guide and part history. Thomas Moran prepared drawings for the book that were converted into engravings.

Pangborn's great triumph came at the Columbian Exposition, where he created a display on the history of railways. It was the largest history display at the Chicago Exposition and attracted thousands of visitors. Full-size relics and wooden reproductions were shown along with photographs, prints, and drawings. Much of this collection is on display today at the B&O Museum in Baltimore. Pangborn also published a deluxe magazine called the *Royal Blue* that was given out freely to promote the B&O's Baltimore-to-New-York train. Photographs for the magazine and other promotional purposes were made by top artists in that field like William H. Jackson. Other railroads hired master photographers like Andrew J.

Russell, whose record of building the Union Pacific Railroad was distributed to the public in the form of stereopticon. These cards were easy to view in the comfort of one's parlor, and prints copied as lantern slides could be projected for the enjoyment of a large audience. Jackson produced a wonderful record of Colorado railroads that stimulated interest in touring the Rockies. Thomas Moran's magnificent painting of the Grand Canyon was reproduced (22 by 38 inches) as sheet-metal lithography by the Santa Fe Railroad passenger department. Such a handsome image was suitable for the downtown ticket office or the family living room.

Another way to sell tickets was to make it easy for the customer. Railroad depots were almost never found in the heart of town, especially in big cities, but the convenience of downtown ticket offices could and did bring in a lot of trade. This idea went back to steamship times, and the railroads were quick to copy it. The New York Central Railroad, for example, had ticket offices on Lower Broadway, on Clark Street in Chicago, and as far west as San Francisco. The B & O Railroad had a similar system of ticket offices. The Washington office was on H Street, only about two blocks from the White House. Uniformed delivery boys would bring tickets directly to a patron's office without charge.

Budgets for advertising were generous; by the 1890s a trunk line would spend 1 or 2 percent of its passenger revenues for promotion. Folders, leaflets, and timetables were standard items offered free to the public and would emphasize fast trains, electric lights, vestibules, steam heat, and dust-free stone ballast. The Santa Fe Railroad promoted Fred Harvey Restaurants and good food. The Michigan Central reminded patrons it was the direct way to Niagara Falls. The Lake Shore line was the fast mail line and used an official leather mailbag as its logo. The Burlington Railroad offered booklets on the scenery in the heart of the continent. It was common to print 500,000–600,000 folders a year as giveaways. It was money well spent that all came back through increased business.

Travel promotion often went beyond advertising and cheap fares. Certain railroads built and operated resort hotels or devised easy access to existing scenic areas. Many New England roads refined this service to serve popular vacation destinations such as Bar Harbor, Maine, and the White Mountains in northern New Hampshire. Obscure towns such as North Conway and Littleton, New Hampshire, became major destinations on the Boston and Maine Railroad from Boston, or the Maine Central Railroad from Portland. During the summer season a dozen trains a day would arrive with tourists eager for the cool mountain air. They stayed at enormous wooden hotels with wide porches for $7 a week. Visitors could wander the trails on foot or horseback to see national wonders such as the Great Stone Face or Franconia Notch in New Hampshire. Special open observation cars were operated on trains so that less athletic souls could ride over the state's Frankenstein Trestle or see the Presidential Mountain Ranges. It was possible to reach the top of Mount Washington, the tallest in this range, by a cog railway. On a clear day – a rather rare occurrence on that stormy peak – you could see as far away as Quebec.

The New York Central Railroad specialized in carrying weary city folks to the Adirondacks in northern New York. It was a forest preserve that was popular with sportsmen and those seeking a spiritual revival from a few days in the remoteness of the woods. By the early 1870s railroads began to invade the area. Resort hotels and a steamship line soon appeared on Blue Mountain Lake. It was not long before Wagner parlor cars were rumbling through the pristine forest. August Belmont and Collis P. Huntington came by private car to escape the summer heat of Wall Street. At the same time, lumbermen and iron miners were extracting nature's gifts that had stood undisturbed since the beginning of time. In 1892 New York created the Adirondack state park to preserve what they could of this splendid land.

The Baltimore and Ohio Railroad devised its own plan for a series of hotels along its route for the comfort of passengers who grew weary of too many days on the cars. Here was an opportunity to get off for a day or two and resume the trip. Or the wayfarer might choose to stay the summer. The first of these hostelries, the Glades, was built on a beautiful mountaintop meadow. A station designated as Oakland, Maryland, was located at the same place. The Glades Hotel was a small, two-story, whitewashed structure famous for its beautiful setting and its locally made whiskey. This amber liquid was said to slip between your teeth as easy as flaxseed tea. Some visitors would take home a barrel of this rare malt beverage – it was that tasty. In 1876 a new less-rustic hotel was built behind the Glades, and an even larger and grander hotel was put up at nearby Deer Park by the B&O in 1873. In a few years, after several remodelings, this hotel was enlarged to 110 rooms. It was near the summit of the railroad, 2,700 feet in elevation, and about 226 miles west of Baltimore. The railroad also had large hotels at Relay, just west of Baltimore and at Cumberland, Maryland.

One hundred thirty or so miles south of the Deer Park Hotel were a series of natural springs along the border of Virginia and West Virginia. They, too, were celebrated for their curative powers in precolonial times. The Chesapeake and Ohio Railroad built through this area in the summer of 1869. A dozen years earlier a hotel built at White Sulphur Springs, West Virginia, became a popular resort. The wood hotel was affectionately known throughout the south as "The White." Plantation owners would come here to escape the summer heat. Many of the first families of the south would gather here to enjoy lawn tennis during the day and sip on mint juleps during the evening; this sweet alcoholic drink was invented at The White. Henry Clay and J. C. Calhoun were regulars there, but Yankees like Martin Van Buren were welcome as well. In 1890 the Chesapeake and Ohio purchased the Homestead Hotel at Warm Springs, Virginia, about thirty miles northeast of White Sulphur Springs. It was a fine traffic generator, so in 1910 the railroad purchased The White as well. A new hotel intended for year-round use was built in 1913.

In 1875 the St. Louis Iron Mountain and Southern Railroad reached Hot Springs, Arkansas. These large mineral springs had been a healing source for the rheumatic since about 1830. The U.S. government created the nation's first federal reserve here, and the area was made a national park in 1921. The railroad purchased part of the property through an act of Congress and operated a restaurant at this place for many years.

In the far West, the Yellowstone, Wyoming, area was long recognized for its hot springs and geysers. Naturalists were convinced the area must be preserved as a natural wonder, but they had little influence with territorial or federal officials. It took a railroad promoter to persuade Congress that setting aside land here was a worthy idea and that fast action was necessary lest the region be destroyed by developers. Jay Cooke was a Wall Street financier and much involved in building and financing the Northern Pacific Railroad. As a devout Christian, Cooke exhibited a bit more soul than the average tycoon of the Gilded Age. He pressed Congress into setting aside this volcanic area in the northwestern corner of Wyoming as the world's first national park. Experts in earth science might plead with congressmen for years about the wisdom of preserving the area, but experts knew too much, and they only confused or annoyed the average politician. However, if a very rich man like Cooke thought it was important, it must be a sensible plan. In time, the Northern Pacific would pass near the entrance of Yellowstone and benefit from the tourist traffic. Americans for generations to come would benefit from the preservation of this 3,400-square-mile park that was a hotbed of springs, including the famous spout Old Faithful.

In a like manner, the Southern Pacific Railroad lobbied for the establishment of Yosemite Park in California. Naturalist John Muir was astonished that this "soulless" railway would help so nobly in preserving this spectacular scenic region on the west slope of the Sierra Nevadas. The western railways were active in establishing tourist hotels catering to well-off tourists. In 1880 the Southern Pacific opened the Del Monte Resort at Monterey, California, an easy commute from San Francisco. The hotel was a decorative Swiss Gothic structure with rooms for five hundred guests. It had glorious gardens with fine trees, lakes, and heliotropes as tall as trees. There was an indoor swimming pool with a glass roof. The climate was semitropical and delighted most visitors.

A larger resort hotel, the Hotel del Coronado, was opened in San Diego in February 1888 by retired railroad executive Elisha S. Babcock. It had its own private railway powered by a dummy locomotive that carried visitors from the ferry wharf to the hotel's front door. The building was constructed of a vast pile of siding and wooden shingles in what might be described as Queen Anne style. There were 379 rooms and a dining hall that could seat one thousand people. Two thousand Chinese carpenters and laborers put the structure up in less than a year and worked for another two years finishing the details. This Victorian giant is still standing and functioning as a hotel.

RENTAL CARS AND RENTAL TRAINS

For those seeking greater exclusivity there was no better way to travel than by a private rail car. The notion of a special car being required for notable persons goes back to the opening of the Liverpool and Manchester Railway in 1830. A very special and decorative car was built for the Duke of Wellington, who rode in the first train. No one would consider seating the prime minister and hero of Waterloo in an ordinary car. In the 1830s private cars were also quickly adopted in America, egalitarian principles aside, for railroad officials. They grew in size, elegance, and complexity that were equal to a small but deluxe hotel on wheels. By 1870 wealthy businessmen felt they deserved and could afford their own railroad car. Because they were persons of influence, their cars were willingly moved by the national rail system.

There is a good record available on a special car constructed for John Garrett, the president of the B&O Railroad, in the late 1850s. It was not a large vehicle, being only about 40 feet long, and was divided into three compartments. The rear platform was built as a viewing platform, in the earliest known mention for what came to be called an observation deck. A high iron railing protected occupants from falling off. It was open and breezy but offered a splendid view of the passing scene. The center compartment was a bedroom, while the rear space was a combination pantry and crew's quarters. The exterior was painted maroon with dark blue panels and highly varnished. The inside was pure white and nicely furnished with rugs, draperies, and gilt mirrors. In 1872 the railroad repair shop at Mt. Clare produced a well-engineered and well-finished car for Garrett named the Maryland. It was larger than the car just described, and its interior was divided into four compartments. The inside paneling was dark and somber, but gilt trim and the use of mirrors brightened it somewhat. Garrett traveled thousands of miles in this luxurious vehicle. He lent it to friends and acquaintances, including several U.S. presidents. Lincoln had traveled in the earlier Garrett car several times, and Grant and other presidents rode in the Maryland. It was so convenient being stationed in Baltimore, just 40 miles from the White House.

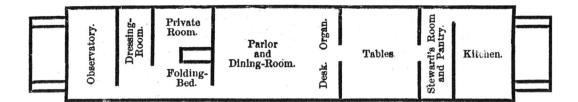

14.16. The floor plan of Pullman's private car, the Pullman Palace Car of 1877. This car carried many U.S. presidents as well as notables to and from every corner of the United States.

(*Harper's Weekly*, October 8, 1887)

Another private car frequented by U.S. presidents was Tom Scott's business car, the 120, a product of the Pennsylvania Railroad's Altoona shops in 1871. It was comfortable and spacious, but not elegant or even pretty. The tops of most of the arched windows were covered over. The exterior was a blood-red color unrelieved by striping or gilt work. The running gear was brown and the wheels a bright green. Most of the interior was paneled in black walnut, except for the large dining room, which was covered in mahogany. One unusual feature was the bathtub, likely one of the first installed on a railway car. Many distinguished persons rode on the 120, including the Grand Duke Alexis, Prince Arthur, presidents Grant and Hayes, and members of all cabinets. James Garfield was transported in the 120 at no charge from his home in Ohio to Washington for his inaugural ceremony.

Commodore Vanderbilt traveled in a fine car befitting his station as a railway king. Considering Vanderbilt's wealth and power, the car was actually rather plain and reserved. It was painted cream with the cornices in a darker shade of cream. The only ornamentation was a keystone lettered with the commodore's monogram. The interior was more lively and featured black walnut woodwork and silver-plated hardware and fittings. Large plate-glass windows offered a fine view of the scenery. The old man had an aversion to gas lighting, so candles were used instead. The commodore was not much given to lending his cars – at least there is no obvious record of its use by others. He did like to go fast, and he would present a $10 gold piece if the train made a particularly fast run. His son and successor as president of the New York Central, William H. Vanderbilt, had one of the largest private cars in the nation. It had a special stateroom for the chief and a card room for his pals. The exterior was decorated with paintings of scenes along the railroad from Grand Central Station to Niagara Falls. William, like his father, liked to travel fast, and all other trains were ordered to stay out of the way when the "president's special" was on the road.

Curiously, George Pullman never had a private car built for his exclusive use. The company had several such cars available as rentals, and Pullman's favorite was the PPC, the initials representing the Pullman Palace Car (Company). He used the PPC so regularly that it became known as Mr. Pullman's car (fig. 14.16). It was built in 1877 with a large central dining room/parlor and bedroom space suitable for ten people. The triple sets of windows – a large central pane flanked by narrow side panes – gave the car a distinctive appearance. Fifteen expert wood-carvers created a delicate and refined oak interior in the Eastlake style. The ceiling was painted to represent ferns, flowers, and hummingbirds. Pullman believed that an elegant room had a profound influence on human behavior. *Put the roughest man in a palatial setting, and somehow it improves his manners. The more refined the surroundings, the more refined the man.* There was a reed organ in the main room. The car was watched over by Arthur Wells, the chief steward and the personal attendant to Mr. Pullman whenever he traveled by rail. The car might be rented for $85 a day, which included a conductor, a cook, and two stewards. In addition, every passenger would have to purchase eighteen first-class tickets for every mile of travel. On some lines an extra charge was made for crossing bridges. Provisions would be provided by Pullman at cost, or the renter could buy his own. If the travelers desired to be pulled by their own locomotive, most railroads would provide one for 25 cents a mile, but it was much cheaper to attach the rented car to a regular train.

In the fall of 1887 the Pullman Company put together a special train for Grover Cleveland and his young wife. It was to be a 4,500-mile goodwill tour of the United States that would include a dozen cities from St. Paul to Atlanta. The PPC was reserved for the president and his wife, with Arthur Wells attending to their care with almost or as much attention as if George Pullman were the sole passenger. The couple had traveled in Robert Garrett's private car on their honeymoon in June 1885. This was a less strenuous journey, ending at the B&O's summer resort of Deer Park in western Maryland, just about 260 miles from Washington.

The opening of the transcontinental railroad in May 1869 created much public excitement by creating a thin line of civilization across a vast, unsettled land. Officials of the Boston Board of Trade found that many of their members were eager to see the wonders of the West. These wealthy merchants could afford such a trip and hoped to establish business relations with their counterparts on the Pacific Coast. George Pullman agreed to furnish an eight-car train for 150 riders. The first two cars would offer space for baggage, supplies, bunks for newspapermen, a smoking and card-playing compartment, plus a barber shop. Two hotel cars offered sleeping berths and a small kitchen for light meals. Two saloon cars offered more berths and a parlor for daytime gatherings – one of these cars was the Palmyra, mentioned earlier in this chapter. The final two cars were commissary cars, which combined a full-size diner and kitchen with enough berths for twenty people.

The trip and its deluxe train generated much interest as far away as Britain, where the magazine *Leisure Hour* commented on the rich and beautiful carpets, the ravishing upholstery and cabinet work, and a kitchen ready to serve up viands in a splendid style. The American press was excited as well, and Pullman was repaid a thousand times over with positive publicity. Just think – traveling 7,000 miles, and it was a pleasant experience and not a dusty ordeal.

The train left Boston on the morning of Monday, May 23, 1870, to travel over the Boston and Albany, New York Central, and Great Western (Canada) Railroads to Chicago. It then followed the Chicago and North Western Railroad to Council Bluffs, Iowa. The special left Omaha on Friday, May 27, and rambled over the Union Pacific and Central Pacific Railroads, stopping only to change engines or pick up water and fuel. At two places open observation cars were added so that passengers might better see the splendor of the Rockies. Special arrangements were made so that the Boston train could enter the city over streetcar tracks, and the locomotive and its cars traveled down Market Street into the very center of San Francisco. The train came to rest at one o'clock in the morning of June 1, 1870. The visitors toured the city and California generally before departing late in June.

Train rentals were fun for passengers and profitable for the Pullman Company. They were not limited to the well-heeled; middle-class folks went in special trains or cars provided from Pullman's reserve fleet. Groups, fraternal and religious, would travel in this manner to meetings and conventions.

Pullman had been in the rental car business since 1870. A few years later two old sleeping cars acquired from the Central Transportation Company were rebuilt and renamed the Davy Crockett and the Izaak Walton. They were less highly finished than the typical Pullman and were meant to appeal to hunting and fishing parties who wanted to rough it in comfort. They came with a cook and waiter at the bargain rate of $35 a day. They had room for up to fifteen people and were equipped with gun racks and dog kennels.

Jerome Marble went on a hunting trip to the Dakota Territory – perhaps on one of Pullman's cars just named – and found it a wonderful experience. The plains were teaming with big game. Millions of buffalo, elk, and antelope could be seen from the car windows. Passengers would lean out of the ordinary coach windows and fire away at whatever passed by. The Kansas Pacific Railroad rented out excursion trains to hunt buffalo. Marble was a banker and businessman from Worcester, Massachusetts, with capital and business experience to compete with Pullman for this specialized part of the rental car market. He organized the Worcester Excursion Car Company in July 1878. The company's first car, named the City of Worcester, took a party of fourteen on a seventy-eight-day 4,000-mile trip for just $203 each. The catch of one trip to Nebraska and Iowa was reported in the December 12, 1879, *Railroad Gazette:* in sixty days a party on one of Marble's cars dispatched 96 geese; 256 ducks; 188 quail; 8 woodcocks; 12 jackrabbits; 2 deer; and no less than 1,557 prairie chickens. Marble added more cars and opened a ticket office in Manhattan on Lower Broadway. By the late 1880s Worcester had nine cars in service and counted notables such as Sarah Bernhardt and Edwin Booth among its customers. The census of 1890 officially declared that the western frontier was closed. The huge herds of buffalo had been all but exterminated a decade earlier. The Worcester Excursion Car Company shut down around 1895. However, the car rental field was prospering as a Pullman monopoly in 1900. They had two dozen cars available and were also leasing parlor cars to wealthy commuter groups in New York and Philadelphia.

The railroad passenger business continued for another seven decades as a private enterprise after Queen Victoria's death in 1901. By 1916 the Interstate Commerce Commission declared the railroads controlled 98 percent of the nation's passenger business. Mileage peaked in the same year at 250,000 miles. The passenger traffic kept growing until the late 1920s. By this time the automobile and motor car had captured much of short-distance travel. Many local trains were eliminated, and suburban service around large cities began to disappear. The hard times following the stock market collapse of 1929 dampened the travel market in general. Tourism suffered, and only the wealthier class could vacation to faraway places.

The primitive condition of interstate highways made long road trips slow. Such roads were paved, but almost none were more than two lanes. All wandered through large and small communities, making trips long in terms of time. Roads through mountainous areas were burdened by steep grades and sharp curves. There were few expressways and almost no beltways around large cities. It was simply faster to take the train to Chicago or New York or Portland if the distance was of any consequence. No driver could hope to match the speed of the Broadway Limited from New York to Chicago in sixteen hours – even if he drove in a very reckless manner well over the speed limits. The same would be true for the New York Central's Cincinnati-to-Chicago train, the James Whitcomb Riley, which made the 302-mile run in five and a half hours over a secondary main line. This schedule could be made regardless of the weather. The trains were reliable, safe, clean, and comfortable.

As late as 1939 railroads continued to handle two-thirds of the long-distance commercial travel. The airlines were beginning to take an increasing bite of the trade, but it was not until the introduction of the jetliner that they really began to cut away the railroad's margin. At the same time, the interstate highway plan was creating excellent roads that permitted cruising speeds of 70 mph and bypasses around most towns and cities. By 1965 the railroads controlled only 20 percent of interstate travel. The prospect of no rail passenger service became very real, so the U.S. Congress created a federal agency, the National Railroad Passenger Corporation, to maintain a skeleton system known as Amtrak. In 1970 President Nixon signed the legislation with the understanding that Amtrak could be made self-sustaining. That has not been the case, but federal subsidies have kept the trains running. Meanwhile, most Western European nations have invested in an excellent system of high-speed rail passenger service.

SUGGESTED READING

Barger, Ralph L. *A Century of Pullman Cars*. Sykesville, Md.: Greenberg, vol. 1, 1988, vol. 2, 1990.

Beebe, Lucius Morris. *20th Century: The Greatest Train in the World*. Berkeley, Calif.: Howell-North, 1962.

———. *Mr. Pullman's Elegant Palace Car: The Railway Carriage That Established a New Dimension of Luxury and Entered the National Lexicon as a Symbol of Splendor*. Garden City, N.Y.: Doubleday, 1961.

———. *Overland Limited*. Berkeley, Calif.: Howell-North, 1963.

Bowen, Eli. *Rambles in the Path of the Steam-Horse: An Off-hand Olla Podrida*. Philadelphia: W. M. Bromwell and Wm. White Smith, 1855.

Douglas, George. *All Aboard the Railroad in American Life*. New York: Smithmark, 1996.

Dubin, Arthur D. *More Classic Trains*. Milwaukee: Kalmbach Books [1974].

———. *Some Classic Trains*. Milwaukee: Kalmbach Books, 1964.

Harwood, Herbert H. *Royal Blue Line*. Sykesville, Md.: Greenberg, 1990.

Hungerford, Edward. *Modern Railroad*. 1st ed. Chicago: McClurg, 1911.

Marshall, Walter Gore. *Through America; or, Nine Months in the United States*, by W. G. Marshall. London: S. Low, Marston, Searle, and Rivington, 1881.

Mencken, August. *Railroad Passenger Car: An Illustrated History of the First Hundred Years, with Accounts by Contemporary Passengers*. Baltimore: Johns Hopkins University Press, 1957.

Muirhead, James F. *Land of Contrasts: A Briton's View of His American Kin*. London: Lane, 1900.

Pangborn, Joseph G. *Picturesque B & O: Historic and Descriptive*. Chicago: Knight and Leonard, 1883.

Post, Robert C. *Technology, Transport, and Travel in American History*. Washington, D.C.: American Historical Association, 2003.

Pratt, Edwin A. *American Railways*. London: Macmillan, 1903.

Reinhardt, Richard. *Out West on the Overland Train, Across the Continent Excursion with Leslie's Magazine in 1877 and the Overland Trip in 1967*. Secaucus, N.J.: Castle Books, 1967.

Runte, Alfred. *Trains of Discovery: Western Railroads and the National Parks*. Boulder, Col.: Roberts Rinehart, 1998.

Soderbere, Lisa. "Western Tourism and the Pullman Car." Unpublished paper. Washington, D.C., 1976.

Sipes, William B. *Pennsylvania Railroad: Its Origin, Construction, Condition, and Connections*. Philadelphia: Pennsylvania Railroad, 1875.

Scudder, Horace Elisha. *Recollections of Samuel Breck, with Passages from His Note-Books (1771–1862)*. London: Low, Marston, Searle, and Rivington, 1877.

Shearer, Frederick E. and Williams, Henry T. *Pacific Tourist: J. R. Bowman's Illustrated Trans-continental Guide of Travel, from the Atlantic to the Pacific Ocean*. New York: Bowman, 1883.

Smith, William Prescott. *The Book of the Great Railway Celebrations of 1857*. New York: D. Appleton and Co., 1858.

Trollope, Anthony. *North America*. 2 volumes. London: Chapman and Hall, 1862.

Tye, Larry. *Rising from the Rails: Pullman Porters and the Making of the Black Middle Class.* New York: Holt, 2004.

Ward, James A. *Railroads and the Character of America, 1820–1887.* Knoxville: University of Tennessee Press, 1986.

Williams, Frederick S. *Our Iron Roads: Their History, Construction, and Social Influences.* London: Ingram, Cooke, 1852.

White, John H., Jr. *American Railroad Passenger Car.* Baltimore: Johns Hopkins University Press, 1978.

Zega, Michael E., and John E. Gruber. *Travel by Train: The American Railroad Poster, 1870–1950.* Bloomington: Indiana University Press, 2002.

Appendix

Travel Words & Tales

THIS APPENDIX COVERS THE ORIGINS OF WORDS CONCERNING travel and, wherever possible, relates some aspect of travel history to those words. For example, when I refer to words relating to roads, I include something about the early road builders, vehicles, or taverns.

Although I spend time discussing words, this is not a vocabulary lesson. The words are commonplace and, for the most part, are in everyday use. You all can identify a ship's hull, an anchor, or a deck. So the point here is not to dwell on the modern meaning but to investigate where the word came from. Origins and original meanings can often be rather startling.

The days of the week are about as commonplace as any words in English. There is no mystery about Sunday, Monday, and so on. We all know Sunday is the first day of the week; it is a day for rest, reflection, and worship. The surprise is that the Lord's Day is named for the sun, that great fireball at the center of our planetary system. It was once avidly worshiped by our pagan ancestors thousands of years ago. And Monday is the moon's day. The moon was also the object of pre-Christian devotions. It doesn't get any better as we move along: Tuesday is named after the Teutonic god of war; Wednesday is Mercury's day; Thursday is named for the Norse god of thunder, or Thor. Saturday is named for Saturn, a very ancient Roman god who ruled the universe before being succeeded by his son, Jupiter. Friday is in some ways the most interesting; it is named for Frigg or Frigga, the Norse goddess of the heavens. She was also the goddess of matrimony and love and the wife of Odin, the supreme Norse god. Frigga was a major goddess, and she was understandably upset when the Nordic tribes abandoned her for Christianity in about 1100. Frigga was not about to become another forgotten has-been, so every Friday she and eleven witches, plus one devil, met to create whatever toil and trouble this group of thirteen could conjure up. Thus Friday the thirteenth has become known as a day of misfortunes.

I hope I have prepared you to understand that many everyday words have complex and unexpected origins. Part of this is because English is such a rich and complex language. It is not pure, nor is it from a single source. It was built up over the centuries as England became home to new groups of people. England was conquered or invaded several times over the past two millenniums. The Romans came about the time of Christ, and Latin became the language of the land. In the fifth century the Anglo-Saxons, a Germanic people, took over Britain after Rome had abandoned it as a colony. So the basics of modern English were established, but you and I would have great difficulty speaking and understanding Old English. In 1066 William of Normandy crossed the channel, and French because the language of the land. We must not forget to mix in a solid dash of Danish, for the Danes controlled a good-size piece of Britain in around AD 900. Modern English appears around 1450.

From this brief review, you can see that English was a linguistic melting pot of four languages. This alloy generated a huge half-million-word vocabulary so that we now have at least forty-three words to express joy and thirty-nine to express sadness. Most languages have only one or two words to express an idea. English is spoken by 20 percent of the world's population, and about another 20 percent use it as a second language. It has become the standard for commerce and technology and is used by international airports.

With this information as a background, we are ready to get on with "Travel Words and Tales." We will start with some of the general words that apply to all forms of transportation from marine to airway. We can do no better than start with the most basic word: *travel*. It's a happy word. People's spirits brighten at the very mention of a trip. We all envision a holiday, our escape from the care of work and the routine of life. We need a break. Let's take trips and leave our troubles behind. Everyone loves to travel!

That is true if you are speaking of recent generations. But your ancestors, well, they likely had misgivings about travel. They felt very differently, for in the past, travel was rarely done for pleasure. It was a painful and dangerous adventure, full of adversity and hardship. The going was not only slow, but also it was often a painful rather than a pleasurable experience.

Why? Well, it was all explained by the root word for *travel,* which is *travail.* The original meaning of travel was just that, a travail. Now, as the rigors of travel lessened, roads and ships improved, regular schedules were established, and better food and lodging were offered, the meaning of *travel* took on a new and more positive meaning. Today it has evolved completely, and most people are enthusiastic travelers. Some folks speak of *going on tour,* or *touring,* as another expression for pleasure travel. Here is another old word that has changed meaning, but in a less dramatic fashion. The word *tour* comes from the ancient Greeks. The Romans picked it up; in Latin it is *tornus,* which means a circle-making tool (or a compass?). In later times a tour meant making a circuit, just as a dramatic company would move from town to town offering a stage production. When the local audience was satisfied, the group would move on, eventually returning to their home base. Now a tour is understood as group travel led by a guide, where the travelers go along on a prearranged journey. All stay in the same hotel, eat the same meal, see the same sights, and enjoy the benefits of a packaged travel experience.

I mentioned the word *holiday* earlier, and I know you are familiar with Holiday Inns, Holiday Spas, Holiday Pools, and Holiday just about everything else. But the original meaning of the word has been much corrupted in modern usage. It once meant something very serious. I need only pronounce it in its original cadence to make the point – holy day. This was a day for reflection and prayer and, to a degree, celebration. But it was not to be taken lightly or treated as "party time." Fortunately, for those of you who have forgotten the serious beginnings of holy day, there is always a plentitude of serious-minded old men around to remind the slackers of their waywardness. I might add that *halibut* was so named because it was a fish to eat on holy or fast days.

There are some other words common to all forms of travel. We talk about *roaming;* this term goes back to early Christian times when pilgrims would wander off in search of Rome, the seat of the mother church. To take an *excursion,* on the other hand, originally meant to run (in Latin). A *journey* started out as a French word for a day's work or a day's march. From this you will understand that a *journeyman* is a day worker. Let us consider *trip* – a word in daily use but vastly different from its original Teutonic meaning of "to dance or to skip."

What about the word *junket*? It's in the newspaper every time a congressman takes a trip. Here is this guy traveling around the world in luxury, at the taxpayers' expense. With such a clear and well-established meaning, it's difficult to believe that the original Latin meaning of *junket* referred to a particular marsh plant. The reeds of the *juncos* plant were used to make containers for a cream cheese. By the 1300s the English used the word to describe any sort of sweet dish from pastries to custards. The word then evolved once again to describe a large picnic, where eating and drinking was part of the entertainment. From this, *junket* came to mean a pleasure trip, and then, in more modern times, it took on a more judgmental and negative meaning.

Resort is another familiar word that has undergone a less dramatic transformation. Today it is a destination, usually a fine hotel on the islands or a famous beach. Most resorts are glamorous and expensive and a place we all long to visit. Resorts are a plush stopover for those on tour, an excursion, a holiday, or a junket! But originally the word meant a place of rest, relief, assistance, or repair – all so different from its modern meaning. I think from these examples you can see why it would be difficult for us to step back into the past, for if we would brightly suggest visiting a resort, then our ancestors would think we needed to go to a hospital.

I can remember my English grandparents talking about *booking* tickets. No one says things like that anymore. You might hear it as a line in a very old play or movie, but no contemporary travelers go to a booking office – unless you are playing the horses. Yet this was once a very common term. What does it mean? Very simply, in a time before tickets you would "book" your passage on a boat or a stagecoach or even a train. You could go to a boat itself, but more often you would go to a harbor-side tavern. They maintained a large, leather-bound ledger book for the purpose of booking a trip. If you wished to sail on the ship *Spring Green* for Liverpool on May the tenth, you would pay your fare and a clerk would record your name, the date, the fare, and other necessary details. A copy of this record was made and given to the ship's captain or the first mate. This sheet was the *manifest* – a term still used in shipping today. You would report to the ship on the day of sailing and be greeted by a clerk who would read down the manifest: "Oh, yes, here you are, Mr. Pierce. You are sharing Cabin 2 with a Mr. Haffner." The same thing went on with stagecoaches and early railways: the big book, the manifest sheet, but no tickets. Yet even years after tickets were issued as proof of payment, old-fashioned people would persist in saying they were going down to the ticket office to book their passage.

Printed tickets for travel began to appear in about 1820 and were fairly common by 1840. The word *ticket* is much, much older. Originally it meant a small slip of paper for short notes. Later, tickets were used as evidence of a right or token of admission to the palace or a ceremony or some other important place or event. In centuries past they were handwritten.

When purchasing passage, the matter of cost was always a basic question: What is the fare? *Fare* is an Anglo-Saxon word that originally had nothing to do with the cost of travel. It meant simply "to go." It was also used as an informal blessing – as in "fare thee well" – or travel safely. And now it simply means the cost of travel.

I have finished talking about general travel words, and so we will move on to the major modes of travel. Let's begin with some marine words and the various parts of a ship. We might as well start at the front. Pretend that I am the *bow* of the ship – what I am doing is bowing to the sea. You will observe this motion even in a small boat as it plows through the water. In the early days of sail, there was often a large structure on the bow called the *forecastle*. This was soon shortened to *focsle* and referred to the place where the crew slept. Focsles have been obsolete for upward of three hundred years, but the word is still around.

If you will look over the ship's side, you will see two anchors hanging down from the bow. Why two anchors? Because you might lose one or, if the wind comes up, you might need two to hold your position and not be blown into the shore. The word *anchor* comes from the Latin word *ank*, which means bent or crooked – just like the shape of an anchor.

Follow me to the *stern* of the boat – you understand we are moving toward the rear of the vessel. In Old English *stern* meant steering. The boat was directed from the *read*. Before around 1250, this was done with a steering board – a large, paddle-like device hung over the right side of the ship. The steering or stern board was replaced by the more modern *rudder*, but the term *stern board* survives to the present day as *starboard* or the right-hand side of the ship. The stern board was on the right because most people are right-handed. *Port* was used for the left side. Port and starboard – unless you are a mariner, you may have heard these two words all your life and wondered what they meant.

Now that we have rudder at the center of the ship's stern, we need someone to man it. The earliest rudders were operated by a *tiller*, or a long post that reached back into the hull's interior at the rear and belowdecks. The *helmsman* was thus belowdecks and could not see where he was going. A lookout on deck shouted orders below, and the helmsman would shift the tiller accordingly. The space where the helmsman stood was called *steerage*. But, as with so many words, it took a more general meaning over succeeding generations, and any space below the main deck became known as steerage. So when we talk about immigrants coming to America in steerage, it means they traveled belowdecks in what was basically the cargo space. There were no portholes and no ventilators other than the main hatch, and that was tightly closed during times of heavy weather. This meant the immigrants sat in the dark with little fresh air and no chance to go up on deck. Think of the smells, the sounds of the ship crashing through the waves, the absence of a cooked meal, and the sheer boredom of being in a dark hole for days on end until the waves settled down. Life in steerage was not pleasant – it was a travail.

You can be sure the captain, the mates (junior officers), and the first-class passengers spent little time in steerage. They were housed in the *stern castle* or, as it more commonly has beencalled in recent centuries, the *cabin*. The cabin was above deck; it had windows or portholes and was laid out as a large, single room. It served as a combination parlor, dining room, and bedchamber. Small, separate bedrooms became common by around 1800. This was the captain's headquarters. The word *captain* is derived from Latin for "head." Hence the captain is the head man or leader, just as the capital – be it London, Rome, or Washington – is headquarters of the government.

We should say a little more about the captain. He was the master of the ship, and when the ship left the shore, he was absolutely in charge. What he said was like the word of God. No sailor would question the captain's word. Passengers who did so were at risk as well. If the captain decided a passenger was undermining his authority by his or her impertinence, the master of the ship might have such a person put in the *brig* for a few days to reconsider their deportment. The U.S. Navy used twin-mast sailing ships, or *brigs,* as prison ships; thus *brig* came to refer to the military prison onboard a ship.

It would be challenging to cover all of the many types of ships in early existence even in a separate book. In considering sailboats alone there are *cutters, brigs, schooners, clippers,* and *windjammers.* However, I am going to explain instead a common seagoing vessel of no particular rig or hull shape, and this is the *packet boat.* The term *packet boat* was a very common description for steamers on American inland waterways. It referred to a vessel used for both freight and passengers. Seagoing packets tended to follow regular routes. For example, *The Royal William* normally ran between Liverpool and New York, whereas *The Eliza* almost always operated between Baltimore and Charleston. But why the name *packet*?

The name comes from something that is really rather incidental to the packet's operation. It involved mail, letters, perhaps even very small packages, but in general, international correspondence. The letters were piled up and tied together, forming small packets. This is how the system worked: If you wished to get a letter to a relative in England, your best bet was to visit a tavern along the New York waterfront. You would inquire of the tavern keeper, who might tell you of a Captain Shaw, master of *The Royal William;* she is a regular trader and goes back and forth to Liverpool as regularly as a ship's chronometer. "The captain's a good man; he will take your letter. I already have a little bundle started for him," the tavern keeper would say. It might take your letter months to reach England, because one-way transit across the Atlantic usually required thirty days. The system was informal, but it seemed to work pretty well. Newspapers were transported back and forth in the same fashion. Papers in London would copy American papers, but of course the news was pretty stale by the time it reached the other side of the big pond.

So far I have tried to keep this subject somewhat light, but, alas, life is not always so. And it's true that even today one of the common features of ocean travel is that dread malady – seasickness. Some people turn green just standing on the dock. Others can bounce around through the mightiest storms without the least ill effects. I served in the navy and must confess I spent some time hanging over the rail paying tribute to old Neptune. *Nausea* is one word used to describe seasickness. We might note that *naus* also inspired the English words *naval* and *nautical.*

You need not be an old sea dog to identify a *ship's log*. We all know it's a daily record of the ship's history. Each day, the captain writes in his book about the weather, his location, a cargo broken loose, a man overboard, an insolent tourist fed to the sharks, or any incidents of importance. The ship's log was not always a book or a diary. Originally it was a device used to calculate the ship's speed. Try to imagine a torpedo-shaped contraption, about two feet long, outfitted with fins, and having a light towline attached. The earliest of these "speedometers" were fashioned from a small log – the same kind you throw in your fireplace. The log was given a pointed end, a few fins, and a line. When thrown into the sea and towed behind the boat, it would spin. The faster it spun, the faster the ship was moving. The captain would look out and say, "I think we're going about four knots." The mate would, of course, agree: "Four knots it is, sir!" A record of this observation was made in a daybook – April 12, 1718, noon, traveling at four knots. From this, a rough calculation of the ship's location could be made. The daybook became known simply as the ship's log. I had best explain that a *knot* is a unit of speed, not distance. Distance at sea is measure in nautical miles, or 6,080 feet, which are somewhat larger than a land mile. Hence, when speed is recorded in knots, you are going faster than if it were recorded in miles per hour.

Now, one last sea word, and then we will move on to highways and other matters. We don't expect large corporations or businesses to receive names in an indirect or haphazard fashion. General Motors and Microsoft are names that were carefully created for major enterprises. Some firms were named after their founders, such as Sears and Roebuck or Allis-Chalmers. *Lloyd's,* the giant insurance underwriting company headquartered in London, began operations in 1688 primarily in the marine insurance business. It was a high-risk business because ships and their cargo are at the mercy of the weather, sea, fire, collisions, and even pirates. The rates were accordingly high. If the ship came through, the partners who had underwritten that vessel profited handsomely. If the boat was lost the underwriters might be ruined, because their risk was unlimited and they might lose everything. This organization, which was not incorporated until 1871, or about two hundred years after it started operations, acquired its name in a most peculiar fashion. It appears the original partners met in a London coffeehouse located on Lombard Street, in old central London, near the Bank of England. Here they haggled over rates and contracts while swilling coffee and pastries. The coffeehouse was their office, their social club, and their bank, and in all ways just a good place to hang out and risk a few million pounds. Their host, the operator of the coffeehouse, was a modest sort of fellow who had no real involvement in the gigantic financial transactions taking place in his small establishment, but his name was important. You see, his name was Edward Lloyd (1648–1713).

※ ※ ※

Highways have surely undergone a dramatic rise and fall over the past decades. Modern man has been around for about one hundred thousand years, and during much of that time about the only way he could travel was over the land. In the beginning, he was more of a follower than a leader. The first roads were picked out by field mice, seeking a path to a creek. Then came the rabbits with wild dogs in hot pursuit, and then deer and perhaps a water buffalo. The path was getting pretty big by now. Trees and vegetation were beaten back, and earth was well trampled. The beasts of the forests had blazed an efficient trail just by following their instincts; they seemed to always find the shortest and most level route between any given points. Some of our modern roads follow these tracks that date well back into antiquity. It is certain that early man ran or walked along these tracks in his search for food, flints, salt, and warfare.

As civilization began to flourish, the ancient Assyrians and Egyptians developed roads for military and trade purposes. And the Romans, a true race of builders and engineers, built some incredibly solid roads to hold their empire together. You can see preserved sections of the Via Appa outside of Rome today. In recent years, I rode along some Roman roads in England; that is, I rode on the path of these primeval roads, separated, I am sure, by several feet of tarmac from the original pavement. The Inca were also skilled and energetic road builders. The Royal Road ran from Chile to Ecuador. It was a fine road with impressive bridges and embankments. The roadway itself was approximately 15 feet wide even though the Inca had no vehicles. Foot soldiers and messengers raced along this pathway as did pack animals. Colonial America made do with vastly inferior roads, and we would do well to remember this superior technology.

Now that I have you thinking in the highway mode, it's time we began a study of related words. *Road* comes from the Anglo Saxon word *rod*, which means the act of riding. This is not riding just to get somewhere – we are not riding to pick blueberries or to visit Aunt Bessie. We are out riding for plunder and booty. We are on a raid. *Raid*, in fact, comes from the same root word as *road*. We normally don't think of roads or riding in a hostile sense, but the Anglo-Saxons were a very warlike people, and raids were the stuff of everyday life. *Street*, on the other hand, reflects the more peaceful side of the old English language. It means a strewn way or, in effect, a road or path that has some sort of crude paving material thrown about. Road building and repairs were conducted in parish systems in

England, a scheme that spread to North America. Members of the parish (each church was a parish) constituted a subdivision of a county or shire. As a member of the parish, you were expected to work a few days each year to keep the roads in good condition. The system did not work well; people would report for duty, but most showed no enthusiasm for the task and many disappeared after a few hours on the job.

In 1663 the notion of toll roads was introduced in England. A private company would build a good road for public use. They would maintain bridges and mileposts. Tollbooths would be set up every five to ten miles. Fees were collected at a graduated level – so much for a wagon, so much for a rider on horseback, and so much for a herd of goats. Free enterprise would save the day and offer good roads. The scheme worked fairly well; roads were certainly improved. In Britain city stagecoaches began rolling as early as 1650 as toll roads came into service. However, some folks would ride around the tollbooth, and a few braver ones would jump the gate and tear down the road, getting a free ride. It did not take long for the turnpike to be invented. We use the term *turnpike* interchangeably with *toll road*, but almost no one knows the literal meaning of a turnpike. Envision a pike – that is, a spear. Next consider a cluster of pikes made into a gate. Now consider some young country rascal attempting to jump the gate made up of pikes. The result – an injured rider and a dead horse. However, riders who stopped to pay their toll watched as the pikes were turned and then passed by unharmed. The meaning of *turnpike* is a very literal one.

The introduction of toll roads generated much interest in improved roads. Several French and British engineers made a study of this new engineering art in the eighteenth century. They were seeking to create a durable, all-weather road. They wanted something that would not fall apart in a heavy thunderstorm or be wrecked by a winter freeze. At the same time, it must be cheaper than the Roman system of road building. They wanted a plan that was practical, not monumental. One of the people involved in the science of road building was John L. Macadam, a native of Ayr, Scotland (see chapter 2). Macadam had always been interested in road building. He came up with a scheme to build highways from crushed stone. The sharp edges of stone kept the surface together. This, plus heavy rolling and side drainage ditches, made a durable but cheap road surface. He went on to build roads throughout England and see his system developed worldwide. We should add that macadam roads today involve a tar or asphalt binder. This is one of the most common road surfaces in use today, but it is not what Macadam proposed. You may sometimes see the word *tarmac* referring to the paving in and around airports. This is derived from *tar* and *mac,* a shorter form of *tar-mac-adam.*

Tavern is a Latin word that means a little house of boards. Most American cities today have Italian restaurants named *Taverna Alberto* or some such name – being derived from *tavern*. Taverns have been around since ancient times; they were a necessity as empires and trade grew. Soldiers, merchants, government officials, pilgrims – all needed a temporary place to eat and sleep. Inns were also a place for locals to gather, gossip, and hear news from far away. They also became a refuge for loafers, drunks, and other folks low on the social ladder.

The Roman poet and soldier Horace left us an early description of tavern life in his narrative *A Journey to Brundisium* in 37 or 38 BC. Horace traveled only in the best circles – Virgil and Caesar Augustus were among his good friends. But this trip was no royal adventure. I should perhaps explain that Brundisium is today the port city of Brindsi in southern Italy. It is on the "heel" of Italy's boot, if you can picture the shape of the country. This original town was at the southern end of the Appian Way and was the main port for vessels going to Greece. So the road was hardly a byway or some lonely country lane. Even so, Horace found the public inns along the way to be wretched places. They were dirty and overrun with bedbugs. The food was poor and the wine was terrible. But his main criticism was the oversupply of ladies of easy virtue who conducted most of their business at taverns.

Horace's picture is surely too harsh for the realities of British and American taverns. Some of these were really fine establishments, though hardly deluxe by modern standards. Some were notable for their food and wine list. The proprietor was often a respectable member of the community: a property owner and sometimes head of the local militia. After all, Martin Van Buren's father was a tavern keeper in New York. Young Martin worked around the tavern as a lad and grew up to become the eighth president of the United States.

There was usually a good size crowd around the tavern. Most of them did not have much to do but wait for the next stage to arrive. This presented an opportunity for traveling salesmen. The most common of these peddlers was the patent medicine salesman. They employed some imaginative techniques to sell their wares. Having a confederate in the audience was a standard trick. The "Professor" begins his spiel on the wonders of his elixir, and then after a suitable time he pulls a live toad from his pocket and displays the poor creature to the crowd. Everyone knew, or at least supposed, that toads were the source of a deadly poison. The salesman then calls for a volunteer to consume the toad so that he can demonstrate his magic curative. No one steps forward but finally the confederate walks up and puts on quite an act. After more persuasion, he takes the toad, bites its head off, and swallows, instantly becoming ill. He collapses – the crowd gasps – the Professor rushes over and administers several good glugs of the medicine. In a few minutes, the confederate is restored to perfect health and a good number of bottles are sold. The salesman and his associate leave town quickly. A particular world came from this specialized fraud. And that world was created to describe the medicine man's assistant. The word is a *toady*. Today we use *toady* to describe anyone who is servile.

I almost forgot to tell you about how *Stilton cheese* got its name. It came from a tavern in the village of Stilton, England, which is just south of Peterborough or about sixty miles due north of London. It was on the Great North Road going to York and Scotland. There was a large amount of traffic on this road during the eighteenth century, and customers at the Bell Inn were looking for something tasty to eat. The proprietor discovered a fine blue cheese made about thirty miles away in the village of Melton Mowbray. The cheese sold so well at the Bell Inn that it became known as Stilton cheese. In 1722 Daniel Defoe visited Bell's Inn, where he was told the cheese was best when it was so well aged that it was crawling with mites and maggots.

The college town of Cambridge is just to the east of Stilton. In the early 1600s there was a livery stable operated by one Thomas (or Tobias) Hobson. Poor Hobson was bedeviled by the students who would insist on renting their favorite horse and no other. There were definite favorites – the fast horse especially. Hobson reminded the various "hotspurs" who came to his door that horses must be rested and that he could not keep sending out the same animal without doing damage to his stock. Finally the tradesman had had enough. The most rested horse was placed next to the door. It was now a house rule: accept this horse or do without. The policy became known as *Hobson's choice*. Today the phrase tends to mean a choice among several undesirable alternatives.

When it comes to horse-drawn vehicles, there are many interesting stories on how they got their names. The *hackney cab* was named after a district in London, the *hearse* for the style of candleholder placed near the coffin, and *Conestoga wagons* for a valley in Pennsylvania. Even the invention of *stagecoaches* conjures up scenes of the American West with John Wayne or some hapless movie star being chased by an ungodly ferocious mob of angry American Indians. This picture is not entirely untrue; however, the American stagecoach was equally at home in the eastern United States and was in fact exported to South America and South Africa. Stagecoaches were also commonly referred to as *Concord* or *Troy coaches*, because the majority of them were made in Concord, New Hampshire, and Troy, New York. These vehicles were introduced around 1825. They were, of course, a variation on European prototypes. The name *coach* is perhaps one of the most interesting words of any associated with horse-drawn vehicles. It is Hungarian, and I can assure you there are very few words in English that come from the land of the Magyars. The first of these four-wheel enclosed passenger-carrying vehicles appeared in around 1450 in the town of Kocs (also spelled Koszi or Koszeg), which is on the Austrian and Hungarian border about fifty miles south of Vienna.

※ ※ ※

Railways have been around since at least Elizabethan times. They remained largely hidden from public view until 1825 when they were adapted for common carrier service in Britain. This was something of a backdoor entrance to the transportation world. All of its basic elements and even its vocabulary were largely borrowed from existing technologies. The word *railroad* is a case in point. *Rail* means a bar in Old French, and *road*, already examined above, is derived from *raid*. Other European languages speak of the railway as an iron way or path. *Train* is based on another Old French word for "to drag or tow," or even "slide along behind." *Track* is of Teutonic origin and means "marks in earth" left by something that was dragged along. Or you might think of animal tracks – bear tracks, deer tracks.

Station is based in Latin and connotes a place to stand or a post. In French this would be *baton,* as in Baton Rouge or "the Red Post." *Depot* is also Latin for "to deposit" and *terminal* once meant a boundary. We tend to use all three words today interchangeably.

When it comes to vehicles, we are back in the borrowing mode: *coach* was just explained, *car* was related to *chariot,* and *carriage* to horse-drawn vehicles, but *car* became an obsolete word and was rarely used until American railway men picked it up in the 1800s. *Locomotive* was a happy find because engineers could not find anything satisfactory for railway engines. *Traveling engines* and *fiery chariots* just would not do. And then in 1825, Stephenson named an engine on the Stockton and Darlington Railway the *Locomotion.* This was formed from two Latin words meaning "place" and "motion."

A *dummy locomotive* meant an engine covered over with a large cab to make it look like a passenger car. This could be explained as a fake engine in the sense of a blank cartridge. But one of the early builders of dummy locomotives devised a special type of engine that did not exhaust its steam, hence it ran silently and was "dumb" in the mute sense of the word.

Freight cars bring up two interesting examples of word origins. A gondola car is a long, low, open-top vehicle used to carry scrap iron or other rustic materials. It was named after the famous gondola boats of Venice; *gondola* means "rock and roll," which goes back several centuries before the birth of Elvis. *Caboose* was the little red car at the end of the train that offered shelter to the trainman. It comes from a Dutch word used to describe a ship's kitchen, not the conventional galley, but a small, open kitchen placed on the main deck. This position eliminated smoke and fire hazards belowdecks. The who and when of applying the word to a railroad car is not known; we can only suppose an ex-sailor-turned-railroader thought it an apt term because cooking was done aboard. *Caboose* first appeared around 1855, and the word came into common usage a few years later. The caboose is now seldom seen in the United States.

In the public transit area, I could find only three words that proved very intriguing. *Omnibus* was by far the oldest. So often these borrowed words are different in pronunciation and spelling from the original, but in this case, the word was lifted directly from the Latin language. What is being described is a horse-drawn bus that first appeared in Paris in about 1660 and was adopted in New York in 1829. Omnibuses became common public transit vehicles in most cities until the modern motor bus replaced them in around 1915. *Omnibus* means "for all."

Tram is the common word for a streetcar in England. It is an old term taken from the Scandinavian word for a shaft or beam that formed part of a wheelbarrow or sled. There was a similar Norse word that was even more ancient. A few popular writers have suggested that the word *tram* was taken from the British engineer and iron maker, Benjamin Outram (1764–1805). This notion, I feel, is clearly wrong, despite the fact that Outram built several wagon ways, including the Peake Forest Tramway, located near Manchester. The horse-powered line opened in 1799 and continued in service, remarkably, until 1926. *Tram* is a word rarely used in America, except when referring to mine cars.

Trolley is another matter. Americans seem to love the word *trolley* and use it to describe everything from electric streetcars to horsecars and cable cars. This includes rubber-tired replicas, which are not only diesel powered but are trackless as well. How many fancy restaurants have you visited where they wheel out the dessert trolley? Here is a word that has been beaten up, in my opinion, and this is one case where I am ready to call in the "word police" to protect it. This is the nature of English – it's wide open for new words and for new uses of old ones. It's a Libertarian's dream of an open and unrestrained society. Not so in France, of course. There, a prestigious and powerful national academy sits in judgment of any additions or changes to language. Its decisions are uniformly conservative, and if *trolley* were a French word, it would be preserved in its pure, original meaning. Actually, *trolley* is a Middle English word (AD 1200–1450) that describes walking, sauntering, or moving with a rolling motion. This rolling motion named the little wheel that rolled along the overhead wire to collect electricity that powered the car. And so the trolley wheel gave its name to the entire vehicle.

SUGGESTED READING

Oxford English Dictionary – A nine-volume set that covers just about every imaginable word. Offers literary sources for first use of words.

MANY BOOKS DEVOTED TO WORD ORIGINS

Webster's Word Histories. Springfield, Mass.: Merriam-Webster Inc. (1989).

A Concise Etymological Dictionary of Modern English by Ernest Weekly revised edition. New York: E. P. Dutton and Company, Inc. (1952).

A Concise Dictionary of English Etymology: Wordsworth Reference by Walter W. Skeat. Darby, Pa.: Diane Publishing (1993).

In a more popular vein are several books by Richard Lederer, including *Crazy English, The Miracle of Language,* and others.

There is always the *American Heritage Dictionary* for home use.

Index

Page numbers in *italics* refer to illustrations.

Abbot, Downing, and Company, 59, 60
Adams, Charles F., 40
Adams, John, ix, xi
Adams, John Q., 170
Adams Express Company, 276
advertising and promotion, 472–478
Africa, 8, 115
African Americans, 95, 169, 469
Albany, N.Y., 76, 80, 157, 174, 463
Albion, Robert, 271
alcoholic beverages. *See* drunks and drinking
Allegheny Mountains, 179, 460
Allegheny Portage Railroad, 160
Altoona curve, 460–461
American Fur Company, 195
American line (steamships), 348
American President lines, 290
American Society for the Prevention of Cruelty to Animals (ASPCA), 118–119
Amtrak, 485
anchor(s), 491
Anchor line (Mississippi River), 220
ancient travel, xiv, 3–6, 488, 494, 496
aqueducts, 159, 160, 162, 168
Asian travel, 290–293
ASPCA, 118–119
Aspinwall, William, 284
Astor, John Jacob, 224, 280, 373
Atchison, Kans., 29
Atlantic Ocean, 297, 310
Audubon, John James, 196
automobiles, 17, 246, 269

baggage, 23, 45, 52, 53, 151, 169, 281, 317, 358

Ballin, Albert, 347, 350
Baltimore, Md., 53, 83, 278, 409, 422, 427, 428, 437
Baltimore and Ohio Railroad, 409, 422, 423, 428, 429, 430, 474–476, 478, 479, 480
Bangor, Maine, 266, 267, 269
barbers and barbershops, 169, 460
Bar Harbor, Maine, 269
basterna (horse litter), 7
baths and bathtubs, 45, 46, 170, 244, 360, 460
Bay State Steamboat Company, 255
beds, berths, and bunks, 46, 47, 167, 169, 184, 185, 188, 192, 194, 199, 217, 220, 244, 252, 287, 302, 304, 306, 308, 316, 347, 382, 383, 448–457
bell punch, 104–106
bells, 11, 454; signal bells, 101, 212
Bergh, Henry, 118, 119
Birch, James E. 27–28
Bird, Isabella L., 229, 268, 269, 352, 354
Black Bart (stagecoach robber), 43, 44
blind horses (ferries), 134
Blue Riband (prize for speed), 342, 345, 348
bob-tail cars. *See* horse cars and street railways
boiler explosions, 89, 146, 195, 203, 206–208
Boise City, Idaho, 29
Bonaparte, Joseph, 308
Bordentown, N.J., 22, 308
Boston, Mass., 7, 78, 79, 93, 94, 132, 265, 267, 269, 278, 408, 447
Boston and Lowell Railroad, 422
Boston Board of Trade, 482
Boston Post Road, 24

brakes and stopping, 101, 412, 413, 433
Breck, Samuel, 447, 448
Bremen, Germany, 357
bridges, highway, 28, 35, 37, 38, 42
bridges, railroad, 412, 427, 429
Bristol, England, 328, 329
British and American Steam Navigation Company, 327
British and North American Royal Mail Steam Packet Company, 330
British Railways, 403, 408
Broadway (street), 68, 75, 91
Broadway Limited (train), 459
Brooklyn, N.Y., 16, 92, 93, 132, 139
Brougham, Henry, 12, 17
Brower, Abraham, 68
Brownsville, Pa., 202
Brunel, Isambard Kingdom, 328, 329
Bryce, James, 410, 411
Bullock, William, 193
Burlington, N.J., 22
Burlington, Vt., 134
Busch, Moritz, 198
Butterfield, John, 27

cable cars, 125, 126
caboose (kitchen), 498, 499
cabriolet (carriage), 11
Cairo, Ill., 180
Calhoun, John C., 34
California, 27, 125, 126, 281, 425
Calyo, Nicolino, 13
Camden and Amboy (C&A) Railroad, 23, 420, 427–429
Canada. *See* Great Lakes boats and shipping; Welland Canal
Canadian Pacific Railway, 400, *401*
canal boat crews: cabin boys, 170; captains, 168, 171, 174; cooks, 169; drivers, 171; steersmen, 166, 171

501

canal boats, 166–168, 175; fares, 175; ladies' cabins, 167, 167; meals, 169; sleeping arrangements, 167, 170; speed, 172–175; use of horses, 171, 172
canals: abandonments, 161, 163; Cape Cod Canal, 269; Chesapeake and Ohio Canal, 156, 162, 163; construction, 158, 159; costs, 157, 162, 164, 167; early canals, 155; Erie Canal, 156–161, 168, 169, 172, 175, 176; James River Canal, 156; Main Line of Public Works, 156, 160, 161; Miami and Erie (M & E) Canal, 163; Middlesex Canal, 156; Ohio and Erie canal, 163; South Hadley Canal, 156; traffic on canals, 164; Wabash and Erie Canal, 156; Wabash Canal, 156
canoes, 224
Cape Cod Canal, 269
Cape Hatteras, N.C., 272, 273
Cape Horn, 288, 289, 295
Cape Horn route (gold rush), 286–289
Cape Race, 297
captains, 303, 304, 307, 311, 314–316, 321, 332, 352, 357, 492
car (word origin), 498
car ferries, 151, 152, 246, 427, 428
Carnegie, Andrew, 373, 451, 452
Castle Garden (emigrant station), 390–393
Catlin, George, xv, 195
Census, U.S., xx, 210, 368, 431
Central Pacific Railroad, 152, 399, 400, 404, 435, 436, 464–468
Central Transportation Company, 450
chamber pots. *See* toilets
Chambers, William, 352, 354
Charleston, S.C., 249, 272, 273, 275
Charlestown, Mass., 132
Chattanooga, Tenn., 136
cheap travel. *See* emigrants
Checker Cab, 17
Chesapeake Bay, 23, 151
Chevalier, Michael, 96
Chicago, 226, 228, 232, 234, 239, 425, 450, 451, 452
Chicago, Burlington, and Quincy Railroad, 397, 402, 414t, 448, 451
Chicago, Rock Island, and Pacific Railroad, 471

Chicago and Alton Railroad, 438, 439, 451
Chicago and North Western Railroad, 435, 443
children: child labor, employees, or workers, xix, 61, 62; child travelers, 13, 134, 194, 214, 231, 241, 342, 356, 404, 467
China, trade with, 263, 280
Chinese, 402, 465, 466, 469
Cincinnati, Ohio, 15, 81, 82, 108–110, 113, 132, 163–166, 185, 186, 190, 191, 214–216
civil engineering, 158
Civil War (U.S.), 30, 429
classes of travel: first class, 447; second class, 447; third class, *see* emigrants
Cleveland, Grover, 482
Cleveland, Ohio, 98, 163, 224, 234, 240
Clinton, DeWitt, 157, 164
clipper ships, 264, 265
Clyde, Thomas, 274
coach horns. *See* horns
coal (as fuel), 255, 284
coastal service (by region): Long Island Sound, 251–263; New England, 263–270; Panama Pacific, 280–290; South America, 293–295; Trans-Pacific, 290–295
coastal ships: accidents, 253, 257, 267, 272, 274; costs, 254, 258, 264, 274, 285, 292; decline, 263; décor, 257, 258, 262; fares, 253, 260, 266, 275, 282, 285, 286; food, 256, 268; fuel, 267. *See also* coastal ships (by name); coastal steamships (by name); coastal steamship service; coastal trade and shipping
coastal ships (by name): *Bay State*, 255; *California*, 282, 284; *City of Lawrence*, 258; *City of Worcester*, 258; *Cleopatra*, 254; *Commonwealth*, 257, 262; *Connecticut*, 267; *Danger*, 267; *Eagle*, 261; *Empire State*, 255; *Home*, 272, 273; *Lexington*, 253; *Massachusetts*, 254, 259; *Metropolis*, 257; *Norfolk*, 268; *Old Colony*, 257; *Ornevorg*, 268; *Patent*, 266; *President*, 254; *Providence*, 258
coastal steamships (by name): *Bristol*, 258; *Chancellor Livingston*,

252, 267; *City of Peking*, 292, 293; *City of Tokio*, 292, 293; *Colorado*, 251; *Commonwealth*, 262; *Firefly*, 252; *Fulton*, 252, 271; *Governor Dudley*, 274; *Humboldt*, 282; *James W. Paige*, 286; *John S. McKim*, 274; *Joseph Whitney*, 278; *J. W. Coffin*, 281; *North Carolina*, 273, 274; *Panama*, 282; *Patent*, 266; *Pegasus*, 277; *Penobscot*, 268; *Pilgrim*, 261; *Plymouth*, 262; *Priscilla*, 262; *Puritan*, 261, 262; *Southerner*, 274; *Tennessee*, 284; *Tom Thumb*, 266; *Unicorn*, 284
coastal steamship service: accidents, 253, 256, 257, 268, 273, 274, 277; boats (early), 252; cost of boats, 254, 257, 258, 266, 292; costs of operation, 274; decline of service, 262, 263; fares, 253, 260, 266, 275, 277, 283, 284, 286, 295; food, 256, 268, 283, 288; iron hulls, 258, 267, 292; number of ships, 250, 251, 260
coastal trade and shipping, 249–296; size, 253–255, 261, 273, 292; speed, 252, 253, 255, 264–266, 271, 274, 275, 277, 286, 295
Collins, Captain Edward K., 314, 315, 232, 236
colonial travel, 179, 249, 264
Columbus, Christopher, 285, 297
Columbus, Ohio, 26
commuters, 65–80, 88–98, 124–128, 139–150, 431, 439
Concord, N.H., 59
conductors, railroad, 419–421
Coney Island excursion, 277, 277, 278
Connecticut River, 427
Conrad, Joseph, 312
construction, 88, 92, 98, 122, 158, 159, 163, 181, 299–301
Cooke, Jay, 479
cooking and kitchens, 45, 48, 49, 133, 168, 169, 465
Cooper, James Fenimore, 301
Council Bluffs, Iowa, 182, 402, 469
counterfeiting: money, 104; tickets, 104, 421
crews. *See* canal boat crews; ferry crews; helmsmen; horse car and street railway crews; omnibus; railroads; riverboat crews; sailing ship crews; stagecoach workers; steamship crews
Cromwell, Henry B., 275

Cromwell line (coastal steamships), 275
Crozet, Claude, 34
Cuba, 276, 280
Cudahy, Brian, 132
Cugnot, Nicolas, 17
Cumberland, Md., 162, 202
Cumberland or National Road, 35, 35
Cumberland River, 200–202
Cumberland Valley Railroad, 449
Cunard, Samuel, 330–337
Cunard line, 330–334, 336, 340, 351–355, 364, 369
customs service, 309, 317, 318, 375, 388

Dana, Richard Henry, 280, 282, 301
Daniels, George H., 473, 474
Dayton, Ohio, 164
Daytona Beach, Fla., 279
deck passengers, 187, 200
decorative treatments, 166, 168, 184, 185, 187–189, 216, 217, 229, 232, 257, 258, 262, 454–456
Delaware, Lackawana, and Western Railroad, 143, 144, 148
Delaware River, 132
democratic notions of travel, 440–442, 447, 448, 471
Denver, Colo., 31, 471, 472
Depew, Chauncey M., 472, 473
depot(s), 498. *See also* stations
Detroit, Mich., 134, 224
Detroit and Cleveland (D&C) Steam Navigation Company, 242, 243
Dickens, Charles, 35, 36, 169, 197, 331, 332, 437
discomforts of travel, xvii, 31–33, 39, 40, 45–47, 166, 217, 218, 440–444
dollar, value of, xix
Dollar Steamship lines, 290
Dramatic line (ships), 315
Drew, Daniel, 90, 411
drivers (vehicles), 14–17, 60, 61
drunks and drinking, 11, 15, 47, 61, 196, 309, 354
Duluth, Minn., 244
dummy locomotives or cars, 93, 498
Dunbar, Seymour, xiii
duty (tax). *See* customs service

earnings and profits, 187, 189, 197, 211, 228
Eastern Steamship Company, 269, 270

Eastland (steam boat), 240
East River ferries, 131, 137, 139
Eaton and Gilbert, 60
Edison, Thomas, 421
electric lighting, 191, 258, 259, 457
electric street cars, 126–128
elevated railways, 126. *See also* street railways
Elkins, William L., 95
Ellis Island, 393–394. *See also* Castle Garden (emigrant station)
embezzlement, 104–107, 420
Emerson, Ralph W., 407
emigrants: aid and help for, 384, 389; bad treatment of, 374, 378, 379, 385, 389; baggage, 375, 389; becoming rich or famous, 373; beds and berths, 375, 376; as a cheap way to go, 381–384; deaths of, 379, 384; destinations, 391, 395–397; fares for, 378, 380, 381; federal involvement with, 293; food, 376, 377, 380, 384; good treatment, 379, 380, 389–394; hardships, 374; health, 379, 389, 393, 394; land sales to, 397; laws regarding, 390; modes of travel, 402t; numbers of, 372, 393; registration, 390, 394; returning home, 394; seasickness, 384, 387; sleeping cars, 399, 400, 404; to the United States, 1820–1910, 372t
– emigrant ships (by name): *Aurania*, 381; *China*, 380; *Egypt*, 379; *Isaac Webb*, 377
– nationality or region of origin of: British, 371, 372; distribution on a single steamship (1897), 387t; Eastern European, 372, 373; 1897, 387t; German, 372, 373, 389; Irish, 372, 384; Scottish, 371
– travel, 121, 199, 200, 227, 228, 229, 256, 312, 338, 359; by railroad, 390, 396–404; by rivers, 375, 396; by sea, 374–389; by wagon, 375, 395
emigration, 371–404
Empire State Express, 473
employees. *See individual modes of travel*
engine room signals, 212
epizootic, 115, 116
Erickson, John, 230, 274
Erie, Pa., 234
Erie and Kalamazoo Rail Road, 424
Erie Canal, 156–159, 168, 175
Erie Railway, 409

Erie Railway ferries, 145, 150
excursion boats, 221
excursion trains, 465–467, 482

Fall River line, 255, 261, 262
Falls of the Ohio, 181, 183, 198, 219, 220
fares, 490; taxi, 10, 14. *See also individual modes of travel*
Fargo, William G., 31
fast or express steamships, 342, 343, 345
federal regulation, 452. *See also* government regulation; riverboats: inspections (federal)
ferry boats: accidents, 132, 133, 145–147; colonial, 132; fares, 132, 135, 137; fog bells, 147; Fulton's, 137, 138; horse-powered, 134, 135; human-bearer ferrymen, 4–5; Lake Champlain, 134, 136; manual, 132, 138; New York/Brooklyn, 138–149; passengers, 138, 140, 146–149; railroad, 140; rope, 136; steam, 137–152; stream powered, 135, 136; Susquehanna River, 150–152; taverns, 133; team boats, 134, 135; traffic, 142; western, 152. *See also* ferry boats (by name); ferry crews
ferry boats (by name): *Baltimore*, 142, 143; *Bergen*, 143; *Cincinnati*, 144; *Elmira*, 150; *Idaho*, 148; *Jersey*, 137; *Maryland*, 152; *Mauch Chunk*, 145; *Nassau*, 137; *Northfield*, 145; *Solano*, 152; *Susquehanna*, 151; *Westfield*, 146; *York*, 137
ferry crews: captains, 134, 138; engineers, 140; pilots, 131, 143, 145
Fifth Avenue (New York City), 12, 75, 76–78
financial panics, xix, 229, 409
fire hazards, 148, 204, 205, 228, 253, 312, 313, 362, 363, 443
firewood. *See* Great Lakes boats and shipping: railroad boats; riverboats
first-class travel, 447–452, 464–470, 480–484
Fisher, Hanna (tavern keeper), 49
Fisk, James C., 255, 411
Fitch, John, 182
Flagler, Henry M., 279, 280
flat boats, 208, 375, 396
floods, 163, 166

Florida, 278–280; as a winter resort, 278–280
Florida East Coast Railway, 279, 280
Flugel, J. G., 184
fogs, 147, 200, 229
food and provisions, 45, 48, 49, 133, 168, 169, 198–200, 217–220, 465, 466, 469, 471
food service. *See* canal boats; riverboats; sailing ships; stagecoaches; steamships (ocean)
forecastle (focsle), 321, 491
freight, carriage of, 31, 53
French Line (Compagnie Générale Transatlantique), 348
fuel: costs and consumption, 185, 186, 187, 228, 231, 255, 267, 274, 284, 291, 328, 334, 357, 462, 463
Fulton, Robert, 137, 138, 157, 182, 183, 252, 253

Gallatin, Albert, xx, 34, 157
Garrett, John, 480
Garrison, Cornelius K., 289, 290
gas lighting, 258, 456
Germany, 372, 373
gold coins, xviii, 54, 306
gold rush, 27, 281–290
gondola, 498
Gooch, Daniel, 441
Goodrich, Albert E., 245, 246
Gould, Jay, 411
government involvement in travel, xx, 181, 182, 374, 408, 414, 452
government regulation, 7, 10, 14, 207, 374, 376, 377, 414, 432
Governors Island, 135, 137
Grant, Ulysses S., 199, 293
Great Lakes boats (by name): *Atlantic,* 229; *Augusta,* 240; *Badger State,* 230; *Charles Townsend,* 226; *Chicago,* 246; *Christopher Columbus,* 233, 245; *City of Cleveland II,* 242; *City of Cleveland III,* 242; *City of Detroit II,* 242; *DeWitt Clinton,* 228; *Eastland,* 240; *Empire,* 229; *Erie,* 227, 228; *Eureka,* 236; *Frontenac,* 225; *Griffin,* 224; *Lady Elgin,* 240; *Mayflower,* 229; *Merchant,* 233; *Northland,* 245; *Northwest,* 233, 245; *Ocean,* 229; *Ontario,* 225; *Oswego,* 224; *Plymouth Rock,* 231; *Samson,* 230; *Seeandbee,* 244; *Vandalia,* 230; *Walk-in-the-Water,*

225; *Western World,* 231, 232
Great Lakes boats and shipping: accidents, 228, 229, 239–242; boats (early), 224; canals, 234, 237–239; cost of boats, 228, 232, 243; costs of operation, 225, 228, 231; crews, 228; decline of passenger service, 232, 243; excursion travel, 231, 240, 242; fares, 226, 227; food, 245; general aspects, 223; ice, 223; iron hulls, 233; monopoly, 227; number of ships, 225, 226; ports, 224, 234; propellers, 230; railroad boats, 229; safety, 226; sailing vessels, 224, 225, 227; shipping season, 223; speed of ships on, 226, 244; St. Lawrence River, 236, 237; storms, 226; whalebacks, 233, 245. *See also* Great Lakes boats (by name)
Great Miami River ferry, 132
Great Northern Railway, 244, 245
Greeley, Horace, 428, 429
Green Bay, Wis., 226, 228
Greene line (riverboats), 221
Green River, 213
guidebooks, 139, 140, 220, 235, 374, 375; for emigrants, 374, 375; general, xxiii, 220
Guion, Stephen B., 340–343
Guion line (Liverpool and Great Western Steamship Company), 340–343
Gulf Stream, 297

hackney coach, 9–11, 497
Halifax, Nova Scotia, 330, 333, 363, 364
Hall, Basil, 38, 193
Hallidie, Andrew, 125, 126
Hansom, Joseph A., 11, 12
Harlan and Hollingsworth (ship and car builders), 142
Harlan and Wolff (ship builder), 344
Harlem, N.Y., 74
harness, 11, 114, 115
Harriman, Edward H., 436
Harrisburg, Pa., 160
Hartford, Conn., 24
Harvey, Charles T., 238
Hathaway, Charles, 97, 98
health inspectors, 317
heating, 40, 197, 204, 258, 440, 441, 457

Hell Gate (East River), 251, 252, 259, 316
helmsmen, 401
Hertz, John D., 17
Hibbett, Theodore, 200, 201
Hill, James J., 244
Hobart, Horace R., 468
Hobson's choice, 497
holdup men. *See* robbers and holdup men
holidays, 489
Holladay, Ben, 31, 468
horns, 44, 45, 133, 170, 171
horse car and street railway crews: boy conductors, 110; conductors, 100, 102–107; drivers, 98, 100, 101; hill boys, 112; stablemen, 115; supervisors, 107
horse cars and street railways, 120–124; accidents, 99, 100; ASPCA and, 118, 119; bell punch, 104; benefits, 104; bobtail cars, 123, 124; Boston, 93, 94; Britain, 97, 98; Brooklyn, 92, 93; city councils and, 91; costs of operation, 114, 115; Fourth Avenue line, 88–91; harness bells, 91; headways, 98; Highland Street Railway, 94, *94*; horses, *see* horses; hours of service, 99, 107, 108, 109; humane societies, *see* horse cars and street railways: ASPCA and; Louisville, 97; mileage, 96, 97; New Orleans, 92, 123, 124; New York and Harlem Railroad, *86,* 88–91; New York City, 88–92, 99; Paris, 91, 92; Philadelphia, 95, 96; praise, 96, 97; Roxbury, 93; San Francisco, 125, 126; schedules, 98, 99; signal bells, 101; spotters, 106, 107; statistics, 96, 97; St. Louis, 97; strikes, 107; taxes, 91, 119; tickets, 91, 104; traffic, 90, 93, 96, 97; two-man crews, 101; uniforms, 107. *See also* horse car and street railway crews; horses
horses, 3, 134, 135, 151, 171, 172; breeds, 61, 62, 110, 111; cost, 112, 114; drivers and their teams, 101; feed, 112, 113; feet, 114; inhumane treatment of, 118–119; manure, 113, 114; old, 111; service life, 111; shoes, 114; size, 111; training, 112
hotels and resorts, 46; Deer Park, 478; Del Monte Resort, 479;

The Glades, 478; Homestead, Va., 479; Hotel del Coronado, 479; Hotel Seminole, 279; Hot Springs, Ark., 479; Key West, Fla. 279; Miami, Fla., 279; St. Augustine, Fla., 279; Tampa Bay, Fla., 279; White Sulphur Springs, Va. and W.Va., 478; Winter Park, Fla., 279
Hot Springs, Ark., 479
Hudson River, 134, 156, 183, 186, 231, 232, 252, 253
Hudson River Railroad, 434
Hudson River steamboats, 231, 232, 327
human burdens, 3–5
Huntington, Collis P., 293

icebergs, 311, 343, 365–367
ice hazards, 148, 152
Illinois Central Railroad, 399
Imlay, Richard, 437
Indians. *See* Native Americans
inland rivers. *See* Cumberland River; Mississippi River; Missouri River; Monongahela River; Ohio River; riverboats
inland seas. *See* Great Lakes boats and shipping
Inman, William, 337–340, 379, 380
Inman line (Liverpool and Philadelphia Steamship Company), 379
inns. *See* taverns
International Mercantile Marine (IMM) Company, 350
Interstate Commerce Commission, 414, 432
Ireland, 371, 372, 379, 387, 389, 395
iron hulls, 233, 234, 258, 261, 272, 277, 278, 292, 325, 329, 342, 347, 360
Ismay, Imrie and Co., 343
Ismay, J. Bruce, 350
Ismay, Thomas H. 343
Ismay line (White Star line), 344, 350

Jackass Mail, 28
Jarrett and Palmer (train trip), 435
Jefferson, Thomas, 37
Jersey City, N.J., 132, 333, 345
Jervis, John B., 433
Jews, 373
John Elder and Co. (shipbuilders), 342

Johnson, Samuel, xiv
journey, definition of, 489
Joy, David, 453
junket, definition of, 389–390

keelboats, 179, 180
keels, 299
Kentucky, 41, 45, 46
Kipling, Rudyard, 293, 461
Kirby, Frank E., 242
Kirkman, Marshall M., 4

labor unions, 15, 108
Lachine Rapids, 236–237
lady travelers. *See* women travelers
LaFollette Seamen's Act, 240
Lake Champlain, 134
Lake Shore and Michigan Southern Railroad, 409
lake travel and ships. *See* Great Lakes boats and shipping
Lancaster, Pa., 35
Lancaster Turnpike, 35
land grants, 164, 397
Lardner, Dionysius, 327
LaSalle, Robert, 224
Latrobe, Benjamin H., 193, 304, 305
Law, George, 92, 283, 284
Leslie, Frank, 464–467
Leslie, Miriam F. (Mrs. Frank Leslie), 465–467
life-saving service, 362
lightning, 42, 121, 143, 149, 188, 189, 191, 204, 205, 213, 229, 456, 457
Lincoln, Abraham, xi
Lincoln, Robert Todd, 452
litters, 5–6
Little River Turnpike, 34
Liverpool, England, 303, 309, 315
Livingston, Robert, 137, 138, 182
Lloyd, Edward, 493, 494
Lloyd's (insurance), 493
locks and dams, 181, 203
locomotives, 415, 417, 434, 435, 462–464, 471, 473, 498
London, England, 8, 10, 11, 66, 67
London General Omnibus Company, 66
Long Island Sound, 251–263
Long Island Sound steamers. *See* sound steamers
lost at sea (ships), 313
Loubat, Alphonse, 91, 92
Louis Philippe. *See* Orléans, Duke of

Louisville, Ky., 27, 117, 181, 187, 189, 190, 206, 215, 219
Louisville and Portland Canal, 181, 219
low water (rivers), 200, 201, 217
Lyell, Charles, 198, 199

Macadam, John L., 36, 37
Madison, James, 157
mail service routes, 24, 28, 53, 283, 291, 303
mail subsidies, 330, 332, 333, 339
Main Line of Public Works (Pennsylvania), 160–161, 173
Majoribanks, Alexander, 231
Manhattan Island, 90, 126, 131, 139, 259
Marble, Jerome, 483, 484
Marietta, Ohio, 135
marine architects: Kirby, Frank, 243; McKay, Donald, 265, 266; Webb, William H., 258, 306
marine disasters (major), 207–208, 240–242, 334–336, 363–364
marine hospitals, 389
Marshall, Charles H., 323
Marshall, John, 33
masts, 300
Maximilian, Prince Alexander Philip, 195, 196
Mayhew, Henry, 66
Maysville, Ky., 97
McKay, Donald, 264, 265
McMillan, James, 242
meals. *See* food and provisions; *and individual modes of travel*
medical care, xxii–xxiii, 310, 322, 323
Meiggs, Henry, xv, 295
Merchant Marine fleet, American, 290, 323, 323t, 325, 336, 351
Merchants and Miners Transportation Company, 278
Mexico City, Mexico, 97
Miami, Fla., 279
Miami and Erie (M&E) Canal, 163–166
Michigan Southern and Northern Indiana Railroad, 444
Middlesex Canal, 156
Milwaukee, Wis., 228, 234, 239
Mississippi River, 180, 198, 409
Missouri River, 180, 182, 195, 196, 409
Mohawk River Valley, 157
money, xviii, 54, 55

Monongahela River, 202, 203
monopoly, 183, 227, 269, 452
Montreal, Quebec, 226, 236
Moore, Thomas (poet), 33
Morgan, Charles, 272, 273, 289, 290
Morgan, J. Pierpont, 255, 350, 351
Morse, Charles W., 269
Morse, Samuel F. B., 226
mules, 117, 172
multiple modes of travel, xviii,
    22, 23, 202, 429–431
music and entertainment, 47, 48,
    149, 221, 259, 359, 360, 467, 468

name trains, 459–462, 470, 473
Napier, Robert, 330
Narragansett Bay, 252, 255
Nashville, Tenn., 200, 201
Natchez Trace, 180
national parks,
    establishment of, 479
Native Americans, 44, 132,
    188, 197, 225, 237
nausea, 493
navigation, 298, 304, 314, 363
navigation lights, 213, 214
Neil, William, 26
Newfoundland, 297
New Jersey, 140
New Jersey Railroad
    and Transportation
    Company, 140, 428
New London, Conn., 426, 427
New Orleans, La., 92, 123,
    124, 183, 430, 431
Newport, R.I., 255, 270, 271
newsboys, railroad, 421, 422
Newton, Isaac, 231
New York, New Haven, and
    Hartford Railroad, 426
New York and Harlem
    Railroad, 421, 422
New York Central Railroad,
    410, 413, 423, 434, 449,
    461–464, 473, 474
New York Central Sleeping
    Car Company, 450
New York City, 13–17, 22–25,
    41, 49, 67–78, 88–92, 115, 122,
    126, 131, 137–150, 159, 249,
    251–263, 270–278, 284, 303,
    306, 314–317, 323, 328, 332–336,
    339, 347, 368, 389–395, 398,
    401, 404, 409, 413, 426–428
New York ferries, 138–149

Niblo, William, 68, 69
Nicaragua, 283, 289, 290, 294
Nicaragua route (Gold
    Rush), 283, 289, 290
Nichols, Thomas L., 228
Norfolk, Va., 224, 304
North Atlantic Ocean, 301, 302, 327
Northeast Corridor
    (railroad), 426, 429
Norwich, Conn., 254

Oakland, Ca., 404, 435, 436, 369
Ocean Steamship Co., 275
Ogden, Utah, 469
Ohio River, 179–181
Old Colony Steamboat Co., 255
Old Dominion Steamboat Co., 275
Olmsted, Frederick L., 36
Omaha, Neb., 468, 471
omnibus: Albany, 80; Baltimore,
    83; bell signal, 73; Boston, 78, 79;
    Cincinnati, 81, 82; conductors,
    77–78; double-deck, 77, 78;
    drivers, 71–75, 77; fare box, 74, 75;
    fares, 72, 78; fees and permits, 76;
    Fifth Avenue line, 75–78; hotels,
    80; London, 66; Mt. Washington,
    81; New York, 67–78; numbers
    of, 70, 76; origins, 65, 499; Paris,
    65–66; Philadelphia, 78; resorts,
    80, 81; roof seats, 77, 78; Saratoga,
    80, 81; sleighs, 75, 76; St. Louis,
    79, 80; traffic, 70, two-man crews,
    77; as vehicle, 83, 84; and wages,
    74; White Sulphur Springs, 81
Orléans, Duke of (Louis
    Philippe), 46, 151
orphan trains, 404
Overland Stage Company, 28
Ox Bow route, 28
Oxford, Ohio, 80

Pacific Mail line, 275, 284, 290–293
Pacific Ocean, 280, 293
Pacific ships (by name): *City of
    Peking*, 292, 293; *City of Tokio*,
    292, 293; *Colorado*, 291
Pacific Steam Navigation
    (PSN) Company, 294, 295
packets, 492
Paducah, Ky., 200
paint, color, and ornamentation,
    7, 58, 84. *See also* decorative
    treatments; *and individual
    modes of travel*

Panama City, Panama, 282, 294
Panama Pacific ships (by name):
    California, 284; *Humboldt*, 282;
    James W. Paige, 286; *J. W. Coffin*,
    281; *Mayflower*, 282; *Pilgrim*, 281;
    Tennessee, 284; *Unicorn*, 284
Panama Railroad, 285, 286
Panama route, 30, 281, 283, 285
Pangborn, Joseph G., 475–476
paper money, 54, 345
Paris, France, 11, 65, 66
Pascal, Blaise, 65
passports, 318
Paulus Hook (Jersey City, N.J.), 137
Pearce, William, 342
Peninsular and Oriental (P&O)
    Steam Navigation Company, 290
Pennsylvania Railroad,
    140–143, 413, 423, 429, 434,
    435, 449, 458–461, 481
pensions, 347
Perth Amboy, N.Y., 22
Philadelphia, 7, 23, 24, 38,
    41, 78, 94–96, 132, 160, 161,
    338, 415, 427–429, 453
Philadelphia, Wilmington,
    and Baltimore Railroad,
    151, 427, 428, 449, 453
pickpockets, 100
Pike, Zebulon, 185
pilot house, 184, 211–214
pilots, 185, 211–214, 316, 317, 328, 354
pirates, 250, 271, 272
Pittsburgh, Pa., 26, 160, 180, 188, 459
Plant, Henry B., 278–279
Point Judith, R.I., 252, 255
Polk, James K., 332
Ponce de Leon, Juan, xv
population, U.S., 22, 371, 415
Portland, Maine, 252, 268, 269
Portland, Ore., 51
postal routes, 28. *See also*
    mail service routes
postilions, 9
Probasco, Henry, 109, 110
prostitutes, 15, 260
Providence, R.I., 252, 253,
    254, 255, 259, 278
public transit. *See* horse cars and
    street railways; omnibus
Pullman, George M., 449–452, 481
Pullman cars, 415, 432, 435,
    450–452, 461, 464, 470
pumps, 312

Queenstown, Ireland, 338

racing, riverboat, 198, 205
railroad cars: baggage, 416, 464; builders, 437, 438, 454, 456; construction and cost, 408, 410, 412; décor, 437; design, 437–440; dining and hotel, 413, 440, 464, 469, 471; heating, 457; hunting and fishing, 483; ladies', 448; library, 460; lounge and smoking, 458–460; mail, 440, 464; palace, 413, 456; parlor, 458; private, 480–482; rental, 480–484; sleeping, 413, 416, 440, 448, 448–457. *See also* railroad cars (by name)
railroad cars (by name): City of Worcester, 483; Davy Crockett, 483; Elkhorn, 456; Izaak Walton, 483; Palmyra, 467; PPC (Pullman Palace Car), 482; President, 464–466; Romulus, 460
railroad crews and employees, 410; barbers, 460; brakemen, 413, 417–419, 433; conductors, 419–421; engineers, 462–464; firemen, 462–464; newsboys, 403, 421, 422; porters, 454, 460, 474
railroad hotels, 477–480
railroad maps, 422, 425
railroad officials and managers, 410, 415, 416
railroad resorts, 477–480
railroads: accidents, 471; British origins of, 407, 408; classes of accommodation, 431, 432, 447; double track, 408, 413, 429; employees, 410, 413, 415, 417–422; fares, 412, 414, 431, 432, 436, 457, 461, 468, 470, 473; federal regulation of, 414; food, 415; free passes, 432; gauge track, 412; mileage, 408, 415; non-U.S., 294, 295; number of passengers, 415, 417, 423–426; operations, 416–422; profits, 413, 414, 415, 452; promotion and advertising, 415, 472–480; speed of, 408, 415, 416, 432–436, 461–464, 469, 472, 473; statistics, 415, 423, 424, 426, 436; train size, 416, 439, 440; transcontinental, 412, 425; travel corridors, 426–428; word origin, 498

railroad systems (by region): Anthracite, 414, 414t; Bridge, 414t; Eastern, 424; Granger, 414, 414t; Middle Atlantic, 422–424, 458–464; Midwestern, 409; New England, 413, 422, 424, 426, 427; Pocahontas, 414; Southern, 408, 409, 414t, 424, 429–431; Transcontinental, 414, 414t; trunk lines, 413; Western, 412, 424, 435, 436, 464–472
Ralph, Julian, 220
redcaps (baggage men), 474, 475
Reeside, John, 53, 54
resorts, 25, 80, 81, 270, 271, 275, 277–280, 293–295, 489. *See also* vacation travel
rheda (carriage), 8
Richmond, Va., 127, 430
Ringwalt, John L., xiii
riverboat crews: bartenders, 185, 209; cabin crews, 185, 218; captain's crews, 211, 219, 220; cooks, 185; deck hands, 185, 201, 219; firemen, 185; pilots, 185, 211, 212, 219; size and salaries of, 208, 208t, 209, 209t, 210
riverboats: accidents, 193, 203–209, 219; arrangement of decks and cabins, 185, 186; bells, 212, 217, 219; berths, 195, 220; boilers, 195; comforts of travel on, 189, 191, 192, 193, 198; cost of, 187, 189, 190; deck passage, 187, 194, 199, 200; decline of, 190, 216–219, 221; décor, 184, 185, 188, 189; earnings, 187, 190; engines, 186; explosions, 106, 195, 207; fares, 185, 187, 188, 217, 218, 220; fires, 190, 204, 205; food, 193, 194, 198, 199, 200, 217, 220; fuel, 185, 186, 187; hulls, 183, 190; inspections (federal), 190, 207; ladies' cabins, 184, 187; low water, 180, 181, 200; main cabin, 188; number of, 216, 216t; operating costs of, 187; passengers, 196, 197, 217; pilot house, 214; racing, 198, 205; and scenery, 191, 194, 197, 202; signals, 191, 202; and snags, 181; speed, 184–186, 188, 193, 200; state rooms, 185, 188, 180, 217, 218, 220; steam pressure, 186; stern wheels, 217; toilets, 188; traffic, 191, 202, 214–216; wages, 185; washstands, 220; whistles, 212, 213, 220

riverboats (by name): *America*, 206; *Arabia*, 203; *Belle Zane*, 204; *Ben Sherrod*, 205; *Buckeye State*, 187, 188; *City of Providence*, 220; *Clipper*, 213; *C. T. Dumont*, 208; *D. A. Tomkins*, 201; *Diana*, 187; *Dr. Franklin*, 213; *Eclipse*, 189; *Fleetwood*, 190; *General Pike*, 185; *General Warren*, 213; *George Washington*, 213; *Grand Republic*, 190; *Great Republic*, 189; *Hinds*, 208; *Homer*, 187; *Iron Queen*, 205; *Jenny Lind*, 200; *J. M. White*, 188; *Louis A. Sherley*, 190; *Magnolia*, 198; *Messenger*, 197; *Moselle*, 206; *Natchez*, 188; *New Orleans*, 183; *New Orleans II*, 184; *Omega*, 196; *Oronoko*, 207; *Pacific*, 205; *Paris C. Brown*, 218; *Patriot*, 195; *Prairie*, 208; *Queen City*, 190, 191; *Revenue*, 112–113; *Rainbow*, 198; *Sultana*, 207, 208; *Tecumseh*, 185, 186; *Thomas Sherlock*, 205, 221; *United States*, 206; *Velocipede*, 194; *Virginia*, 190; *Waverly*, 190
roads, 24, 27, 31–37, 494, 495
roaming, 489
robbers and holdup men, 26, 42–44
Rogers, Captain Moses, 134, 135
Roosevelt, Nicholas, 183
rope ferries, 136
Rouses Point, N.Y., 134, 136
runners (dock side ticket agents), 218, 260, 261

Sacramento, Calif., 27, 30, 31, 281
safety. *See individual modes of travel*
sailing ship crews: cabin boys, 305, 318; captains, 302, 304, 305, 314, 315, 318; cooks, 318; mates, 318–320; sail makers, 318; sailors, 302, 306, 319–323; size of, 304, 319
sailing ships: accidents, 310; beds, 302, 304, 306, 308; Black Ball line, 303, 304, 310, 323; cabins, 302, 304, 306, 308; clipper ships, 264; construction, 299–301, 322; copper bottoms, 300; decline, 323–325; fares, 305, 308; food, 305, 307, 308, 321; iron/steel hulls, 325; masts, 300; navigation, 298; packets, 303, 305; pilots, 316, 317; retirement, 318, 322; safety, 310–314; sails, 300, 301, 304, 310, 319; size of, 302, 303; sounds, 297; speeds of, 265, 271, 304, 316;

storms, 310; traffic, 309; watches, 314, 318, 319; windjammers, 325; wine, 307. *See also* sailing ship crews; sailing ships (by name)
sailing ships (by name), *Albion,* 310; *Bounty,* 314; *Charles H. Marshall,* 323; *Cornelius Grinnel,* 308; *Cortez,* 307; *Dirigo,* 325; *Dreadnought,* 315; *Eliza,* 304; *Hottinguer,* 315; *Independence,* 323; *James Monroe,* 306; *Liverpool,* 311; *Maria,* 324; *Mediator,* 306; *Mississippi,* 315; *Montezuma,* 311; *Poland,* 313; *Shakespeare,* 315; *St. Denis,* 309; *Tornado,* 312; *Victoria,* 306
sailors. *See* sailing ship crews; steamship crews (ocean)
Salem, Mass., 22, 264
Samuels, Captain Samuel, 315, 316
San Diego, Calif., 28, 280, 479, 480
Sandusky, Ohio, 36, 234, 240
Sandy Hook, N.Y., 251, 277, 316, 317, 328
San Francisco, Calif., 96, 125, 126, 280, 283, 290–293, 404, 435, 469, 470, 479
sanitation, 304, 321
Sault Ste. Marie Canal, 238, 239
Savannah, Ga., 22, 274, 275, 278
Savannah line (Ocean Steamship Company), 275
scenery, 197, 202, 245, 463, 465, 476, 477, 479
Schurz, Carl, 373
Scott, Thomas, 481
screw propellers, 230, 231, 338, 346, 348
seasickness, 305, 310, 354
sea travel as a health cure, 293–295
sedan chairs, 6–8
separation of the sexes, 47, 140, 168, 309, 310
sextants, 298
Shillibeer, George, 66
shipbuilding, 299–301, 330–332
ships, coastal and other U.S. (1851, 1880), 250t, 251t. *See also individual types of ships*
ship's log, 493
shipwrecks. *See* ferry boats; riverboats; sailing ships; steamships (ocean)
Shreve, Henry, 183
signal cannons and guns, 185

Singapore, 292
slaves, 229, 270
Slawson, John, 75, 123, 124
sleighs, 75, 76
Smith, Frank Hill (interior decorator), 262
Smith, Junius, 327, 328
smoking, 448, 458–460
snags, 181, 203
snowsheds, 465
sounds and noises of travel, 297, 309, 444, 454, 462, 463
sound steamers, 253, 254, 254, 258, 258, 263
South America, coastal service in, 294, 295
Southampton, England, 356
South Carolina Railroad, 408, 409, 424
sparks, as fire hazards, 443
speed, comparable (by mode of transportation): canal boats, 172–175; coastal ships, 249, 252, 255, 264–266, 271, 274, 275, 277, 286, 295; ocean sail, 265, 271, 304, 316; ocean steam, 329, 330, 332, 334, 342, 356; railroad, 408, 415, 432–436, 461–464, 469, 472, 473; river boats, 184–186, 188, 193, 200; stagecoach, 22, 24, 26, 29, 31, 35, 41, 42, 55
speed as a cost factor, 360, 433. *See also* speed, comparable (by mode of transportation); *and individual modes of transportation*
stagecoaches: accidents, 41, 61; baggage, 23, 45, 52, 53; bridges, 38; colonial, 22; decline of, 55, 56; discomforts of travel in, 21, 32, 33, 39–41; early U.S. (eastern), 33–36l; employees (number), 29, 31; European origins of, 57; fares, 29, 31, 51, 52; ferries, 37, 38; food, 29, 30, 31, 47–49; Gallatin's plan, 34; heat, 40; horns, 44, 45; horses, 41, 42; Indians, 44; Macadam and roads for, 36, 37; mail, 30, 36, 45, 53; Midwestern, 26; money, 54, 55; mules, 29, 42; overland, 28; Ox Bow, 28; speed of, 22, 26, 29, 31, 35, 41, 42, 55; turnpikes, 35; western, 27–31; windows, 39, 40. *See also* stagecoach workers
stagecoach workers: drivers, 22, 42, 60, 61; hostlers, 22

Staten Island Ferry, 138, 146
station restaurants, 403, 469
stations, 410, 415, 426, 428, 429, 448, 498; railroad, 140–142, 410, 428, 429
St. Charles, Mo., 182
stealing of fares, 74, 104–107
steamboat inspection. *See* riverboats: inspections (federal)
steamboats. *See* ferry boats; riverboats; steamships (ocean)
steam dummies, 93, 125
steam heating, 258
steamship crews (ocean): captains, 352, 353, 357, 363; engineers, 362; firemen, 360; stewards, 352, 355, 359
steamship lines (North Atlantic): American, 348; Anchor, 351; British and North American, *see* steamship lines: Cunard; Collins, 332–336; Cunard, 331–337, 351; Guion, 340–343; Hamburg-American, 346, 347; Inman, 337–340, 349; International Mercantile Marine, 350, 351; North German Lloyd, 346, 348, 356; Red Star, 349; White Star, 343–345
steamships (ocean): accidents, 334, 358, 360, 362; British domination of, 327, 336; cost of, 329, 333; décor, 329, 331, 333, 334, 351; engine rooms, 360; express service, 342; fares, 332, 338, 342, 345, 359; food, 333, 334, 351, 354, 355, 359; fuel, 334, 345, 360, 363; harbors, 352; iron hulls, 329; life saving service, 362; operations, 352; passengers, 333, 339, 340, 343, 367; profits, 334, 338; safety, 336, 340, 360, 362, 364; sea lanes, 362; speed, 329, 330, 332, 334, 342, 356; Sunday service, 356; tenders, 352, 358; traffic, 367–369. *See also* steamships, ocean (by name)
steamships, ocean (by name): *Adriatic,* 336; *Arabia,* 334; *Arctic,* 333; *Arizona,* 342, 366; *Austria,* 347; *Baltic,* 333, 345; *Borussia,* 346; *Britannia,* 331; *British Queen,* 328; *Chicago,* 342; *City of Boston,* 340; *City of Brussels,* 345; *City of Glasgow,* 338; *City of Manchester,* 338; *City of New*

York, 340; *City of Paris,* 350, 365; *City of Philadelphia,* 340; *City of Rome,* 342; *City of Washington,* 340; *Colorado,* 342; *Columbia,* 342; *Dakota,* 342; *Deutschland,* 347; *Elbe,* 348, 356; *Germanic,* 345; *Great Britain,* 329; *Great Western,* 328; *Hammonia,* 346; *Kaiser Wilhelm der Grosse,* 347, 348; *Manhattan,* 342; *Minnesota,* 342; *Montana,* 342; *Nevada,* 342; *Normandie,* 369; *Oceanic,* 344; *Oregon,* 343, 364; *Pacific,* 333; *President,* 330; *Queen Elizabeth,* 265; *Queen Mary,* 369; *Savannah,* 327; *Saxonia,* 347; *Servia,* 342; *Sirus,* 328; *Washington,* 348; *Wyoming,* 342
steerage, 491. *See also* emigrants
Stephenson, John, 69, 70, 81, 122, 437
stern, 491
Stevenson, David, *188,* 226, 227
Stevenson, Robert Louis, xiv, 401–404
St. John's, Newfoundland, 367
St. John's River, 274
St. Lawrence River, 236, 237
St. Louis, Mo., 79, 80, 132, 182, 220
St. Mary's River, 238
Stockton, Calif., 60
Stonington line, 253
storms, 208, 239, 268, 272, 273, 289, 295, 310, 312, 357, 358
St. Paul, Minn., 180, 220
Strader, Jacob, 211
Straits of Magellan and Cape Horn, 288, 289, 295
stream or current boats (ferries), 135–136
street cleaning, 114
street railways: operating costs (1865), 114t; U.S. system, 96t, 97t. *See also* cable cars; electric street cars; elevated railways; horsecars and street railways; steam dummies; subways
Strickland, William, 408
strikes, 107, 108
Strong, George T., 254, 255
subways, 94, 126
Suez Canal, 290
summer resorts. *See* resorts; vacation travel
Sunday service (railroads), 121, 419
Susquehanna River, 37, 38, 150–152, 428–429, 453

Svinin, Paul, 150
Swallowtail line, 323

taverns, 45–51; 495–497
tax, xix
taxis, 8–19
Taylor, George A., xiii
team boats (ferries), 134, 135
Thoreau, Henry D., 407
tickets, 23, 51, 91, 104–106, 110, 431, 432, 490
Tiffany, Louis, 450
Tipton, Mo., 28
Titanic (ocean liner), 208
toady, 497
toilets, 46, 49, 170, 188
Toledo, 163, 232
toll roads. *See* roads
tonnage ratings (ships), 325
tours, 293, 489
Towne, Alban N., 399
track: railroad, 408, 413, 429, 469, 471, 498; street railway, 87–89
trains: boys (news boys), 403, 421, 422; operations and safety, 410–413, 415–422, 433; size and number of cars, 416, 437, 439, 440; travel promotion and advertising, 472–480. *See also* trains (by name)
trains (by name): Black Diamond Express, 458; Broadway Limited, 459; Chicago Limited, 459; Empire State Express, 473; Fast Flying Virginian, 461; Golden Gate Special, 470; James Whitcomb Riley, 484; Overland Limited, 461; Pacific Express, 461; Pennsylvania Limited, 459; Twentieth Century Limited, 474; White Train, 461
trams and tramways, 499
travail, 488
travel: promotion and advertising, 472–480; reasons not to, xvi–xxi; reasons to, xiv–xvi
Twain, Mark, x, 21, 39, 214, 275

Union Pacific Railroad, 403, 435, 436, 464, 465, 468, 469
unions. *See* strikes
upper berths (railroad), 453, 454
urban travel. *See* horse cars and street railways; omnibus
U.S. Mail Steamship Company. *See* steamship lines: Collins

vacation travel, xiv–xvi, 25, 80, 81, 231, 240–242, 277–280, 293–295
Van Buren, Martin, 332
Vanderbilt, Cornelius, 138, 253, 267, 289, 290, 423, 450, 472, 481
vendors, 421, 467
ventilation, 232
Vicksburg, Miss., 180
Victorian era, xxi–xxiii, 108, 109, 128; as the Age of Steam, 110; charities for sailors in, 322–323; crew or employee salaries in, 318, 420; railroads in, 442; ships lost during, 360, 362; travel in, 261, 293, 295, 310, 352–360
Vincennes, ferries across the Wabash, 37, 133
Vincennes, Ind., 37, 133
Virginia Board of Public Works, 34
Virginia City, Nev., 30
von Gerstner, Franz, 89, 186, 227, 228

Wabash and Erie Canal, 164
wages, xix, 15, 74, 110, 187, 208–210, 321, 322. *See also individual crews or mode of transport*
Wagner, Webster, 450
Wagner sleeping cars, 450
Walker, William, 290
walking, 3–8, 26
Ward, James O., 276
War of 1812, 225, 252, 306
Warsaw, Ky., 206
wash basins, 188, 191, 192, 220, 232, 302
Washington, D.C., ix, xv, 162, 427–430
Washington, George, 117
Wason Car Company, 451
water: drinking, 189, 198, 288, 305, 379; supply for ships, 288, 305, 379
Webb, Walter S., 450
Webb, William H., 258
Weldon, N.C., 48
Welland Canal, 226, 235, 236
Wells, Fargo and Co., 31
Western and Atlantic Railroad, 431
Western Railroad (Mass.), 426
western settlement, 224, 227
West Indies, 274–277
West Point Foundry, 229
Widener, Peter A. B., 95
Wilde, Oscar, 415, 416
whaleback steamers. *See* Great Lakes boats and shipping: whalebacks

INDEX 509

Wheeling, Va. and W.Va., 26, 34, 46, 193, 217
Wheelwright, William, 294
whistles, 145, 417
White Mountains, 477, 478
White Sulphur Springs, Va. and W.Va., 478
Whitman, Walt, 74, 131, 197, 198, 407
Wilmington, N.C., 273
Wilmington and Weldon Railroad, 430
windjammers, 325
winds, 208, 239, 297, 312
Winthrop, John, 7
wire-rope-cable ferries, 136
women travelers, xx–xxi, 47, 103, 140, 184, 185, 186, 194, 196, 197, 198, 220, 229, 256, 268, 309, 310, 352, 354, 448, 453, 465
Wood, James R., 458
wooden hulls, 299, 300, 312, 323
Woodruff, Theodore T., 449
Worcester Excursion Car Company, 483, 484
workers. *See individual modes of travel*
Wright, Isaac, 306
Wright's Ferry, 150

Yellow Cab, 17
Yellowstone Park, 479
Yerkes, Charles T., 95, 96
Yokohama, 293
Yosemite, Calif., 479

Books in the Railroads Past & Present Series

**Landmarks on the Iron Road:
Two Centuries of North American
Railroad Engineering**
William D. Middleton

South Shore: The Last Interurban
(revised second edition)
William D. Middleton

**Katy Northwest:
The Story of a Branch Line Railroad**
Donovan L. Hofsommer

**"Yet there isn't a train I wouldn't
take": Railway Journeys**
William D. Middleton

**The Pennsylvania
Railroad in Indiana**
William J. Watt

**In the Traces:
Railroad Paintings of Ted Rose**
Ted Rose

**A Sampling of Penn Central:
Southern Region on Display**
Jerry Taylor

**The Lake Shore
Electric Railway Story**
Herbert H. Harwood Jr.
& Robert S. Korach

**The Pennsylvania Railroad at Bay:
William Riley McKeen and the
Terre Haute & Indianapolis
Railroad**
Richard T. Wallis

The Bridge at Québec
William D. Middleton

History of the J. G. Brill Company
Debra Brill

**Uncle Sam's Locomotives: The
USRA and the Nation's Railroads**
Eugene L. Huddleston

**Metropolitan Railways:
Rapid Transit in America**
William D. Middleton

**Perfecting the American
Steam Locomotive**
J. Parker Lamb

**From Small Town to Downtown:
A History of the Jewett Car
Company, 1893–1919**
Lawrence A. Brough &
James H. Graebner

**Limiteds, Locals, and Expresses in
Indiana, 1838-1971**
Craig Sanders

**Steel Trails of Hawkeyeland:
Iowa's Railroad Experience**
Don L. Hofsommer

Amtrak in the Heartland
Craig Sanders

**When the Steam
Railroads Electrified**
(revised second edition)
William D. Middleton

**The GrandLuxe Express:
Traveling in High Style**
Karl Zimmermann

**Still Standing: A Century of
Urban Train Station Design**
Christopher Brown

**The Indiana Rail Road Company:
America's New Regional Railroad**
Christopher Rund

**Evolution of the American
Diesel Locomotive**
J. Parker Lamb

**The Men Who Loved Trains:
The Story of Men Who Battled
Greed to Save an Ailing Industry**
Rush Loving Jr.

The Train of Tomorrow
Ric Morgan

**Built to Move Millions:
Streetcar Building in Ohio**
Craig R. Semsel

**The New York, Westchester &
Boston Railway: J. P. Morgan's
Magnificent Mistake**
Herbert H. Harwood Jr.

**Iron Rails in the Garden State:
Tales of New Jersey Railroading**
Anthony J. Bianculli

**Visionary Railroader:
Jervis Langdon Jr. and the
Transportation Revolution**
H. Roger Grant

Iowa's Railroads: An Album
H. Roger Grant & Donovan Hofsommer

The Duluth South Shore & Atlantic Railway: A History of the Lake Superior District's Pioneer Iron Ore Hauler
John Gaertner

Frank Julian Sprague: Electrical Inventor and Engineer
William D. Middleton & William D. Middleton III

The Indiana Rail Road Company: America's New Regional Railroad
(revised and expanded edition)
Christopher Rund, Fred W. Frailey, & Eric Powell

Little Trains to Faraway Places
Karl Zimmermann

Twilight of the Great Trains
(expanded edition)
Fred W. Frailey

Railroad Noir: The American West at the End of the Twentieth Century
Linda Grant Niemann

From Telegrapher to Titan: The Life of William C. Van Horne
Valerie Knowles

The Railroad That Never Was: Vanderbilt, Morgan, and the South Pennsylvania Railroad
Herbert H. Harwood Jr.

Boomer: Railroad Memoirs
Linda Grant Niemann

Indiana Railroad Lines
Graydon M. Meints

The CSX Clinchfield Route in the 21st Century
(now in paperback)
Jerry Taylor & Ray Poteat

Wet Britches and Muddy Boots: A History of Travel in Victorian America
John H. White Jr.

Landmarks on the Iron Road: Two Centuries of North American Railroad Engineering
(now in paperback)
William D. Middleton

On Railways Far Away
William D. Middleton

Railroads of Meridian
J. Parker Lamb, with contributions by David H. Bridges & David S. Price

JOHN H. WHITE, JR., has written fourteen books, including this one, and his *American Railroad Passenger Car* was nominated for the 1980 National Book Award. White was curator of the Smithsonian Institution's Museum of American History from 1958 to 1990.

This book was designed by Jamison Cockerham and set in type by Tony Brewer at Indiana University Press, and printed by Thompson Shore, Inc.

The typefaces are Arno, designed by Robert Slimbach in 2007, and Caecilia, designed by Peter Matthias Noordzij in 1990, both issued by Adobe Systems, Inc.; LHF Billhead 1910, designed and issued by Tom Kennedy in 2004; and IM FELL DW Pica Pro, designed and issued by Igino Marini 2007.

THE MOST RELIABLE ROUTE
TO
NASHVILLE, MAMMOTH CAVE & GRAYSON SPRINGS,
VIA
Louisville & Nashville Railroad
AND
Stage Lines.

Six Daily Lines of Stages

TWO DAILY LINES OF COACHES,
TO
NASHVILLE.

Messrs. CARTER & THOMAS are now running, in connection with the 6.35 A. M. EXPRESS TRAIN on the above Railroad, Coaches for Russellville, Clarksville, Hopkinsville, &c. By this Route Passengers can reach Nashville in 24 hours, and connect there with Trains for all the Southern cities.

They are also running, in connection with the same Train,
Two Daily Lines to the Mammoth Cave,
AND A
DAILY TO BOWLING GREEN,

Connecting at Franklin, Ky., with
THE GRAYSON SPRINGS LINE.

Connects at Upton with the same Train as above, and arrives at the Springs at 3 o'clock P. M., with only 18 miles staging, being 10 miles less than by the Elizabethtown route.

By this arrangement Passengers can reach the CAVE the same day to dinner.

Passengers by this line can dine either at Hilltown or the Springs, as they may prefer.

All of the above lines are stocked in a style unsurpassed by any lines in the country, and in charge of careful and accommodating

---

United States Mail line of Coaches

For Baltimore, Washington City and Philadelphia
Via National Road.

THE NATIONAL ROAD STAGE COMPANY respectfully inform their patrons and travellers generally, that the above lines are in GOOD order and run as follows:

THE FAST MAIL leaves Wheeling every day precisely at 1 o'clock, reaching Frederick in Forty Six Hours, thence to Baltimore or Washington by Rail Road, to or from Washington City by Coaches.

THE RELIANCE LINE also leaves Wheeling daily, and travels the same route.

NEW COACHES of the best kind are placed on these Lines, and the whole stock cannot be surpassed by any in the Union. "They are the only Lines in connection with the BALTIMORE AND OHIO RAIL ROAD.

Passengers wishing to branch off from the Main Road into any of our Cross Lines, are informed that they have the preference over any others. Seats will always be secured for them.

NEW LINE FOR BALTIMORE

CITIZENS LINE—NO NIGHT TRAVEL.

The National Road Stage Company have established a new line called "Citizens Line," between Wheeling and Baltimore, running as follows: Leaves Wheeling every other morning, (Sundays excepted,) lodges first night, Cumberland second night, Winchester third night, giving passengers a full nights rest, at the end of the journey.

For seats apply to the Offices, on Water Street, and at Virginia Hotel in Wheeling.

W. K. NEWMAN, Agent.

Wheeling, May 3, 1855.

N.B. Travellers will please take notice that the above lines do actually run the National Road and not branch off at Washington, Pa., through Mount Pleasant &c., nor over did.

SOMETHING TO REMEMBER!

BIG OAK FLAT DIRECT ROUTE

NEVADA STAGE CO'S LINES
-THE-
BIG OAK FLAT & CALAVERAS GROVE

To Yosemite and Big Trees!

BY LEAVING YOSEMITE VALLEY BY THE
BIG OAK FLAT ROUTE
REMEMBER,
You arrive in Stockton or San Francisco
Twenty-Four Hours ahead of any other Route!

SPEED, COMFORT AND SAFETY!

THE ONLY ROUTE

Passing through the Historical Gold Fields of California, and the scenes of "Bret Harte" and "Mining Camps" made famous through the Big Bonanza Times of Big Oak Flat, (the route passes through the Dutch Flats and Tuolumne Dam of Big Bonanza fame) giving the coach riders a view of a fast changing population, which in a short time will be taken the place of the old and become a memory of history, crossing the spur of the Sierras going East of West.

And starting from the Valley the same day as Modern and Moved Routes, you arrive in STOCKTON or SAN FRANCISCO the SECOND DAY, in time for the Trains going East or West. The Oak line is over a being well appointed line, do so on the saddle of carriage journey on this line, say not over did.

Any information or the folder or otherwise, on application.

No. 6 MONTGOMERY STREET (BOOKSTORE).

T. T. WALTON, Agent,
cheerfully furnished by letter or otherwise.

BOSTON.

U. S. MAIL COACH, via New Haven and Hartford, starts from the York House, No. 5 Courtlandt street, every morning at half past eight o'clock, and arrives at Boston next evening at eleven o'clock.

Fare, from New York to New Haven $4 00
do   New Haven to Hartford   2 50
do   Hartford to Boston   5 50

For seats apply to WM. B. JAQUES, at York House, No. 5 Courtlandt street, second office from Broadway.

††† Expresses and extra coaches furnished at the shortest notice.

N. B. All baggage at the risk of the owners thereof.

MOTT, DAVENPORT, LOVEJOY & Co.
Proprietors.

a 17 2w

FRINK, WALKER & CO'S
POST COACH LINES.

MAIL COACH leaves Peru six times a week for Chicago, in connection with the mail Steamboat from Peoria. Extra Coaches always in readiness when Boats arrive at Peru. Daily line (Sundays excepted,) from Hennepin and Peru for Dixon and Galena. Also—Tri-weekly from Dixon to Rockford and Freeport. Tri-weekly line leaves Galena for Madison and Milwaukie via Platteville and Mineral Point on Monday, Wednesday and Friday mornings. Also—Tri-weekly for Prairie du Chien same day and same time.

Newark Stage for New-York.

A FOUR HORSE STAGE will leave Archer Gifford's, in Newark, every morning (except Sunday) at half past five o'clock, and will leave Fowler Hook at 5 o'clock in the afternoon for Newark—This arrangement gives time for doing business in the city, and the cool of hours for travelling. Passengers desiring this conveyance may apply for seats to John Bond at A. Gifford's.

J. N. Cumming.

tf

STAGE LINES.

NEIL, MOORE & CO'S STAGES,
LEAVE DAILY FOR
Columbus, Zanesville & Wheeling
At 8 1-2 - 2 A. M.
ALSO,
For Dayton and Piqua,
At 2 P.M.
Through to Dayton in 7 hours,   Fare to Dayton
Two Dollars.

P. CAMPBELL, Ag't.
Office in CINCINNATI,
On Front Street,
Two doors below Cincinnati Hotel.

New Line of Stages.

THE PROPRIETORS
OF THE
NEW LINE OF STAGES
CALLED THE
RICHMOND
AND
Washington Dispatch,

IN CONNECTION with the line called the Richmond and Fredericksburg Dispatch, have the pleasure to inform the Public that this line above said, which formerly ran every other day from the City of Richmond and from the City of Washington, now run from each of those Cities every Richmond and the City of Washington every morning at 5 o'clock, the above named Stages, through Fredericksburg, will leave the City of Richmond and the City of Washington every morning at 5 o'clock, and arrive at each of those Cities about 5 o'clock the following evening, which is much cheaper, and equally as good as the old road. These considerations, it is presumed will secure to the proprietors of the Richmond and Washington Dispatch, as much of the public patronage as they can accommodate.

The road from which the mail coaches run is one of the best our country can boast, and this mail line route is two of the best one, and takes in the villages of Ruther's Tavern in the same town, and McAvoy's, in the City of Washington, Messrs. O'Neal, McLeod, and McAvoy's, on the routes, call at the respective Taverns in Georgetown, and will, on its routes, call at the passengers at Mr. Crawford's Tavern in the same town, but the approbation of the Public generally, and that which rode from Mr. Washington shall form the Rail Tavern, rally—The Stages leaving Richmond will start from the Bell Tavern, and that which leaves from Mr. Washington starts from Mr. Joseph Skinner's Tavern, Georgetown.

For seats, apply at Patton's Courtlandt street, New York; at Chandler's or Cook's Newark and at Drake's Morris-Town.

JOHN DRAKE,
Morristown,
CHARLES HOPPING.

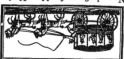

MORRIS-TOWN AND NEW-YORK
STAGE.

Through Hanover, Orange and Newark,
DAILY.

THE public are respectfully informed that a new arrangement has been made on this route, whereby a DAILY LINE, which has long been wanted, will be run from Morristown, Whippany and Hanover to Orange, at which place passengers will take the Car for New-ark. The company will spare no pains to accommodate the public, as excellent teams and coaches, and careful drivers, are in requisition to serve them.

This line will leave Morris-Town at 9 o'clock in the morning, and arrive at Orange in season for the Rail-road Car which arrives at New York at 2 o'clock P.M.

Passengers for Morristown must take the 11 o'clock car at Newark for Orange.

For seats, apply at Patton's Courtlandt street, New York; at Chandler's or Cook's Newark and at Drake's Morris-Town.

JOHN DRAKE,
Morristown,
CHARLES HOPPING.